★★★ AMBUSHED ★★★

AMBUSHED

Why
George Herbert Walker Bush
Really Lost in 1992

Anne DuBose Joslin

Anne DuBose Joslin
26 October 2003

Henley & Luce
BOSTON

1090

Web site: www.7Omega.com
E-mail: info@7Omega.com

ISBN: 0-9744516-0-6

To my Son and to my Daughter . . .
It is because of their values,
their integrity,
their honorableness and
their commitment to sharing their talents with the world
that I have had the courage
to write these words.

To Lance and Joslin, who set the standard.

INTEGRITY

Man's most precious attribute is his integrity. It is a very private quality, but it is the very rock upon which character is built. If, when you say you will do a thing, you do it; if honesty is a matter of fairness with you; if you feel the privilege of living involves a moral responsibility—you have in you the seeds of integrity. You develop integrity by consistently daring to do what seems to you to be the honorable thing to do.

—Source unknown
[Given to me by my Father when I was fifteen years old]

THE GODS OF THE MIND

The means by which one person is able to rule others is a fascinating subject of study. Invariably, the explanation of such control is that it is a matter of the mind. Any ruler, no matter how numerous his weapons or great his wealth, must finally rule by others means. He must rule by persuasion, the ultimate weapon through which influence on a culture is produced and sustained. The truly powerful leader must influence the minds of men.

To do this, he must produce in the minds of others something more, something stronger, something more compelling than what we call an idea. This "thing" he must produce in the minds of others actually exists, but in the form of a mental construct. It is an image the influencer sets up in the minds of others, an image that can become an object of occupation, then of concentration, and then—dare we say it—of veneration. The influencer must produce in the minds of those he influences a kind of little god. This god of the mind is a "real thing" he plants in the mentality of unsuspecting people.

—Dave Breese
Seven Men Who Rule the World from the Grave

★★★ CONTENTS ★★★

Part 5:
Acts of Courage

Part 6:
A Promise Is Forever

Part 7:
Off with the Rose-Colored Glasses

Part 8:
The Light Brigade

During the summer of 1987, when Vice President George Herbert Walker Bush was preparing to run for President of the United States, I decided to become a part of his campaign. Already of the opinion that Mr. Bush was a Jeffersonian-type of man, a gentleman of character, family values and patriotic ideals, I hoped that by joining his team at the national headquarters in Washington, D.C., I might be able to contribute in some way. And although George Bush was the reason for my foray into politics, Barbara Bush also served as inspiration.

At different times, Mrs. Bush and I had been young girls living in New England when our families sent us south to attend Ashley Hall, a small boarding school in Charleston, South Carolina. Mrs. Bush in the 1940s and I in the 1960s. Over the years, I read numerous articles in the Ashley Hall newsletter pertaining to Mrs. Bush . . . as the wife of a congressman, ambassador, and the Vice President and, through the written word, I followed the highlights of her life, always admiring her accomplishments and vivacity.

In 1987, when Vice President Bush formalized his run for the presidency, I was living in the D.C. area, and it seemed only natural to support his candidacy. I just happened to be in the right place at the right time, and in September of that year, I signed up as a volunteer. My two children and I were living in McLean, Virginia, close enough to the District for me to commute by car to the Bush national campaign headquarters. Inexperienced in Washington customs and crusades, I had no ulterior motive or illusion about gaining anything from my work other than helping the Vice President become President. My choice was strictly personal, not political.

AMBUSHED, although political in nature, *is not* about political Parties or Party affiliation, but personal character and moral integrity. It chronicles the Bush "players" and their proceedings between September 1987 (when the national Bush campaign started) and November of 1992 (when Bush was defeated in the reelection). As I became more involved with the 1988 campaign, the Transition team, and later the administration, I found that my foremost interest was in observing those serving in the highest levels of our nations government, including some of Bush's most trusted advisors and friends. Among these individuals were aides and counselors with more interest in amassing power for themselves than in serving their Party, their country or their President.

Over nearly six years of working in the Nation's Capital, I discovered that greed and self-serving purposes often prevailed over ideology and merit; for those persons to whom winning was everything, *not anything nor any one* would stand in their way! My political status was nowhere near the Cabinet level, but in geographic proximity, I was mightily close to those who were.

While placed among the all-powerful in myriad circumstances, I had to make difficult choices, decisions that not only defined who I was and what I believed in, but also identified where my priorities lay. Continually, and often ruthlessly, my convictions were tested by the Washington "system."

More often than not, my attitude and actions were analogous to the military mind-set that was so familiar to me; naval tradition ran deep within seven generations of my family. As the daughter, granddaughter, niece and sister of captains, colonels, commodores and admirals, love for America was instilled in me from the time I was born—which happened to be on the grounds of the United States Naval Academy. Serving the commander in chief had begun in 1799 when my great, great, great-grandfather Denison became a midshipman. His daughter would marry Stephen Bleecker Luce, founder of the Naval War College in Newport, Rhode Island, my father's hometown.

Consequently, with names like Bleecker, Luce, Henley, Higbee and Kane, as well as Joslin and DuBose in my ancestral past, I grew up steeped in two centuries of Navy ritual. No practice was more highly regarded than protecting the freedoms of the United States, and no individuals more esteemed than the brave and true naval officers who kept Americans safe from harm. For me, these honorable men who wore uniforms of rich blue-black with gold braid trim on their shoulders and multicolored ribbons on their chests stood tall, though none were as tall as my Father, who stood at a striking six feet, four inches.

During much of my childhood, Father was either at sea in the Far East or teaching ordinance engineering at the Naval Academy. Some of my happiest days were in the late 1950s when I was a teenager and the

★★★

Academy "campus" was my backyard. Across the street from our quarters on Upshur Road was the midshipman's parade ground—Warden Field—and only yards beyond was the Chesapeake Bay. For four years, Annapolis was a paradise for a family of seven (I was the eldest of five children) and a German Shepherd. These years left their imprint and, although I was not aware of it at the time, served as a constant filter through which I viewed my life and the world around me. Many decades later, these Navy Days provided me with the underpinnings and insights to first "see" and then write *AMBUSHED*.

The opening scene of this book could have been taken from a novel. However, this writing is nonfiction, a memoir and only my truth as best I know it. Throughout my five-year labor, I did not write to impress, be praised or be judged. As a statistician and researcher, I simply related an unforgettable experience, one that, from the beginning, wove its own assumptions and suggestions, eventually leading me to what I believed was a feasible conclusion. It was in my last revision of the book that I coined the phrase, my "Crazy Conspiracy Theory," and it is this axiom that becomes the premise upon which *AMBUSHED* is based.

I *had* to write *AMBUSHED*. It is a story I lived with for fifteen years. My hope is that this memoir might encourage others to make their voices heard, whether it be in politics or in some other facet of life. For it is only through sharing our realities that we come closer to revealing the truth. Fact allows us the opportunity to understand and, if need be, initiate change. Nothing is more powerful in building a strong democracy than truthful communication, and as Americans, we need to know our leaders are being honest with us. And as a responsible society, we must make it our duty to fight for candid, forthright representatives. If the American citizenship does not take an active role in establishing the fitness of their nation, I am afraid that they, The People, will soon find themselves among those already *AMBUSHED*.

★★★ AMBUSHED ★★★

Vice Presidential Residence, June 17, 1988
With V.P. Bush while attending the campaign staff picnic.

★   ★

PART 1

I Want to Be President

★   ★

Symbols and mythology of power are predominately male-oriented. Our ultimate image of power is the President, a man surrounded by men in a male-oriented world and sustained by artifacts and trappings of a masculine society and technology—soldiers, lavish jet aircraft, secret servicemen, helicopters . . .

—Michael Korda

★★★ ━━━━━ ★★★
CHAPTER

1

POTOMAC FEVER

Only the weak believe they possess answers to all the questions; only the weak mount the public stage swelled with swagger, filled with cant. Only the weak tell others what to think and how to act, based on their ideology: only the weak aspire to be demagogues.
—Richard Bode

SEPTEMBER–DECEMBER 1987

This is a story about power, politics, and the President of the United States.

It begins on the sixteenth of December 1987 on a snowy evening in Washington, D.C. The frosty night air felt extraordinarily invigorating that night. And a brilliant moon shone down upon the Capital City and onto the residence of Vice President and Mrs. George Herbert Walker Bush.

I and my colleagues—members of the Vice President's 1988 presidential campaign staff—arrived at the Bush home for a holiday party. The stately quarters, referred to as the Admiralty, were situated on the grounds of the Naval Observatory in Northwest Washington and, on this evening, were dressed in greens and candles. It glowed in the richness of the Christmas season.

Inside the house, it was warm and inviting; an understated elegance enveloped the entire first floor of the Victorian manor. In the mistletoe-adorned foyer, an enormous Christmas tree, fully decorated with a lifetime collection of family ornaments, was the first thing to catch my eye. Not far from it stood an oversized dining room table filled with festive treats and cocktail hors d'oeuvres.

Of all the rooms on the first floor, the one I remember best is a small drawing room in the back of the house where, on top of a long, narrow console, the Bushes had amassed a large grouping of photographs. Set inside a variety of silver, glass, and wooden frames were pictures of celebrities and sports figures, as well as politicians and world leaders. The display was indicative of the family's vast number of friends and acquaintances—they were known for having the largest Rolodex in Washington. Adding to the cozy and homelike atmosphere of the sitting room were overstuffed, multicolored, chintz-covered chairs and ample windows overlooking the dormant gardens. It was only after the receiving line was well underway that I hesitantly put down my glass of chardonnay and joined my fellow campaigners in the front of the house, where a string quartet was playing Bach's *Christmas Oratorio*.

The music added to the ambiance of the occasion, but it was the energy of the people that gave the evening its significance.

Before arriving, I had been certain the celebratory gathering at the Bush home would be an ideal way to get to know some of my fellow staffers, who, like myself, had been working in the Vice President's campaign headquarters for only a few short months. While standing in the receiving line—which looped its way through several rooms—I made a point to notice the men and women encircling me. They displayed a confidence beyond what was normally exhibited when we were at headquarters in downtown Washington.

As the photographer snapped pictures of the Bushes shaking hands with their guests, nearly one hundred staffers smiled and laughed and made conversation with one another just as people would at any party during the Christmas season. Nevertheless, unlike other groups, their collective attitude could best be described as invincible. The self assurance—almost haughtiness—of those mingling with Vice President and Mrs. Bush on that frosty December evening perplexed me. I found their air of superiority and poise somewhat intimidating, yet at the same time, infectious and enticing.

Not unlike a "moth drawn to the flame," I was charmed by their charisma, feeling something I could not then define. It is clear now that the elusive commodity was power.

This was my first real glimpse of how power, or the perception of having power, or the chance to be near someone with power could alter one's awareness of reality. Like accumulating wealth and sexual prowess, attaining political power can be seductive. And exceedingly alluring.

Being in close proximity to the center of command carries with it the capacity to make a person feel as if he were the center of the universe. Such is the ego of the Power Elite. In such an atmosphere, I would learn, it is easy to lose perspective.

Despite my rudimentary observations at the Bush residence, I viewed those of us on the national team as bound by a similar purpose, tied together like brothers and sisters. I believed that devotion to country and self-sacrifice for principle were the goals that had brought us together. I imagined that we had put our personal interests aside for the "common good," and were here to help an honorable man be elected President of the United States.

Little did I know that this—my first political contest—would turn out to be a once-in-a-lifetime education. And *not* the political instruction I thought it would be.

It had all started just three months earlier, at the Bush national campaign headquarters.

ON a late summer morning, I signed up to be a volunteer in Vice President Bush's quest for the presidency. It was September 15, 1987.

Before arriving at headquarters, I had to make my way up 15th Street with all the other Washingtonians. As always, the traffic going toward Thomas Circle was snarled and noisy. The sidewalks were filled with young people—mostly men—scurrying to their next appointments. In gray pinstriped suits, carrying leather briefcases, each appeared to be on his way to a meeting so significant that, should he not arrive on time, he, and he alone, would be responsible for the fate of humankind. As I marched alongside them, only yards away from the White House and just two blocks from Vice President Bush's office, I got a taste of this intoxicating thing called Potomac Fever.

Referring to the business card I held in my hand, I checked the address I was looking for: 733 15th Street, NW, Suite 800, Washington, D.C. In blue print, above the campaign address, was Lee Atwater's name, along with his title: Campaign Manager, George Bush for President. Two days earlier, Atwater had handwritten the name of his deputy, Ed Rogers, above his own, and told me to contact the former attorney from Birmingham, Alabama, for assistance in finding volunteer work at the 1988 Bush headquarters. A small staff had already formed.

Thus, I found myself approaching the Woodward Building, a structure that on this particular overcast morning looked as gray and drab as the sky above; after the campaign was over, the Woodward was targeted for demolition. As I entered, I noticed a little newsstand—part deli—nestled to the right of the front door. In the lobby, I saw sections of the walls plastered, without paint, and the oak trim around the windows untreated and not securely attached. All this made for a less than desirable first impression. The lobby elevator reminded me of one in a department store back in the fifties; I took it up to the sixth floor, where a young man in khaki pants, a Brooks Brothers' shirt and a striped tie informed me—in a hushed voice—that I was in the wrong place. The eighth floor was for Bush senior staff only.

I was quickly rerouted to the sixth floor, the second of the two floors housing the Bush campaign.

As the elevator doors opened, I could see above the receptionist's desk a vibrant blue and white banner with "George Bush for President" printed across the middle. Immediately, a young man, Alvin Williams, who was sitting behind the receptionist's desk, greeted and escorted me to the office of the director of volunteers, Greg Mendez. Arrangements apparently had already been made by Rogers, the former regional political director in Reagan's 1984 reelection.

Shabby and cluttered, Mendez's office reeked of stale coffee in Styrofoam cups and cigarette butts; he was a chain smoker. Outside his window loomed a dark alleyway, and a fake owl was perched on the ledge, presumably to scare away the District pigeons. The room was indicative of the other offices on the eighth floor of the Woodward Building, where space was at a premium, one-person-offices scarce, and equipment almost nonexistent.

I explained to Mendez that I wanted to work on a part-time basis, but that I had no previous campaign experience. For six years, I had been in Washington working in the corporate world, and from what I had heard in conversations, thought a presidential race would be fun—not that time-consuming or demanding. All those rallies with balloons and flags came to mind.

Yet, at the same time, coming from a multigenerational family of Naval officers, I projected that I would be able to immerse myself in the values, philosophies, and convictions of our Founding Fathers, the

★★★

ideological truths upon which the United States and our democracy were created. To someone with a better understanding of politics, my way of thinking may sound naïve or pretentious, but for me it was genuine. Patriotism took a high priority in my family (a long line of Naval Academy graduates) and I had been taught to feel passionately about my country. Trying to reconcile these ingrained military values with a civilian life style and national politics would cause me conflict and uncertainty over the next six years. I had no idea that the journey on which I was about to embark would defy every belief I held concerning power, presidents, politics and personal integrity. It would challenge me to find my center and force me to define my priorities as well as identify my passions. In other words, my Bush "experience" would provide me with another lens to view the world.

On that first visit to headquarters, I conveyed to Mendez that what I was lacking in political skills, I would make up in motivation, and I offered to work wherever he needed me. In response, Mendez looked around his office—where papers were strewn across black metal filing cabinets and manila folders lay scattered on the floor—turned to me, and asked if I would be willing to come in three days a week and work as a coordinator in the volunteer office. He desperately needed the help, and I excitedly agreed to take the job.

The next day, September 16, 1987, I became a part of the machine that would turn out the winning candidate for the office of President. The election was more than thirteen months away; in political circles, where events move at supersonic speed, that was light-years from the present. The Bush campaign roster was short, no more than fifteen names, including politicals Rich Bond, Janet Mullins and Jim Pinkerton as well as Pete Teeley, Roger Ailes, Bob Teeter, Mendez and Rogers. George Walker Bush (some mistakenly referred to him as George Junior), known to those of us in the campaign as "G.W.," the eldest son of the Vice President, served as liaison to his father and the Office of the Vice President (OVP). Having left Texas to help with his father's campaign, George W. was given the official title of senior advisor and resided on the sixth floor with the other senior staff members.

The life of all the Bush aides was in high gear, but none was more fired-up and ready to go than Lee Atwater, chairman. Although small in stature, Atwater was bigger than life itself, and once met, was never forgotten. One's first impression could be as powerfully negative as it could be positive. The South Carolina political strategist, trained under Senator Strom Thurmond (R-SC), had a reputation for performing "horrible deeds, symbolizing the dark side of American politics." In a March 30, 1991, *Washington Post* article written by Thomas Edsall, Atwater was depicted this way: "In 1980, Atwater's instinct for the jugular sent a chill down the spines of even some of his friends and supporters, and it was with Strom Thurmond . . . that Atwater began to earn his reputation as a tough, and in the minds of some, dirty and negative campaigner."

Adversaries represented Atwater as a southern redneck who, while playing on people's uncertainties and insecurities, had used race as an integral part of his strategy. He was portrayed as an evil man, and his harshest critics referred to him as a "racist pig."

However, there was another side to Lee Atwater: he was a superb strategist and campaign leader. With his finger always on America's pulse, he intuitively knew which way the wind was blowing at all times. Because I was there to witness Atwater's ability to command—even under the most difficult of times—I choose to write from this perspective.

Atwater had a reputation for eating hamburgers, pizza, and fried chicken for breakfast, for sleeping five hours a night, and for jogging no fewer than six miles a day; he and George W. were fanatics about their noontime run around the city. Atwater, who played guitar, claimed the book *Combat Tactics from the Sword and the Mind,* written by three Japanese sword masters, to be one of his favorites.

While attending Newberry College in South Carolina, Atwater started his political career as an aide to Senator Strom Thurmond. He was also chairman of the South Carolina College Republicans at that time and, in 1973, became executive director of the College Republicans in Washington, where he began his friendship with Bush Senior, then Republican National Committee chairman. Atwater later ran Texan Carl Rove's race for chair of the College Republicans. Rove, who won the contest but never finished college, would go on to become a state advisor to George Herbert Walker Bush.

In 1974, Atwater returned to Columbia, South Carolina, and managed his first statewide race, that of General William C. Westmoreland; the Vietnam War commander lost his gubernatorial bid, but Atwater was now hooked on campaigning. In the South, an almost

★★★

nonexistent Republican Party was beginning to flourish, and in 1978, Atwater rejoined the team of Strom Thurmond, again running for South Carolina's Senate seat. Shortly after Thurmond's victory, in 1980, Atwater managed Reagan's South Carolina primary victory, going on to become a regional director for his campaign. Reagan won and Atwater was appointed to the White House political office. In 1984, James Baker, Reagan's chief of staff and chairman of the reelection committee, chose Atwater to be deputy manager, overseeing all fifty state campaigns.

Just after the Reagan win in 1984, Baker brought Atwater back into the White House, selecting him to be Vice President Bush's chief political strategist and manager of his 1988 presidential campaign. Atwater accepted, and at thirty-six years of age, Young Lee was in his third presidential campaign. Baker, who had initiated the 1988 Bush run, had also appointed himself as chairman. Since the fall of 1984, he had been strategizing, working behind the scenes, either from the White House (from which he ran Reagan's 1984 campaign), or his secretarial office in the department of the Treasury. Jim Baker had kept his thumb on both "presidencies."

Years before the Bush campaign was a formal organization, there was an influential force serving the Vice President. Just after Reagan's reelection victory in 1984, Baker chose Atwater, Craig Fuller, Nicholas Brady, Robert Teeter (who had also been on Reagan's 1984 senior campaign staff), Peter Teeley, and Roger Ailes to be part of a "new" Bush team. These individuals made up what was called the Group of Six, or the G-6 (taken from the organization known as the G-7, a group of the seven economically superior nations). Also part of this inner circle were Richard Darman, Baker's deputy at the White House and at Treasury, and Robert Mosbacher, the long-time Texas friend of Bush who, although not part of the day-to-day G-6 operations, was in charge of fundraising.

Many of the individuals from Reagan 1984 were involved in Bush 1988.

And to comprehend the Bush 1988 campaign constitution, it is important to take into account the Reagan 1984 reelection organization. I was at a distinct disadvantage while working in the campaign, having not grasped the past roles of the present players. Here is what I learned.

At the top of the 1984 Power Pyramid was Jim Baker, chief of staff to Reagan and chairman of his reelection committee. Baker's aides were Ed Rollins (campaign manager), who directed the Reagan White House political office and reported directly to Baker; Lee Atwater (deputy campaign manager), who reported to Rollins; Michael Deaver, President and Mrs. Reagan's long-time friend and a top advisor in the Reagan White House; and Stewart Spencer, a confidante and advisor to Reagan since the 1960s (yet had defected in 1976 and joined Baker to secure Gerald Ford's defeat of Reagan).

Baker also chose two pollsters: Richard Wirthlin, a Mormon from Salt Lake City, Utah, who had been Reagan's 1980 pollster, and Robert Teeter, from Detroit, Michigan, who had been a pollster for Richard Nixon and, like Spencer, had gone with Baker when he ran Ford's 1976 campaign. It was by Baker's personal request that Teeter joined the 1984 Reagan senior campaign staff.

Baker's closest aide in the 1984 campaign was Richard Darman, deputy for presidential appointments and correspondence. Baker's scheduler and confidante, Margaret Tutwiler, was moved to the White House political office and became a key link between Baker and the rest of the 1984 campaign staff. (Ed Rogers would be assigned to this office at the beginning of Reagan's second term.)

Predictably, Reagan won the reelection in November 1984, and within a month's time, Baker, having just completed his responsibilities as Reagan's campaign chairman—and while still chief of staff—called together the first G-6 meeting and started planning the presidency of George Bush. Atwater had been appointed Baker's key contact and was tapped to lay the groundwork for the campaign.

Unlike the majority of his compatriots from Reagan '84, Atwater swiftly shifted political energy from Reagan to Bush. He relished the challenge of a campaign fight, and had a tendency to become lost in the love of the game. Having established the Fund for America's Future (a Republican political action committee—PAC), Atwater was given credit for raising over $2 million during the summer of 1987. By September, when I arrived, the campaign had raised a record-breaking $10 million more than any Republican presidential candidate in that short of a time.

Fund-raising strategy gave way to election strategy, and Atwater, above everyone else, drove the Bush 1988 campaign team. "George Bush for President," the official name of the operation, was underway.

Despite questions surrounding Atwater's personal life (he was sometimes known as a renegade and a womanizer), his innate sense of political direction and tenacious personality colored the entire campaign.

And although few predicted Bush to be the victor in 1988, Atwater seemed hell-bent on taking the "underdog" to 1600 Pennsylvania Avenue. He was our leader; we followed, no questions asked. Still, the fact was, Bush's outlook was rather grim. On October 10, 1987, from the *Congressional Quarterly*, I read:

> Clearly, Bush's large campaign apparatus is girding itself to withstand an early defeat. But others are not so sure he could survive. "He's an exceptionally weak front-runner," says John Sears, a veteran Republican consultant and one-time Reagan campaign manager. "He doesn't have a personal constituency." In Sears' view, Bush is a weaker front-runner than former Vice President Walter F. Mondale was…in 1984.

Throughout the autumn of 1987, the idea of a Bush victory was considered a long shot. The Vice President was known to be too nice, too much of a good guy, with not enough "fire in his belly" to be a winner. Another article, from the *Baltimore Sun*, October 18, 1987, was written by Richard Vatz (assistant professor at Towson State University) and Lee Weinberg (assistant professor at the University of Pittsburgh), and it stated: "Indisputably around Washington there has been the suspicion that Mr. Bush is perceived as weak. In fact, 'wimp' is the new buzzword, the rhetorical switch with which his opponents hope to derail his front running train."

A few days later, on October 22, 1987, the *New York Times* came out with Bernard Weinraub's piece, "Compassion Becomes a Republican Theme," in which Bush was quoted: "Our whole history was protecting those who needed protection and making this a kinder nation. Prosperity with a purpose means helping your brothers and sisters, whoever they are, wherever they are, and whatever their needs." However, rather than following a positive theme, the press corps chose to denigrate Bush's softer sentiments and give him the "wimp" image.

The so-called wimp factor started to take on a life of its own.

Newsweek, in October, published what became known as the "Wimp Issue." In the cover story, entitled "Fighting the Wimp Factor," it claimed: "Bush suffers from a potentially crippling handicap, a perception that he isn't strong enough or tough enough for the challenges of the Oval Office. That he is, in a single, mean word, a wimp." I wondered why a national publication would come out with something so critical. I believed the office of the Vice President—and Bush himself—deserved more respect.

Robert Joseph Dole, the then sixty-five-year old Senator from Russell, Kansas, was predicted to win the Republican nomination. Dole had many relationships with the wealthy and the politically powerful, yet he preferred to present himself as the man from Middle America, one who grew up in poverty on the Kansas prairie. (One of Dole's grandfathers was a tenant farmer, the other a butcher, and his father a manager of a grain elevator.) With all the press attacking Bush, Dole had good reason to believe that he would easily beat his opponent.

I had been working in the volunteer office for almost a month when, on October 12, the staff gathered around a television to watch Bush officially announce that he was running for President. In his speech, given in Houston, Texas, Bush declared: "The presidency isn't like anything else. A presidency can shape an era—and it can change our lives. A successful presidency can give meaning to an age; a failed presidency can give us problems it takes generations to undo."

Life inside campaign headquarters, like a fast-moving train, picked up steam as it moved along. As a result of Atwater's zeal over Bush's candidacy announcement, momentum started to build inside the camp. A more spirited team evolved, while the number of players steadily increased. By the end of October, the official Bush campaign apparatus was in place, and the activity had intensified to the point where it could be described as having "come alive."

There was a discernible heartbeat.

During the fall months, a campaign roster including staff and volunteers came out every other day, with ten to twenty names added each week. No one had a title except Atwater and Rogers. Those of us who had established some seniority due to position or longevity (a week was considered a long time) were issued business cards, a practice discontinued after the first of the year.

My part-time position turned full-time as I coordinated the rapidly expanding volunteer organization. Without computers to help facilitate the work, my job of placing new volunteers in the headquarters and tracking their work hours was challenging. In need of structure, I taped large sheets of graph paper (on which I penciled in the days of the week, one month at a time) to one of the concrete walls in the volunteer office. Next to the hour coordinates, I wrote the name of the volunteer, noting the

★★★

staff member to whom he or she was reporting. I recorded the volunteers' time on the premises down to the quarter hour. A master schedule quickly evolved.

By determining who was working, where they were, and for how long they were in the headquarters, every day, twenty-four hours a day and seven days a week, I became familiar with the chain of command as well as with the staff and volunteers. In fact, at this early stage in the campaign, I got to know everyone at headquarters. This would prove to be valuable information to me in the future. And, too, I was beginning to feel like an effective member of the team.

During the first week in November, while continuing to coordinate the volunteer operation with Mendez, I started working part-time for the campaign research group. A number of volunteers already had been assigned to the research staff, most of them politically well-connected males in their late twenties. More often than not, their daddies had found them slots in the campaign. Because of the link between research and "policy" (everyone's favorite), finding a position in the division was difficult. An entire wing of the sixth floor was reserved for the research staff, and those who worked there not only enjoyed special status, but also benefited from having an office with a private telephone line. Very few people outside the senior staff were allotted such rewards.

The Boys in research were cocky, but they had been groomed to be charming, and they had politely requested my assistance with collating campaign issues. I worked on what was known as the Issues Log, several loose-leaf binders organized alphabetically in which I filed Bush's views on the controversial and not-so-controversial issues of the day. After pasting volumes of political statements into the quick-reference book, I selectively grouped and highlighted the policy issues that had the most promise of becoming the basis for the Republican platform in 1988.

During the early months of the campaign, Bush usually addressed issues in generic terms. The staff believed the less he said, the better, deferring the possibility of controversy. In coming months, when the issue of abortion struck and Bush, previously pro-choice, reversed his stance, there would be a dispute among Republicans whether that was an appropriate move to make. Personally, I was disappointed in the Vice President's decision. It was easy to understand the wisdom of a "wait and share" approach to "issue" statements.

Despite my displeasure over the pro-choice/life matter, early on, I believed Bush had a clear picture of how he wanted the country to move forward into the twenty-first century. His plan for a New World Order made sense to me, as did his idea of a peaceful world where compatible nations honored each other's differences and embraced their likenesses—somewhat similar to what Franklin Delano Roosevelt had envisioned after World War II: fewer global barriers and fewer multinational conflicts. Of the many Bush quotes I pasted into the Issues Log, one that I particularly liked was the Vice President's statement concerning the United States's role in the world:

> The challenge before us in the future is to continue to defend freedom and champion democracy around the world. We must keep the peace. That's what it is all about. In the future, if we don't turn our backs on the world, but remain engaged; if we resist the temptations of isolationism and protectionism; if we remain true to our values and ideals and resist paralyzing self-doubt; then I believe we can look at the years ahead with confidence and hope. We can set foreign policy goals that include resolving some of the major conflicts of the world affairs—not simply managing them, but actually resolving them. (University of New Hampshire, May, 23, 1987)

When the holiday season arrived in Washington, the volunteer office became my focus once again. We were responsible for addressing and mailing Vice President and Mrs. Bush's twenty thousand Christmas cards. On the front of the 1987 card was a picture of the entire Bush family—children and grandchildren—sitting on the rocks overlooking the Atlantic Ocean outside their home in Kennebunkport, Maine. It was shortly after the multitude of cards had been delivered to the D.C. Post Office that the Vice President's holiday party on the grounds of the Naval Observatory had taken place.

During the same week in December, another gathering was held for the campaign staff, this time at the Vice President's office in the Old Executive Office Building (OEOB) adjacent to the West Wing of the White House. Of all the buildings in the District, the OEOB is truly one of the most magnificent in its architecture and design. Built in 1871 by the architect Alfred Mullet, the OEOB had previously been called Mullet's State, War, and Navy Building. In the 1960s, it had almost been torn down. Luckily, President John F. Kennedy had preserved and restored the building as part of the nation's architectural heritage. The six-story, gray granite facade all but overpowered the simple beauty of the presidential mansion next door.

However, on this wintry evening in 1987, with its magnificent stone pillars and ornate porticos, the OEOB seemed less an imposing structure than a warm, welcoming retreat. Once inside the building, complete with thousands of square feet of marble and mahogany, the Bush campaign members and the Vice President's personal staff celebrated the campaign's newfound momentum. All one hundred-some of us took time to applaud Bush on his rebound in the political polls. In his honor, a political skit was presented; afterwards, eggnog was served in paper cups and toasts were made. In between the chatter, we all wondered where we would be this time the following year. Our future or, more importantly, the future of George Bush, was still anyone's guess.

Little did I know then that I would be back in the OEOB in January 1989 under very different circumstances.

Right now, I was preparing for a mini-holiday. As indicated by a memorandum sent out by Atwater, the campaign headquarters would be closed on Thursday, December 23, and reopen on Sunday, December 27. The staff was given three days off for rest and relaxation, the first official break since September.

Just before leaving, I received an unexpected call from Tony Lopez, one of the coordinators on the research staff. Not anticipating the call, I was surprised—and pleased—to find out he was contacting me to see if I would join his group on a full-time basis, managing the Policy Issue Groups. In order for me to accept the position, I had to find a replacement for my slot in the volunteer office. Someone came to mind. I was grateful when Barbara Jaroka agreed to replace me so that I could start my position in research. The job—another volunteer position—would begin the first Monday in January.

★★★ ▬▬▬▬ ★★★

CHAPTER

2

WIMP NO MORE

Mountain forests, rugged steeps, marshes and fens—all country that is hard to traverse: this is "difficult ground."

—Sun Tzu

JANUARY–FEBRUARY 1988

January the fourth turned out to be a cold, blustery winter day in the nation's capital. Snow was coming down hard as I made my way to the Woodward Building. One hundred thousand commuters and I slowly entered the District, a city of many hills, traffic circles, and one-way streets. Washington is a challenge on most storm days, but with diplomats from around the world who had never driven in snow, the problems compounded. Even a light sprinkling caused chaos for those of us who were more accustomed to tempestuous weather. Navigating my way to Pennsylvania Avenue took an hour longer than usual.

Once at headquarters, I attended the first of many early morning staff meetings headed by Jim Pinkerton, campaign research director. For the rest of the winter, Pinkerton's team would meet in his corner office every morning—Monday through Friday—at 7:30 sharp to pursue the constant task of keeping up with whatever was newsworthy on the political scene. Before anyone else.

"Pink," as he was referred to, stood a towering six feet, nine inches tall, and he already had his sights set on an office in the West Wing in 1989. On one occasion, he brought in a table-sized paper replica of the interior of the White House and pointed out where he intended to work once Bush was elected President. Pinkerton's present mission was to

16

remind us *every* day that it was our responsibility to locate meaningful news on the contenders for the presidency.

After settling into my space in the research wing, complete with desk, telephone and a window overlooking 15th Street, I realized how fortunate I was to be one of the few with such an office. My first impression, though, had been that it looked rather sparse compared to the corporate world. It was basic; however, weighed against the other working areas at headquarters, it was plush.

As I began my work with the Policy Issue Groups, I started going through the files of some six hundred men and a few women—all from the private sector—who sat on the foreign and domestic policy committees. Among the twenty-three group titles—all topics that had been included in the Issues Log—were crime, education, health, defense, housing, energy, telecommunications, environment and international economics. The official objective of the high-profile members was to assist in formulating policy for the anticipated Bush administration. Once a month they came from across the country to headquarters to debate political events, design policy statements and present opposing Party ideas, generating reams of briefing papers.

In March 1988, Russell Rockwell joined me in managing the policy groups; the two of us were charged with overseeing the candidate selection process, as well as coordinating the monthly meetings and ensuring that members kept in contact with headquarters. Although the group members came with impressive résumés and were known to be captains of industry, finance, law and the arts, in reality, they sat on committees used as holding tanks for individuals who desired to contribute to the Bush cause. It was too early in the election cycle for determining policy. Documents and position papers submitted by the members were seldom seen and, to my knowledge, never used by the campaign; however, it was important that the staff acknowledge only one reason for these volunteers being on board: they were vital to the success of the campaign. Rockwell and I served as diplomatic liaisons between these private sector representatives and the Vice President's office, always being careful to show our (Bush's) appreciation for their input.

During the first week of January, while I was getting to know the names of the policy advisors, there was an unexpected visit from Bush. Because security dogs were brought over in advance to sniff out the offices, we knew when the Vice President was coming, but on this particular day, there had been no dogs. Bush quietly had come to headquarters to practice for the upcoming presidential debate in Des Moines, Iowa, on January 8. In a mock debate, he was to play the part of himself while campaign staff took on the roles of the other Republican candidates. This was an attempt to prepare him for the unexpected comments or questions, particularly character attacks, that are inherent in the contests.

So far, Bush had displayed an unusual amount of confidence in the Republican debates; he also had experienced his fair share of disappointments, suffering an embarrassing loss to Pat Robertson and Bob Dole in the September Iowa straw poll. But later, he sustained a landslide vote on the Maryland ballot, receiving 67 percent of the votes. However, it was the first GOP debate in Houston, on October 29, that put Bush out in front of the Republican pack. The candidates with whom he shared the debate stage numbered five: Pat Robertson, Virginia Southern Baptist minister and television evangelist; Robert Dole, Senate minority leader; Jack Kemp, New York representative; Pierre (Pete) duPont, governor of Delaware from 1975 to 1985; and General (retired) Alexander Haig, former secretary of State under Reagan.

In advance of the debate, each candidate was allowed to pass out two hundred tickets to supporters, and on the evening of the broadcast, these cliques were evenly distributed about the auditorium "to prevent formation of cheering sections." The debaters were given ninety seconds for their initial replies to questions posed by Bill Buckley and Robert Strauss, and forty-five seconds for rebuttals.

The Houston debate, which was a special edition of William F. Buckley, Jr.'s "Firing Line" program, was broadcast by nearly 270 public television stations live from Houston's four thousand–seat George Brown Convention Center. It was the first time the voters had a chance to see all the Republican candidates for president on stage together. In anticipation of the political premiere, Atwater had been quoted in a *Washington Post* (October 22, 1987) article, "GOP Presidential Hopefuls Prepare for Premiere Debate," by Lloyd Grove: "The vice president's opponents have been throwing spitballs at him every chance they get. It'll be interesting to see if they do it themselves at the debate, or leave it to their henchmen and flunkies."

★★★

Nothing in the Houston debate exemplified Bush's ability to be assertive more than his retort to du Pont after the former governor accused Bush of having "no vision, principle or policy of his own, but just slavish acceptance of anything that President Reagan wanted." Du Pont, a Princeton University and Harvard Law School graduate, complained that he was "waiting for details." Bush blasted back with, "Pierre, let me help you." For the next sixty seconds, Bush outlined the reasons why the intermediate-range nuclear forces agreement was good for Europe, the United States, and the military balance of power. He attacked du Pont for criticizing those who were responsible for making "the tough calls," suggesting that du Pont was an ignorant "outsider." Then, before his time ran out, Bush called du Pont's idea to offer young people an alternative to Social Security "nutty."

By the end of the evening, Bush had delivered a persuasive message, proving that he could fight back when under fire. The press corps raved that the Vice President was the best he had ever been, and that the Houston debate had been the ideal forum for Bush to bury the "wimp" image. It was reported that Bush had a "full grasp" of his material while at the same time managing to exploit his opponents' weaknesses. More importantly, the media and the country had seen Bush looking "presidential."

Ten days after the *Baltimore Sun* article had come out describing Bush as a wimp, headlines in the *New York Post* on October 30, 1987, read: "Macho Bush Hits Hard in GOP Slugfest."

While Bush was pulling ahead of Dole and Robertson in the Republican race, Al Gore was gaining on front-runner Jesse Jackson in the Democratic chase. The opposing line-up numbered one more than the Republicans: Al Gore, senator from Tennessee; Jesse Jackson, reverend from South Carolina; Michael Dukakis, governor of Massachusetts; Bruce Babbitt, former governor of Arizona; Richard Gephardt, representative from Missouri; Paul Simon, senator from Illinois; and Gary Hart, former senator from Colorado.

Under a scandal, Hart had dropped out of the race in May. Although he had taken the Democratic lead back in the spring, he had been caught in an affair with Miami model Donna Rice while aboard the cruise boat *Monkey Business*. In December—the day before the deadline for entering the New Hampshire primary contest—Hart, without Democratic Party counsel, reentered the primary. With his reentry, a total of thirteen Republican and Democratic candidates were running for the highest office in the land.

When debate season had first started, there had been some uncertainty as to how well Bush would do in that arena; he was known for jumbling his words and speaking in a high-pitched voice. However, he performed successfully not only in Houston, but also Washington, D.C., and Boston, holding his ground with the other contenders.

As the new year began, there was a feeling at headquarters of cautious optimism. Thus far, the Vice President's newfound strength and poise had the effect of transforming a rather doubtful candidate into a promising one, and one man in particular received most of the credit for Bush's image turnaround: Roger Ailes.

The forty-eight-year-old, generously proportioned, mustached Ailes, always with a devilish twinkle in his eyes, had a long history of political image making. The master of the "new" Nixon and the "ageless" Reagan was now Bush's media consultant and debate coach. When it came to dialogue theory, Ailes preferred a combative approach, and he encouraged his clients to attack hard and often. In the Houston debate, he had suggested that Bush refer to du Pont by his given name, Pierre, meaning for it to be a putdown. He had also suggested ways to slow down Bush's speech and lower his voice. Ailes knew how to heighten his candidate's self-confidence so that he would go on the offensive, rather than waiting to defend himself.

Like Atwater, Ailes was instrumental in setting the tone and pace of the 1988 campaign. Ailes labored more behind the scenes, Atwater out in front. They both were exceptionally good at what they did, and neither was accustomed to mediocrity in their work, nor did they enjoy taking orders from others.

Atwater and Ailes worked in tandem, yet because of their opposing styles, their dual effort was not always complementary. The young, uncontainable Atwater, driven by gut instinct, and the older, seasoned Ailes, who methodically made his decisions based upon years of experience with men of preeminence, were different and yet alike in one way: they both savored their power.

Purely by coincidence, while cleaning out my desk at campaign headquarters that first week in January, I came across a Xeroxed copy of a book by Roger Ailes; the title was *You Are the Message: Secrets of the Master Communicator*. A month later, when I met Ailes in the hallway with a cup of coffee in his hand, waiting for the elevator, I introduced myself and told him that I had found a rough copy of his book in my desk drawer.

After I asked where I could find a hardback edition, he responded, "In the bookstore up the street," adding, "If you buy one, I will be glad to sign it for you." I did, and a week later, after chatting with me about my research work at the campaign, he wrote on the inside page of *You Are the Message*, in large, legible script: "To Anne Joslin, You are doing a great job. Best wishes, Roger Ailes." At the time, I knew very little about Ailes, and had no idea about his prestigious history working with presidents and political champions. The words on the pages of *You Are the Message* were what had caught my attention. Ailes's book intrigued me, and his theme became more and more captivating as I continued my work in the campaign: power, who has it and who does not.

In the first chapter of Ailes's book, entitled "The First Seven Seconds," Ailes points out that we, as individuals, make up our minds about someone within the first seven seconds of meeting them, and that much of one's first impression centers on the unspoken. During the first seven seconds of introduction, Ailes claims, you either lose control to your new acquaintance or take control.

With respect to the Republican candidates during the early months of the campaign, Bush was learning how to take control. For two months after the Houston debate, the polls showed Bush in front of his competitors; by the end of January, he had a twenty-point lead.

Then a turn of fate.

By mid-February, Bush fell behind by a significant margin; being Reagan's Vice President was paying few political dividends for Bush during the early winter of 1988. Reagan's programs regarding farm policy had hurt Bush in Iowa. Reminiscent of the September straw poll, the Iowa precinct caucuses on February 8—the first big challenge—reflected the Vice President's poor standing among his farming constituents. Bush finished a humiliating third place (4 percent), behind Dole (12 percent) and Robertson (6 percent). On the Democratic side, Gephardt came away from Iowa as the front-runner. The caucus, in which Bush scored nearly 20,000 fewer votes than he had in 1980, ended his significant lead in the polls, and the campaign team took it as a personal defeat.

After the loss, Atwater held a meeting for "all staff" in the only large conference room at headquarters. With his habitual optimism, he tried to put the emphasis on what lay ahead, not on what had just happened. That was difficult. It was especially hard for Rich Bond, who had directed the Iowa caucuses. Bond, with Atwater, stood front-and-center at the meeting; later, he would find himself in a diminished role. In fact, he would not resurface in a major capacity with the Bush troops until the 1992 campaign. However, Bond would always be a part of the Bush Family, and for that reason, I reflect back to how he made his entrance.

The Bond-Atwater story had actually begun in 1980. Bond, an attorney from Long Island, had led Bush's Iowa victory over Reagan, and he, not Atwater, had been crowned hero of the Bush Task Force. In 1980, Bond had moved to Ames, Iowa, and organized the statewide Bush Brigade in preparation for the caucuses. He had done a splendid job, and Bush had gone on to beat Reagan by a good margin. As his reward, Bond was made deputy chief of staff to the Vice President, reporting to Admiral Daniel Murphy, Bush's chief of staff. However, due to some internal power struggles, Bond was not happy in that job, and with the help of Jim Baker, reestablished himself as deputy to Republican National Committee chairman Richard Richards.

When Bond moved to the RNC, Atwater remained in the White House political shop. These two operatives—both obsessed with victory—became involved in an ongoing feud competing with each other for the number-one political spot, each wanting to be *the* Republican guru.

When Richards left the RNC a year later (Frank Farenkopf, Nevada State chairman, was brought in to replace him), so did Bond. In 1982, Bond crossed the Potomac River to Alexandria, Virginia, and set up the lobbying firm of Bond, Buck and Donatelli. Atwater remained in the Reagan White House. The competitors' story ends there, until 1985, when Baker, forming the 1988 Bush campaign team, pulled Bond back into the circle of influence.

During the meeting at headquarters in February 1988, I wondered what the two *really* were thinking as they stood there in front of us. Despite what Atwater said, Bond was clearly being held responsible for Iowa's loss and therefore had lost any possibility of promotion. And *because* of the loss, Atwater, "defeating" Bond, had taken the winner's position. The double-edged loss for Bond must have made his presence on stage with Atwater excruciatingly painful.

On top of the Iowa loss in January, Bush was being hounded by the press and his rivals about his involvement in the Iran-Contra Affair—the biggest scandal of the Reagan administration. In fact, since early 1987, the Reagan White House had been buried under accusations involving the U.S. sale of arms to Iran and the resulting diversion of profits to the Nicaraguan contras. Bush's critics continually brought up the possibility of the Vice President's having played a more substantive role in the matter than he admitted. At headquarters, we worried that the issue could cause a fatal blow to Bush.

Over the fall of 1987, I heard many different rumblings about the Reagan-Iran situation—both pro and con—and finally decided to learn something more about "that time," something that went beyond my memory of Oliver North on trial in the television version.

My research of current Bush campaign members, revealing many intertwining backgrounds, also exposed their interconnecting experiences in Iran-Contra. Once again, in order to comprehend the significance of present events, it was necessary to do some digging. Based on the resulting excavation, I present this version of my Iran-Contra investigation. The mundane facts become relevant when remembering that these events taking place in Reagan's 1981 White House would boomerang not only into Bush's '88 campaign, but also into his 1992 one.

The Iran-Contra ordeal actually had its roots beginning in 1979 in Nicaragua, the small, poverty-stricken Central American nation, when a band of rebels—the Sandinistas—seized control of the government, establishing ties to the Soviet Union and Cuba. At the time, Reagan was a strong opponent of communism, and in 1981, he authorized $20 million in U.S. aid to form the rebel group referred to as the contras, in hopes that they would overthrow the socialist Sandinista government in Nicaragua. Very few Washington government officials (including members of Congress) knew about the buildup.

Unexpectedly, in 1982, the press uncovered the contra story, exposing the fact that thousands of civilians had been killed by the rebel forces trying to bring down the Sandinistas. Upon learning the news, Congress voted 411–0 (The Boland Amendment) to stop all aid. Nonetheless, Reagan's covert actions continued until 1984, until the *Wall Street Journal* wrote about the continuing support of the freedom fighters. Congress, irate, then passed a tougher version of Boland, now mandating *absolutely* no aid to the contras.

However, Reagan ordered his national security advisor (from 1983 to 1985), Robert C. McFarlane, to find a way to continue U.S. support to the contras, *and* McFarlane did as he was ordered. In 1985, with Reagan's approval, McFarlane made a deal with Iran whereby Iranian terrorists would exchange U.S. hostages for U.S. weapons; the missiles were delivered, but the Iranians refused to release the hostages.

In the early weeks of the 1988 primary season, the media pushed the Iran story. They were always looking for ways to quiz the Vice President about his *real* involvement. CBS news anchor Dan Rather, who had known Bush from their days together in Houston, hit him the hardest. In a live, nationally telecast interview, Bush and Rather appeared in the most confrontational dialogue of the campaign.

As directed by Roger Ailes, Bush's campaign media team insisted the Rather interview—advertised to be a campaign promotional—be live, not taped. On January 25, 1988, in a suite at the Capitol building, Bush readied for his interview with Rather, who remained in his anchor chair in New York. Reports from some of the staff on the Hill with Bush that evening said that Ailes appeared overly belligerent and ready for a fight. Several of Bush's senior staff knew ahead of time that the CBS spot was more than a personal profile. In fact, they had been made aware that Rather was intending to put the heat on Bush in regard to his contra involvement. Almost before the introductions took place, Rather took command of the television show, and in a lengthy report, pointed a scornful finger at Bush for his participation in the affair.

Bush, surprisingly, took the offensive as well. Angrily chastising Rather for his preliminary presentation and accusing him of judging his career by "one incident," Bush compared his own situation to Rather's when he'd walked off the network because of being preempted by a U.S. Open tennis match. The interview went this way: "Rather: Mr. Vice President, these questions are designed . . . Bush: to judge a whole career; it's not fair to judge my whole career by a rehash on Iran. How would you like it if I judged your career by those seven minutes when you walked off the set in New York?" Ailes, sitting next to Bush at the interview, had extemporaneously scripted Bush's stinging response regarding the "seven minutes" on a cue card. After a few more heated exchanges, the Rather-Bush meeting ended.

The Iran issue not only disappeared after the Rather interview, it certified what earlier had been established: Bush could fight back, and he

★★★

was no wimp. Yet, despite the contra situation being a "closed" case in 1988, the Iran affair would not disappear altogether. A full four years later, in the critical moments of the 1992 campaign, to the detriment of Bush, the past circumstances surrounding the affair would cause irreparable damage to his reelection. And now, in February 1988, in spite of the brief comeback, Bush's campaign started to collapse. It was assumed that the Iowa vote had proved devastating.

With Bush's loss of momentum, Robert Dole began to flourish. Known for his toughness and sharp wit—and equipped with "a will of iron"—Dole was expected to take the New Hampshire primary. Unless some miracle occurred. And no one was expecting one.

The Granite State primary, the first true presidential contest of 1988, required everyone at the Bush headquarters to temporarily relocate to the campaign site in Nashua. Atwater wanted all of us there. And he meant *everyone*. It was now a matter of life and death.

★★★ ▬▬▬▬▬ ★★★

CHAPTER

3

ONE SHINING MOMENT

It was five hundred Englishmen,
Were treading the purple heather,
Five hundred of Lord Loudon's men,
Marching softly together.

—*Unnamed*

FEBRUARY 1988

The week before the New Hampshire primary, a steady stream of buses filled with Bush volunteers left the Woodward Building and started moving north. Rather than make the trip by bus, however, I decided to join the staff members and fly.

We traveled from National Airport by plane, then car, until we arrived at the Bush campaign headquarters, a low-lying, nondescript building, the kind often seen in a strip mall. The weather was bitter cold with fourteen inches of snow on the ground and driving winds. Everyone was bundled in his or her warmest winter parkas and snow gear.

Huddled into small conversation groups, campaign workers were scattered outside the Nashua headquarters. Once inside, I was met by a staffer who assigned me to one of the working teams. There were nine in my group; some I knew (from Washington), others I did not. Nonetheless, we all became instant comrades in battle. With my new companions, I spent the next two days preparing for a campaign rally given in Bush's honor on February 13. The event was being held in the local high school gymnasium, and it was promoted as the most visible pre-primary event in New Hampshire. More of an echo chamber than a prime rally site, the gym was in dire need of a quick transformation before Bush arrived on Saturday.

Several of the volunteer teams, totaling over two hundred, spent the next forty-eight hours decorating the massive, gray, concrete cavity, turning two adjacent basketball courts into a political art gallery. Scores of posters and banners were designed to cover the walls: "We Love Bush," "New Hampshire is Where it Begins," "Roll over Dole," and "George and Barbara to the White House in '88" were just a sampling. Hundreds of red, white, and blue balloons hung from the ceiling in oversized sheets, waiting to be dropped onto the stage during the grand finale, just as Bush completed his address.

All went as planned, yet during the preparation for the rally, I had noticed factions evolving. It was evident that not everyone in New Hampshire was from D.C. headquarters; some supporters had turned up in Nashua for the first time. Many of the newcomers were seasoned politicos, including those from the Reagan ranks, and, surprising to me, they readily took the leadership roles, which immediately put them in conflict with "our" campaign commanders. From the first hour together, hostility, control disputes, and general disarray erupted, becoming loud and vocal. Shouting matches became part of the exercise. Feeling uncomfortable, I kept my focus on the work and remained quiet.

At my four-month point in the campaign, I was witnessing what I thought was a one-time event, an outburst caused by people's nerves being frayed. Staying in motels with eight to a room, we were not getting much sleep. We were eating burgers and fries on the run. Inside the gym, it was *cold*; we worked with our coats and gloves on. In addition, the pressure to have the site ready for the Vice President just compounded our frustrations. Overall, it was not a relaxed environment, but, to me, the squabbles seemed extremely childish. Stress between the political groups in New Hampshire—which I attributed to "extenuating circumstances"— may have been aggravated by the outside factors, but what occurred, I found out, was not so unusual between Bush and Reagan troops. It would become clearer as time went by that the turf battle between the two legions had been established years earlier.

In fact, what I observed in the gymnasium in 1988 was quite similar to a flare-up in a previous New Hampshire primary. Eight years earlier, the basis for an eruption between the Reagan and Bush squads also had been territorial. At a like rally, Reagan had grabbed the microphone from Bush, claiming that *he* "had paid for this." The Reagan campaign *had* funded the New Hampshire rally, and Reagan's comment meant to imply that only *he* would decide how the event schedule should unfold; Reagan had wanted more Republican primary candidates admitted to the affair and Bush had not. Reagan won. In February 1988, I was observing just "one more" skirmish between two groups that had been in a power struggle for almost a decade. It would not be the last.

The day after the 1988 Bush rally was Valentine's Day. No one mentioned the occasion—too busy. All day Saturday, campaign workers had been in the blizzard-like conditions in the field, combing the highways and byways, knocking on doors, covering every square mile of the Granite State, trying to convince the electorate to cast their vote for the Vice President. During the early morning hours the next day, on Sunday, we came together to enjoy the warmth of the Nashua headquarters. Cold and exhausted, a group of us gathered on the floor to read the early editions of the out-of-state newspapers. The press reported that Dole still had the upper hand.

According to the *Washington Post* tracking poll, after taking a twenty-two point drop between February 7 and February 12, Bush was predicted—with a high probability—to be the losing candidate. It was said that despite his fall recovery, Bush would be out of the race in a matter of days. Those of us on the campaign staff felt a deep sense of discouragement as we read about—"our" future, drank hot coffee and devoured donuts. Outside, the winds continued to howl.

Then, as that Sunday progressed, a strange thing happened. Along with a glorious red-purple sunset that evening, there was—without warning—a noticeable change in the political momentum. With no explanation, in a matter of two or three hours, the political energy (and there is such a phenomenon) had shifted from Dole to Bush. Before the polls and the press had told the real story, we knew that Bush would win. Down in the polls at lunchtime but surging ahead by the supper hour, Bush, we predicted, was about to make an extraordinary reappearance on the political stage!

Before we left Washington, paying no heed to the earlier doom and gloom of the media, Atwater had assured the staff that we *would* win New Hampshire. And that we did. Bush won the primary vote over Dole with a resounding ten-point lead and regained the entire twenty-two-point drop he had just recently suffered.

★★★

Because the press has a less-than-qualified way of interpreting statistics (thereby making it difficult for the reader to understand), I will simplify "the numbers" surrounding Bush's comeback. In ten days, Bush had gone from a ten-point lead (on February 7) to a twelve-point disadvantage (February 12) and back to a ten-point lead (February 16). Between Friday, February 12, when he was down twelve points, and Primary Day (Tuesday, February 16), Bush rallied an amazing twenty points. A bona fide political miracle had taken place.

On February 29, 1989, in a *Washington Post* article, Paul Taylor described the occurrence this way:

> The various tracking polls in New Hampshire all caught the last minute shift in momentum, but not its magnitude. Even now, pollsters are mystified that sentiment could have moved so sharply in one direction then doubled back just as sharply in the other . . . without the intervention of a major news event. "I've studied data from thousands of elections," said one pollster, who asked not to be identified. "This is the most unique finish I've ever seen."

If there were one time in the campaign that I could relive, it would be during the windswept, whiteout days of the New Hampshire primary. That is when we were at our best, and when I got my first real taste of what it feels like to win an election—being part of a winning team, and not just *any* political team. In early 1988, the D.C. headquarters crew was a small unit, and those of us who traveled to New Hampshire would always feel we were the Real Team. Anyone joining after that was looked upon as a latecomer. In the Bush '88 campaign, the dividing line between The Team and the Come-Lately group was the New Hampshire primary. February 16, 1988, was a defining day.

In New Hampshire, the candidate either finds his impetus or loses it. The Bush win was one of the most significant competitions in any presidential primary and, by far, the most important in the 1988 Republican election cycle. No candidate who lost New Hampshire had ever gone on to win the presidency. In addition, the victory in February 1988 was that much sweeter because *we were not supposed to win!* Since that time, I have looked for ways to explain the event and have found it almost impossible to find something that adequately describes the experience. My son wrote a paper while he was in graduate school that comes as close to describing the New Hampshire win as anything I have found. And although, as a Duke alumnus, he wrote about high-stakes basketball rivalry, the elements of success as he portrays them are the same as in political competition. A portion of "One Shining Moment":

> Shining moments... are what we, as human beings, hold as our ultimate destinations. What creates a shining moment? For sixty-four college basketball teams, March Madness provides the opportunity for one special team to enjoy not only what is called "the world's greatest sporting event," but the opportunity to find their shining moment. There are seven "rules" for creating such moments: *One:* you need a skillful coach. *Two:* adversity strikes; things never go as planned. *Three:* there is always a crunch time when panic sets in. *Four:* there is always a form of luck or fate involved. *Five:* dedication, patience, and teamwork are attributes of teams that reach their final destination. *Six:* success is followed by recognition from those who appreciate the magnitude of what the team has accomplished. And lastly, *Seven:* the best shining moments are those that are unexpected.

As the make-or-break event for Bush in 1988, the New Hampshire primary would forever be referred to as our one shining moment of the campaign. Without that win, there would have been little promise of a Bush presidency, and because of the weight of that win, there would always be a debate about who or what was responsible for the unexpected turn of events.

What occurred in snowy New Hampshire can be attributed to a combination of events and people, a mix resulting in just the right amount at just the right time. Hundreds of campaign workers (volunteers who took the all-night bus ride from D.C. to Nashua) had placed "Vote Bush" signs across the state the weekend before the election. The governor of New Hampshire, John Sununu, showed an inordinate amount of leadership and loyalty as he fought for Bush; for that reason, he would go on to become Bush's chief of staff. The senior campaign staff, headed by Atwater and the two Massachusetts brother-in-law politicals, Andrew Card and Ron Kaufman (all three destined for the Bush administration), did a spectacular job with strategy. And, of course, the infamous, last minute "straddle" advertisement should not be overlooked. The weekend before the election, Roger Ailes televised an ad presenting Dole as a candidate who refused to take a firm stand on the national tax issue, implying that he favored a tax increase. Bush had not wanted the advertisement to go forward, but he was persuaded by his staff to run it for seventy-two hours.

Everyone, in his or her own way, had "seized the day," but there was no mistaking the fact that Bush himself had been the foremost reason for the triumph. He had done an excellent job in reaching out to the people in the state, talking to them in their own backyards, whether that meant a lumberyard or a truck stop. This was not his usual mode of campaigning, but it *was* Atwater's style. And too, Bush's down-home appearance at the informal press conference Saturday night (after the rally) was breezy and informative. He had connected with his audience.

Back in Washington, after the New Hampshire primary, I read several articles attributing Bush's win to his participatory management style. Having let the captains of his campaign call their own shots, Bush had appeared confident in their judgment and had followed along with their strategy and tactical decisions. On February 21, 1988, Chicago newswoman Sallie Gains addressed the issue of Bush's delegation of authority this way: "George Bush's campaign is successful because he has learned the simplest rule of management: how to delegate authority." Gains quoted Eugene Jennings, a professor of leadership and management at Michigan State University's graduate school, as saying: "Bush knows what responsibilities to keep and what to delegate, and he doesn't take back that which he delegates. Bush holds on to very few things—the overall strategy—but all the other stuff he delegates, and he doesn't second guess."

This character attribute of Bush—the willingness to delegate— seemed to give him his strength as a leader in the 1980s and as a candidate in 1988. I believe this trait, although advantageous at certain times, would turn out to be one of the key reasons for Bush's ultimate downfall. Unfortunately, those to whom Bush gave his confidence did not always merit—nor return—the trust. I believe this quality that propelled Bush toward success in February 1988 would later prove to be his greatest weakness as President.

After the New Hampshire primary, when Bush won 38 percent of the vote, the campaign staff, with fingers crossed, were hoping he would not lose his edge before the Super Tuesday primaries scheduled for March 8.

With twenty southern states voting, there would be enough delegate votes at large for Bush to lock up the Republican nomination. Predicting Bush to sweep the South, the polls had us feeling sanguine, but Atwater made sure we did not become overly confident, calculating that the road ahead was still a rough one. In his coarse voice, he threatened at staff gatherings: "If you don't like being in the white water, then you should get out!" Our tactical visionary relished the rough times, with all its rumble and tumble, and he wanted a staff around him who enjoyed the ride just as much. I did not notice anyone leaving.

Of the three trailing Republican contenders—Dole, Kemp, and Robertson—it was Dole whom we still had our eye on, and it was predicted that, in time, with his intemperate demeanor, Dole would be his own worst enemy. We waited and watched.

In '88, Dole presented himself as the People's Choice. The Kansas senator, an Army veteran of World War II who had been wounded in Italy, had, in 1945, returned home from the battle and gone on to receive a law degree from Washburn University of Topeka. Years later, after having taken on a political career, Dole, in 1976, became the vice presidential running mate to Gerald Ford. Jimmy Carter, winning over Reagan in the primaries, defeated Ford and Dole.

As described by the media, Dole was an amalgam of conservative and partisan, moderate and pragmatic, sarcastic and hotheaded. He had a narrow circle of friends. Of no particular philosophical leaning and without any group to which he was overtly loyal, Bob Dole liked being his own-man, and his disdain for Bush was well known. Bush, the Aristocrat, had been handed everything on a silver platter, while he, the Populist, had made it the hard way.

Dole's greatest advocate and asset during the '88 run was his wife, Elizabeth Hanford Dole (whom we called Liddy). Married in 1975, the Doles were pictured as Washington's ultimate power couple. Identified for her polished charm, Mrs. Dole was a former Democrat now turned Republican. Recognized in Washington circles as a strong-minded politico in her own right, Elizabeth Dole had served on the Cabinets of several previous presidents, and had given up her five-year tenure as Reagan's secretary of Transportation to take on the role of her husband's '88 political strategist. From Salisbury, North Carolina, she knew the southern ways, and she aptly prepared her husband for the Super Tuesday clash.

Opposite to his wife's charming manner was Senator Dole's mean streak. His temper would often flare when his back was against the wall, a tendency that had given rise to his reputation for having a "dark side." Immediately after the New Hampshire primary, I saw for myself an example of this darker Dole. Becoming angry about his primary defeat (which was understandable, since he most assuredly had seen himself as victor of that contest), the Senate minority leader made a bad situation even worse.

In an interview with NBC's Tom Brokaw on national television the night after the primary, Dole suddenly exposed his more volatile side. While expressing his displeasure over the New Hampshire loss, Dole had been interrupted by Brokaw, who asked him if he had anything to say to Bush. Dole lashed back, "Yea, tell him to stop lying about my record." With that, while still on the air, Dole kicked a New Hampshire voter's dog . . . in clear view of everyone there as well as the television cameras. Those of us gathered back in D.C., meeting in Pinkerton's office for our 7:30 a.m. briefing, ran and reran the clip of Dole "attacking" the dog. Jim Pinkerton just smiled as he announced, "We got him!"

In terms of political reality, the 1988 fight between Dole and Bush was over in New Hampshire, yet Dole, with Richard Wirthlin, Reagan's pollster, and Bill Brock, his campaign manager, continued to denounce Bush, hoping to restore his own credibility. One such attempt during the months to come was a Dole television commercial showing "someone" (not recognizable) trudging through the snow, but leaving no footprints behind; it was meant to imply that Bush had been an invisible Vice President. Dole dismissed Bush's advantage as being a mere reflection of Reagan's popularity, saying, "I can beat George Bush, but not Ronald Reagan." The implication that Bush was in Reagan's shadow, on the President's coattails, would be a controversial topic, not only during the 1988 campaign, but also during the four years of the Bush administration.

It did not help matters to have Candidate/Vice President Bush (with his followers) and Outgoing President Reagan (and his loyalists)— constantly in opposition with one another. Despite an upcoming string of victories for Bush, some larger issues were still being defined. It seemed that Reagan's shadow was longer than just his coattails.

★★★ ══════ ★★★
CHAPTER

4

SHOTGUN MARRIAGE

In general, the presidential image is the product of craft, deception, legerdemain, and the calculated manipulation of words and pictures.

—Forrest McDonald

MARCH–MAY 1988

In spite of his New Hampshire win, in the newspapers it was said that Bush was running a themeless campaign.

William Murchison, associate editor of the Dallas Morning News, questioned, "What are the things he wants to do for America? Mr. Bush has lately given few hints. Bush is for President Reagan's programs—no doubt of that, but in ten months Mr. Reagan will be gone. We need a Bush program. What will it be?" In his article, Murchison alluded to the fact that most citizens wanted an extension of the Reagan presidency, yet at the same time, they wanted a distinct Bush program.

It was a Catch-22.

For the most part, the populace equated conservatism with Reaganism because that was the talk Reagan talked, but it was a false conclusion when surveying the policy direction of Reagan's administration. Reagan epitomized the ideological conservative values in his speeches; however, he willingly consented to the whims of his principal counselors to carry out a contradictory political agenda. Some of these advisors were more seasoned than others, and some had more integrity than others, but most were diametrically opposed to Reagan's views.

This left Reagan (and his communications crew) in the position of maintaining his popularity through illusion. In politics, where perception

★★★

is truth, Reagan often won out. But in reality, Reagan's Conservative Presidency was really based on a Moderate Plan. The fact often overlooked is that the Reagan Plan—often credited with being traditional—was not executed in accordance with right-wing principles.

The Reagan program—before he took office—was designed by the old-line conservative guard from California. All that changed once Reagan became president and Baker was chosen chief of staff. Jim Baker was the power broker. Not Reagan. Yet, the potency of Reagan lay in his promises, not his accomplishments. For eight years he was packaged as the definitive conservative.

Central to this book is the theory that the conservatives never did have control in the Reagan White House. Although Reagan and his California elite promoted that agenda—cut government programs, decrease taxes, and fight communism—Reagan's administration actually had gone in the opposite direction. The communist cause, although not embraced, was tolerated, taxes were increased, the federal agenda grew exponentially, and the pro-choice case *Roe v. Wade* was never overturned. Reagan supposedly loathed these moderate measures, yet they flourished during his presidency.

One of Reagan's earliest reversals occurred when Baker, with his closest aide, Richard Darman, presented to the President a plan that increased taxes by almost $1 billion. Moreover, because Reagan saw national defense as a security issue, not a government program, the Pentagon expense account expanded mightily for eight years. And the national deficit, likewise, grew.

In 1988, if Bush—on his own and outside the Reagan ranks—stood by the Reagan agenda as it was being managed (with Baker's influence), he would be viewed as a supporter of the moderate Republicans and a traitor to the conservative cause—the Reagan Old Line. Yet, if he stood behind the conservative agenda—doing what Reagan said he would do, yet never did—Bush would be seen as a believer of the "cause," advocating programs in keeping with the Reagan rhetoric; however, the irony of the situation was that, if Bush followed the perceived ideological Reaganism (conservative), it made him appear weak, not his own man. On the other hand, not following the Reagan philosophy made Bush appear disloyal, not only to the President, but also to all conservatives and most of America.

It should be noted that Baker, responsible for implementing the Reagan moderate plan, was seldom referred to as a defector. Yet Bush, supporting the same policies, was referred to as a turncoat. The press presented him as not owning his own set of ideas and of obsequious loyalty to Reagan. No matter what the Vice President proposed, it was hopeless for him to try to voice a clear mandate. His connection to the President—his mere proximity to Ronald Reagan—made it impossible for Bush to carve out a well-received agenda.

Despite his flaws, Reagan was the symbolic conservative, whose vision of a brighter America had captured the imagination of the country. The Teflon President held the country under his spell in a way Bush never could. Yet, unlike so many who surrounded him, Reagan himself was not politically motivated. He had a laissez-faire attitude toward life and a hands-off policy toward the agenda developed by those under his authority. While in the White House, Reagan seldom questioned or challenged the content of material brought to him for approval. In fact, there was a remoteness associated with the President, and his understanding about what was going on in the real world was uncertain. Nevertheless, news accounts seldom made note of Reagan's inability to distinguish fact from fiction; instead, they made light of the situation by portraying "the slips" to be some kind of personal idiosyncrasy.

On his watch, Reagan saw his share of political turmoil, particularly during his second term, including the Iran-Contra Affair, the Republican loss of the Senate (now run by the Democrats), and the spiraling federal debt. The deficit had grown from $1 trillion to nearly $4 trillion in less than eight years! Through it all, Reagan seemed unaffected, responding almost as if the occurrences never happened. Always calm and cheerful, he masked—or never understood—the serious nature of the problems facing the country, and he never shared the truth with its citizens. The Bush team had to face these facts without seeming to betray Reagan.

For decades, Reagan had expressed his strong beliefs about patriotism, communism, and business, and as the leading conservative voice of the Republican Party, along with the help of many influential and wealthy Republican conservatives, he was elected governor of California in 1966. With his Midwest, small-town American values, Reagan had become an adamant anti-communist advocate, standing behind Joseph McCarthy in his efforts to expose communists in

★★★

the Hollywood infrastructure. Contrarily, Reagan was an anti government man; he had seen Washington take what he described as an unfair portion of his paycheck. He also had been a strong supporter of a woman's right to choose, signing into California law in 1967 legislation legalizing abortion.

These conflicting directions begged the question, "Just what did Reagan stand for?" If Reagan believed in Republican conservatism so strongly, why—when he became President—did he betray his beliefs by installing a government that went against his core values? Was this just politics as usual: trying to please everyone at the same time and ending up with no truths of his own? Through the power of illusion only, Americans kept believing what Reagan said, and for that reason the President remained popular. Reagan's charisma carried him through politically. Significant to keeping this false image of Reagan alive was the finely tuned White House communications and public relations team. These handlers, when joined with a complacent press corps, enabled the President to keep his reputation intact. Hollywood came to D.C.

Reagan, accustomed to West Coast living, lived in the White House in quiet seclusion, away from the frenzy of Washington's political core. His political appointees had been given free rein to do as they pleased. All except his Vice President. Bush had no such freedom. Reagan kept Bush on a tight leash, seldom allowing him to make a move without his authority. The roots of the tepid Reagan-Bush relationship went back to the time when Bush ran against Reagan in the 1980 presidential primaries.

After winning the 1980 nomination, Reagan had surprisingly chosen Bush as his vice presidential running mate. It had not been a personal choice, but a last-minute effort to fill an unexpected void. Reagan placed Bush on the ticket without really knowing him, and what Reagan did know about him had not impressed him.

As Reagan's 1980 chief challenger, Bush, to the ire of the Reaganites, had continued to campaign even when it was obvious he would not carry the nomination (he lost twenty-nine out of thirty-three primaries). At the Republican convention in Detroit in 1980, Reagan was the shoe-in nominee; however, his running mate had not been decided. At the top of the list was former President Gerald Ford; Henry Kissinger, former secretary of State, was on the convention scene to negotiate a deal for America's 38th president.

The Reagan-Ford ticket was promoted as the "Dream Team." Chairman of the Republican National Committee at the time, Bill Brock, was in favor of the Reagan-Ford alliance and threw his weight in that direction. Furthermore, a nationwide survey taken by Richard Wirthlin had found Ford to be the strongest of the running mates in contention. Bush was number two on the list, and Jack Kemp and Paul Laxalt took the third and fourth positions. Ford, whose political views closely resembled those of Bush, represented the more moderate Eastern wing of the Republican Party. Kemp, more conservative in philosophy and closer to Reagan, was considered by some to be the most conservative Republican since Barry Goldwater.

On the third day of the Detroit convention, Ford made two mistakes. The first was going on television, and the second was telling Walter Cronkite, in a live interview, his "conditions" should he be chosen. In Ford's mind, the powers of the presidential office would be evenly divided, a dual-presidency. While publicly announcing this "setup," Ford had prematurely alluded to the fact that he was the one who was going to get the nod for vice president. While there had been in-depth talks between the two camps about what amounted to a possible Reagan-Ford co-presidency, within hours of Ford's television disclosure, Reagan eliminated Ford.

At the eleventh hour, and with no one else waiting in the wings, the Reagan advisors suggested George Bush simply because they thought that he would be best at rallying voters.

After giving a Reagan endorsement speech on the convention floor, and not expecting to have any further role in the '80 campaign, Bush went back to his hotel room, where he received a phone call. His campaign manager, Jim Baker, answered and was told that the Reagan-Ford idea was collapsing. There followed a second phone call, this time from a member of the Secret Service. Then a third call, again from the Secret Service; this time Bush answered. Later, while recounting that night at the convention, Bush, with the help of Victor Gold, wrote an article entitled "Bush Becomes Running Mate of Ronald Reagan." Taken from the Houston Chronicle on Tuesday, December 1, 1987—months before I had joined the campaign, but published a year later in the Campaign News Clips—was Bush's account of that night:

The voice couldn't be mistaken, though the tone was different from the one I remembered from our pre-convention primary debates. "Hello, George, this is Ron Reagan." There was a pause. "I'd like to go over to the convention and announce that you're my choice for vice president . . . if that's alright with you." The truth is that the flow of events had reversed so quickly that I wasn't completely focused on what was taking place. But I was focused enough to know the answer to Reagan's question: "I'd be honored, governor." Then there was a momentary pause on the other end of the line. Then: "George, is there anything at all . . . about the platform or anything else . . . anything that might make you uncomfortable down the road?". . . I told him that I had no serious problem with either the platform or his position on any of the issues, that I was sure we could work together, and that the important thing was that he win the election in November. "Fine," he said. "I'll head over to the convention, then we'll get together in the morning." I thanked him, then slowly put the receiver back into its cradle. Barbara and the kids rushed across the room and we exchanged hugs. Jim Baker and Dean Burch shook my hand. Someone turned up the TV set. "Not Ford . . ." the network reporter was shouting from the convention floor. "It's Bush."

The 1980 Reagan-Bush ticket had been described as a "shotgun marriage," consummated for political reasons only. Many on Reagan's staff had balked at the addition of Bush, not only because he had been their campaign foe, but because Bush was not trusted to hold the so-called conservative line. Reagan's choice was looked upon as a betrayal to the cause. Reagan supporters viewed their President as more than a person in political office; for them, Reagan embodied the foundation upon which they fought. Bush did not. Accordingly, the Bush selection made Reagan's people angry. There were rumors of a revolt on the Detroit convention floor: "Down with Bush!" In fact, the rebellion that broke out within the Republican ranks in 1980 in Detroit had continued in presidential politics over the next twelve years.

Bush was placed on the '80 ticket, but to those on the Reagan team, he would always be the opponent. He was the one who had lashed out at Reagan's "voodoo" economics, faulting the President for his ideas regarding the cutting of the federal deficit, slashing taxes and eliminating government programs while increasing military spending. Bush became an outsider inside the Reagan White House. And despite being the best friend of Jim Baker—the mastermind of the Reagan administration—Bush never was allowed on the Power Pyramid. As Vice President, he played a minor role in the Reagan policies and programs devised and schemed by Baker.

This long-running feud between Reaganites and Bushites made working in the 1988 Bush campaign an uphill climb, and the cool relationship between the Hollywood movie star and the New England–bred politician had only escalated with the assistance of Nancy Reagan. I believe that, because President Reagan was so uninterested in and unaffected by White House matters, Mrs. Reagan had more influence over his decisions than was healthy for the presidency or for the country. Nancy Reagan's interests usually lay in promoting Nancy Reagan, and she was not well-versed in the philosophy of following in your husband's silhouette. At great lengths, Anne Frances Robbins had redefined herself and her world to be one in which she felt in control and comfortable.

From the day they married, Mr. and Mrs. Reagan focused on their public image: what they looked like to their observers. Beginning in 1976, when the group of influential California entrepreneurs (Holmes Tuttle and the "Kitchen Cabinet") had put up the financial base for Governor Reagan to run for president, the Reagans had been a political team. Having set aside their souls, they found their identity on stage, in their acquired power, whether that was in Hollywood or in Washington, not believing that times of yore had anything to do with who they were in the present.

There is simply no way to grasp political events during the Bush Years without full knowledge of events during the Reagan Years, and Nancy Reagan, I have learned, put her imprint on the Reagan White House as much as any presidential aide or program. "Mommy," as President Reagan often called his wife, had made sure the "right" people were always by her husband's side. From the beginning of Ronnie's political career, Nancy had the deciding vote, and as such, endorsed Reagan's California benefactors whose mission it was to "sell the president." With Mrs. Reagan's approval, Mr. Reagan had been transformed from actor to governor to presidential candidate. And from candidate to President. All with Nancy's approval.

Given that Mrs. Reagan had not encouraged a congenial relationship between her husband and the Bushes, it made sense that, in the presidential campaign of 1988, Nancy Reagan supported another candidate: Paul Laxalt (R-NV), Reagan's close friend and ally in the Senate. She encouraged her husband to follow her lead. Mrs. Reagan's attitude had not worked in favor of the Bushes in the past, and it certainly did not heighten Bush's status in the spring of 1988.

At the time, I had assumed that the sitting president would (should) endorse the man who was in his eighth year serving as his vice president. Today, more than a decade later, I choose to believe that Reagan was a man of good intentions and, therefore, not fully aware of the negative impact he had on Bush's 1988 presidential campaign. Yet, the lack of affirmation on his part was, and remains, unsettling.

In retrospect, Reagan's blasé nature may have been attributed to a variety of causes, including the onset of poor health (Alzheimer's was later diagnosed) or, as mentioned, his personal dislike or even envy of Bush, or it may have been that Reagan did not want to be upstaged by his "second man." Still, I was perplexed as to how Reagan could get by without endorsing his Vice President. As the campaign unfolded, his aloofness became glaringly obvious, and it was clear to me that Reagan never emotionally passed on the baton to Bush.

On the other hand, Bush had grown up in a family in which loyalty was not only a virtue, but a matter of social etiquette; following this teaching, the Vice President had learned how to place his own ambitions second to the needs of the person he served. In 1987 and 1988, when Reagan appeared non-supportive of his candidacy, Bush never hinted at an identity dilemma or disappointment. I assume Bush responded to Reagan in this manner because he believed that loyalty to the office of the president—more important than the person—was one of highest priority and that it warranted self-sacrifice.

In my military family, I had been taught to obey the commander's orders for no other reason than because the orders came from the commander. Today, I wonder about the judiciousness regarding the laws of loyalty. In the late '80s, although I never questioned the "do as told" mentality, I wished that Bush had not been quite so restrained. I felt the cool and detached Reagan team had avoided him too long and was convinced that the Reagan staff was fully aware of the Bush campaign's submissive role. Enjoying their superiority, they continued to toy with us for as long as possible. By springtime, the Bush team said, "Enough is enough." Everyone was fuming and became disheartened over the fact that Reagan was not forthcoming with an endorsement. We now believed that being "the heir to the Reagan estate" was nothing more than a pretense. The campaign had proceeded throughout the fall and winter months without the approval of the White House, and in May, we were still wondering when the official backing would come.

Finally, there were rumors that the moment we had been waiting for was about to arrive. First, we were told Reagan's "approval" would take place at a cocktail party on Capitol Hill, then it changed to an afternoon affair in the Rose Garden at the White House, and before long, we were told Reagan would make his announcement at a dinner at the headquarters of the National Republican Senatorial Committee. All these plans were canceled due to what the White House unofficially said were scheduling problems.

By now, Dole's campaign had collapsed, and Bush's was likened to Patton racing across Europe. The Vice President had swept through the Super Tuesday elections on March 8, leaving nothing in his wake but victories. Super Tuesday, originally the brainchild of the southern Democrats, was, in 1988, the first of its kind. Starting in 1985, Atwater had mapped out a southern strategy for Bush—as he had for Reagan in 1984—forming a power base and grooming Bush for a whopping victory. What was planned came to be. Winning more than 57 percent of the total votes cast, Bush lost only Washington State, and the percentage of voters describing him as "strong and forceful" rose substantially. Never before had so many states simultaneously held a presidential primary contest. It was the closest this country had ever come to having a national primary. And afterward, Bush had glided to what seemed like a safe landing spot on the campaign trail.

Although it was important, Super Tuesday did not hold the same significance for Democrats as it did for Republicans. Massachusetts Governor Michael Dukakis appeared to be the victor, but despite his wins, it was the Reverend Jesse Jackson, the charismatic black leader of the Rainbow Coalition, who gained momentum in the Party. He and his band of followers, which included a group of diverse, disillusioned Americans—environmentalists, feminists, homosexuals and civil rights advocates—thrust Dukakis into a tailspin.

With the Pennsylvania primary vote on April 26, Bush received over 1,139 convention delegate votes and wrapped up the Republican nomination earlier than any non-incumbent in more than forty years. Two weeks later, in celebration of the victory, staff at campaign headquarters were invited to an Over the Top rally in the Constitution Ballroom at the Grand Hyatt Hotel in downtown D.C. We were told that Reagan was *now* going to endorse Bush. Never planning an event of their own, the White House waited until our victory party to make an appearance.

On May 3, at the Hyatt, campaign staff filled the hotel's largest ballroom. Police security was tight, and the Secret Service agents traveling with the President were stationed in every corner of the room. In crammed quarters, we stood shoulder to shoulder, while Reagan was escorted onto the stage to "say a few words." From behind the podium, his comments came across as cold and impersonal. He was barely audible from where I stood, only feet away.

The President did not direct a single statement to the many political accomplishments of Bush, who happened to have the most impressive résumé of any presidential nominee in history. In addition to being Vice President, Bush had twice served as a member of the House of Representatives; he had been United States ambassador to the United Nations, chairman of the Republican National Committee, chief of the U.S. Liaison Office in the People's Republic of China, and director of the Central Intelligence Agency. During the Reagan administration, he had worked on the Anti-Terrorism Program, the Task Force on Regulatory Relief, and the National Narcotics Board Interdiction System.

Ten days after the rally, on May 13, Reagan again attempted to endorse the Vice President, this time at a banquet given in Bush's honor. Once again, there was a lot lacking, and, so, a third effort was made to send a positive message. On the day following the third try, May 14, 1988, I read an editorial titled "The Presidential Nod," published in the Washington Post, describing Reagan's comments from the night before. It seemed the writer and I agreed on the President's tone:

> President Reagan finally made it public Wednesday night at George Bush's big fund-raiser: he endorsed Mr. Bush for president. The president's endorsement was terse, even curt; he did not utter a single sentence praising the vice president's accomplishments and skills. The faintness of his embrace instantly became more of a political item than the embrace itself, so much so that the president was moved to issue a second endorsement, describing himself as "enthusiastic" and "fully committed," the next day.

Approval from Reagan, by now, had lost its meaning. For Bush, it could be compared to being an Olympian gold medal winner and having the presenter discredit the achievement before congratulating you. To many of us, Reagan's support—lukewarm, at best—was both disappointing and maddening; Bush, however, appeared grateful for whatever came from the White House and remained unruffled by the snub. Those of us on the front lines who felt awkward and embarrassed about the White House rebuff decided to try to follow the Vice President's lead and remain silent. From then on, inside headquarters, little mention was made regarding our frustrations.

Nonetheless, the strained Reagan-Bush relationship would bring further tension inside the campaign, resulting in several tussles between Reagan (and his White House staff) and Bush (and his campaign team). These struggles, which ran long and deep, would continue to sever the two camps.

On May 16, 1988, Washington Times writer Donald Lambro wrote a commentary entitled "Bush Ignoring Conservatives in Staffing Campaign Cadre." In it, Lambro gave his opinion about why there was a great divide between the President and the Vice President:

> Part of the problem is that the Bush campaign is dominated by non-philosophical campaign professionals who have not sought to draw the party's rank-and-file conservative activists directly into the Bush operation, said a number of conservative officials. Said a former top Reagan campaign official, "There's a real resentment, as I talk to people around the country, that there is not a policy of inclusion [in the Bush campaign]. To these people it's the '80 [primary] race all over again and their attitude is 'we've been shut out in the cold for eight years and we are going to do it our way this time."
>
> "If you were asked to search for old line Reaganites in the Bush campaign organization, outside of (campaign manager Lee) Atwater, you wouldn't find any," said GOP political consultant David Keene, who was a campaign advisor to Senate GOP leader Robert Dole. "He has wrapped himself in Reagan, but it's the flag and not the substance."

Assuming Lambro's observations correct—that "conservative activists" were not prominent in the Bush camp—I disagree with his conclusion as to why. I theorize that the reason for the conservative "block out" was due to the management of Jim Baker.

Bush's most senior advisor, who served as chairman of the Bush campaign while remaining the most powerful operative in the Reagan presidency, was James Baker. He was in a win-win situation. That may have been due—in part—to the fact that he was not a conservative, not a moderate, not a liberal. Baker was a political chameleon; he chose whatever political persuasion was most advantageous to him at the moment. And since he rarely demonstrated any particular loyalty to one cause or contingency, he had been able to woo individuals throughout the entire Republican political spectrum. And as such, he had amassed more power than any other Party member.

Baker, "the outsider," was more of an "insider" in the Reagan administration than any Old Line Reaganite. If a conservative had been closed out of the Bush '88 campaign, it was because Baker wanted it that way. Chances were those individuals who were excluded in 1988 were the same individuals excluded by Baker eight years prior, at the beginning of the Reagan presidency. Baker unilaterally ruled the Washington Power Pyramid.

During the spring months, it was reported that the Bush campaign would have to cut its spending budget to less than $1 million. Presidential candidates were allowed to spend $23.3 million throughout the primary season, until such time as they were officially nominated at their respective convention. Because the Democratic convention was scheduled one month sooner than the Republican, the Democratic nominee would receive the allotted federal campaign funds (totaling $46 million) a month earlier, giving them the advantage.

By April, Dukakis had overcome Jackson's front-runner status, and by mid-May, he was actually leading Bush by 48 to 39 percent. Even though Dukakis did not yet have the 2,082 delegate votes he needed to win his Party's favor, he was doing well, and Bush was back in a slump. Bush had spent $20 million of the specified federal funds, compared to $18 million spent by Dukakis, leaving the Bush moneybag almost empty. It would remain that way until mid-August. The wait for the Republican convention seemed endless.

In March '88, I had been told by the campaign staff that I would start receiving a paycheck by June; along with the majority of staff, I was still a volunteer. However, the chance that I would become a paid member looked slim. Even senior campaign members were working without paychecks. Those of us at the lower levels were seldom told what was going on, but we knew that the campaign's sense of direction was unclear. Bush had secured the nomination, but we were left short on finances and with too much time on our hands. This situation bred dissatisfaction and uncertainty. The more ambiguity we experienced, the more the gossip inside the campaign headquarters spread. In a presidential campaign, where rumors inside the camp fly easily, it is hard to know what is true, yet we did know that what the press was reporting in regard to the staff being cut in half since Super Tuesday was not true. Still, it was evident that some kind of shift in the upper ranks was going on.

A shake-up in the top command came with the forced resignation of Bush's communications director, Peter Teeley. An English expatriate, known in press circles as the Sultan of Spin, Teeley had been the chief spokesman for Bush in three previous national campaigns. He also had been tapped by Baker to be a member of the G-6 in 1984, working on the Bush '88 campaign. Teeley had been recruited as press secretary by Bush's son George W. in the fall of 1987, to fill the spot vacated by Marlin Fitzwater (press secretary to Reagan).

Now, in the spring of 1988, Teeley was fired. As communications director for the campaign, Teeley had been directly responsible for dealing with the press and for overseeing how the Vice President communicated his political messages to the public. However, Teeley said that he was not being allowed to do his job. In the *Washington Post,* he was quoted as saying he "had been deliberately excluded from critical decisions about Bush speeches and strategy, making it impossible to perform his job."

There had been weeks of conflict leading up to the Teeley dismissal. It seems arguments had flared between Teeley and some of the other senior Bush advisors, most notably Craig Fuller, Bush's chief of staff. These disagreements had centered on whether Teeley should be invited to attend senior staff meetings and whether he should be privy to campaign strategy. Teeley argued that for him to write speeches, he needed full access to Bush and full knowledge of what was happening in the Vice President's office. With Fuller as gatekeeper, he had not even been able to get advance copies of Bush's speeches.

Teeley felt that Bush needed to be more aggressive in his campaign style, and had recommended that instead of targeting just local news

★★★

stations, Bush use national networks to get out his message, hoping that this strategy might help Bush in his tumbling public opinion polls. While trying to fight for a more vocal candidate and, at the same time, salvage Bush from being enmeshed in Reagan's domestic problems, Teeley had let the White House know they were creating troubles for Bush, and that the present administration was limiting Bush's ability to define his differences with Reagan. On his own, Teeley had taken a stance regarding Bush versus Reagan. And for *supporting* Bush, the communication director's situation grew worse, until finally he was cut out of the senior loop and the campaign.

Ironically, it was Teeley's loyalty to Bush that had compromised his political position. Fuller charged just the opposite, saying that Teeley had not been loyal to Bush. He blamed him for submitting anonymous statements about Bush to the press and called him "combative" in his approach. It was clear that Fuller wanted Teeley dismissed, and although there was nothing to substantiate Fuller's charges, Teeley was fired.

Within twenty-four hours, it was announced that a new communications advisor would begin work immediately. Jim Baker appointed Jim Lake, a Reagan Man to the position. Lake had worked in Reagan's California state lobbying office in Washington, D.C., when Reagan was governor, and he had served as press secretary to Reagan in his 1976, 1980 and 1984 campaigns.

I mention the Teeley episode for two reasons. First, because it serves as an example of a much-used, unfair method for getting rid of an "undesirable" team member by placing blame on that person and accusing him or her of being disloyal without any evidence. Most often the accused was the most loyal. The second reason is to point out the amount of clout Fuller possessed at the time. Fuller had first acquired his leverage when appointed as chief of staff to Bush by Baker in 1985. During the first G-6 meeting called by Baker in 1984 (with the intent to jump-start the Bush 1988 campaign), Atwater had been tapped as manager, and Fuller had been designated as Bush's new chief of staff, replacing retired Admiral Dan Murphy.

As of April 1, 1985, Fuller, at thirty-something, became not only the chief advisor to Vice President Bush and a key aide to campaign chairman Baker, he also became the liaison between Baker, Bush and Reagan's chief of staff, Donald Regan. This allowed him untold right of entry into the

Oval Office and immediate access to Baker. With direct lines to Bush, Baker and Regan, Fuller held more than a considerable amount of power in the Reagan White House as well as the Bush campaign. He had virtually unlimited authority.

Craig Fuller's ascent to the top of the Power Pyramid had been rapid. Having come to Washington from California with Michael Deaver, he had been a Reagan White House aide to Edwin Meese before being tapped by Baker to become the Cabinet secretary. Fuller had first worked down in the basement of the White House in an office next to Richard Darman, where they were both paper pushers: Darman the experienced one, Fuller the novice.

In 1984, Fuller accepted the assignment to be Bush's chief of staff, with the provision (demand) that he would report directly to Baker. Atwater also had stipulated immediate access to Baker. There would be no intermediary for either Fuller or Atwater. Although not under Baker's direct command (neither Fuller nor Atwater worked at the department of the Treasury, where Baker was secretary from 1985 to 1988), these two young men turned to Baker for instructions. During Reagan's last term and while the Bush campaign was gaining ground, Fuller had "laid down the law" in the Office of the Vice President (OVP).

When I was dealing with the OVP—while handling the Policy Issue Groups in the winter of 1988—I had found it to be an ordeal. The one reliable person I met was Charlie Greenleaf, Bush's deputy chief of staff, and often I coordinated my efforts with Jean Balestrieri, Greenleaf's secretary. Nevertheless, getting Vice President Bush's signature on a letter, which I had to finesse on more than a few occasions, had proved to be one hassle after another. And for no apparent reason. Several times, I walked over to OVP and camped out in the hallway until I received the completed document. This lack of accessibility to Bush's vice presidential office and to Bush himself was indicative of Fuller's administrative style and foreshadowed the way he, at Baker's instruction, would handle things regarding Bush in the future. No access to the Vice President.

In late March, it had been announced that Secretary Baker would leave Reagan's Cabinet to become the official chairman of the Bush campaign, but not until late summer. (This had been planned much earlier, in the December 1984 G-6 meeting.) Some were hoping Baker would come sooner, speculating that he could "turn things around."

★★★

But that did not happen. It seems, the time was not right for the secretary of the Treasury.

Little happened while we all waited for May to turn to August and the Republican convention. Bush continued to fade in popularity, and Dukakis continued to gain in the polls. During these months, the Democrats were still engaged in their primary season, which kept them on the front page of the newspapers and, therefore, very much in the public spotlight. Jackson and Gore remained in the race behind Dukakis, while all the other Democrats fell by the wayside. With a greater degree of certainty now, our research team predicted that Dukakis would be the nominee.

At campaign headquarters, we tried to keep up our spirits and maintain our camaraderie by engaging in outside-the-office social activities. Taking advantage of the wide-open fields just to the south of the White House, we organized softball teams, and games were played each week on the field at the Ellipse. And at headquarters, we looked for ways to stay engaged.

I became involved in several campaign projects. The first of these endeavors was working with the newly formed Platform Committee that was preparing for the August convention. Organizing the Policy Issues Log and managing the Issue Groups had provided me with a good background for this newly formed committee. I also managed the interns assigned to the research division over the summer and remained determined to harness the young flock in as pleasant a manner as possible, but that was not always easy. Having a slew of eighteen and nineteen year-olds on the premises, running up and down the halls with raised voices and eating cheese-and-sausage pizza from Dominoes, was a distraction, to say the least.

My third and last assignment came by way of being appointed to the opposition group doing research on Dukakis (who was by now the shoe-in nominee). It was this assignment that proved to be the most challenging. Initially, I looked at the project more as a way to fill time rather than to contribute, and considered it nothing more than busy work. Unknowingly, it would lead me to write a paper on a subject that turned out to be one of the major issues in the 1988 presidential campaign: Boston Harbor.

★★★ ════════ ★★★
CHAPTER

5

$6 BILLION CLEAN-UP

If conflicts arise between the individual and the hierarchy, we regard these very conflicts as touchstone for the stature of a personality.

—Herman Hesse

JUNE–JULY 1988

Seven of us at Bush headquarters were selected to do "comparative research." I was first introduced to the Bush campaign opposition group on Wednesday, June 1, 1988. At the request of Jim Pinkerton, research director, a meeting was called to discuss political issues as they pertained to the Dukakis campaign. After the April 5 Wisconsin primary, the polls showed that Massachusetts Governor Dukakis had clearly established himself over Jackson and was going to be the Democratic nominee.

As we sat squeezed into the small office of Don Iloff for our first gathering, we were presented with seven political subjects, presumably ones to be used in the general election. The topics were chalk-written on a small blackboard mounted to the wall, and we were asked to choose the topic that most interested us and to begin thinking about how to research the issue with Dukakis as the target. I waited longer than anyone in the room to respond (probably because I was not that familiar with the choices), so by default, I ended up with the last and least favorite subject of the day—the environment.

Under Reagan, the Washington politicians had not been receptive to the idea of slowing down business development for the sake of environmental progress, and on the national level, discussion regarding environmental issues paled in comparison to crime, labor and foreign

★★★

policy. I obviously had drawn the least consequential of the lot, but I decided to make the most of it. I was fortunate to have any assignment; so few in the campaign were working on any project.

Boston Harbor had been tagged by the Bush senior staff as a possible topic to use against Dukakis. At the time, the idea of making the harbor into something considered newsworthy seemed absurd. As I tackled my work, I was fully aware that it most likely would end up in some black hole. However, as a statistician and researcher by trade (I had a Master of Science degree in industrial/organizational psychology, with a major in statistics), I felt it to be a challenge. Almost a decade earlier, I had been compelled to do my best in graduate school (as wife and mother of two) and had worked hard and finished first in my class, with a 4.0 grade point average. Researching—scientific or not—with the goal of coming that much closer to the truth had been and would remain a passion of mine. In the spring of 1988, the skills I had attained in class were the basis of my data gathering for the harbor project.

During the first week, while working alone and starting from scratch, I pulled together as much information on Boston Harbor as possible. The campaign had given me no instructions as to what I should include in my report, where to focus my attention, or how to go about sourcing my material. I had only three weeks to build a case; my completed study, which I decided would entail the history and management of the harbor, was due by June 20. I was given complete autonomy to do whatever I wished.

In the first week or so, I submitted a brief on my initial findings. It caught the interest of not only the campaign research staff, but also some of the senior advisors. Suddenly, they wanted more information *now*. I was told to start addressing my memos to Roger Ailes, Bush's media consultant, who had signed my book and whom I had been observing from a distance over the past eight months. Ailes was responsible for weaving Bush's message into commercials and sound bites to be aired on television in the fall. The directive to send my material to him seemed a bit unusual, but no explanations were given. Because of the extra workload, I asked for some research assistance.

A Washington lawyer who supposedly had an inside track to the Environmental Protection Agency (EPA) agreed to provide me with some statistics, and the Republican National Committee (RNC) research staff, which collected and computerized newspaper articles on the opposition candidates, started doing Dukakis computer searches for me. Then, I heard that two RNC researchers, Don Senese and John Shilling, had gone to the Massachusetts state archives in Boston to look at public documents. While they were talking to Republican leaders, I thought they might have picked up something pertaining to the harbor. Negative. Nothing from either the EPA or RNC was forthcoming, and because I was counting on that data, I was in worse shape than when I had started. My pleas for administrative support from the campaign staff went unheeded, as well.

At this point, I thought about politely bowing out of the project but ultimately reconsidered. A true researcher finds it hard to stop in the middle of tackling a problem or proving/disproving a case. I decided, in spite of the frustrations, to work at full-throttle every day, including weekends, until I finished.

There were no typewriters on hand, and because the four computers in the research wing were always out of order, the draft of my final paper had to be handwritten. Even when I could find a working computer—set up in the hallway outside my office—the noise level from the many summer interns congregating in the corridors made it impossible to concentrate. I stayed in my office and wrote and wrote and wrote, condensing almost one hundred legal-sized sheets of raw data to a mere eight. My copy index read: "Boston Harbor—The Present Status, the History, the Costs, and the Conclusions." In my final draft, I stated:

> Prior to Governor Dukakis, the only famous dumping activity in Boston Harbor was the Boston Tea Party. Now Boston Harbor is famous, or infamous, as the dirtiest harbor in the nation. Every day at high tide, tons of sewage sludge and millions of gallons of wastewater are dumped into the harbor. It took a lawsuit by the Environmental Protection Agency in 1985 to get Massachusetts to agree to stop this dumping. Even so, Massachusetts will be out of compliance with federal standards until 1999. Dukakis's stall tactics on harbor cleanup have cost Boston residents millions of dollars. The current estimate for the cost of the cleanup is $6 billion, and the local water and sewer rates will quadruple—from $300 per year to $1200 per year. The Boston Harbor mess is a continuing testament to Dukakis's fiscal and environmental mismanagement. Dukakis is wrong when he says he is not the guy who polluted Boston Harbor. He was governor when almost all the critical decisions that have delayed the harbor cleanup were made.

I learned that when Dukakis first took office in 1975 he had promised to clean the harbor, yet in 1988, it was considered by many environmentalists to be "the dirtiest harbor in the nation." The governor's emphasis on environmental issues did not accord with his neglect of Boston's premiere waterfront. His lack of authority, I concluded, had resulted in the mismanagement of millions of federal dollars allocated for the cleanup. Whether it had been through oversight or conscious neglect, I believed that Dukakis's mishandling of the harbor was his most expensive mistake as governor. He clearly had been asleep at the switch when it came to overseeing environmental policy.

I felt confident that I had built a tight case against the governor, and on June 20, when I submitted my paper, I was pleased. With its completion, I found an intrinsic satisfaction. Although this project had not involved inferential methods or variance analysis, it proved reminiscent of the basic investigative skills and analyzing abilities I had utilized in grad school. The final data were measurable and verifiable, and my conclusions sound. With the project behind me, I was looking forward to involving myself in other campaign activities, something less intense.

But that did not seem to be in the cards.

Immediately after I submitted my report, I was pressured for yet more material from the research staff and "invited" to attend a series of early morning critique sessions headed by a large group of senior advisors, none of whom I knew. Most of the individuals in attendance were considered outsiders, for they did not have offices on the premises. As a group—although they carried little weight with those of us who had been working in the trenches for twelve months—they acquired a rather elitist attitude, and they focused more on interrogating me and scrutinizing my every statistic than giving me constructive criticism.

I became annoyed and expressed my feelings to Don Iloff, who was coordinating the opposition effort at the lowest staff level. I had been working with Iloff since the fall of 1987 and considered him not only a peer, but a friend; we were both approaching our one-year mark in the campaign. However, Iloff was no help to me in trying to understand the review committee's over-interest in my study; I surmised that he did not know any more than I.

DURING the month of June, despite Bush's victories in California, Montana, New Jersey and New Mexico, the campaign still seemed lost and confused, and Atwater had been unusually quiet. We were pleasantly surprised, therefore, to be called to a staff meeting on Friday, June 17. Atwater knew his team had lost its spunk, and hoping to put some zip back into the organization, he invited us to the Bush residence at 34th and Massachusetts Avenues for a picnic that same evening. My last occasion at the Bush home had been the Christmas party six months earlier. That cold winter night in December 1987 seemed long ago when contrasted to the warm June day in 1988. To a campaign for which victory looked questionable, the evening suggested hope and newfound resolve.

The gathering at the Naval Observatory could not have come at a better time for a group of floundering campaign workers and ultimately turned out to be the highlight of the summer. On this one occasion, there was no evidence of power plays in action; in fact, it was one of the only times I remember being together while everyone was relaxed and just themselves.

As I entered from the south side of the Bush residence, I could see an array of cotton quilts in vibrant shades of apricot, lavender, and rose, in appealing motifs of leaves, flowers, and patchwork, strewn across the lush green lawn. A traditional summer supper of pork barbecue, baked beans, and keg beer added to the casual and familial setting. After dinner and before the party commenced, rumor was that Atwater was going to make a debut appearance on his guitar. And that he did.

Taking center stage, he was clad in a royal blue, short-sleeved Hawaiian shirt with apple-green palm trees and peppermint-pink parrots (not tucked in, with collar open), baggy white jeans, and brown leather woven loafers with no socks. Shaggy, sandy-brown hair hung down over his ears, giving him a Jimmy Buffett weathered look. And despite the silver and gold Rolex watch on his left wrist, the way he had his electric guitar slung over his shoulder, he could have been in some country bar or on a remote island in the South Pacific.

From the white-pillared porch of the residence, Atwater put on a rhythm and blues show at its best. It was, to say the least, an unusual sight: the redneck political strategist leading the blue-blooded Vice President of the United States in a medley of get-down-and-dirty tunes. Accompanied by three black musicians and a white drummer, and standing in front of a microphone, Atwater sang feel-good, let's-have-another-margarita soul music with song titles like "Ya Ya," "Te-ni-nee-ni-nu," and "Bad Boy." Quite different from the Republican pinstriped set who would later take over the Bush White House.

Vice President and Mrs. Bush joined the campaign staff crowded around the residence porch to sing the choruses. George W., his wife, Laura, and their twin girls, Barbara and Jenna (age seven), were standing in the front row; George W. was attired in a T-shirt inscribed with "Don't Mess with George" on the front.

Sally Dunbar Atwater, Lee's wife, with the two young Atwater girls in tow (Ashley Page, age two, and Sara Lee, eight) sang along with the rest of us well into the evening. In matching turquoise shirt and pedal pushers and big white-looped earrings, Sally beamed as her husband belted out the blues.

Never again would the campaign staff enjoy informality and good times with the Bush family as we did on that special occasion. Before leaving the Vice President's residence, and with camera in hand, I took what turned out to be my favorite photograph of Bush. He was wearing a blue denim shirt, looking relaxed yet still in command of the troops that surrounded him. For me, the companionship I enjoyed that summer evening was short-lived, and the good times soon—much too soon—would take a 180-degree turn for the worse.

A little over two weeks later, on July 5, I went to the campaign headquarters as usual. As I got off the elevator, I was met by another research member who hurriedly escorted me to the office of Tony Lopez, the staff member to whom I had reported while managing the private sector Policy Issue Groups. Lopez's office was next to mine on research row. Because he was not involved in opposition work, I had seen little of him while working on Boston Harbor. Three other researchers (colleagues and friends) were present while Lopez, seemingly reluctant, told me that I was being dismissed from the campaign.

A mumbled reference was made about the press, the media, and Boston Harbor, and how I had wrongly advised one of my harbor sources of my affiliation or, more correctly, my lack of affiliation with the Bush campaign. I could not make sense out of what was happening. It was all so bizarre and unexpected. I felt as if I were free-falling off a cliff; everything was spinning. My first reaction was to insist on speaking to

Pinkerton, the head of the research group. My request was denied, and in
harsh tones, I was told that I was not allowed to make any statements or
ask any questions. In five minutes, I was fired from the campaign and
ushered out of the building.

Later, I would find out that there were several White House
campaign staff meetings held over the Fourth of July weekend in regard
to the press's uncovering my research work. I queried, without answers,
"How had the press ever connected me to the campaign?" "How did the
story about my working on the Boston Harbor research ever get outside
headquarters into suspicious hands?"

Days after my being fired, I saw, with astonishment, a copy of the
newspaper article Lopez had alluded to during my dismissal meeting. The
July 2, 1988, Quincy *Patriot Ledger* article had been published three days
before the scene in Lopez's office. Under the section called "Tracking the
Campaign," State House Bureau reporter Eve Epstein had written "Bush
Volunteer Dismissed." (Daniel Schnur, who was quoted in the piece, was
assistant press secretary for the '88 Bush campaign and later would
become Pete Wilson's '92 communications director—and even later, John
McCain's 2000 campaign spokesman.) Epstein's article read in part:

> A George Bush campaign worker who hid her affiliation while
> seeking information from Massachusetts officials was dismissed
> after the Bush campaign learned of the incident yesterday. Bush
> spokesman Daniel Schnur said Anne Joslin was dismissed "because
> her failure to identify herself was contrary to campaign policy. We
> do not condone that type of behavior," Schnur said. [Quoting a
> spokesman from the Massachusetts Water Authority,] "It is one of
> the oldest of dirty tricks in the campaign lexicon to send folks into
> the opponent's camp. I am not surprised if the Bush people would
> do that.". . . Schnur confirmed Joslin was working on a Boston
> Harbor project for the campaign's research department as a
> volunteer. But Schnur said the Vice President doesn't want
> researchers misrepresenting themselves.

Four days later, on July 6, the *Patriot Ledger* came out with a second
article regarding my research, and again it was written by Eve Epstein,
only this time it was a longer piece and it came under the heading
"Campaigns Encourage Staffers to be Honest." It is my opinion that the
only thing correct in the Epstein article was the description of what was
driving the new Bush momentum:

Information about Dukakis's record in Massachusetts has become a key element in the Vice President's campaign strategy. Bush has gone on the offensive about Dukakis's record recently, criticizing him for everything from the state's furlough policy to the Governor's budget problems this year. Observers credit the Vice President's offensive with narrowing Dukakis's lead as the favored candidate in public opinion polls. Although George Bush and Michael Dukakis expect their campaign staffers to identify themselves when conducting opposition research, neither appears to have a formal system to ensure workers comply. State officials said Joslin did not need to hide her identity when she called for information.

The article went on to enumerate all the reasons why campaign researchers should divulge their identity while sourcing material, and it concluded by saying how "receptive" the camps were to their oppositions' requests. Obvious to me was the fact that Epstein had never worked in a political campaign and was either covering up something or creating a smoke screen. She appeared to be under the mistaken assumption that opposing camps were on friendly terms when it came to intelligence gathering. But more importantly, I had never made any attempt to obtain information from any Boston source—or any other—that was not already available to the general public.

In fact, I had been prompted by staff "to lie," if necessary, but I had not. With my educational training in research, I was fluent in data collection, assimilation and conclusions. I was not trained in, nor had any inclinations toward, political skullduggery. Moreover, there had been no reason for me to misrepresent the truth, for no one ever asked where I worked or in what way the information would be used. I had found the easiest and most honest way to proceed while doing my work was simply to state my name and say nothing more than I was working on a research paper. Period.

I had called Massachusetts state agencies requesting public documents, true, but never was I asked if I worked for the George Bush campaign, or any "company" for that matter. Had they done so, it would have been odd, for it was their job to distribute the documents to callers. Never did I ask for any information that was not already available for public dissemination, so when I did make a request, the assistants just *assumed*—that like the rest of those inquiring—I wanted the papers to be mailed. In several cases, they even offered before I asked. I gave my home address; there simply was no occasion when anyone questioned me about a work address.

In the July 6 *Patriot Ledger* article, there was another quote from Bush campaign spokesperson Dan Schnur, saying, "Joslin's superiors have gone out of their way to say 'you are not to make any misleading statements.'"

At the initial opposition research meeting I attended in Iloff's office, the only instructions I had been given were that, "should we be queried by a source about where we worked, we were to *misrepresent* the truth." Before starting our research, the directives given by staffer Iloff and attorney Bret Wacker were to use any name and affiliation we wished, but not at any time to say that we were working for the Bush campaign. Clear enough. No other guidelines for securing data had been given. The people I spoke to in Massachusetts, as well as elsewhere, were always cordial and most helpful. In fact, gathering information had been the least of my worries; it had been presenting the multitude of facts in a meaningful way that had been so problematic.

Unbeknownst to me, if an "agent" was found out, the campaign would simply blame him or her for wrongdoing, exclaim how unbelievable it was for such a thing to occur, and fling the accused off the premises. This out-the-door method is easier, safer, and far less time consuming for the staff than defending the suspected party. The same individuals who had instructed me never to let it be known that I worked for the campaign held me up as an example of "conduct unbecoming," thereby preserving their own integrity, and their jobs. I wondered to whom at a higher level I could appeal my case and realized there was no one. However, the episode continued with a rather strange twist.

Hours after my dismissal on July 5, and not yet knowing about the *Patriot Ledger* articles, I returned home only to receive a phone call from campaign headquarters. Obviously having been tagged by the Bush senior staff to contact me, Iloff, in a rather sheepish voice, asked if I would continue doing work on Boston Harbor from my home. "They" needed a one-page spin summary and a two-page executive brief as a follow-up to the research I had submitted on June 20, and they needed these reports in the next forty-eight hours.

My thought was that if "they" wanted to fire me, fine; they could find someone else to do the summaries. Then, maybe because I still

wanted to claim ownership of my work, or maybe because I did not want
to bring any unfavorable attention to the campaign or to Bush, or maybe
because I still saw it as my job (or maybe all three—obligation, loyalty,
and responsibility), I agreed to do the papers. Two days later, July 7, I had
a courier deliver the material to Iloff.

At the same time I was completing the brief and summary at home—
as a favor to the individuals who had just dismissed me—a memo was
being circulated at campaign headquarters. I found out about it by way of
an anonymous campaign member, who sent it to me in the mail several
days later. I surmised that senior staff had threatened the research group,
suggesting that, if it was found out that they were communicating with
me, they, too, would be reprimanded.

The memorandum was written by Bret Wacker, the man who had
instructed me, while I was doing my research, not to make any reference
to working in the Bush campaign. Dated July 6, 1988, Wacker's brief had
been distributed to the campaign research staff the same day the second
Patriot Ledger article had come out. Attached was a copy of the July 2
article by Epstien, taken from the *Presidential Hotline,* a campaign
publication circulated to the White House and everyone in the
administration. Wacker's memo read:

> Attached is a piece from today's *Presidential Campaign Hotline.* The
> attached is a clip everyone should take note of for two reasons 1. It
> is true, and 2. It is very unfortunate because it involves one of our
> best researchers. Andy Warhol once said that everyone will be
> famous for fifteen minutes. I cannot emphasize enough that being
> famous is not a goal of yours while associated with this Division.
> Please, everyone, make a greater effort to consider the
> consequences of your actions.

I had been working with Wacker for almost a year; he knew that I
pursued my tasks with diligence and as a team player and that I kept
pretty much to myself. I was forty-three years old—while most of the
others in research were in their twenties and early thirties. Fame and
glory were the last things on my mind; I was a divorced mother, solely
responsible for raising two teenage children. His accusations were
ridiculous, and Wacker knew they were.

Weeks after having been taken off research, I learned that the
campaign was using my Boston Harbor work for their environmental

offensive against Dukakis *and* as a way to defend the poor Reagan-Bush record. The material I had submitted to Ailes in June and July had become key for the campaign's upcoming ads.

The reason I had been pressured for more and more material was that the campaign was working under such a tight deadline. When the Bush advertisements first started to be aired in August (and then later for the general election), the urgency would begin to make sense to me. At the present, it did not. By the time I was fired on July 5, the senior staff had most of what they needed from me in order to use the harbor as a symbol for their environmental platform. With the final papers I submitted on July 7, they were confident enough to begin planning their Boston Harbor blitz, which would include a three-day Vice Presidential campaign swing through several states, starting the first week of September. The objective of Bush's September trip would be to portray him as an environmentalist and show him breaking from the traditional no-hands-on Reagan record. Dukakis was depicted as the anti-environmentalist.

Considering that this issue had been a sleeping dog for many years and that Bush, during the Reagan administration, had actually worked to weaken environmental regulations, this was a politically risky leap for the Republicans. My work was helping Bush orchestrate a turnaround on these less-than-successful past efforts.

On September 1, 1988, I found an article in the *Los Angeles Times* titled "Bush Vows 'Zero Tolerance' of Environmental Polluters." John Balzar quoted Dukakis and Senator George Mitchell:

> "Talk about an election-year conversion," the Massachusetts governor snorted at a press conference in Boston. "He and the Administration he's been part of have done everything they could to eliminate environmental programs." Joining Dukakis at the press conference was Sen. George J. Mitchell (D-Me.), chairman of a Senate environmental protection subcommittee, who added: "Where has Vice President Bush been for the last seven years? The record of the Reagan-Bush Administration on water pollution, indeed on environmental questions in general, has been an unmitigated disaster."

On September 2, midway through Bush's environmental tour, the Vice President took a boat cruise on Boston Harbor, pointing out the harbor's unhealthy state and setting the stage for other attempts to paint Dukakis as guilty of neglect.

In June and even July, I had worked without knowing what was happening in the upper levels of the campaign and had little comprehension of how significant opposition research could be in establishing the direction of a presidential election. In the years to come, I would read about the major role opposition played in the 1988 election, much of it praising the Republicans for their creativity and chiding the Democrats for not using the same tactics. Jim Pinkerton headed our team, while John Podesta led the Dukakis group. Attempting to look more closely at the Democratic side of things, I found a back-dated (May 12, 1988) commentary from the *Boston Herald* titled "Dem, GOP Do their Homework: Researchers Prepare for Battle." Wayne Woodlief described the Dukakis research team this way:

> The Democrats "Bush Whackers" are up against the GOP's Joe Friday "gumshoes," scouring for bombshells to drop on the opposition in the upcoming Michael Dukakis-George Bush battle for president. "We'd try to find out what Bush did at the CIA (when he was director), but I don't think we'd be too welcome at agency headquarters [in] Langley Va." quipped DNC spokesman Mike McCurry. McCurry, with a verbal play on the White House astrology craze, said Bush has a built-in excuse if he doesn't win in November: "He'd just say it wasn't in the tarot cards."

Another article, entitled "Evolution of the TV Era's Nastiest Presidential Race," and subtitled "Bush Team Test-Marketed Negative Themes," gave me the first real clue as to how my research had been linked to the chronology of campaign events as they unfolded in the summer of 1988. Paul Taylor and David Broder, *Washington Post* staff writers, had their piece published on October 28, 1988, and in it, they described two Bush campaign strategy meetings: one was held in Paramus, New Jersey, on May 26, and the other—starting a day later and continuing over Memorial Day weekend—in Kennebunkport, Maine, at the Bush summer home.

According to the Taylor/Broder article, in late spring of 1988, Baker, as campaign chairman, and Lee Atwater, as manager, had determined that Bush needed a new strategy. Bush was trailing Dukakis by a substantial fifteen points. The Paramus team was made up of Baker, Atwater, Roger Ailes, Stu Spencer, and Bob Teeter. Before going to Paramus, Baker and Atwater had tentatively decided to use a reverse campaign strategy: they needed something with quick results and pondered the idea of accentuating Dukakis's negatives rather than portraying Bush's affirmative side. Launching an offensive assault, they projected, might be more efficient and effective than "remaking" their candidate's positives. Before kicking off a blitz, though, it was decided that a feasibility study was necessary, and campaign pollster Teeter, the Republican Party's tribal leader, would lead the investigation.

Teeter was not just another pollster; he was a renowned presidential advisor and consultant. Having started out in college working for George Romney, governor of his home state of Michigan, Teeter began his advisory role to the political elite when he joined Romney's 1967 (abortive) race for the White House. He first met George Bush when Bush served as RNC chairman under Nixon and Teeter was an advisor and pollster to Nixon. Bush and Teeter had stood together while fighting to keep the GOP from coming apart during the dark days of Watergate. Then, in 1976, Teeter became a member of the Ford campaign, channeling information from his polls to Jim Baker (campaign chairman) and Dick Cheney (Ford's chief of staff) and acting as one of Ford's chief strategists. Eight years later, Baker brought Teeter into the 1984 Reagan campaign as his pollster and, in 1988, had requested that Teeter come back on board for yet his third presidential race.

In Paramus, with Teeter instructing, The Guys carried out a test market study on political issues that had been gathered by Jim Pinkerton and his research group at the campaign. They used a marketing technique first employed to "sell" Reagan in the mid-1960s. A newer version had been improvised and updated by the Bush team, but it remained a method that played on people's fears. To determine the most disturbing national issues (to be used in the candidate's campaign ads), the focus group would be told facts about several social/political "evils" and then asked which were the most disturbing.

On May 26, a focus group of thirty Democrats who had backed Reagan in 1984 but were now Dukakis supporters were asked by the Bush team to listen to selections from Pinkerton's anti-Dukakis research material and respond. The issues included the Massachusetts furlough program, the Pledge of Allegiance, and the pollution of Boston Harbor. At the end of the session, after having heard Dukakis's stance regarding crime, patriotism and the environment, an amazing fifteen of the thirty individuals had changed their minds about voting for Dukakis.

With Teeter-inspired glee, the Bush squad had found their strategy, and the Paramus group decided their new line of attack. Now, they needed to convince Bush to go negative. Five campaign aides— Atwater, Ailes, Teeter, Craig Fuller and Nick Brady—hastily journeyed to Bush's summer home in Maine. Over Memorial Day weekend, while President Reagan attended the Moscow Summit with Mikhail Gorbachev, Bush was being persuaded to take a negative posture and launch an offensive on Dukakis as soon as possible. With resolute desire, using the three top issues—crime, patriotism and the environment—the team deliberated about how to paint Dukakis as a flaming liberal, the candidate who marched out of step with the rest of America.

Just before the Taylor/Broder article, on October 27, in the *Wall Street Journal,* another report provided details regarding the use of my research. In "Bush Thrives on One-A-Day TV-Message Capsules Prescribed by His Skilled Poli-Tech Image Makers," James Perry and Monica Langley described the Kennebunkport rendezvous this way:

> The senior staff and the image-makers, led by Mr. Ailes, had lunch with Mr. Bush in June [in Kennebunkport]. All of the negative material gathered by the research staff was spelled out. By the time of the June luncheon, Mr. Ailes already had chosen Frankenberry, Laughlin and Constable, Inc., an advertising agency based in Milwaukee (and up until then best known for its efforts on behalf of Oshkosh B'Gosh, Inc., a manufacturer of kids overalls) to produce the campaign ads. Keeping in mind that the polls indicated that the best issue for Mr. Dukakis might turn out to be the environment and that the worst one might turn out to be crime, the Milwaukee agency was told to come up with two ads—one about the pollution in Boston Harbor and one about the failures in the furlough program.

The Bush senior campaign staff had needed to be absolutely sure that the data I presented on Dukakis and the harbor was airtight so it could be used as one of the central focuses of the campaign. That is why every fact, number, statistic and quotation had been under such microscopic scrutiny. When the *Patriot Ledger* mysteriously picked up on my work, the Bush campaign had panicked out of fear that the story might get into a more significant newspaper. If that happened, they would not have been able to use the material for their planned strike.

Having to dump the research and ruin an opportunity to paint the Massachusetts governor as an anti-environmentalist would significantly hurt their game plan.

However, the write-ups in the *Patriot Ledger* had not been significant enough to do any real damage; for that, the Bush staff was thankful. Because word never leaked out to the rest of the world, it allowed those in the campaign to remain on their chosen path. Pinkerton, Wacker, Lopez, and Iloff, to name a few, all stayed in the campaign ranks, knowing that my termination had saved them as well as the critical research they were protecting.

Ten days after I was dismissed from headquarters, and after I had written the executive brief and spin summary, the campaign called me and offered me a deal: a paid position working in opposition research at the Republican National Committee. Three conditions came with the verbal proposal: first, I could not mention my research work on Boston Harbor to anyone, second, I would have to sever all ties with campaign headquarters and with everyone who worked there, and third, I would be moved to the RNC research staff and continue doing opposition research—quietly.

I thought it all sounded so clandestine, and although they were not generous terms, I agreed to them and took the job. My one demand was that they honor a previous agreement with me, assigning me to the campaign's research team traveling to the National Convention. It was decided that I would be given all the necessary credentials to be temporarily reinstated on the campaign staff while in New Orleans. Looking back on it, I do not think the campaign offer to go the RNC was extended as a generous gesture to "include" me, but as a way to ensure that I was silenced during the critical weeks before the environmental ads came out. From my perspective, I had put a full year into the campaign, and I wanted to see it through to the election, just three months away.

Once driven out of the Bush headquarters and sent to the Committee, I never breathed a word about my Boston Harbor opposition work, and with the exception of one good friend and coworker, Russell Rockwell, I never heard from anyone at the campaign until after the election. Even then, relationships were strained, at best.

In the years to come, I would be reminded of my time in opposition research. Sometimes it felt fine; other times it felt as though I had sold my soul to the devil. In spite of my personal mindset, the 1988 Bush opposition team would continue to intrigue people. In the first issue of *George* published by John F. Kennedy, Jr., in December 1995, William Saletan gave an account on comparative research as it applied to political candidates and elections. Referring to the 1988 election in his "Spy versus Spy" article, he said:

> In 1988, opposition research changed the course of a presidential election. The GOP detailed its legendary squad of self-described excellent nerds—35 oppo agents—to dredge up the unsavory parts of Michael Dukakis's gubernatorial record. They devoured newspaper clips, budget books and debate transcripts. Their most damaging findings were quickly translated into George Bush's speeches and attack ads. One month Dukakis was winning a race about Iran-Contra, Manuel Noriega and the Massachusetts Miracle; the next, Dukakis was getting whipsawed on Willie Horton, Boston Harbor and the pledge of allegiance.

Although I do have a love for crunching numbers and delineating fact from fiction, I would not describe myself as a nerd, and if there were a legendary squad of thirty-five, I did not know anything about them. The newspapers were always claiming the campaign had agents in every state; that was not the case. Although the college kids clipped articles and copied material into computers (at the RNC), only a few individuals actually worked on stories.

To say that the Bush opposition research team changed the course of the presidential election is debatable, but no doubt, it did play a part in turning the tide just weeks before the Bush victory. According to most experts, Bush's offensive attack on Boston Harbor was perceived as one of his strongest and most effective assaults against Dukakis. As *Boston Globe* staff writer Chris Black put it:

> In the crucial 24 hours after the first presidential debate, the campaign of Vice President George Bush whacked Governor Michael S. Dukakis with the first negative advertising of the General Election campaign to be shown on network television—a critical advertisement on polluted Boston Harbor…The 30-second advertisement, highlighting the "Dirtiest Harbor in America," aired on NBC during its Olympics coverage. … In the spot, the camera pans polluted water and an announcer says, "As a candidate, Michael Dukakis called Boston Harbor an open sewer.

As governor, he had an opportunity to do something about it but chose not to." The announcer continues, "The Environmental Protection Agency called his lack of action the most expensive public policy mistake in the history of New England. Now Boston Harbor, the dirtiest harbor in America, will cost residents $6 billion to clear. And Michael Dukakis promises to do for America what he has done for Massachusetts."

The Harbor Ad made its debut on network television just after the first presidential debate, held on September 25. Shortly after the initial airing, I watched a rerun in the RNC sound room. The words accompanying the clip sounded very familiar.

They should have; they were mine.

New Orleans, Louisiana, August 16, 1988
V.P. Bush arrives by riverboat for the Republican convention.

★   ★

PART 2

Drinking Champagne

★   ★

Campaign rhetoric derogates the very skills of compromise and give-and-take that are essential to the successful functioning of government. Yet, the public obviously warms to the partisan sport of black-and-white, good-versus-evil posturing, even if it defies common sense.

—Hendrick Smith

★★★ ═══════ ★★★

CHAPTER

6

QUAYLE HUNT

The Federalists professed disdain for the "detestable practice of electioneering" and haughtily dismissed the campaign methods developed by Jefferson's followers in the 1790's (parades, barbecues, posters, handbills) as "forensic degladiation."
—Paul Boller, Jr.

AUGUST 1988

The next event for the Republicans was the National Convention, scheduled for mid-August, just a month before the first Boston Harbor ad aired. Going to New Orleans was what I had been waiting for since the New Hampshire primary win, and I was going as campaign staff, as planned. Upon my termination, I had gotten this one thing.

But first came the Democratic National Convention. In mid-July, at the Omni Center in Atlanta, Michael Dukakis accepted his Party's nomination and announced his running mate as Lloyd Millard Bentsen, Jr., a private man who led a public life. Having made his fortune in the insurance business, Bentsen had established strong ties to the Democratic Party. For forty years, the senator and chairman of the Senate Finance Committee had been an influencing factor in political circles throughout the nation and Texas. Bentsen had run for the Senate in 1970, defeating fellow Texan George Bush, and he was still in office. In the campaign of 1988, Bentsen was predicted to bring the Reagan Democrats back to the ticket. Ironically, while fortifying the Democratic Party base, Bentsen's appeal would serve to accentuate the political shortcomings of Dukakis.

On the same day that Dukakis announced Bentsen as his running mate, I drove to the Republican National Committee headquarters on Capitol Hill to start my new job. It was raining and terribly humid. As the arm responsible for raising money for national political candidates, the RNC was housed in what was officially referred to as the Dwight D. Eisenhower Republican Center, and located at 310 First Street, SE, just a few blocks away from the Capitol.

As I entered the main reception area, I found the decor old-fashioned but pleasing, with a few antique reproductions, including a Chippendale sofa at one end of the room and three walls of presidential campaign memorabilia. Elephant replicas abounded, in bronze, silver, crystal and pewter, from desk-sized to nearly life-sized. After signing in at the front desk, I was escorted by a security guard to the opposition research center located on the main floor, not far from the reception area. The first thing that caught my eye upon entering the large research room was a three-foot-square poster tacked to the left of the door. It read: "There is only one tactical principle which is not subject to change. It is to use the means at hand to inflict the maximum amount of wounds, death, and destruction on the enemy in the minimum amount of time. [Signed] General George S. Patton, Jr."

The room was partitioned into two sections. The first was teeming with fifteen or so twenty-year-olds sitting at desks in schoolroom fashion The second was arranged with numerous dividers, behind which the senior research staff—probably another dozen persons in their thirties— sat doing work on their computers.

At the desks, college kids referred to as "fast-trackers" input hundreds of political newspaper articles—going back to the 1960s—into the computer system. Working on the highly complex RNC Opposition Research Quotes Program—more commonly known as the "fast track"— was tedious, non-stop and maintained twenty-four hours a day. It was set up for the benefit of the senior campaign staff, who, at any time, were at liberty to request information on an opposition candidate. By computer search, the fast track could locate the intelligence. At least, that was the intent. The fast-trackers, or should I say their system, had been no help to me when I requested information on Dukakis and Boston Harbor just two months earlier.

The general atmosphere in the RNC opposition room was one of controlled chaos, as in the research wing at campaign headquarters, but something here was different. To begin with, the RNC research budget for the 1988 election was $1 million, which enabled them to buy more and

★★★

better office equipment and pay salaries to their staff. With far fewer funds, the campaign had acquired only outdated computers and was manned by volunteers. Those of us in opposition at the campaign had worked exclusively on our own, and some of us were fortunate enough to have an office. At the RNC it was just the opposite; everyone worked together in one room, twenty-some people in a space not much larger than a high school classroom. The RNC also differed in that, after the November election, it would still be alive. The campaign, on the other hand, was a house of cards, designed to collapse in three months.

Of all the disparities between the two, none was as significant as the political makeup. The Committee members had spent the last eight years supporting President Reagan, who had appointed Frank Fahrenkopf chairman and Maureen Reagan, his daughter, co-chair. This allegiance to Reagan from the RNC staff was understandable, and it was logical that Bush, considered by Reagan standards as a lightweight Vice President, had not won the respect of the RNC workforce. Despite Bush's having been Committee chairman in the past, he was still thought to be an incapable leader. The RNC cheered for Reagan, the campaign for Bush, making them arch rivals.

The intelligence edge helped give RNC research members their air of superiority. Nevertheless, and despite the fact that the RNC had information resources that were far beyond the campaign's limited reach, they remained second to campaign staff in status. Although Atwater and the campaign often took issue with the RNC, they paid little heed to it. As manager, Atwater was in charge until Election Day. This made for serious tension between the two camps, and very few individuals successfully crossed the line between Campaign and Committee.

On my first day working on the Hill, I reported to Don Todd, head of RNC research. I told him that I hoped to work as an independent, as I had at the campaign. For control reasons, he did not like the idea of my not being under his wing; however, he assigned me to RNC senior researcher Gary Maloney, whom I had known from research days at campaign headquarters back in the winter months.

Now one of the Committee's premiere researchers, Maloney did the majority of his labor out of the RNC. In a one-man office on the second floor, he was with the other higher-ranking staff, yet he still was tied into 15th Street operations. As one of the rare individuals who had successfully forged the campaign/RNC divide, Maloney had friends in both places. Aware of my Boston Harbor situation, he was willing to pull me back into the loop as best he could. For that, I was grateful. No one breathed a word about my "past"; it was awkward, and I was never completely comfortable there. Working out of the RNC library, I began my new job while sharing an office with Doug Campbell, a long-time Republican and Bush "Fund for America's Future" member.

During the first few weeks, I started several projects involving investigative work, mostly on Dukakis, but it was late in the game for doing opposition. Campbell scoured twenty newspapers a day for Bush-related articles, which he then published in the *RNC Daily News Clips*. Constantly in the proximity of Campbell's "news room," I was always asking him questions; he enlightened me about how often political news is dictated by the media's presentation. Because of those few weeks of being inundated with news and newspapers, my propensity for collecting data increased.

Then, just before my flight to Louisiana, I received a phone call from a long-time friend, R. Carter Sanders, a former Reagan appointee at the department of Housing and Urban Development (HUD) and Washington lobbyist. As a transplanted Californian, Sanders had worked on Reagan's 1980 campaign. He was now at the convention site, but on his own, not working with either the Bush or the Reagan entourage. In our phone conversation, Sanders passed on to me that the platform committee had already arrived in New Orleans and that in the pre-convention stages, a flurry of activity had begun. He also relayed to me that, curiously enough, a division was evident in the Party. Two distinct groups were in attendance: supporters of George Bush and followers of Ronald Reagan. There seemed to be no middle ground between them. In fact, Sanders said he had observed outright hostility between the opposing camps.

Such was the scene when I arrived at the Marriott Hotel on the evening of August 13. As the campaign had promised, I was reinstated to their research division, and for a brief seven days, I joined the staff I had been expelled from a month earlier.

During the week of the convention, the Marriott was temporarily set up as the site for Bush campaign headquarters, and my first stop in the hotel was to the staff room to pick up my "credentials," or identifying badges.

★★★

The three-by-five-inch identifiers served as our status cards over the ensuing six days and were assigned by access code. Each color specified a certain security level—one to five, with five being the highest. The badges read, "Bush '88 Campaign Staff" and were worn around our necks on a chain at all times, day and night, no matter where we went in the Crescent City. Well aware of the unusual circumstances regarding my campaign status, I was quite surprised to learn that I had been assigned a level five, "all access." I wondered who had granted me admittance to *all* the campaign sites and events. Like most everything else that had to do with my venture in the campaign, I would never find out.

Our first research staff meeting was held at 7:00 Sunday morning at the Marriott. We were each given a one-inch-thick master calendar of convention events that listed what was happening in New Orleans hour by hour, day by day, and delegation by delegation. Most state teams were situated in one of the numerous downtown hotels. Two of the most popular were the Avenue Plaza (Arizona) and the Royal Sonesta (Tennessee).

The small committee to which I had been assigned—Media Coverage—was responsible for assembling the campaign newsletter, a package of relevant political articles from as many national newspapers as we could put our hands on. Similar to the campaign's and the RNC's *Daily News Summary*, the publication was adequate, but not professionally published. Finding newspapers early in the morning on the streets of New Orleans turned out to be a challenge; the resources for cutting, pasting and copying, all necessary for production, were scarce. Despite the limited equipment, we managed to put out a decent-looking document of approximately fifty pages, which we distributed to the Bush senior personnel staff each morning before the breakfast hour. As ad hoc publishers, our days in New Orleans were busy, and as a reward for our efforts, we had evenings off to attend the events at the Superdome, where most of the Republican Party's official activities took place.

From the New Orleans town center, buses chauffeured campaign staff to and from the huge football stadium-turned-convention hall. The ground floor, representing the Republican nerve center, was off limits to everyone except state-elected delegates and the press corps; the balconies were open to onlookers. News correspondents (including anchors from the four major networks), with their booths set up in the middle portion of the Superdome, covered the convention site like locusts.

It is my contention that the media took the 1988 Republican convention to a place no one could have predicted. It all started on Tuesday afternoon, with the arrival of Bush by riverboat.

That morning, by chance, at the last moment, I received an invitation to the arrival ceremony. The invitation read: "The City of New Orleans and the Louisiana Host Committee cordially invite you to be our special guest at the Grand New Orleans Welcome, honoring the Vice President of the United States, Mrs. Bush and the Bush family. Please present this invitation for Special Viewing Area."

The welcome took place at 3:00 on August 16 at the Spanish Plaza-Canal Street Dock in the center of town. Although it was the official arrival of the Vice President, the event had received little publicity; a relatively small crowd of maybe three hundred was on hand. Another reason for the low turnout was the weather: it had been dreadfully hot and humid for the previous three days, and the one hundred-degree temperatures seemed to bear down on the Big Easy that afternoon. Most conventioneers, staff, and press stayed in cool, air-conditioned hotels, shops and restaurants on the afternoon of Bush's arrival. I decided to brave the heat and go down to the docks to see what was happening.

Standing in the front row of the throng and taking advantage of my viewing-area pass, I watched a huge riverboat, with Bush and his staff aboard, come closer and closer. I could see the Bush family standing on one of the open decks among red, white and blue half-circle banners tied to the Mississippi paddleboat's railings. The Bushes were smiling and waving to the crowd.

After pulling up to the dock, the Vice President's family disembarked from the *Natchez* and made their way to a platform at the river's edge. I was standing directly next to this stage when another gentleman, whom I first thought to be a Bush relative, ran onto the raised deck with Bush. Then, something caught my eye. Ailes, the Bush media coordinator, was circling the platform from down below, at my level, while Bush and the others spilled onto it up above. Ailes was looking unusually concerned, I would say even flustered, which was not his style. Seconds after I noticed Ailes's curious behavior, Bush blurted: "I want you to meet my vice presidential running mate, Senator Dan Quayle." It all happened in a matter of seconds.

★★★

In the sun-drenched plaza, the crowd, stunned by the unexpected announcement, was silent for a second or two before applauding. I asked myself, "Who is Dan Quayle?"

Those of us on the research staff had been expecting Bush to announce his vice presidential choice on the night of his acceptance speech, two days away. While in New Orleans, we had been working with a long and short list of possible running mates, and for months, the pundits had been mulling over the challenge Bush faced in picking a Vice President who would not hurt the ticket and would pick up votes: a conservative such as Jack Kemp, a moderate such as Thomas Kean, a regional asset such as Lamar Alexander, someone to bridge the gender gap such as Sandra Day O'Connor and a charismatic running mate like Bob Dole were all thought to be viable choices. Dan Quayle's name had not been on any of the lists that I had seen. The Indiana senator was an unknown not only to those who were supposed to be "in the know," but also to most of America. However, that was *no* reason for the furor that followed Bush's announcement.

Beginning on the afternoon of August 16, Quayle, like a misguided cannonball, was thrust into the national limelight—completely unprepared. A political catastrophe. A communications calamity. Bush's introduction of Quayle was national politics turned awry. Big time. The entire dockside arrival was so opposite of the professionally orchestrated events we had grown accustomed to seeing when Bush was in the public eye, it was hard to believe this was part of the same campaign.

The Indiana senator's first five minutes as the Republican Party's candidate were without any professional orchestration. He came across as a high school cheerleader at his first football game, jumping up and down on stage while he spoke—no, while he yelled—into the microphone, laughing, clapping, exuberance overflowing. In light of the moment, Quayle was understandably experiencing a reflex reaction, but this was not the right time or place for such a response. He should have been briefed on the Ailes "first seven seconds" theory: We make up our minds about other people within the first seven seconds of meeting them.

The manner in which Quayle was presented to the public was exceedingly important to the success of the ticket. From the first moment he set foot onto the riverfront stand, he needed to come across as vice presidential and in command. Quayle's boyish charm and unbridled

enthusiasm on this day did not portray a man in control, and because of
that, he lost all credibility. Within twenty-four hours after Quayle met
America, the press corps did just what one would predict they would do
with a vulnerable candidate: they chewed him up, inch by square inch,
and spat him out. Whether or not it was an accurate portrayal of Quayle
(I personally do not believe it was) was not the issue; it was how he was
perceived. As I have said before, one's political power—or lack of it— is
almost always a matter of perception. Not fact.

Later that afternoon, the same day as Bush's arrival, the research staff
was called together to view the first media accounts of the Quayle
announcement, which were already coming in over national radio and
television. Back at the Marriott, we watched the clips on a full-size movie
screen; this technique only seemed to exaggerate Quayle's inexperience
and flaws. We watched the reporters assault Quayle . . . on everything
from his congressional record on civil rights to his college performance at
DePaw University, and from his supposedly "rich and famous" family
with their millions of dollars to his stint with the National Guard during
the Vietnam War (it was seldom mentioned that Bush's son George W. had
been in the Texas Air National Guard and never spent a day in Vietnam).
The attacks, unmerciful and relentless, were only the beginning of what
would be an ongoing condemnation of Quayle for years to come, making
him one of the country's most criticized figures in U.S. history.

Seemingly, the only possible solution to a Quayle "reversal" was to
send in a first-rate rescue squad. By Tuesday evening, hours after the
dockside arrival and the first media reviews, I expected to see some sign
of damage control from the campaign spin doctors, something that would
bring Quayle back to life.

To my amazement, nothing was forthcoming, and, predictably,
things got progressively worse over the next three days of the convention,
not because of anything Quayle did, but because of what Quayle's
handlers and advisors did *not* do. They sat on their haunches and
watched Senator Quayle go down in flames. Why?

I think a great deal of the blame for the fiasco lay with the chairman
of the campaign, Jim Baker. The just-retired secretary of Treasury was
finally "out-in-front," holding the reins of power. Because Baker
controlled both campaign and vice presidential communications, his
authority had increased two-fold during the week of the convention.

The day after the Quayle announcement, on Wednesday morning, Baker planned a Bush-Quayle joint news conference. Bob Kimmit, Baker's aide, who worked at Treasury and who had headed the vice presidential search committee, thought it wise to put off the news conference so that the campaign could "buy" time and distribute some positive press on Quayle. Baker vetoed the idea.

It should be noted that Jim Lake, who had replaced Teeley as Bush's senior communications advisor in June 1988, was senior convention spokesman, and he reported to his longtime friend Baker. In June, when Lake was appointed communications advisor (after the Teeley firing), Sheila Tate had been tapped campaign press secretary. But, with Lake always out in front, Tate essentially played a supporting role (if that).

All communications positions are crucial during campaign season and even more essential during convention time. In this regard, Bush had been in a precarious position since 1987 and was now on the verge of a total communications collapse. What was happening in New Orleans was indicative of what had been going on for months. Why?

In April 1985, Jim Baker had appointed Marlin Fitzwater as Bush's vice presidential (OVP) press secretary. Earlier, as a former bureaucrat at the department of the Treasury (under Donald Regan), Fitzwater had been brought to the Reagan White House as assistant to Larry Speakes (Reagan's press secretary after Jim Brady was shot). Shortly after Regan became Reagan's chief of staff, Fitzwater left Speakes's office and joined Craig Fuller and Bush. Baker was gearing up for the 1988 campaign, and while Fitzwater reported to Bush in OVP, he also reported to Jim Baker.

Almost two years later, in January 1987, Fitzwater was pulled back to the White House to serve as press secretary to President Reagan, replacing Speakes. This left Bush without a press secretary. Larry Thomas held the position briefly, but then, because no one had filled it nine months later, George W. called in Pete Teeley. With Teeley's departure in May 1988, Steven Hart had served as acting press secretary until Sheila Tate (previously Mrs. Reagan's press secretary) was appointed in June 1988. Under Sheila Tate, Daniel C. Schnur (the Bush spokesman quoted in the Boston Harbor articles) was first assistant press secretary and then field press director reporting to Tate. Bottom line: Bush had no one to properly promote him or his campaign. *No one.* Having a talented press secretary is imperative for a Vice President, not to mention a presidential candidate. And from January 1987 until June 1988 (eighteen months of crucial campaigning and vice presidential responsibilities), Bush was without a capable spokesperson. This void, still evident during the time of the convention, put Bush in a vulnerable position.

To appreciate the impact Jim Baker and Jim Lake had on Dan Quayle and George Bush in New Orleans, I turn the clock back to the mid-1970s, when Lake headed then-Governor Reagan's state lobbying office in D.C. Following that stint, Lake signed on with Reagan's 1980 presidential campaign as press secretary, replacing Lyn Nofziger. John Sears, a member of Richard Nixon's New York law firm, was also new to the Reagan inner circle (Holmes Tuttle, Ed Meese, Mike Deaver and Nofziger), and he became Reagan's 1980 campaign manager. However, when a power struggle emerged between Meese and Deaver—after the 1980 New Hampshire primary—Meese emerged victorious over Deaver, Sears and Sears's two aides, Jim Lake and Charlie Black. Meese was appointed campaign manager, while the other four were exiled from the Reagan camp. After the Reagan victory, Sears, Lake and Black were left outside the administration walls, while Deaver, Meese and Nofziger went into the White House with the new President.

Sears never would make a comeback, but at Jim Baker's request, Black and Lake were called to work on Reagan's 1984 reelection and Bush's 1988 campaign. In 1984, Baker had appointed Lake to be Reagan's campaign press secretary; in 1988, as already mentioned, Baker had tapped Lake as senior communications aide despite the fact that Sheila Tate was Bush's new press secretary.

Complicated? Yes and no.

Understanding past interrelationships of key players was the only way for me to understand what was happening in the present; without that background, there was no way to assess who had the power and who did not. Political titles, I realized, were not necessarily transparent when trying to equate authority on the Power Pyramid.

Back to New Orleans 1988.

During the final two days of the convention, the research division tried to stay on top of the avalanche of Quayle press. My newsletter team was inundated with anti-Quayle articles in papers from Los Angeles to New York. A *Washington Post* headline by Helen Dewar, "Battle Lines Form Over Quayle's Record," was typical of the hundreds sweeping the country. Battle lines had been drawn, and another meeting of the research staff was called to assess the extent of Day Two fallout.

Again, we viewed tapes of Quayle's television appearances, watching him respond to attacks by reporters who questioned every detail of his life and seemed concerned only with criticizing him, not listening to his answers. The press, having taken over in the "first seven seconds," seemed to have left Senator Quayle without any chance of a rally, and the idea of his being replaced—taken off the Republican ticket—had begun to surface as soon as his name was announced. And it was Jim Baker, campaign chairman, who had helped promote this notion! Baker had made it clear to the press (through Lake) that Quayle was not *his* choice, and that he was "going to do what he could with a bad situation." This attitude of Baker's, of course, was opposite to the message Bush was trying to communicate, and it set a negative tone for the rest of the campaign.

On Thursday night, August 18, 1988, the Republicans, all four thousand plus, gathered at the Superdome to nominate Bush as their candidate for President. For this last scheduled event of the convention, I had secured a floor pass, which entitled me access to where the state delegates were seated: I joined the Virginia delegation. The noise from where I sat was overwhelming and mesmerizing at the same time. Among flags flying, banners waving, horns sounding and delegates cheering, Bush walked onto center stage in the mammoth sporting arena to deliver his address.

Caught up in the whirlwind of energy, and standing only a few feet away from the podium, I listened to Bush give one of his most remarkable speeches. From behind the TelePrompTer shield, the Republican presidential nominee spoke boldly: "This has been called the American Century, because in it we were the dominant force for good in the world. We saved Europe, cured polio, we went to the moon, and lit the world with our culture. Now we are on the verge of a new century, and what country's name will it bear? I say it will be another American Century."

Despite the turmoil Bush had suffered in the two days prior to the convention finale, this evening managed to maintain its luster and dignity. Nonetheless, one phrase above every other would have unimagined ramifications. On acceptance night in New Orleans, Bush declared: "The Congress will push me to raise taxes, and I'll say no, and they'll push, and I'll say no, and they'll push again. And all I can say to them is *read my lips:*

No new taxes!" With time, this line would take on a life of its own, remembered by some as the most unfortunate choice of words a Republican presidential candidate had included in an acceptance speech.

Bush's New Orleans address had been written by Peggy Noonan, Reagan's speechwriter. The former CBS journalist talked openly about her previous obsession to find a way to write speeches for Reagan, a man she worshipped. After leaving his administration, she had telephoned Bush and volunteered to help him with his October 1987 candidacy acceptance speech. And then his 1988 convention speech.

In her 1989 memoir, Noonan tells about how Jack Kemp, another ultra-conservative Republican and staunch supporter of Reagan, had strong opinions regarding the issue of not raising taxes. According to Noonan, Kemp wanted to be sure the no-new-tax idea was included in Bush's convention discourse. He had told her to "Hit hard on taxes. Bush will be pressured to raise them as soon as he is elected, and he has to make clear he won't budge."

In the New Orleans speech, Noonan had emphasized concepts around the ideas of faith in God, family, decency, honor, pride, loyalty, freedom, faith, service to country, fair play, and strength… themes given to her by Bush, who also had scripted a personal remark about himself: "Others may speak better, look better, be smoother, more creative but I must be myself. I want you to know my heartbeat—this is where I'd lead." Such terms had led Noonan to write "kinder, gentler nation," and "This is America . . . a brilliant diversity spread like stars, like a thousand points of light in a broad and peaceful sky."

Standing in the Superdome on the evening of August 18, I reveled in the grand finale: a storm of confetti and balloons floating from the ceiling onto the convention floor. The scene reminded me of the rally in New Hampshire just hours before Bush won his first primary. As the memory of a frosty New Hampshire quickly melted away in the steamy Louisiana Superdome, speculation about what lay ahead was uppermost in my thoughts. With the conclusion of the Republican convention, a new phase of the Bush campaign had begun.

The final phase.

CHAPTER

7

THE FABULOUS BAKER BOYS

Part of his strength appeared to be his capacity to seem indifferent, to seem almost naïve about questions of power.

—Michael Korda

AUGUST 1988

Having been declared their Party's choice, George Bush and Dan Quayle, trailing Michael Dukakis and Lloyd Bentsen by almost 20 percentage points, faced an incredible uphill battle if they hoped to secure a Republican victory. The plan to assail Dukakis as a candidate who was soft on crime, lacking in patriotism, weak on defense, and negligent about his responsibility to the environment was about to be put into full gear. The first tactical exercises had been hailed a success; the results, however, were yet to be seen.

In August 1988, the most significant turn of events in the Bush camp was the downgrading of Lee Atwater as campaign manager and the elevation of Jim Baker as chairman. Baker stepped out of his "ivory tower" at Treasury and joined the Bush troops as their chief. Having appointed himself—more than three years earlier—campaign chairman, Baker was in charge of readying the campaign for the general election.

I had been at headquarters on several occasions when Baker glided through, and as he passed along the campaign hallways there had always been someone who asked: "Was that really Him?" Behind the patrician reserve, Baker was a lethal politician. No one questioned his authority, and his presence had—and would—remain towering in the campaign organization.

Bush's strong ties to Baker were somewhat of a mystery to me; I found the Bush-Baker friendship and political story both complex and out-of-the-ordinary. Bottom line was that Bush and Baker had defined each other's lives. More importantly, their individual personas were entirely different. The events taking place between 1958 and 1988—the times shared between these two men, politically and as friends—were fascinating. Their contrary, yet interwoven, relationship, more than any other factor, embodied the divergent limbs on the Republican family tree.

More than thirty years earlier, before moving to Texas, Bush had easily developed friends and begun new relationships, at prep school at Andover Academy, in the Navy, and at Yale University. After graduation from Andover, during the summer of 1943, Bush had been commissioned a Navy ensign and served aboard the aircraft carrier *San Jacinto*. Discharged as Lieutenant J.G. in September 1945, and after marrying Barbara, he enrolled at Yale in a class of eight thousand students, of whom five thousand were returning service men. His father, great-grandfather, uncle and brother also had attended Yale. After being voted "Most Respected" by his classmates and being captain of the Yale baseball team, Bush graduated in 1948 with a Phi Beta Kappa key and a degree in economics.

Soon afterward, a young George Bush, with his wife and first son, left Yale and the East Coast and headed West—to the flat plains where he was to work for Dresser Industries. Drawing on the diligent work values instilled in him by his New England family, Bush worked hard to establish himself. Midland, a city known for its oil wells, oilrigs, and tall bank buildings, became home for the Bushes, and in 1951, out in the middle of the West Texas brush, Bush became a cofounder of Bush-Overby Oil Development Company. In 1953, he cofounded Zapata Petroleum Corporation— named after a Marlon Brando film that was playing in town—and a year later, Bush became a pioneer in offshore drilling platforms with Zapata Offshore Company.

Looking back on his days in Midland, Bush had said: "There was unique warmth and camaraderie to the friendships Barbara and I made in those years, a lot like the attachment I felt to my shipmates and the members of my squadron during the war." The close ties Bush had established early on were indicative of the high priority he gave to his relations and associations throughout his life. Including Baker. On

★★★

Reagan sabotaged Carter's efforts to win the release of the hostages before the November election. Nonetheless, and in spite of a quarrelling campaign staff, Reagan won resoundingly over Carter in 1980. And Baker's stock rose.

The most unforeseen twist of the 1980 campaign was not that George Bush went on the ticket, but that Jim Baker was tapped as Reagan's chief of staff. Baker was a complete outsider to the Reagan clan and a vicious antagonist of Reagan's political dogma.

George Bush had created Jimmy's (as Bush called him) *entire* political career, starting with his change in Party affiliation from Democrat to Republican. The fourth-generation Texan and Princeton graduate (a few years younger than Bush) had followed Bush's political lead every step of the way . . . *until* he became Reagan's chief of staff.

In 1981, for the first time, the Bush-Baker momentum started to reverse itself, and Bush, as Vice President, started to turn toward Baker, as chief of staff, to see which way the political course would turn. During Reagan's first term, Baker would unilaterally orchestrate the Reagan presidency. All the while, the Vice President watched more than he participated. And during Reagan's second term, Baker, who chose to be Treasury secretary, continued giving orders. Despite the various Reagan chiefs of staff who would come and go after his departure (Donald Regan, 1985–86; Howard Baker, 1986–88; Kenneth Duberstein, 1988–89), Baker remained the dominant force behind the President.

Beginning in late 1984, with all his sharp instincts intact, Baker continued to be Reagan's most authoritative voice, while he simultaneously worked behind the scenes to establish a 1988 campaign organization for Bush. Baker often seemed more enthusiastic about the prospect of that run than did the Vice President.

Until August 1988, everything progressed as Baker planned.

Prior to the convention, there had been talk about Baker, the "900-pound gorilla," saving the Bush campaign ("Can Baker Rescue Bush? A Campaign Mr. Fixit" published in *Newsweek,* June 13, 1988). Predictions were that Baker would bring order to the splintered campaign by squelching the Republican infighting *and* suppressing the Dukakis forces. HE would save Bush from "going under."

In March 1988, it had been announced that Baker (who had learned the importance of timing) would finally quit his Cabinet post and make his entrance in the campaign in August. This was the schedule Baker had scoped out for himself during the first G-6 meeting in the Reagan White House during December 1984. Like clockwork, that is what took place. As a member of the original G-6 group and as campaign manager, Atwater had known for almost four years that Baker would appear on the scene just at the time of the convention.

Before arriving in New Orleans, Baker surprised most of us by announcing that he had appointed himself as Bush's chief public spokesman, and it was expected that would create some problems with the previously designated communication aides. In his all-encompassing role, Baker brought *his* staff to the convention. This was reasonable. What did not seem as sensible was that Baker's men all outranked Atwater and The Team. Baker's Guys, not Atwater's, were accountable for the way the convention unfolded, including the vice presidential announcement.

Many on Bush's senior staff were not in favor of Quayle for Vice President; however, Fuller and Atwater had thrown their support in his direction. Bob Teeter had conducted the polls for Quayle in his 1996 senatorial campaign against Jill Long (that showed Quayle did not suffer from a gender gap), and he, too, had backed Ailes's idea of Quayle being the number-two person. But never Baker.

Although Baker had not been in favor of Quayle, it was his staffer, Robert M. Kimmitt, who had orchestrated the search for a vice presidential candidate *and* who had run background checks and FBI clearances on Quayle before clearing him for the slot. Baker even called Quayle in New Orleans on August 16 and conveyed to him Bush's desire to make him his running mate. Naturally, Quayle had some reservations about his first introduction to the nation, and it was Baker who assured him that he would be in "good hands" with seasoned political strategists when it came to interacting with the media forces.

Baker knew firsthand about the anxiety Quayle was experiencing, for he had been with Bush when Reagan had tapped him for Vice President some eight years earlier. Now, Baker was on the other side of the phone, and he clearly understood the way the game was played. No time was quite as important as the first twenty-four hours after the vice presidential announcement—to Quayle, Bush and the Republican Party.

Baker botched the Quayle introduction.

I do not think that what happened to Quayle in New Orleans was unintentional, or some sort of fluke. Baker was too seasoned and too smart to let something so central to the Party happen without his authorization. As early as August 20, the last day of the convention, Baker made arrangements to keep Quayle under wraps for the remainder of the campaign. Quayle was actually locked out of key cities when it came to working the campaign circuit. In September, it became well known among those at the campaign and at the RNC that Baker was making sure Quayle was not heard from and was seen as little as possible. Soon, this situation was noticeable to the entire nation; Bush seldom mentioned his running mate's name. In a campaign update in the *National Journal*, published on October 29, 1988, the "Missing Quayle" situation was addressed this way:

> On a recent ABC News *Nightline* broadcast, when reporter Jackie Judd was asked by host Ted Koppel whether she had ever reported on the substance of his [Quayle's] views "rather than the issue of Dan Quayle" during her coverage of the campaign, Judd said "Give me a moment to think about that. I have to tell you I think not."

In describing the Baker-Bush relationship, the name Richard Darman, a man who had been by Baker's side for more than twelve years, has to be addressed. Having been Baker's deputy in the White House during Reagan's first term, Darman followed Baker to Treasury, again serving as his closest aide and confidante. Upon leaving his Treasury post for the Bush campaign, Baker had brought Darman with him.

This was not the first presidential campaign in which Darman had worked for Baker; he had been Baker's most senior aide in Reagan's 1984 campaign, when Baker was campaign chairman and Ed Rollins was campaign manager. After that win, Darman was placed at the top of Baker's G-6 organizational chart. Like the man he worked for, Dick Darman had remained behind the scenes of the 1988 campaign until convention time. Having already played a pivotal role in the Bush ranks for the previous four years, Darman now publicly joined the lineup, outranking Atwater.

Since his arrival in Washington in 1971, Darman had climbed the Political Ladder slowly, but persistently. The New England elitist had been an aide to Elliot Richardson (the attorney general fired by Nixon for refusing to carry out his orders to fire Archibald Cox—the special prosecutor investigating Watergate) not once, but four consecutive times.

He had been his senior aide when Richardson was secretary of Defense, attorney general, secretary of Health, Education and Welfare, and secretary of Commerce! Darman had made a reputation for himself as being a staunch anti-Reagan, anti-conservative liberal. Although his philosophies were "against the grain," he had quite an impressive political résumé for a youngster.

Baker had first met Darman in 1975 at the department of Commerce when Baker was appointed deputy secretary and Darman was there to supervise the transition from Secretary Morton to his boss, Richardson. Since arriving in Washington—beginning with his position at the White House in 1981 as chief of staff to Reagan—Baker had relied on Darman more than any other individual. During the early weeks of the 1980 Reagan transition (before inauguration and before he had been officially appointed as chief of staff), Baker, unassumingly and with a purposely low profile, assembled a group to work with him in the upcoming administration. He looked for people who knew the ropes in and around Washington and—most importantly—those who would remain loyal to him; loyalty, he knew, was the key to establishing power.

As a rogue Republican, Darman was one of the few Nelson Rockefeller followers in the administration; his ideas were diametrically opposed to those of the California conservatives surrounding Reagan. While Baker's deputy in the Reagan White House, Darman had managed all presidential scheduling, appointments, messages and correspondence. In other words, Darman, under Baker's management, controlled the flow of all information going into and out of the Oval Office. The pecking order in the Reagan White House stood as such: Jim Baker, Edwin Meese and Michael Deaver; they were referred to as The Troika. Although not on the official org chart, Dick Darman was situated between Baker and Meese.

During the 1987-88 campaign season—as Baker's deputy at Treasury—Darman had unofficially become the economic advisor to Vice President Bush. Known for embracing the idea of tax increases, Darman (an arch rival of Kemp), had vehemently disagreed with Bush's campaign tax pledge not to increase taxes. He raised serious doubts about Bush being able to keep his promise of no-new-taxes once in office, and was bitterly opposed to the idea of including the phrase in Bush's convention speech.

However, the pollster Teeter and his aide Bob Zoellick (a former aide to Baker at Treasury who, in 1989, would be one of his top aides at State) were also included on Noonan's tax "advisor" list while she was crafting the convention address. Before submitting the speech to Bush and Baker for final approval, Teeter and Zoellick—over Darman's disapproval—decided to keep the "no new taxes" slogan. So it was that on the last night of the convention, Bush had spoken those emphatic words. Darman had seemingly lost the fight. Only temporarily.

With reference to Quayle's situation, I believe that Baker, with his two buddies, Dick Darman and Jim Lake, played a central role in the mishandling of Quayle in New Orleans. I also believe that there were two other individuals with enough political seniority, savvy and proximity to Quayle to also have had a major influence on how the vice presidential nominee was introduced to the nation. Roger Ailes and Stuart K. Spencer should be held partly accountable for the Quayle debacle and the concurrent blow to Bush.

First, Roger Ailes. As the political and media consultant to Bush, Ailes had taken on an increasingly influential role in the quest for the Bush presidency, ever since the fall of 1987. He held one of the highest positions in the campaign and commanded the highest salary—$25,000 a month, twice that of Atwater. It was Ailes's job to prep the vice presidential candidate before he met the world; however, Ailes had not followed through with his responsibilities.

This was an unusual situation for several reasons. No one on the Bush team knew Quayle better than Roger Ailes; he had coached Quayle in his 1986 bid for the Senate, *and* Ailes had been the one to recommend Quayle be placed on the Republican ticket. What really made the 1988 circumstances perplexing was that Ailes knew more about political image making than *anyone*. He had learned at a young age.

At twenty-three, Ailes started out as an associate producer of the *Mike Douglas Show* in Cleveland, Ohio, where the then-local show was produced (later the television program was sold into national syndication). Next, he became a celebrity in his own right, as a New York advertising agent specializing in media techniques for candidates running for high office, including President.

Ailes had come to the rescue of Richard Nixon after his debilitating debate with John Kennedy in 1960, and he had revived Ronald Reagan in

1980 after his disastrous first debate with Walter Mondale. He had also come to the aid of Nicholas Brady, long-time friend of Bush, when Brady had turned to him for public speaking advice. Based on his experience with Ailes, Brady had subsequently brought Ailes into the G-6 in 1984, thereby creating a place for him in the Bush inner circle. By 1988, Ailes had a long, impressive history of "turning around" the politician. He was almost as much of a mythical figure as Jim Baker.

Although not a member of the G-6, Stuart Spencer was on Baker's short list. In the spring of 1988, Spencer had volunteered to manage the campaign for the second in command—long before Quayle was chosen. As the primary handler, he was responsible for making sure that the vice presidential nominee, at all times, was presented in the best possible light. When Baker told Quayle that he would "be in good hands," it was Spencer whom he had in mind.

Known as a slick California strategist, Spencer, like several others in 1988, came from the Nixon era. In 1966, he had been "loaned" to Reagan to assist him with his first run for governor. Afterward, Spencer had served as an advisor to Reagan on every one of his campaigns except for 1976, when he worked with Baker on Jerry Ford's team. Nonetheless, Spencer rejoined Reagan in his 1980 campaign, and after the Republican convention that year, along with Michael Deaver, Spencer recommended that should Reagan win, Jim Baker be appointed the new president's chief of staff!

While remaining a close personal and professional advisor to Reagan (in a few months' time, he would be on the plane with the Reagans as they made their way back to California), Spencer kept up with those staffers with whom he had started in the Nixon administration. For that reason alone, not surprisingly, Spencer and Baker had formed a political alliance, and this relationship had introduced Baker to those in the Old Nixon Line. And in 1984, Baker had put Spencer on Reagan's reelection team, right at the top with Darman, Ailes, and his two senior deputies, Rollins and Atwater.

While at the RNC in the fall months, I read an article about Spencer, a disconcerting piece in the September 21, 1988, *New York Times* entitled "Image: The Packaging of a President." After trying to digest the contents of the commentary by Lars-Erik Nelson, I came away with an unenthusiastic feeling about Spencer. Based on taped conversations in

Jane Mayer and Doyle McManus's book *Landslide,* Nelson quotes Spencer as he reflects on Reagan's 1984 campaign team:

> "They've run out of ammunition. The most striking thing I discovered is that they [Reagan's aides] don't have a goddam thing in the pipeline. They don't have an idea." Undaunted, Spencer then repackaged this intellectually unburdened Reagan crowd and sold it to the American public as "Morning in America." To his colleagues, Spencer explained Reagan's phenomenal success: "He ran against the ——ing government he was running. I mean, he believes he's above it all. He believes it. That's why they believe it. I can't believe it. But they do."

Spencer had been in Paramus, with Baker and The Boys in May when they decided to launch the attack against Dukakis. It was about that time that Spencer requested the position of managing the vice presidential campaign; he was looking for a job that he had not held before. Stu Spencer knew how to climb the political ropes as well as anyone, and so did the man he brought with him in 1988. Joseph Canzari was another individual out of the Nixon generation and a former public relations veteran with both Nelson Rockefeller and Ronald Reagan.

Quayle did not know Spencer, Canzari, or any of the others on his newly appointed staff. And once he became the vice presidential candidate, he had been cut off from his senatorial office aides, and had to trust what Spencer and Canzari told him. As it turned out, this was unfortunate for Quayle. The two former Nixon men had an agenda of their own, one that clearly did not include the best interests of Quayle, or, for that matter, Bush.

Under normal circumstances, Bush's choice of Quayle would have been an excellent one. Quayle had a reputation for being an astute politician and committed statesman; he was respected on the Senate floor and had distinguished himself on the Hill. As a solid conservative for eight years, he still managed to befriend the moderates and the liberals. And with his sense of humor and command of the podium, he had built relationships on both sides of the aisle, sometimes being described as an unorthodox conservative. At forty-one, he looked thirty; he was said to resemble Robert Redford, but this ambitious politician was more than just a Hollywood look-alike. He had been elected to Congress for two terms and had won a seat in the Senate. In his eight-year Senate tenure, he had served on three key committees: the Armed Services Committee, the Budget Committee, and the Labor and Human Resources Committee. These facts were seldom mentioned in 1988.

As the third-ranking Republican on the Labor and Human Resources Committee, Quayle had served as the senior minority member on its Subcommittee on Labor. He also served on the Subcommittee on Employment and Productivity (where, in 1982, he authored and won unanimous passage of the Job Training Partnership Act), and the Subcommittee on Education, Arts and Humanities. Through his first six years in the Senate, the young statesman had a cumulative voting attendance of over 98 percent, one of the highest. In and out of Senate circles, Washingtonians and constituents alike thought him to be bright, inquisitive and innovative. Whether the subject pertained to foreign policy or a domestic initiative, people listened to what Quayle said. In fact, few other politicians had achieved so much so soon.

Even Quayle realized that fact, as was evident in his quote in *The Making of a Senator* by Richard Fenno: "I haven't had many failures. So I just keep going on the theory that when you're hot you're hot. Now what will happen when the roof caves in on me, I don't know. It hasn't yet. And I never think of it doing so." In the 100th Congress, which convened in January 1987, Quayle was the ranking Republican on the Armed Services Subcommittee on Conventional Forces and Alliance Defense. He also served on the Subcommittee on Strategic Forces and Nuclear Deterrence and the Subcommittee on Defense Industry and Technology. A strong supporter of Reagan's Strategic Defense Initiative (SDI), he was also pro-business, pro-job training for the unemployed, and pro-abortion rights.

The left-wing liberals viewed Quayle as "not crossing over the line far enough." And the conservatives sometimes viewed Quayle as a traitor. The funny thing was that Roger Ailes knew how the right-wing Reagan Republicans felt about Quayle when he suggested him as Bush's running mate. I assume Bush, also, was aware.

Bush's relationship with Quayle dated back to 1978, when he was preparing to run against Reagan. Bush called Quayle, who was then seeking election to a second term in the House, to ask if he would campaign for him in Indiana. Quayle accepted eagerly. It could have been that Bush saw in Quayle the potential for loyalty and reserve, not unlike what he displayed in the Vice President's seat. And too, Quayle appeared to be a man faithful to ideals, taking positions based on principle. Bush and Quayle were even related. *The Washington Times* on November 11, 1988, published an article by genealogist Gary Boyd Roberts—a specialist in the lineage of presidents—showing that Vice President Bush and Senator Quayle were tenth cousins, once removed.

With the proper handling (incumbent upon his political advisors— Baker, Ailes, Spencer and Canzari) Quayle should have won the hearts of America. Instead, he had fallen victim to a political disaster. Again, I state, that in my opinion, the events surrounding Quayle in New Orleans—and beyond—*could not* have happened the way they did by accident. The Power Players were just too experienced in this area to allow the events to unfold so untidily.

The unraveling of Quayle's public image proved to be the first significant event in the demise of the Bush legacy; forty-eight hours *before* Bush accepted his Party's nomination, the present and outgoing administration was at work to bring Bush down.

Kernels of political discord were firmly planted in New Orleans, and in time, these seeds would give growth to a web of tangled vines, eventually choking and destroying the President and the Vice President of the United States. Quayle never would recover from that sizzling day in New Orleans when he ran down the gangway of the *Natchez* onto the riverside docks. And although Bush would experience an unexpected and sudden rise in popularity after the convention, afterward, he would suffer as well.

Irrevocable damage had been done.

The G-6, always in place, had arrived.

CHAPTER

8

THIRTY-SEVEN MURDERERS

While I nodded, nearly napping, suddenly there came a tapping
As of some one gently rapping, rapping at my chamber door.
                                        —Edgar Allan Poe

SEPTEMBER–OCTOBER 1988

Just before the Republican National Convention, surveys showed that Bush was rapidly losing ground. California, New York, even Texas were turning toward Dukakis. With a huge seventeen-point lead, the Democrats were controlling the campaign agenda and the gender gap was widening (Bush trailed three-to-one with women voters), a disparity made all the more significant because 10 million more women than men were projected to vote.

Dukakis was expected to take 278 Electoral College votes, leaving Bush with 128. Shortly after the Republicans met in New Orleans, however, the political tide reversed itself. By the first of September, Bush, amazingly, was ahead of Dukakis by a margin of 46 percent to 40 percent.

Back at my desk in the RNC library, I was reading the articles clipped by Doug Campbell from the previous day, September 14, 1988, and an article in the NEA written by Robert J. Wagman caught my eye:

> Take a tour of Dukakis's headquarters these days and the feeling you get is less of a campaign in panic than of one shell-shocked by the turn of events since the Republican Convention. Going into the third week of August, almost every poll showed Dukakis with a double digit lead. Most national polls now show Bush with a small lead. For the last three weeks the Dukakis camp has allowed George Bush to completely set the campaign agenda. The Democratic

campaign has been forced into the role of responding to Bush, and this has allowed the Vice President to dominate the nightly news and turn things around.

Three days earlier, on September 11, 1988, in the *Washington Post,* Mary McGrory had written an article titled "The Bush Barrage," which had captured pretty much the same details outlined by Wagman: "As they wait every day for the shells to come over, the people in the Michael Dukakis encampment get their few and hollow laughs by remembering what George Bush said about wanting 'a kinder, gentler, nation' in his acceptance speech. Obviously, he doesn't want it to happen any time soon."

In the fall of 1988, one of the reasons for the amazing change in political surge was the use of television advertising. Close to 50 million viewers tuned in each evening to watch the political "line of the day." The way Bush and Dukakis were portrayed on the national news stations had an impact on their respective rise and fall in the polls.

The Bush campaign was accused of running a deplorable negative assault against Dukakis. Successful though the Bush advertising seemed to be, the ads were attacked for being filled with partial truths and clever distortions, and one of those cited was Boston Harbor. Although faulted for being harsh and unfair to Dukakis, the Boston Harbor ad could not be criticized for untruths or for misrepresenting the facts. It was not some hasty sound bite. I can attest to that. Drawn from weeks of research and data crunching, my conclusions had been turned into a smart thirty second commercial by Ailes.

My feeling was that the news media should have picked up on Dukakis's harbor oversight before I did. But they had not; I was the first to uncover it. Granted, while I conducted my research, I was not completely impartial, and I looked at the governor as an attorney would making a case against a defendant—from only one angle. But my job had been to find a way to discredit Dukakis, and I had simply used the available data to form my deductions, never knowing Dukakis would ever see or hear what I had written.

In 1989, Christine Black and Thomas Oliphant came out with a book, *All by Myself: The Unmaking of a Presidential Campaign,* about the 1988 campaign of Michael Dukakis. In that tome there is a chapter in which the authors refer to Boston Harbor. Little did I know in 1988 that what I "unearthed" would one day appear in a book about the campaign—from the Dukakis point of view:

> In one of the truly remarkable campaign moves, Bush succeeded in putting Dukakis on the defensive with the environmental issue. The weapon was Boston's historic harbor, which had been a repository for garbage and other detritus since the American Colonists pitched tea into it two hundred years ago. Harbor cleanup did not become a government or widespread public issue until well after a more environmentally sensitive era dawned. Boston Harbor is still filthy; it was a fissure in Dukakis's record, and the Bush campaign turned it into a political San Andreas Fault; and most important, Dukakis let it happen.

The Ailes-produced Boston Harbor advertisement, which aired nationally the third week of September, spotlighted Dukakis's mishandled pollution restrictions by showing a video of some of the 48 million gallons of sludge and foul water that ran daily into Boston's harbor. Using quotes and statistics from my research, Ailes had included a statement from Michael Deland, EPA regional administrator (who would head Bush's White House Council on Environmental Quality), as saying: "The harbor cleanup delay was one of the most expensive public policy mistakes in the history of New England."

During September and October, stories pertaining to Boston's muddy waters were on the rise, including a comical one from San Francisco that was written up in the *Campaign Newsletter*. For some reason, when I read it, I did not find it that amusing. Maybe the issue had turned too serious for me to appreciate the humor:

> This week's mail in some newspaper offices in San Francisco included an unusual campaign package: a small vial of water described by one recipient as "clearish with little things floating around in it." Accompanying the water is a statement saying, "In Massachusetts this might pass for Perrier, but we suggest you don't drink it. This is genuine Boston harbor water, bottled especially for the California Bush-Quayle campaign. We don't recommend it with fish. We don't recommend it with chicken. We don't recommend it with pasta. In fact, we simply don't recommend it."

Despite the joking associated with the vial of water, the harbor commercial drew as many critics as fans. It was labeled one of the two

★★★

most recognized negative campaign ads in the election. The Willie Horton "Furlough" clip, also know as the "Revolving Door" ad, was deemed the most heinous and indecent and was the most controversial of the Ailes ads. There were many inaccurate accusations and interpretations connected with the Bush Horton ad.

Filmed at Utah State Prison, the black-and-white commercial centered on criminals and crime, showing black, white and Hispanic prisoners leaving through a made-for-Ailes revolving prison door. The set was accompanied by a voiceover giving information to an "official" authorizing furloughs to murderers not yet eligible for parole. No names were mentioned. However, the message was that Dukakis was soft on crime. Many saw the ad as offensive, but going a step further, some chose racism as the overwhelming issue.

The basis of the Furlough ad was a true story about Willie Horton, a black man convicted of the murder and dismemberment of a teenage gas station attendant in Massachusetts in 1974. In 1988, Horton was one of four prisoners at the New England Correctional Center in Concord, Massachusetts, who were ineligible for parole. Having committed a first-degree crime, he was sentenced to life in prison. Then, in 1987, Governor Dukakis decided to issue the four men a weekend furlough. Upon being released, Horton fled to Oxen Hill, Maryland, where he broke into a home, stabbed a twenty-eight-year-old man named Clifford Barnes twenty-two times and then raped Barnes's fiancé twice.

On December 2, 1987, CBS News had presented an account of the Horton horror on television. And over a period of almost a year, hundreds of articles had been written about the episode, fueling popular outrage in Massachusetts and pressuring Dukakis to end the furlough program. Neither I nor anyone else I knew in the campaign had read the article in *Business Week* magazine (March 28, 1988) in which all the Horton particulars had been spelled out, including this quip:

> According to the *Boston Herald* article of January 6, 1988, Dukakis granted commutations to 37 murderers during his first term. Moreover, he has strongly defended a policy granting convicted murderers weekend furloughs, though his staff says he is reconsidering his position in light of a recent tragedy (the Horton story).

Dukakis had been presented with a bill that would have eliminated furloughs for first-degree murderers sentenced to life without parole; however, he decided to pocket veto it. The Massachusetts program, which was unique in releasing felons early in their sentences rather than at the end, continued. Due to public outcry, Dukakis finally reversed his decision, but not without a fight and not any too soon; it was late spring 1988 before he did so. By then, the whole country had been exposed to the Horton story—*before* it came to the attention of the Bush campaign.

In April '88, a week before the New York primary and directly after the *Business Week* article, Senator Al Gore used the Horton story to embarrass Dukakis during the last Democratic primary debate. At the *New York Daily News* debate at Madison Square Garden, Gore was hoping to show Dukakis "soft on crime" and get the edge he needed to stay in the race. In the debate, he asked: "If you were elected President, would you allow a similar program for federal penitentiaries?" Never responding, Dukakis went on to another subject, and the murder incident was ignored. Gore's question had not done anything to boost his ratings; in fact, Gore was out of the race after the New York primary. Nonetheless, Bush campaign research director Jim Pinkerton had noticed that Dukakis appeared uneasy with Gore's question on the furlough issue.

In July, nearly three months after the Gore-Dukakis debate and two months after the Bush team first got wind of the story, *Reader's Digest* ran a lengthy article entitled "Getting Away with Murder." The Horton story was now everywhere and, it should be noted, at no time had there been any mention of the Horton furlough/murder having racial overtones. By now, Pinkerton had determined the Horton incident was one way to paint Dukakis as a liberal. Coupled with Dukakis's opposition to capital punishment, the Bush squad could portray the Massachusetts governor as sympathetic to criminals. This was even better.

The Paramus focus groups and test-marketing study conducted by Teeter and company in late May confirmed Pinkerton's suspicions that the furlough issue was weighty material. Starting on Memorial Day weekend, Willie Horton (although never named directly) and his furlough tale had taken on a significant role in the campaign—way before other issues evolved.

However, what made "the furlough" both confusing and disturbing was the fact that several outside campaign organizations, with no

★★★

connection to the Bush campaign, used the Horton material in a much more explicit manner. A contributing factor to the mix-up was that one of the groups was the Republican National Committee. A fellow researcher at the RNC, Peter Borranao, had worked on collecting information on the Horton account, and his material mailed to state offices had helped expose the story.

The chairman of the Maryland Republican Party, Daniel E. Fleming, was one of the individuals requesting RNC information. He was in the process of preparing a mailing for a state fund-raising campaign. Included with his letter were photographs of Dukakis and Horton and a statement saying, "You, your spouse, your children, your parents and your friends can have the opportunity to receive a visit from someone like Willie Horton if Mike Dukakis becomes President." The headline on Fleming's letter read: "Is this Your Pro-Family Team for 1988?"

Clearly, the Maryland propaganda had crossed the line. But the RNC staff had not participated in the writing of the flyer nor had they approved it before its mailing. It was a Maryland-initiated project, specifically designed by a Maryland Republican team to be circulated to Maryland residents, and had no connection to the Bush national campaign. Yet despite the explanations, it was thought to be Bush-related. (As an aside, in 1989, Borranao received an appointment to the department of State—one of the few to be assigned there—yet, because of bragging about "his" RNC work regarding Horton, he was fired and would never return to the administration.)

Jim Baker went on the CBS News program *Face the Nation* to denounce the Maryland fund-raising letter, saying it was "totally out of bounds, totally unauthorized, [and] not authorized by this campaign."

As soon as he did that, another organization, hoping to exploit Willie Horton, appeared on the scene; this one was named the National Security Political Action Committee.

NSPAC also had ties to the Republican Party. Three of their production people—Larry McCarthy, Jesse Raiford and Floyd Brown— just happened to be former employees of Roger Ailes at Ailes Communications. The connection did not look good for the campaign, especially since the NSPAC ads were far too graphic and descriptive, citing the names of both Horton and Dukakis. I cringed when I read the thirty-second script for "Weekend Passes," as published in the *New York Times* on November 11, 1988:

Side-by-side photographs of Bush and Dukakis (were on the screen) while an announcer said "Bush and Dukakis on crime." Then flash to a picture of Bush. "Bush supports the death penalty for first degree murderers." Then a picture of Dukakis. "Dukakis not only opposes the death penalty, he allowed first degree murderers to have weekend passes from prison." Flash to a mug shot of a glaring Willie Horton. "One was Willie Horton, who murdered a boy in a robbery, stabbing him nineteen times." Flash to another blurred black-and-white photograph of the convict, looking enraged as he is being arrested by a police officer. "Despite a life sentence, Horton received ten weekend passes from prison," the announcer says. "Horton fled, kidnapped a young couple, stabbing the man and repeatedly raping his girlfriend." As the announcer gives these details, the words "kidnapping," "stabbing," and "raping" flash on the screen. The last photo is of Dukakis. The announcer says: "Weekend prison passes. Dukakis on crime."

As campaign chairman, Baker was supposed to approve all advertisements before they aired. Upon first learning about the NSPAC commercials, he had the right to veto them. Whether or not he tried to stop the Horton commercials is not clear, but Brown, with or without the campaign's blessing, proceeded with his rendering.

The Willie Horton advertisements and the ensuing negative backlash were a large reason for the dubbing of the 1988 campaign as the "Smear Campaign," the "Down-and-Dirty Campaign," and the "Sleaze Campaign." News media reported that the country was "disgusted, disappointed and mistrustful" of both the campaign and the candidates. According to an October 20-21, 1988, *Newsweek* poll, voters were fed up with all the election hype and found the advertising to be "dirtier" than in past campaigns. Quite simply, Americans felt that better-qualified candidates should have been selected, and they did not believe the men running for president were giving honest views on the issues.

Yet, when the public was asked, "Who is most responsible for the negative aspects of 1988's campaign?" the vast majority of respondents to the poll answered, "The way news organizations are covering the campaign." The press corps and journalists played up the *un*constructive issues and constantly referred to the "Dirty Campaign." No doubt, advertising played an important role in determining the way individuals viewed the presidential race of 1988. Although the press (and, therefore, the public) focused on the off-putting ads, there were actually more positive than negative commercials in 1988.

The two most popular feel-good Bush ads were the one of the Vice President throwing his granddaughter up in the air and catching her . . . and the one of Bush with his wife as he was being sworn in as Vice President in 1981. The first was meant to convey warmth; the second expressed majesty and humility. The favorite positive Dukakis ad was the one that showed him relaxed, talking about his family and the problems young parents faced. In this clip, the Massachusetts governor promised—in a tag line that closed many of his ads—"The best America is yet to come."

For the most part, the positive message communicated by the Democratic and Republican contenders in these visually pleasant moments were tossed aside in the fall of 1988, and the electorate, ironically, chose to remember the ads they approved of least. In the Bush camp, this response was unexpected.

In the early spring of 1988, when Bush advisors first came up with the idea to paint Dukakis as a Massachusetts liberal—a man who did not hold the values of most Americans—they did not anticipate much success, just enough to keep them in the race. In fact, the Paramus Attack Plan had been launched during the summer months—only because Bush had been straggling behind Dukakis by such a wide margin. It was an act of desperation. Bush was in a defensive position, and the ads were devised to create a more level playing field. The Bush team had hoped to move into a less-combative mode by fall after the general election campaign officially would have started.

But by Labor Day, the blueprint they had set in motion just weeks earlier had been so successful and had made such an impact, that a second plan to use positive Bush advertising was never necessary. Everyone, including Bush, went with what was working. The Bush themes, along with the symbols they represented, were all the Vice President needed to surge ahead.

With no discredit to Roger Ailes—he and his media crew were the best—I do not believe his ads were compelling enough to turn the campaign around and win the election. Nor do I believe that Ailes's negative media blitz against Dukakis, which most often was publicized to be the reason for the Bush turn-around, was the distinguishing factor for the change in the public opinion polls. What gave Bush his advantage— and what won the election for him— was Dukakis's response. Or more to the point, his lack of response.

Not fully understanding how compelling the Ailes-produced images behind the Bush ads were (e.g., the harbor, the convict), Dukakis never refuted the attacks. He did not feel "they" were the real issues to be dealt with. Nor did he think the American public would buy into them. These were Bush's issues. Dukakis wanted to bring *his own* to the table. So, while Dukakis and his staff waited for the real issues in the real campaign to begin, they lost complete control. As a result, they never brought anything substantive to the competition.

Thinking that their team was still playing an offensive game (relying on the fact that they had been ahead seventeen points), the Dukakis war room made the mistake of underestimating the blows of the Bush attack. Consequently, they misread the public's response. Because Dukakis never fought back—other than with a knee jerk reaction—the Vice President enjoyed a political match without any real opposition. The Bush successes were played out on the evening news in televised appearances; Dukakis trudged on while Bush breezed through.

During the first week in September, Bush made his promotional environmental splash in a boat tour of the Boston Harbor. In the near-perfect national television airing, Bush appeared strong and invigorated. On September 2, aboard the ferryboat the *Bay State*—complete with brilliant blue skies and gentle breezes as a backdrop—Bush looked presidential, relaxed, and strong. The ad worked. In the words of Christine Black in *All by Myself*, "Bush literally sailed into Boston's harbor at the end of the summer and used the murky ocean water to deliver a scathing indictment of Dukakis's record as governor." Accompanying her text was a photograph of an exuberant Bush, standing aboard the *Bay State*.

In contrast to Bush, Dukakis, when on television, was cast indoors, looking like a college professor lecturing, appearing clumsy and unprofessional. Seldom was an affirmative image of Dukakis seen on national news, and when his media crew finally shot him outside, it was disastrous.

Dukakis either looked diminutive in an M-1 tank wearing an Army helmet (with his name across the front) careening across the lawn or was depicted standing among charred ruins of fire-ravaged Yellowstone

National Park. The Tank Ride clip was supposed to show Dukakis's support for conventional forces, but it backfired, and the Yellowstone shot, an attempt to portray his interest in the environment, gave the opposite message. These images of Dukakis, showing an almost comical rather than commanding figure, were broadcast across the nation for all to witness.

Dukakis and his crew made many mistakes during the fall of 1988; however, I conclude today that he is an honest and decent man who, with his academically oriented staff, fell victim to overconfidence. His gubernatorial expertise—other than harbor management—was not something I explored in 1988, but since then, I have taken an interest. I regret not having had a broader biography of Dukakis during the time I was unknowingly fighting him. Dukakis, who grew up in affluent Brookline, Massachusetts (on the Western border of Boston—overwhelmingly Democratic and extremely Catholic), came from a strict Greek-immigrant background. He had been taught, as had George Bush, the principles of duty, honor and the intrinsic value of hard work. An intelligent and scholarly man, well educated at Harvard, Dukakis surrounded himself with people of similar abilities. Presidential politics almost always involves hurting good people. I realize now that I contributed to doing that in 1988, but it was never my intent.

In the Bush campaign and at the Committee, we constantly compared our senior leaders to those in the Dukakis lineup. I learned that these star players were often more telling about a candidate's campaign than the candidate himself. At the RNC, I studied up on Dukakis's three strategists, all lawyers. Thirty-two-year-old Susan Estrich was a professor at Harvard Law School and the first woman to hold the title of campaign manager for a major Party's presidential nominee; in title, she was equivalent to Lee Atwater. Paul Brountas was a longtime confidante and former Dukakis college classmate. As national chairman, he was our Jim Baker. And John Sasso had "made" the political Dukakis; he was the one to suggest that Dukakis run for President in 1988.

Sasso had become Dukakis's top political strategist, serving in the same capacity as Lee Atwater, until September 1987. After spearheading Dukakis's presidential campaign as manager and national political director, Sasso had left. He had clandestinely supplied the news media with a videotape accusing Senator Joseph Biden of plagiarism, which resulted in Biden's departure from the race. In the fall of 1988, a year later and a year too late, Sasso returned to the Dukakis campaign just in time to witness the collapse of his forces. Headquartered on Chauncy Street in Boston, Sasso, Estrich and Brountas were left in a sinking ship.

A prime example of the Dukakis team's inability to rally was captured in how they responded to the Pledge of Allegiance issue. During Bush's acceptance speech in New Orleans, he had asked: "Should public school teachers be required to lead our children in the Pledge of Allegiance?" Bush answered his own question, "My opponent says no, but I say yes." In fact, Dukakis had said "No" when he vetoed a Massachusetts state bill requiring teachers to lead their students in the pledge while facing the American flag mounted in their classrooms. In an overreaction to Bush, Dukakis had started reciting the pledge at all of his campaign rallies; the more he brought attention to the subject, the worse it got.

With bad news steadily coming out of Boston, Jim Baker began to act as if the recent Bush successes were all his own doing. Displaying his chameleon-like characteristics, he no longer was of the opinion that Bush would never win with Quayle on the ticket. From my vantage point, Baker was far removed from the driving forces of the Bush campaign in the fall of '88, yet, without a bit of difficulty, he managed to quickly assume the lead role, taking all the credit when the political current started to flow in Bush's direction. In September and October, his contribution to the troops was not much more than keeping the cruise-control switch turned on; he gave his line-of-the-day, promoting the already-in-place negative advertisements. That's it.

Baker's principal job, it appeared, had been to keep everybody away from Vice President Bush, ensuring that The Team was kept at bay, including Quayle. While decreasing Bush supporters' access, Baker significantly enhanced his own. This tactic—assuming that Bush won—would give Jim Baker the command position, and with it, he could continue giving all the orders.

Politics—the insatiable quest for power and prestige—was sometimes capable of bringing out the best in human nature, but it could also promote the worst. I sometimes think that there is a direct correlation between our leaders and inflated egos, and when winning has to do with assuming the world's most powerful job, egos are in overdrive.

Unfortunately, what I observed happening at headquarters was also apparent at the Republican National Committee. With just over a month until the election, the Bush campaign, once again, reeled in a rush of internal rivalries.

★★★ ═══════ ★★★
CHAPTER

9

WHILE BOSTON SLEPT

"The opportunity of defeating the enemy is provided by the enemy himself."
—*Chin-Ning Chu*

OCTOBER 1988

Autumn 1988 was unusually magnificent, with warm, sun-filled, crystal-blue-sky days. While I remained mindful of my precarious situation at the Republican National Committee, being there had allowed me to continue research efforts and also afforded me the opportunity to enjoy life on the Hill during one of Washington's finest fall seasons. Being covertly housed at the RNC worked to my advantage: I became familiar with a section of the city I had not known before.

Politely positioned between several other white-brick buildings on First Street, almost at the corner of C Street, the Committee was just a block away from Independence Avenue, the Capitol Building, and the Supreme Court. It stood across the street from the Cannon House Office Building, with the Longworth and Rayburn buildings just down the street on Independence Avenue. The Capitol Hill Club next door was frequented by many congresspersons and senators as well as those of us on staff at the RNC. The most popular restaurant and bar within blocks, Bullfeathers, was at the south end of the street.

Sometimes, after sitting at my desk for hours at a time, I found it a welcome relief to stroll through the tree-lined streets of the neighborhood. Most of the quaint townhouses on Capitol Hill had seen better days, but they still maintained their splendor, and the small gardens that graced their historic entryways were now ablaze in autumn's jewel-colored hues.

A quiet, cohesive community, the Hill appeared almost rural when compared to downtown Washington, home of the Woodward Building and campaign headquarters.

Despite the residential feel outside the front door of the Committee, life inside was anything but tranquil. While the Dukakis campaign was self-destructing, the Republicans appeared more involved with fighting one another than assailing the opponent.

Frank Farenkopf, appointed by Reagan, was presently chairman of the RNC and had been in that position since 1983, and Maureen Reagan, the President's daughter, was co-chair. With Ms. Reagan and Fahrenkopf on their way out, Bush had appointed Frederic Malek to take over, making him deputy chairman. Having just managed the Republican convention in New Orleans, Malek had a career as a businessman and was a former top executive with Marriott Corp. Previously, he had been a White House appointee in the Nixon administration. By chairing the 1988 convention—at the personal invitation of Bush—Malek had made his comeback into politics.

As the recent convention chairman, Malek had performed admirably, but often, he was out of his league, especially when it came to dealing with individuals like Jim Baker and Jim Lake. Despite Malek's top position in New Orleans, Baker had run the show. And because Malek had been out of politics for some time and had few connections to the Reagan White House, he was considered an outsider by those in the administration, including the individuals at the RNC.

Presumably, the Committee job would give the able businessman an opportunity to stand on his own. Responsible for directing the day-to-day RNC campaign operations, Malek would act as the link between the five hundred-member organization and the senior staff at campaign headquarters. It was predicted that he would quickly take over Fahrenkopf's command and essentially have all the control that was assigned to the chairmanship station.

But, there was a glitch in the plan.

Just as Malek started his new job, several newspaper articles came out relating to him during his Nixon White House days. As the former personnel director to Nixon and one of John Mitchell's senior deputies in the 1972 campaign for reelection, Malek had come under fire in 1973 for having compiled figures for Nixon regarding the number of Jewish

Democrats serving as top officials at the Bureau of Labor and Statistics (BLS). These accusations of anti-Semitism now resurfaced in 1988, and Malek was denigrated for his past transgressions. Within days, accounts about Malek and his involvement with Nixon, going back to 1968, were placed in every Washington newspaper. According to the reports, Nixon had relied on secret internal polling for personnel selections as well as policy decisions, and based on his private 1971 polls, he believed a Jewish cabal was inside the BLS trying to undermine his economic programs. From covert poll results—which Nixon did not share even with his own pollster, Robert Teeter—the President developed an Enemies List, and he needed someone to confirm just how many individuals of Jewish heritage worked in the BLS. Malek was assigned the job.

After being pressured by Nixon for the personnel count, Malek (previously having declined to follow the order four times), finally responded that there were twenty-four Democrats in twenty-five positions at the BLS, and about half were Jewish. Malek also related that the statistics being used at the BLS were fair and not skewed. Still, Nixon wanted more of "his own" in the career ranks—thus, the drafting of the Malek Manual. This plan, drawn up in 1971, concerned the hiring and firing of civil service employees, and was said to be the cause of two individuals being moved to less senior positions in the BLS. There was some initial speculation as to the reasons for their demotion, but before the issue got out of control, it came to an abrupt end. The turmoil revolving around the Watergate affair took precedence, and the "almost-scandal" was forgotten.

This incident seventeen years earlier, now resurrected, was leaked to the *Washington Post* in October 1988. Dubbing Malek one of Nixon's former "Hatchet Men," the *Post* took the position that Malek's previous actions (his tolerance of anti-Semitism) was an "embarrassment" for the Bush campaign and was cause to dismiss him from the RNC. The campaign spokesperson responding to the *Post's* accusations said, "We are very troubled by the story." After that, Malek was abruptly fired. But, before leaving, Malek composed a personal note to the RNC staff, and on his last day, he posted it in the RNC elevator. As I went to my office on the day after his firing, I read it: "The story in the *Washington Post* was offensive and incorrect and my 'resignation' is difficult because all my instincts say to stay on and defend myself against the outrageous charges."

True or not, relevant or not, the BLS story had tainted the RNC chief, and because the accounts had hit the newspapers *(How? By whom?* I asked myself), the campaign could no longer afford to keep him. Malek was publicly exiled in the name of saving face for the senior Bush advisors and the good name of the Committee. This likeable and accessible man, whom I often saw in his rolled-up shirtsleeves walking the labyrinthine RNC hallways, was gone. Just like that.

I felt a tremor of recognition. I had been there myself, only I had not had the insight or instinct to fight back. Now, just weeks before the election, the Vice President's aides ousted the RNC deputy chairman.

How suddenly a person in a political position, at any level, could be discarded by another with more power. This element of hidden peril— never knowing what the next day would bring—gave working in politics its edge; it kept adrenaline pumping and hearts pounding. Like the climber making his way to the top of Everest, the politico knows that with just one misstep (not always within his control), he could land at the bottom of a crevasse. Just surviving, when so few actually do, is part of the attraction of being in politics. The odds are against you. The risks necessary to attain the summit are what make the challenge of the political climb both exhilarating . . . and lethal.

Reflecting on the saneness of my own trek, I realized I had started the ascent without knowing there was a peak to reach, not to mention how incredibly difficult it was just to remain on the trail. I saw how rivalry intensified ruthlessness. Nonetheless, there was the lure. For myself, once I experienced the "misstep" of Boston Harbor and thought I had been too injured to go on, I fought to stay and continue the climb.

The individual who, years ago, had claimed the highest rung on the political ladder—the Power Pyramid—was, of course, Jim Baker. After the convention, once he became a visible chairman, I thought there would be rousing news pertaining to his finally being with "us." Just the opposite. I hardly heard anything about our leader. And although I always kept my eyes and ears open, I seldom found any out-of-the-ordinary news tidbits pertaining to his latest heroics. Baker had received so much attention before New Orleans—about what he was doing and what he was going to do—that his lower profile in the fall was that much more noticeable.

There was the usual conversation about Baker's line of the day, his message of the day or week or whatever, but besides that, little else seemed to come from the captain's quarters. Baker may have been taken by surprise when Bush made a rebound in the polls and actually had a chance at winning. And I imagine with the turn of events, Baker was rearranging his plans for the future, a future in a Bush administration. With the campaign on cruise control and Atwater still close by to manage, Baker kept Bush severed from his team, allowing him (Baker) plenty of time to think about what was important: Jim Baker. Just as he had in 1980 and 1984. Baker did not have to make front-page news every day to remain significant. Silent or not, he was the chief.

At campaign headquarters, the Bush staff prepared for the upcoming Bush-Dukakis debates. Ninety-minute face-offs were set for September 25 at Wake Forest University in Winston Salem, North Carolina, and on October 13 at the Pauley Pavilion in Los Angeles. Before the first debate aired, some feuding occurred that involved whether or not the candidates would sit or stand. Bush wanted to sit, while Dukakis preferred to stand. They ended up standing, which proved advantageous for Bush, who was a half-foot taller than Dukakis.

It is hard to say who wins a presidential debate, but the press later wrote that, in North Carolina, Bush outperformed Dukakis; the Massachusetts governor was portrayed as rather chilly and dispassionate. Also making the news was the October 13 debate, in which Bush did well presenting his attack and defense positions, while the governor failed miserably. The Dukakis breakdown had to do with one reply in particular. CNN's Bernard Shaw (with a panel of journalists), asked Dukakis the first question of the evening. It was a personal question: "Governor, if Kitty Dukakis were raped and murdered, would you favor an irrevocable death penalty for the killer?"

Dukakis, in a very professional manner, as if he had been asked to explain farm subsidies, said: "No, I don't, Bernard, and I think you know that I have opposed the death penalty all of my life. I don't see any evidence that it is a deterrent, and I think there are better and more effective ways to deal with violent crime." From there, Dukakis went on to talk about the crime rate and drugs and on and on and on. Realizing what had happened, Bush struck with a tactful yet direct response and quickly turned the issue of crime into one of values: "You see, I do believe that some crimes are so heinous, so brutal, so outrageous—and I'd say particularly those that result in the death of a police officer—those real brutal crimes, I do believe in the death penalty."

Although Dukakis's reply was not what the public was expecting nor desiring to hear, I identified with Dukakis. It was clear to me that while under the pressure of television cameras, he had answered philosophically and generically, not because he was not devoted to his wife, Kitty, but because, beneath the lights, he was answering in terms of the politician, not the husband. Nonetheless, in doing so, Dukakis had left out the all-important human element, not referring to how he would *feel* about his wife being harmed.

Politics seldom encourages the politician to be himself. The more accepted route is to say what the *listener* wants to hear. Dukakis thought he had done this. He had given an honest, straightforward answer, and a political one; however, in this case, it would have been to his benefit to have given a more personal one. A heartfelt comeback—usually not a politician's first response—was what the people, in this case, wanted to hear. Watching the debate in the RNC research room, I realized that Bush had successfully connected with the American viewer. Dukakis had not.

The one vice presidential debate between Dan Quayle and Lloyd Bentsen was held on October 5 at the Omaha Civic Auditorium in Nebraska. It had been hailed as the "Senator versus Senator" debate. Still bridled by his handlers and still distanced from the American electorate due to Baker's power, Quayle had gathered more than his fair share of critics. Recently he had been accused of being admitted into Indiana University Law School under a program designed for the economically disadvantaged; the question of preferential treatment had come up, and it was expected to cause trouble for Quayle at the debate.

Yet, it was Bentsen's one-liner regarding another topic that was best remembered for doing harm to the young vice presidential nominee. Quayle began: "I have far more experience than many others who sought the office of vice president...I have as much experience in the Congress as Jack Kennedy did when he sought the presidency." Then Bentsen zinged: "Senator, I served with Jack Kennedy. Jack Kennedy was a friend of mine. Senator, you're no Jack Kennedy." A cutting remark regarding Quayle's lack of qualifications. After the match was over, Quayle's performance was tagged controversial, and consensus was that Bentsen won.

Although I did not like Bentsen's attack, I felt it was within the lines of normal debate confrontation. There was little Quayle could do to rectify the situation—his ongoing story. Quayle's senior political advisors had taken over his life, and beginning with his live television interviews in New Orleans, he had been surgically unraveled and removed from the campaign circuit. Based on what I heard about Quayle inside the Bush campaign during September and October, I believe that his Republican supporters were attacking him more viciously than his Democratic opponents. These assaults proved to diminish Quayle's character and advance Baker's strategy for creating an invisible VP candidate. Quayle's predicament was summed up in "Quayle Role As Phantom Of Campaign" in the *New York Times* on November 7, 1988. Richard Berke wrote:

> The disappearance of Dan Quayle is apparent. Call up a local Bush-Quayle office and there is a good chance the telephone will be answered "Bush headquarters." Many Republican bumper stickers do not include Mr. Quayle's name. In fact, the most attention given Mr. Quayle is from Governor Dukakis and Mr. Bentsen. Mr. Bush's aides have employed a simple strategy throughout the campaign: act as if Mr. Quayle did not exist.

Quayle was too new to the national political structure to balk when instructed to "do it this way," even when it was detrimental to the success of his candidacy. What is bizarre is that this "harnessing" of Quayle was no secret; all of us in the campaign saw what was happening, and we knew that Quayle's staff was the reason for most of his woes. Campaign friends of mine assigned to Quayle's advance team who accompanied him on political trips brought back stories about the appalling way Quayle was treated by his own aides.

Quayle's senior staff, starting with his chief of staff, Stuart Spencer, was unsupportive and critical of him in public and in the press, often making reference to Quayle being "more than they could cope with." Stu Spencer's aides in Quayle's office were Joseph Canzari, David Prosperi and James Cicconi.

Cicconi was the young Texan whom Baker had brought into the Reagan administration as Cabinet secretary and then appointed as one of his personal aides. (In the Bush White House, Cicconi would serve in the same capacity as Darman when Baker was chief of staff—one of *the most* critical jobs—deputy to the chief of staff for presidential appointments and correspondence.) Since August 1988, Prosperi had worked as Quayle's press secretary, having served as assistant press secretary under

Fitzwater in the Reagan White House before becoming the director of public affairs at the department of the Interior. In the Bush administration, Prosperi initially stayed with Quayle in OVP before being selected as assistant secretary of public affairs at the department of Transportation with Sam Skinner.

With experts such as Spencer and Canzari (and now Cicconi and Prosperi), how could it be that Quayle's "presentation" remained such a calamity? I surmise, as I did during the convention, it was no slip up. By portraying Quayle as the comic fool, Spencer intended to embarrass and humiliate Quayle. And Bush.

Coming from the ranks of the right-wing conservatives, Spencer was considered an insider to Nixon's old crowd as well as Reagan's present one (he accompanied Baker to Paramus). Spencer viewed George Bush as not being worthy of high office. Nonetheless, this was not going to keep politicos like Spencer out of the action. Politics ran in their blood, and they did not need to respect a candidate to work for him. Quayle's staff members used Bush and Quayle to put forward their own agenda and maintain *their* egos. It had nothing to do with loyalty to the candidate. Self-aggrandizement was part of the Power Game, a sport that Spencer aptly played, even after being fired by Quayle.

Spencer's former Los Angeles-based Republican consulting firm, the Dolphin Group, "coincidentally" formed the Committee for the Presidency during the Bush-Dukakis battle, and the group functioned under the pretense of being part of the Bush campaign. In October 1988, Spencer's company released two unauthorized Willie Horton commercials (without any endorsement by Baker or Atwater, so it was reported in the newspapers). The thirty-second spots featured Donna Fournier Cuomo, sister of the man Horton murdered, and Cliff Barnes, the man Horton had terrorized. Both of these commercials, being Horton ads, caused just that much more confusion regarding what was *really* coming out of the campaign ranks.

After the vice presidential debate, and contrary to what was predicted, Quayle seemed to take on a revitalized stance. He seemed renewed, even confident, during the last weeks of the race. For the first time, Quayle was doing things his way. Angered by reports that he was a robot and a drag on the Republican ticket, he decided to break ranks from his own staff (Spencer and Canzari) and be his own man. He had come out with, "There's not going to be any more handler stories because *I am the handler*." (Tom Sherwood, October 11, 1988, *Washington Post*.)

Baker, who had successfully kept campaign staff away from Bush during the months following the Republican convention, had kept Quayle isolated from both Bush and the public as best he could. Those who should have been Quayle advocates had turned out to be his enemies. Not having previously known the men assigned to him as "protectors," Quayle still was able to figure out—in less than two months' time—that he did not want these men on his staff. Having been subjected to their less-than-adequate behavior, he made the only decision he could: he fired Spencer, Canzari, and Cicconi! He left the experts behind and resolutely took charge of his own political welfare.

While Quayle let go of his handlers, he also put himself in a vulnerable place. For now, though, following in Bush's wake, his position was tolerable, especially while Bush continued to grow in popularity.

In mid-October, a hopeful and confident Bush made a five-day West Coast tour: the theme song aboard Air Force II was "Don't Worry, Be Happy," a song in the Top 40 at the time. According to a *Washington Post*–ABC News Voters Presidential Preference Poll, Bush was leading 52 percent to Dukakis's 44 percent. With a strong advantage, the Vice President held solid leads in twenty-one states and had a predicted 220 electoral votes—just 50 short of the 270 needed to win. The gap would narrow right before the election. But not by much. With Dukakis somewhere in the wings and his staff appearing befuddled, the Bush contingent seemed unstoppable.

Back at headquarters, the significant gain did not change Atwater's orders; his strategy remained the same. In his shrill voice, he would shout, "I don't want complacency. I don't want anyone acting smug, and I don't want anyone pulling any punches." The staff was instructed to keep the heat on every hour of every day. "I want everyone to run like we are ten points behind," Atwater would bark. Fifteen points up or fifteen points down, Atwater had held the campaign ship steady and had managed to weather the many storms over the previous fourteen months. He was always out in front and always accountable. Beginning in September 1987, I had seen him under every imaginable condition. Despite his fiery outbursts, he had always kept cool enough to lead the campaign to the next challenge, and the next, always appearing to be focused on the moment, determined to win.

When Baker officially became chairman in August, it was assumed Atwater would be much less in touch with the campaign staff. Not so. Because of Baker's absorption in other matters (such as whether he wanted to be secretary of State or Vice President), Atwater had continued to shepherd the flock, albeit in a less glorified and less assuming manner. On the public front, Baker always liked to meet the press, making the appropriate statements at the proper time, and when the campaign needed either a spokesman or someone to receive a pat on the back, Baker was there front and center. Atwater was made responsible for everything that went wrong, and seldom was commended when they went according to plan.

During the home stretch, I remained at the RNC doing research, but it was really past the time for doing much investigating. Because I had become well instructed on how to run the RNC's Lexus/Nexus system, I did some of the more complex searches on stories not yet in the news. And more often than not, I was beginning to think about my move back into the private sector. I had decided that I wanted to work in the District, doing opinion research.

Despite the distractions of job hunting, I always stayed on top of the political news. On my desk each morning were clips from the *White House Daily News,* the *RNC News Summary* and the *Campaign News,* containing hundreds of the latest articles, which I quickly skimmed when I arrived. On October 13, I read an article in the *New York Times* by R. W. Apple, Jr. Addressing the failing Dukakis campaign, Apple quoted Governor Bill Clinton as saying that Dukakis had hurt himself by permitting the Bush campaign to "savage him on television for four or five weeks, unanswered, on issues important to Southern rural voters." The Clinton quotation continued:

> You don't have to be all broke out with brilliance to know what to do. You need some blunt, no-nonsense, hard-hitting television that responds to their charges and makes positive points about Dukakis. You need to scrape off some of the barnacles Bush has put on his image. But you can't do that now with those awful commercials they're running now, with the fake Bush strategy meetings.

At the time, the Apple piece hit me as amusing. Maybe because of the way Clinton (about whom I had no previous knowledge) came across

★★★

as such an unpolished politician ("barnacles"?). Odd that, in spite of his coarse manner, Clinton was chosen by Dukakis to introduce him at the Democratic convention, a day that should have been one of the most memorable in Dukakis's career.

I wondered why the well-read, articulate Massachusetts governor, surrounded by Harvard-types, would tap Clinton to set the tone. After a long-winded, unpopular nominating speech, Clinton suffered politically, both nationally and in his home state. The Arkansas governor's role in the 1988 election had come to an abrupt end after convention time, to the point of his not being received inside the Dukakis camp. Little did anyone anticipate that, in four years' time, Clinton—the man cast out by the Democrats for a speech introducing the nominee—would *be* the nominee.

On November 2, in the final hours of the campaign, the *Washington Post,* which maintained a lukewarm position for both Bush and Dukakis, came out with what they called a "No Endorsement" editorial. Historically, the *Post* was more pro-Republican, but whatever their stance in 1988, they were not forthcoming. Part of their editorial read: "The *Washington Post* does not have a candidate in this campaign. Neither man running has established claim to the office that we find compelling. So far as endorsing either of their candidacies is concerned, each is, by our standards, too deeply flawed."

With another point of view—somewhat cynical but not enough so to make it offensive—Everett Carll Ladd at the University of Connecticut made these observations in his November 4, 1988, article in the *Christian Science Monitor:* "Of course there are problems this year in the 'making of the president,' but it would be both unfounded and unfortunate to pass through our 51st presidential election without seeing it for what it is—an impressive spectacle."

Many of the transformations in the 1988 election cycle were due to changes in the voters' interests. According to a Wirthlin poll in 1984, 77 percent of the voters considered either an economic or foreign policy concern as the most important problem facing the country; that figure was down to 35 percent in '88, and of those, only 8 percent named a specific foreign policy issue.

Crime, drugs and the environment were on the minds of the people of the Republic. Times were shifting, and in spite of last-minute disputes in the media about who should or would win, the bottom line was that

Bush had an undefeatable lead. Dukakis never would be able to scrape off those "barnacles."

An ABC poll taken the day before the election showed Bush in the lead by thirteen points. Newspapers described him as being assured of a win with an "insurmountable advantage." It was suggested by some that there could be a landslide victory.

Looking back over the previous fourteen months of the campaign, I felt as if I had been on a nonstop roller coaster.

Bush was down in the fall of 1987. He was ahead by year's end. The Vice President was crushed in Iowa. Bush was a wimp; he would never win over a heavyweight like Bob Dole; his political career was over. Then Bush rebounded in the New Hampshire primary, and after Super Tuesday, we knew that Bush was going to be the Republican nominee. Al Gore looked to be the opposition. Then a few weeks later, it seemed as if Jesse Jackson was going to be the opponent.

There had been four long months during the spring and early summer when it looked as if there were no way Bush could pull ahead. Our thoughts were confirmed in July, just before the Democratic convention. Dukakis had it locked up. In mid-August, Bush was the underdog by seventeen points, struggling for recognition in a race that seemed already over. California was predicted to throw its huge block of forty-seven electoral votes to Dukakis. The press and the polls said there was no way.

On top of that, Bush had been hit with the Quayle-Thing.

It all seemed so hopeless—until September.

Dukakis dropped the ball and left an opening for Bush not only to catch up but also pass him.

The Bush campaign staff had been there to take benefit from the unexpected opportunity. The anti-Dukakis material Baker and Atwater and Ailes and Pinkerton used during the summer months, predicted to be outdated by summer's end, lived on into the fall, never losing its punch. Dukakis turned out to be "the issue," not Bush, leaving Dukakis to defend his position.

The Dukakis strike squad had hurled just as many attacks at Bush (Iran-Contra, Noriega, and the environment) as the Bush team had hurled at Dukakis, and they were just as negative. Just not as effective. Roger Ailes, as always, had been brilliant in his use of images. The right ones delivered at the right time. That was not by coincidence. Ailes was a master of his craft, and upon reflection, I wish that while working on *my* craft with Boston Harbor, I could have had the opportunity to labor directly with the master rather than incognito. The Bush advertisements produced in 1988, including the furlough, the flag and the harbor, were accomplished in a proficient and skillful manner. The material was accurate, the sourcing ethical. Nonetheless, the journalists in 1988 coined the phrase "negative campaigning," and *that* is how the campaign would be remembered.

During the weeks leading up to the election, the Bush team sat back on their haunches and simply watched their candidate roll into the winner's circle. At this point, the only strategy they needed was to keep doing what they already were doing. Replay the commercials. It was working without being refueled. *Without effort.* It could have been likened to the perfect wave a surfer catches at just the perfect moment. The one that, with a thrust and momentum all its own, takes the rider safely to shore, while all he has to do is remain onboard. Jim Baker and company were riding the wave.

After what was described as a volatile last week on the stump and a grueling last weekend of whistle-stop campaigning, Dukakis finally was back in Brookline, and Bush in Houston. On the day of the election, Tuesday, November 8, the work of the campaigns came to an abrupt halt. The strategists, schedulers, pollsters, advertising sages, press agents, media mongers and researchers all put their vocations aside. Baker, Atwater, Brady, Teeter, Fuller, Spencer and Darman closed shop. Bush, Dukakis and the rest of the country waited for the returns.

As for those of us remaining in Washington, including hundreds of Bush campaign workers, their spouses, escorts and families, we gathered for a victory party at the Washington Hilton Hotel on election evening. Dan and Marilyn Quayle joined us. When the major television networks declared Bush the winner (with the exit-poll projection of more than 270 electoral votes), the usually sedate ballroom at the Hilton turned into a circus scene. Women in shimmering cocktail dresses and men in dark suits sang the victor's song while the champagne flowed. We celebrated a conquest that just two months earlier had not been foreseen.

As masters of the universe, we marveled at our splendid political strategy, forgetting about the claims from the press of having run a campaign that was "issueless" and having conducted ourselves in an "unworthy" manner. That night in the Hilton, the campaign staff chose to believe that the issues had been real and that the Bush victory represented a well-informed choice by the American people.

Although it had not been a landslide (and the Republicans lost seats in both the House and the Senate, making for another Democratic Congress), Bush swept every region in the country and won by more than seven million votes. With 426 electoral votes, he thrashed Dukakis, who totaled only 111. An estimated 94 million Americans had voted. Bush obtained 54 percent of the popular vote to Dukakis's 46 percent.

Until just weeks ago, it was a feat no one had forecast—not even Atwater, who always *said* we would win. The Vice President had been guaranteed to lose; in spite of that, he won. And the triumph, though significant, was a mishap, leaving the Democrats disillusioned and the Reagan Republicans thwarted. They never had planned—nor desired—a win by George Bush. Truth be told, the Bush campaign had won on luck more than anything else. Not the most noble way to win a political battle, but that is the way it was. Bush had successfully attacked Dukakis, but the opponent simply had not responded. Having said that, I give Bush, Ailes and Atwater credit where credit is due. Bush was an honorable candidate; Ailes a superlative media artist; and Atwater the committed campaign manager, without whom we may have lost even with the last-minute advantage.

Nevertheless, it was due to the mistakes of the Dukakis team—both in the offensive and defensive lines—that Bush was delivered the crown of victory on Tuesday, November 8, 1988, and was elected the nation's 41st President.

The day following the election was declared a holiday for all Republican National Committee members and campaign staff. I was invited to Andrews Air Force Base for the arrival ceremony in honor of the Bushes, who were flying back to Washington, D.C., from Houston. My former officemate in research at headquarters, Russell Rockwell, asked me to ride out with him and his wife. On the morning of the President-elect's return to the Capital City, the Rockwells and I jubilantly left the District and headed for Andrews. The crowd was small in comparison with the one the night before and, for that reason, seemed much more personal and less remote from the nominee-turned-winner. I

★★★

liked the feeling of closeness, as if I were part of a large family in which one of the members had just won a stupendous award. Vicariously, I experienced the moment as my victory, too.

The hangar that usually housed Air Force One had been transformed into an arrival site and greeting area. Bleachers filled the space in which sleek presidential jets usually parked. Out on the tarmac, the imposing Boeing 707, flying the Bushes home, made a smooth landing. The plane, with its football-field-length fuselage painted white and an underbelly in blue, slowly taxied toward the hangar where we were seated. I could see on the upper portion of Air Force Two the words "The United States of America" distinctly written in bold, jet-black letters; the American flag was emblazoned on the tail with the numbers 56974 inscribed directly underneath.

Upon arriving at Andrews, I had received, as had the other guests, a small American flag to be waved when the Bushes and Quayles appeared. When the Bushes deplaned Air Force Two to join the Quayles, hundreds of flags went into the air along with a multitude of cheers. It may sound like a cliché, but at that moment I felt overwhelmingly proud to be an American. On that unusually warm November afternoon, as I waved my flag, I wished that my Father—maybe in his Navy dress blues—could have been standing there beside me. Father, the patriot, coming from seven generations of military loyalists, would have known exactly how I felt, and he also would have been pleased.

All the disappointments, anger, surprises and delights that I had undergone in the previous fourteen months drifted through me, leaving me with a dual sense of exhaustion and gratitude. He made it! We made it! I made it! I was confident that President-elect Bush would bring with him to the White House the pride, loyalty, and service to country upon which our nation was founded, virtues that I felt he so aptly represented. More than ever, I believed he *was* the decent, honorable man I thought him to be when I first set foot in the Woodward Building in September 1987 to work in his presidential campaign. Now Bush returned to Washington to claim his prize. He deserved it; *the* shining moment in a year of many blemished ones.

Balloons and American flags covered the makeshift campaign platform adjacent to the mammoth plane, from which George Bush, with Barbara and the Quayles standing next to him, delivered the requisite remarks and congratulations. After Bush thanked us for contributing to his conquest, he paid tribute to Reagan, saying that the former President "was one of the great heroes of the modern era." While standing among the banners and crepe paper, I remembered something Bush had said about himself not so long ago at the Republican convention in New Orleans, "I may not be the most eloquent. I may sometimes be a little awkward, but there is nothing self-conscious in my love of country."

George Herbert Walker Bush, who started his presidential campaign amid charges that he was "too nice" to win, celebrated the fact that he had proven them wrong. His dream of a triumph had become a reality. The statesman had won the presidency by a throw of the dice. A lucky pitch. But nevertheless, he had won. Now he was starting a new game. With the 1988 campaign over, the seventy-three-day transition to take the President-elect to the White House had begun. Forces were presumably already in place to ensure that it happened efficiently and without delay. I would find out sooner than most just how ready they were.

Washington, D.C., Summer 1988
Are they Reagan troops or on the Bush team?

★   ★

PART 3

In Sheep's Clothing

★   ★

All warfare is based on deception. Hence, when able to attack, we must seem unable; when using our forces, we must seem inactive; when we are near, we must make the enemy believe we are far; when we are far away, we must make him believe we are near.

—Sun Tzu

★★★ ▬▬▬▬ ★★★
CHAPTER

10

FORM BATTLE LINE!

It is important to bear in mind that all Presidents make serious mistakes. That is guaranteed by the shear speed of events, the difficulty of the job, and human fallibility.
—*Carl M. Brauer*

NOVEMBER 1988

Four days before the election, November 4, 1988, I clipped an article by Jean Becker from *U.S.A. Today*. Included in "He . . . seemed Energized, Brought to Life by the Loss" were comments from Bush's eldest son about his father's setting his own agenda. I disagree with his observations; nevertheless, this is what George W. had to say regarding his dad:

> I think the explanation is simple. This is a man who is in the autumn of a highly successful career. He recognizes this is his final foray into politics. It's given him a sense of peace. I remember a point in June when things were looking really bad. I had a long talk with Dad. The campaign was fairly dispirited. But not dad. He was confident. He knew what he wanted to do and how he was going to do it. He was going to be the one setting the agenda.

Now that the campaign was over and the election won, setting an agenda for the incoming administration was foremost on everyone's mind, not just Bush's. Even President Reagan had begun to think in terms of transferring his presidential authority. On November 10 in the *Washington Post*, Lou Cannon wrote the commentary, "President Reagan, Passing the Torch, Has Praise for the Victor and Vanquished":

> President Reagan passed the torch of leadership in the sunlight of the White House Rose Garden yesterday, with words of praise for victor and vanquished and the hope that the next four years will extend and deepen the legacy of his two-term presidency. "This is not the end of an era, but a time to refresh and strengthen our new beginning," said Reagan, with President-elect Bush and his running mate Dan Quayle standing by his side. "In fact, to those who sometimes flatter me with talk of a Reagan revolution, today my hope is this: You ain't seen nothing yet."

At 10:30 on the evening of the election—after the networks had declared Bush the winner (and not a moment before) Reagan had made the congratulatory call, and shortly thereafter, he had asked his top aides to submit their resignations. A presidential team organized under the leadership of Ken Duberstein, Reagan's chief of staff, planned to assist Bush with the White House part of the transition. Despite what many people assume happens when one Party inherits an administration from members of the same Party, there is an enormous amount of work to accomplish.

The changeover from Ronald Reagan to George Bush would prove to be one of the most problematic and bewildering transitions *ever*.

From the time a President-elect wins an election to when he has established himself as President—usually about six months—his administration is in the transition *"period."* However, the seventy-three days, (or approximately ten weeks), immediately following the election and before inauguration is most often referred to as *"the"* transition. The president-elect sets the agenda for his new administration, and his transition team launches the Office of the President-elect or Transition Office or simply Transition.

The goal of this select group of advisors is to help guide the President-to-be in setting his new course. Given a seventy-three day window in which to do the impossible, these individuals formulate policy and personnel actions for the new administration. The work they accomplish during these ten weeks, hasty though it must be, sets the tone for the next four years. No single period of time in a President's administration is as significant or as telling as the pre-inaugural transition days.

This is the moment when the power and direction of the incoming president is either established or lost!

What is at stake is momentum. If the incoming President loses his authority at this point—usually due to mistakes made in personnel selection—there is seldom opportunity to reestablish himself. For a brief period during the transition days, presidential power hangs in the balance, waiting to be obtained, and not always by the individual for whom it was intended. Although filled with the chance for individual gain, transitions are equally filled with possibilities for loss. Still euphoric about claiming one of America's greatest accomplishments—winning the presidency—the victor must simultaneously be composed and levelheaded enough to make senior-level appointment decisions.

In the late fall of 1988, Bush, who had scored a bigger popular win than Reagan, Nixon, Kennedy or Carter, was forced to decide who would be his most high-ranking aides. Almost three decades earlier, while reflecting on his own transition, former President John F. Kennedy had said, "For the last four years I spent so much time getting to know people who could help me get elected that I didn't have any time to get to know people who could help me, after I was elected, to be a good president."

George Bush's problem was not the same as Kennedy's; Bush had known the individuals who helped elect him *before the campaign started.* He had been in the Reagan White House with most of them since the beginning of his political career. Still there was a problem: Bush made the mistake of assuming that those who had supported Reagan in his presidency would shift their allegiance to him. That would not happen.

WHEN critical personnel for the Bush administration were starting to be selected, I received a letter dated November 9, 1988, from President-elect George Bush. It read:

> Dear Anne:
> From the snows of New Hampshire to the Convention in New Orleans to our victory on November 8th, I have been helped and inspired by the untiring efforts of people like you. This mission could not have been accomplished without the time and effort that you and other loyal supporters brought to this campaign. Our great team gave me strength to meet the challenge. I share this victory with you and thank you for all your help.
> Warmest personal regards,
> George Bush.

This may have been a form letter, but for me, that did not matter. In fact, of all the many personal and political items I collected and received during my years in politics, this remains the most meaningful.

During this same week in November, I returned to my office at the Republican National Committee. An eerie calm permeated the hallways and the offices of the usually vibrant committee headquarters. Because I had not been issued a termination date, I stayed on a few days to clear out my desk, and on November 10, I received a phone call from Dave Dawson at Bush campaign headquarters. I knew Dawson from my days in the campaign volunteer office, but his call—the first I had received from anyone at headquarters since I moved to the RNC in July—took me by surprise. Before I had time to make small talk, he asked if I would consider taking an unspecified job with the Bush-Quayle Transition Team. It would start the next day.

I had never planned to stay with the Bush organization beyond Election Day. No one at the RNC had said anything to me about continuing, and I had just assumed my banishment had ended all ties with the campaign. I had looked into joining a research-marketing firm in the District. But, out of curiosity—and a little excitement—I accepted Dawson's offer and agreed to be at campaign headquarters the following morning. The call was over before I could ask how my name came to be on the list. That question would never be answered. My assignment to Transition was as swift and mysterious as my exile from the campaign staff some four months earlier. It just happened, with no explanation. No matter the details, I was thrilled to be placed in one of the most sought-after assignments in Washington: the Transition Team.

The next day, I nostalgically entered the Woodward Building to fill out a standard set of security clearance papers, and while doing so, I observed the final dismantling of the brain of the 1988 Bush campaign. Computers, tables, chairs, and packed boxes were stacked in piles waiting to be hauled away, thrown out or sold; U-Haul trucks were waiting outside. The sight of everything being removed from the premises gave me a strange and empty feeling.

As I sat at a desk in a corner of the busy first floor and surveyed the chaos, I reflected on the many times my family had moved from one home to the next. Always off to yet another homestead. I had watched the moving crew of Mayflower or United Van Line's loading the furniture

★★★

and boxes into the back of twelve by thirty-foot "container," shoving all the family objects inside a fourteen-wheel truck. The good with the not so good, the old as well as the recent, packed in a brown box or wrapped in a brown canvas cover. The finality of it all. Another ending. Another goodbye. It was never easy to leave behind the familiar and go into the unknown.

Now, sitting among the bundled campaign boxes, I felt the same way. I was still emotionally attached to those offices where it had all begun fourteen months earlier, the place where I had first entered the world of "political intrigue." Pulling myself together, I completed my security papers, and then took the Metro train uptown to 1825 Connecticut Avenue, the headquarters of the Bush Transition Team. It was the end of the second week in November and of another phase of my Bush years.

The Universal Building, a 1950s-style white marble office building sandwiched in between the Bank of Pakistan and a Roy Rogers franchise, was what we now called the Transition Building. Of the five floors in the Universal Building, four belonged to Bush The office complex was half a block down from the Washington Hilton Hotel, the sight of the Victory Party earlier in the week and the hotel in front of which President Reagan had been shot in 1981, just seventy days into his first term.

On the same day that I filled out my security papers, a group of eight of us was asked to scope out Universal. When we arrived, I was astonished to find hardly anyone there. Except for the security guards stationed inside the building, there was mostly unoccupied office space, professionally decorated and nicely furnished, but no one sitting behind the desks and no one to answer the telephones.

In one of the larger office complexes, workers were installing access for a fifteen-line phone bank. When they finished their work—and because the phones started to ring—I gathered four or five teammates together and started answering incoming calls. We told the callers that the office had not officially opened and to call back. By Tuesday, the makeshift phone bank had evolved into the Transition's information hub. The center was now handling hundreds of incoming calls a day. Without any formal management, the Transition Team had begun to take shape. Staff filled the once-empty offices.

Although from the outside, the building did not appear that much different from any other five-story building in northwest Washington,

access to it was indeed unique. An unusually large number of security
police stood watch and patrolled the locale day and night. Behind the
three sets of glass doors at the entrance and in front of the red ropes that
secured the first floor area, there was a large sign that read: "Presidential
Transition Visitors Must Register at Security Desk." Unauthorized
visitors were not welcome.

Getting into the building was difficult enough; getting onto a
designated floor was much more of a challenge. The police force lined each
story, standing one officer to every fifteen feet or so in the hallways,
making sure no one without the proper credentials entered. Those of us
"assigned" wore identifying badges around our necks, allowing access
only to the floor on which we worked. Going from one level to another was
prohibited without special clearance, and even then, security agents met
us at the elevator door. For the next ten weeks, while going about our daily
duties, we were hermetically sealed inside this fortress.

There were no more than 150 paid members and almost an equal
number of volunteers. The paid staff drew on the $3.5 million that
Congress had appropriated for the Bush Transition. In 1980, Reagan had
one thousand more members on his team than did Bush in 1988. Where
Reagan had spent almost all of his $2 million (as well as hundreds of
thousands of dollars in private funds), Bush, who raised no private
money, would return almost $1 million to the taxpayers. Surprisingly,
some of Bush's unpaid staff included Lee Atwater, John Sununu, and
George W. Bush. The President-elect's chief of staff, and now Transition
chairman, Craig Fuller, was still on the payroll of the office of the Vice
President. The team that established George Bush as President was one of
the smallest of any President-elect.

Once the information center was in place, I was asked to take a
position with the Résumé Management Group under the leadership of
Ted Lewis in the office of presidential personnel. Lewis reported to Chase
Untermeyer, director of Transition presidential personnel and soon to be
director of personnel in the Bush White House.

My new job began on November 16. With twelve others, also
reporting to Lewis, I started to review the more than one thousand
résumés that arrived each day; there would be over 100,000 applications
by inauguration time. People from all across the country sent in their bios
hoping to find jobs in the administration, either in one of the 3,000

★★★

positions dispersed "at the pleasure of the president," or in one of the hundreds of part-time positions on boards or commissions. Included with their applications, they attached everything from photographs of their pets to their children's latest swimming awards, not to mention copies of their birth certificates and even wrapped pieces of chocolate candy. However, there was no time for emotional reactions to these highly personal packages.

Having worked in corporate executive search for two years, I should have had the advantage of knowing something about personnel systems, but nothing I was familiar with was very useful. Because there was no administrative support, we had to arrange the huge amount of incoming mail ourselves. Quickly, I designed a sorting matrix and a set of criteria to guide us. On each résumé, we either recommended an individual for "further evaluation" (separately tagging the "must hire" individuals) or cut him or her out of the system. And we did it all by hand. Our office had no computers. In 1992, Clinton would implement a highly sophisticated Resumix computer system that processed, stored, and acknowledged (by letter to the sender) the résumés received every day. What would take the 1992 Resumix three seconds to scan took us fifteen minutes.

After all the initial processing was completed and candidates were determined, we sent the applications down the hallway to be entered into one of the four or five desktop computers in the data-entry office. The few computers and computer programs at Transition were not much more sophisticated than those that we had struggled with at the campaign. Due to the archaic process, added to the large number of candidates, we just hoped that the résumés would safely make their way into the Transition computer. Without a tracking system, we had no way to either retrieve them or track them. They were gone, supposedly transferred to our sister personnel organization at the Reagan White House.

Crucial to the biographical data relocation was the combining of our files at Transition headquarters with the files in the White House. This was vital to getting an appointment system up and running after inauguration. In fact, the successful merging of résumés was *imperative* to running the new administration.

Unless our records at Transition were properly input to the computers at 1600 Pennsylvania Avenue by January 20, Bush would not have his team in place. Absolutely everything hinged on the computer transfer. Those of us in Lewis's office were logging in long hours, relying on the fact that the transmission was taking place.

Lunchtime became our get-away-from-it-all time, and Dupont Circle with its countless restaurants became our daily retreat. We often unwound at Suzanne's down the street, a small, quiet place where, over a bowl of pasta, we would review the day's events. Or we might go to Timberlake's across the street, where the atmosphere was not quite as sedate but the club sandwiches and French fries were terrific. On several occasions, we ordered take-out food from the Red, Hot and Blue Restaurant (where Lee Atwater played with his band) and feasted on southern barbecue inside the headquarters.

Another boost to morale involved two unannounced visits. During the first part of December, Bush came to the offices, and went from room to room, meeting each person. Shortly after the Vice President's visit, Arnold Schwarzenegger came by to introduce himself. The Austrian-born movie star—tan and thinner than I thought he would be—was wearing a khaki suit and was all smiles as he went from office to office shaking hands, giving pats on the back and expressing his appreciation for a job well done. Bush would later tag Schwarzenegger to head up the Council on Physical Fitness.

Right before Schwarzenegger's "house call," I was transferred to yet another office in Transition, still in presidential personnel, but this time in the office of Detailed Evaluation. By now, it was difficult for me to keep track of the various jobs I had had since campaign days. Over a period of sixteen months, I had seven jobs: four in the campaign and three in Transition. Unlike most other working environments, political positions come and go quickly, with no rhyme or reason. I never knew who recommended me for a job, including my newest one with Ted Bureaux.

Detailed Evaluation was part of Lewis's résumé management organization, but in a separate division headed by Bureaux. This small group of men and women marched to their own drum, and because they were so few in number and held more senior positions than most in presidential personnel, they came and went as they saw fit. Some worked long hours while others came in only a few hours a day; however, most were putting in the requisite six-day week. The work was not anything we could do hurriedly. Assigning specific senior-level jobs (in an agency) to the "must hires" took time and personal consideration. While doing so, the Plum Book *(The United States Government Book of Policy and Supporting Positions)* became our bible. The 230-page softbound tome was the granddaddy of all publications. Because it listed the most sought after and best paying federal jobs—with over 7,000 positions and a pay scale that ran from $30,000 to more than $100,000—it was the hottest-selling book in Washington.

No matter what source one used, locating the most appropriate and promising political job for any one individual was never easy. Of the more than 100,000 applications predicted to come our way, fewer than 3,000 would move into the administration. This realization sometimes made our job discouraging. Challenged by the immensity of it all, I nevertheless found the opportunity to learn about the agencies, job titles, and pay structure to be absorbing. It was a civil service personnel education in itself.

My work with Bureaux lasted a relatively short time, and before long, I received my last and fourth duty in presidential personnel. I moved to the office of Scott Bush, the President-elect's nephew. For the most part, Scott's office was undisclosed, and what he did was kept top secret. This made me somewhat curious about my newest assignment, which I forecasted to be my last before returning to the private sector. As always, nothing would happen as I planned.

11

POLITICAL RIPTIDE

Those individuals who seem most resolute, who seem so sure of themselves, are often the ones who have lost their way.

—Richard Bode

<u>DECEMBER 1988</u>

While still at the Office of Presidential Personnel (which used the reverse acronym PPO), I started my work with Scott Bush, a young man in his twenties and nephew of George Bush.

Scott was at a disadvantage in his job because he had no previous knowledge of—or experience in—his uncle's 1988 campaign organization. He simply had not been there. Surprisingly few on the Transition team had worked in the campaign, and no one from the campaign was in presidential personnel. Jim Pinkerton and some others from the research staff were appointed to the Transition policy development group, but because I never saw them, I concluded they did not have offices inside headquarters. Or maybe, with the offices so isolated from one another and guarded so closely, I just missed them.

By title, and because of his name, Scott Bush held one of the most senior personnel positions in Transition. He and his small staff were responsible not only for obtaining Bush-specific campaign background information on the candidates but also for verifying that what these individuals put on their résumés was factual. Thinking that in order to get an appointment it was important to have campaign experience, many applicants misspoke regarding their history. My job entailed running campaign background checks on the "must hire" applicants.

Having worked at both campaign headquarters and the RNC, I knew staff and campaign positions better than anyone at Transition. Recalling names and staff assignments from my days in the volunteer office during the fall of 1987 allowed me to tell immediately if someone was being truthful about where he or she had worked. If I had any doubt about one's experience, I knew who to call and find out about the names, dates, and locations cited on the résumé. As the Transition's "personnel historian," I became consumed with not only my own work, but also the work of others in Scott's office. I enjoyed having an authoritative position, yet I was bothered as to why there were not others with campaign experience to assist.

Another strange twist was that we in Transition personnel were not given any support by our "sister" in the Reagan White House. Legally, it was their responsibility to make sure everything was running smoothly before the new President and his team arrived in January. And, too, they were aware that no office was more important in establishing a new administration than personnel.

The Reagan personnel staff never came forward. They never offered a hand. Robert Tuttle, grandson of Holmes Tuttle (the California millionaire who had first sponsored Reagan for presidential office) headed Reagan's presidential personnel office. His deputy was Ross Starek, and together Tuttle and Starek sat in their posh offices on Pennsylvania Avenue, seemingly oblivious of us.

Craig Fuller, Bush's vice presidential chief of staff, directed the Transition group, and his co-director was Robert Teeter, Bush's campaign pollster. Previously, both of these men had been on Baker's G-6; presently they led the 300-member Transition. On Fuller and Teeter's senior staff were Jim Baker, Fred Bush (no relation), George W. Bush, Tom Collamore, Dave Demarest, Mike Farren, Fred Fielding, Bob Grady, Boyden Gray, Mary Lukens, Janet Mullins, Jim Pinkerton, Dennis Ross, David Ryder, Sheila Tate, Diane Terpeluk, Margaret Tutwiler, Chase Untermeyer, Fred Zeder and Governor John Sununu.

Later I would realize that the very individuals Bush trusted most during his transition—his top aides—would chart a less than straightforward course for the President-to-be. Fuller, as linchpin in this underhanded endeavor and as Transition chairman, was serving under the most unusual of circumstances.

As noted, in 1985, Fuller was appointed as Bush's chief of staff by Jim Baker. Since that time, Fuller had sought sovereign powers, and his strategically positioned jobs had immeasurably increased his opportunities for direct access to Bush, Reagan's top aides and Baker. Before being assigned to OVP, Fuller was Cabinet affairs aide for four years and had proficiently learned about the workings of the White House. Nevertheless, while serving Bush, Fuller's personal ambitions had sometimes gotten in the way.

Over the previous eight years—since arriving in Washington from California with Michael Deaver and while under the protective wing of Baker—Fuller had been the ascending young star in the Reagan-Bush administration. From Cabinet affairs aide to Bush chief of staff, the thirty-something Californian had evolved into a dominant political figure. Not only had he been Bush's liaison to the Baker wing of the Reagan White House, he was also the link between Baker and Bush in the 1988 campaign effort.

Apparently, Fuller had made up his mind that he was the *only* one who deserved the position of chief of staff in the Bush White House. He felt entitled to this most influential position. During Transition days, while Bush was at his oceanfront vacation spot in Gulf Stream, Florida, Fuller stayed in Washington to make sure that no one pilfered "his" job. He was a shoo-in—or so he thought until Bush picked John Sununu. After several days of jockeying and much speculation about a possible three-person senior position, made up of Fuller, Teeter, and Sununu (versus a single chief of staff), Bush named the three-term governor of New Hampshire, forty-nine-year-old Sununu to be his COS. The man who had been credited with "the" primary victory would be the number-one administrator in the White House, not Fuller.

What I heard via the grapevine was that Fuller had been passed-over due to loyalty problems. Rumors were that Fuller had been more loyal to Fuller than to Bush. Still, the California native was offered other senior jobs in the administration. Not wanting any position if he could not be chief of staff, he turned down all of them.

It probably did not help matters that Fuller's co-chair at Transition, Bob Teeter, was offered the deputy chief of staff position. After consideration, Teeter replied to Bush that he may have been tempted to accept the job had Fuller been tapped, but that he did not want to work with Sununu. The fact that Teeter stood by Fuller was much publicized, for it appeared that Teeter was more committed to Fuller than the future President.

Then again, Teeter already had established his place in political history. Having started his odyssey under the tutelage of former President Nixon, he had gone on to advise both Ford and Reagan. Yet, with his home in Michigan, Teeter had never been on staff in the White House. His choice. Whether or not he went into the Bush West Wing made little difference to Teeter. Although not placed formally in the administration, he would not be forgotten by Bush. After all, it had been the Detroit-based pollster who had organized the focus groups in Paramus, giving the Bush team its winning edge in the election. (In the spring of 1989, Teeter would form a political consulting firm with an office in Washington and, under contract with the Republican National Committee, would provide polling analysis and advice to the Bush White House as an outside consultant.)

Fuller, on the other hand, saw himself as just beginning his political stardom and wanted to start at the top—in the White House with the President. Not having been selected COS, he decided that before going back into the Washington mainstream, he would stay in place as chairman of the Transition team. No longer preparing himself to be chief of staff, Fuller was forced to change his course of action, and he only had so much time. He seized the reins of authority while he had the chance and took control of the new administration before the new administration began. Not a happy man, and enraged over the Sununu selection, Fuller wanted revenge. I believe he wanted a Bush payback. Putting two together with two—but having no hard evidence—I theorize that Fuller saw things as very black and white. If he were going to be ousted by Bush, then he would return the "favor." And as director of Transition, he had no one standing in his way.

Since 1985, Fuller had been turning to Baker for his marching orders, and during Transition, nothing would change. While managing headquarters, Fuller was given a long leash, not only by Baker, but also by Bush. The President-designate, somewhat obliging to Fuller in his last days, was generous to the point of allowing his outgoing COS to keep the level of command to which he was accustomed. However, constructing a successful Bush regime was not foremost on Fuller's mind. No longer feeling any allegiance toward Bush, Fuller turned toward those he *did* remain loyal to: Baker and the Reagan appointees who had been his friends and peers for eight years.

While Fuller was enjoying his last fifteen minutes of fame, it made sense that he would use it to his advantage, and if he had his druthers, he would prefer that those already in authority in the White House remain there rather than turning the control over to a Bush regime. Why not have a ninth year of the Reagan administration?

Like Baker, Fuller had worked hard to keep the Bush loyalists away from "the candidate" during the campaign, allowing the Reagan appointees to hold the reins for the duration. And because it was supposed to be a changeover between friendly armies, for Bush to appear "suspicious" of the outgoing group's actions would have looked less than trusting. Bush was a trusting man. This made it convenient for the Reaganites. Why change things now just because there was a different man in the White House? There was no reason for Bushies (as called by Reagan men and women) to partake in the political spoils. Why should they? It was Reagan's White House.

I had thought that after the election, by virtue of "becoming" President, Bush would finally rule. Instead, from my perch in Transition headquarters, I witnessed the effects of Fuller taking control of what was erroneously called the "Friendly Transition." The Bush Transition team was going in the wrong direction . . . backwards!

It was my belief then, and is still today, that with the assistance of Fuller at Transition (along with Baker's nod of approval), the Reagan appointees stayed where they were, doing what they had been doing since 1981. Quietly, but with the influence already conferred upon them by Reagan, they would continue to be "in power." The idea that Fuller, by way of Baker, would crusade against Bush just to maintain his own authority was, at first, difficult for me to digest. In fact, it seemed crazy. And when I suggested it to other people, they confirmed I *was* crazy.

But, what if?

Should my hunches be correct, I wondered if this constituted a conspiracy? I judge there was "intent." I also judge that on the part of Baker and Fuller (and, to a lesser degree, Teeter) there was a secret scheme powerful enough to shape history. Going further, I believe that this molding was executed in order to meet the needs of these power-hungry men.

Ludicrous? Maybe. Still, in this writing, I am advancing what I will

★★★

call my Crazy Conspiracy Theory. And along with this supposition, I also promote the idea that Jim Baker, as the individual at the top of the Power Pyramid, was the only one who could have carried out this foolish scheme.

Baker was the Number One Guy in Washington politics. Atwater referred to Baker as "Numero Uno," and he was right. Although, in title, Fuller was at the top of the Bush Transition team—just as Atwater had been the manager of the Bush campaign—he, like Atwater, knew that the one who operated the levers of power was Baker. Supremacy *was* James A. Baker, III. And during the Bush Transition, with Baker's blessing, Reaganites were being installed in pivotal positions in the *Bush* administration.

In the November 11, 1988, *Washington Times,* an article by Ralph Hallow and Jeremiah O'Leary entitled "Bush Taps Baker for State, Names Transition Team" referred to Baker: "Mr. Baker is expected to loom large in the transition process, and Mr. Bush acknowledged as much yesterday, saying the former Treasury secretary and White House chief of staff will be his 'advisor on key aspects of the transition.'" The press had earlier reported there might be a Bush-Baker co-presidency, or maybe—the media pundits speculated—Baker would be "deputy president" to Bush. That is how much power Baker had.

As the head of the senior advisors to the Bush Transition team (Atwater, Rogers, Sununu and George W. Bush), Baker had predictably been the first to secure a position on the Bush Cabinet. Having previously said he preferred the role of statesman to political operative, Baker was awarded the premiere appointment, that of secretary of State. It was what Baker had most desired, and according to the man himself, he deserved it, for he was the one most responsible for securing the presidency for Bush.

During the fall, and well into the following year, many did credit Baker with the 1988 victory. He had been referred to as the Rescuer, the man who saved George Bush from losing the presidency. With his "message of the day," he had salvaged a losing nominee. For giving Bush the momentum to overcome Dukakis, he was showered with accolades. Baker never had trouble taking the honors. And most often he did so at the expense of his campaign manager. Atwater was the one condemned for running a negative and themeless campaign. Baker was the high flier.

However, not everybody fell for the misleading dualism. Mark

★★★

Shields wrote in the *Washington Post* on November 15, 1988, the following:

> For being the crafty hands-on manager of a campaign that has been
> called one of the worst in modern history, which left his victorious
> candidate without a mandate and that was based more on rejecting
> Dukakis and perpetuating Ronald Reagan than electing George
> Bush, Jim Baker is a unanimous selection as the Best Campaign
> Manager Ever.

Baker had learned how to situate himself at the apex, not only during presidential campaigns but also during Transitions. Realizing the significance of "ten weeks" in the Reagan transitions of 1980 and 1984, he had successfully engineered a plan that placed himself at the center of power. Without bringing it to anyone's attention, he placed himself at the peak of the Power Pyramid.

And through it all, always by Baker's side, was Margaret Tutwiler whose political career started in 1978 as assistant to Baker when he was chairman of Gerald Ford's presidential campaign. She had been with Baker when he was campaign chairman of George Bush's 1980 presidential race. In both these campaigns, she was scheduler. When Baker went to the Reagan White House as chief of staff, Tutwiler, predictably, followed; in 1985, when Baker left the West Wing to direct Treasury, Tutwiler once again assumed the master scheduler position, a station that by now gave her renowned status in Washington. Looking back on the time between 1978 and 1989, Tutwiler had been with Baker during each one of his strategic moves on the political chess board.

Starting in the Reagan White House, Baker established his authority by positioning himself as the *closest* aide to the President. During the fall of 1980, just after Reagan beat Carter, Baker cunningly crafted his responsibilities as chief of staff. During the Transition—which he was not a part of—he carved out what became known as the Baker Wing of the White House, and he learned that he did not have to be a member of the President's inner circle to accomplish this.

As a Reagan insider and 1980 Transition chairman, Attorney General-elect Edwin Meese had planned on becoming White House chief of staff (as had Fuller). But in an unforeseen move by Reagan, Baker was chosen instead. Michael Deaver and Stu Spencer, who had not wanted Meese in the chief of staff position, had recommended Baker—Reagan's adversary—for the job. Baker accepted, and to everyone's satisfaction, Meese went on to assume the Cabinet-level post of counselor to the President for policy.

During the early days of the 1980 Transition, Baker cleverly designed Meese's position, and Meese was led to believe (by Baker and Reagan) that *he* had the more authoritative spot. Actually, by way of an informal, one-page agreement with Meese, typed by Baker on November 13, 1980, Baker formulated an arrangement that gave himself the authority to rule the White House agenda. Meese would *develop* policy, but Baker had the power to *regulate* policy.

During that fall, Baker drafted what was called the "First One Hundred Days," a planning document for Reagan's first three months in office. The thrust was short and simple: balance the federal budget by cutting taxes, yet increase defense spending. All other domestic and foreign policy issues were put on hold. Reagan pollster Richard Wirthlin found that Baker had correctly read the mood of the country and that Americans would "buy into" his One Hundred Days idea. Despite the backlash that occurred less than a year later, when the deficit was larger than ever, Baker was repetitively referred to as "brilliant" and "shrewd" for his aggressive move.

Baker had taken advantage of that narrow window of chance during the seventy-three days of Transition. Within months of assuming his position of chief of staff in the White House, he had become Reagan's superior aide, wielding power over both Meese and Deaver. By knowing which presidential jobs carried the most weight—and by overseeing those jobs—Baker held the keys to the White House kingdom.

From the first day of Reagan's presidency, Baker had the authority to determine what briefs reached Reagan, what paper Reagan sent out, who saw Reagan, and for how long a guest would see him. Baker knew that to maintain his influence, he must keep an eye on everything and everyone going into and out of the Oval Office. He also had included in his job description oversight of the essential offices: the press office, the congressional liaison office, the political office, and the speechwriters office. All these White House domains were secured by Baker in the document he had drawn up for Meese's signature in November 1980.

Key to implementing Baker's plan was his choice of deputy. He selected Dick Darman, and gave him reign over presidential appointments, presidential scheduling and presidential correspondence.

Darman, the gatekeeper to President Reagan's office, reported only to Baker and served as his eyes and ears in the West Wing.

Darman understood how Washington worked. Having just arrived in town, Sununu did not. In fact, I doubt that Governor Sununu was doing any kind of strategizing in November of 1988, let alone figuring out who he would place in his position for presidential appointments. The outcome was predictable. Sununu had his deputy selected by Baker.

Jim Cicconi, the young man from Texas whom Baker had brought into the White House four years earlier, would serve in Sununu's top position. An unusual state of affairs seeing that most senior aides prefer to have deputies whom they know and trust. Cicconi had served with neither Sununu nor Bush; he had been in the Reagan White House at the pleasure of Baker, as both Cabinet secretary— replacing Fuller when Fuller went to the office of the Vice President—and Baker's personal aide. In the summer of 1988, at Baker's urging, Cicconi had gone to work on Quayle's vice presidential campaign staff, and was one of the staffers (along with Spencer and Canzari) Quayle had fired.

Jim Baker relied on individuals such as Darman and Cicconi, who he felt knew the Washington infrastructure and who also would be loyal to him . . . *only*. Political affiliation, for Baker, was a second priority, if that. In 1980, with Darman's acceptance of the deputy position, Baker ensured his sovereignty during the Reagan Years. And whether or not he was in the White House (between 1985 and 1988, he had moved across East Executive Avenue to the Treasury department), Baker's power never waned. In fact, with his sophisticated, ever-growing personnel lineup, Baker's prominence increased with each ensuing year of the Reagan presidency.

In November 1988, as the senior advisor to Bush, Baker planned to do what he had done in 1980: appoint *his* person to the key position in the West Wing. Only this time it was not Dick Darman, but Jim Cicconi. With Cicconi as deputy to Sununu, Baker immediately established an ally who had total access to the comings and goings inside the Oval Office.

Previously anticipating a Democratic victory, Baker had to rethink his situation with a Bush victory; nonetheless, he had landed on "both feet." He was perfectly positioned, and by using the same strategy that had worked so well for him in the past, he realized he could extend his power for another four years.

Once in the department of State, Baker would be in a world of his own, no longer burdened with the petty political details that were part of working in a campaign and at the White House; the presidency hinged on politics, not diplomacy. As *the* American statesman, he was where he wanted to be. Outside or, more aptly, above the political fray. Baker's diplomatic splash would prove to be more important to him than helping his "friend" George Bush be President.

As the wheels of appointing continued to turn at Transition headquarters, another series of disconcerting events took place in the Reagan White House. Ignoring the personnel work at Transition head-quarters, Bob Tuttle, Reagan's personnel director, was busy making White House appointments of his own. In the month of November, more than thirty *Reagan* appointments were made—placing individuals in the *present* administration! These individuals took their jobs with the understanding that their term would last only until Inauguration Day, two months away. It was highly unusual for an outgoing President to be making last minute appointments, especially while the Transition team was trying to fill the same ones. Even more bizarre was the fact that these men being placed were senior-ranking officials—including the ambassadors to Israel and India—who needed congressional confirmation. Because of the length of time it took for Senate approval (three to four months), it was impossible for the candidates to be confirmed before Reagan left office. They would become *Bush* appointees.

Also during the November-December period, Reagan made several controversial policy decisions, none of which had a positive effect on the President-elect. He signed an executive order that limited states' authority to approve disaster evacuation plans before a nuclear power plant could become operational—not congruent with Bush policy. Another move involved Reagan pocket vetoing an ethics bill, one that Bush had earlier indicated he supported. And too, the Justice department, in December 1988, decided, without Bush's approval, to intervene in a case before the Supreme Court to seek a reversal of the 1973 decision Roe v. Wade. One last move involved Reagan's secretary of State George Shultz who was in a United Nations dispute that resulted in refusing Yasir Arafat a visa needed to enter the United States. As chairman of the Palestine Liberation Organization (PLO), Arafat did not take the shun lightly.

Concerning these Reagan White House actions, the *National Journal* printed a telling article on December 3, 1988. Jack Germond and Jules Witcover wrote "Administration Moves Complicate Bush's Life," in which they described Bush's present predicament this way:

> If you consider the treatment President-elect Bush has been getting
> from the Reagan Administration, you have to wonder what would
> have happened if the incoming president had been a Democrat. In
> the first three weeks after the November 8 election, President
> Reagan and his appointees have taken a whole series of steps that
> seem likely to make life complicated for Bush. Presidential
> transitions are often awkward periods because they usually involve
> one party's surrendering power and perquisites to the other. There
> are often hard feelings left over from the campaign just ended. This
> case is different: an orderly transfer of authority from one
> Republican to his natural successor. It should have been a piece of
> cake. Instead, George Bush has a right to be asking whether, with
> friends like Reagan and Shultz, he needs any enemies.

While working in the office of Scott Bush, I did not have much time
to read the newspapers. To compensate, I developed a system of saving
articles to read later. I created a chronological filing system, with a new
folder for every month, and continued the practice of clipping Bush-
related newspaper articles throughout the administration. While still at
Transition, I especially tried to follow the news reports regarding the
Reagan White House's drafting of a new federal budget. The financial
plan for fiscal year 1989–90 (beginning in October 1989) was submitted to
Congress before January 10, 1989—and before the Bush inauguration.
Although it was said that Bush would have some input, the new
budget would bear only Reagan's stamp of approval. Bush would have to
wait until the following year.

Michael Boskin was the principal economic advisor to Bush during
Transition. A Stanford University economist and present director of a
West Coast economic think-tank, he was brought onto the team at the
invitation of Jim Baker. Boskin was the author of Bush's "flexible freeze"
proposal to balance the federal budget, and as a middle-line conservative,
he was against using tax increases as a way of bringing the deficits
under control.

After the election, Bush, who agreed with Boskin's theories,
reiterated that he was adamant about not increasing taxes: "I'm talking
about holding the line on taxes, and I don't plan to deviate, and I think the
American people must have understood that when they elected me." In

January 1990, however, Bush would submit his fiscal plan for 1990–91, and only four months later make an atypical decision regarding his idea about "holding the line."

In the late fall and early winter of '88, the silent war between Bush Transition headquarters and the Reagan White House continued. Trying to understand the mindset of the Reagan appointees, I reminded myself that they had been working for a President who with an aloof, indifferent and disengaged style had abdicated his leadership role eight years earlier. Reagan's "hands off" policy had encouraged his aides to chart their own political courses. As best as I could determine . . . they had turned greedy. With their latitude from Reagan—during the Transition—they held the Bush infantry at bay. With a nod from Fuller at headquarters, Baker's endorsement, and many years of accumulated autonomy and resentment toward Bush, the Reagan ranks held their ground, not giving an inch. While some of us thought we were setting up a new administration, members of the present one had figured out a way to keep theirs intact. Their goal was a "Reagan III," not a "Bush I." There never was an "orderly transfer of authority."

Bush's chief personnel aide, Chase Untermeyer, did not help the situation. The *New York Times* (November 12, 1988) printed an article by Steven Roberts, "Bush Personnel Team Aims for Stiff Scrutiny," that showed Untermeyer's apparent lack of motivation to place Bush supporters:

> The Administration's announcement on Thursday that all Presidential appointees would be asked for their resignations sent a wave of jitters through the capital today as officials tried to calculate their prospects for survival.

> "What happens now [re: resignations] is extremely sensitive and delicate [said Chase Untermeyer]. Undoubtedly there is potential here for wrenched feelings, but it is far preferable to sending a letter sacking somebody."

If fired, the Reaganites could not be reappointed. If they resigned, they could be. It was customary practice to have the outgoing appointees resign, and it was just as routine not to reinstate them, whether in the same Party or the opposition. That was the tradition. However, this was not true in the Reagan-Bush turnover. The Reagan resignations soon would turn into Bush appointments. Rumor at Transition headquarters was that previous Reagan appointees might assume as many as three-quarters of the 3,000 positions. If that proved true, I knew Bush would never build a loyal political base upon which to run his administration.

Throughout Transition days, I held on to the thought that what I was doing at headquarters was going to make a difference somewhere down the line. I kept moving, trying to stay within the eye of the invisible hurricane. Although I sensed an imbalance of authority while working there, I had no one to speak to about my concerns, and I hoped my intuitions would prove incorrect or at least would be corrected with time.

The personnel climate in the political arena—especially a presidential crusade—is different from the private sector. The stakes are so high, and most often workers have volunteered to do a job, which is not the same as being an employee on someone's payroll. In politics one is at the mercy of everyone in a more senior position, and can be let go at any time, for no reason. There is no hierarchy to turn to. No vice president of human resources to complain to. No system of justice, so to speak. In this sense, politics is highly unruly.

You are "in" because someone likes you, trusts your loyalty, needs your particular expertise or is obliged to do someone else a favor. Conversely, you are "out" if someone does not like you, feels threatened by you, no longer needs your expertise, or is doing a favor for someone who holds a grudge against you. The probability of coming into a presidential campaign with no mentor and still being in the system six months later was slim...there were just too many opportunities for failure, few of which actually had to do with competency or qualifications. Playing politics is like playing a game of musical chairs; everyday someone is left without a place. With this arrangement, we the troops, were left feeling constantly on edge.

At my level on the Political Ladder, no one dared to complain or ask a question. It could be directed to the wrong person or be used as evidence to get rid of potential "trouble," in other words, *you*. And to be labeled "not loyal" was ruinous. For this reason, most of us on the Transition team—at least the foot soldiers—never voiced a complaint, asked a question or inquired about securing an appointment of our own. I realize this description of the work environment does not paint an appealing picture. In fact, it often leaves me wondering about my own motivations. My only explanation is that politics is like a drug. It is addictive. The more you are involved, the more you want.

Although we did not say so aloud, those of us working at Transition headquarters could not help but question whom, if any, from our ranks would find a position in the "new" government—jobs like the ones we had been selecting for everybody but ourselves. Not knowing what would happen on January 23—the first day of the Bush administration— and still looking forward to the inaugural celebrations that lay ahead, I anxiously waited to find out. Oddly enough, the Reagan White House already knew our fate.

★★★ ═══════ ★★★

CHAPTER

12

HIGH NOON AT THE CAPITOL

Perhaps this sounds simple, but simple things are always the most difficult. In actual life it requires the greatest of discipline to be simple, and acceptance of self is the essence of the moral problem and the epitome of a whole outlook upon life.

—Carl G. Jung

JANUARY 1989

At last. January 1989 was upon us, the month in which the country celebrated the American Bicentennial Presidential Inaugural. It was the two hundredth anniversary of the inauguration of the first President of the United States, George Washington, who, wearing a brown suit with silver buttons and standing on the balcony of the Federal Building in New York City (serving as the Capitol), was sworn into office on April 30, 1789. For two hundred years, the transition of American governmental authority from one President to the next—the Eternal Government—had followed the same orderly and commanding course.

On January 20, 1989, during a ceremony that had taken place only fifty times previously, George Bush would recite the same thirty-five word oath that George Washington had pledged two centuries earlier: "I, George Herbert Walker Bush, do solemnly swear that I will faithfully execute the office of President of the United States, and will to the best of my ability preserve, protect, and defend the Constitution of the United States."

In less than fifteen minutes, in front of a throng of thousands gathered before the Capitol Building, Chief Justice William Rehnquist would swear-in Bush as the forty-first President. Dan Quayle would be sworn in as the forty-fourth Vice President by Justice Sandra Day

146

O'Connor. Following a twenty-one-gun salute, Bush, not Reagan, would hold the highest office in the land.

Unlike two hundred years ago, when there was no press corps and no television, in January 1989, the whole country and millions of people from around the world observed the chain of events from their living rooms. Under the microscopic scrutiny of the media crews, Bush and his entourage would feed the public's appetite for a meticulous news account.

The presidential inaugural committee was the organization responsible for ensuring that every detail was taken care of and that all the fine points of the weeklong festivities unfolded without a misstep. Housed on Capitol Hill—the opposite side of town from Transition headquarters and not that far from the Republican National Committee— the inaugural group had a staff three times the size of Transition's. Unlike the office of the President-elect—in which campaign workers had been shut out—the inaugural committee had let campaign workers slip into its ranks. All of this meant that it was overstaffed and unwieldy, and considered "second cousin" to the Transition. A November 21, 1988, *New Republic* article titled "White House Watch: Job Creation" noted the difference between the two groups:

> The experienced political operatives, some issue nerds, and a few others will make it to the transition staff. Most of the munchkins, junior campaign aides, won't. They'll have to settle for jobs at the inaugural committee, which offers a more circuitous and less certain route to permanent employment on Bush's team. But at least they'll gain the single most important asset in getting a sub-Cabinet or lower post: a Bush credential.

David Herron, assigned to the inaugural committee as liaison to the diplomatic corps, was a former campaign member and friend of mine from research days. I had not been in touch with him for five months. Without any forewarning, Herron contacted me and asked if I would like to join his committee. It seemed that the diplomatic staff, while finalizing its member list, realized they needed one more person to serve as liaison. The job required escorting the ambassadors (and other high-ranking foreign dignitaries) to the various events and festivities during inaugural week, which sounded like a terrific opportunity, but what pleased me the most was talking to one of my friends from the campaign.

With the Bush victory, I realized how much I missed the people I started out with in the Woodward Building, when the idea of George Bush overcoming Bob Dole was a distant and uncertain dream. My isolation from The Team had been, and still was, difficult. With pleasure, I accepted Herron's invitation. I then requested a leave of absence from Transition, agreeing to report back at the end of the week, before the headquarters closed on Friday, January 20.

On Monday, January 16, I met the other members of the liaison staff at the Lincoln Memorial, the site of the inaugural opening celebration. Serving as a backdrop to the makeshift performance stage was the imposing nineteen-foot statue of Abraham Lincoln in all of his twenty-eight blocks of white-marbled splendor. Arriving ahead of the thousands of other spectators were one hundred or so diplomats. And as at all the upcoming events, the diplomatic corps received VIP treatment, including front-row seats, hot coffee and—when the weather dictated—lap blankets.

Live from California, the Beach Boys were among the first on stage; they sang a medley of their ever-popular songs from the 1960s, including "California Girls." However, it was "Kokomo" from the movie *Cocktail* (the number-one song in November 1988) that stole the show. In fact, the multitude went wild. Gloved hands clapping in the air and hundreds—if not thousands—of voices chiming in with the Beach Boys. The contrast between the bitter cold evening and the words of a song fantasizing about "bodies in the sand" on some warm, sunny island filled the crowd with energy.

As part of the evening's grand finale, fireworks were set off over the Reflecting Pool. One by one, the discharges burst into a shower of color and light against a wintry, iron gray sky. In the distance to the east, I could see the illuminated Washington Monument surrounded by fifty American flags; the marble and granite obelisk situated in the center of the Mall, midway between the Capitol Building and the Lincoln Memorial, dominated the skyline.

Tuesday and Wednesday were crammed with luncheons, coffees, and sightseeing events. Then on Thursday night the Inaugural Gala was telecast from the arena inside the Washington Convention Center. The black-tie celebration, concluding the pre-inaugural parties, was the highlight of the week. It was the Hollywood-in-Washington affair and, like the Oscars, was made for television. I was there early to meet the diplomats and their spouses as they were being dropped off from their chauffeur-driven cars.

Once our VIP guests had gone through the magnetometers at the front entrance, they were escorted into the Great Hall and seated to the right of the President-elect—and his wife—and the Vice President-elect—and his wife. From here, only feet away and under the spotlights, was a circular stage set up in Cirque-du-Soleil style. The opulently clothed diplomats, many wearing dress from their native lands, were seated within feet of the Bushes and the Quayles and practically able to touch the various actors, actresses, singers, dancers and comedians performing on stage. As delightful as the show was, I found myself distracted, watching such celebrity guests as Brooke Shields, wearing a champagne-color dress and walking down the aisle next to my seat.

The next day was Inaugural Day, and for me, it began at Blair House.

The presidential guest house on Jackson Place (adjacent to Lafayette Park and across the street from the White House) was actually a set of eighteenth-century Georgetown townhouses strung together to form one exceptionally large home, where, in 1861, Robert E. Lee committed himself to the Confederacy and declined command of the Union armies. The well-appointed quarters had recently been redecorated and now was full of handsome mahogany chests and tables, colorful silk fabrics, fine Chinese hand-painted porcelain, as well as a collection of early-nineteenth-century paintings.

For the past three days, during the inaugural festivities, Blair House had been home to the Bush family. Having already packed up their belongings at the Naval Observatory (where they had resided for eight years), the Bushes had come into the city for the final events. The entire family—including children (George W., Jeb, Marvin, Neil, and Doro) and grandchildren—had been at Blair House until this morning, when they left to meet the Reagans at the White House. Together, the two First Families were to proceed to Capitol Hill for the inauguration. I arrived at the emptied home just after the Bushes had left.

The Secret Service escorted me to the side entrance of the house, and once inside, I found only a few people on the premises; the diplomats and most of the inaugural staff were on Capitol Hill, waiting for the swearing in ceremony. Before the luncheon started, I was instructed to familiarize myself with the layout of the rooms. One of the more exquisite ones I found was on the first floor. Upon entering the Blair Drawing Room, my attention went straight to a mahogany oval table placed under a crystal chandelier; on the surface was a fine-looking, sizeable green glass vase, arranged with a bouquet of six dozen white lilies. Adding to the décor were the ceiling-to-floor damask draperies, a large gilded-frame mirror over the fireplace and Chinese rugs woven in time-worn colors of salmon pink, navy blue and beige.

In the Garden Room—an informal, yet large, dining room—the house staff was busy preparing for a reception to be given later that afternoon. Because of numerous French doors opening out onto flowerbeds, the room was filled with sunlight; however, there was no furniture in it. While the Bush family was in residence, the space had been turned into a playroom for the grandchildren, and toys still were strewn across the floor. As I walked around the room, almost stumbling on blocks and balls, I realized how fortunate I was to be here, a place so full of history, and I was reminded of an editorial I recently read in the *Wall Street Journal*; "Whither Democracy?" had been published on Election Day 1988:

> By long tradition Americans take their blessings for granted. So it is perhaps fitting to pause on this Election Day and reflect for a moment on what a rare spectacle we are witnessing. Today the American people pick the most powerful human being on earth. Some ninety million of them will flock to the polls to name their choice; and for that brief moment in the voting booth the freshest teenager or most ordinary toiler counts for as much as a Roosevelt, an Einstein or a Rockefeller. When it is done, whatever the momentary sulking by the defeated, the result will be accepted by all as right and just. In all of this the most amazing thing is that so few Americans find it amazing.

Meanwhile, the Bushes and the Reagans were leaving the White House and making the one and one-half mile ride up Pennsylvania Avenue by limousine to arrive at the Capitol just before the swearing-in. And at high noon, not a second before or after, the ceremony would begin. I looked for a television in Blair House to watch the proceedings.

In the Truman Study I found a small group gathered, and assuming they were inaugural staff, I joined them. I sat quietly in the back of the room while they talked among themselves. Then, on the television screen came pictures from the Capitol's West Terrace—a panoramic view of the city's parks and monuments. I could almost see Arlington Cemetery across the Potomac. Governors, diplomats, congressional representatives, presidential guests and the news media all surrounded the podium where Bush was to take the oath. Hundreds of thousands of others, nearly a half-million people in all, stood beyond the Reflecting Pool on the Mall, waiting for the ceremony to begin.

The temperature was way below freezing, but the sun was shining and the skies were clear. At the noon hour, Bush raised his right hand and placed his left on two Bibles, while Chief Justice Rehnquist administered the oath. Barbara Bush, dressed in an aqua-blue coat, was holding a Bush family Bible; the second one had been used by George Washington at the first inaugural in 1789. Immediately following the presidential pledge, the cannons fired the requisite twenty-one-gun salute, signifying the transfer of power, and the Marine band played "Hail to the Chief." Reagan was the first President in sixty years to turn over the office to a man in his own Party.

In his inaugural address, President Bush spoke about America enjoying the longest peacetime economic expansion in its history; the Dow Jones industrial average stood at 2,235. He spoke about the good times: "We live in a peaceful, prosperous time, but we can make it better," he said. Moreover, after talking about the environment, education, drugs, and his hope that Americans would learn how to help one another, Bush referred to "the age of the outstretched hand," and he promised to work with Congress. Stressing his desire for bipartisanship, he promised to reconcile with the Democrats: "The people did not send me here to bicker . . . I am putting out my hand to you." The new President spoke forcefully yet laced his words with just enough gentle tones to support genuine warmth.

Inauguration, the hallmark of our democracy, is an inspiring event, yet what I was to witness at Blair House would bear down on me whenever I recalled the 1989 Bush inaugural.

The reaction of the group in the Truman Study caught me off guard—the men and women supposed to be celebrating the transfer of power from Reagan to Bush had no such interest. To the contrary, their attitude was one of sarcasm as Bush took the oath of office. They laughingly referred to him as the "wimp." With smirks on their faces, they ridiculed and made disparaging comments about him. Their comments left me with a chill. Jubilation should have filled me that day. Instead, fury brewed.

While still watching the television, I saw the new President and First Lady escort the Reagans to a helicopter waiting for them on he Capitol lawn. Just before the Reagans climbed on board, and with the military honor guard standing at attention nearby, the two men who had been working together for eight years exchanged salutes. After the Reagans departed, the television network followed the Bushes as they walked from the heliport to the Capitol entrance. Then, unexpectedly one of my companions in the Truman Study jumped up and changed the network to the one following the Reagans in the helicopter. I was not sure how to react. Should I say, "Please turn back the channel," or should I yell, "What are you doing?" I felt this burning anger inside, but I just sat there. I sat there not saying a word and stared at the swirling rotors of the Reagan's helicopter as it swirled down on the West Front of the Capitol.

I watched the Reagans arrive at Andrews Air Force Base, where thousands of supporters were on hand to greet them; one held a placard that said, "So Long, Gipper." Bands were playing, honor guards were marching and another twenty-one gun salute was fired. Reagan gave his last review of the troops before boarding the giant 707 jet with his wife. I observed that everyone in the Truman Study was crying unabashedly. I actually felt sick to my stomach.

I later found out that my cohorts were, indeed, on the Bush inaugural committee *and* they were also members of Reagan's staff. They had placed themselves at Blair House. These appointees were only a few of the three thousand in Reagan's administration, but their attitude was typical—Bush had won simply because of Reagan's popularity. *They* viewed themselves as the "winners." *We* were the "losers." Literally as well as figuratively.

Taking leave of the Truman Study, I joined the diplomats who had returned from the Hill. A lavish buffet luncheon of sandwiches, salads and desserts was served in the Lee Drawing Room, Jackson Place Dining Room, and the Garden Room.

At Blair House, the Coca-Cola Company was the official host; a company or companies, depending upon the cost, sponsored each inaugural event. The Atlanta executives brought with them gifts of Cross pens (a tiny Coca-Cola bottle was attached to the upper portion), woolen lap blankets and umbrellas. With the newly acquired blankets in hand, we readied ourselves for the parade and then progressed outside to the front of Blair House.

The sun slowly crossed behind the Jefferson Memorial, to the south, as our guests climbed onto the bleachers that had been erected diagonally across Pennsylvania Avenue from where President and Mrs. Bush's reviewing box was located. Flags representing the countries of the one hundred-or-so individuals in the diplomatic corps—Poland, Italy, Greece, New Zealand, Peru and Switzerland, to name a few—were on tall poles behind the stands. With strong winds prevailing that day, the multicolored flags made loud flapping noises as they billowed above the seated visitors bundled in their lap blankets. Because the parade started at the top of Pennsylvania Avenue (at the Capitol) and ended at the White House (with the President), the diplomats would be the last to view the procession. There was a waiting period.

Before the parade arrived, I decided to venture back inside the residence, where it was delightfully warm. While the house was vacant, I set off on another self-directed tour. Starting on the lowest level, with its labyrinth of hallways resembling underground tunnels, I made my way up to the second floor, where Vice President and Mrs. Bush had stayed the night before. The Eisenhower Sitting Room and Library was the first room I came to, a warmly lit, book-lined retreat for family and friends. Across the long hallway, I discovered an unoccupied bedroom, and decided to make it my parade viewing spot.

From the room's floor-to-ceiling windows, I could see directly out over Pennsylvania Avenue, and as I stood at one of the windowpanes, waiting for the parade to arrive, my thoughts went back to when my Father had taken me and my two younger siblings to Eisenhower's inauguration in 1957. That was thirty-two years in the past. I had been twelve years old, not able to see above the crowd that surrounded me. Today, from the Blair House window, I could see with no encumbrances; the military personnel and D.C. police lined the parade route for as far as the eye could see.

At last, the caissons, motorcades, horses and high school bands came marching down the center of Pennsylvania Avenue, past the White House and Blair House. Quite a sight. Quite a day. However, because of my next assignment, I could only stay and watch the first part of the parade before I had to gather my things together and make a quick escape.

Outside, north of the park, by the Church of the President's, I hailed a taxicab and went uptown to the Washington Hilton Hotel. I was to be one of the hostesses at the Diplomatic Inaugural Ball.

In 1989, twelve inaugural balls were held throughout the District, (a ticket cost $175), and depending upon state of origin, guests were assigned to specified locations. For instance, individuals from Oklahoma, Nebraska, Wyoming and Florida attended the ball at the National Air and Space Museum, while other groups visited sites including the Kennedy Center, the Pension Building, and almost all of the major hotels. The Diplomats' Ball—being the smallest of all, and the only one not designated by state—received special media attention. Because of the seniority of the attendees, including ambassadors and Cabinet members, there was an unusually bountiful supply of gourmet foods and an open bar. Tables were filled with platters of shrimp, lobster, salmon, beef tenderloin, fruits and cheeses, all helping to make this party the favorite among those who had previously attended inaugural balls.

Most balls were not what they were built up to be. With nothing more than peanuts for hors d'oeuvres and a cash bar, a lot is lacking. The crowds are excessively large for the space allotted, with hundreds of over dressed people standing shoulder-to-shoulder with one another. It is too warm and too stilted, and extremely noisy. It is impossible to carry on a conversation even with the person next to you. The fact is these balls are dreadful. Nevertheless, when the new President and Vice President arrive with their wives, everyone forgets the less-than-desirable aspects of the evening.

As President and Mrs. Bush and the Quayles partied their way across the city into the wee hours of the morning, attending each of the twelve balls, the guests—most from out of town and many in Washington for the first time—reveled in the resplendent moment and were thrilled to be part of the superficial merriment. They would go home to be the envy of their friends.

A review of the Bush inaugural balls would not be complete without mentioning what perhaps was the most engaging of all in 1989: the Bush Blues Bash. This all-star rhythm and blues concert was sponsored and hosted by Lee Atwater and co-hosted by the Bush's son Marvin. Bush not only made an appearance, he was one of the entertainers. On a guitar named "The Prez," and complete in black tie, President Bush joined

Atwater, in a sport jacket, on center stage. Together, they strummed their guitars and sang with soul singer Sam Moore of the Sam and Dave Duo. The crowd went wild. Bush still looked noble-enough—in fact, I dare say, charming, with tuxedo and guitar—and he laughed, as if he were genuinely having a really good time. Atwater, of course, beamed.

Although some wondered just how smart Atwater was, given his southern ways and sometimes-outlandish behavior, I think that his court-jester-like performances were a cover for a very bright man who sometimes felt out of place with the elite. Music helped him "fit in" a social class he had not grown up in. A lover of soul music and rhythm and blues, Atwater was particularly fond of the blues-style music called stax, a sound played in Memphis. This bad boy of politics, who owned six guitars and always kept one in his campaign headquarters office, referred to stax as being the "most totally American music."

On inaugural night, Atwater had the opportunity to share some of these sounds with the President and the guests, those there to celebrate a victory the South Carolinian had orchestrated. Later, Atwater claimed that seeing Bush sworn in as President was the "highlight of his life." Nonetheless, he admitted he had skipped the inaugural parade so that he could jam in a warehouse with Joe Cocker, Sam Moore, Ron Wood, Percy Sledge and Billy Preston, all performers who had accompanied him to the Blues Bash.

On the night following the celebrations, when most of the out-of-town guests had returned home and the City of Monuments again belonged to its residents, the diplomatic corps was invited to a final reception given in honor of Vice President and Mrs. Quayle. The Quayles had been adhering to a frenzied schedule during inaugural week and had spent most of the day with the Bushes, meeting them at the White House before the festivities started and attending the parties with them that night. Yet they arrived for this occasion in the Benjamin Franklin Room at the State department looking rested and relaxed.

Outside the State windows was a dazzling array of star-like beams that spread from the Capitol Building to the Lincoln Memorial. A perfect winter scene. Within the gilded confines of the department of State—on the eighth floor—the Quayles were introduced to diplomats representing countries from every corner of the globe. And amidst one of America's finest collections of antique furnishings (the Americana Collection, valued at more than $35 million), the Vice President and his wife shook hands with everyone who had waited in the long receiving line, making some personal comment to each, and appearing as pleased with the small talk as their guests.

While observing Vice President Quayle in the role of honoree this evening, I sensed, once again, but more adamantly, that he had not been fairly represented by the press. And although I did not personally know the Quayles, I was somewhat familiar with who they were simply because they lived in the same town as I: McLean, Virginia. Their children went to the public schools, and I knew that their neighbors thought of them more as Dan and Marilyn than "Senator and Mrs." At the diplomatic party, Quayle's demeanor seemed so incongruous with the newspaper caricatures of him as a juvenile and robot. The past five months had not been kind to this politician; the moderates had accused him of being too conservative, and the conservatives had berated him for being too moderate. Both political camps, as well as his own campaign team, had damaged him. Unfairly. Conversely, on the evening of the State reception, he was eagerly embraced by scores of diplomats from around the world. With grace and aplomb and just the right amount of self-confidence, he impressed them all. I knew that because I could hear the comments of others as I made my way around the room.

The last inaugural event was the Sunday morning prayer service held at the Washington National Cathedral, the home of the Presiding Bishop of the Protestant Episcopal Church. On another chilly day in Washington, we united in prayer and thanksgiving on the inauguration of President George Herbert Walker Bush and Vice President James Danforth Quayle. In this marvelous, massive superstructure, the diplomatic corps sat clustered together in the first twenty rows of the nave, close to the south transept of the main sanctuary. I with them. The President, Vice President and their families were seated to our left, and out of the corner of my eye, I could see my favorite news anchorman, Peter Jennings, whom I watched religiously every night.

The Right Reverend John T. Walker, Bishop of Washington, presided over the service. As he entered, the thousands of us in attendance stood and sang the National Hymn. In front of the choir that marched with him were the crucifers, who proceeded in slow motion, carrying the cross and torches and they made their way down the long, narrow center aisle.

The service was solemn, but filled with optimism, joy, and a touch of religious beauty. A quote from the cathedral service program read: "As we worship here today, congregations across the land will share with us in this liturgy. As we depart, bells across the country will peal in a national expression of joy, denoting our praise and thanksgiving to the Lord for His blessing on our people, our land, and our government."

For the recessional, we sang "Eternal Father," known as the Navy Hymn. A brass ensemble from the U.S. Marine Corps Band joined in during the final verses, filling every square inch of the cathedral with the thunderous sound of trumpets. Accompanying the music were voices singing: "Eternal Father, strong to save, Whose arm hath bound the restless wave, Who bidd'st the mighty ocean deep, Its own appointed limits keep: O hear us when we cry to thee For those in peril on the sea." And with the sound of the trumpets, I was reminded of what Bush said at his inaugural address, given less than twenty-four hours earlier, "Some see leadership as high drama and the sound of trumpets calling; and sometimes it is that. But I see history as a book of many pages."

AMERICA had a new chief and leader of the Free World who would help usher the nation into the twenty-first century. President Bush would take the United States out of the industrial era into the generation of the computer or what would be referred to as the age of information technology. As usual with times of development and change, both joy and turbulence lay ahead, yet for Americans, what appeared to be a promising and definitive new administration under a competent and accomplished commander would turn out to be something incredibly different.

The precarious days of Transition were over, and President Bush was scheduled to cross the threshold of 1600 Pennsylvania Avenue the next morning.

13

WHITE HOUSE CAMOUFLAGED

To "roll" someone is Washington tough talk for overturning, toppling them, bringing them down, as a wrestler or a street mugger might.

—Hedrick Smith

FEBRUARY 1989

Two days after the cathedral service and the second day of the Bush administration, I was asked to report to the White House. At 8:30 in the morning on Tuesday, January 24, 1989, I received a call from Bob Davis, whom I did not know, and was instructed to be at the Old Executive Office Building (OEOB) by noon. After checking in with White House security, I was to proceed to the office of Scott Bush.

Davis told me that Scott, for whom I had worked at Transition headquarters, was going to head the personnel office of Schedule C appointments. As mentioned, he was the President's nephew, and the lone relative of Bush to follow him into the administration. At first, there was some question as to whether Scott's being a member of his uncle's administration violated rules against nepotism, but it was found that he could stay, first on staff in presidential personnel and later in a position at the Overseas Private Investment Corporation. Bush's eldest son, George W., had been the only one of the five Bush children who had worked at the campaign headquarters (as well as at Transition), but he had returned to Texas after the inauguration.

Not a soul was in sight when I drove up Pennsylvania Avenue. The city was unusually quiet, and none of the normal commotion so much a part of downtown Washington was evident. It is wonderful to drive block upon city block without a long backup of cars at the stoplights. Everyone was taking one last deep breath before the wheels of the new administration started turning.

Emerging fortress-like, with its nine hundred freestanding exterior columns of pink and tan marble, the Old Executive Office Building (OEOB) was hard to miss. I parked in a garage on Pennsylvania Avenue, crossed the street and walked up the unusually wide flight of steps to the front entrance of the building. Sitting adjacent to the White House, the OEOB housed the offices of the Vice President as well as a majority of the White House staff, including those in presidential personnel. Referred to as the White House Annex in years past, the OEOB (one hundred years old) remained one of the most handsome and ornately designed structures in Washington.

Staff members housed in the Old Executive Office most often considered themselves to work "in the White House." Although they were not lodged in the actual building, they were a part of the White House workforce and were included in the White House Phone Directory. Most senior aides to the President (and the office of the Vice President) were not housed in the West Wing; they were in the OEOB. Seldom was the distinction made between those working in the Executive Mansion and those working in the OEOB . . . except for members of the West Wing, who did not consider *them* a part of the real White House. Still, most senior aides to the President were not housed next to the Oval Office; they were in the OEOB.

As I arrived at the front door on the west side of Exec Drive—a few lackadaisical-looking security guards at the main entrance to the OEOB waved me through with hardly a glance. Once inside I took my time to look at the striking curved staircases, the four-foot granite walls, the eighteen-foot-high ceilings and some of the two miles of white and black marble corridors. As I walked down the spacious and immaculate hallways, I could hear my footsteps resounding off the marble and tile interior; the polished mahogany doors did not give a clue that it was an office complex.

On this one day only, I and the few others there had access to all the nooks and crannies of the building, which until two days earlier had been in the hands of Reagan's outgoing staff. In twenty-four hours time, word would hit the streets that the OEOB housed presidential personnel, and the heavy black metal doors at the entranceway would be closed to intruders. Starting on Wednesday, the police guards would tighten their security procedures: metal detectors would be back in operation, and incoming staff would need the appropriate badges and clearances to enter and depart. Visitors would have to be cleared in, and the guards would need to be notified in advance of their arrival.

Today was different. On the first floor, not too far from the main entrance, I found room no. 139, Scott's office; he met me and welcomed me back to his team, explaining that I would share an office just down the hall with several others on his staff, most of whom were arriving the same time as I. After being introduced, my coworkers immediately informed me that being first in the building had its privileges. We could secure furniture from the five hundred-some vacant offices for our own use, taking advantage of the "first come, first served" policy.

Collecting furniture, however, is not my most vivid memory; the devastation of the offices in which we found the furniture is what I will never forget. Behind each handsome ten-foot door was a room looking as if a bomb had gone off in it. In the turnover of one administration to the next, some disarray was to be expected, but there was nothing civil about the Reagan team's departure. Their debris gave the appearance of an irate and bitter out-going staff. These former tenants had ravaged their own offices, and what remained was a shameful display of personal disregard, not only for the furniture and objects themselves, but also for the Office of the President.

Desk drawers were thrown open, revealing handfuls of broken pencils, damaged pens and torn index cards. Reams of paper in opened packages were scattered everywhere, as were briefing papers and magazines. Trash baskets were filled with crumpled paper. Dozens of soda bottles and half-empty Dunkin' Donuts boxes were lying on top of the desks, bookcases and tables. Walls were full of large, gaping holes where nails had been carelessly torn from the plaster. The hardwood floors, many previously shiny parquet, were dusty and scratched, and telephones were out of order.

From the wreckage, I salvaged a few of the many remaining eight-by-ten color pictures of Mr. and Mrs. Reagan...standing by a pond, sitting on a fence and riding horseback. I feel sure that Ronald Reagan, who left the presidency with a 90 percent approval rating from his own Party, and whose public decorum always seemed dictated by a touch of class, had no idea how his staff had left their offices upon his departure.

The only offices we found locked on our first-day tour were those in the presidential personnel suite. Obviously, the Reagan appointees who had occupied them had not planned to go anywhere other than back to *their* offices. They had left and taken their keys with them. As a group, White House personnel is responsible for submitting the paperwork on all incoming appointments and all outgoing resignations. With that authority, these staffers had resigned from their positions and *then* reappointed themselves before Bush was inaugurated!

Reagan resignations, effective January 20, had quickly turned into appointments on January 26, a scheme implemented while Fuller was heading the Transition team, and while Baker was senior advisor to President-elect Bush. Reagan was still president while this self-directed rehiring took place. This situation, a Bush refutation, would prove to be the crux of many problems that lay ahead for the Bush administration.

In the fall of 1988, Bush had assured those of us at the Transition headquarters that there would be a decisive personnel change in his administration, promising that it would not be a Reagan III. While I was still at the Republican National Committee on November 6, (the day before Election Day), I had read a *USA Today* article by Jessica Lee, "Bush Says He'll Appoint New Faces," stating this:

> Bush, reluctant to detail his plans, said he "could well" retain some of Reagan's appointees. But he said, "There's no commitment to anyone of any kind." When asked would his election represent the ninth year of the Reagan administration, he replied, "I hope it will be that successful, but in terms of people, it will be a lot of new faces. A lot of change."

Now, sitting in the near-empty OEOB on the third day of the administration, I questioned if what Bush said were true.

Months ago, (Charles G.) Chase Untermeyer had been assigned the job of finding individuals to fill Bush's political positions. Having assumed one of the major jobs on Bush's team—heading the office of personnel during the campaign *and* Transition—Untermeyer, as expected, had been selected the new director of the Office of Presidential Personnel. A critical position. He replaced Reagan's top personnel man, Robert Tuttle.

Untermeyer's history with President Bush went back to his college days in Houston, Texas, in the mid-1960s, when he had spent two

summers as an intern for then-Congressman Bush. After graduating from
Harvard in 1968, Untermeyer was commissioned an officer in the Naval
ROTC program, leading him to serve on a destroyer in the Tonkin Gulf
during the Vietnam War. Back at home in the early 1970s, he found a job
as a reporter for the *Houston Chronicle,* and in 1978 and 1979, he worked
on a George Bush autobiography, one that was never completed.
Untermeyer was a Republican member of the Texas House of
Representatives from 1977 to 1981 and, in 1982, was called by Bush to be
his executive assistant in the Vice President's office.

Shortly after arriving in Washington in March 1983, Untermeyer left
Vice President Bush and assumed a Reagan appointment at the
department of Defense as deputy assistant secretary of manpower and
reserve affairs, responsible for recruiting and training Navy and Marine
personnel. Promoted in May 1984 to assistant secretary of that same
organization, he stayed at the Pentagon until April 1988, when he left his
billet and, once again, joined forces with Bush. This time, his job included
the staffing of a predicted-to-be Bush administration.

Untermeyer had set up an office at the RNC, where I recalled seeing
him briefly during the fall of 1988; I knew his assistant, Helen Mobley,
from early campaign days. It was well known that the personnel chief
kept mostly to himself. Unlike Fred Malek, who was a hands-on manager,
Untermeyer remained removed from the troops and was seldom seen in
the corridors of the RNC. Now in January 1989, with his office in the West
Wing, I seldom saw him in the hallways of the OEOB.

While holding such a central position in the new White House,
Untermeyer oversaw a directive of many offices and staffs.
Comprehending the organizational structure of the office of presidential
personnel, with its different levels and job titles, could be intimidating
even to those like myself who worked in the organization. To help
understand the personnel directorships (and associated authority that
came with those positions), I share this clarification.

Except for Cabinet positions and ambassadorships, staffed solely by
Untermeyer, all political appointments were managed by his deputy, Ross
(Roscoe B.) Starek. Untermeyer may have had the prestigious title, but
Starek had the authority. A key member of the former Reagan White
House, Starek had been the number-one deputy in presidential personnel
under Bob Tuttle. Remaining in that slot under Untermeyer, he had made

sure he retained his OEOB office, one of the largest, just down the hall from mine. His staff of associate directors (called ADs) was responsible for filling the several thousand White House/agency positions.

Each AD handled appointments specific to a given number of government departments. For instance, there was an AD for Finance, one for Social Services, another for Trade, and so forth. The AD in charge of filling positions for National Security represented all the agencies falling under the national security umbrella (State, Defense, CIA, and the National Security Council). There were eight ADs in all.

On a daily basis, the ADs were kept informed about who was and was not being considered for a possible appointment to one of the fourteen agencies or one of the numerous committees and boards. By handling all the paperwork and necessary approvals, Starek and his ADs could easily make or break a candidate's chance to find a position. Receiving an appointment in an agency without Starek's stamp of approval was almost impossible. And although the ADs could not always assign a candidate to a specific agency, they *could* keep him out. This is what gave them their power. They could stall a potential appointment whenever they wanted. Under the leadership of Starek, the ADs would appoint as many individuals as possible from Reagan's previous crew to positions in the Bush administration.

From personal experience, before going to the White House, I knew something about Starek and the associate directors. While at 1825 Connecticut Avenue, at the urging of a Transition staffer, I was approached about becoming a candidate for an assistant AD job. On December 30, while at the Transition headquarters, I was interviewed, on site, for the position of assistant to Martha Goodwin, who handled several domestic agencies. Almost immediately after the meeting, I was informed by someone on her staff that no one from the Bush team would be assigned to presidential personnel during the first year of the administration. All the Reagan ADs were going to keep their positions "to help smooth things over." I was told to reapply for the job the following year.

Because the Reagan ADs kept their jobs for *all four years* of the Bush presidency, I never had an opportunity to reapply. Had I been chosen for the slot in '88, Goodwin would have kept her job for one year, and then I would have replaced her. As it was, Martha Goodwin kept her job, as did all the others in her office, for the entire time Bush was in office. Reagan personnel ran the northwest corner of the White House. For four years! Without missing a beat from one administration to the next, they continued to pass out their business cards that read simply, "Special Assistant to the President."

By the end of January 1989, the full White House personnel staff numbered close to seventy-five. Some were "detailed" to the West Wing with Untermeyer, but most resided in the OEOB under the direction of Starek. Those of us in Scott Bush's office were considered temporary, and not part of the Starek team. Nevertheless, we were on Untermeyer's roster, and for the time we worked there, we were officially part of presidential personnel. To Starek's chagrin, we were more of a parallel team than a junior one.

Scott Bush, like Ross Starek, reported directly to Untermeyer; this gave Scott instant influence. But because we worked unilaterally, not under Starek, we were viewed as a threat. The Reaganites kept their distance from us, and even though we were within feet of each other (and bumped into one another from time to time), the friction was played out in dead silence. No one spoke to anyone else on the "other" team. This experience, although uncomfortable, later on would help clarify many of the bizarre administration happenings. Already I knew there were two distinct groups, "We" and "They," rooting against the other. Now I was certain it had been Reagan versus Bush from Day One.

On the fourth day of the administration, Untermeyer called a staff meeting in the Indian Treaty Room, the most ornate room in the OEOB, where presidential news conferences were sometimes held. He gave a pep talk, much like one he had given us before we departed Transition headquarters, saying, "This is going to be a great administration, and we are lucky to be a part of it." The thirty-some individuals who attended Untermeyer's meeting on January 26 received a roster of "who's who" in presidential personnel. After quickly surveying the list, I noticed that a couple of names were from Transition, but not one name was from the Bush campaign or even the Republican Committee. Despite my having been in the system for eighteen months (and now working in the hub of the new presidency), I did not know anyone other than Scott Bush. He (who had no campaign experience) and I were the only ones in presidential personnel from the Transition personnel office.

With me in Scott's group, were six political rookies, including a thirty-five-year-old homemaker, a seventy-eight-year-old department of

★★★

Defense retiree and the son of a Congressman, Bob Davis, the person who had requested me to report to the OEOB. My peers were personable and hardworking individuals. I liked all of them, yet I never understood how, without any national campaign experience, they were chosen. Unlike my teammates, who came together from unrelated backgrounds, the ADs under Untermeyer's command all knew each other from earlier times. During Transition days, Fuller had guaranteed Starek and his squad untold supremacy for as long as they wanted.

After the Treaty Room meeting, I would not see Untermeyer until eight months later at a two-day orientation for new appointees. The September 27 meeting would be held back in the OEOB, and Untermeyer would comment on the "responsibility" appointees were assuming in their new positions, pointing out that egos should be kept "in check" and that we should never "embarrass the President."

In January 1989, I soon realized that placing nominees was a difficult task, especially in view of the elaborate executive job structure; in 1989, the federal civilian workforce numbered just below three million. The three thousand presidential appointments included a wide range of positions: Senate-confirmed Cabinet and sub-Cabinet; Senior Executive Service; and Schedule C (personal and confidential assistants). At his pleasure, the President also appointed several thousand to advisory boards, commissions and special councils, as well as hundreds of federal judges.

Learning the government system helped me not only execute my job, but appreciate the complexity of the well-defined political hierarchy. However, grasping the intricacies of the various job levels was daunting, especially when trying to understand the correlation (or lack thereof) between job positions and political power. This was the pecking order: Cabinet posts, of course, were at the top, as were ambassadorships. The Executive level, with five grades, followed. The Senior Executive level (SES), with six grades, included such titles as under secretary (highest), assistant secretary and deputy assistant secretary, and lastly came the Schedule C level, with eighteen grades (eighteen being the highest).

Of all the political appointments assigned in an administration, the vast majority are low-level jobs. Two thousand are Schedule C; seven hundred Senior Executive; and two to three hundred are reserved for the Executive ranks. The higher-ranking positions at the SES and Executive level, as well as Cabinet positions, require Senate confirmation. It was the

Schedule C slots that, with far less authority and no confirmation requirement, made up two-thirds of the appointments.

Untermeyer did not bother with the Cs; he focused his attention on finding nominees for the weighty Cabinet and ambassadorship posts. More significantly, Starek was the one who kept his eye on the other *two thousand nine hundred and fifty* positions. When that number was combined with Starek's previous experience in the Reagan White House, it was easy to see that he had far more influence than Untermeyer.

Starek's ADs carried out their work from spacious, well-furnished offices. They had staffs of assistants, plenty of administrative backup, and computer access. In Scott Bush's office, we proceeded without any of these perks. During the first few weeks in February, while the ADs concentrated on filling the SES and higher positions, we worked only on the Schedule C slots. However, our mission came with a caveat: we were given an undefined amount of time in which to fill the positions. According to the OEOB grapevine, Scott's office would close by April 1.

Given the small window of opportunity—two months—to process as many candidates as we could, the eight of us persevered nonstop day and night. We worked ten-hour days every day except Sunday, and our only break was when we took turns to run to the OEOB cafeteria for a hamburger and a bag of potato chips. We took calls from people all over the country. We were besieged with phone calls. Our six phone lines never stopped ringing. Most of those calling wanted to know if their résumés had been received, and, more importantly, if they would soon get their appointments. We never let them know how slim their chances were or how overloaded the system was. The April 1 cutoff was always in the back of our minds.

As at Transition (without access to computers) our work in Scott's group was accomplished by hand. What made it so difficult was the daily avalanche of mail that filled our offices (spaces the size of closets). With literally thousands of sheets of biographical data stacked everywhere, we painstakingly divided them alphabetically and then filed them into large steel cabinets.

Once an applicant was selected to be a nominee, we marked his or her file according to a number system (1 to 5). If the nominee was tagged "must hire," we assigned him or her to the agency we thought he or she would be most qualified to work. For example, someone who had

★★★

experience working in a state park might be sent to the department of Interior. The background checks were just as extensive as they had been at Transition. By telephone, we checked on the individuals' political campaign experience, education (a college degree was mandatory), present job, area of expertise, and voting record—before recommending him for an appointment.

Not until mid-February did the agencies finally start to communicate with us and request candidates. Our list (with the nominee's completed file) was hand-carried to the White House liaison office in the receiving government agency. Once a nominee's file left our office, it was no longer our responsibility to track it; we had to focus our attention on the hundreds of individuals still pursuing positions. As soon as fifty names were sent to the White House liaison, another two thousand were waiting for us to process, and out of those, maybe another fifty would be lucky enough to reach the agency level. Only a certain percentage of the fifty would actually find jobs.

Those who received a blessing from the White House and got their names (résumés) in departments during February or March were given what was referred to as a 120-day temporary assignment, *not* a specific job. The nominees had approximately four months inside the department to find one for themselves. And because there were more names submitted to the agencies (Transportation, Labor, Interior, Education, and so on) than there were available positions, many never did find an appointment and were lost in what we called the "wasteland." There turned out to be more of these individuals than anticipated. I would soon realize why so few slots were opening for our candidates. Reagan appointees had already filled them.

To my horror, thousands of résumés had arrived at the White House *before* we, on Scott's staff, assumed our positions. From November '88 to January '89, the Reagan personnel staff had been putting them in boxes unprocessed. But far worse, none of the résumés from Transition headquarters had been transferred to the White House! The computer transfer—the merging of résumé data that was so vital—had never taken place. All the untold hours of work over the three-month Transition period, whereby thousands of applicants were politically screened and tagged, had been for naught. According to the Reagan ADs, the data was simply "lost." No explanations were forthcoming, and as far as I know, Scott Bush never pursued an answer as to why this happened.

The Reaganites had blatantly and with intent sabotaged our efforts . . . in order to protect their own. Even in February 1989, located three doors down from data entry, we were told that the White House computers were "off limits." The essential office—computer management—had kept, and would continue to keep, us at bay. The only data to be input was from the Reagan associate directors, who, without that service, would never have been able to proceed the way they did.

White House ADs were reassigning Reagan appointees from their present agencies to other agencies across town (e.g., from Interior to Education), thus severely minimizing the available positions for new Bush-credentialed appointees. The system became jammed in every direction. Not only was Starek filling the higher-level positions (deputy assistant secretary, assistant secretary, and under secretary), he was shuffling old appointees at the lower levels into new Schedule C jobs. He was filling our slots as well as his own!

From the time I first entered the OEOB, I had sensed that something was terribly amiss, and I reflected on the notes I had written in my personal diary:

> *January 25*—All the AD positions are filled!
> *February 1*—Is Chase supporting us?
> *February 2*—Feel the pressure . . . what's happening? . . . I realize I am surrounded by Reagan people . . . they have filled *all the jobs* in presidential personnel. *No* Bush people here . . . why? Why?!
> *February 7*—Not sure what is going on in presidential personnel . . . is Chase calling the shots? . . . work never stops . . . constant all day.
> *February 8*—In Lanny Griffith's office, stories abound about Bush moving in and Reagan people leaving their jobs furious. Absolutely furious!
> *February 21*—Working *long* days . . . so many calls . . . are we really getting Bush people in the administration?
> *March 2*—I'm not sure who is friend or foe!

To my knowledge, no one ever questioned what transpired between the White House Personnel Office and the Transition Personnel Office, but because the candidate files on those with Bush credentials were neither acknowledged nor accepted, hundreds of potential Bush appointees never found political positions. The battle for authority between the previous administration and the present one had unfolded neatly and smoothly. Without notice.

★★★ ═══════ ★★★

CHAPTER

14

MY FATHER'S DAUGHTER

The Bridge Coat was made of navy-blue Melton cloth and came down almost to the ankles . . .it had a double row of gold buttons down the front and loops for shoulder boards, big beautiful belly-cut collar and lapels, deep turnbacks on the sleeves, a tailored waist, and a center vent in the back that ran from the waistline to the bottom of the coat.
—Tom Wolf

<u>FEBRUARY 1989</u>

Few comprehended how significant the decisions made in the Office of Presidential Personnel really are. Appointment choices determine the management of the administration. The presidential aides represent either power for the President or, in Bush's case, lack of power.

By controlling the Bush appointment list, the previous Reagan staff—now the Bush staff—was able to shape the administration and manage the Bush agenda. This was accomplished during the Transition. Before the presidency was ever formalized.

Although Chase Untermeyer knew the Reaganites, I do not believe that he understood the magnitude of what was happening. Under Reagan, he had been in a position at the Defense department, which in Washington spheres is "outside" the political ballpark. Seldom are those who work at DOD considered to be on The Team. A different story for Starek. He and the ADs—having continued to be in charge of recruiting during Transition—easily kept former Reagan appointees in the loop, quickly building a system that secured them their power base. Previous to Bush's arriving at 1600 Pennsylvania Avenue and *before* those of us on Scott's team appeared, the Bush supporters had been purged from the system. In the ADs' way of thinking, our short intrusion on their turf was insignificant; we would be out of their way in no time.

169

Ross Starek was not the only one who had shored up his previous clout during Transition days. Jim Baker, having masterminded his authority in Reagan's 1980 and 1984 transitions, knew what he wanted and he knew how to get it. The department of State—the premiere Washington agency—was now Baker's.

Schmoozing his way past the Senate confirmation hearings, Baker impressed those on Jenkins Hill with what he was best known for— finesse. Not familiar with nor having experience in foreign policy matters, Baker, once coronated, had turned to his hefty circle of contacts and acquaintances to fill his political appointments. None were experts in the field—with the exception of his deputy, Lawrence Eagleburger.

In the paper and on television, Eagleburger did not appear to be the former Harvard professor he was, but more like a wrestler, emerging scary, big, heavyset and always frowning. Maybe he had reason to scowl—he had been in the political game a long time.

Eagleburger gave Baker his influence in the international affairs field during the Bush administration. Beginning in the Nixon White House, Eagleburger had been an aide to Henry Kissinger, the former national security advisor. Kissinger had been despised by the Republican right for his foreign policy principles, especially his handling of the Soviets and the Chinese. Yet, not one to be deterred, Kissinger relished in his fame, and single-handedly took over the foreign affairs domain. In 1973, when he became secretary of State (ousting Dean Rusk), Kissinger refused to give up his position as director of the National Security Agency. Therefore, for two years, under Nixon, he simultaneously held *both* positions. When President Ford assumed office, he agreed to keep the liberal Kissinger as State secretary but gave the national security advisor job to Brent Scowcroft (chief deputy to Kissinger while he was national security advisor).

When Kissinger took over State, Eagleburger had gone with him, and when he stayed on with Ford, Eagleburger also remained. While at State, Kissinger's fiercest adversary and most threatening competitor had been Ford's Defense secretary, an archconservative, Donald Rumsfeld. During the Reagan administration, Kissinger went back to the private sector in New York, and Eagleburger was appointed an assistant secretary at State, ultimately taking on an undersecretary position, one of the highest ranks outside deputy secretary. In 1984, at the end of Reagan's first term, Eagleburger, then sixty-three years old, joined his mentor in the New York consulting firm Kissinger Associates and was made president. Eagleburger had been at the lobbying firm, dealing with everything from Soviet affairs to the world price of oil until 1989, when tapped by Baker for deputy secretary of State. Luckily for Baker, the savvy Eagleburger had joined his camp.

Jim Baker kept unilateral control over his dominion on C Street. No one was invited to work at the State department without his personal invitation. Of all the federal agencies Scott Bush's staff worked with during those first two months of the administration, State was the only one that never requested a list of Schedule Cs. Baker, we were told, did not want interference from White House personnel. He shunned the entire presidential staff, intentionally alienating himself while building his own domain.

The opposite situation existed at the DOD.

In February 1989, the department of Defense became the first agency to open its doors and give 120-day temporary assignments to Schedule Cs. In fact, starting the first week of the administration, DOD was the only department actively pursuing candidates. Pentagon White House liaison, Ted Lewis, for whom I had worked briefly in my first personnel job at Transition, actually begged Scott's office for candidates. It was well known in the hallways of the OEOB that things were a bit unsettled at the Pentagon; this had not helped us as we tried to fill Lewis's appointments.

The Defense department remained a dilemma for us. The five-sided building across the Potomac River in Virginia was not a location where most political applicants wanted to work; their sights were set on one of the agencies in the District. For them, the military ranks were considered outside the political power circle, and seldom did someone who had not had previous military experience mix well with the rank-and-file serving in the armed forces. In staffing Defense, I learned something about the great divide between politicians and soldiers. While growing up in my Navy family, I had assumed the two camps were of the same ilk. Not so. I discovered two dissimilar brands of "patriots."

It seemed ironic to me that politicians used military language in their everyday talk (he's "on board," see you at "1700-hours"), and too, they loved having officers in uniform visit their premises and were known for playing military marching music at official events. Many offices of the senior aides in the West Wing, including the Oval Office, had paintings on their walls of Naval ships in battle. Many of these men did not choose to be part of the armed services themselves, but, I supposed, felt military customs added to their bravado. Despite their use of the trappings, politicians did not like the military mentality. Too rigid. Too shipshape. Too squared away, and too black-and-white. Politicians preferred the slap on the back, a pale handshake, and a wink of the eye.

On the other side, military men were not that fond of politicians. Politicians were too smooth. Too slick. Too schmoozy, and too self-promoting. They never stood on principle. When aboard ship, in a fighter jet or in the field, officers were told not to appear "too inside the Beltway." One lost credibility if he were thought to be cavorting with the Washington crowd.

The military officer and the politician, not cut from the same mold, had different agendas, and it looked to me like they did not trust one another. Seeing these differences while working in the White House, I wondered if I had been treading on foreign soil for eighteen months, thinking that all the while I was on familiar ground.

In February, just after arriving the OEOB, Ted Lewis had offered me a position at Defense, and I had declined. Like the majority of administration hopefuls, I did not imagine myself "over there." I too had come to see the DOD as far removed from the power center of political life, and understood why applicants offered a slot at the Pentagon refused and took their chances elsewhere.

Sometimes those wait-and-see individuals received other positions and sometimes not. For those who did accept jobs at Defense in January or February of 1989, they found their appointments short-lived. This situation was due to the aborted appointment of John G. Tower as secretary of Defense. Tower's nomination shook the administration and the Office of Presidential Personnel like no other event in Bush's first one hundred days. It ultimately weakened the presidency.

As a Bush nominee, Tower ultimately relied upon Untermeyer to shepherd his nomination through the Senate to confirmation. And so did the President rely on him. The personnel chief had the responsibility of ensuring that Cabinet nominees were "clean" before submitting their names to the Senate for approval. Untermeyer should have thoroughly investigated all the negatives associated with Tower *before* Bush nominated him. It was not as if Bush and Tower had not known one another—they went way back.

With the help of George Bush, the former senator and chairman of the Senate Armed Services Committee had built the Republican Party in Texas. Having left Southwestern University to serve in the Navy during World War II, Tower went on to be defeated by Lyndon Johnson in his run for the Senate, but then came back victorious in 1961. By 1970, Tower was chairman of the Republican Senate Campaign Committee, and he supported Bush financially and otherwise in his campaigns for senator and congressman.

Tower played a part in Bush's 1980 run for the presidency, and he was in Houston in 1987 to introduce the Vice President on the day Bush announced he was again running. A loyal follower and friend of Bush for many years, Tower—as chairman of Reagan's joint House-Senate special review board on the Iran-Contra Affair—had been lenient in his assessment of Bush's role, exonerating him from any illegal involvement in the exchange of arms for hostages.

The same had not been true for Reagan. In the 500-plus page Tower Commission Report, John Tower had accused many of those in the Reagan White House of wrongdoing, including the President himself. The Texas bulldog found Reagan accountable; however, he did give him some benefit of the doubt by characterizing him as a "detached leader." Never fully admitting his involvement, Reagan did acknowledge later that he had written in his diary, dated January 1986, "I agree to sell TOW's [anti-tank missiles] to Iran."

Then Reagan ran into more trouble. When the one hundredth Congress convened in January 1987, the Democrats controlled the Senate for the first time in Reagan's presidency (with a ten-vote majority; and an eighty-nine-vote majority in the House). With newfound momentum, Congress set out to defy Reagan's previous six years (1981–87) of unilateral authority in the Senate. Having had to bow to the President's wishes in the past, the Democrats made it clear that *they* were now the directors of the legislative agenda.

Before the Tower selection, the Robert H. Bork nomination was a prime example of how Democratic power was used against presidential nominees. In July 1987, President Reagan designated Bork as Supreme Court Justice, filling the vacancy left by Lewis Powell. Not without warning, Bork was opposed by the Congressional members who found the outspoken, conservative Yale legal scholar to be radical in his ideas and theories. Douglas Ginsburg was nominated in Bork's place. Yet, after allegations of drug use, he withdrew his nomination. Finally, Anthony Kennedy was selected and unanimously confirmed. Still the harm inflicted upon Reagan's authority was permanent and extremely damaging, and with the Ginsburg nomination, Congress gained in stature while President Reagan lost some.

Americans had already showed their disapproval of Reagan's handling of Iran-Contra in the favorability polls. In one month's time, his public approval had fallen from 67 percent to 46 percent. The 1987 Tower Report had cost Reagan a great deal of public support, and with his plummeting popularity, he accomplished little in the domestic area during his second term. The Democrat-controlled House and Senate passed dozens of laws regarding housing, civil rights, and education—all going against the conservative cause, and the congressional-executive relationship was irreparably injured. Behind the pretentious media curtain, Reagan limped his way into the final years of his presidency.

The fact that Reagan had been reprimanded over Iran-Contra while Bush had not inflamed the Reaganites *and* disgusted many congressional members. The verdict was looked upon as favoritism; Tower had saved him. However, instead of working to Bush's advantage, the "conclusions" had forced just the opposite. And *because* Bush was found innocent, Congress (which never believed in the Vice President's not-guilty verdict) ended up disliking Bush more than Reagan!

For John Tower, none of the Iran-Contra events had made him a well-liked figure, either with the Reagan White House or with Congress, and since that time, not much had changed for Tower in regard to his popularity.

In the winter of 1988-89, President Bush and Chase Untermeyer severely underestimated the wrath of the Senate, and to make matters more complicated, during some of the most crucial hours of the Tower nomination, Bush was in the Far East attending the State funeral of Japanese Emperor Hirohito. Regardless of the allure of rubbing elbows with heads of state, the President should have been at home trying to counteract the surge of criticism breaking over the nation's capital like a tsunami wave.

★★★

The American press ran with the ensuing hassle. An article from the *New York Times* on December 7, 1988, had given a hint that there were going to be "challenges" with Tower. In "Bush Keeps Webster in CIA Post; Appoints 3 to Economic Team," it was written:

> In making his announcements, Mr. Bush left unfilled the key job of Secretary of Defense...Former Texas Senator John G. Tower is widely believed to be the frontrunner for the job, but his appointment has been held up apparently because Mr. Bush wants to select a Defense team together with Mr. Tower that would be committed to streamlining the Pentagon. Speaking at a conference sponsored by *Defense Week,* John McCain (R-AZ) was quoted saying, "If the process goes on any longer, it could harm Senator Tower's effectiveness. All of us are working for him, from Senate Minority Leader Bob Dole all the way down."

Walter Pincus, in the *Washington Post* on November 23, 1988, described the situation this way: "Some Capitol Hill Republican sources critical of Tower's possible nomination have raised questions about the possibility that Tower's private life could become an issue in any confirmation process. Tower recently went through a bitter divorce battle. In court papers, his former wife sought records that she said would show expenditures on other women."

A recent divorcé, Tower was said to have a history of excessive drinking and some womanizing, and during Transition days, these "weaknesses" were the talk of the town. Debates regarding Tower's character were held throughout the Senate and House buildings, as well as in downtown hotels and restaurants. Before the confirmation vote took place, the Senate was led to believe that Tower had a serious alcohol problem, and Senator Ernest Hollings (D-SC) released an FBI file confirming "a prior pattern of alcohol abuse." This data was supposed to prove Tower was unqualified for the Cabinet job. Whether or not that was a reasonable argument, the Hill members used it to weaken both Tower and the Bush presidency. (Later, a background check would disprove Hollings's charges.)

Sam Nunn, a senator from Georgia, also did what he could to squelch the Tower nomination. As the ranking Democrat on the Armed Services Committee, Nunn was regarded by Democrats and Republicans alike as the foremost defense authority in Congress. Although the press had already contributed more than necessary to the Tower brouhaha, Nunn arrogantly pushed it along a bit further, denouncing Tower's integrity.

This was the same Congress that Bush had turned to in his Inaugural Address and said, "I am putting out my hand to you." The President had known that, in order to be successful, he would have to take a bipartisan approach with Congress. Yet, if the first few weeks in office were any indication of things to come, Bush could assume the Democrats were not willingly going to accept his "open hand." Bitterness that lingered from the Reagan days had deepened during the fall months of the '88 campaign; the Democrats felt that Bush had mistreated Dukakis. With Tower, the House and Senate were letting President Bush know—in no uncertain terms—that they were an entity to be reckoned with. They did not have to accept Bush's "open hand" because they had the "upper hand."

Fred McClure was the White House director for legislative affairs and responsible for ensuring quality communication between the Hill and the Oval Office. Despite the fact that this former Republican Texas steering committee vice chairman received one of the highest salaries in the White House ($125,000) and despite the warning signs posted early on regarding John Tower, once his name was submitted to the Senate as the President's choice for Defense secretary, McClure could neither engineer a win nor retrieve the ballot. In January 1989, Bush's young congressional aide concluded that all attempts to salvage the nomination were for naught and realized that his mission to ensure a Tower appointment was impossible. Bush, still trying to push Tower through, called the character attacks on his nominee "nothing more than allegations and rumors." To no avail.

Instead of moving the Tower nomination forward in an expeditious manner, Untermeyer (or maybe it was Bush?) sat on the recommendation way too long, letting rumors fly and dissension grow. Then, it was too late. On March 9, the Senate unanimously voted down Tower for secretary of Defense.

One of the few to throw his support behind Tower had been Dan Quayle, and, surprisingly, it was he who recommended to Bush the new Defense nominee: Richard Cheney. Quayle had known Cheney (who presently held the number-two Republican spot in the House, as Party whip) from their days in Congress together. I suspect that Quayle hoped Cheney could bring a more civilized President-Congress relationship to the table. Cheney had served five terms in Congress and was a staunch conservative, supporting the Reagan arms buildup and backing the Nicaraguan contras, serving as the ranking Republican on the House committee that investigated the affair.

Little did any one suspect *then* that the new secretary of Defense, a staunch conservative, would play a noteworthy role in the Bush presidency—as the antagonist. No one—not even Dick Darman—had the political experience and hubris of Dick Cheney, and it was widely known in political rings that if it were not for three heart attacks and a quadruple bypass, Cheney would have preferred to be president. Secretary of Defense was close enough for now.

The forty-eight-year-old Wyoming congressman, known for his ability to get things done, had once served as Gerald Ford's chief of staff. Later, during the time of Ford's run for the presidency in 1976, at Bush's request, Dick Cheney had brought Jim Baker into President Ford's campaign. Cheney's ties to Baker both politically and personally had remained firm since the Ford days. Two other "friends" to both Cheney and Baker were Stu Spencer, Reagan's advisor and confidante, and Brent Scowcroft, Ford's national security advisor.

Both Cheney and Scowcroft were serving in the Bush White House in positions unusually similar to those they had assumed in the Ford administration. By naming Scowcroft—the sixty-two year-old retired Air Force general and former West Point graduate—as his national security advisor, Bush brought together two men with recognizable foreign affairs skills. However, they would not see eye-to-eye. Their political points of view were diametrically opposed.

With pleasure, Scowcroft, who had started out as a National Security Council aide to Nixon, accepted the position as Bush's top security advisor. The former general had been an outspoken critic of Reagan's foreign policy measures, and during Iran-Contra, he was a member of the 1986-87 investigation and the Tower Commission. Unlike Tower, who was cast out by the very body in which he had served as a robust leader, Scowcroft emerged from the affair unscathed.

As secretary of Defense, Cheney now would be working not only with his cohort Baker at State, but also with Scowcroft in the White House. Although he was a Bush outsider, by having previously befriended Baker and Scowcroft, Cheney was given an immediate inside track. Having successfully made the transitions from political aide *to* Ford

White House chief of staff *to* congressman *to* secretary of Defense, Cheney had one man to thank: Donald Rumsfeld. In fact, Cheney owed his entire political career to Rumsfeld.

Nixon-appointee Rumsfeld, the director of the Cost of Living Council and the Office of Economic Opportunity (OEO), had hired Cheney (as well as Frank Carlucci and Ken Adleman, the latter of whom became chief of the Arms Control and Disarmament Agency under Reagan and one of Cheney's closest friends) to be his aide when the youthful Cheney was on a congressional fellowship working in Representative Bill Steiger's (R-WI) office. In 1973, Rumsfeld became Nixon's ambassador to NATO; after Nixon's resignation in 1974, Ford asked him to be his chief of staff. One thing led to another, and Rumsfeld accepted the COS position, once again bringing with him his loyal aide, Dick Cheney.

In the Ford White House, Don Rumsfeld held the seat of power, overseeing the entire White House staff and controlling the Oval Office operations office. As deputy to the chief of staff, Cheney was second in command, and when Rumsfeld left to become secretary of Defense (during the last year of the Ford administration), Cheney, not surprisingly, filled Rumsfeld's shoes and became Ford's chief of staff. Cheney had control over the Ford White House *and* the ensuing 1976 Ford presidential campaign. What many people do not realize is that the Nixon staff serving in the Ford presidency had a far stronger bond with Rumsfeld and Cheney than they ever did with President Ford.

Now, on March 17, 1989, the Senate confirmed Cheney by a 92 to 0 vote as Defense secretary. The ballot came just eight days after the formal rejection of John Tower. Although the Defense nominee story seemed to have a winning conclusion, the fact that up until Tower's rejection no new President in two hundred years had ever been denied his choice for a Cabinet position could not—and would not—be forgotten anytime soon. According to the *Washington Post,* the Tower nomination was "the most bungled political disaster in memory." (Within a couple of years after the nomination battle, Tower was killed in a plane crash.)

POLITICS rolled on, and so did I. By the end of February, I received a 120-day assignment to the department of Commerce. This was extremely welcome news for me. Making it that much more exceptional, the day before leaving presidential personnel, I, along with my six teammates and Scott Bush, had lunch in the White House senior staff dining room.

★★★

With only a driveway separating our offices from those in the West Wing, we easily traversed West Executive Avenue (where dignitaries' limousines lined up) and arrived at the diplomatic entrance. An aide met us and escorted us to the dining room. Dark wood paneling and dim lighting in the White House "mess" made the room appear smaller than it was. Low ceilings contributed to the aboard-ship feeling, and the stewards, suited in white jackets, attended to us with military precision and flawless politeness. White linen tablecloths and napkins, along with flat silver and white china, provided the ideal touch of refinement. My mind wandered; something in the setting was reminiscent of times past.

The White House ward room reminded me of springtime in 1961 when Father, in command of the cruiser *Galveston*, sailed into the naval port of Charleston, South Carolina. I was in my junior year boarding at Ashley Hall, far from home in Newport, RI, and Father had invited me to give a small dinner party aboard his ship. Three other Ashley Hall classmates and four cadets from the Citadel completed the guest list. With Father, I hosted (with the help of the Filipino stewards) an elegant five-course meal in the private dining room reserved for the captain. A well-dressed table and formal place settings, including two silver candelabra and fourteen-inch candles, made for an impressive scene. The cadets wore gray and black uniforms with stiff upper collars, and I wore a white chiffon dress with a bodice made entirely of white beads. Father was in dress uniform, with blue and gold loops (aiguillettes) over his left shoulder and a bow tie. When we came aboard the ship and when we departed—over the gangway—in recognition of the captain and his party, the bosin's mate blew his pipe. As a sixteen-year-old, I felt so grown up that night aboard ship in Charleston Harbor and so proud to be with Father. I *was* my father's daughter.

Now, many years later, with my workmates, I sat in the West Wing dining room lingering over lunch, in no hurry to leave. After the last course was served, we were invited to tour the White House unchaperoned and at our leisure and, in an unusual gesture by the President's staff, were given permission to use our cameras. Photography is not permitted in the White House, and certainly never in the West Wing.

Our first stop was the notorious Press Room. It was compact and much smaller than I had expected. One by one, we stood behind the press podium photographing each other as we pretended to be press secretary.

Of all the rooms on the State Floor, none compared to the North Entrance Hall, the area one enters when attending a formal or ceremonial event. The first things to catch my eye were the President's flag and the flag of the United States flanking the door to the Blue Room. The expansive North Hall and Cross Hall, separated by an arcade, were part of James Hoban's original plans for the White House, as was the Grand Staircase to the left of the front door. Red carpet covered the marble floors of the Cross Hall, which led from the State Dining Room to the East Room.

As the North Entrance Hall had captured my attention on the first floor, on the ground floor, the Diplomatic Reception Room (Mural Room) did so. Designed as a drawing room of the early nineteenth century, the room served as a gathering place for the President and his guests at state functions. A handsome oval French Aubusson rug was woven to fit the dimensions of the room. Within the wide blue border were the seals of the fifty states. Covering the curved walls of the large room was a hand-painted, panoramic wallpaper depicting various images of our nation. Called "Scenic America" and printed in 1834, the wall covering showed scenes of American landscapes, including Niagara Falls, West Point and Boston Harbor. The scene portraying the bustling port of Boston triggered thoughts of the previous July . . . and my research project.

Outside and near the South Portico, we found ourselves in the now-dormant Rose Garden, which adjoined the Oval Office. Walking the same brick pathway the President used to come and go from the family quarters, we turned into one of the corridors outside the Cabinet room and found ourselves heading back into the West Wing, where the staff was busy at work. West Wing staffers were usually attired in the standard uniform: men in gray or blue suits and women in street dresses, never pants. Like in the OEOB, most work was done behind closed doors. Everyone moved about efficiently and quietly, with a certain air of urgency. There is definitely a mystique surrounding the West Wing.

As I left the White House grounds to go back to my office in the OEOB, I stopped to survey the 108-year-old presidential mansion, with all its 132 rooms. On the sloping South Lawn (President's Park) were an array of majestic trees, and over to the left was the department of Commerce, the building in which I would start my assignment the following morning.

Department of Commerce, Washington, D.C.
Beginning my appointment at the International Trade Administration.

★ ★

PART 4

We Call It "Spin"

★ ★

It is from numberless, diverse acts of courage and belief that human history is shaped. Each time a man stands up for an ideal, or acts to improve the lot of others, or strikes out against injustice, he sends forth a tiny ripple of hope; and crossing each other from a million centers of energy and daring, those ripples build a current that can sweep down the mightiest walls of oppression and resistance.

—Arlington National Cemetery

15

DARLING OF THE CABINET

To be a player is to have power or influence on some issue. Not to be a player is to be out of the power loop and without influence.

—Hedrick Smith

MARCH–MAY 1989

Within the city of Washington, D.C., snuggled between the Capitol Building to the east and the majestic Potomac River to the west, lies the Federal District. It is the heart of Washington and the hub of political life. Most agencies, including the department of Commerce (DOC), are located here.

Commerce was one of the smaller—some would say obsolete—departments in the federal bureaucracy, yet it maintains territorial strength. Located between Pennsylvania and Constitution Avenues and a block away from the White House, it takes up an entire city block. Situated within the massive six-floor structure, complete with remarkable mosaic floors and a medley of courtyards, were five thousand of the forty thousand employees. And with its own peculiar charm, the DOC was laid out in quadrangles, where neither the floors nor the corridors connected on the same level; in many ways, Commerce was difficult to navigate.

Approximately one hundred DOC employees were political appointees, of whom I was now one. All of us reported to Robert Adam Mosbacher, who sat on the Bush Cabinet as secretary of Commerce. Mosbacher was one of Bush's oldest friends, and upon his nomination, Bush had said, "I will be glad to have his wise counsel in my Cabinet."

Born in Mount Vernon, New York, in 1927, Mosbacher was the son of Emil Mosbacher, a wealthy New York financier and stockbroker. After attending the Choate School in Wallingford, Connecticut, and Washington and Lee University in Lexington, Virginia, Bob Mosbacher moved to Houston to manage his father's oil investments. His first wife, and mother of his four children, Jane Pennybacker, forty-nine, died of leukemia in 1970 at age forty-nine. By that time, Mosbacher had forged a friendship with George Bush, whom he had first met in Houston in the early 1960s when both were starting their careers in the oil business. Mosbacher as a wildcatter, Bush in offshore drilling.

After his wife's death, Mosbacher headed the fund-raising effort for Bush in his Senate campaign against Lloyd Bentsen. When Ford ran in the 1976 presidential campaign (and Jim Baker was chairman) Mosbacher had become finance chairman, as he had for Bush in his presidential campaigns of 1980 and 1988. As Bush's chief fund-raiser in the 1988 Bush campaign, Mosbacher had brought in $25 million and headed Team 100, the program for contributors of more than $100,000. During the eighties, Mosbacher was partner with Bush in a tugboat and barge company servicing the oil industry and, up until his recent appointment, had been chairman and chief executive officer of the Mosbacher Energy Company, started by his father some forty years earlier.

On December 1, 1988, a *Washington Post* article entitled "Suave Oilman, Pragmatic Conservative" by Paul Blustein described Mosbacher this way:

> In a Cabinet that is rapidly filling with pragmatic Republicans, Robert A. Mosbacher is the epitome of the breed. A wealthy, suave oilman from Houston, who has gained something of a jet-setter reputation by dint of his yachting skill and socialite wife, Mosbacher is one of the GOP's most successful fund-raisers. And the Commerce-secretary-designate is a thoroughly non-ideological conservative who is likely to push for an active government role in promoting business interests.

Mosbacher did have a penchant for the extravagant and for having a good time, and he was a world-class sailor, as was his brother Emil (Bus, as he was called, was winner of the America's Cup in 1962 and chief of protocol in the Nixon administration). More important was the fact that Mosbacher had spent a lifetime as a successful independent businessman, supporting business groups active in global trade endeavors—beyond the realm of oil. Expecting to bring his entrepreneurial expertise to Washington, the energy executive planned to promote U.S. business interests abroad in a major way. However, in the first few weeks of the new administration, instead of focusing on the more professional side of the new Commerce secretary, the Washington press chose instead to scrutinize the more glamorous side.

In the winter of 1989, reports about the Mosbachers' trips to Europe and their invitations to Hollywood captured the imagination of Washingtonians. Secretary and Mrs. Mosbacher were seen more as a novelty rather than a political force.

For Mosbacher's efforts in Bush's 1988 campaign (and all the campaigns before) his was one of the first Cabinet posts awarded in the administration. The Senate unanimously (100-0) confirmed his nomination on January 31, 1989. On April 11, 1990, Jack Anderson and Dale Van Atta wrote about the Commerce secretary in the *Washington Post:*

> In a sense, he earned the Cabinet job. He raised millions of dollars as finance director of George Bush's 1988 campaign. Mosbacher doesn't apologize for winning a Cabinet post because he is a generous Republican Party supporter who can wring big bucks out of his friends.

The Texas oil baron, known to have a net worth of over $170 million, was the wealthiest member on the Bush Cabinet. Ironically, he directed the department that had long been considered one of the "poorest," one with little authority and even less impact on policy. Secretary of Commerce was not a position of influence; still, it was quite visible. Without having previously lived in Washington, and therefore unfamiliar with how The System worked, Mosbacher jumped into the job feet first. As a savvy tycoon with a firm grasp on economic theory and international trade principles, Mosbacher applied his intellectual energies to Commerce's agenda without much forethought. When he saw green lights, he just kept going, not stopping to get "permission" and without checking in with the Oval Office. In the April 30, 1989, *Washington Post,* with reference to his friendship with Bush, Mosbacher said, "I try not to, and I don't believe I do, play on being a friend of the President's. I don't look for any extra edge. We have been friends for a long time. But I don't play on it. I won't say that under dire circumstances I might not sometime. But I have not."

Without formal authorization, Mosbacher put Commerce on the Washington political map in a way no one could have predicted. During February and March, his name was in the *Post* every other day. He was the darling of the Cabinet, unexpectedly emerging as a commanding force in designing the administration's economic policies; he even attended Tuesday meetings at Treasury with Jim Baker, Dick Darman, and Nicholas Brady. The sexiest and the hottest issues of the day were on *his* plate: high definition television (HDTV), supercomputers, semiconductors, and Airbus were but a few of the initiatives with the secretary's name attached to them. Nevertheless, no project under his purview would compare in significance to the joint U.S.-Japanese venture to produce the Fighter Support Experimental plane (FSX). The FSX and the evolving power plays surrounding this endeavor represent the severity of the political battles within the Bush presidency, those between Bush's most senior advisors, underscoring the veiled hostility between members of Bush's senior staff. These in-house struggles that bloomed early in 1989 would pervade the White House for the remainder of the Bush administration.

The $7 billion warplane program, which had been developed by Reagan's advisors and dumped into Bush's lap, still needed congressional approval, and the unusual circumstances that enveloped the plane's production highlight the enormous lengths to which men caught up in a territorial battle will go.

Originally a fighter jet that Japan intended to build independently, the FSX had a controversial history. Only after pressure from the Reagan White House did former Prime Minister Yasuhiro Nakasone agree to produce the plane in a joint venture with the United States. The team that rallied around the President in support of the FSX viewed the agreement as a big win.

During the winter of 1989, with President Bush in the White House, the FSX issue was heralded not as a triumph, but as the first "significant" policy dispute among Bush Cabinet members. The negotiations over the FSX had been going on for more than four years, and a signed contract was thought to be a done deal . . . until Mosbacher became involved.

Bruce Stokes, in the *National Journal* on February 25, 1989, wrote a six-page article titled "Beat 'Em or Join 'Em," in which he described the FSX situation this way:

Like a punt returner who had eluded pursuers on the football field,

broken several tackles and reversed field several times, the FSX
deal—Washington's controversial four-year-old-plan to co-develop
a tactical jet fighter with Tokyo—finally broke into the clear late last
year and streaked toward the goal line. Only yards from pay dirt,
however, in what seemingly was an open field, the agreement was
blindsided by opponents.

Also in the *Washington Post* was the article "FSX Becomes Symbol of
a New Age: Aircraft Dispute Shows Technology Is Now Political Tool," in
which Evelyn Richards reported:

> Almost overnight, the plane has become a symbol of a new age in
> which technology is used as a hot political tool, when the global
> balance of political and economic power can be affected by a faster
> computer or a denser semiconductor chip. Just as suddenly, the FSX
> has become a cause celebre for critics who say it's time for America
> to end a habit of giving away vital technologies that come back later
> in products irresistible to American consumers and devastating to
> U.S. industry.

Previous to the Bush presidency, the United States had agreed to
permit Japan to produce the FSX with U.S. assistance. The negotiations
had ended in a "memorandum of understanding" (MOU, in trade lingo)
in November 1988, just as Reagan was leaving office. Negotiated by
Reagan's department of Defense team (with no input from Commerce or
State), the joint venture allowed and *encouraged* Japan to participate in the
building of the FSX. General Dynamics Corporation, the principal
American industrial participant, which made the F-16, had been chosen to
be subcontractor—and would get 40 percent of the $1.2 billion cost of
developing six prototypes. Japan's Mitsubishi Heavy Industries, the
prime contractor, would receive the remaining 60 percent. Two other
American companies would continue with their present Japan aerospace
contracts while the FSX project was underway: Fairchild Industries, and
McDonnell Douglas.

In February 1989, Secretary Mosbacher took the offensive and joined
with Congress (which during the fall months had criticized the FSX
accord) to voice his opinion that the agreement infringed upon the
commercial rights of U.S. business interests. He believed that the transfer
of aerospace technology to Japan could hurt American competitiveness.
At first, he suggested Japan buy American F-16s off the shelf, later, he

softened his decision and determined that imposing restrictions would prove more beneficial to U.S.-Japan trade relations in the future.

Mosbacher's desire to be influential during the Bush presidency went beyond the FSX project. He hoped that when a similar issue arose, he—not just Cheney (Defense) and/or Baker (State)—would be granted decision-making authority. He, unlike his peers, perceived technology transfer issues as important to protecting American business. The foremost issue raised by the FSX accord was how much of a role U.S. economic security and job protection should have in foreign policy and defense security matters. Mosbacher's ideas differed from those of Baker and Cheney; he was more interested in guarding jobs and the economy—preserving the country's industrial base. Baker and Cheney were *supposedly* more worried about building America's national defense.

It was hard to believe that by bestowing contracts to favored American companies such as General Dynamics, Cheney and Baker were *really* thinking about shielding the United States from enemy attacks. In my opinion, by adding to the coffers of their own departments (Defense and State), Baker and Cheney protected their political authority and their personal clout, which allowed them to remain on the higher rungs of the Political Ladder. Defense, in particular, had a lot to gain by remaining in charge.

Past military agreements designed by the Pentagon had established Japan as a primary manufacturer, producing all or part of an aircraft, according to American specifications. For that privilege, Japan had paid the U.S. well, though hardly enough to make up for the fact that America allowed Japan five times the amount of imports Japan accepted from the U.S. It appeared to me that Mosbacher, by viewing American business as a whole (not just the portion that included the larger companies), was able to appreciate the need to give smaller firms a voice. The original intent in establishing the Commerce department was to serve the "little guy."

For Republicans in 1989, this was a novel way of thinking. However, a new wind was blowing through American foreign policy, and economic security concerns were becoming just as legitimate as national defense. In a briefing paper later distributed at Commerce, Mosbacher insisted, "international trade is really going to be a key aspect of international politics in the new administration." In the brief, he also said that he was determined to protect against foreign commercial applications of

FSX technology: "If this nation surrenders to complacency, if we lose control of industries and production of products vital to our defense and way of life, at stake is not just American jobs and prosperity, but America's freedom."

While striving to gain support for renegotiation of the FSX contract, Mosbacher appeared to have the President's support, but the Cabinet was split. National Security Council meetings, headed by Brent Scowcroft—who had taken a hands-off position—ended in further argument and disagreement. Having earlier promised Japan that he would work to win approval of the FSX accord, Baker, siding with Cheney, gave the Defense department his full endorsement. I noticed that the *Washington Post*, on March 17, 1989, took a "middle-road" stance in the debate:

> In the Reagan administration, the Defense Department was much involved in civilian export licensing on grounds that the technology could have military applications. Now, in the Bush administration, the Commerce Department is challenging a military export on grounds that it could have civilian applications. Each has a point, but it is up to the White House to keep these struggles under control. The Defense Department should not be allowed to choke down the flow of American exports unless the national security implications are overwhelming. Nor should the Commerce Department be allowed to disrupt a reasonable foreign policy to which the country is already committed.

The *Washington Times*, on March 22, 1989, wrote: "Sources said that Commerce Secretary Robert Mosbacher, who favored tighter controls on the project, appears to be the victor in a Cabinet tug-of-war with the Defense and State departments, which had supported the project with fewer reservations."

On March 21, President Bush decided to go forward with a revised FSX agreement, including clarifications and specific limits on software source codes (that dealt with advanced aerodynamic and avionic concepts). Once Bush made a decision, Commerce, Defense and State officials held a series of meetings: they concluded in an agreement. On April 30, as front-page news, it was announced that Bush had signed a U.S.-Japanese agreement to jointly design and build a new-generation fighter plane, a pact that Bush said would protect both American jobs and sensitive technology.

Seeing the American FSX dispute as ominous and feeling rebuffed,

Japan unhappily, but finally, accepted the U.S. "clarifications." The administration, having done its part in securing the accord, now turned the matter over to Congress, which had not been involved with the previous Reagan-FSX issues. The majority of congressional members wanted to scrap the Japanese transaction, and they held the power to veto the Washington-Tokyo agreement.

In support of Mosbacher, Congress would later introduce several bills requiring Pentagon officials to consult with the Commerce secretary on existing and future arms deals having "significant adverse impact on the international competitiveness position of U.S. industry" (DOC *Daily News Distribution*). Some congressional members looked at the FSX Japanese accord from the other perspective and chose to back Baker and Cheney. John McCain, an Arizona Republican who sat on the Senate Armed Services Committee, was one of these individuals. He strongly promoted the idea that the agreement should be completed as intended under Reagan, going so far as to telephone Scowcroft at the White House and say, "To go back on the Reagan deal is damn foolishness." McCain and his collaborators feared that if Congress could pressure its President out of a signed agreement it would leave a disastrous image.

However, the forces against the FSX outnumbered those advocating it, and a fight was imminent. Mosbacher, Cheney and Lawrence Eagleburger went to Capital Hill to represent the administration's viewpoint. At the hearings, the three men spoke in front of a packed House Foreign Affairs Committee hearing. Mosbacher said, "In clarifying the terms of the FSX co-development with Japan, we have found it possible to proceed with defense cooperation without compromising our economic security."

With Mosbacher's endorsement, the accord passed the Senate Foreign Relations Committee, but barely (by a 9 to 8 vote), before going to the full Senate; the House was unable to complete its vote before the Senate. On May 17, the Senate narrowly (52-47) approved the Bush-revised accord. "The vote provided a congressional go-ahead to an agreement that [had] been mired in controversy since it was announced in the last months of the Reagan administration," the *Washington Post* reported on May 17, 1989.

Because of Mosbacher's contribution, President Bush gained the congressional support he needed to pass the agreement. Chances were that, had the Commerce chief not taken such a firm stand on outlining the qualifiers, the accord never would have passed in Congress. All the way around, Mosbacher enjoyed the biggest political gain from the FSX project, and it seemed he was guaranteed a place in future technology decisions—those that had previously fallen only under the authority of State and Defense. In the earlier months of the administration, Commerce—known for little more than its Census Bureau and National Weather Service—was taking charge of some of the highest-priority items in the Bush presidency.

Having assumed power in early 1989, Mosbacher—by virtue of being first on the scene—had "seized the day" when no one expected him to, and he had done so, it seemed, with President Bush's blessing. Because Mosbacher was so new and presided over one of the least influential agencies in the executive branch, he at first was perceived by the Washington in-crowd as unlikely to make political headway. Even after the FSX issue arose, he continued to be portrayed as the rich Texan on the Cabinet because he was the friend of Bush and was in town so that he and his wife could enjoy the "society."

But Mosbacher had come to the city with a working agenda: increasing America's competitiveness. Stuart Auerbach wrote in the *Washington Post* an article on April 30, 1989, "Asserting Himself Swiftly, Mosbacher Dashes 'Party Boy' Reputation":

> By becoming a major player during the first hundred days of the Bush administration, Mosbacher has confounded conventional Washington wisdom. He arrived here bearing the reputation of a rich Texas party boy, confidante and chief fundraiser for President Bush, and husband of Georgette Mosbacher, who was labeled "curvy" and "nervy" by Women's Wear Daily. "Is the Commerce Department ready for her?" the publication asked. In fact, Georgette Mosbacher has been conspicuous by her absence on the Washington scene and her husband has been working six-day weeks, 12 to 14 hours a day.

In the same *Post* article, Mosbacher was quoted, "I hate to ruin a wonderful image. Being a party boy sounds like so much fun. But if you check in Houston, you will find I can't live up to that image. I've been a reasonably serious player there for a long, long time."

The Commerce secretary's ability to take control "in the first seven seconds" worked well as long as no one was there to challenge him. In Washington, what seemed to be a sure thing one day could always reverse itself the next. If someone with more clout wants what someone else has, or thinks that someone has too much, or simply does not like that someone, the scenario can change drastically, often before the other person realizes what has happened. Mosbacher found himself in this predicament in the late spring and early summer of 1989, just five months into his appointment.

As time went by, others in the Bush White House had a chance to watch Mosbacher's level of authority take on unusual proportions. And the President's "Most Prestigious" swiftly singled out Mosbacher for claiming too much of the political pie. Having set his sights high, with visions wider in scope than even he may have believed possible, Mosbacher must have felt pleased that he had aggressively moved forward and staked out what he thought to be rightfully his. But, Mosbacher had claimed jurisdiction over areas not previously allocated to the DOC. He had overstepped his political bounds, and President's friend or not, he was going to have to learn his place as a newcomer to the Washington community.

Almost overnight, Mosbacher lost most of his political agenda and personal clout to "someone" who most assuredly had more strength and savvy than he. By July 1989, Mosbacher's role in the administration had gone from darling to defeated. Someone on the "inside" had made sure the Texas multimillionaire was out of the limelight and out of what was appearing to be the most interesting position on the Cabinet. The newspaper columnists follow the leads given to them by the White House press secretary; now, instead of writing about how successful Mosbacher was with his initiatives (as in their earlier upbeat articles), they said the administration was willing to "consider" his proposals "after studying them more closely." These phrases are ill omens in politics.

Predictably, there were no explanations for the turnaround. The press never mentioned that Mosbacher's job description had been rewritten. And unless one had been in the administration early on—and had been paying close attention to what Mosbacher did during that time—one would never have known he had taken a tumble. Publicly, his loss of power was either ignored or forgotten.

Watching both Mosbacher's rise in power and his fall helped me understand yet another principle of politics: the Good Guys do not always win. No matter how admirable one's ideas, the best, albeit regrettable, way to survive the political game is to lay low. Even for the idealist, there is some wisdom in knowing how to keep out of the line of fire. Mosbacher had to find out the hard way.

Bush, Baker, and Mosbacher, all Texans, had known each other for years. However, Bush and Baker had been the political players; Mosbacher had never held a government job before arriving in Washington in 1989. Could it have been that James A. Baker, III—the secretary of State, Reagan's former chief of staff and friend to both Bush and Mosbacher—felt a twinge of jealousy when he saw the Honorable Robert A. Mosbacher take Washington by storm? I doubt that Baker had anticipated Mosbacher's instant rise in power and popularity. When he saw some of State's national policy issues being turned over to Commerce, he could have felt threatened.

In the spring of 1989, rivalry between Baker and Mosbacher began to show up in publications such as *Time* magazine; one with Baker's picture on the cover and was headlined: "A Gentleman Who Hates to Lose." The *Washington Post,* on April 30, 1989, carried a piece by Stuart Auerbach referencing the cover and the Baker-Mosbacher relationship. Auerbach wrote, "The competition between the two is well recognized." Then Auerbach quoted what Baker had written on the autographed copy he gave to Mosbacher, "To Bob, who hates to lose even more [than I do]."

Or could it have been Baker's friend, secretary of Defense, Dick Cheney, who had become uncomfortable with Mosbacher's newfound role? Commerce had tried to acquire the FSX fighter aircraft issue, which had been a Defense Only matter. The Defense budget, of $275 billion, was larger than all the other agencies put together. Defense was 25 percent of the federal budget; all the agencies *combined* made up only 6 percent. For Cheney, there was a lot at stake.

Based on these statistics alone, it was easy to see why—when it came to the construction of airplanes and telecommunications systems—and such—Cheney towered over Mosbacher in influence and authority. And too, Cheney had been "rubbing elbows" with the most influential in Washington for fifteen years. He had been Reagan's "senior aide" in Congress. Cheney's situation in the Bush White House was unique—he fit in with all the other conservative Reaganites, with only Bush and

Scowcroft to harness him.

Nonetheless, in terms of family money, Bob Mosbacher was the wealthiest on the Bush Cabinet and therefore had some sway; yet, as long as Cheney had Baker on his side, he held the political edge. Chances were that, together, Cheney and Baker had a lot to do with Mosbacher being brought down several rungs. I doubt this was with Bush's sanction.

Past Presidents, instead of soliciting advice from Cabinet members, often had taken liberty to turn to their senior advisors. Over the years, the clout of the White House staff—regarding drafting policy and appointing personnel—had become more and more concentrated at the top. Fewer individuals were included in the inner circle. Cabinet members that the public assumed to have significant power sometimes did not. In the Executive Office of the President, the chief of staff, budget director, national security advisor, and secretary of State held the most weight. Frequently, the most authoritative advisor of all would be the chief of staff.

With Bush's COS, John Sununu, this was not the case. Although the former New Hampshire governor knew how to lead a state-level political campaign, in the White House, he was not on a familiar course. Without directions on how to successfully navigate the terrain of the West Wing and concurrently smooth the ruffled feathers of Congress, Sununu would eventually find himself overextended. Because Bush lacked both a Washington-smart chief of staff *and* tough Cabinet advisors, there was plenty of opportunity for Baker to step forward and claim more than a generous portion of authority. In his mind, he had won the presidency for Bush and the President owed him. No one was going to make an end-run around Baker. Certainly not Bob Mosbacher.

Articles such as the one written in the *Washington Post* on August 10, 1989, must have sent Baker reeling:

> How could someone so new to the Washington power game, overshadowed by his dazzling socialite wife, possibly become a mover and shaker, the skeptics asked. Perhaps no other member of the Bush Cabinet took office with lower expectations than the president's choice for Commerce Secretary. But in just five months in office, George Bush's longtime friend has run up a string of successes.

By August, Mosbacher, having lost his battle for control, made the

Post article outdated. Still, what was intriguing about this story was that it had been accurate just weeks earlier.

While the struggles in the Bush White House were ongoing, a second agenda for Mosbacher and the department of Commerce was drafted. It no longer included cutting-edge computer technology, state-of-the-art military aircraft or high-definition television.

Another one of Mosbacher's highest-priority items, HDTV, had been taken out of his hands and turned over to Cheney at Defense. Although the press would allude to the possibility that the administration was going to drop the HDTV/ initiative, in fact, it would not. Up front, there was a $30 million commitment to HDTV from the Defense Advanced Research Projects Agency (DARPA), the Pentagon's research and development office. Despite millions of dollars appropriated for HDTV, the U.S. never went forward with the proposal that Mosbacher had strongly advocated, and the reason was never fully explained; it was "suggested" that it would take too long and cost too much to catch up with Japan. I wonder who decided that.

Mosbacher ambivalently accepted his situation and persevered on the Bush Cabinet. He continued to be part of the Washington scene. One of the last articles touting Mosbacher's remarkable "first inning hits" was published in the same August 10, issue of the *Post*. This one was entitled "Mosbacher Scores High in Capital Power Game." A picture of Mosbacher was captioned "Secretary of Commerce Mosbacher Has Proven a Deft and Skillful Player in the Game of Politics"; below it was written:

> Mr. Mosbacher's early successes have made the Commerce Department, long considered a backwater agency with little impact on big decisions, a player in Washington. He is careful not to define his proposals as industrial policy, but rather an industry-led business-government partnership; he has come out in favor of government support in the race to develop high-definition television; he favors relaxation of antitrust laws to allow high-technology industries to join forces to promote research and development; he would like to ease government regulations to aid industry.

Simultaneously, during the months of Mosbacher's demotion, stories in the press related to strife among some of the Bush Cabinet members. The aforementioned *Post* article described the White House "family" conflict in these terms:

> Those views [industry-led] are far from universally held
> throughout the Cabinet. Mr. Mosbacher says he was unhappy that
> reports of the internal disagreement found their way into print . . .
> news leaks, the time-honored way for opposing forces to sway
> public opinion in Washington, leave Mr. Mosbacher "horrified."
> "You go to a meeting with the president of the United States and
> you come out and the next day you read about everything that you
> said and what everyone else said. If that were my company, I would
> fire whoever did that."

In Washington circles, it was well known that during the Reagan days, Baker was notorious for leaking information to the press, especially when someone threatened him and he wanted to nudge them out of the way. Unfortunately, if Baker were the guilty party in Mosbacher's case, he would never be fired. Baker would stay just where he always stayed, untarnished and at the top. With the FSX, Jim Baker had put Bob Mosbacher "in his place." After having suffered the fall, Mosbacher learned that he could remain in Washington if he so desired, but when it came to joining those on Baker's Power Pyramid, he should *never again* presume to take an uninvited step.

★★★ ══════ ★★★
CHAPTER

16

HONEYMOON BOUNCE

As you might have guessed, fishing is my favorite source of relaxation. It is with a rod and reel in my hand that I tend to count my blessings.
                                                        —*George Herbert Walker Bush*

JUNE–AUGUST 1989

L unch is an event in the Federal City.
        With the onset of warm, balmy days and cool, clear nights, the appointees were feeling the effects of both Potomac fever and Spring fever. The days of three-martini lunches had disappeared, but many of us took time during the lunch hour to meet and greet fellow politicals and swap stories about what we knew concerning the President's agenda. It would be difficult, if not impossible, to stay in the administration without keeping up with the latest from the White House. And in a town where those in the administration always looked for a reason to gather, no time was better to get together with a friend or colleague than when the forsythia bushes, cherry trees and crab apples were in bloom. Whether we ate a turkey-on-rye at a grassy park or ordered shrimp scampi at the Willard, whether we were reclining on a bench in Lafayette Park or sitting on Queen Anne chairs in the dining room at the Hay Adams, we loved seeing each other and exchanging the latest scoop.

        A favorite was the Washington Hotel, with its open-air, porch-like rooftop restaurant located on the twelfth floor. Less than a block away from the White House, at 15th and Pennsylvania, it had a view comparable to that of the department of State, but facing the west. Nevertheless, neither an alluring view nor tasty food accounted for the popularity of the Washington lunch. The giving and taking of information was the primary reason for meeting. Engaging in the talk of the day was part of a springtime ritual. Because the exchange of news in political circles is almost always empowering, the luncheon date in the District was known as the Power Lunch. Right now, because I was among the first to be sent to the Commerce department, *I* was news.

While spring was in the air and Mosbacher was still the rising star of the Cabinet, I arrived at Commerce to start my 120-day assignment. I was eager to start and optimistic that my appointment would somehow prove my observations at the White House to be wrong. I wanted to believe that the personnel situation was not as dire as I had thought—despite the fact that friends and acquaintances of mine from the campaign were grumbling about not getting jobs.

The Commerce building loomed large as I approached it. Managing to navigate my way through the maze of floors and hallways, I was instructed to check into the office of the White House liaison. My first meeting did not bode well. The office director, Maryann Fish, was part of the leftover Reagan personnel group, and like her colleagues, she was not planning to leave. Fish reported to Starek's team, and the associate directors had made sure that all White House liaisons remained on-site, with their previous powers preserved.

Fish was not there to do any favors for the Bush people, especially those being sent to *her* building. Being the first Schedule C to arrive, I saw more of Fish than did the others who followed me, and unfortunately, because the beginning of a administration usually moves more slowly in processing appointees, she had some time on her hands. I got to know Fish better than I would have wished. Her demeanor was chilling, and as gatekeeper to the political positions, she had learned how to make the most of her clout: she had reserved as many of the Commerce jobs as she could for individuals with Reagan credentials. It would not be unfair to say that she could terminate my appointment, or anyone else's—either through intimidation or by making things uncomfortable—whenever she wished. She soon would gain a reputation for putting a good number of 120-day candidates back on the street.

Responsible for selecting my own job—in this organization of forty thousand—I shuffled through books that gave descriptions of the various divisions until I chose the International Trade Administration. The ITA, with two thousand members, I read, supported American industries that

★★★

imported or exported goods or services. In graduate school, I had studied management theory and the evolution of successful U.S. corporations; having learned how these companies vied with one another domestically, I was intrigued by the thought of learning how they competed in the world market.

In the ITA, only one or two senior-level individuals were in place; therefore, in March 1989, my choice of offices in which to work was limited. Fortunately, the incoming assistant secretary for trade development (TD) was on the premises; I hoped that Michael Skarzynski would have slots to fill. He did, and I applied for one of his four positions, and shortly thereafter received an invitation to join his staff. It was a temporary job; I would have the requisite four months to find a permanent one.

Skarzynski was a friend of Secretary Mosbacher. From 1970 to 1980, he had been an associate with the Center for Strategic and International Studies (CSIS) in Washington, where Mosbacher had been a director. At Mosbacher's request, in 1989, Skarzynski had left his job as head of business development with Motorola in Schaumburg, Illinois, and come to Washington to be one of four assistant secretaries (the other three headed the Import Administration, International Economic Policy, and U.S. and Foreign Commercial Service). Skarzynski's Trade Development group was responsible for expanding American international business and regulating trade policy. It was considered one of the premiere bureaus in Washington, and the position came with a plush office (number 3832) on the third floor. Large, steel-framed windows looked out over the Ellipse and the Washington Monument; the flight path of the President's helicopter was within feet. Skarzynski's maps, globes and flags were all in place; the only thing missing was the collection of personal pictures on the wall. Complete with mahogany desk, conference table and chairs, couches, and a telephone on every table, the office was being reserved for him until he was confirmed by the Senate. It was rumored Skarzynski's confirmation would take place "soon." For the time being, he was in a holding pattern, with only one on his staff: me.

I occupied an office—much less grand—two doors down from his, one of several that made up the assistant secretary's suite. During March, while Skarzynski was waiting for his confirmation and the trade development offices were in the throes of reorganization, I became involved in a research project relating to Total Quality Management (TQM) and the Baldrige National Quality Award. Secretary Mosbacher, in hopes of becoming more informed regarding government quality management, had asked Skarzynski to compile previous TQM programs used in the federal agencies.

For several weeks, I gathered information from reports and papers and interviewed Commerce employees. My resulting twelve-page account outlined ways the secretary could implement TQM into the Commerce environment. At the time, most programs were carried out in public and private institutions, not government circles. In fact, except for the four branches of the military, the system was almost unknown; a federal version of TQM had been created by Congress in 1987, and the department of the Navy at the Pentagon had successfully used it. For the past three years, the Commerce department had awarded American organizations—those using the highest quality standards—with the Baldrige Quality Award, named after former Commerce secretary Malcolm Baldrige. The National Institute of Standards and Technology (NIST), the technical arm of government that oversaw the Baldrige Award, was in Commerce and under the direction of Mosbacher.

An article by Karen Riley in the *Washington Times* on December 14, 1990, titled "4 Companies Revel in Glory of Receiving a 'Baldrige'" described the prestigious award and some of its recipients:

> President Bush yesterday gave the Baldrige Award to four U.S. companies the government judged to be doing the most to improve quality and satisfy customers: GM's Cadillac Division, Federal Express Corp., IBM's Rochester, N.Y., plant, and Wallace Co. of Houston. "In just a few years, the national quality award has literally become the standard of business excellence," Mr. Bush said at the award presentation at the Commerce Department, [showing that] America *can* compete with Japan on a quality basis.

The issue of quality would not become as much of a recognized theme during the Bush administration as was planned, but Mosbacher did turn out to be a noted flag bearer for the cause, and by integrating quality standards into the DOC organization, it was his intent to make Commerce the federal TQM flagship. The secretary had already grasped the importance of quality in regard to international success. "We've got to realize that it's a shrinking world and, if we want to do more than flip the

hamburgers for the world, we've got to come out with *quality* products,"
Mosbacher said at a news conference before meeting with the Economic
Club of Detroit.

During his first months in office, Mosbacher was always looking for
new ways to put Commerce out in front. He gave the department vigor.
Along with his political gains, he invigorated the employees under his
command. It was fun to see what was going to happen next. I loved going
to work.

THE chitchat during the spring and early summer was encouraging. On
April 29, President Bush celebrated his first one hundred days in office,
what was referred to as the Honeymoon Period.

Since the administration of Franklin D. Roosevelt, the press had
taken note of the Presidents' early accomplishments, and records showed
that during this pace-setting time, Eisenhower had agreed to a U.S.-North
Korea prisoner-of-war exchange, Nixon had directed the Defense
department to develop a plan to end the draft, Kennedy had approved the
unsuccessful Bay of Pigs invasion and held the first live television news
conference and Carter had pardoned draft evaders and banned playing
"Hail to the Chief" in his honor, and Reagan had signed legislation to
raise the national debt limit and reinstated playing "Hail to the Chief."
Bush was credited with having approved legislation to overhaul the
Savings and Loans, accepted a contra aid accord with Congress,
proceeded with the development of MX and Midgetman missile systems
and traveled to four nations and twenty states; he had held nine news
conferences. Only Kennedy, with ten, had topped that. And, only
Kennedy, with 83 percent, had exceeded Bush in the "honeymoon"
Gallup poll approval ratings.

According to a May 1989 *Washington Post*-ABC News national
survey, Bush's approval rating, holding at 73 percent, gave him a seven-
point increase since the April polls. He was just three points below his
inaugural high of 76. In 1981, at the five-month mark, Reagan held his
highest approval rating, 68 percent; two months earlier, he had been shot
by would-be assassin John Hinckley, Jr.. Within Bush's first five months,
he matched and surpassed Reagan's high.

With the energy flowing from the White House, those of us in the
administration were feeling as zealous as the President, and I put the

worries I had while working in the Office of Presidential Personnel behind me. These were good times, and I was going to celebrate like everyone else. I felt sure that if anything got out of hand, Atwater would take notice.

Leading the National Committee, Atwater's primary responsibility was to raise money for the Republican Party. One indicator by which Bush's public approval was gauged was the success of the RNC's fund-raising. Under Atwater's tutelage, the RNC was raising money at a rate of more than ten times that of the Democratic National Committee. Contrary to earlier predictions, it was collecting contributions in record amounts, and the person given credit for the handsome treasury was Lee Atwater. After the election, he had his pick of any job in the administration, and he had chosen the RNC leadership, "I've already done the White House thing," he said. (He originally had made this statement during the summer of 1987, and the quote had been used since then in articles referring to his not wanting a West Wing job.) All Atwater wanted to do was run political races, and what better place to do that than at the RNC.

The Bush campaign manager had replaced Reagan-appointee Frank Fahrenkopf, a former Reno lawyer who, with seven years in the post, was the longest-serving GOP chief in the twentieth century. Fahrenkopf had catered to the state Republican leaders, those now raving over Atwater's style. They liked his hardball, do-whatever-it-takes methods he had used during campaign days. The RNC chief's efforts were producing a ready cash flow, and the Party leaders, whose coffers he was filling, were both indebted and thrilled.

Atwater had willingly accepted the criticism for the negative ads of the1988 campaign, never pointing his finger at anyone else. In spite of the "bad boy" image, there remained one well-known truth about Atwater: he instinctively looked beyond the moment. And with his incredible intuitive sense about people and politics, he understood the "nature of the beast" better than most. In May, when the rest of Bush's political aides were enjoying the good life, Atwater was already focusing on 1992, and had spotted someone he thought might try to challenge Bush. He was convinced that the Democratic candidate would be a conservative southerner, and he had been searching the horizon for possible contenders. Governor Bill Clinton of Arkansas was first on his list.

On May 19, 1989, I came across an editorial from the Arkansas *Pine Bluff Commercial* written by Paul Greenberg and titled "Lee the Terrible vs.

★★★

Willie the Slick." It had been reproduced in the *Washington Times:* "Out here on the Arkansas frontier, the infighting has started early for—can you bear it?—the presidential campaign of 1992. Only three years in advance, and the first skirmish has been recorded . . . Lee Atwater, to nobody's surprise, started it. In the course of speculating about presidential politics, he dismissed Arkansas Gov. Bill Clinton as a serious possibility in 1992."

Believing that, in 1992, Bush could beat any Democratic contender, Atwater rejected the idea that the Arkansas governor could be a threat, and according to the Greenberg article, he had made a comment about Clinton, saying that "Clinton comes across more as Dale Bumpers than Sam Nunn. Bill Clinton doesn't *feel* like an authentic conservative, no matter how dutifully he recites the lines." The Arkansas editor agreed with Atwater's conclusion. "The Boy Governor," as Greenberg referred to Clinton, simply did not have what it took to be President.

The *Washington Times* publication of the Greenberg article—six columns long, including pictures of both Clinton and Atwater—was telling because it showed that in May of 1989, Atwater had already determined that he could wage a successful campaign against William Jefferson Clinton. Connected to President Bush and protective of him, Atwater, I believe, looked out for Bush's political welfare; recognizing that Clinton was on the scene was evidence that he was still watching for potential difficulties down the road ahead.

Two other 1988 senior campaign advisors, both now working under independent contracts with the RNC, had not felt as obligated toward Bush as Atwater. Ailes had declined to work with Bush in 1989 yet gladly accepted a contract with the RNC so that he might work with "other" clients. Teeter also had turned down the President and formed a Washington consulting agency.

Atwater continued with his allegiance to Bush. As RNC chair and number-one operative, he continued to be the President's political eyes and ears. And Bush, with his patrician reserve, listened to what the non-aristocrat Atwater had to say.

The office of political affairs at the White House should have taken the lead in all political matters, especially because of reelection contingencies. But that was not the case. Atwater was, by far, the most experienced in these matters. The director of political affairs was not.

Washington Post columnist Ann Devroy wrote a piece on March 19, 1989, regarding this very subject. In "For White House Political Operation, Focus Will Be Popularity, Not Policy," she reported:

> Political management has a lesser status in this White House than in the last one. Sununu, who helped win the pivotal primary in New Hampshire last year, but did not play a major strategic role in the overall campaign, said in an interview last week that "we are not doing very much on the political side at the White House but that the political team exists, but at a different geography than it did in previous administrations." Although the Bush White House has a political director, Jim Wray, his role is aimed more at pleasing and servicing Bush loyalists and campaigners from around the country than at giving political content to White House decisions on policy, scheduling and the like.

The arrangement of the political office in the Bush White House was quite unusual. The relationship between Atwater and Wray had been a solid one, but something here appeared to be amiss. I remembered Jim Wray's name from September 1987; he had been a regional field director in the campaign along with Andy Card, Eileen Padburg, Jim Shearer, Lanny Griffith, Tom Hockaday, Mary Matalin, and Ron Kaufman. Having been under Atwater's command, Wray was accustomed to taking orders, and now, as the White House political director (the job Atwater previously occupied under Reagan), Wray still looked to Atwater for direction. Nothing was wrong with this in itself, but without a strong political advocate in White House, Bush doubled the burden on Atwater. In essence, the political office, which usually plays a vital role in framing the direction of an administration, did not do so in under Bush. This was a critically weak link in the chain of command. Without proper representation, the office was not effective, and more importantly its vulnerability gave other White House offices the opportunity to become quite influential.

One of those ready to pounce on the "empty space" was the White House press secretary, Marlin Fitzwater. It should be remembered that Craig Fuller, with Jim Baker's seal of approval, had suggested Fitzwater be Bush's press secretary. In fact, he was the only candidate for spokesperson they had brought to Bush for approval, making Bush the only President ever to retain his predecessor's press secretary. Once Bush agreed, Baker and Fuller had ousted Sheila Tate, Bush's campaign press secretary.

★★★

Fitzwater was a personal favorite of Baker's. In 1985, Baker had placed him in the Office of the Vice President as Bush's press secretary when Fuller was chief of staff. Baker had worked closely with Fitzwater in that office during the pre-1988 campaign days and time of the G-6. During the 1980s, Fitzwater had worked well with Baker and Fuller and the whole Reagan team, and as a previous career civil servant, he already had learned how to take orders. While concurrently representing Reagan—with Baker-crafted messages—Fitzwater had a trouble-free job, for Reagan too, did as instructed. However, with Bush wanting to be himself and not wanting to be "created," Fitzwater found his job more challenging.

In trying to determine Fitzwater's political persuasion, I found data scattered in bits and pieces, always incomplete, almost as if the facts were purposely jumbled. This is what I finally put together.

Fitzwater received a bachelor's degree from Kansas State University in 1965, and after serving as a sergeant in the Air National Guard, he worked as a reporter and advertising executive for several Kansas newspapers. Then he came to Washington and started his government service as a spokesman for the Environmental Protection Agency (EPA). During the early years of the Reagan administration, and at the request of Ann McLaughlin (Treasury Secretary Donald Regan's press advisor), Fitzwater was brought to Treasury to assist Regan with his speeches and press matters. In September 1983, he left Treasury and began working as deputy press secretary to Larry Speakes in the Reagan White House. Speakes had needed someone to help with formulating domestic policy.

Just as Baker was leaving as Reagan's chief of staff, he pulled Fitzwater out of the White House press office and assigned him to Bush. From April 1985 to February 1987, Fitzwater worked with Craig Fuller in the VP's office, reporting to both Bush and Baker—as did Fuller. After serving time with Bush, Fitzwater returned to the West Wing to be Reagan's press secretary, claiming the title of assistant to the President for press relations (title of press secretary was still reserved for Jim Brady, who had been shot during the attempt on Reagan's life in 1981). From 1987 until 1989, until Reagan left the presidency, Fitzwater directed the office of the press secretary under three different chiefs of staff: Don Regan, Howard Baker, and Ken Duberstein. However, Fitzwater always remained loyal to the first COS, Jim Baker.

In 1987, after Fitzwater had left the Vice President's office, Bush had difficulty replacing his spokesperson, and a succession of mishaps over the ensuing campaign months regarding the selection of a suitable press secretary severely damaged the Bush communications operation.

Larry Thomas finally succeeded Fitzwater, but only briefly, and without anyone to fill the slot, in the fall of 1987, George W. finally assigned Pete Teeley—who had worked as press secretary to Bush in two of his previous campaigns—to be communications director and chief spokesman for the 1988 campaign. As has been recounted, Teeley was fired by Craig Fuller and Jim Baker in May 1988, and replaced by Jim Lake. Lake, the Washington lobbyist and former Reagan campaign press secretary (exiled in 1980), came aboard as communications director with acting press secretary Steven Hart.

Sheila Tate replaced Hart in June 1988; she was Bush's first official press secretary in over eighteen months. However, she did not stay long. Immediately after the Bush victory in November, Fuller fired Tate, charging her with being "too remote" with the press corps and not being available for questions. (Tate returned to Hill and Knowlton, the public relations firm from which she soon represented Georgette Mosbacher and her cosmetics firm, La Prairie).

After Tate was dismissed, Fuller and Baker extended the invitation to Fitzwater to return to the White House as press secretary to Bush. Although it had not been his idea, Bush went along with the appointment.

During the Reagan administration, Fitzwater had gained a reputation for being fair and honest with the press corps. He knew the ways of the White House as well as anyone. Under Reagan, he had been endowed with substantial influence, with almost unlimited access to Reagan—including admittance to presidential meetings that had not been given to press secretary's in the past. Fitzwater's unusual clout was a first, and it had been Bush, as Vice President, who authorized most of it.

Now working for Bush as President, Fitzwater wanted to ensure he had the same privileges he enjoyed under Reagan. After accepting the job in November 1988, Fitzwater's first question to Bush was, "Will I have access to you and all your meetings, including the National Security Council?" He demanded the same access and level of authority as he'd had previously. This veteran of the White House press office for six years was no dummy. And with the extremely ineffective political and communications offices in the Bush White House, Fitzwater's powers would expand exponentially. Before the administration was over, he would assume the prestigious rank of presidential counselor. Another "first" for a press secretary.

BUSH had especially high approval ratings during the summer of 1989 and was still being compared to Reagan. Bob Levey of the *Washington Post,* on July 25, 1989, was one of a few who chose not to match up the two:

> "What difference does it make if Mr. Bush is more popular at this stage of his presidency than Mr. Reagan was? The issues are mostly different, the leaders on the Hill are totally different, the economic situation is totally different, our relationship with Russia is totally different and the style of the two presidents is totally different. It's apples and oranges."

Despite his popularity, most of the media attacked Bush for not following the Reagan agenda. They accused him of abandoning Reagan policies and painted him as "one that is closer to what one might have expected from a Democratic President than the bearer of the Reagan legacy." George Bush was likened to former President Jimmy Carter.

A Washington attorney and former chief domestic policy advisor to Carter, Stuart Eizenstat said in a June 1989 *Washington Post* article, "How Bush Abandoned Reagan," that "Democrats should beware." He cited areas in which Bush had broken ranks: the war in Nicaragua, defense spending, the environment, and industrial policy. He pointed out that the Bush administration, which boasted of having many people with appropriate conservative pedigree, was not what it said it was. Eizenstat queried, "What are they contributing when the people who really count, Budget Director Dick Darman, Treasury Secretary Nicolas Brady, Secretary of State Jim Baker, and Bush himself don't believe in conservative principles?"

As I continued to read Eizenstat's piece, I detected he was not necessarily criticizing Bush, but advancing the idea that Bush was alienating himself from his own Party:

> By moving sharply away from the conservative Reagan doctrine to more centrist positions, he has both achieved a significant measure of bipartisan Democratic support and effectively cut the ability of Hill Democrats to define an appealing alternative agenda. By sitting astride the broad middle of the American political system, even at

the expense of potentially alienating true-blue Reagan loyalists on
the right, he has put the Democratic Party on the defensive and
positioned himself as the dominant figure in the public policy
arena, which a President of the United States must be to succeed. In
the process, Bush may actually prove to be a more difficult target
for Congressional Democrats than Ronald Reagan, who, though
personally popular, had a polarizing policy agenda.

Most Presidents want to be remembered after they leave office. With
that as a goal, they are not always as interested in being politically correct
as they are in surviving. Reagan had accomplished this goal . . . or more
truthfully stated, Reagan *and those who served in his administration* had
achieved that goal. And these men and women of the Reagan Regime
continued to make sure that their voices were heard and that they were
not forgotten.

During the first five months of the Bush administration, the
Washington Reagan alumni hosted four parties in Reagan's honor. "It's as
if the ex-president were Elvis, and the fans want him back so much they
can't believe he's really gone," said *Washington Post* staff writer Kara
Swisher in her June 20, 1989, article "Never Say Goodbye." In the same
article, Liz Cordia was quoted as saying, "We're here to keep the Reagan
agenda alive. I mean, George Bush would not be President without
Ronald Reagan." A deputy assistant in the Reagan White House, Liz was
the wife of Lou Cordia, who had been a Reagan special assistant at the
Environmental Protection Agency.

In 1988, Cordia had appointed himself executive director of the
Reagan Appointees Alumni Association. Not so surprisingly, Cordia—
who would continue to publish a Reagan-Bush alumni directory—also
became the self-appointed director of the Bush-Quayle Alumni
Association and publisher of its directory.

Swisher's write-up pointed out that not only did Bush have Reagan
to thank for being elected President, but that, "He'd also be out of help."
According to Swisher, the Reagan Alumni directory, which gave a where-
are-they-now inventory, listed half the Bush Cabinet and thirteen
assistants to President Bush as Reagan alums. Actually, eight of the
fourteen Bush Cabinet members were previously high-ranking
Reagan officials: Baker (State), Brady (Treasury), Elizabeth Dole (Labor),
Richard Thornburg (Justice), Edward Derwinski (Veterans), Clayton

Yeutter (Agriculture), Carla Hills (U.S. Trade Representative), and Laura Cavazos (Education).

It was also accurate to say that, except for Baker, Cheney and Scowcroft (and what should have been Mosbacher), Bush did not have a strong Cabinet. Bush *himself* was the one with a robust political agenda and a voice capable of setting him apart from his predecessor. In five months, Bush had rejected Reagan's unpopular war in Nicaragua, cut back Reagan's defense budget, abandoned Reagan's idea that there was no role for the federal government in promoting U.S. business, and advocated a clean environment. Bush *was* prepared for the job of being President—he had spent a lifetime preparing—and, despite prevailing suggestions to the contrary, he had assumed the office with a clear idea of where America should be in the twenty-first century!

That said, while attempting to build his Republic, Bush found himself in the same quandary he had been in during the campaign. Although many wanted to see him as his own man, the strong conservative right wanted to see a continuation of Reagan (his rhetoric), and a more conservative agenda. What the country did not grasp, nor had it for the previous eight years, was that Reagan *never* did deliver what he had promised. Unlike his predecessor, Bush said what aptly coincided with his actions. He spoke about what he believed and tried to back up his convictions with appropriate action. In the process, he alienated himself from Reagan supporters and the conservative loyalists. In essence, he was battling those now running *his* White House.

This begs the question, "Why had these staffers kept quiet, seemingly content, when Reagan's policies drifted from the right to a more moderate position under Baker?" There was only one reason. Personal greed.

When it came to policy, Reagan had relinquished his presidential powers to others in his White House, most notably Jim Baker. And depending upon which was the more politically advantageous to Baker at the moment, he resorted to either conservative or moderate leanings— even liberal, when pushed. An example of Baker's wishy-washy stance was revealed in the way Dick Darman influenced him (and thereby Reagan) on fiscal issues. Darman, Bush's director of the Office of Management and Budget, was anything *but* conservative. Yet, he had been Baker's Man from the first day of the Reagan administration in 1981.

With neither the desire nor the time to watch every appointee, Baker had carefully picked Darman to manage those on the lower rungs of the Political Ladder. Baker chose to focus his attention only on key policy and personnel arenas, and often turned the other way when it came to managing the second-level troops. This system had allowed those holding appointments in Reagan's administration enormous latitude when setting their own agendas. The consequences did not always result in such good form. Ethics violations had been a recurring problem during the Reagan presidency, and the press continued to investigate matters after Reagan left office.

One of the most flagrant examples of misused power on Reagan's watch (which Bush was left to deal with), was a case involving the department of Housing and Urban Development (HUD). The scandal resurfaced during the summer of 1989.

Bush appointee Jack Kemp served as HUD secretary and was an extreme right-winger and originator of supply-side tax cuts. The congressman's predecessor was Sam Pierce. Shortly after Pierce had departed, charges of theft, influence peddling, and perjury were brought against HUD, and Pierce was accused of being negligent in his responsibilities as secretary. The most stinging accusation involved his misdirection of the agency's "moderate rehabilitation grant program," more commonly known as Section 8. Grants under this section were set up for the purpose of rehabilitating housing for lower-and middle-income families.

Using a mortgage loan from HUD, along with millions of dollars in tax credits, a developer could acquire a property, divide it into multiple housing units, and after rehabilitation, rent the units to low-income families. HUD would subsidize the tenants' rent for fifteen years. The system was risk-free to the developer, luring hordes of avaricious speculators to the table. Secretary Pierce's executive assistant, Deborah Gore Dean, was the disperser of the Section 8 funds.

With little if any supervision by Pierce, the thirty-year-old former Georgetown bartender was responsible for the approval of hundreds of millions of dollars, and as gatekeeper to the HUD treasury, she illegally dispersed more than $2 billion in government funding to former Reagan and Nixon appointees. The court case in which Dean was finally found guilty took place during the summer of 1989 in D.C.. Press coverage of the trial highlighted the issue of exploitation of influence under Reagan. A column by James Kilpatrick in the August 11, 1989, *Washington Post* summed up the HUD affair this way:

> For the eight years of his administration, it now seems evident, the president paid virtually no attention to this huge, costly department. For political reasons that are understandable, if not altogether admirable, he named a token black to be HUD secretary. This was "Silent Sam" Pierce, the invisible man. What a choice! Reagan did nothing. Pierce did nothing—or less than nothing. He filled top executive positions with political has-beens or never-weres. He named as his chief deputy a pretty young thing whose talents lay principally in tending bar. She in turn brought in her buddies. At HUD the career people called them the "Brat Pack."

The Reagan appointees had good reason for supporting their President, and had motive for keeping silent even when his policies took a more moderate and less conservative bent. The reason was . . . Reagan had made them all "little presidents!" With that kind of authority, individual fiefdoms had sprouted throughout the administration complex. Because of the actions taken during the Transition, whereby Craig Fuller and Jim Baker ruled, under Bush, each of the Reagan "landholders" (i.e., appointees) continued to reign supreme over their own province.

ALTHOUGH the media's spin on the first months of the Bush administration had been kind to the President, it had not done any favors for his Vice President. Odd but true. Quayle's damage control team had never tried to improve his negative standing. Adding to his difficulties, at the six-month point in the presidency, Quayle experienced a senior staff shake-up. His chief of staff, Robert Guttman, was leaving.

Having previously held a staff position in Congress, Guttman had worked with Quayle while he was formulating a jobs training and employment program—Quayle's major legislative initiative as a senator. Guttman was the *one* person on his staff whom Quayle had known before. But because Guttman found the job "too political," he resigned. I have a feeling that Guttman did not like Darman and Sununu maneuvering *his* work and *his* people in the Vice President's office, usurping Guttman's control and undercutting *his* authority as chief of staff.

William Kristol replaced Guttman. Harvard educated and of Jewish decent, Kristol was the thirty-six-year-old son of neoconservative writer Irving Kristol. A former assistant professor of public policy at Harvard, Kristol had come to Washington in 1985 to serve on the staff of William Bennett at the Education department. As Reagan was preparing to leave office in 1988, Kristol worked as campaign manager for Alan Keyes in his unsuccessful bid for the Senate. With ideas of his own about how the federal government should be run, Kristol, I believe, used Quayle's office as his pulpit to carry out his ultra-conservative mission.

The second staffer to leave Quayle was David Prosperi, who had been assigned as Quayle's press secretary during the campaign. He had started his career as assistant press secretary for Reagan (with Fitzwater), and had gone on to the department of the Interior before taking the job with Quayle. Prosperi now accepted an appointment as assistant secretary at Transportation with Samuel Skinner.

Quayle's new press secretary, David Beckwith, was a former *Time* correspondent. A University of Texas law student in the late 1960s, Beckwith, for twenty-five years, had been a political and legal reporter, covering the Watergate hearings, the Reagan White House, and the 1988 Bush campaign. During the summer of '89, he had been preparing to move to South America on assignment with *Time* magazine, but he changed his mind and accepted the Quayle job. Queried about what he thought of Quayle at the time of his appointment, Beckwith had told the media crews, "I probably had an opinion, but it was like everyone else's: he was a drag to the ticket." Beckwith's ties to the press, particularly *Time*, would be a continuous source of trouble for Quayle, but the former reporter's lack of loyalty to the Vice President would become an even bigger problem.

On top of his staff shakeup, Quayle had to endure more personal humiliation. During the summer of 1989, the book *Whose Broad Stripes and Bright Stars?—The Trivial Pursuit of the Presidency of 1988*, written by Jack Germond and Jules Witcover, was published. It flooded Washington bookstores and was avidly read by people in the administration. I got my first taste of the book in July 16, 1989, in a *Washington Post* article written by Ann Devroy titled "Candidate Quayle Recalled Harshly in New Book." Devroy's recap described the book as bordering on the obscene:

Joseph Canzeri, a Quayle "handler" last year who once worked for Nelson A. Rockefeller and served in several national campaigns and in the Reagan White House, describes Quayle's immaturity and lack of attention: "He was like a kid. Ask him to turn off a light switch, and by the time he gets to the switch, he's forgotten what he went for." Canzeri concludes: "We knew we were going to have to script him." Stuart Spencer, who spent three previous presidential campaigns traveling with the Republican nominee as a key advisor [and who headed the Quayle vice presidential campaign], offers a more colorful, if less printable, account. Explaining one of the few occasions when Quayle departed from his prepared text and spoke extemporaneously, Canzeri is quoted as asking Spencer why he had "let" the candidate do that. "I want him to step on his own (anatomical part deleted), and then we'll own him again," Spencer replied.

Canzeri and Spencer, both of whom were fired by Quayle from his campaign staff, were among the many to criticize the Vice President, and they did so, as this article shows, unabashedly.

Similar to Dan Quayle, Secretary Mosbacher had lost authority over his sphere of influence. And, like Quayle who suffered from press derision, Mosbacher was beginning to be publicly ridiculed—beyond being just a "party boy." With technology issues having been taken off his agenda, Mosbacher found himself promoting the administration's Green Theme.

A year earlier, during the campaign, the environmental platform had been chiseled out—if you could call it that—for the first time. Before I discovered the facts about Boston Harbor, there had been no expectation that such issues would ever gather any momentum. Twelve months had changed that, and during the early summer of 1989, Bush worked closely with his Cabinet preparing for the Economic Summit in Paris; the environment was labeled as a top priority.

In mid-July, Bush joined the other leaders of the world's largest industrialized nations, and for the first time, the agenda included effects of global warming, ocean dumping, deforestation, acid rain and ozone depletion. With fewer economic issues to contend with—thanks to the continued economic expansion and comparatively low unemployment rate—the heads of state of Great Britain, Canada, France, Italy, Japan and West Germany focused their attention on the planet's newly recognized ecological concerns.

Bush declared the environment a major political issue of the 1990s, and once back home, he began to follow through with his declaration. He appointed the secretary of Commerce as one of his point men, involving Mosbacher in Gulf Coast turtles and Texas shrimp. The multimillionaire from Houston made his first "green" decision when he decided to let shrimpers trawl without trapdoor devices (which kept endangered sea turtles from drowning in their nets). It turned out to be a huge mistake. The media conveyed Mosbacher's actions as wreaking havoc on the turtle population and the public jumped all over his ruling. Later, the courts would overturn his decision, and the shrimpers would be required to use the devices, but in the meantime, Mosbacher was mocked and given the nickname of "Cap'n Mossback." The *Teenage Mutant Ninja Turtles* comic book featured him as the villainous shrimper with a peg leg and an eye patch. Transitioning from high tech to low tech was not so easy for the secretary of Commerce.

I, too, entered my own transition.

Michael Skarzynski, for whom I had been working since March, officially became the assistant secretary of Trade Development in the International Trade Administration; he predictably breezed through his Senate confirmation. My position with him had been a good place to start assimilating the complexities of a political job. I had been in an area closely connected to Mosbacher's office and gotten to know the issues from the top. I thought of approaching Skarzynski to see if there might be an opportunity for me to stay on his staff, but before I had time to inquire, I was offered another position. Alan Dunn asked me to be his confidential assistant.

In passing, I had known Dunn at the campaign headquarters; he was an outside advisor on one of my policy issue groups. Now he joined Skarzynski's staff as deputy assistant secretary of Basic Industries, or BI (energy, paper, chemicals and metal), a position low enough not to warrant Senate confirmation. I gladly accepted his offer. Because Dunn was in the export division, I could continue to work with many of the people I had already met and also remain focused on the competitiveness of U.S. industries in the international market. I felt fortunate to have secured a permanent position, for more than a few of the 120-day temporary appointees had been purged from the system during their search at Commerce and elsewhere. I celebrated having found a real job— finally. My letter of appointment from the White House read:

★★★

June 8, 1989
Dear Ms. Joslin [crossed out, with Anne inserted],
Today your paperwork crossed my desk. I am pleased to know that
you will be a Confidential Assistant to the Deputy Assistant
Secretary for Trade Development at the Department of Commerce.

These next few years are going to be very exciting ones for all of us.
The honor of serving the President is something I know that we will
always cherish. There is not any doubt that you will be a strong
asset to the Bush Administration. If there is anything I can do to
help you, please don't hesitate to call.

Congratulations on your new job!
Sincerely, Ron
Ronald C. Kaufman
Deputy Assistant to the President

At the top, Kaufman had written, "The next four years are going to
be great ones for all of us lucky enough to be part of the Bush team."

Dunn was a bright, attractive, thirty-six-year-old Washington
attorney and son of an Army general. He was well connected, and knew
how to land on his feet no matter how rough the spill. Always wearing a
charcoal gray, pinstriped suit and a white button-down shirt with a
conservative tie, Dunn could talk his way into or out of anything. Unlike
some who were new to administration politics, Dunn did not have to
worry about "falling through the cracks." He came into his position with
all the correct tickets punched, and he knew how to schmooze as well as
anyone I knew. Although I thought it silly when he referred to his male
friends as "Doctor So-and-So" or "Professor So-and-So," just to upgrade
their status, I wondered why women never received these professional
titles. For sure, Dunn represented the "man" in a "man's world."

Before I started working for him, I read his résumé and found that
after he graduated from George Mason College in Fairfax, Virginia, and
the University of Virginia Law School in Charlottesville, he spent five
years with the Foreign Service. Afterward, he had practiced
environmental law at a Washington law firm before joining the Product
and Safety Commission. Finally, he had been propelled back into law, this
time specializing in maritime and shipping law at O'Conner and
Hanahan. With little international trade experience, per se, Dunn, I feared,

was in over his head, but it turned out that he was a quick study and eager to move up in the hierarchy. The phrase "making a mistake" was not in his vocabulary. "Getting to the top" was.

Once when an industry magazine reporter asked him, "How often do you go over to the White House, and who there do you meet with?" Dunn swiftly replied, "It depends on what issues are hot over at the Domestic Policy Council. I deal a lot with Cabinet Affairs, to some extent with the Office of Policy Development, and with National Security Council working groups with less regularity. Sometimes I'm at the White House three times a week and sometimes I won't make it over there for three weeks."

Along with his other talents, Dunn could talk a good game. Relatively speaking, Dunn was not that much higher on the political ladder than I, and for three years, my office was within ten feet of his. I never saw any evidence of his weekly and/or daily journeys to the White House, nor did I ever hear Dunn mention his attending these meetings. Before the administration terminated, and to no one's surprise, Dunn would marry Deborah Romash, who worked in Bush's White House visitors' office. From Texas, Debbie had worked in the 1988 campaign as assistant to the then–Vice President's son George W., and she was popular with everyone. Debbie was genuinely warm, affable and unpretentious. On the few occasions I was in her company, I always found her fun to be with.

In spite of our differences in style, Dunn and I, with a degree of professional respect for one another, joined the ranks of the federal government in June 1988. Most of the fifty-seven bureaucrats working in Basic Industries had been in Commerce for many years and planned to be there many more after the two of us left. We were "temporary." Upon first walking into the office complex, we experienced the anticipated chilly reception, which was quite normal for new appointees intruding upon careerists' turf.

After a week or so, Dunn and I seemed to have made a good first impression and quickly became involved in the dynamics of the office. Before long, the bureaucrats not only accepted us, but also seemed to support us. In fact, before I left the administration, I actually made more friends in the civil service ranks than I did with my fellow appointees. Toward the end of the Bush presidency, some of the careerists approached me and said they would like to help me find a permanent job in their office. That gesture was a high compliment. Over the term of my stay at Commerce, I would seldom have difficulty working with the bureaucrats. I *would* have problems working with Dunn.

When I started my job, I had not realized the degree to which Dunn (who always called me "A.J.") would expect complete loyalty from me— or, more importantly, the measure to which he did not intend to return that allegiance.

I was not into the Power Game; Dunn was, and he was not about to consider me a rival for his supremacy. From the beginning, he simply dismissed me as being inconsequential, paying little attention to me or to my endeavors, including several instances when I produced work with significant results. By ignoring me, Dunn let me know he had no intention of "singing my praises." And if it meant sacrificing my job for his, so be it. He had assigned to me his one political appointment, and in his mind, he owed me nothing more. In the future, this implicit arrangement would have unsuspected consequences for my professional career and an eye-opening effect on my understanding about political players and their perpetual craving for control.

I would also learn that women seldom—if ever—were seen as equals. The possible exception may have been for women without any personal identity or status of their own. "The Wife" of a powerful or wealthy man most likely would be respected and made to feel included—for a married woman represented a dependency on the male, often assigning him the superior status. On the other hand, I can say unequivocally that, for a female in Washington, standing independently and on one's own was the "kiss of death." Never would she be invited into the circle of influence. The Washington All-Men's Club would stay the way it had always been. The set of laws regarding Washington power would be no different *with* women in the system than it had been, some years earlier, without women.

17

RUN SILENT, RUN DEEP

The Reagan appointee is an entirely different breed of appointee than in the Carter, Nixon, and Ford administrations. They are ideologically committed. There is no allegiance to the department, only to the Oval Office or the conservative cause. No other administration has penetrated so deeply.

—Paul Light

SEPTEMBER–OCTOBER 1989

With their insatiable need to get in one more attraction, tourists invade downtown Washington in droves every summer. However, as the steamy temperatures of July and August 1989 turned into the cooler breezes of September, the families headed back to their homes and The City was ours once again. The Reflection Pool at the Lincoln Memorial, the Tidal Basin at the Jefferson Memorial, and the Smithsonian Museum on the Mall (the "Grand Avenue" as L'Enfant referred to it) were no longer adorned with long serpentine lines of sightseers. Washington turned inward. And the Power Game began in earnest.

Shortly after Labor Day, the temporary appointees either had found permanent positions in the administration or had been eliminated. The "process," a long and drawn-out procedure, was an aggravation to many appointees, not so much because of complications with personal or professional background checks, but because of inefficient government procedures. An endless sea of red tape. Investigations could go on and on, with the feds looking at every facet of the candidate's life. A multitude of questions pertaining to bankruptcies, lawsuits, traffic offenses, tax liens, alimony and child support, as well as the indecorous side of one's family were all fair game. The FBI verified places lived, schools attended, where and when employed, and what the neighbors had to say about matters relating to drugs, alcohol, firearms, explosives, mental health, and the cops. Nothing was off limits, and nothing was left out.

Having received my White House security papers while working in presidential personnel, I obtained my secret credentials sooner than most and, by October, was on Secretary Mosbacher's official roster.

Upon first arriving at Commerce, I had been required to spend two weeks in the secretary's office to familiarize myself with his organization. Starting in the late spring—when there were only thirty appointees at the department—120-day appointees met for an hour once a week for two months. This period could be likened to a midshipman's plebe summer or a shakedown cruise. An intensive initiation of sorts.

Within Mosbacher's inner sanctum there was a young political staff, and they were known for their demanding demeanor and intimidating style. Of all the personal aides, Craig Helsing used his authority most unabashedly to "straighten out" the new recruits. Helsing welcomed the appointees as a drill sergeant might embrace new soldiers at Fort Bragg. Accordingly, in the spring of '89, he chaired the Schedule C initiation meetings before we started our workday. At precisely 8:00, from inside the room, Helsing locked the door, and anyone late in attendance would be excluded from the meeting.

For the first few weeks—until people caught on— the "tardy" would bang on the door trying to get in. Helsing responded to their knocking with silence. The rest of us, sitting around the table, were frozen in our chairs. Finally, the unsuspecting party would leave, assuming they were at the wrong conference room. Those of us who remained with Helsing would be subjected to one of his lectures on some political aspect of our job or listen to him read the biographical background on one of the Cabinet members or one of the presidential aides. We were there to learn, and Helsing made it clear that we were "at his mercy" while at Commerce and that he could make life miserable for us if he wished. While showing off his authority, he always had a gleam in his eye and a grin on his face. Helsing was hell.

Maryann Fish was Helsing's partner in crime, and as White House liaison, she attended all our meetings. I have always remembered something she said at one of our meetings, something she had learned from her husband, a Republican congressman and a staunch supporter of

Reagan: "Whenever you are in a room, always count the number of people present; using that number you can calculate the number required for a majority." "Remember," Fish pontificated, "you need a majority to carry a vote . . . you need a majority to win. It is important to always be aware of your position of strength in a group."

Secretary Mosbacher's fifth-floor compound was run like a mini-West Wing. During my break-in period, I was instructed in everything from how to properly answer the telephone to how to escort a visitor to one of the conference rooms or dining rooms. On one occasion, Robert Redford came through the door without any forewarning. He was just *there*. After accompanying him into the secretary's office, I tried to stay composed, but do not remember a word he—or I—said.

I do recall standing in Mosbacher's office for the first time, which was as large as the Oval Office and complete with all the trimmings. In the center of the room, under glass, was a large model of a nineteenth-century sailing ship. Against the left wall, over a splendid fireplace, was a portrait of President Herbert Hoover, former Commerce secretary. Directly behind Mosbacher's desk was a bigger-than-life, black-and-white picture of his wife, Georgette, that took up one entire wall. Known for her flaming red hair and tailored designer suits, Georgette Mosbacher, fed up with Washington, had gone to New York City. Still, she had left behind an aura. The secretary's picture was proof of that.

Few who were not on Mosbacher's immediate staff visited his office suite, and the inner sanctum was somewhat a place of mystery. The majority of the forty thousand careerists in DOC would never see it, and for that reason, the people I worked with were curious about what I saw on my trips to the Fifth Floor. Most in the civil service spent their day working in four-by-four-foot cubicles, never coming in touch with secretary or his staff, except indirectly through what was called the "tasker."

This communiqué or work order, sent out to the individual Commerce offices, usually requested a written "position paper" on a subject of interest to the secretary. In a month's time, hundreds of taskers would be issued; most often, they were distributed several days before Mosbacher met with an industry executive coming into town. Essentially, they served as his briefing papers. What bothered me was that after the completed tasker was submitted back to Mosbacher's staff, seldom was there any notification that the work had been received, let alone appreciated. The memoranda seemed to fall into a black hole, and although it may not have been Mosbacher's intent to distance himself from his employees, this is what occurred. It eventually had a debilitating effect on the spirit of the career employees.

For a different reason, morale among the 120-day appointees was suffering more than ever. Many who thought they would have received their appointments by now had not; the staffing of the administration failed to move along as quickly as had been forecast. The media attributed the delay to a variety of reasons, namely the wrong candidates for the wrong jobs. The newspapers reported that there was no leadership at the senior executive (SES) level. When jobs were left open, it had a crippling effect on management. Untermeyer, who continued as director of presidential personnel, was constantly in the news defending himself and the work of his office.

Of the close to three million civil servants, (three hundred thousand in D.C.), political appointees accounted for less than one-tenth of one percent, and among the senior level positions on which Untermeyer focused, it was one-fifth less than that. These 600-some top policymaking jobs received most of the negative publicity, and by November, the White House divided the 600 positions into five categories: confirmed (401); awaiting confirmation (42); undergoing clearance (99); Reagan holdovers (33), and vacancies (34). Assuming these numbers correct, the breakdown by category was somewhat deceiving. Those confirmed were almost all previous appointees under Reagan receiving new positions; the holdovers were those few Reagan appointees who remained in the same jobs; and those awaiting confirmation and undergoing security clearance were—also— mostly individuals who came from the Reagan ranks and were being reappointed.

Inasmuch as the majority of Reagan appointees had waited in their previous positions before being reassigned into the Bush administration, the entire personnel system had been blocked for months and had kept new Bush appointees out. As has already been cited, presidential personnel, having accepted the mandatory resignations of the Reagan appointees, had turned the resignations into new appointments, thereby successfully reappointing hundreds of former Reagan appointees.

Examples of this "political reinvention" (going from Reagan to Bush) were announced in the Washington Post's column "In the Loop." Some of the reassignments mentioned included: Catherine Bertini, Bush nominee for assistant secretary for Food and Consumer Services at the department of Agriculture (Reagan's assistant secretary for the Family Support Administration at the department of Health and Human Services); Adis Vila, Bush nominee for assistant secretary for administration at Health and Human Services (Reagan White House aide, assistant at State and Commerce); and Paul Adams, Bush nominee for inspector general at the department of Housing and Urban Development (retaining the Reagan appointment he had since 1985).

The personnel list of previous Reagan members now in the Bush administration was long, and nowhere was this shuffle more obvious than at Commerce. Reagan reappointees cascaded into an agency that already had a reputation for being a political haven. In an article in the *National Journal,* dated March 13, 1989, titled "Washington's Movers and Shakers," I read about the Reagan blitz at Commerce:

> A veritable blizzard of announcements about high-level nominees and prospective nominees is spewing from the White House these days. *Michael Darby* will be nominated as Commerce undersecretary for economic affairs (Reagan assistant Treasury secretary for economic policy). *Dennis Kloske* will be nominated as Commerce undersecretary for export administration (Reagan deputy Defense undersecretary). *Eric Garfinkel* will be nominated as assistant Commerce secretary of import administration (Reagan vice president and general counsel at the Overseas Private Investment Corp.). *Wendell Wilkie* will be nominated as general counsel at the Commerce department (Reagan general counsel at the Education department from 1985–89).

To offset the possible onslaught of Bush candidates, the Reaganites had built an even mightier organization. They had masterminded their own bureaucracy! And because Commerce had been taken advantage of and had more than its fair-share of Reaganites, it also had more senior positions filled by former Reagan-types. One of the classic cases was the appointment of Michael Farren, the undersecretary of my organization, the International Trade Administration (ITA). The Farren "rebirth" is a marvelous illustration of the sophisticated personnel operation run by Reagan personnel before the Bush inauguration.

★★★

As chief of the two thousand-member ITA, Farren had reached a political apex. His climb onto the Power Pyramid was not unusual, but because of the high level of his position and the deftness necessary to make this particular move, it was extreme and significant. The circumstances had captured my attention because of Farren's association with the law firm Wiggin and Dana in New Haven, Connecticut, where my sister and brother-in-law practiced as trial attorneys. They knew Farren, but not that well.

In July 1988, when Farren resigned from his three-year appointment as deputy undersecretary of ITA, he left Washington to practice law at Wiggin and Dana. Within a month, he departed his new job and returned to Washington to enlist as a volunteer at the Bush campaign headquarters. By now, it was August, and Bush, beginning to gain some momentum after the convention, was attracting last-minute well-wishers by the hundreds, all thinking maybe Bush *did* have a chance. Farren, one of these individuals, said he wanted to "contribute" and explained to the campaign staff that he had left his appointment in ITA to take a legal position at Wiggin and Dana, *and* that he would be returning to his practice in New Haven as soon as the election was over, win or lose.

If Bush were defeated, all Farren would lose would be a couple of months on the job. However, Bush won, and—surprise—Farren did not return to New Haven. He was appointed to the second highest position on the Transition team, as deputy director, working at the top with Fuller. And after the administration began, Farren was one of the first to receive his appointment—back in Commerce, promoted from deputy under-secretary to undersecretary of the ITA, one of the premiere appointments in Washington. When I first arrived at Commerce, I had heard from several bureaucrats in Trade Development that Farren had always wanted that position. Now that he had it, he would stay there until the 1992 campaign geared up, and at such time, he would leave his position at Commerce *again* to be on Bush's reelection committee *again* and start the cycle all over. However, this time, it would have a different outcome.

Farren's plan to climb the political ladder was more complicated than that of other Reagan appointees reincarnated in the Bush administration: he had quit his job before Bush won, but the bigger risk had endowed him with the bigger gain. Farren's selection to the Transition team was not some fluke, nor was his reappointment to DOC;

both had to be orchestrated by the Craig Fuller crowd. Everything had worked perfectly—for Farren and all the others who had not risked as much, and by December 1989, almost a year into the presidency, Reagan candidates had filled the majority of Bush appointments.

The person working the other side of the personnel aisle, supposedly taking care of Bush Loyals, was Ron Kaufman, deputy director of presidential personnel, reporting directly to Chase Untermeyer and serving in a lateral capacity with Ross Starek.

The man who would—could—and should—have held the most significant post in employing the Bush administration was Kaufman. As a former Massachusetts GOP committee member, he had been a field director in the 1980 Bush campaign, and in 1988, was elevated to national field director for Illinois, Michigan, Pennsylvania and Connecticut; during primary season, he served as regional political director for the northeast. In Reagan's first term, Kaufman had been political director at the Republican National Committee. When it came time for the 1984 Reagan reelection, he had joined Bush's vice presidential campaign.

Along with his brother-in-law Andy Card (deputy to Sununu), Kaufman and Sununu had received much of the credit for the New Hampshire primary win. After the election, and before going to the White House, he worked on the Bush Inaugural committee. Although he seemed loyal to Bush and knew strategy in the field, Kaufman knew nothing about personnel and even less about generating presidential appointments.

I was in the Old Executive Office Building when Kaufman came to the White House in February 1989. Actually, almost everyone had been at work for a couple of weeks before Kaufman joined the team. It took him a long time to claim his office, a suite on the west side of the OEOB and one of the largest and most ornate in the building. Scott Bush's staff had made use of the empty space, spreading out hand-collated résumés across Kaufman's office furniture. Once he arrived, it was impossible not to know he was there. He was loud, arrogant and seemingly impressed with himself and his title. I was unimpressed, and for good reason. I never saw any evidence that Kaufman successfully promoted the cause of Bush followers while he served in the White House. In his current job— carrying out the work Scott Bush's office had started—Kaufman was supposed to look out for the interests of Bush supporters seeking jobs.

Under another set of circumstances, this job would have been crucial in staffing the Bush presidency; however, because Starek was the gatekeeper to appointments, Kaufman was little more than a figurehead.

From Bush's public announcements, it was difficult to tell whether he knew what had transpired in his personnel operation. On the anniversary of Election Day 1988—one year after his presidential victory—the President held a news conference; I and some of my friends listened on CNN. Among other issues, Bush touched on personnel, and then he talked about the country's economic status:

> I believe that we've had, so far, a successful first year in office...I'm very pleased that our administration has come together rapidly with good people, with good ideas, and with a quiet sense of purpose that promises great progress in the year ahead. . . .One area that has not changed is the underlying strength of the American economy. We have the longest peacetime economic expansion in history, 119 million Americans at work, the creation of over 20 million new jobs since 1982. The unemployment rate is only 5.3 percent, a rate that we've not achieved for a full year since 1970. Inflation remains moderate. I'm not happy with it, but it's moderate and appears to be under control.

The nine-month polls showed Bush maintaining a 76 percent approval rating, and some were surprised that he held high approval among the black community. Pollsters pointed out the overall support was "shallow," meaning many people *approved*, but they did not *strongly approve*. The fact still stood that the American people agreed with the way Bush was handling his job regarding the nation's environment, foreign affairs and illegal-drugs. However, Bush did not receive such high marks when it came to resolving problems regarding the economy and the budget deficit.

For eight years, Reagan had carefully kept issues surrounding the spiraling federal shortfall under wraps, and Jim Baker, as COS and secretary of the Treasury, had made sure it stayed that way. Although he did not fully understand economic doctrine, Baker was aware that despite low unemployment, low inflation and low interest rates, there never would be a Reagan Revolution. The deficit that soared during Reagan's eight years had wiped out any chance of economic recovery once Bush took office.

Supply-side theory held that cutting the taxes of the rich would improve the country's business climate; by giving a tax break to wealthier Americans, benefits would accrue to those in the lower economic brackets. The hope was to eliminate tax preferences, subsidies and economic regulations—all thought to strangle capitalism. However, the supply-siders were scorned by their adversaries as "defenders of the wealthy," and they were accused of promoting "trickle-down" economics.

In Reagan's first term, his budget director and former congressman from Michigan, David Stockman, had revealed that the President's supply-side economic program (proposed by Jim Baker) was not workable when cross-matched with increased defense spending. However, Reagan resolutely stated his goal: cut taxes for the wealthy while reducing government spending—*except* for the increase of military expenditures. Reagan was adamant. Expecting the treasury to be large enough to cover a military buildup *while simultaneously cutting taxes*—was ludicrous. Yet this was the basis for the so-called Reagan Revolution.

Statistics from 1982 to 1989 included the following: overall government spending increased to $2.130 trillion, non-military spending increased to $1.365 trillion and military spending increased to $765 billion. Compared to the previous decade, revenues decreased and spending increased. Substantially. During the Reagan presidency, the deficit was massive. Under Bush, it would continue to grow.

The "revolution" promoted by Baker and launched in the early months of Reagan's first term failed before it ever began. David Stockman solely took issue with Reagan's unconventional thinking and made it public. On November 12, 1981, *Atlantic Monthly* published an article that quoted Stockman saying it was *not* possible to cut taxes and concurrently increase military spending. The press twisted the critique into an overnight phenomenon, accusing Stockman of turning against Reagan's economic program and undermining the presidency.

For his role in "exposing" Reagan, Stockman would have been fired were it not for Baker. As Reagan's chief of staff and the originator of the Reagan Revolution, Baker depended on Stockman for his own financial counseling, and because he did not want that to change, he made sure Stockman remained in the White House. After a perfunctory reprimand, Baker told him that in order to keep his job he would have to keep his economic analyses to himself. Stockman agreed to the terms and

★★★

remained as Reagan's budget director. Although the White House organizational charts had Stockman reporting to Meese, he now promised his full allegiance to Baker.

Other senior aides had financial interests and economic authority in the Reagan administration, one of whom was secretary of the Treasury (during Reagan's first term) Don Regan. However, Regan, the former chief executive of Merrill Lynch, plummeted from power once Baker and Stockman were in control. At the beginning of Reagan's second term— when Baker swapped jobs with Regan—Baker continued doing what he had always done regarding the economy: nothing. And, too, from 1981 to 1988, Jim Baker kept silent on the subject of balancing the budget, making sure *he* did not open Pandora's Box.

Subsequently, during the '80s, the economy had steadily grown. Yet, on Bush's watch, in late 1989, there was talk of a possible recession, and, by those "who knew," it was strongly suggested that the United States reduce the deficit post haste, by taking such actions as holding back consumption, reducing dependence on foreign capital and goods and augmenting the domestic savings rate.

Over the previous decade, foreigners had injected more than $800 billion into the United States economy. And Americans had consumed and borrowed at record levels. For the first time in years, the country's long-term prosperity appeared endangered. Dependent on foreign investment, the nation simply had failed to generate from within the capital necessary for expansion, and toward the end of 1989, it was predicted that the 1990 growth rate would slow to around 2.6 percent. Not that significant of a decrease, still, the standard economic indicators (employment, inflation, interest rates, and production) showed a sluggish and unstable economy. Bush was being forewarned that he should expect the worst. The Big Three auto companies announced temporary plant closings, and IBM and AT&T announced layoffs. People had started to worry about their *own* jobs.

Inheriting nearly a decade of overspending and not having enough revenue to keep the country in the black, President Bush was expected to turn things around. Magically if need be. And the sooner the better. Pandora's Box had been opened.

★★★ ━━━━━━ ★★★
CHAPTER

18

THE CASH CUSTODIANS

The general who wins a battle makes many calculations in his temple before the battle is fought. The general who loses a battle makes but few calculations beforehand. It is by attention to this point that I can foresee who is likely to win or lose.

—Sun Tzu

NOVEMBER–DECEMBER 1989

While trying to reassure the nation that financial markets were secure and that his administration was on top of the deficit problem, Bush was simultaneously negotiating the upcoming budget with Congress.

In 1980, Reagan had promised to wipe out the federal deficit and balance the budget. Neither had occurred. Because the mid-1980s were comfortable "on the surface," the country had gone along with Reagan, who overlooked the underlying reasons why America was overdrawn, and never pressed the White House to rectify the overspending. Unemployment was low, interest rates were low and inflation was low. Most Americans had jobs. Most were bringing in paychecks. Things were relatively pleasant.

In addition, most Americans had problems with grasping the ramifications of national debt, which are complex at best and always problematic upon interpretation. To tie the nation's debt problem to one's personal financial situation was a leap most were unable to make. Under the impression that the country was financially well off, the public was given no incentive to try and understand debt as it related to the nation or to themselves.

What actually took place was a different story. The economic expansion perpetuated by President Reagan and Jim Baker was not

228

completely true. On top of every tax dollar collected, the government had also spent $75,000 of future tax dollars expected from each family of four! Federal revenues were declining and expenses were increasing. The economy may have been expanding, but so was the deficit. As a country, we either had to stop appropriating so much or start increasing revenues.

From the time Bush was elected President, he had to deal with this escalating deficit; by the time of the inaugural, spending was out of control. In addition to the inherited problems, part of the reason for the fiscal failure in the first year of the Bush presidency had to do with bad counsel.

Because economic issues had taken on more and more significance as the country approached the 1990s, Bush increasingly turned to his economic policy team for advice. Included were Nicholas Brady, secretary of the Treasury; Richard Darman, director of the Office of Management and Budget (OMB); and Michael Boskin, chief economist and chairman of the Council of Economic Advisors (CEA). Each had his own story.

Michael Boskin, known as an anti-government interventionist, came to the Bush White House from academia. Like others, Boskin "owed" Baker for bringing him into the White House. As with so many on the Bush team, Boskin had originally been brought into the 1988 campaign by Baker, who had appointed him principal economic advisor and chosen him after the election to be the President's chief economist.

A former Stanford professor and director of the Center of Economic Policy Research, Boskin had a B.A. from the University of California at Berkeley (1967) followed by an M.A. and a Ph.D. in economics from Stanford. Referred to as a "reasonable conservative," Boskin was capable of presenting a fiscal argument in relatively straightforward, understandable terms. In 1987, he had written a book titled *Reagan and the Economy,* in which he cited the budget deficits as a serious blot on the legacy of Reaganomics. According to Boskin, the deficit had required the government to borrow hundreds of billions of dollars, diverting funds from private investment.

In his capacity as chief financial advisor to Bush, Boskin proposed a "flexible freeze," a budget plan that called for economic growth, lower interest rates and a major cutback in domestic spending. The strategy was geared to balance the budget over a five-year period, whereby government spending—except for Social Security—would be held to the inflation rate. Boskin claimed that his plan would create a balanced budget by 1993—without any tax increases. Although a vital member of the Bush economic troika, Boskin would hold a stance geared more toward "let's wait and see what happens" than "let's tackle the problem now." His blasé attitude would later hurt the President.

Nicholas Brady was second on the Bush economic team, holding the position Don Regan and Jim Baker once had as secretary of the Treasury. He was Bush's ultimate defender and promoter, an old, close friend of the President. Brady was an understated fellow and while in the limelight, always managed to keep a low profile. Having grown up on a four thousand acre farm in Far Hills, New Jersey, he knew, as did George Bush, what it was like to be a member of an affluent family. While at Yale, Brady had been the captain of most every sporting team, and after getting his M.B.A. from Harvard, made his career as head of a Wall Street brokerage firm. He had met Bush in 1975, and worked in his 1980 presidential campaign. In late 1984, Baker tapped him to be member of the G-6, making him an insider during the 1988 campaign.

While the '88 campaign was underway—and in his final months of the presidency—Reagan appointed Brady to serve as chairman of the task force on the stock market, and the ensuing Brady Commission was responsible for looking into reasons for the 1987 stock market crash. In August, when Baker left to chair the Bush campaign, Brady took over his Treasury post, and when Bush became President, understandably, he had kept Brady in the position. Unfortunately for Brady, his appointment at Treasury had a shaky start under Reagan. Things had not gone so well for the gentleman from New Jersey. It would be my guess that Baker had something to do with this.

As Bush's Treasury secretary, Brady made it one of his top priorities to explore ways to reduce Third World debt. A *Washington Post* commentary by Hobart Rowan on May 11, 1989, "Nicholas Brady, After a Slow Start," addressed the Brady Plan in these words: "Brady's boldest move so far was the initiation of a new Third World debt plan, calling for debt relief—an approach that had been rejected by his predecessor, Jim Baker. Despite some delays, Brady feels his plan already has provided 'hope, energy and momentum' for change." Brady should have had an opportunity to "spread his wings" in the Bush administration; he was enthusiastic about his job on the Cabinet. But as the administration

★★★

unfolded, Brady, the consensus builder, continued to struggle in an uphill battle. On April 25, 1989 an article by Lois Romano in the *Washington Post*, "The Casual Force of Nick Brady," stated:

> Certain Reagan administration holdovers let it be known that there was no direction at Treasury. At meetings, Brady came across as bumbling and uninformed. During a conference of foreign economic leaders just a few weeks ago, he began reading a statement not germane to the question he'd been asked—and realized it only when interrupted. Capitol Hill observers were taken aback by his reticence during hearings . . . a far cry from his predecessor, the savvy and controlled James Baker, they said. "Jim Baker absorbed paper," says one former Treasury official. "This guy doesn't read."

When interpreting economic indicators, Brady preferred graphics to words, yet no matter what the differences, he would never overcome the constant comparisons made between himself and Baker, and being dyslexic did not help his cause. No matter how good intentioned he was, or how hard he worked for George Bush, Brady was left with little clout and even less influence.

Actually, only one individual on the President's financial team held any authority: Dick Darman, director of the OMB. Although Darman was Bush's economic advisor, he was Baker's protégé, and while sitting comfortably in the White House under the protection of Baker, Darman knew that he could throw as much weight around as he wished. Taking over the budget job (that once had been the domain of David Stockman), meant that Darman reported directly to Sununu, but he remained "obliged" to Secretary Baker . . . similar to the arrangement Stockman had with Baker in 1981. Darman, the ultra-liberal, was the force behind President Bush's economic agenda.

As former deputy to Elliot Richardson, Darman had worked at the departments of Defense, Justice, Health, Education and Welfare, and Commerce; he had been the number-two operative at four different federal agencies. Even by Washington standards, that was as impressive as one's résumé got. With instruction from Richardson and later Baker, Darman became as savvy and knowledgeable in the nuances of political power in Washington as anyone; he had learned to use this sway to his advantage and, simultaneously, to Baker's benefit. The two stood at the top of the Power Pyramid.

If Bush wanted Baker, he would have to take Darman, too. It was as simple as that. Yet, what resulted was a Baker-Darman coalition that reigned supreme in the White House, one that left Bush in a precarious position. To me, the relationship between Bush and Darman was perplexing: these two men had so little in common—other than their devotion to Jim Baker. Ideologically, Bush and Darman stood miles apart. On the issue of taxes, they were diametrically opposed. Bush had vowed to cut taxes; Darman was determined to increase them. In the Reagan White House, Darman was there when Baker convinced the President to go against his beliefs and (for the greater cause) increase taxes during his first term.

Based on the tax issue alone, Darman had not befriended the Republican conservatives. Nevertheless, during the early days of the Bush administration—analogous to the early days of the Reagan administration—the tax increase "scenario" followed the same course with Bush as it had with Reagan. Strangely enough, once Darman became Management and Budget chief, no one seemed to raise a red flag. And when the Bush administration began in full earnest in 1989, the President's ability to keep his no-new-taxes campaign pledge depended entirely on Darman's skill in dealing with the budget. However, it was no secret that Darman would *never* promote cutting taxes—for any reason, let alone for keeping a campaign pledge. By the end of the year, I heard it rumored that as early as November 1988, Darman had been out to sabotage Bush's program to lower taxes. I believed it.

The roster of the Bush financial team would not be complete without mentioning Federal Reserve Chairman Alan Greenspan. Before becoming Fed chairman, Greenspan had been an outside economic advisor to President Reagan, originally drafted into the President's economic circle by David Stockman. Greenspan had been chairman of President Ford's Council of Economic Advisors, though not by Ford's choosing. Nixon had nominated Greenspan for the CEA job but the tainted President had resigned before the Senate had time to confirm him. Ford had kept Greenspan—as he had almost all the Nixon White House staff —and made him his senior economic advisor.

In August 1987, when Paul Volcker retired as Federal Reserve chairman (having held the position for eight years and having not been

★★★

asked to serve another four-year term), Reagan appointed the "supposed" conservative Greenspan. Unlike Volcker, Greenspan was known to be a friend to Wall Street as well as to President Reagan, and was expected to collaborate more closely with the White House than his predecessor. He was also thought to be more sensitive to the risks of a possible recession. Greenspan had been in office just over a year when Bush won the presidency. With so much emphasis on what happens in White House circles, one tends to forget that no institution has more control and more regulatory authority to affect the nation's economy than the independent bank established by Congress in 1913: the Federal Reserve. Greenspan held *that* kind of influence.

Since the 1988 election, Greenspan had been thwarting Bush's efforts to decrease the deficit without a tax increase. In fact, with his "sky-is-falling" pronouncements, he nearly sank the presidency before Bush got into the White House. Greenspan had advised Bush that the only solution for decreasing the deficit was to reverse his no-new-taxes promise. On November 11, I clipped the article "Trying to Push Bush Around" by Paul Roberts from the *Washington Times* and remembered taking note of its ominous message:

> In no uncertain terms, Mr. Greenspan has told George Bush to reduce the deficit at all costs, including the political cost of eating his no-tax pledge. If Mr. Bush wants to make Mr. Greenspan the most powerful federal official for the next four years, all he has to do is follow his advice. If, on the other hand, Mr. Bush wants to demonstrate that he intends to be in charge of the government and keep faith with the electorate, he should respond to Mr. Greenspan's challenge to his authority by requesting his resignation.

Shortly thereafter, in those heady times of the Big Win, the *New York Times,* on November 23, 1988, published Rowland Evans and Robert Novak's "Fed's Greenspan Blamed for Manufacturing Budget Crisis over Deficit." They agreed that Greenspan had been the President-elect's biggest headache:

> No sooner was Bush elected than relatively stable markets went haywire. The dollar plunged, sending down stock prices amid lamentations over a deficit that had not overly concerned anybody

during the campaign. The Fed chairman's testimony before the
National Economic Commission implicitly complained about
Bush's failure to engage the budget issue two months before
Inauguration Day. Greenspan's threatened boost in interest rates
triggered an unnecessary budget crisis. Even though the chairman
prefers spending cuts to tax increases, his doomsday statements
opened the door to the taxes. Bush insiders believe that for Bush to
break his campaign promise and opt for higher taxes would court
economic and political disaster.

I have always felt there was more than some truth to the idea that
Greenspan, with his incessant talk about how poorly the economy was
doing, was directly involved in plotting a recession or, at least, planting
the idea of a recession in America's mind. If one believed Greenspan
during the Bush years, it was hard not to think a huge economic
weakening was going to hit the country. A weakening in 1989 and '90?
Yes. A recession in '91? No.

Adding to the Bush-Greenspan dilemma was another Reagan-
inherited problem: the savings and loan disaster. Thrift lobbying had been
going on for years in the Reagan administration, unchecked and without
government intervention. In the fall of 1989, the shakedown of the
banking and the savings and loan industries became headline news,
mostly due to one investor, Charles Keating.

Keating had been battling federal regulators for five years, and along
with five other U.S. senators, was accused of "unethical conduct" and
became the subject of a $1 billion civil fraud and racketeering suit. The
Lincoln Savings and Loan, which Keating owned, ended up costing
Americans $2.5 billion, the principal loss in the S&L scandal. This event
proved to be one big wake-up call for me.

Arizona land developer Charles Keating had bought the California-
based Lincoln S&L only to have it collapse shortly thereafter because of
high-risk speculation. The demise gave rise to a group known as "The
Keating Five," made up of one Republican senator, John McCain, and four
Democratic senators, Dennis DeConcini (McCain's colleague from
Arizona); Alan Cranston of California; John Glenn of Ohio and Donald
Riegle of Michigan. These men were accused of pressuring Edwin J. Gray
(former Reagan chief regulator of the savings and loan industry and
chairman of the Federal Home Loan Bank Board) to go easy on Mr.
Keating. For their part in intervening, Keating and company had rewarded

★★★

the senators with $1.3 million in contributions to their political campaigns. Before the end of Bush's first year in office, the disclosure of the campaign financing deal was in all the newspaper headlines. In a November 19, 1989, *Washington Post* article titled "The Lincoln Mess: Let's Say Goodbye to Keating Five," I read Hobart Rowan's take on the scandal:

> So long as politicians accept huge blobs of political campaign money—some of which under present law, they are able to pocket after leaving—those giving the money will expect to have political influence, and those getting the money will be expected to snap to attention when the donors have business with the government. "It's the way the system works, and it is wrong," says an insider. "That's why, when an angel like Keating comes along, senators just love him. But it is a lousy system: once you take their money, you can't tell them to get lost."

And so, my political schooling continued. With McCain as one of the Keating Five, I was seeing that political involvement did not always equate with honorable intentions, and, too, I was learning that a military background did not necessarily ensure patriotic inclinations. Sometimes I felt as if my moral compass was broken, particularly with the events regarding Navy junior and Naval officer himself, John McCain. Because of family parallels, McCain's unscrupulous involvement bothered me more than usual. In the Navy, especially multi-generational Navy, it seems everyone relates to everyone else in some way, and this was true in the case of McCain's family and mine. As a high school student in the 1950s, John McCain had attended the boys' boarding school Episcopal High School, in Alexandria, Virginia; my son had graduated from The High School (as they called it) in 1987. In addition, McCain had followed his father and grandfather to graduate from the Naval Academy in 1958; my brother had followed Father and Grandfather, graduating in 1969. McCain and my brother were naval veterans of Vietnam. McCain's father had graduated from the Naval Academy in 1931, my father in 1940. His grandfather graduated in the class of 1906, my grandfather in 1913.

I do not know if our fathers crossed paths, but I do know our grandfathers had. Even though my grandfather, Admiral DuBose, was seven years junior to Admiral McCain, because it was wartime, the class of 1913 (of which my grandfather was president) moved up faster in the ranks than previous classes and had caught up with the more senior officers. McCain's grandfather (nicknamed Slew) was an aviator who flew planes off aircraft carriers, and my grandfather captained battleships and cruisers. They both served in leadership positions in the South Pacific during World War II. Later, my grandfather held the job of Chief of Naval Operations at the Pentagon; at another time, McCain's father was Deputy Chief of Naval Operations.

Although I had never met John McCain, the McCain-Keating scandal left me feeling as though the senator had personally let me down; before the Keating scandal he had represented the forging of the honorable naval officer with the principled politician. There were not that many of us with military heritage in the Washington political mainstream, and McCain had a chance to "rise above," yet, in my opinion, he had let people down.

The Lincoln Savings exposé played on throughout the fall and into the next year. Because Baker, as previous Treasury secretary, had failed to fix the savings and loan crisis, Nicholas Brady would issue Brady Bonds and clean up the mess. It cost taxpayers over $600 million, and the Federal Deposit Insurance Corp. and the Resolution Trust Corp. would pay a hefty percentage of that figure to outside law firms.

Despite the high public approval ratings the President received during late 1989, I am convinced the savings and loan incident, among the controversies over the deficit, distracted Bush from essential matters at home and abroad. Nonetheless, as the first year came to a close and the end of the decade was approaching, two international events took center stage: the invasion of Panama and the collapse of the Berlin Wall. These incidents gave Bush some positive publicity at a time when his domestic appeal was just beginning to wane.

The first event, yet another Reagan-inherited imbroglio, involved the U.S. face-off with Panama's President Manuel Antonio Noriega. For years, the Reagan staff had been game-playing with Noriega, indicting him on drug charges, but without any visible consequences. Noriega's relationship with the U.S. went back to the 1960s when he was put on the CIA's payroll for reporting on the moves of the Panamanian leftists. By the early 1970s, Noriega was involved with drug trafficking, and his rise to power was fueled by American support. The U.S. seemed to look the other way when it came to the Panamanian general's criminal activities.

In 1976, Bush, as director of the CIA, had met with Noriega. As Vice President and director of the National Narcotics Board Interdiction

System, he again met with the foreign leader. However, Bush always maintained he never knew about the mounting evidence that Noriega was protecting major drug traffickers. Bush critics alleged he knew more. Still, there had never been any proof he had played a direct part in maintaining ties with Noriega.

In February 1988, two federal grand juries indicted Noriega, and Bush who believed that dropping the drug indictments would set a bad precedent for an administration locked in a war on drugs urged Reagan to be skeptical. It was promoted in the press that Noriega—powerful, wealthy, and formerly well protected by U.S. connections—had become "the enemy" of President Reagan, Vice President Bush and the national security team.

Then in the fall of 1989, Panama had a new president, Guillermo Endara, and Bush had a new chairman of the Joint Chiefs of Staff, General Colin Powell. Only weeks after Powell was sworn in, an unsuccessful internal coup was waged against Noriega, and shortly thereafter, several Americans were ambushed by General Noriega's army; one of them was killed. Bush immediately approved troop intervention, and on December 20, 1989, American paratroopers landed in Panama City. Close to five hundred Americans were either killed or wounded, and thousands of Panamanian civilians perished. Noriega had yet to be captured.

Although some criticized Bush for waging an illegal invasion (going against international law, the U.N. Charter, and the U.S. Constitution) and causing a military debacle, his move was recorded in the press as a victory. The day after the invasion, the *Washington Post* came out with an editorial, "The Panama Intervention," in which it applauded Bush's attack:

> President Bush did the right thing in ordering American forces into Panama. General Noriega's latest provocations—the declaring of a "state of war," the murder and harassment of Americans—altered the situation on the ground and created a new and sufficient cause for the concern about the safety of U.S. citizens, the workings of the canal, and the integrity of the canal treaties.

Noriega finally surrendered during the first week in January 1990 and was brought to the United States to stand trial, but not until April 1992 was he found guilty of cocaine trafficking, racketeering and money laundering. Ironically (?), two years after that, in 1994, his former military musclemen would be politically reinstated.

Thousands of miles from Panama, on the other side of the globe, Eastern Europe was reverberating from another, more momentous, kind of fall. Soviet President Mikhail Gorbachev and his Communist rulers were losing control of their empire, and ultimately, all fifteen Soviet Republics would claim sovereignty over themselves. The Eastern European countries of Bulgaria, Czechoslovakia, Hungary, Poland and Romania were showing signs of political and economic reform and beginning to unshackle themselves from the superiority of the Soviet Union. By late fall of 1989, nowhere was this breakdown of the Communist Bloc more evident than in East Germany. Six million people, living in an area no larger than the state of Virginia, were holding massive demonstrations.

Hundreds of thousands of demonstrators marched in a pro-democracy protest through Leipzig on October 16, 1989, the fortieth anniversary of the creation of the East German state. Two days later, Erich Honecker, the country's seventy-seven-year-old Communist leader, was removed and replaced by Egon Krenz. The crowning moment, which marked the end of the Cold War, came on November 9, 1989. The Berlin Wall collapsed. For the first time in forty years, hordes of East Germans freely walked through Checkpoint Charlie into West Germany. The barbed wire fences of the Iron Curtain were dismantled, and the Brandenburg Gate was opened. Hans Modrow became the new East German premier, and West German Chancellor Helmut Kohl proposed a plan to unite the two Germanys.

It would take years for the people from the East to reestablish themselves with the people from the West, and vice-versa. Billions of dollars, much of it from the U.S., would be poured into the East German economy—with limited success. Nonetheless, the reunification of East and West Germany heralded a remarkable turn in world history and global politics. The manifestation of freedom was felt and observed worldwide. President Bush—if for no other reason than because he was President of the most democratic and most powerful country in the Free World—also won a victory. Just two days before the wall came down, Bush, who later refused to gloat over the wall's collapse, commented on the German situation in his November 7 news conference:

> Around the world we've seen the most dramatic moves toward
> democracy in at least 40 years, as people of one country after

another have expressed their yearning for freedom. And we have
supported those efforts with substantial aid . . . in addition, we've
set the time frame for a summit with the Soviets, and we're on the
verge of an informal meeting with President Gorbachev.

The informal meeting with Gorbachev that Bush referred to in his
press conference turned out to be the Malta Summit. Just weeks after the
cave-in of the Berlin Wall (December 1-3), Gorbachev and Bush met
aboard the Soviet cruise ship *Maxim Gorky*. During the three-day meeting,
Bush, who kept quarters aboard the U.S.S. *Belknap*, met with those in his
presidential party, representatives from the State department, the Joint
Chiefs of Staff and the National Security Council. Standing in for Brent
Scowcroft was Condoleezza Rice, Bush's Soviet Union expert. Scowcroft
had known Rice before he appointed her to his staff and was responsible
for bringing her into the Bush upper echelon, commissioning her to find
a way to balance U.S. support between the political interests of the
emerging free Eastern European countries and those of Mikhail
Gorbachev. Rice assisted Bush in his effort to smooth the way for the
Soviet president, who was now in the throes of expanding his political
system while relinquishing control of Eastern Europe.

The American and Soviet presidents experienced what would be one
of their most engaging and productive rendezvous. During the Summit at
Sea, Bush laid the groundwork for what would come to be known as the
"post–Cold War world." Having already had his sights set on America's
becoming an economic powerhouse, Bush realized that with Gorbachev
as his ally, his dream had a better chance of becoming a reality. In Malta,
he agreed to support Perestroika, and Gorbachev—having surrendered
Soviet control of Eastern Europe—willingly endorsed the United States
presence in Europe.

Over the next couple of years, the Malta Summit would set the tone
for the Soviet-American relationship, and Bush and Gorbachev would
work in concert, rather than in conflict. Although it was more than a year
before the Communist empire would crumble, these two world powers
had charted the New World Order before most leaders of their time.
Nonetheless, like heroes in a Shakespearean drama, they would both,
within a relatively short period of time, experience a similar and
unexpected political unraveling.

In the first year of his presidency, Bush, who confidently embraced the Soviet situation and took an aggressive stance against Noriega, suggested to those who witnessed him on the world stage that he was a tough and decisive leader. The problems associated with the budget and the deficit seemed to pale in the glow of the foreign affairs victories, and by year's end, Bush managed to hold on to his unparalleled twelve-month 76 percent approval rating. December 1989 arrived. The next decade was going to take America to the millennium; the year 2000 was but a short ten years away.

One of the buzzwords associated with predictions for the future was "integration." The world was forecast to grow smaller as the population grew larger, making it difficult for anyone who lived on the planet to plead isolation. It was calculated that the global population would become intricately engaged with one another—integrated by way of the personal computer (PC).

If you believed the communication experts at the time, the computer would become a way of life for all of us, connecting the man in Florida with his daughter working in Thailand and the businessperson in Texas with his client in Italy, all in a matter of seconds. The Internet, an electronic superhighway of computer networks, would physically connect sites thousands of miles apart, creating a system of boundless information. Developed by Tim Berners-Lee for the department of Defense and used almost exclusively by the military and universities up until now, the World Wide Web was introduced to the public, and only the satellites circling the planet determined its communication boundaries.

With the emerging Internet in place in the 1990s, people would begin accessing and exchanging more data than thought possible. Computers built on the assembly lines of IBM, the world's largest information company in 1989 (with revenues of $55 billion), and Macintosh, the world's twelfth-largest company (with $5 billion), would paint a new face on the old globe. With the flick of a switch, the gathering and sharing of information would change the way people looked at themselves, their neighbors, and the world.

Bush was Commander in Chief at a time when all countries, particularly the United States, were going through this communications metamorphosis. Soon, employees throughout the federal government as well as private industry would have an "e-mail" address, and "dot-com" would become standard lingo as we learned to surf the Net. But, at present, most of us in Washington still relied on newspapers for gathering information. The *Washington Post* never ceased to be my lifeline to my job, the world and the political arena on which I focused everyday. On December 26, 1989, I read the defining moments of the previous decade; among the many listed for each year, I refer to one significant one:

> *Under President Carter:*
>   1980: The prime lending rate rose to 21.5%.
> *Under President Reagan:*
>   1981: Air traffic controllers began an illegal strike and were fired.
>   1982: Unemployment hit 10.8%—highest in 42 years.
>   1983: The national debt topped $1 billion.
>   1984: The breakup of AT&T took effect.
>   1985: Coca-Cola brought back the original formula after consumer protest.
>   1986: Stock speculator Ivan Boesky paid $100 million in fines and restitution and agreed to plead guilty to a single felony count.
>   1987: The stock market suffered the biggest single-day drop in history as Dow Jones industrial average fell 508 points.
>   1988: RJR Nabisco Inc. agreed to a $25 billion buyout—biggest in history.
> *Under President Bush:*
>   1989: The longest peacetime economic expansion in U.S. history reached its 7th anniversary

On Monday, January 1, 1990, on the front page of the *Post* Style Section, was an article incorporating predictions for the coming year. The writers, filled with a sense of lightheartedness and optimism, suggested that: "In the face of global upheavals, or because of them, things are becoming more sentimental—and softer—all the time. Lace is preferred over leather. Brocade has replaced beading. Matchmakers are back, not personal ads. Simple, cozy, homey things continue to be popular—Dads and staying married are in, trophy wives and divorces are out. Calm. Things seem to be calming down."

★★★ ═══ ★★★
CHAPTER
19
GOVERNMENT MEANS CONTRACTS

I'm nobody! Who are you?
Are you nobody, too?
Then there is a pair of us—don't tell!
They'd banish us, you know.
How dreary to be somebody!
How public, like a frog.
To tell your name the livelong day to an admiring bog!
—Emily Dickenson

JANUARY–MARCH 1990

During the winter of 1990, several storms hit Washington in a matter of weeks. Snow and high winds complicated the morning commute into the city, and traffic backups on the George Washington Parkway and the 14th Street Bridge were neverending. The bad weather in January and February brought with it an infectious flu that seemed to catch everyone off guard—except those in the legislative branch. After having worked for a little more than a month, the new 101st Congress fortuitously had left frigid Washington and were sunning themselves in Aruba and the Seychelles, leaving the rest of us to keep the wheels of the nation turning.

While Congress was on recess and in the midst of our wintry assault, I attended a luncheon at the Capitol Hill Club, just up the street from the Republican National Committee, where I had spent three months before the '88 election. As a member of the Republican Women's Forum, I was invited each month to the club for lunch and to hear one of the Cabinet members or White House aides speak. What always made the affair entertaining were the introductory comments by the speaker's spouse, often with references to personal habits or traits, such as when Lynn Cheney mentioned that her husband liked to raid the kitchen late at night and eat peanut butter straight out of the jar.

On January 11, we gathered at round tables of eight on the upper floor dining room to hear John Sununu give the address. A shy Nancy Sununu avoided the usual personal references and quickly turned the meeting over to her husband. Bush's chief of staff told us what we already knew: things could not be better for the President. It was Sununu's feeling that the predicted recession was already over and the Bush presidency was running as "smooth as cream." He reported that the latest White House poll showed Bush with an 80 percent approval rating, up four points in two weeks and extraordinarily high after one year in office. The chief of staff assured us that Bush, without any doubt, would have an eight-year term.

Shortly after I heard Sununu speak, Mary McGrory published an article in the *Washington Post* that aptly summed up "Bush's Charmed Presidency":

> Ronald Reagan seemed to enjoy himself most of the time. But Reagan was St. Sebastian compared to George Bush, for whom every day in the Oval Office is Christmas. The president's palpable delight in being where he always wanted to be has not waned in the 15 months since he took office. Plainly it was worth it all, the slavish service to the Reagans, the kow-tows to the right, the lacerating interview with Dan Rather, the snide magazine covers, the sneering predictions that he would never make it. In large things as in small, Bush has been touched by magic. Things keep falling into his lap.

With previous economic worries now attributed to nothing more than a "jumpy" stock market, Bush continued to tout that the country was enjoying its longest economic expansion in history. (Although the deficit problem would not subside during Bush's term, 1990 was the first year in what would *later* be a ten-year economic boom.) White House talk was upbeat and centered around the prosperous economy at home, including several technological advances.

The bureau overseeing the most advanced of the high-tech trials was the White House Office of Science and Technology, directed by physicist D. Allan Bromley of Yale University. Unlike his predecessors, Bromley was quite influential; he sat on the Domestic Policy Council, the Space

Council, and the Competitiveness Council, all of them carried a great deal of prestige. With a range of interests—from global warming to the superconducting supercollider—Bromley oversaw the commercial space industry, including the SR-71 Blackbird spy plane. As the world's fastest airplane, it recently had made a record-breaking sixty-eight minute flight from Los Angeles to Washington, D.C. This feat was considered a real coup for the United States. And so was the Hubble space telescope.

Carried aloft by the shuttle *Discovery*, Hubble turned out to be a true American success story. Thousands of scientists and engineers, in both government and industry in the United States and Europe, had spent almost two decades struggling to design and refine it. The most expensive scientific instrument ever built was launched into orbit in early 1990. At a hefty price tag of over $2 billion, Hubble, with its telescopic magic, was expected to transform astronomy, and bring back to earth unprecedented views of the farthest reaches of the universe.

Nevertheless the most important of all the space-age technologies in 1990 was the 41,000-pound Pegasus rocket, sent into space from an airborne plane over the Pacific Ocean near Monterey, California. Because launch pad usage was susceptible to the government's schedule, Pegasus gave aerospace companies hope for more-timely launches. To help rectify the situation, "the winged rocket" was projected to make at least twelve launches per year. Pegasus had been built in only two years (1988–90), but it would change the course of satellite operations for the next decade.

Created and developed by Fairfax, Virginia–based Orbital Sciences Corp. under a $60 million contract from the Pentagon's Defense Advanced Research Projects Agency, Pegasus was the first project in DARPA's Advanced Space Technology program. As a joint effort by private industry and government to jump-start space projects, and with the expertise of Orbital as the prime contractor (Hercules Aerospace Company won the secondary contract), the Defense department had successfully navigated the building of the nation's "winged rocket."

The Orbital-Defense venture, along with other military-industrial complex largesse, may help explain why Cheney had so forcefully fought Mosbacher regarding the FSX and HDTV projects. DARPA was *his* agency, making him influential in parceling out tech contracts, as had been the case for his predecessor, Frank Carlucci, presently of the Carlyle Group, a prime military contractor. (Baker and Darman would later join

Carlyle; Cheney would found Halliburton, another defense contractor.) Technology funding held a high priority for those on the Power Pyramid, and Cheney who reached far beyond the authority of other Bush agency secretaries, held in his hand the largest and most pricey contracts. His desire was to single-handedly determine which companies won technology contracts and which therefore competed in the international race for economic superiority. Cheney wanted to be the one to choose the winners and the losers. He did not want Mosbacher to interfere with projects (such as the FSX) that had always been in the Defense domain . . . multi-billion dollar programs that had tremendous muscle in government ranks, and even more in the private sector.

It is as evident in the D.C. area as anywhere in the nation, that defense contracts can make or break a company. The Pentagon's dollars make up an incredible amount, and without them, many people in metropolitan Washington would be "without." Federal contracting has its less-than-desirable parts that run through the heart of conservative and liberal legions alike. The common denominator is often greed. Despite what people say about "industrial policy" (government choosing company winners) being unfair, government-industry partnerships run rampant throughout the country. What is unjust about the system is that the contracts go to those individuals with the personal contacts and who already run successful businesses. Those who have a product or service of merit, but are without connections, almost always lose out.

Mosbacher had triggered my initial interest in understanding industrial policy. Before he started talking about it in reference to the "little guy," conversation on the subject had not gained my attention. Once privy to gossip in the back offices of Commerce, I started to take notice. Just from the tones of people's voices, I could tell the subject was hush-hush. One day, a coworker whispered, "It is not a good idea to talk about industrial policy at work." I was spurred on to find out more, and I discovered DARPA.

The obscure office at DOD, unknown to most in and out of government, was the Pentagon's secret. Very hush-hush. Dr. Craig I. Fields, who, in 1989, headed DARPA and its 140-person office at the Pentagon had previously been its deputy director of research. Fields had the authority to decide which technologies America would pursue, which company(ies) would be tapped to do the development, and which would follow through with the manufacturing.

Congress had allocated over $1 billion to DARPA and charged its staff with channeling their monies into American universities and organizations at their discretion, whether projects were defense related or not. Controversy regarding the direction of this sort of "behind the scene" maneuvering in the Bush administration, having begun with the FSX-Mosbacher-Baker-Cheney struggle, erupted again a year later, during the spring of 1990. An article by Evelyn Richards in the *Washington Post* on April 29, 1990, "Uncle Sam As Venture Capitalist," read in part:

> Popular on Capitol Hill, but anathema to the Bush administration, is the notion that government should somehow help shore up certain key industries—not specific companies, but underlying commercial technologies like the making of computer chips and advanced materials—in the same way that it played a role in building a national transportation system of highways and railroads. With the worldwide easing of military tensions, the simmering debate over whether government should play a larger role in key areas of the private sector—so-called industrial policy— is growing more complex. More than ever, economic competitiveness is an important factor in the global balance of power, blurring the lines between what is good for the military and what is good for the economy. The Bush administration would generally prefer that the government stick to weapons, period.

If the White House, which gave the appearance of "no industrial policy in this administration," was going to promote weapons only, then DARPA at Defense was the natural choice to manage the contracts. However, if the administration, with Congress pushing, and Mosbacher supporting, was going to fund non-defense-related technologies, then the department of Commerce should have received these funds. As it stood, Defense held a firm grip on all the financial assets allocated to both defense and non-defense technologies—which approached $50 billion. Commerce, the agency working most closely with the smaller high-technology companies, was, most often left out of the loop.

One of the exceptions was a Congressional non-military grant awarded to Iowa State University's R&D program—a boost to technology that I knew something about. Under the authorization of Commerce, a $7.3 million grant was overseen by my office of Basic Industries (BI), and Alan Dunn held the purse strings. For this reason, he and I played a major role in administering the Iowa grant.

Congress had tagged funds for technological projects that had the potential for rapid development and commercialization. The $7.3 million appropriated to ISU's materials research lab was one of these ventures; in fact, ISU held the reputation of being one of the country's best working models. The goal was to successfully integrate completed scientific and engineering research projects with a full-scale marketing program. The prerequisite for ISU's continuation of the Iowa grant was an annual inspection by a representative from Commerce, followed by a report submitted to Congress. In other words, a recommendation from Basic Industries—in this case, Dunn—was necessary before ISU could receive another year's dose of federal money.

So that he could report back to Congress on how well the lab was performing, in February 1990, Dunn, with me accompanying him, made a visit to Ames, Iowa. For two days, in the snow-covered hinterlands of Iowa, we observed the newest in laboratory technology. On the first evening, Dunn and I joined the president of the university and a few of his board members for dinner. Afterward while looking at the graduate school yearbook, I noticed an overwhelming majority of the students to be of a foreign nationality, many were of Asian and Hispanic heritage. That surprised me.

The morning of the second day started early, and after several briefings and a tour of the facilities, Dunn and I met with the research scientists who developed the into-the-future technologies. Their projects were astounding. The scientists enlightened us with the working backgrounds of their schemes, detailing their discovery methods, explaining the far-reaching consequences of their creations, and showing us amazing prototypes constructed from twenty-first-century designs. In one instance, we were given a sample of a magnet—the size of a nickel— with a force potent enough, when used in adequate proportions, to suspend a bridge.

I became aware of how significant the effects of federal dollars were on our country's competitiveness, particularly as it pertained to the "winners." I decided that the federal process of choosing the frontrunners and dispersing billions of dollars could cut two–ways. The funding could be used to build a stronger America and a thriving democracy (that included a fair method of tagging the smaller, qualified, yet unknown companies), or it could become riddled with corruption, incorporating only the successfully elite companies, those that had a "friend" in the administration.

Upon my return to Washington, I reread the article, previously mentioned, from the *Washington Times*, "Mosbacher Scores High in Capital Power Game." The issue of industrial policy, which I had ignored on first reading, was addressed. I read it more carefully this time:

> Mr. Mosbacher portrays the competitiveness issue in almost life and death terms. But, within the administration there is intense debate over the proper role of government in assisting American businesses to compete internationally. One view holds that anything that smacks of an industrial policy, where government singles out certain industries for assistance, is anathema to the Republican free-market views on economic issues. But, Mr. Mosbacher has been campaigning for a much more activist approach.

Mosbacher's views had not been in harmony with some of those in Bush's White House, including the true conservatives. However, Nick Brady, at Treasury, had wholeheartedly agreed with him. And in the spring of 1989, when Baker and Cheney were trying to wrestle away the technology projects from Mosbacher, they had done so because they felt Commerce had usurped *their* power.

Power, the kind that Mosbacher lost, is assumed in one of two ways: by *amassing it,* or by *taking it away.* If one used the second method, it was advantageous to compete with weaker individuals, those who could be easily wrestled to the ground. Contrarily, when the second technique was required, a much more forceful tactic was necessary. When Baker and Cheney decided to "take out" Mosbacher, they had to use maximum force, because Mosbacher turned out not to be one of the weaker ones—Baker had underestimated his strength.

In the end, after the FSX haggle was over, Baker and Cheney had fortified their authority and a coalition between the two had been established. With Baker as the preeminent weapon, both men had emerged victorious over Mosbacher.

Today I ask myself, why did Bush—whose beliefs coincided more closely with Mosbacher's than Baker's or Cheney's—not defend his Commerce secretary? I have to assume it was because Bush owed more to

Baker than he did to Mosbacher. And, too, Bush needed Baker more than he needed Mosbacher.

Without Bush's support, and having been entirely stripped of his more prestigious functions, Mosbacher had become more involved in the environmental theater. But before he had been dethroned, he had been thrust into a national environmental catastrophe.

On Bush's watch, one particular ecological disaster caught everyone's attention: the oil spill in Prince William Sound. On March 24, 1989, the Exxon oil tanker *Valdez* had collided with Bligh Reef off Alaska, spewing an estimated 240,000 barrels (11 million gallons) of crude over the pristine Alaska coastline, almost ruining the lives of 33,000 fishermen and native villagers. The cleanup of the sound would last for more than a decade, and even then, almost none of the wounded species (animals and ecosystems) would be considered fully recovered.

Because Mosbacher was appointed federal trustee of the oil spill cleanup, I paid closer attention to the events in the aftermath of the collision. A special *Valdez* Office was set up in the DOC just down the hall from mine, and remained there, fully staffed, for over two years. Exxon mounted an enormous buildup of equipment and personnel to help with the cleanup, but the job was way too massive for the company to undertake, and it ultimately depended upon Mosbacher's assistance. Charged with managing the overall rescue effort, Mosbacher, over time, became more and more immersed in the effort. Scientists in Commerce's National Oceanic and Atmospheric Administration took on the primary role in the Bligh Reef rehabilitation, and the NOAA crew provided extensive damage assessment for months.

Alaskan fish, shellfish and marine mammals harvested near native subsistence villages and commercial fisheries had been contaminated beyond anything ever seen. Two hundred fifty bald eagles died; thirty thousand birds were killed; almost the entire population of clams, mussels, salmon, and herring perished; the whale community, the seals, the ducks, even the common loon all but disappeared from the area.

After a series of contested court cases, involving an endless fight over the appropriate amount of damages to be paid by Exxon, the "injured" people were never rewarded the way they were told they would be, and life for them barely improved, financially or environmentally. The skipper of the *Valdez*, Joseph J. Hazelwood (who failed an initial blood-alcohol test given by the Coast Guard), was charged with nothing more than a state misdemeanor conviction of "negligent discharge of oil." How could that be? The *Valdez* incident, involving over 1,300 miles of Alaskan shoreline and costing over $4 billion in cleanup costs, would later be described as the worst environmental disaster in United States history.

As horrible as the Alaskan catastrophe was, President Bush, with an escalating approval rating at 80 percent in late March 1990, remained relatively unscathed. His triumphs, now numerous, were beginning to be routine. The feel-good warmth of success and the springtime sunshine once again flooded Washington's parks, ponds and pathways, and after a horrifically cold winter, the Federal City bloomed.

For the first time in a long time, I started to feel confident and content about the future. Yet, there still was that part of me that said, "Don't get too comfortable." I knew that in politics it was never a good idea to take things for granted. Atwater had taught me that.

★★★ ═══════ ★★★
CHAPTER

20

DEADEN THE SPIRIT

The world of political spin is one in which no one can dare take another's word at face value. War can be peace, freedom can be slavery, and ignorance strength, if a source close to the White House deems it so.

—Eric Alterman

MARCH–APRIL 1990

On a gossamer spring day, I sat on one of the black wrought-iron benches in Lafayette Park to eat my turkey club sandwich. With the newspaper in my lap, I surveyed the wide-open spaces around me. As I looked south across Pennsylvania Avenue, I could see the White House. To the West was the presidential guesthouse, Blair House. Looking over to the East, I saw the top of the Woodward Building, the 1988 Bush campaign headquarters (it had not been demolished), and on the Northern rim, the church that had remained in continuous use since 1816, St. John's Episcopal Church, referred to as the Church of the Presidents.

I marveled at the view before returning to my newspaper. According to several articles in the *Washington Post* that day (April 16), the country, encouraged by Bush's first fifteen months in office, also remained enamored with the First Lady. Barbara Bush, more familiarly known as Bar, had found her own identity while living in the White House, which went beyond being the wife of the President. But then, Barbara Pierce Bush had always maintained her sense of self, no matter what the situation or position of her husband.

I imagined Mrs. Bush's position as wife and mother with many responsibilities being somewhat analogous to the life of a Navy wife; she had dedicated herself to supporting her husband's career, all the while raising a large family and keeping on the move year after year. By the time she arrived at the White House, she had lived in some twenty-nine homes.

In an article printed in the *Atlanta Constitution* on October 16, 1987, "Barbara Bush Chooses to Take a Back Seat," there was a quote: "'I'm at peace with myself about it,' Mrs. Bush said when asked about her husband's bid for the Republican nomination for president. Even if the man she married more than forty years ago is not elected, she added, 'it won't be the end of the world. Either way is all right for me.'" Barbara Bush had flourished as First Lady, and because of her down-to-earth manner, her appeal had an even broader base. Most often adorned with three strings of pearls around her neck, Mrs. Bush developed her own style and her own rapport with America. The nation loved her.

Mrs. Bush was the mother of six: George Walker, Pauline "Robin" Robinson (who had died at age four), John "Jeb" Ellis, Neil Mallon, Marvin Pierce and Dorothy "Doro" Walker. And she was the grandmother of twelve. Nevertheless, she found time to contribute to many worthy causes. Mrs. Bush was involved with organizations that helped people with AIDS; she assisted groups that fed, clothed, and comforted homeless women and children; she gave her support to child abuse prevention programs; and for the ninth year, she served as national chairwoman of the fundraising effort for leukemia, the disease to which she and the President had lost their daughter.

Barbara Bush even found time to write the best-seller *Millie's Book,* a tale about the family Springer Spaniel living in the White House; the proceeds went to the Barbara Bush Foundation for Family Literacy. Mrs. Bush gave a great deal of her time and energy to breaking the intergenerational cycle of illiteracy and to establishing education as a value in every American family. Since her childhood, reading had been an inspiration to her, and her empathy for people, especially children in less fortunate circumstances, had propelled her into her work. In her own words, she explained:

> I'm concerned about every living human who hurts. It is never easy to say "no" because there are so many causes that deserve attention. But since no one can do everything, I try to focus my energies where they'll do the most good. That's why I chose literacy as my primary project. Years ago, when George was considering running for higher office, I realized I had a wonderful opportunity to make a difference as well.

In constant demand and with invitations overflowing, Barbara Bush needed a staff to keep her on schedule. Two women in particular assisted her with her busy days in the White House: Anna Perez and Susan Porter Rose.

Barbara Bush's press secretary, Anna Perez, had worked her way up on the Hill as deputy press secretary, and then as press secretary for several Republicans. After the 1988 election, Perez lobbied for the job with Mrs. Bush, and got it. Married with three children, Perez had faced her fair share of challenges during the first year of the administration but had landed on her feet. She was involved in all of Mrs. Bush's domestic and international engagements, as well as her soon-to-be reelection events. Brought up in Manhattan and Queens, she knew how to handle the clamoring press. She also had a sense of humor. At a White House Correspondents' Dinner, Perez had her picture taken—attired with a pair of Ray-Ban sunglasses—with Donald Trump's significant other, Marla Maples. The photo, showing the other side of Perez, ended up in newspapers all across the country. And caused quite a stir.

Susan Porter Rose served as the First Lady's chief of staff. At fifty years of age, Rose was well known in White House circles; she had been Pat Nixon's appointment secretary and Betty Ford's scheduler. Her husband served as special assistant to Nixon before becoming assistant attorney general in the Reagan administration. Having gone to work for Barbara Bush in 1981, Rose was on staff when Vice President Bush announced his candidacy in 1988, which put her in the right place at the right time. The chief of staff job with Mrs. Bush had fallen easily into her hands. With her fifteen-person staff, Rose screened all requests for the First Lady's public appearances and media interviews, as well as causes and events to which Mrs. Bush was asked to lend her name.

With the First Lady in no need of image boosting, the personal-enhancement function fell more toward her husband's image-makers, those responsible for how Americans viewed their President, than hers. One of these individuals was Sigmund Rogich, better known as Sig, who was the builder and owner of a $40 million Las Vegas-based advertising business, R&R Advertising. Accustomed to rubbing elbows with casino owners and show business celebrities as well as politicians, Rogich—a forty-five-year-old divorced father of two teenage girls—was an ally of former Senator Paul Laxalt of Nevada. Laxalt had brought Rogich into the

1984 Reagan campaign to work on the Tuesday Team, a group of political advertising executives. During the 1988 primary season, Rogich had joined Laxalt's presidential campaign team, and when the senator aborted during the primaries, Rogich was invited to work with Roger Ailes at the national Bush campaign headquarters.

I remembered Rogich from those days. On a bracing March morning in 1988, he had come to headquarters to spend the day, and I was assigned to be his liaison, making sure he kept to his demanding schedule. Before returning to Las Vegas that evening, he was slated to make a visit to Capitol Hill, and because the campaign had neither drivers nor cars for guests, I was asked to drive him (in my two-door 300ZX Nissan.) to the Hill. While there—as the stage was being set up for advertising commercials—I was able to observe Rogich in action. The former ad man to Frank Sinatra had a pleasing smile and a personable way about him. On this particular afternoon, as he made his way from office to congressional office in the Cannon Building, it was evident that people felt relaxed in his company. A lot of lively conversation and good-humored joking went on as his work progressed.

Before joining Bush, Rogich had a reputation as one of the best in the advertising business. He was known as "the man with the camera." Instrumental in fine-tuning Ailes's television ads during the final months of the '88 campaign, he had gone on to become a key Bush advisor, helping to produce several of the more significant ads, including Boston Harbor and the Furlough.

But of all his accomplishments, Rogich was most recognized for conceiving and producing the infamous Dukakis Tank commercial, in which the candidate, wearing a heavy Army helmet and riding in an onerous tank (on an Army base), appeared on screen, with the voiceover saying: "And now he wants to be our commander in chief... America can't afford that risk." Ailes, who took most of the credit for advertising in 1988, most assuredly had relied on Rogich, who did not seem to complain about his lack of recognition.

After Bush won, Rogich returned to Nevada. Then, in the fall of 1989, he was asked to take a job in the White House, a position that first had been filled by Steve Studdert. Eased out because of (I heard) poor job performance and an inability to be a team player, Studdert became the first on Bush's senior staff to leave, paving the way for Rogich.

★★★

While accepting his new position as assistant to the President for events and activities, Rogich said, "I know it sounds corny for someone to tell you that they're patriotic and that they feel honored to do something like this, but I believe deeply in this President because he is a good guy." In spite of all the glitz and glamour inherent in his life, Rogich—responsible for locating and staging the President's events—seemed to be indeed patriotic and genuinely respectful of Bush.

Six months into the job, Rogich was being compared to Michael Deaver, the aide who devised the theme-of-the-week and message-of-the-day for Reagan. With some curiosity, I read a column by my preferred journalist, Ann Devroy, titled "The President's Public-Events Man: Attempting 'Moments,' Not Messages." Devroy touched on the Rogich-Deaver comparison:

> If Deaver's job was to make sure Reagan got on television with a message scripted for him, Rogich's job is to make sure that when Bush has something to say, the setting enhances the message. Rogich, the man who holds what could be called the "Deaver job," says that what he does are "moments," not messages. "I oversee and coordinate events for the president. I make sure that the setting is right so that it amplifies what he is going to say or do. The president, after all, is the one who decides the message and delivers it. This administration does not contrive events to get coverage."

To some degree, it was correct to say that the President decided what message he wanted conveyed and how that message was going to be delivered. Nonetheless, no President, including Bush, "conversed" with the public without guidance from his communications experts. This team, which decides the content of the message, is an important group; they take the material given to them by the domestic and foreign affairs policymakers and spin a story for the public. They should have the expertise to make the President look presidential at all times, especially when he or the White House is going through tough times. Conversely, this group can make the President look dreadful, even in good times. These spin-makers have the wherewithal to project the nation's commander in either a favorable or an unfavorable light, creating an image of the President just as Hollywood does its actors and actresses. However, in movies, the viewer knows he is viewing fiction; when watching the President on the television screen, America assumes what they are seeing is nonfiction—the real thing. It usually is not.

Opposite of Reagan, Bush did not enjoy having image-makers "spin" him, nor did he take pleasure in reading prepared scripts. Not withstanding, the President's communications director was responsible for making sure Bush appeared strong and in command. David F. Demarest, Jr., former Reagan assistant secretary of public affairs at the department of Labor (1985–1988) was Bush's communications chief. He held one of the most influential jobs in the West Wing. Even the press secretary was to take cues from his instruction. Demarest *should have been* the President's most senior advisor on what would and would not work in front of the camera, yet, in the first year of the administration, the craft he and his crew produced had been almost invisible.

In the Bush White House, Demarest had an immediate staff of four. Three of these individuals were designated to public liaison and one to communications: Doug Wead, Bobbi Kilberg, Sichan Siv and Chriss Winston, respectively. In the summer of 1990, Wead, a friend of George W., was fired from Demarest's staff "because of his conservative religious views." I had known Wead informally at the campaign; in fact, he had given me a copy of his 1988 book titled *George Bush: Man of Integrity*, a compilation of Bush family stories, a well-written and intimate collection told in "their own words."

Demarest also directed the five White House speechwriters: Mark Davis, Mark Lange, Daniel McGroarty, Edward McNally and Curt Smith. All five had previously been speechwriters for Reagan officials. With the exception of Davis, the writers had come from Cabinet-level offices: Lange with Ann McLaughlin and Elizabeth Dole at Labor; McGroarty with Casper Weinberger and Frank Carlucci at Defense; McNally at Justice; and Smith with Sam Pierce at Housing and Urban Development. Davis had been with Frank Fahrenkopf at the Republican National Committee.

Although these young men, between the ages of twenty-seven and thirty-eight, were not known for possessing an unusual flair for the written word, they had listened and learned from those who scripted the weighty words of Reagan's speeches. And if the Reagan speech-writing operation had been able to perfect the consummate phrase and the crucial word—capturing Reagan's ideals—then one would assume they would be able to do so for Bush. Yet symbolism and inspiration did not appear to be in Bush's presentations. I say "appear" because there may have been an explanation as to why the public never had a chance to hear a Demarest oration.

Once a speech was completed by Demarest (or one of his writers), it rarely made the cut as written; revisions were the standard next step. The draft was edited by Darman or Sununu and passed on to several others on their staffs who would each rewrite what had already been rewritten. These many revisions made for diluted dialogue, and seldom (if ever?) did a Demarest speech make it into the Oval Office. I doubt this always was based on inadequate scripts. Nonetheless, by way of the spoken word, a bond was never forged between Bush and America. The manner in which the Bush communications team carried out its mission (or, more correctly, was stopped from carrying out its mission) was a large part of the reason why Bush, particularly with domestic issues, never made a personal connection with the public. Because Sununu and/or Darman wanted to control the President's message, they dismissed the speeches coming out of the communications director's office. And too, the press secretary's office had something to do with this arrangement.

More often than not, Bush—who never relished the idea of a prepackaged speech and who seemingly did not have a staff that could assist in making the speech-giving process less grueling—turned to the press conference for channeling his ideas. Since Fitzwater had been taken off Bush's vice presidential staff and pulled back into the Reagan White House in the winter of '88, Bush had been without a spokesperson. Once Baker placed Fitzwater on the Bush presidential team, Fitzwater took charge of scripting President Bush's message. He was unilaterally responsible for the *manner* in which the President was heard (versus Demarest who focussed on the *content)*, playing a critical role in determining how the public perceived him.

Although Fitzwater could appear unthreatening (he looked like a jolly guy, rather robust, balding and pink-cheeked), he was a shrewd man. In addition, he had an enormous advantage over his superior, chief of staff Sununu. Having spent the last five years in the Reagan White House, Fitzwater knew the way the system worked, and although Bush had not been the one to tap him for the job of press secretary, Fitzwater seemed to have gained his trust, having been endowed with the ultimate tool: access. The one-time Environmental Protection Agency bureaucrat had become *the* Bush advisor. Jim Baker was the man to whom Fitzwater was indebted for this privilege.

In the not-too-distant future, Fitzwater would not only be the President's top communication's advisor, he would also be his top domestic policy advisor—taking away authority from both David Demarest (communications) and Roger Porter (policy) and eliminating their responsibilities. Because the White House communications and domestic policy offices appeared ineffective, Fitzwater would take on that much more seniority. With Sununu still trying to orient himself to Washington—not to mention the West Wing—and with Darman, Fitzwater's "old friend" in the Baker League, Fitzwater, because he had Baker's blessing, was permitted to prevail during the Bush presidency.

Fitzwater and Darman were buddies from their Reagan days, which made finessing the underground power structure in the Bush White House that much easier for both; Darman did not interfere with Fitzwater's "setup," and vice-versa. Under this arrangement, Fitzwater's role as press secretary took on a more multifaceted dimension than the one he assumed with Reagan. He definitely was now on one of the top rungs of the Political Ladder.

With Reagan, Fitzwater had aptly portrayed the President as the committed conservative; with Bush, he portrayed him in much less vibrant terms, seldom aligning him with the conservative cause. With Reagan, Fitzwater had concealed the essence of the man, who said one thing and did another; with Bush, he also skewed the story, but in a different way and with different results. Fitzwater's former distortions had worked in favor of President Reagan; his misrepresentations worked against President Bush. Instead of portraying Bush as having vision, readying the United States for the Great Tomorrow—as he did with Reagan—he painted Bush as devoid of an agenda. Fitzwater, who had judiciously, but not truthfully, carved out a positive image for Reagan, cunningly created a downbeat message for Bush, who, in reality, had a much more tantalizing message than Reagan.

To be fair, Fitzwater had allowed himself to be put in an impossible position. The necessary advice and counsel of others—communications experts, skilled media consultants, passionate speechwriters, and perceptive policy makers—were missing in the Bush White House. Given the conflicts that occurred among those on Bush's staff, it sometimes made sense that Bush would rely on other means than the speech to communicate. But not always, and it seldom helped his situation when he allowed his Cabinet members to disclose major policy events; he should have given the victory announcements. When Dick Cheney announced a compromise vis-à-vis deploying both the MX and Midgetman missiles,

President Bush missed a chance to take credit for a major defense move. The deflection approach works well when announcing bad news, but it is an opportunity missed when broadcasting good news.

Despite the skewed communications infrastructure in the White House, Bush actually had managed quite well in the beginning of his presidency, creating an affirmative portrait of himself. One of the ways he kept his image positive had little to do with the skills of his communications team; it had to do with the manner in which Bush presented himself in international situations, those times when he dealt with foreign heads of state. He was in a natural in this environment. Media events involving Bush and other dignitaries had a special appeal, and the country repeatedly saw the President of the United States looking and acting as the premiere statesman.

Bush kept his eye on overseas events more than any previous president, taking many more trips out of the country than Reagan; his foreign policy decisions, unlike his predecessor, were given a top priority. These factors had worked mightily in Bush's favor. By early 1990, the Cold War was over, communism was dying, and Violeta Chamorro had won the election in Nicaragua. Yet nothing was as gratifying as observing Eastern Europe embrace Western democracy.

Poland was predicted to play a vital role in the democratization process of other European countries. The thinking was that if Poland succeeded with its experiment of free markets and Western-style democracy, then other nations might follow suit more rapidly. All the Central European countries were in need of economic and political guidance and financial aid; estimates of such support approached $30 billion a year, for up to four years. This amount was projected to make a significant difference in whether or not a country could establish a capitalistic state. As one of the first to obtain U.S. support, Poland was receiving $1 billion in economic assistance from Congress, with another $736 million set aside to help both Poland and Hungary. This U.S.–Polish alliance culminated in a State Visit by Prime Minister Tadeusz Mazowiecki in late March 1990.

Upon Mazowiecki's arrival, President Bush held a State Dinner in his honor. At the ceremonial affair, Bush recalled his last trip to Poland (the previous summer) and repeated something he had said at that time: "Once more Poland holds its destiny in its hands. The time has come that Poland can live in freedom and for Europe to be whole and free." On the day following the dinner, in the March 22, 1990, *Washington Post,* a commentary by Donnie Radcliffe and Barbara Feinman described the occasion. Surprisingly, there were more annotations about the cuisine than interpretations of policy. Comments regarding the President's dislike for one particular vegetable abounded:

> Holding forth in the Blue Room after the meal, President Bush stood his ground. "I do not like broccoli," he said, adamant despite broccoli growers' 10-ton shipment of the vegetable to Washington in protest of his earlier comment that henceforth Air Force One would ban broccoli from its menu. When asked what he would do with the broccoli headed here, he turned to Barbara Bush, standing nearby, and said it was her problem. The First Lady, who often admonishes her husband, "Now George, eat your vegetables," rose to the bait when asked if she likes broccoli. "You're darn right I do. I love broccoli. We're going to have broccoli soup, broccoli main dish, broccoli salad and broccoli ice cream," she said.

At this juncture in his presidency, the real problem for Bush was that his administration appeared to be running too harmoniously. With the confidence level so high, I contend that President Bush forgot to remain on guard. However, visible trouble occurred on March 8, 1990. What was seen then as a "personal" crisis (an aide's health) would become something far greater.

On March 8, while making a speech in a hotel in downtown Washington, Lee Atwater suddenly collapsed and was taken to the hospital. Afterward, he told everyone that it was "nothing" and that his tests were inconclusive.

No one was in better shape physically than the thirty-nine-year-old Atwater. He had never been sick a day in his life. He never missed a day jogging. He needed little sleep. In general, he was a health freak.

Until March 8, 1990.

Shortly after March 8, Atwater admitted to having a small, non-malignant growth. The media crews staked out his hospital and discovered the truth: a massive, inoperable tumor on the right side of his brain. It was the worst news one could get: a grade-4 brain tumor.

In typical Atwater style, the hardball campaign leader chose the most aggressive medical treatments offered, dousing himself with large amounts of radiation and steroids, but he paid a price for trying to have "one more day." Ten holes were drilled into his head. His body swelled to twice its normal size, and all his hair fell out. Lee no longer looked like Lee. From pictures I saw, he was unrecognizable.

But this did not stop Atwater. He just kept on going and going, like the Energizer bunny, a testament to his internal strength and determination. A brain tumor was not going to stop him. Not yet.

What kept him wanting to believe in medical miracles—besides his wife, two little girls and a baby on the way—was his job as RNC chairman. He still saw himself as the Big Man on Campus. I remembered—as I often did—the Atwater quote published in the *Christian Science Monitor* on April 17, 1988, by political editor Steve Neal: "People say if Bush wins, I'll be chief of staff or something. No way. I've done the White House thing. There's nothing there for me. I've done it once. I just want to keep doing races until I can't do them anymore." I had been there in the trenches with Atwater before the '88 games really started, and had witnessed his management of the campaign for over a year. He knew how to "do" races.

Atwater did not need the aura of the White House to experience the ecstasy of power. This man, with his uncanny ability to sniff out what was politically significant—along with all his craziness and crassness—was a man of earthy charm who made a difference in how the big picture of politics was painted and played.

Politics *was* Atwater.

Now his capacity to strategize, spin and seduce was severely limited by the horrific disease. I thought the time would come when Lee would admit that fighting for his life was all he could manage. But he didn't. For months, he would not give up the fight for his life *or* his RNC chairmanship. At nearly forty, Atwater had lived the life of an eighty-year-old, he had packed as much into his half life as was humanly possible. He knew what made him tick. He knew his passions and obsessions. Always in motion, always moving, twitching, and fidgeting, Lee thought and spoke faster than anyone I knew. A 45-RPM record played at 78 speed. Maybe that is why he died so young; he lived at twice the normal rate.

Lee had missed little along the way. As the "most devoted soldier" to George Bush, he could not be replaced. There was only one head of the troops. Those of us who believed in George Bush believed in Lee Atwater. We needed Atwater now and for the 1992 reelection. I had already imagined what it would be like hearing him talk about the second-round campaign. A chance to do it again!

In March 1990, Atwater's metastasized cancer not only diminished his own strength, it weakened the entire Bush administration and the Republican Party. Looking back, it was more than just a coincidence that as soon as Atwater became ill, the White House began a slow but perceptible demise. I experienced a sense of apprehension as I reread an article by William Safire in which he reminded his readers that history often repeats itself.

In the November 10, 1988, *New York Times* (two days after Bush had won), in "The Voter's Message," Safire wrote: "The last sitting Vice President to win the Presidency, Martin Van Buren, lasted only one term; and the last time the Republican Party won the White House for the third time in a row, it nose-dived into 1932."

Bush's presidency was the first since 1837 in which the standing Vice President had assumed the presidency after eight years of his Party holding office. Having been personally groomed by Andrew Jackson to assume office, Van Buren had lost the support of the voters when he did nothing to solve the economic panic of 1837. Lacking Jackson's magnetism and personal appeal, Van Buren was unable to unite the diverse factions in the country, and lost to William Henry Harrison in 1840, to the tune of "Van! Van! is a used-up man."

The President who had won the White House for the Republicans for the third time in a row was Herbert Hoover (1928–32). An Iowa Republican and former secretary of Commerce, Hoover was elected President by the largest majority since George Washington (444 electoral votes). Just a year later, in 1929, came the economic crash and the Great Depression, and the wheels of industry stopped turning. Millions were unemployed, thousands of banks closed and thirty thousand businesses a year failed. All the while, Hoover promised, "Prosperity is just around the corner." He did not believe in federal welfare programs and held off on providing a helping hand. When the Reconstruction Finance Corporation came on the scene, it was too little, too late.

In 1932, when Hoover ran against New York Governor Franklin Delano Roosevelt, he received 59 electoral votes to Roosevelt's 472, fewer than any incumbent except for Taft. In his memoirs, President Hoover stated that he had found the Vice President to President succession "a handicap" because "he had inherited too much policy and personnel deadwood" from the previous administration.

As Safire said, "history repeats itself."

The West Wing and the OEOB, March 1989
After lunch in the West Wing with the Presidential Personnel staff.

PART 5

Acts of Courage

Whether as warrior-leader, father of his people, or protector, the president during his tenure is the living embodiment of a nation. It is not enough to merely govern well; the president must also seem presidential. He must inspire confidence in his integrity, compassion, competence, and capacity to take charge in any conceivable situation.

—*George Reedy*

★★★ ═══════ ★★★
CHAPTER
21
ROLL OUT THE RED CARPET

If you can talk with crowds and keep your virtue,
Or walk with kings—nor lose the common touch;
If neither foes nor loving friends can hurt you;
If all men count with you, but none too much . . .
—Rudyard Kipling

MAY–JUNE 1990

In December 1988, just a month after the election of George Bush, Mexico also elected a new president, Carlos Salinas de Gortari. Under his leadership, some surprising measures had begun to take place, including talk of a revolution, albeit a peaceful one. Mexico, a sleeping giant of a nation with 81 million residents, was in the throes of some major changes, and its young president was the reason. As the leader of a country where drugs and political upheaval ran rampant, Salinas had decided he was going to upgrade Mexico's second-class status. And he had called on the United States to lend a hand.

Into this climate, on May 14, 1990, Alan Dunn and I, and twenty-three U.S. oil and chemical executives, arrived in Mexico City for a five-day trade mission. It had taken us several months to get ready for the trip, and because of all the preparation, a cordial Mexican Cabinet, and an efficient American Embassy, the team would accomplish far more than had been anticipated.

Charged with assembling the briefing book for the mission, I had collected volumes of information on the men who now ruled from their capital in Mexico City. Salinas directed the charge. The soft-spoken, fifty-year-old Salinas was knowledgeable in American ways; the son of a former Cabinet minister, he had been raised as part of Mexico's elite. His father had sent him to Harvard, where he earned two M.A.s, in political economy and government, and a Ph.D. in public administration.

Like their president, most of Mexico's Cabinet members were educated at America's finest institutions, graduating from Harvard, M.I.T. and Yale. Enthusiastic and well-informed, these politicians, (who spoke fluent English) envisioned Mexico as a global market and were determined to put Mexico on the world map. Four months after my trip, in September 1991, the *Washington Post* had this to say about the Mexican leader:

> The changes that Mexican president Carlos Salinas has brought about in the first two years of his government define the profile of a leader who has learned to be on time for his appointment with history. ...In a short time, he has climbed through the government hierarchy in Mexico, to place himself at the forefront of the international scene.

Having already slashed inflation, reprivatized banks and renegotiated foreign debt during his first year in office, Salinas now proposed forging a common market with the United States. He had made a State Visit to Washington during the fall of October 1989.

Commerce Secretary Mosbacher, who was a part of the Bush-Salinas negotiations at the White House, returned from the talks and issued a memo to the International Trade Administration staff. The summary report, dated October 3, 1989, read, in part: "In demonstration of U.S. commitment to greater economic cooperation between the United States and Mexico, U.S. Secretary of Commerce Robert A. Mosbacher and Mexican Secretary of Commerce and Industrial Development James Serra Puche today signed an understanding establishing the Joint Committee for Investment and Trade (JCIT) between their two countries."

Shortly thereafter, the White House announced that the JCIT would meet semiannually in sub-Cabinet level consultations to identify trade and investment opportunities. The bilateral initiative called for a series of four Business Development Missions to Mexico City, the first scheduled for May 15, 1990. Because Mexico's domestic production of petrochemicals (goods including hundreds of products, from ammonia to xylenes) was insufficient to satisfy internal demands, it was decided that

★★★

oil would be the focus of the first trade mission. And on behalf of the Mexican government-owned oil conglomerate, Petroeos Mexicanos (PEMEX), President Salinas invited a group of American petrochemical representatives to visit. The Commerce department, housing the U.S. private sector oil authorities, was chosen as the sponsoring agency, and the office of Basic Industries (with the chemical and petroleum experts) was tapped as the supporting bureau. Dunn would head the mission and I would act as liaison to the business executives journeying with us. May 14 was our scheduled date of departure.

Beautiful, crisis-filled Mexico City was a metropolis of great contrasts. Alongside the wealth, beauty and sophistication was a capital as poverty-stricken as I had witnessed. Men and women lined the streets with nothing more to their name than the shirts on their backs; the young children who scampered at their feet wore few, if any, clothes and appeared extremely malnourished. Like their parents, they spent hours every day in the hot sun begging for money while rough-looking men armed with loaded machine guns stood alert on almost every street corner.

On the morning after our arrival, we made our way from the Maria Isabel Sheraton Hotel to our central operating hub, the U.S. Embassy. Located across the street from our accommodations, the Embassy had set up a mission control room wired for dedicated phone lines and fax machines. Our first event was a meeting with John Negroponte, the U.S. Ambassador to Mexico; after he addressed the delegation, Dunn introduced to him, one-by-one, the twenty-three American executives— an impressive line-up of men from such companies as Dow, Exxon, Eastman Chemical, Union Carbide, Ethyl and General Electric.

For five days, Mexican officials wined and dined the U.S. delegation in Cabinet offices, professional suites and some of their finest corporate headquarters. We enjoyed a five-course luncheon at a prominent downtown office building and an evening cocktail party on the twenty-fifth floor of an apartment complex. Our hosts orchestrated these lavish affairs with impeccable social aplomb and decorum, enhancing the opportunity for socializing as well as conducting business. The Bank de Serfin meeting was the most protocol-correct assembly I had attended— or would attend. A scene I would never forget.

In a skyscraper in downtown Mexico City, we gathered inside one of *the* most splendid conference rooms: recessed lighting, walls of beige raw silk, with a twenty-foot-long mahogany table and chairs in the middle of the room. Original works of art hung on the walls, as well as a theater-sized movie screen for presentations; a public address system was equipped with microphones and headsets for each person, and interpreters were stationed every six feet around the exterior of the room. Food and drink were served every fifteen minutes. Opulence abounded. Service was impeccable. Nothing was out of place or mismanaged—for three hours. We were witnessing the most lavish side of Mexico, and one could not help but be impressed.

At the meeting with Negroponte, we had received invitations to visit Salinas's Cabinet ministers in their government headquarters; and during the ensuing three days, we called on five: Secretary of Energy Fernando Hiriart, Secretary of Commerce Jaime Serra Puche, Secretary of Finance Pedro Aspe, Undersecretary of Ecology and Urban Development Sergio Reyes Lujan, and Secretary of Labor and Social Welfare Arsenio Farell.

On the evening of the second day, we met with Secretary Farell, the longest-serving Cabinet officer, having held his position since 1982. He spoke directly, citing Mexico's most significant problem with American companies to be the unwillingness of Americans to understand Mexican culture. If U.S. businesspersons were more willing to accept the customs and mores of the Mexican labor force (something as simple, for example, as recognizing Mexican holidays), he said, that would go a long way in establishing a better business climate.

After his talk, Farell opened the floor for discussion; dialogue went on late into the evening. Although some of the oilmen there that evening took issue with Farell's comments, I agreed with his perspective, having observed that Americans often wanted the world to do it "their way," overlooking the other country's rituals. I left hoping that what Farell said might somehow improve the association between American executives and their neighbors to the south.

On the last night of our stay, the U.S. officials gave a cocktail party in the Embassy ballroom. The following morning, the mission concluded with a visit to Mexico's two largest and most modern petrochemical complexes, Cangrejera and Moreles, in southern Mexico. By private plane, we flew down for a site tour, returning to Mexico City just in time to dash to the midtown marketplace and purchase some Mexican trinkets. I bought silver jewelry to take home for presents.

A month after the mission, several chemical trade magazines wrote about the U.S. trip to Mexico in glowing terms, noting that Mexico had acquired over $3 billion in U.S. petrochemical investment. The U.S. team had returned with both a financial stake in Mexico's growing oil business and several signed agreements for the purchase of American products.

In less than six months, the United States Congress would begin talking about a U.S.–Mexico Free Trade Agreement and, soon afterward, an all-encompassing North American Free Trade Agreement (NAFTA), tying together the United States, Canada and Mexico. Earlier, in 1987, the United States had concluded a Free Trade Agreement with Canada; through President Bush's efforts—and his personal relationship's with Canadian Prime Minister Brian Mulroney and Mexican President Carlos Salinas—NAFTA would ultimately come to be. Soon, many would agree that Bush was the most influential figure in building the commercial bridge to the north, with Canada, and to the south, with Mexico, making North America a truly united continent.

Nevertheless, in the short term, the accord with Mexico would become more and more problematic; in fact, NAFTA would become a blistering issue in the last two years of the Bush administration and in the 1992 campaign. At present, Mexico appeared of little interest to most of the country, while the White House focused its attention on another part of the world: the Soviet Union.

President Bush was preparing for a visit from Soviet President and Mrs. Gorbachev, who were arriving in Washington on May 30. Just over six months earlier, the two presidents had been at the Malta Summit, and eighteen months had passed since Bush had met Gorbachev on December 7, 1988, with President Reagan in New York City. For the most part, before his presidency, Bush, an observer, had stood by while Reagan had made a great "to-do" over his Soviet "friend."

Reagan, who had made campaign promises to launch a military build-up *against* the Soviet Union, radically changed his foreign policy ideas and military philosophies once in office. In 1980, the Republican Right had applauded him for his strong and tough stance with the Soviets; later, the same conservatives admonished him for conceding too much to Gorbachev. In New York, Reagan (now referred to as a "detentenik") had signed a U.S.–Soviet treaty with Gorbachev eliminating intermediate-range nuclear forces (INF). The man who had once supported a U.S. military buildup against the Communists, had made a 180-degree turn. Ultimately, he was viewed by conservatives as a coward, and they mobilized in the Senate and around the country for a full-scale offensive against him.

When Bush met Gorbachev during the fall of 1989 in Malta, at the Summit by the Sea, he was no longer shackled by the Reagan presidency and he took his time to establish a relationship with the Soviet president. The conservatives who denounced Reagan saw Bush moving in the same direction: relying on negotiation more than force. The right-wingers portrayed the Bush-Gorbachev tie as a disgrace to the American way, and described Bush's public embrace of Gorbachev as indicative of a "crumbling coalition of the ideological conservatives and main-stream Republicans."

Although the relationship between Bush and Gorbachev spurred negative reactions, the overwhelming response to their 1990 Washington meeting was positive, mostly due to the optimistic views reported in U.S. newspapers regarding the revolutionary changes taking place in the Soviet bloc. Despite public demonstrations held on the streets of D.C. during Gorbachev's visit, pollsters found that 73 percent of Americans had a positive impression of him. A stunning shift in opinion regarding the ruler of the once "Evil Empire." On several occasions, Gorbachev stepped out of his Zil limousine to touch the crowds as he toured the nation's capital. The press reported him as appearing "more than mortal" and "almost heroic."

On the evening of Thursday, May 31, just two weeks after the Mexico City trip, President and Mrs. Bush hosted a State Dinner in honor of the Gorbachevs, one of the most lavish affairs of the Bush presidency. The extensive guest list printed in the *Washington Post* included Vice President and Mrs. Quayle, most of the Cabinet members and their wives, presidential politicos, several Democrats, corporate CEO's, news commentator Tom Brokaw, actors Jessica Tandy and Morgan Freeman, and the Reverend Billy Graham, to name a few.

A banquet was served in the State Dining Room, the most elegant room in the Executive Mansion. Encircling the room, round tables were set for ten and filled with the best of everything—china, silver, crystal, candles, and arrangements of fresh-cut flowers. The center of the room was reserved for dancing after dinner. Close to the table where

President and Mrs. Bush sat was a large fireplace, and carved into its mantle was an inscription taken from a letter written by John Adams in 1880 on his second night in the White House: "I Pray Heaven to Bestow the best of Blessings on THIS HOUSE and on all that shall hereafter inhabit it. May none but Honest and Wise Men ever rule under this Roof." Over this mantle hung a portrait of Abraham Lincoln, painted in 1869 by George P. A. Healy.

The day following the dinner, Gorbachev met with Bush at the White House to begin formal discussions on atomic energy, intellectual property rights, most-favored nation (MFN) trade status, chemical weapons, and cultural exchanges. A signed accord would take place before Gorbachev left Washington.

Despite his present popularity in the U.S., the international press wrote about Gorbachev as a "doomed" man. As head of state since 1985, he was out of favor in his own country; Soviets were angry with their deteriorating economic situation. It was reported that political turmoil had seized Russia, and the newly elected president of the Russian Republic, Boris Yeltsin, one of Gorbachev's former protégés, was speaking out against the Soviet president.

On the Friday evening following the State Dinner, the Gorbachevs, who had flown their best china into Washington from Moscow, hosted a dinner for President and Mrs. Bush at the Soviet Embassy, and on Saturday morning, the two world leaders departed by helicopter to Camp David, while their wives traveled by plane to Wellesley, Massachusetts.

Barbara Bush and Raisa Gorbachev were to give the graduation speech at Wellesley College, an all-female institution. Earlier, there had been concern about Mrs. Bush not having graduated from college (she had left Smith in her freshman year to marry her husband), and some of the students had protested her appearance. Later, the problem was resolved and the two First Ladies were graciously welcomed. The *Washington Post* published the full text of Mrs. Bush's speech, in which she made three suggestions to the graduates: believe in something larger than oneself; find joy in life, and cherish relationships with family and friends. Mrs. Bush challenged the young women of Wellesley to realize their own personal dreams, not society's. Mrs. Gorbachev, who had received her doctorate in philosophical sciences from Moscow State University, reportedly "charmed" the Wellesley graduates, as she did most of her Western audiences. Bright, fashionable and articulate, she never had been that well received at home; the Soviets resented the fact that she had carved out a public/political role for herself.

Finally, on Sunday, June 3, the Gorbachevs and their 250 aides left Washington. Escorted by 35 U.S. security vehicles, the local SWAT team and an air shield of Secret Service helicopters, they made their way to Andrews Air Force Base for their flight back to Moscow. Upon conclusion of the Summit, the media proclaimed the East-West rendezvous an historic achievement, describing Bush "as astute and as articulate as they could remember" . . . his "reasonableness" seeming to "transform" Gorbachev. An article in the *Washington Post* explained the state visit this way: "The leaders are tackling different and sensitive subjects, touching the vital interests of their countries. Not that Mr. Bush is unmindful of political pressures at home, but the fact is, moreover, that the Soviet Union is in tumultuous internal transition—so tumultuous as to have finally reduced Mr. Gorbachev, in America's eyes, to the proportions of a mortal politician."

Unfortunately for the Soviet President, he had to return to Moscow.

★★★ ══════ ★★★

CHAPTER

22

FLIPPIN' AND FLOPPIN'

For Ptolemy, the great Egyptian astronomer, the earth was the center of the universe. But Copernicus created a paradigm shift, and a great deal of resistance and persecution as well, by placing the sun at the center. Suddenly, everything took on a different interpretation.

—Stephen Covey

MAY–JUNE 1990

Of all the newspapers in the country, the *Washington Post* ranked fifth. In terms of circulation, it fell below the *Wall Street Journal, USA Today,* the *Los Angeles Times,* and the *New York Times.* However, and as noted previously, for those of us in Washington, there was a tendency to think the *Post* was gospel. Devoted readers felt fairly sure they were well-informed of events both in and out of the capital city, and strange as it may sound, more often than not, life was lived according to the articles written in the *Washington Post.*

No one would dare start his or her day without reading the *Post.* A symbiotic bond between presidential politics and news reporting gave the *Post* influence beyond the usual scope of exposure. In fact, we "on the inside" would not have known what was happening "on the inside" without it. No one wanted to be out of the loop when attending the 8:00 staff meeting.

Habitually, each morning, I devoured four papers: the *Post,* the *Washington Times, USA Today,* and the *New York Times,* before my first cup of coffee. Since working in research at the campaign and the Republican National Committee, I had acquired a passion for getting the latest news the soonest.

273

Then there were those infrequent times when one mistakenly assumed that if the *Post* did not cover "it," then "it" was not important. Such was the case in June 1990, with Bush and the tax issue. Tax concerns had been an up-and-down item since pre-election days. Right after the win, the *Washington Times* on November 10, 1988, published Ralph Z. Hallow's article, "Bush Seeks Help of Congress to 'Obtain Will of the People.'" An excerpt read:

> The issue of taxes, the federal budget, and trade deficits are expected to be a major, ongoing point of contention between the new president and Congress next year. But yesterday Mr. Bush reiterated his determination not to raise federal taxes, implying he would wield his veto power to counter major new spending proposals that require tax increases. "I'm talking about holding the line on taxes and I don't plan to deviate," he said.

Since the time Reagan speechwriter Peggy Noonan had included the tax phrase in Bush's candidate announcement in October 1987, Bush had continued to vow "no new taxes." The slogan received top billing throughout Bush's campaign trek. And as presidential nominee, from the convention floor, Bush authoritatively reiterated his promise to America. The *New York Times*, on November 11, 1990, printed "Challenges for Bush: An Uncertain Agenda and a Wary Congress," in which R. W. Apple, Jr., wrote:

> Money will be a central problem. The Vice President made ironclad promises during his campaign that he would not raise taxes. Indeed, he promised to cut capital gains taxes. And he made those pledges so often and so vividly—"read my lips," he would say in his best Clint Eastwood manner—that Republicans concede that he would destroy his credibility if he changed his mind, at least in the first phase of his administration.

Michael Boskin, Bush's chairman of the Council of Economic Advisors (CEA) was adamant against raising taxes. In the *Times* on December 7, 1988, he stated, "I am absolutely convinced in my heart of hearts that the budget deficit can be brought under control without a tax increase and that the surest, safest way to get the budget deficit under control is to slow the growth of government spending."

In the role of CEA leader, Boskin's job was to ignore politics *per se* and focus on what was economically good for the country; his financial assessments were crucial in assisting Bush in trying to determine fiscal policy. Boskin believed in the "flexible freeze" approach that advocated spending growth only at the rate of inflation except for certain exempted programs such as Social Security. This, Boskin crowed, would reduce federal spending by nearly $60 billion. *Without* a tax increase. And the deficit would be cut in half by 1993.

Immediately following the '88 election, there had been dire predictions about what would happen should Bush reverse his decision; nevertheless, on June 26, 1990—just seventeen months into his presidency—Bush broke his campaign pledge not to increase taxes. The strange thing was that he did so with almost no publicity.

The press did not immediately pick-up on the story. Those news-papers that did, attributed the President's endorsement of new taxes as little more than "a change of mind." No accusation of any wrongdoing. No explanation about what kind of tax increase was being levied. And no reference to the "read my lips, no new taxes" quote. An exception was a critique printed in the *Washington Post* the day after the tax announcement. On June 27, 1990, Wesley Pruden wrote:

> Poor Marlin Fitzwater, looking like the man sent out to announce that the warden had accidentally executed the priest instead of the prisoner, couldn't bring himself to answer the usual questions about what the president actually meant by what he had said. "We are not willing to give it any definition," Fitzwater said. "That's a matter for the negotiators." He'll never persuade prospective allies again that he'll fight for anything. Overnight, he transformed the party of tax-cutting into the party of the big double-cross.

Bush often stated that he wanted to work with the Democrat-controlled Congress, yet during his four-year term, he would use his veto power forty-six times to stop its legislation. He had experienced the lingering wrath of the opposition Party with his Tower nomination. For the first six years of the Reagan presidency, the Democrats had been overstepped and outvoted by the Republican-ruled White House, time and time again. And their feeling was that Bush had gotten off too easy in the Iran-Contra Affair *and* had mistreated Michael Dukakis in the final months of the 1988 campaign.

Unlike the years between 1981 and 1987, beginning in 1988, the Hill—*not* the White House—was the powerhouse. In the 1988 Congress, 99 percent of the 408 incumbents seeking reelection in the House were brought back; in the Senate, a single Democrat incumbent was defeated while the GOP lost three seats. At the state level, the Democrats had picked up one governorship, outnumbering Republicans twenty-eight to twenty-two.

After Bush had been elected, Bob Dole was quoted as saying that, with the Congressional imbalance, "Bush was in for a battle," and on the morning after the election, he said, "This situation is going to spell trouble right from day one for George Bush." In the *New York Times* on November 11, 1988, R. W. Apple wrote, "The division of power portends at best a protracted struggle, at worst a stalemate."

Having been convinced by his own staff to raise taxes, President Bush appeared weak, but more importantly, he had broken the trust between himself and the American people. The ultimate political blunder.

Should Lee Atwater not have been suffering from brain cancer, I am convinced he *never* would have let Bush make this move. The RNC Committee chairman and number-one political strategist would not have let the President back off from his campaign pledge. Bush had given his word. That was sacrosanct. Under no terms would Atwater have let Dick Darman (who converted John Sununu) covertly talk Bush into giving the Democrats that win. Never.

But, Atwater was not there to marshal the President from Harm's Way. In June 1990, he was fighting for his life and was outside the political mainstream. In fact, he had been out of the decision making circle and off the Power Pyramid for months.

In Atwater's absence, there was only one other person who could have looked out for Bush during this critical time: Jim Pinkerton, deputy assistant to the President for policy planning, a high-status job, reporting to Roger Porter (economic and domestic policy director). In early 1989, Pinkerton had taken some of the other campaign researchers with him to the OEOB. All these "policy guys" were talented, yet none were brighter than Pinkerton, the researcher who wrote the substantive stuff for his boss, Atwater. The Californian and conservative issues junkie had credentials, smarts, and Atwater's okay. In 1988, Pinkerton had delivered the furlough, the American Civil Liberties Union (ACLU), Boston Harbor, and the Pledge of Allegiance to Atwater, all *the* key issues of the campaign.

★★★

With his nose for what could make-or-break a presidential candidate, Pinkerton *had* to have known that, if Bush went back on his promise of no-new-taxes, it would shatter his presidency. Pinkerton also would have known that without issues showing Bush as a "man of the future"—a visionary—he never would be reelected.

I was interested in following the newspaper articles about Pinkerton, and after the tax reversal and Atwater's continued illness, I concluded that somehow he had been taken out of the Bush circle of influence. Early on. And at someone's urging.

In the winter of 1990, Pinkerton had written a thesis, "The New Paradigm," in which he proposed a program outlining ways Bush could lead the country forward. "Paradigm" comes from the Greek word meaning a model, theory, or frame of reference, and was originally used as a scientific term to describe the way humans see the world, not in the visual sense, but in perceiving, understanding and interpreting. Bush was disparaged for his inability to deliver a clear message about the future. Pinkerton's paper had been designed to change that.

On April 13, 1990, Donald Lambro, chief political correspondent of the *Washington Times,* referred to Pinkerton in his article "A New Paradigm for Bush":

> What he has done here is to take a variety of emerging political, economic and social movements and ideas and bring them together into one cohesive philosophical structure—a structure that can give some identifiable shape and vision to Mr. Bush's proposals and offer a blueprint for creating new ones. It is exactly what Bush needs at this juncture in his presidency.

The "visualization thing" was important, and, no doubt, Pinkerton's treatise could have served as the bridge between Bush, who *wanted* to talk about his principles and convictions, and a country that was eager to listen. However, Pinkerton's blueprint, giving Bush a platform upon which he could unite America, never did what it was intended to do. One of the reasons was that Pinkerton worked for a man with little authority in White House circles.

Roger Porter was the White House domestic policy advisor, and his influence—or lack thereof—was similar to Demarest's in the communications office and. Under Porter's authority (assistant to the

President for economic and domestic policy) were two powerful Cabinet councils: the domestic policy council and the economic policy council. If the number-one command position in the White House is chief of staff, then Porter held the number-two position. His responsibilities were all encompassing with infinite possibilities for expansion. Under his directorship came *all* the government agencies except for the National Security Council, State, Defense and the CIA.

Because Porter was deficient in interest, ability or finesse—or all three—he never took charge of his office, and while reminiscing about his days as an aide in the Nixon/Ford White House, he rested on his laurels (few though they were) and became enmeshed in petty, showy details rather than focusing on the presidency. As a result, strategy from his office never was forthcoming.

The office that was responsible for making all domestic policy (the one Meese held when Baker was chief of staff to Reagan and Darman held with Baker) was almost an unknown while Bush was President, and those who worked for Porter, such as Pinkerton, never had a chance to inspire or affect the administration the way they should have. And too, in the Bush White House, it would have taken a strong individual to mold the job of domestic advisor into one of influence, most significantly because the senior aide (in this case Porter) would have had to wrestle his responsibilities away from the man who had seized them. The appointed person would have had to enjoy doing battle with one of the most powerful men in the Bush White House, quite possibly *the* most powerful: Richard Darman, director of the OMB. The budget guy.

During the days of the Reagan White House, while under the tutelage of Baker, Darman led the Legislative Strategy Group, *the* authoritative policy voice in Reagan's administration. As dictated by Baker in the 1980 pre-inaugural Meese agreement, the Cabinet councils, which fell under the purview of Meese, were purely token, without any ability to legislate. For four years, Darman, as deputy to Baker, overshadowed Meese. In the Bush administration, Darman, as director of the Office of Management and Budget, did the same with Porter. Only this time it was easier.

Meese had been one of President Reagan's upfront soldiers; Porter came with no such credentials. Still, as a member of the Nixon/Ford group, Porter was not unidentified when appointed to the top policy job;

★★★

Baker had known Porter by virtue of having been Ford campaign manager in 1976. My guess is that Baker realized Porter lacked qualifications and appointed him for just that reason.

Darman, as Bush's budget director, assumed the same unilateral control in 1989 that he had in 1981, deciding that he, not Porter, would take on the role of domestic policy advisor. Darman easily usurped the responsibilities of Porter (and his Cabinet councils), just as he did Sununu. However, he would have to put forth a little extra effort when it came to subduing Pinkerton. A feud between Darman and Pinkerton was to be expected. On December 5, 1990, on the front page of the Style Section of the *Washington Post*, "The Idea Man With A 'Vision Thing,'" by E.J. Dionne, Jr., described the Darman-Pinkerton tussle this way:

> When one of Washington's most formidable political figures goes after a junior White House aide when their struggle is over *ideas*—not just over office space or staffing—and when top members of Congress defend not the big guy but the junior aide, you know something important is going on. That's the story of Washington's newest imbroglio, a turf battle of the most elevated sort. It's about defining the zeitgeist of the Bush years. On the one side: Richard Darman, President Bush's budget director, one of this city's premier inside operators, someone who bids regularly for the title of "the smartest man in town." On the other side: James P. Pinkerton, deputy assistant to the president for policy planning, who is bidding for his place in history with something he calls "the New Paradigm," a free-market, anti-bureaucratic approach to public policy that he would like to see displace the more artfully named "New Deal."

This article confirmed my suspicions.

Whether or not Pinkerton could have made a difference in the Bush administration with his "New Paradigm" is not the main issue here; the fact that he never *got the chance to try* is.

WHILE the Darman-Pinkerton dispute was going on, my boss, Alan Dunn, made a move in the Trade Development division to the office of Science and Electronics (S&E). I left Basic Industries and joined him. It was a step up for both of us.

The S&E group (about sixty-five members) was impressive. With strong technological backgrounds, they worked on some of the most sophisticated projects and papers in government, and were referred to by others in Commerce as the "sexy" division. Because the staff dealt with trade policy involving many of the high-tech issues, they had under their domain many of the issues that Mosbacher prematurely claimed when he first became secretary.

The office directors reporting to Dunn were Jack McPhee, director of computer and business equipment; Jack Clifford, director of microelectronics; and Roger Stechschulte, director of telecommunications—all three had reputations for knowing their stuff. Throughout the first few weeks in the office, Dunn and I sat through briefings that amounted to a crash course in Technology 101: subjects related to computer systems and computer chips; electronics and software programs; semiconductors, satellites and telecom services.

McPhee, Stechschulte and Clifford were known well enough in the private sector to attract the attention of some senior executives in the corporate arena. On one occasion, representatives of Motorola came to Commerce to enlighten our staff on the Iridium project—years before the company invested $750 million in the multi-nation satellite network. Whether it was Motorola's plan for a seventy-seven satellite cellular phone network, or IBM's new generation of Enterprise System 9000 mainframes (costing up to $22.8 million apiece), the S&E staff kept up with America's cutting-edge projects, and I had the opportunity to meet some of those who were designing them.

Just as I was settling into my job at S&E, the White House announced that 90 percent of all political positions had been filled, but that eighty thousand applications still remained in the hopper. In the August 6 *White House Bulletin*, Ron Kaufman, deputy director of presidential personnel, was asked: "If you could shout one thing from the mountaintop to people seeking political appointments, what would it be?" In response, he answered, "Don't call me. Just kidding. Patience is important. Be persistent, but not overbearing. People who are overbearing and don't get jobs probably shouldn't get jobs. I have found that if you truly want to work for the Administration, and are willing to be open about what you want to do, then there is probably a place for you at some point in the remaining seven years."

As previously pointed out, Ron Kaufman (brother-in-law of Andy Card, Sununu's deputy), reported directly to Untermeyer and served in a lateral position to Ross Starek. His effort to look out for Bush supporters over the past year and a half had been negligible, and the "cause" of the Bush loyalists had been lost. Even if Kaufman had attempted to place a Bush team, Starek would have easily outmaneuvered him. In the Reagan presidency, Baker had taken on so much authority that he unilaterally controlled the staffing of the White House *and* the thirteen principal agencies, many of Baker's people were now in the Bush administration.

Starting in 1981, Baker had placed his cronies in key positions throughout the executive branch, with a contact in every bureau. This network enabled him to set the Reagan agenda—whether with the Congress or with the Cabinet—and execute policy the way *he* desired. Overriding the authority of Reagan's Cabinet members—even to place their own undersecretaries, assistant secretaries and deputy assistant secretaries—Baker managed to appoint the person who was most advantageous to *his* job of monitoring and managing the presidency.

Although this aspect of the Reagan presidency has often been overlooked, some writers have occasionally remarked on the staffing of Reagan's administration. A book that points out the infiltration of White House–directed nominees in that administration is Hedrick Smith's *The Power Game.* One paragraph in particular is most revealing:

> It was in the realm of political appointments that the Reagan White House penetrated most deeply into the province of cabinet secretaries. Presidents such as Nixon, Ford, and Carter had a process for reviewing high-level political appointments, but in practice left much discretion to cabinet secretaries in filling sub-cabinet positions. The Reagan White House aggressively centralized the appointment process. It insisted on the litmus of Reaganite conservative ideology, pushed names from Reagan's conservative movement onto cabinet secretaries, and required White House political screening of all appointees. Out of roughly three thousand high-level appointments, earlier administrations were content to review about one tenth; the Reagan team reviewed and approved the full slate, often causing long delays that left agencies decapitated and thus even more susceptible to control. In the process they provided the White House with a political network for monitoring and managing the executive branch.

Those appointees from 1981 were still in place in 1989 and 1990; that is why the Bush Loyals were seldom seen in the appointment mainstream. With Baker's and Fuller's help, in the crucial seventy-three days of the Bush transition, Starek and his workforce had maximized their plan to remain in control of personnel. Nevertheless, at the eighteen-month point of every administration, a predictable turnover begins, and this was true in the Bush years. Some of the casualties were anticipated; others were not.

One of the more fated was that of Education Secretary Lauro Cavazos, the first Hispanic ever to be on a President's Cabinet. As the former president of Texas Tech University, Cavazos had joined the Reagan administration as secretary in September 1988, a month before the Bush victory. With a temperament the opposite of the man he replaced (outspoken conservative William Bennett, the Bush "drug czar"), Cavazos was described as a quiet man, and in the fall of 1988, having just started his appointment, he campaigned for Bush in Texas, California, Colorado and Arizona. In fact, he had been with Bush in Houston for a fundraiser the day after being sworn in to the Reagan Cabinet.

While proclaiming himself as the Education President, Bush had proposed that parents should be able to choose the public schools their children attended, a reform, he believed, that would contain minimal costs to the federal government. He also vowed to wipe out illiteracy, expand education programs and increase education spending. Cavazos followed the President's lead, citing a need for the plan Bush had outlined, by pointing to the deficiencies of American students. On December 6, 1988, at the Council of Scientific Society Presidents, Cavazos stated, "Science and mathematics achievement of American students is truly dismal, and can be blamed in part on inadequate instructional time, poor textbooks, and improperly trained teachers. The nation is facing a shortage of a half-million scientists and engineers by the turn of the century."

When it came to supporting the Bush agenda, Cavazos was well-intentioned, but that was not enough to remain on the Cabinet. Loyalty to President Bush was rarely rewarded. For anyone. In Cavazos's case, during the first eighteen months of the administration, he was blamed for the President's inability to advance educational issues—a failure that the press pointed out was impairing the American educational system. Moreover, it was rumored that because Cavazos had never learned how to "play the Washington game," he was a liability to the President. Most of this grumbling came from the Reagan appointees who had begrudgingly resigned from their positions at Education in 1989, with Cavazos's encouragement.

A strong advocate of Bush, even during the Reagan years, Cavazos had not always followed the so-called Reagan doctrine, and he shared the President's belief that "new people can be invaluable in reinvigorating and revitalizing quality government, bringing with them new perspectives and fresh ideas." When it came time to staff the Bush administration, the secretary had no difficulty asking for the resignations of the Reagan appointees at Education. Now having been judged inept and not charismatic enough, Cavazos was forced to tender his own resignation. It would be my guess the decision was orchestrated by someone other than Bush.

Another Cabinet member nudged out of office was the Energy secretary, James D. Watkins. Like Cavazos, Watkins had difficulty convincing the White House that he should stay. During the Reagan administration, the retired admiral was at the Pentagon as chief of naval operations. A former nuclear engineer and a committed Catholic, Watkins had moral qualms about the doctrine of deterrence with the Soviet Union, and he had viewed the MX land-based missile system as ineffective. Eventually, Watkins, with the other chiefs of staff, led the way for a strategic space defense initiative (*against* ICBM's—intercontinental ballistic missiles) that was non-nuclear, similar to the Strategic Defense Initiative (SDI) Reagan favored. Bush's Energy secretary favored a new technology missile defense rather than an offensive land-based rocket exchange, and in his first year in office, Watkins proclaimed he would transform the culture of the nation's nuclear weapons manufacturing plants by placing safety over production. Supporting Bush's views.

At Watkins's formal swearing-in ceremony on March 9, 1989, Bush made reference to Reagan having wanted to dismantle the Energy department and was quoted in the next day's *Washington Post* as saying: "You are on the cutting edge now, and this department is here to stay. The most pressing challenge is to manage the modernization of America's nuclear weapons complex. We need to clean up the pollution that's been created at these plants."

Early on, Watkins, following Bush's lead, obtained favorable press. He also received Congressional approval for his environmentally progressive ideas. However, Admiral Watkins was in a double bind.

Written in his job description were directives that made him responsible for the manufacturing and delivery of all weapon systems approved by the White House. Under that requirement, he was *not* to stop or slow down nuclear weapons production. To keep assembly running on schedule, it would be impossible for Watkins to introduce the new safety measures he had been touting. Faced with this dilemma, he was pressured by someone to pay less heed to environmental laws, particularly those involving waste cleanup compliance. Soon, Watkins, in a complete reversal, was attending to weapons production, forgetting his original plea for environmental cleanup procedures. Coincidentally, in 1990, the nuclear power industry employed more than one hundred thousand people nationwide. This statistic, when combined with the vigor of the Republican conservatives in and out of the Bush White House (particularly Richard Cheney, who loved every kind of weapons program), may have had something to do with Watkin's turnaround.

Quite blatantly, Watkins was pushed off the Political Ladder, and reading from scripted lines, he told a *Washington Post* reporter, "We were a little naive about how difficult it would be to change operations and attitudes that have prevailed in the nuclear complex for forty years." Someone had to take the fall. This time it was Watkins.

Despite Bush's plan to "clean up the pollution that's been created at these plants," nuclear defense related issues took precedence over environmental ones. The department of Defense won the battle with the Energy department (as it had with Commerce), and this reversal of Bush's previous agenda substantiated the growing impression of an indecisive and non-environmental President.

OVER the summer months, while the *Washington Post* ran several unflattering articles on Cavazos and Watkins (just before they left their posts), Vice President Quayle also suffered image problems. As he always had. It seemed odd to me that Dick Darman, the ultra-liberal, had been the one to select William Kristol, the ultra-conservative, to be Quayle's chief of staff. The Vice President's beliefs ran more middle of the road. Quayle's press secretary, David Beckwith, now made the problem worse. Having decided that the media had never properly met Quayle in New Orleans, Beckwith devised a plan whereby reporters, editors and bureau chiefs would have full access to the Vice President whenever they wanted.

Quayle was continually thrust in front of the media with no prepping; not rehearsing before taking the public stage is disastrous. The more the public and press saw of Quayle, as orchestrated by Beckwith and Kristol, the more they had to criticize. A sampling of Quayle's bad image was put forth in "Dan Quayle's Defensive Lineman: Press Secretary David Beckwith, Tackling the Image Problem," published in the *Washington Post:*

> David Beckwith has a tough job, some would say the toughest in town: trying to turn around the image of the most ridiculed public figure in Washington. After 16 months as Dan Quayle's press secretary, the lanky, intense former Time correspondent never figured he'd still be struggling to put the best face on the vice president's misstatements and misadventures.

As already recounted, Beckwith had a strong legal and political background, having covered the Watergate hearings, the Reagan White House and the Bush 1988 campaign; he certainly should have had more expertise when presenting Quayle. The blame for Quayle's atrocious press always seemed to fall in Quayle's lap, not Beckwith's. The press secretary always managed to make himself the "one everyone felt sorry for."

Finally, Beckwith came up with the idea to stage verbal assaults on the media so that he could accuse them of writing uncomplimentary articles. By harassing reporters such as Maureen Dowd of the *New York Times*, Howell Raines, the *Times* bureau chief in Washington, and Ann McDaniel, staff correspondent with *Newsweek,* Beckwith drew more attention to himself than to Quayle, making positive headline news for himself, not for the Vice President.

A March 1990 Gallup poll reported that 54 percent of the public did not believe Quayle was qualified to be President, and 49 percent thought Bush should select a new running mate in 1992. Still, Bush never considered anyone other than Quayle, and he stood firm.

That decision may not have been the smartest one, but the President's loyalty appeared to be the determining factor. Bush remained faithful to his number-two man; however, he had not supported Teeley, Malek, Mosbacher, Cavazo or Watkins.

How can these dismissals be explained?

My interpretation is that loyalty, because it inherently involves priorities, makes for a rank-listing if need be, and Bush placed Baker (and Baker's flock) at the top of his list. Supporting Quayle was representative of one of those times Bush made a decision based on *his* terms, not Baker's. Baker hated Quayle. But, Bush *was* President, and he could and would choose his own vice president. Of course, in the "tit for tat" mode, Baker saw to it that Quayle (who, I believe, threatened Baker, as did Mosbacher) would never rise to his potential. Moreover, Quayle would never get anywhere near the Power Pyramid.

I think Bush understood what precipitated Cavazos and Watkins's firing, just as he had Mosbacher's demotion, and I doubt he liked it. He agreed to these decisions for one reason: someone more powerful than Mosbacher and Watkins and Cavazos had bullied him. As loyal as Bush appeared to be—to all his friends and followers—he seemed most loyal to one in particular: Jim Baker. In this relationship, Bush sold out when Baker's opinions were contrary to his own.

Baker and Bush may have been old friends, but they were dissimilar in nature and character. Their priorities were different: Baker wanted to win—at all costs; Bush wanted to please. The problem for Bush was that it is simply impossible to follow one's heart and at the same time always please others. Caving in to another's opinion in lieu of one's own—just to keep the peace—puts one in a compromising position, and for that reason, I judge Bush to have been more in conflict with himself than with anyone else.

Men such as Baker, whose motive is to amass as much power as possible, make decisions based on what is most gainful to them and rarely consider another's perspective. Eventually, they leave friends, associates, peers and so on, when these people no longer prove useful. Accruing power is their only goal. In regard to the Bush/Baker "pleasing" versus "winning" scenario, a question comes to mind: "If Bush had not remained loyal to Baker, would he have had an equally dreadful situation on his hands?" I believe the answer is yes. Baker and the few core members at the top of the Power Pyramid had devised such a savvy and seamless network of "agents" (Reagan appointees), the Bush administration never would have been able to stand on its own. Before Bush was elected President, the Reagan Brigade (aka, Baker) had locked him out.

★★★ ═══════ ★★★
CHAPTER

23

BRUISED CHIEF OF STAFF

The great commitment all too easily obscures the little one. But without humility and warmth which you have to develop in your relations to the few with whom you are personally involved, you will never be able to do anything for the many.
—Dag Hammarskjold

FALL 1990

During the months of early and late fall, Bush was not in such a comfortable place. He was confronted with both domestic and out of country crises; the nation's attention was focused on the brewing crisis in the Persian Gulf. Iraq had invaded Kuwait in August, and it looked as though the United States of America was going to war. Just when, no one knew.

The President was beginning to see some cracks on the walls of the Oval Office. For some time, the White House domestic agenda had begun to lose its punch, and now the economy, once again, turned its head to its bad side. On top of these problems, Sununu was losing popularity, and people were beginning to wonder if he would be replaced. A year earlier, the press had reported about Sununu's "uncontrolled temper and belligerent personality." On January 10, 1990, a *Post* commentary by David Hoffman and Ann Devroy (the White House reporter I followed most closely) titled "Chief of Staff Sununu: Bush's Fiery Enforcer" stated:

> In contrast to the kinder, gentler image cultivated by his boss in his first year of office, White House Chief of Staff John H. Sununu has emerged as a bare-knuckles, partisan slugger with a volcanic temper and an aversion to conciliation and compromise. In the

name of the president, he has unleashed a fiery anger at senators and House members, often giving misleading information to reporters, and chewed out political appointees and staff aides, according to several dozen officials in government and politics.

Hoffman and Devroy went on to describe Sununu as not being either the skilled negotiator or the congressional conciliator Jim Baker had been in that position; in their opinion, Sununu had left many lawmakers with a sense that he was "looking down his nose on them."

As Chairman of the National Governors Association in 1988, Sununu had promised to help state governors regain their sovereignty and power, something he felt Washington had usurped. During the 1988 New Hampshire primary season, Sununu had pushed Bush to promise no new taxes. Yet, two short years later, the self-described staunch conservative was persuaded by Darman to reverse his original thinking and join him in advising Bush to overturn his campaign pledge. Through the lens of the Republican conservatives, Sununu had forsaken them.

Actually, it was questionable as to how much sway Sununu really had in shaping political strategy and domestic policy. Through Baker, Darman had assumed the authority in the Bush White House. He knew that to rule the presidential palace was a lot easier *with* Sununu than *without* him. Consequently, he appeared to work in unison with the chief of staff, but it was always to his benefit and on his terms.

From the day he arrived at 1600 Pennsylvania Avenue, Sununu had been kept away from the Power Pyramid. His manner was cold New England—not Washington polished. He had a cynical personality, often using practical jokes as icebreakers; in Washington, talk is smooth and charm cultivated. Sununu had neither.

Baker, Darman and Fitzwater had recognized these weaknesses in Sununu before Bush chose him as his most senior advisor, and taking advantage of Sununu's naïveté, they had dismissed him before he took office. On December 12, 1990, Devroy wrote another piece: "Citing Year of Triumph, Sununu Defends Actions." This time—eleven months after her "Fiery Enforcer" article—she quoted the chief of staff:

> Asked whether his highly publicized fights with members of Congress, party figures and other Republicans did not end up hurting the president, Sununu replied, "If the situation were as

described, I assure you, we would not have been able to put together the first multi-year budget and have the success in areas such as clean air, child care and across the board. I guarantee you that contrary to the legend, any strong statements on my part are both controlled, deliberate and designed to achieve an effect. There is no random outburst. It all is designed for a purpose."

By mid-1990, Sununu's approach was not helping matters inside or out of the Oval Office. The Republicans appeared to dislike the chief of staff even more than some of the Democrats; the Bush staffers had a big problem with the way he directed the West Wing. If it were not for the three White House alums managing his office, Sununu would have been in political trouble much sooner. Andy Card, deputy; Jim Cicconi, junior deputy; and Ed Rogers, executive assistant were The Guys who handled Sununu—whether he knew it or not.

The most senior aide, Andrew H. Card, Jr., was from Holbrook, Massachusetts, and an ardent, long-time supporter of George Bush. Andy, known for his gentle yet persuasive management style, was everyone's favorite. I had Card's name written in my September '87 "George Bush for President" campaign roster; he was a regional political director, along with Jim Wray, Lanny Griffith, Tom Hockaday, and Mary Matalin. Even back then, when you mentioned Card's name, everyone said what a great guy he was.

Card had attended the Merchant Marine Academy from 1966 to 1967, where he was a member of the naval ROTC; from there, he went on to receive a bachelor's degree in engineering from the University of South Carolina in 1971. In 1975, leaving behind a structural/design engineering career, he won a seat in the Massachusetts legislature when Michael Dukakis was in his first term as governor. Card knew Dukakis, agreeing with him on some issues.

As a fairly progressive Republican, Card had been a member of the Party since the Nixon days; he supported Bush in the 1980 presidential campaign by running his winning primary in Massachusetts. That same year, Card was a state delegate for Bush at the Republican convention. After seven years as a legislator (1975 to 1982), Card launched a long-shot campaign to win the Massachusetts Republican gubernatorial nomination. He lost to the incumbent, Dukakis. For a short time afterward, he was vice president of CMIS Corp., in Vienna, Virginia, and then in 1983, he joined the Reagan White House as special assistant for intergovernmental affairs, becoming its director, a post that gave him ties to state elected officials around the country. In 1987, joining another Bush presidential campaign, he worked with Sununu in New Hampshire to win that significant primary.

After the 1988 New Hampshire victory, Card directed opposition research for Bush-Quayle at both the campaign headquarters with Jim Pinkerton and the Republican National Committee with Don Todd. It was during this time, while I was working in research at the RNC, that I had the opportunity to have lunch with Card at the Capitol Hill Club; two other researchers joined us in the club's tavern.

Andy Card had a way about him that put me at ease... immediately. He impressed me as one of those rare gems in politics, someone who had many interests and was engaged in life beyond his work. I remember him talking about his wife, Kathleene, and his three children. Card and I were about the same age, and his children were close in age to mine; with this in common, we discussed Virginia schools and what it was like to live and work in Washington. I did not think to ask at the time, but later I was curious to know if he, being from the Boston area, had any thoughts about the Boston Harbor ad.

When the Bush administration first began, there had been talk about Card forming a political action committee and going back into Massachusetts politics. When his brother-in-law, Ron Kaufman, first arrived in presidential personnel, he had discussed the prospect of Andy running for governor. Word was, if Card left, Kaufman would leave to run his campaign. Card decided to stay, and so did Kaufman. Having spent five years in the Reagan White House had not hurt Card. He knew everyone, and everyone knew him. And he liked his job in the Bush West Wing, even if it meant defending Sununu. In the January 1, 1990, *Washington Post,* Devroy and Hoffman collaborated again, writing an article that included a quote by Card:

> "I like people, so I like to make myself available. I can have a schedule with two or three meetings taking place at the same time. This sounds hokey, I know, but I love my job. I pinch myself sometimes. He [Sununu] is not a gatekeeper as much as he is the funnel into which everything is poured . . . [Sununu] has an open door policy with a lot of unstructured time and no rigid meeting schedules. He does not like regimented meetings, either by time slot

or title, so you have legislative strategy meetings all the time when you need them, but you don't have a legislative strategy group that meets every Tuesday."

Despite the differences in style between Sununu and his senior advisor, Card's easy-to-get-along-with attitude enabled them to work together. Card maintained a sense of balance and was the nice guy everyone gravitated toward, cutting across all lines when it came to political leanings and personal disagreements. Sununu benefited from the fact that Card was "his."

Although Card had been schooled in the Reagan doctrine, his first commitment was to Bush. Like Atwater, he managed to be both ambitious and loyal, the difference being that Atwater was boisterous and enjoyed the limelight; Card was reserved and usually behind the scenes. If I could have worked with any *one* person in the Bush administration, it would have been Andy Card. I imagine quite a few appointees would have said the same thing.

The second individual on Sununu's immediate staff was Edward M. Rogers, Jr., executive assistant to the chief of staff, the man who had set up the meeting for me with the director of volunteers in September '87. The former Birmingham, Alabama, attorney had found his way to Washington by serving on Reagan's 1980 advance team; later, Atwater asked him to join Reagan's '84 campaign, working as his southeastern regional political director. In 1985, Rogers went into the office of political affairs as deputy to Atwater, and in 1987, when Atwater left to work in the 1988 Bush campaign, Rogers replaced him as director. Shortly thereafter, he united with Atwater at campaign headquarters.

In the Bush White House, Rogers was responsible for communications between Sununu and the White House staff; he was also the COS's media coordinator. Rogers was known for playing hardball (Atwater was his mentor) and for being gruff; however, even though it cost him some popularity, he did plug some of the leaks to the press and was fairly successful as Sununu's "enforcer," pouncing on an unsuspecting staffer when he saw him out of line. Rogers said of his boss, "the chief of staff does not suffer gladly those he considers inadequately prepared or intellectually inferior."

The third Sununu deputy, James W. Cicconi, held the same position as had Darman when he was deputy to Jim Baker in the Reagan White

House: director of presidential appointments, scheduling, messages and correspondence. Cicconi had a good-sized staff to help him with the massive amount of paperwork his office coordinated; one of those on his team was John Gardner, with whom I had worked while in research in '88. Cicconi, through his close ties to Baker, earlier had secured a slot on Quayle's vice presidential campaign staff, only to be fired by Quayle a short time later.

As mentioned, Baker initially brought Cicconi, the young attorney and fellow Texan, to Washington to fill the job of Cabinet secretary, later making him his aide and part of the Baker-Darman team. When Baker left the COS job in 1985, Cicconi departed as well, going into private practice with the Washington law firm of Akin, Gump, Strauss, Haur and Feld. Then when Bush won, Baker brought Cicconi back to the White House, strategically placing him as gatekeeper to the Oval Office, as the one channeling every piece of paper sent to and received from President Bush. His colleagues called him "Mr. Paperflow." On the White House organizational chart, Cicconi's job had less visibility and authority than Card's, yet, for those in the know, it was *no less* influential. The Sununu-Cicconi relationship would surely have been volatile (as might have the Sununu-Card one), except for the fact that Andy was so diplomatic and very secure in his job abilities.

In 1980, Cicconi's station (then filled by Darman) had given COS Baker his unprecedented power in the Reagan White House. In 1990, as secretary of State and working in Foggy Bottom, situated several blocks west of the White House, Baker once again had strong ties to the office of the chief of staff, this time through Jim Cicconi. "Numero uno" had not forgotten how to make relationships work for *him,* as demonstrated by the Boyden Gray-Jim Baker "Leak Story."

Having previously served as personal counsel to Vice President Bush, C. Boyden Gray, a Harvard graduate, was presently Bush's White House counsel and ethics czar. He was the son of Gordon Gray, the tobacco fortune magnate who was President Dwight David Eisenhower's chief of staff. Boyden was a member—as was President Bush—of Washington's secretive and historic Alibi Club. (My great-uncle, Admiral John (Jack) Henley Dandridge Kane was also a member, and every time I heard Gray's name, I recalled the club in which we celebrated our 1986 family reunion.)

As ethics director, Gray presided over what was referred to as the "sleaze factor," a term derived by those who observed the numerous Reagan officials accused of unethical behavior. During the fall of 1988, Bush had said he would make conduct a principal theme during his presidency; the Reaganites looked upon this initiative as a form of criticism of "their" administration. During Transition days, Gray was appointed as counsel to Bush's personal office as well as to the team at large. While I was there, Gray issued two lengthy documents, "Transition Standards of Conduct" and "Guidance on Ethical Conduct for Transition Staff." The message from his office was clear: conduct was to be taken *very* seriously.

In an effort to ensure these standards, Gray had set up a team, headed by a panel of lawyers, to screen the accused. Subsequently, regarding *his own* personal financial investments, Gray became subject to his own committee. Although the Gray story had been revealed through unsubstantiated leaks to the press, all that was needed to create a furor in Washington was the appearance of improper behavior. Convinced that he was betrayed, Gray determined the leak had come from one of Baker's people in the White House; Baker, with the reputation for being a master "leaker," used stories he sent to the press as a way to control policy as well as personnel.

Gray fought back, disclosing an account about Baker's involvement with Chemical Bank while he was Treasury secretary. Because no one interceded on Baker's behalf, the clash was taken to another level.

Angered by Gray's retaliation—as well as his lack of support from Bush—Baker made another move. He withheld from Gray (and thereby President Bush) privileged State department information concerning a recently negotiated congressional agreement that ended the Nicaragua contra fighting. Not an insignificant action: the directive went directly against the conservative cause. Always deciding where his allegiances lay based on what was most advantageous to him, Baker had no trouble in making this decision. However, by doing so he had angered the Far Right, and hurt the President—not to mention Gray. The true Reaganites (after years of fighting communism in Nicaragua) felt Baker, *and therefore Bush,* had sold them out.

Gray went on the offensive for the second time, again turning to the *New York Times.* He blamed Baker for stepping beyond his bounds by not reporting the Congressional agreement and accused him of usurping the President's authority over foreign affairs.

The White House was now in an uproar over the private-turned-public feud, and for a moment, it appeared that Baker was going to come away the loser. This is when the Baker-Cicconi alliance came into full play. Baker's third blow to Gray was the knockout.

With the support of Sununu, Baker made sure that *all* paperwork, including policy papers originally channeled through Gray's office before circulating elsewhere in the White House, were rerouted so that Gray received only legal documents. Through Cicconi, who reported to Sununu but remained loyal to Baker, Baker was able to "substantially reduce" Gray's duties and involvement in the White House organization. Essentially, the counsel's ability to influence domestic policy was dissolved, and C. Boyden Gray, having learned his lesson, I assume, never again went to the press regarding James A. Baker III.

Although those on the outside believed that Sununu was placed at the center of power in the Bush White House, I believe these three cameos of his assistants serve to show that he was not. Everything that went on inside the White House complex, outside the realm of foreign policy (Baker, Scowcroft, Cheney and Powell), had Richard Darman's (Baker's) imprint on it. Yes, Sununu was close by, but he did not rule. He was not on the Power Pyramid.

As for his informed and seasoned deputies—Card, Cicconi and Rogers—they, by virtue of Baker, remained inside the power curve. But Darman controlled White House domestic policy in the Cabinet and in the Congress. Buoyed by the ever-present Baker Factor, Darman determined the rules by which the West Wing were run. Despite his book-smarts, Sununu, not nearly as close to The Elite and outside Baker's flock, might have looked as if he were dictating policy, but usually he was not.

Those areas where Sununu loved to "stir the pot" were numerous, and the environment was among his favorites. Because of Sununu's snobish attitude, the environmental community despised him. For good reason. Sununu did not have a great deal of patience or finesse when it came to rubbing shoulders with folks such as those in the Wilderness Society. With his "I-could-care-less" attitude, the chief of staff repeatedly raised the ire of conservationists, and each time, problems for President Bush compounded.

Unexpectedly, the environmentalists had taken the country by storm in 1989. In truth, concerns surrounding the natural world had snowballed following the 1988 election, and activists had taken Bush seriously when he said he wanted to be the Environmental President. They threatened to harass him if he did not keep his word.

The White House aide responsible for environmental issues was Michael Deland, chairman of the President's Council on Environmental Quality (CEQ). As Reagan's administrator of the Environmental Protection Agency (EPA), Deland (whose quotes I included in my Boston Harbor research) had developed an excellent reputation. With his office now housed in the OEOB, Deland reported to Sununu. (All the offices within the White House complex reported to Sununu except for national security—Brent Scowcroft reported directly to Bush.) Accordingly, all environmental policy "white paper" went through the chief of staff's office before reaching the President's desk. This had its consequences.

With an engineering and science background, Sununu delighted in debating the pros and cons of environmental dogma, and he spoke heatedly as he challenged scientific data, particularly that supporting global warming. It was an intellectual game to him. Many thought Sununu had too much influence over the issue. Anyone with a differing opinion from his was regarded with disdain, and in his belligerent and argumentative manner, he showed little empathy for ecological cliques. With his condescending nature, Sununu repeatedly poked jokes at the Green People. None of this assisted Bush's campaign for ecological justice.

In Paris at the 1989 Global Economic Summit there had been a great deal of enthusiasm and optimism regarding a new era for environmental consciousness. The leaders of the seven most influential democracies in the world (the G-7) agreed that the earth's bounty was endangered and action was necessary. Almost one-half of the final Paris communiqué was devoted to environmental issues, and at the conclusion of the conference, Bush said, "This summit marked a watershed. We agreed that decisive action is urgently needed to preserve the earth" (*Washington Post*, July 9, 1990). However, since that time, protesters felt the United States had failed to follow through on its commitment, and they blamed the President (and his chief of staff) for the poor showing, accusing him of forfeiting his leadership role.

In Houston—a year later—at the 1990 Global Economic Summit there had been little interest in environmental issues. Solving Eastern

European trade concerns and finding ways to augment aid to the Soviet Union were given top priority; the world leaders did not exhibit the same level of zeal for cleanup matters. The one exception was the issue of global warming and the need for the elimination of carbon dioxide emissions from fossil-fueled power plants. The greenhouse gases that many scientists believed were causing the earth to warm were addressed with the same sense of urgency they had been previously.

Global warming disputes involved two groups: the business community (adversely affected by regulations regarding carbon dioxide) and the environmental community (wanting to preserve and protect the Earth's natural resources.) To determine the rate of planet warming, atmospheric factors—far more complex than those found in the ocean—needed to be added to the equation, taking, literally, thousands of hours on a computer to calculate. Trying to show how atmospheric variables influenced the oceans made for an almost impossible job. In short, the best global warming theories (if you could call them that) were far from convincing, and because of gaps in the studies, no one could prove anyone else *right or wrong*. This allowed one group to repudiate another's hypothesis at whim. With no scientific data to prove or disprove global warming, supposition on both sides of the debate were inconclusive. In addition, fossil fuel, having been deemed a menace only when applied to concerns about global warming, had never been classified as a pollutant under the Clean Air Act. There was no evidence to suggest the Earth's warming was detrimental to human health or that it had a negative impact on the environment. Before any conclusions could be made, much more research was necessary.

While most heads of state at the G-7 strongly supported global warming preventative measures, President Bush, with U.S. data to support him, did not. Believing that "more study" was needed to determine the causes of the greenhouse effect, Bush was not popular among environmentalists in America or with the other world leaders. He may not have been *the* Environmental President, and he may have been working from a more pro-business stance than he wanted to admit, but he *was* doing something about the nation's conservation concerns.

Regard for the safety and preservation of our natural resources was unheard of in the Reagan administration, and Bush's support for clean air legislation (in a House-Senate conference committee in 1990), and his ban

★★★

of oil drilling off the coasts of California and Florida should have earned him more recognition. In spite of the fact that he did push for reform, Bush was constantly criticized by protesters.

Often extreme in their tactics, these activists hassled Bush over global warming, the spotted owl/timber industry debate (Endangered Species Act), asbestos, off-shore drilling, carbon dioxide emissions, clean air legislation, chlorofluorocarbons (CFCs), forest devastation, marine pollution and the wetlands. Added to their list of complaints was that Bush was not doing enough to help Europe, China and the Soviet Union with *their* environmental problems. They pushed and pushed until they became annoying.

Because of the array of technological and political problems involved in these ecological efforts to preserve our land and water, the White House simply could not come up with a position that pleased everyone. I do not believe that the environmentalists and the Congress (environmentally compassionate) gave President Bush the credit he was due.

In a White House brief that crossed my desk at Commerce, I found a quote by Bush, in which I could feel his frustrations, "We cannot govern by listening to the loudest voice on the extreme of an environmental movement. I did not rely heavily on them for support in getting elected President of the United States. And I'm not going to be persuaded that I can get some brownie point by appealing to one of these groups or the other."

It is true that a presidential campaign is neither won nor lost solely on environmental issues; on the other hand, a nominee *could* win or lose based on economic conditions. Bush, who had broken his campaign promise and increased taxes, had not yet felt the ramifications of that decision. News had been diverted elsewhere during the summer months—the threat of war had taken center stage. But, before the year was over, We, The People, with righteous indignation, wanted to know what happened in regard to the "no new taxes" pledge.

★★★ ═══════ ★★★
CHAPTER
24
ALL THE KING'S MEN

If that flow'r with base infection meet,
The basest weed outbraves his dignity.
For sweetest things turn sourest by their deeds;
Lilies that fester smell far worse than weeds.
                                        —William Shakespeare

DECEMBER 1990

Since the time of Atwater's physical decline in the spring of 1990, political protocol—if you could call it that—had taken a different course. During the five months after Atwater's diagnosis, power had been realigned, and the White House had grabbed the RNC from Atwater as soon as he fell ill. Managing the upcoming races (specifically the 1992 reelection—Atwater's domain) was taken over by Sununu, leaving no one at the Committee to plan for the President's political future. During the ensuing years of the Bush administration, it became every man for himself.

Without Lee Atwater as a moderating influence, Dick Darman reigned in the Bush White House. As the friend, confidante and closest aide to Jim Baker, he served as the link between the secretary of State and the West Wing, just as Cicconi did in Sununu's office. Darman and Cicconi kept Baker fully aware of Oval Office endeavors.

By promoting the idea that any real deficit disaster was years away, Darman went ahead with his plan to revolutionize the way government spent its money. He advocated an immediate reduction in federal borrowing for things such as healthcare and retirement benefits, telling Bush that with the augmented cash flow, not only would the deficit be cut in half in five years, but as President he would control both spending and the restructuring of the federal revenue system. All this, Darman said, would come about if, and only if, Bush would make a covenant with Congress to raise taxes. In other words, break his campaign promise.

Congressional budget negotiations had started in May 1990, and a few select Democrats and Republicans had been invited to a summit at the White House. While Sununu allied himself with Republican members, Darman kept the Democrats happy. The tax increase was approved.

Then, in mid-June, Darman raised his 1991 deficit estimate to $159 billion, up from the $138 billion he had forecast a month earlier. Simultaneously, spending cuts required by the Gramm-Rudman Act forced the government to consider laying off thousands of workers. Shortly thereafter, following a Democratic leader's breakfast, Speaker of the House Tom Foley suggested to Bush that he make his tax reversal decision public. On the spot, Darman hastily drafted a version of an official statement for Bush to read to those gathered for the breakfast. Later that day, after Bush made his announcement on the Hill, there was a White House press conference in which Fitzwater delivered the news to the nation. On June 26 President Bush had announced the new tax increase.

Convinced by Darman that he was going to have control over *all* federal expenditures, Bush took the risk of breaking his campaign promise for the bigger gain. Darman had told Bush that the Democrats, having gotten their tax increase, would return the favor and quickly conclude the budget talks . . . to Bush's liking. He also declared that, although the Republicans at first might be unhappy with his move, when they saw the whole package and realized how much ground the Party had gained, they would be forgiving. Bush had counted on this happening.

In spite of the escalating deficit and having agreed to cut it by $500 billion (over five years), Bush still wanted to reduce the capital gains tax. Michael Boskin's trickle-down theory—tax breaks for the wealthy, benefiting mostly those earning $200,000 or more—was not favorably received on the Hill. Democrats such as Senate Majority Leader George J. Mitchell (D-Maine) vehemently opposed Bush's proposal, and so did many Republicans, including Robert Dole. Bush and his few congressional allies were on tenuous ground.

The capital gains tax–cut proposal, along with the unwillingness of both Republicans and Democrats to give up their federally funded programs, crushed any hopes that the White House may have had for a negotiated budget plan. Predictably, in a congressional vote, Bush was defeated, and the standard cuts—ones that came with non-resolution—were issued. Fiscal and tax issues not solved through bipartisan cooperation are looked upon as a failure on the part of the President. In Bush's case, what resulted was increased government spending, and instead of being reduced, the deficit reached its height during the summer of 1991.

Before selling President Bush on the idea to increase taxes, Darman had persuaded Sununu to buy into the plan; later, the chief of staff described Bush's decision to renege on his pledge in an article by Ann Devroy: "It was a payment of ransom to save this country's economy. Bush was forced to pay the tax ransom once. He will not be forced to pay the tax ransom again." ("Citing Year of Triumph, Sununu Defends Actions," *Washington Post,* December 12, 1990).

Although, at first, the Bush sell-out was not portrayed as a scandalous move, Bush's decision would prove to be the Achilles heel of his presidency, and Dick Darman, alone, was responsible for this tax fiasco. He was also to blame for the bungled budget debates. Raising taxes had *not* helped with solving the negotiations deadlock, and, far worse, the Republicans (and the country) never forgave Bush for the deed.

Both baffling and vile—although typical of a Darman strategy—was that, by the end of the bilateral tax negotiations, Darman *himself* decided to go *against* the tax increase—the increase that *he* initiated and that *he* sold to President Bush. Ultimately, Darman fought against Bush, saying that the President should never have "caved" to the Democrats.

As previously pointed out, twenty years earlier, Darman, under the tutelage of Elliot Richardson (known as Nixon's "Whiz Kid"), had begun his political schooling, serving in both the Nixon and Ford White Houses. Because Richardson had been secretary of four agencies—and Darman had served as his deputy—Baker's protégé had experience working at Defense, Justice, Health, Education and Welfare, and Commerce. Baker had picked Darman to be his deputy in 1980 because Darman understood better than anyone, the nature of power in Washington. He was a planner and a schemer. If Plan A did not work as he intended, Darman would devise Plan B, C and D, and if those failed, he would come up with five others. Richardson had taught him the importance of never having a defeatist attitude.

Had Darman not been so skilled and shrewd, Michael J. Boskin may have played a larger role in Bush's budgetary planning. As head of President Bush's Council of Economic Advisors (an elite group of financial experts that, in the past, had held a low profile), Boskin should have taken on a much more active role. As Bush's economic advisor, he had opposed the tax hike.

However, Boskin, with his team of twenty-four staffers (who advised only the President), also subscribed to the idea that the economy was on the decline, and he forecast that America was in for a turn for the worse. Boskin agreed with Alan Greenspan that the country was heading into a recession.

This threat of an economic downturn, having gone on for years, was enhanced during the summer of 1990 by the possibility of an increase in oil prices stemming from the Iraqi invasion. In some ways the Middle East had been a distraction from the country's economic problems, but by the fall, serious talk arose about an imminent recession, and the citizens, rather than pay attention to a President they no longer seemed to trust, chose to believe the doomsayers. They started to worry.

Acknowledging the bad news, Bush promised that he would meet with his economic advisors to discuss a strategy for settling the problem. Nothing was forthcoming, and as with other domestic issues, Bush simply did not convey he was on top of the situation. He appeared indecisive. Why? Was he a weak and uncaring president? I am not convinced of that. I think the opposite. I believe that Bush was "projected" as being aloof. Those responsible for the President's negative image were the senior staffers surrounding him.

From the time Atwater fell ill, in-house rivalries had caused turmoil in the White House. As Atwater's physical strength and political muscle diminished, Bush's ability to navigate the course weakened. Without at least one loyal advisor, the President was left in a state of uncertainty and confusion, and the aides themselves, I propose, created this situation, resulting in an unmanaged and unruly West Wing. As President, Bush was in no position to facilitate the various fighting factions within the White House, and this lack of supervision in the very organization he commanded, caused him to emerge ineffectual.

One of the individuals who enhanced this fractured and non-conciliatory environment was William Kristol, the journalist and

intellectual acting as Quayle's chief of staff. Kristol believed Bush was
insensitive to Jewish concerns and that he favored Arab oil interests over
Israeli ideals. This issue put the two at odds.

Darman had handpicked Kristol, Bill Bennett's protégé, to lead the
conservative cause, and as one of the few to be accepted into Sununu's
inner circle, Kristol had found himself in an upgraded position. Unusual
for a Vice President's chief of staff, especially one who served an
unpopular Vice President (Quayle), to cross over West Exec Avenue into
the West Wing.

Kristol had used his situation to advance the ultra-conservative
cause and build his own sphere of influence, seldom reflecting on how his
actions were affecting Quayle or Bush. Although the methods he used to
portray Quayle as a True Right Believer had not worked, his attempts to
dethrone Sununu were becoming fairly successful.

At the beginning of the administration, Kristol and Sununu enjoyed
a congenial relationship, but by the fall of 1990, they were constantly at
odds with one another. While faulting Bush for appointing an inept and
unqualified chief of staff, Kristol attacked not only Sununu, but the
President as well. Turning to the press, hoping to undermine the
administration's domestic policy initiatives, Kristol leaked stories about
Sununu and Bush. Embittered over the President's decision to renege on
his tax pledge, Kristol used the issue to wage battle with Sununu,
thinking that if he could initiate enough disparaging comments from
inside the Bush camp, it might assist him in deposing the chief of staff.

Usurpation of Sununu's position by Kristol, however, never
materialized. Once the press began reporting that Kristol had his eye on
Sununu's job, Kristol was banned from the White House. This news,
nevertheless, had led to reports of a White House in turmoil.

As often happens, once chaos erupts in one location, it appears in
another. Divisiveness and feuding, having already been absorbed into the
Bush political bloodstream many months earlier, were now openly
manifested both in the White House and at the RNC. Nothing conveyed
this situation more adroitly than when Sununu, in a surprise statement,
announced that Atwater was leaving the RNC and someone else was
being appointed chairman.

Over the summer and fall months, while Atwater underwent cancer
treatment, Charlie Black (of the public relations firm of Black, Manafort
and Stone, where Atwater was a partner) had stood in at the RNC

for Atwater. November 1990 was RNC reelection time, and Atwater optimistically declared that he soon would be capable enough to get back into the political fray. Atwater *needed* the chairmanship; having the position was helping to keep him alive. He needed to think that one day he would be back doing what he did best—running political races. But, Sununu had been plotting against Atwater. Immediately after Atwater declared he wanted to continue as chairman, it was publicized in the press that RNC fundraising had been "rather slow," and the reason cited for the sluggishness was the failed budget agreement and Bush's abandoning his no-new-taxes pledge. With bad news in hand, Sununu announced that the Committee staff would be reduced by one-third and *he* was going to run the RNC operations from his office in the West Wing.

What was unfair (uncivil) about this was that Atwater found out he was being let go in the *Washington Post*, where he also read that William Bennett had been tapped to replace him. He had not been told in advance. And neither had Bush. The President, on a week-long European/Persian Gulf trip, was spending Thanksgiving Day with the U.S. and Allied troops in Dhahran, and when the Bennett news broke (on November 19), Bush—not forewarned—had given no response. Not even Baker or Darman had been notified. It was Sununu's little surprise.

The new RNC chair, Bennett (who received a great deal of publicity for giving up smoking before taking the position) was a leading proponent of the anti-tax, pro-growth policies of the conservatives. He previously had served as Reagan's secretary of Education (Bill Kristol was his chief of staff), and as chairman of the National Endowment for the Humanities. With a doctorate in political philosophy from the University of Texas and a law degree from Harvard, Bennett, like Kristol, had been publicly critical of Bush's domestic policies. In fact, he resigned from the Bush White House sub-Cabinet position as director of the office of National Drug Control Policy for this reason. On November 8, immediately after Kristol was banned from the White House, Bennett had resigned as Drug Czar. Just days later, Sununu asked him to become RNC chairperson.

Bennett had not wanted the RNC position in the Bush administration, but Sununu had promised that he would be included in all the important senior-level White House decisions, and Bennett finally agreed. Less than a month later, though, Bennett announced he was turning the job down, "fearing it might put him in violation of the federal ethics law"—referring to his previous contacts in the White House.

With Bennett out, some time would pass before a new chairman was assigned. Meanwhile, the most important fundraising arm of the Republican Party was left without a leader. Not helping matters, the Republican National Congressional Committee (the RNC's sister organization) was in an uproar. In 1989, Edward Rollins had been appointed co-chair with Guy Vander Jagt, who had run the institution for eighteen years. It was widely known in political circles that Rollins was a troublemaker. Rollins's job was to secure Republican seats in Congress. In the fall of 1990, he was doing just the opposite.

A former amateur boxer, Teamster (from Vallejo, California) and Democrat, Rollins had been on Reagan's 1980 campaign, serving as his communications director. Following that win—yet after a time lapse—he had gone to the White House office of political affairs where Atwater earlier had been assigned. In January '82, Rollins succeeded Lyn Nofziger as White House political affairs director, making Atwater his deputy, but shortly thereafter, he suffered a stroke. Returning to his job a year later, Rollins, in December '82, went on to manage Reagan's 1984 reelection victory with Baker, but *not* at Baker's choosing. Baker (and Stu Spencer) had wanted Paul Manafort, Baker's closest political aide in the 1976 Ford campaign, for the job.

In June 1982, Rollins had moved into the Reagan-Bush 1984 campaign headquarters on Capitol Hill and chosen Atwater as his deputy campaign manager. After the 1984 victory, the new chief of staff, Don Regan, finally asked Rollins to take over his old job in political affairs. Rollins, who really had wanted a Cabinet seat, reluctantly agreed in October 1985. Once there, he expanded his position to include the intergovernmental affairs office; still, Rollins remained arrogant and angry, and the White House finally had urged him to leave. Rollins quit.

Because of his political fallout with the Reaganites (and because he despised Bush), it made sense that Rollins had not been in the 1988 Bush campaign. No longer at the White House when the campaign started, Rollins was not on Baker's list, either short or long. Nonetheless, Rollins thought that, by having been former deputy in the Reagan political office and an aide in the 1984 campaign, he should have been included, and in his view, Atwater, as manager of the '88 campaign, was obligated to put him in a senior position. If Atwater were arrogant enough to lock him out, he would go to an opposing camp. He did. He joined the campaign of Jack Kemp. Charlie Black, who along with John Sears and Jim Lake had been dismissed from the 1980 Reagan campaign and, in 1988, headed Kemp's, asked Rollins to join him. With delight, Rollins accepted the position of chairman, and fought with unusual gusto against the Bush camp, punching Bush and jabbing Quayle.

Incredibly, at the recommendation of Republican advisors Steve Stockmeyer and Nancy Sinnot, Rollins was included in the Bush '89 lineup as NRCC chairman (a post that worked closely with the RNC chairman, who, in 1989, had been Lee Atwater). He accepted the job, but with the stipulation that the assignment would last four years and pay $250,000, far above the usual $150,000 salary.

Rollins's first year in the position had been a good one for fundraising. The second year had not. Pointing to Bush's tax reversal as the reason for the drop, Rollins, in the middle of the 1990 Congressional campaign, sent a memorandum to the Republican House candidates encouraging them to *oppose* the tax hikes the President was supporting. In his memo, he urged the representatives to be "consistent." If they had not already agreed with the tax pledge and taken their views to their constituents, Rollins urged them to "go with their conscience." If they had not already agreed, he told them to not hesitate "to distance yourselves from the President," maintaining that, because Bush had betrayed them, he no longer deserved their support.

Rollins, going even further, publicly predicted that if Bush were not careful with his handling of the Persian Gulf (pertaining to financial obligations and further tax increases), the presidency would come "crumbling down around him." Having always viewed Bush as someone who could not stand on his own politically, Rollins now represented him as a traitor to the Republican Party and referred to Bush's handling of the budget as having caused "open and festering wounds" with Congress. Rollins took on both Darman and Sununu, saying:

> They just weren't sensitive to all that's going on, and they're still not sensitive to it. Fortunately for Darman, Sununu has been more abrasive. It would be a close vote as to who is liked less." [About Darman specifically, Rollins said], "Among conservative GOP lawmakers, Darman is the most despised figure in the administration; the drumbeat to get Darman to resign is only going to get louder and louder."

Given the possibility that the Rollins Factor could have had a substantial impact on the November 1990 election of the 102nd Congress, the results were not that bad. In the House, Republicans lost nine seats—protecting the Democrat's majority status. In the Senate, Republicans won fourteen seats, and Democrats sixteen. The Democratic Party continued to control both the Senate and the House; however, voting percentages remained almost the same as they had been in the 101st Congress. There was little reason to believe that the Republicans were any less secure now than they had been before the 1988 election.

Not until spring '91 would Rollins resign from his NRCC post, saying, "I don't expect to be invited to the White House in the next two years. I don't expect to have any communication."

THE influential men surrounding the President in 1990 had one thing in common: each served to weaken the Republican Party and the presidency. Darman, Sununu, Kristol, Dole, Bennett, Boskin, and Rollins pursued their own agendas while diminishing the role of Bush. One by one, the President's Men were able to undermine their leader and compromise his position. After the tax blunder, in rapid succession, came the John Sununu-Bill Kristol fallout, the Bill Bennett-RNC fiasco, and the Ed Rollins foul-up. All these events occurred in Atwater's absence, and all would have a profound effect on the unraveling of the Oval Office.

Again, I can prove no illegal conspiracy here—no plot to disengage the President from office—nonetheless, only a few at the top of the Power Pyramid knew what was really happening during the administration of George Herbert Walker Bush. Baker, Fuller, Darman, Cicconi and Fitzwater were trying to dictate the presidency according to *their* needs, and the media reported from *their* perspective. There was no one higher in the government to rein them in, and the former lower-level Reaganites, now positioned throughout the Bush administration, did not cause them concern, because they were happy with their lot; they just followed their superiors. My Crazy Conspiracy Theory.

During the Bush presidency, wars were being waged on many fronts. Between the liberals and the conservatives. Between the Congress and the Executive Office. Between the West Wing and the Vice President's office. Between grown men with grudges and spoiled men who acted like children. These conflicts were fought inside the administration between individuals purportedly playing on the same team, and because of all the in-house bickering, a faltering administration was *created* according to the Baker plan.

If one looked behind the White House walls, one could see that Bush was not himself. He had navigated the honeymoon beautifully, but that had taken little effort—similar to the momentum that evolved on its own during the last two months of the 1988 campaign when Bush surged ahead of Dukakis by just *being there*. But by the end of 1990, the Bush administration began to reverse itself. The year had been one of gathering storm clouds, for Bush and for the world. The European Community had struggled to become unified; the Soviet Union, and its fifteen republics, had taken an economic dive while transitioning from communism to capitalism; and Iraq had invaded Kuwait. In twelve months' time, international relationships had become strained and chances for establishing the New World Order, of which Bush dreamed, looked unlikely.

We in the administration, needing a break, celebrated the holiday season with a ball at the French Embassy, the first event of its kind for appointees and one that I helped to organize. On the evening of the affair, in the glass-walled rooms of the modern French Embassy, several bands were on hand, and tables overflowed with luscious gourmet foods. Cramming the elegant embassy were people dressed in their most formal attire, enjoying the moment, munching, chatting, and, later on, whirling across the dance floor. As guests at our own party, we took pleasure in enjoying the most festive time of the year.

The featured speaker was Edward Derwinski, the first secretary of the Veteran's Administration, who now oversaw the largest of the fourteen federal agencies, employing 245,000 workers and serving 27 million veterans. He encouraged us to continue doing our best to support the President, pointing out that better days were ahead.

The French Embassy Ball was one of those occasions when we, those privileged to serve the President, temporarily forgot about who was doing what to whom. And on that night, we were each given a gift, a white Christmas tree ornament with "Bush/Quayle Ball 1990" embossed in red. Each year when I take out the fragile glass souvenir to place it on the tree, I think back to that night when hundreds of us partied until two in the morning, convinced for the moment that we were invincible. The fantasy of having unlimited boundaries allows for an illusionary self, poised and arrogant, but also, quite often, unable to foresee the future— or contemplate failure. Few, if any of us, were prepared for the war that was about to begin.

★★★ ═══════ ★★★
CHAPTER

25

SACK SADDAM; FREE KUWAIT

All he wanted in this life was to be executive officer of a battleship, then a captain, then an admiral with a BatDiv flag. He could see no further. He thought a BatDiv flag was as fine a thing as being a president, a king, or a pope.

—Herman Wouk

AUGUST 1990–MARCH 1991

In August 1990, thousands of foreigners had been held hostage in Baghdad while Saddam Hussein and his armies invaded oil-rich Kuwait. Saddam claimed that Kuwait had been pumping billions of dollars worth of oil from underneath *Iraqi* territory. The assault set off a worldwide military alert, making the invasion—as selected by 327 Associated Press newspaper editors and broadcast news directors—the top news story of 1990.

The Iranian region, vital for its oil and renowned for its political instability, had been a British sphere of influence until 1971, when the Royal Navy squadron withdrew and the way was open for a realignment of forces. While the United States was preoccupied with overpowering the Soviet Union, it had built a relationship with the shah of Iran, a leader who hoped to dominate the region militarily and was purported to desire a westernized Iranian society.

With a large and growing income from oil, the shah could afford to buy the latest weapons; however, he and his leaders insisted that suppliers share their technical secrets. The U.S. agreed, and as long as Americans kept supplying Iran with their latest fighter-bomber aircraft, the camaraderie between the two nations continued. At one time, U.S. officials even studied the Iranian request for nuclear weapons. In 1980, the

★★★

year after Saddam Hussein claimed leadership of Iraq, he invaded Iran and started the Eight-Year War, and, in that effort, the United States, now going to the other side, provided Iraq with billions of dollars worth of arms. Finally, in 1988, a cease-fire was negotiated. By then, the shah of Iran (with whom the U.S. formerly had been friendly) had fled, and the revolutionary Ayatollah Khomeini (with whom the U.S. previously had fought) returned. Khomeini proclaimed Iran an Islamic Republic.

On February 24, 1990, Hussein outlined a major offensive against the United States; he was determined to be leader of the Arab world *without* any U.S. involvement. The U.S.—seemingly—had agreed to that understanding. In fact, just days before his August invasion of Kuwait, Saddam had met with April Glaspie (U.S. ambassador to Iraq) and Margaret Tutwiler (Baker's spokeswoman), and Glaspie had told him that the U.S. would not take a position on Iraq's dispute with Kuwait. Saddam took this position as a gesture of support.

Hussein, having never served in the military before becoming president, still knew war as a way of life, and he did not consider *any* behavior out of bounds if it resulted in satisfying his agenda and gratifying his ego. His thinking was indicative of the region's mindset to lie if it gained one's persuasion; Iraqi businessmen and government leaders routinely said one thing and did another. The United States recognized there was little if any hope in trying to negotiate with a man who could not be trusted, and for some time, it had relied on President Hosni Mubarak of Egypt to be the linchpin of the American position in the Middle East. Once Saddam tried to take control of Kuwait, that path no longer was sufficient.

Upon entering Kuwait, Saddam reported that the Kuwaiti government had been overthrown by revolution and that his troops were there to "help" the new rulers. The United Nations Security Council came back condemning the invasion, and, instantly, a U.S.-Soviet statement was issued calling for immediate Iraqi withdrawal.

U.S. trade with Iraq was banned. But Saddam did not retreat.

On the second day of August, at 2:00 (7:00 EDT), Bush made the decision to send 130,000 troops and 1,800 tanks into Kuwait. In retaliation, Iraq closed its frontiers to foreigners, stranding hundreds of Americans. Within hours, those trapped inside the country were held captive by the Baghdad government. Lives were in danger, and Americans were told that without Kuwait's 1.5 million barrels of oil a day, so was the world's oil supply. A U.S. aircraft carrier from the Indian Ocean was diverted to evaluate the situation.

Because there was no evidence of Iraq's claimed withdrawal, Bush prepared for an attack, ordering combat troops and warplanes to Saudi Arabia. The 24th Armored Division at Fort Stewart, Georgia, the 28th Airborne Corps at Fort Bragg, North Carolina, and the 7th Light Infantry Division at Fort Ord, California, were put on alert.

On August 9, the day after Iraq annexed Kuwait, U.S. Operation Desert Shield commenced, and President Bush addressed the nation:

> In the life of a nation, we are called upon to define who we are and what we believe. Sometimes these choices are not easy. But today, as president, I ask for your support in a decision I've made to stand up for what is right and condemn what's wrong, all in the cause of peace. We see in Saddam Hussein an aggressive dictator threatening his neighbors. Only 14 days ago, Saddam Hussein promised his friends he would not invade Kuwait. And only four days ago, he promised the world he would withdraw. And twice we have seen what his promises mean. His promises mean nothing.
>
> [Continuing, Bush said] No one commits American armed forces to a dangerous mission lightly, but after perhaps unparalleled international consultation and exhausting every alternative, it became necessary to take action. Standing up for our principles is an American tradition. As it has so many times before, it may take time and tremendous effort, but most of all, it will take unity of purpose. As I have witnessed throughout my life in both war and peace, America has never wavered when her purpose is driven by principle, and on this August day, at home and abroad, I know she will do no less. Thank you, and God bless the United States of America.

Seven days later (on August 16), the U. S. began a naval blockade of Iraq, and along with French and British warships, U.S. ships steamed toward the Persian Gulf. The aircraft carrier, U.S.S. *Independence*, heading a battle group in the Arabian Sea (escorted by the command and control ship of the Joint Task Force Middle East, U.S.S. *La Salle*), made its way toward the emergency area. These two ships, accompanied by thirteen others—including a cruiser, a destroyer and five frigates—were deployed to convey the message that U.S. force remained an option. Cautiously, the United States and the world waited to see what would happen next.

It was not until almost six months later that the U.S. made a full rally for war. In the meantime, the White House kept their options open, making it clear the President was not going to take any action pending Hussein's willingness to comply with the United Nations Resolutions. Of these decrees, No. 660 demanded Iraqi withdrawal from Kuwait; No. 661 called for the embargo of economic and financial resources to Iraq; and No. 662 referred to Iraq's illegal annexation of Kuwait.

On Tuesday, September 11, in another address to the nation, the U.S. commander in chief spoke in more emphatic tones:

> A hundred generations have searched for this elusive path to peace, while a thousand wars raged across the span of human endeavor. Today that new world is struggling to be born . . . a world where the rule of law supplants the rule of the jungle. A world in which nations recognize the shared responsibility for freedom and justice. A world where the strong respect the rights of the weak.

Operation Desert Shield—the U.S.-led initiative devised to stop Hussein from overcoming Kuwait and to prevent the possible Iraqi invasion of Saudi Arabia—had built momentum over the fall months. Bush had conducted a highly successful diplomatic initiative to ensure that should war be declared, other nations (primarily France and Great Britain) would follow. Wanting multilateral support, Bush gathered a global alliance of Chancellor Helmut Kohl of Germany, Prime Minister John Major of Great Britain, President Francois Mitterrand of France, and President Gorbachev of the U.S.S.R. (formerly an ally of Iraq). And on August 27, 1990, Hugh Sidey wrote a *Time* magazine article, "Networking Pays Off," in which he commented: "Bush has devised his own leadership constellation. It has a core of aides who meet, travel, eat and drink with them. There are Cabinet officers and diplomats who come in and out of the circle, flung to distant points for crucial negotiations. Familiarity with the byways of this planet pervades all levels of this operation."

PRESIDENT Jimmy Carter had declared in the Carter Doctrine of January 23, 1980, that: "An attempt by any outside force to gain control of the Persian Gulf region will be regarded as an assault on the vital interests of the United States of America. And such an assault will be repelled by any means necessary, including military force."

A decade later, on November 29, 1990, the United Nations Security Council passed Resolution 678, authorizing President Bush to "use force" in dealing with Saddam, designating January 15 as the deadline for Iraqi withdrawal.

At the same time President Bush proclaimed his intent to send forces to the Gulf, *Time* magazine (January 7, 1991) came out with its "Man of the Year" issue—and George Bush, having won, was on the cover; yet, there was a distortion in the honor. The title on the front read, "Men of the Year; Two George Bushes," with a singular picture of Bush from two opposite angles merged. The President was simultaneously looking to the right and to the left. The inside article, "A Tale of Two Bushes," stated, "One finds vision on the global stage; the other still displays none at home. George Bush seemed like two Presidents last year: one displayed a commanding vision of a new world order; the other showed little vision for his own country." As time went by, these distinctive yet contrasting faces of Bush would be promoted as even more divergent and more negative. Unfortunately, the two-faced image would shadow Bush's remaining presidency until it was only one icon: the one without vision.

In my office on Friday January 11, 1991, I read an editorial in the *Washington Post,* part of which said: "We do support putting in the hands of the President—a President who personally knows something about war—the authority to make a more plausible threat in these eleventh-hour circumstances of President Hussein's pre-deadline countdown." The *Post* was not calling for Bush to launch an attack on Hussein, but it was giving him the nod to do so if that was what was needed to end the Iraqi dictator's aggression.

The next day, the Senate gave Bush authority to wage war by the slight margin of 52-47, the House approving by 250 to 183. Congress granted President Bush the right to "use force if necessary," although it did *not* pronounce an official declaration of war. With this authorization and with the support of several United Nations mandates, Bush felt confident to take more-aggressive action. He pledged to free Kuwait.

With the situation growing more ominous, the State department issued a specially prepared briefing book regarding the history of Iraq and some biographical material on Saddam. Each political appointee in

Washington was given a copy. One of the chapters I remember best pertained to prisoners of war and Iraqi torture. The descriptions and accompanying pictures of persecution techniques (also written in graphic terms) were beyond anything I ever imagined. Unable to finish the reading, I wondered how insane one had to be to inflict such suffering on another human being. I asked myself the question most every American was asking: Is Kuwait worth being tortured . . . or killed . . . for? A pompous and undemocratic country, Kuwait was rich in oil, with almost 100 billion barrels in reserve. The emir, Sheik Jaber al-Ahmand al-Sabah, who now lived and ran the government in exile from a Sheraton Hotel near Taif, Saudi Arabia, boasted that his tiny nation held the world's third-largest petroleum supply, with an overseas investment portfolio showing over $100 billion. With these kinds of riches, Kuwait was a sitting target for someone like Hussein, who desired nothing more than controlling the world's oil reserves.

The Organization of the Petroleum Exporting Countries (OPEC), comprising Nigeria, Iraq, Venezuela, and Saudi Arabia, was the source of nearly half of American oil imports. Saudi Arabia, the largest contributor, supplied nearly three quarters of OPEC petroleum and Iraq contributed approximately 12 percent of the total. This meant that Iraq produced *less than 3 percent* of the world's total oil supply! The number-one single source of oil for the U.S. was Saudi Arabia. Iraq was the lowest.

More than 75 percent of the oil brought into the United States came from a combination of four countries: two OPEC countries, Venezuela and Saudi Arabia, and two non-OPEC countries, Canada and Mexico. The rest came from Angola, Britain, Nigeria, Norway and Iraq. If Saddam took Kuwait, he would control the Arabian Peninsula, and that would give him power, but certainly not enough to take over the world's oil supply.

Although the United States had feared that events taking place in the Gulf region would harm the world economy (Wall Street and Tokyo), that alarm had subsided by early September. OPEC had agreed to suspend quotas limiting world production, and this had settled the markets. As provisions were made for higher oil production, pressure on the global market eased. The U.S. oil supply would not suffer and prices would not be raised.

On the day of the U.N. deadline—January 15th—Paul Bedard of the *Washington Times* wrote, "The White House has posted 'On Hold' signs around the government as President Bush approaches the decision he has spent his life preparing for—war, possibly tonight. While Congress and the public nervously watch the events in the Persian Gulf, Mr. Bush and his top advisors remain outwardly calm, sending signals to the nation that all is under control."

The Persian Gulf War started only eighteen hours after the imposed deadline. At 4:50 P. M. EST on January 16, 1991, F-15E fighter-bombers, armed with Sidewinder and Sparrow air-to-air missiles, took off from the largest U.S. air base in central Saudi Arabia. The war had begun, although the ground war would not begin for another six weeks. What started as a defense of Kuwait and Saudi Arabia was now a full military attack against Iraq.

Earlier, on November 8, 1990, Bush had deployed an additional 200,000 troops to insure "an adequate offensive option." A U.S. fleet of over 100 battleships, aircraft carriers, cruisers, destroyers, frigates and nuclear submarines had already made their way to Kuwait. By January, the Persian Gulf region was overflowing with U.S. air power, troops, tanks, missiles and Naval forces: 1,500 war planes, 415,000 troops, thousands of tanks, and missiles of all kinds, including the Patriot, Chaparral, Hawk, Stinger, Maverick and Tomahawk.

Operation Desert Shield had turned into Operation Desert Storm, and the U.S. bombing campaign, targeting Iraqi's capital of Baghdad, shook both the city and its leader. Saddam, whose whereabouts were unknown, spoke on Baghdad radio:

> When they begin to die and when the message of the Iraqi soldiers reaches the farthest corner of the world, the unjust will die and the "God is Great" banner will flutter with great victory in the mother of all battles. Then the skies in the Arab homeland will appear in a new color and a sun of new hope will shine over them and over our nation and on all the good men whose bright lights will not be overcome by darkness in the hearts of the infidels, the Zionists, and the treacherous, shameful rulers, such as the traitor Fahd [King of Saudi Arabia].

U.S. and allied forces had successfully gone on the offensive with their first attack. Baghdad had been hit, with no reported U.S.-allied casualties. The predawn attacks, which caused heavy destruction of Iraq's missile firing capability, destroyed Hussein's Presidential Palace, but not the president. On January 17, the *Washington Times* stated, "The strikes marked the unveiling of American air power modernized over the past decade with more maneuverable supersonic jets, sophisticated night-flying and target systems and bombs that can follow a laser beam to the heart of a target."

The American press corps covered the conflict with more detail than any other event in recent history, sometimes outdating and overriding the official reports coming out of the department of Defense. CNN broadcast the hour-by-hour, day-by-day "television war," to a worldwide audience that included President Bush and President Hussein. Even the military divisions in the field carried CNN satellite dishes and portable televisions to gain perspective of what was what on the battlefield. Occasionally, reports appeared to be more in favor of the enemy than the U.S. soldier.

With strategically placed reporters on the scene, CNN, as the other networks, told *their* War Story as *they* saw it unfold, often before the military leaders had a chance to communicate the events to the public. This was thought by some to breach national security objectives. During the Gulf War, journalism evolved into more than just reporting the news; it was no longer broadcast in an objective way. Personal beliefs and impressions were tossed in with the data, and often journalists would mold stories to their own satisfaction. In my view, influencing public opinion in this way should never be part of news reporting; the press corps overstepped their boundaries.

All the major networks described in detail the weapons that gave the U.S. troops their technological advantage—the most often mentioned was the Patriot missile. Pentagon officials chimed in, announcing that Patriot technology had performed above what had been expected. Some of this intelligence was later disputed, and rumors circulated after the war that the missile had many more problems than were ever reported back home.

Two hours after the initial attack on Baghdad and before Iraq retaliated, on the evening of January 16, Bush gave a twelve-minute address to the nation. From the Oval Office, he announced he had "ordered air strikes to destroy Iraqi President Hussein's ability to make war, not just to force him out of Kuwait," and he added, "We will not fail." Bush spoke confidently, and conveyed how strongly he felt about keeping the troops safe, bringing them home to their dependents and loved ones as soon as possible.

An estimated one thousand military couples and more than sixteen thousand single parents—all with children in the States—were part of the Gulf force. The forty thousand females who took part in the conflict marked a turning point for women in the military; many served in combat positions, aboard ships and on planes. Two women became prisoners of war, and eleven were killed in action.

As the war progressed and the Iraqi militia continued to blow up buildings and kill civilians in Kuwait, they also set fire to hundreds of oil wells and storage tanks, causing massive black clouds to choke the skies. Saddam's troops dumped millions of gallons of Kuwaiti oil into the Persian Gulf, resulting in dreadful oil slicks; land was devastated beyond recognition, and President Bush *again* demanded the Iraqi dictator withdraw his forces, threatening that if he did not do so, the United States would begin a ground war. Saddam *again* refused to retreat, leaving Bush no other choice than to follow with action.

The Gulf War was the first major crisis in the post–Cold War era, and it marked the first time that military and civilians alike had seriously considered the possibility of air power alone winning a war. However, that did not come to be. During the sixth week of the battle (the thirty-eighth day), the Gulf ground offensive began.

Allied troops, having conducted a nonstop air war on Iraqi troops, tanks and planes, had already destroyed twenty-nine Iraqi divisions, more than half of their entire army. Now, thousands of U.S. ground troops tromped into bomb-shaken Iraq, and, in a matter of hours, turned the area into an Iraqi bloodbath.

On February 26, Saddam announced the withdrawal of Iraqi troops from Kuwait. The war was over.

Allied Forces had driven the enemy troops back behind the Iraqi border, culminating in the surrender of tens of thousands of Iraqi soldiers. After four days of land fighting—February 24–27—Iraqi and Allied military leaders agreed to a tentative cease-fire and to a quick release of the war prisoners. Immediately, Defense secretary Cheney, referring back to Hussein's earlier comment on the Iraqi radio broadcast, remarked: "The mother of all battles has turned into the mother of all retreats."

The Persian Gulf War had lasted forty-two days. Air bombing continued for the duration; however, the ground war lasted only one hundred hours. Although the U.S. had full support abroad, only British and French soldiers fought alongside American troops.

During the first month of the war, it was reported that 11 U.S. marines had been killed (seven from friendly fire), and that several planes and helicopters had crashed, killing U.S. airmen. And according to some of the earlier intelligence, U.S. losses for the six-week war tallied 94 killed in action, 50 killed in non-combat, 213 wounded, 9 prisoners of war, 31 missing in action, 30 aircraft lost in combat, and 21 aircraft lost in non-combat. As time went by, the initial casualty numbers grew to some 400 Americans having been killed and an equal number wounded. Allied casualties numbered close to the same.

Iraqi troops suffered the most in terms of lost lives: more than 20,000 troops and civilians were reported dead. According to U.S. military experts, if the ground war had continued any longer, the United States, with its overwhelmingly powerful military force, would have massacred the population of not one, but two nations, Kuwait and Iraq. But, that had never been President Bush's intent. Nor had it been the goal of his Cabinet, the National Security Counsel, the Congress or the U.S. allies.

On Wednesday, February 27, after nearly eight months in exile, the emir returned to Kuwait from Saudi Arabia, the United States claimed victory over Iraq and President Bush declared Kuwait liberated. Saddam said that he willingly would accept all twelve of the United Nations resolutions.

That evening, I met with several of my political friends and listened to Bush give his "Address to the Nation on the Suspension of Allied and Offensive Combat Operations in the Persian Gulf." As we gathered around the television set, like most others in the country, a feeling of relief swept through us. Some of what the President said included:

> Kuwait is liberated. Iraq's army is defeated. Our military objectives are met. Kuwait is once more in the hands of Kuwaitis in control of their own destiny. We share in their joy, a joy tempered only by our compassion for their ordeal. Tonight, the Kuwaiti flag once again flies above the capital of a free and sovereign nation, and the American flag flies above our embassy. Seven months ago, America and the world drew a line in the sand. We declared that the aggression against Kuwait would not stand. And tonight America and the world have kept their word . . . This war is now behind us. Ahead of us is the difficult task of securing a potentially historic peace.

The return of the U.S. forces in 1991 reminded me of another homecoming. In 1954, thirty-seven years earlier, I had gone down to the ship docks at Pearl Harbor in Hawaii to meet my father coming home, not from war but from spending eighteen months at sea. As a ten-year-old waiting for his return, that time had seemed like an eternity. While Father was captain of the destroyer U.S.S. *Carpenter,* I was in elementary school, living on the island of Oahu, running barefoot on the white-sand beaches of Kailua, taking hula lessons and tanning dark as a native. During his voyages to the South Seas, Father had sent presents and postcards from Japan, Okinawa and the Philippines, and each day I had crossed off another date on my hand-made calendar. Finally, when the *Carpenter* came back to homeport, I, with my mother, younger sister and brother, joined the other families clustered on the steamy wooden pier in Honolulu to welcome back the crew.

In my white sundress and blue sandals, I watched the steel-gray vessel, deck laden with men standing rigid in stiff white uniforms, come closer and closer to shore. As captain of the ship, Father stood on the flying bridge, and with the bright Hawaiian sun overhead, I squinted my eyes, trying to be the first to see him. In keeping with the Hawaiian custom for a returning loved one, we had layers of fragrant flower leis— my favorites were orchids and carnations—over our arms, ready to be placed around the neck of the returning "sailor." I can remember crying because I was so happy.

The 1991 homecoming of the soldiers, aviators and sailors from the Gulf, was, I imagine, as poignant for each family member as it had been for me many years before.

One of the Gulf War declarations, signed on April 2, 1991, officially referred to as Resolution 687, was called the "Mother of All Resolutions." The decree stipulated that [1] Iraq was to be punished for the invasion, [2] Saddam's efforts to produce weapons of mass destruction would be kept in check, and [3] there were not to be any future challenges against Kuwait. If Baghdad did not abide by the declaration's terms, retaliatory economic and military conditions would be imposed. Most of the sanctions against Iraq were lifted; however, the country was prohibited from selling oil until it met the conditions of the cease-fire.

Most of the U.S. posturing over the resolutions was for press reasons only; Iraq would never agree to unconditional weapon inspections by

★★★

American agents, nor would United Nations agents find biological and chemical weapons sitting in Saddam's backyard. Hussein was too clever for that to happen. As leader of 20 million Arab-nation inhabitants, Saddam, now militarily defeated and economically distressed, still saw himself as victorious. His most important objective during the war had been to remain alive, and with his personal military force, the Guard—equipped with the best weaponry and finest soldiers—he had accomplished this goal.

In spite of a global blockade, Security Council threats, having many opponents in the Arab League, and half a million U.S. troops on his heels, Hussein had not flinched. He survived and his resentment toward the United States was more intense than ever. Saddam Hussein felt betrayed. Did he have reason? Had Ambassador April Glaspie known about Saddam's intended invasion, and had she implied that the United States would not interfere?

In the August 27, 1990, issue of *Time* magazine, in "He Gives Us a Ray of Hope," by Otto Friedrich, Saddam was described from a non-American point of view:

> In Western eyes, Saddam Hussein is a killer, a bloodthirsty tyrant, a new Hitler. But to many Arabs he is a hero, the charismatic champion of pan-Arab nationalism, the resolute foe of "imperialist" interventions they long for. His confrontation with America has stirred strong pride among people bitter over generations of Arab humiliation and foreign interference. Saddam and his fellow Arabs hated the United States and Americans "who have long divided, despoiled and dishonored the once powerful Arab world in World War I and World War II with Israel and the Jews."

The Bush White House would continue to bicker and feud with Saddam. Never had the Middle East been an easy territory to deal with, and with Iraq still a nation "to be reckoned with," friction would continue. War would continue to be a way of life for Iraq.

Luckily, for Americans, the same was not true. War had ended. Yet, the men who were influential in the Gulf War—those in the highest commands under President Bush—the leaders of the Foreign Affairs, Defense, State and National Security staffs were required to "stand watch" over the situation. Brent Scowcroft, national security advisor; Colin Powell, chairman of the Joint Chiefs of Staff; Norman Schwarzkopf;

Commander in the Persian Gulf; Richard Cheney, secretary of Defense; and James Baker, secretary of State all would play a role in the aftermath of the Persian Gulf War.

It is sometimes said that politicians are the *leaders* of war, while the military comprises the *mechanics* of war, but whatever the organizational dynamics, with every war come the war champions. The Persian Gulf War was no exception.

After the war ended, General H. Norman Schwarzkopf was the most highly decorated military officer, having been in command of Operation Desert Storm. Known as Stormin' Norman, he received more media coverage and national/international attention after the Gulf Crisis than anyone else on Bush's war team. As commander of U.S. and allied troops in both Desert Storm and Desert Shield, he was awarded the highest honors. The 1956 West Point graduate and son of an Army officer, was fifty-six years old, six-foot, three-inches tall, and weighed 240-pounds. He was affectionately called "the Bear" by his troops and was the commander to more than 650,000 U.S. and allied troops in the Gulf.

Schwarzkopf was determined that the Gulf Crisis would not be another poorly managed Vietnam War, and the military leader of German descent was cautious in his approach to waging battle against Hussein, suggesting that Bush make plans to lead the Gulf army into and out of the field as soon and as safely as possible. Schwarzkopf knew that he had no authorization to invade Iraq for capturing Baghdad *or* Saddam.

When all was said and done, it was not the West Pointer but the ROTC general, Colin L. Powell, who would become the best known of the Gulf War military heroes. And with that honor, Powell, who commanded the battle from Washington, was most often mentioned by opinion polls as the favorite to be Bush's running mate in 1992. During the months of the conflict, Schwarzkopf had received the most notice and had been on television every night. Powell's notoriety would evolve more gradually.

The son of Jamaican immigrant parents and a "C student," General Powell had grown up in the South Bronx, New York, joining the Army ROTC at City College in Harlem. He went on to distinguish himself as one of a few in the military to receive the rank of four-star general, and only the fourth black man in the U.S. armed forces history to attain that rank. Powell had acquired top military billets in three presidential administrations, establishing himself within the highest levels of the Republican and Democratic Parties. He had started in the Nixon White House in 1972

★★★

working as a "fellow" and reporting to Frank Carlucci, who was then deputy director of the Office of Management and Budget. When Carlucci became national security advisor to Reagan, Powell became his deputy.

While on active duty as a Lt. General in November 1987, and at the recommendation of Howard Baker (then chief of staff), Powell became Reagan's sixth national security advisor, a post he kept during the last year of the administration. (Carlucci, coincidentally, was appointed secretary of Defense at the same time.) Before being appointed to the Joint Chiefs of Staff by President Bush, Powell was commander of FORSCOM (250,000 active duty troops and 250,000 reservists) at Fort McPherson, Georgia.

Overlooking fourteen other four-stars legally eligible for the Joint Chiefs post, secretary of Defense Cheney handpicked the most junior member—Colin Powell—and submitted his name to President Bush. When Admiral William Crowe's second term as chairman ended in September 1989—and after Crowe declined a nomination for another two-year term—Bush put Powell in the position, starting on October 3, 1989. According to the *Washington Post* (September 25, 1989), Powell was "the first black officer to hold the position, and at fifty-two, the youngest officer named to the job." Less than one year later, in August 1990, Powell had found himself embroiled in Desert Shield operations, heading 80,000 coalition troops in Saudi Arabia. By November, Bush had engaged 400,000 U.S. troops, the largest American deployment since the Vietnam War.

Before the Gulf War started, Powell had said that he wanted to isolate the Iraqi army and then "kill it." But, while believing that the only way to win was with a full-scale, massive attack, he was also concerned about killing civilians and wanted to avoid the impression that the U.S. was fighting just for the sake of being in a war. Powell counseled Bush *against* continuing the Gulf war on the "Highway of Death" and *against* killing Saddam. He was the first to suggest that Bush should not focus on capturing all of Hussein's army, or Hussein himself, and to be wary of any unnecessary killing of civilians. And too, it was Powell who approached Saudi Prince Bandar about U.S. troops being allowed to have religious services while on Islamic sacred ground.

Over Cheney's opposition, Bush agreed with Powell that the combat operations should cease on February 27, ending the war before going into Baghdad, and before capturing or killing Hussein. Bush kept his promise to not put the troops "in harm's way" any more than what was required to restore Kuwait's freedom.

This had always been the mission, yet, later, Bush would be disparaged for not taking the war further into Iraq and eliminating Saddam. His critics would say that his call to end the war was premature. What was missing from this argument was an important piece of data: the United Nations resolutions had *not* granted the President that course of action. Nor had Congress. Additionally, at the time of the crisis, all other presidential advisors, including Schwarzkopf, agreed with Bush's decision to end the war! Even Cheney—the most ardent of those promoting more aggressive action—agreed not to continue the invasion.

On top of the more-legal reasons for not continuing, Bush did not want the United States to be viewed negatively by world powers, which could have been the case if he was seen using disproportionate military force to destroy the country of Iraq in order to capture or kill Saddam. To flaunt the strength of the U.S. forces on the Iraqi battlefield, where the opponent was so undersized and so much weaker, was not the President's goal. Some news reports likened the imbalance of Iraqi-U.S. troop strength to "killing an ant with a sledgehammer." In an "about face," later, Schwarzkopf and Cheney would change their tunes and join those who criticized President Bush for ending the war too soon.

Despite the glamour surrounding Schwarzkopf and Powell and the U.S. troops in the spring of 1991, Bush remained the true national hero, and the nation that had "tied a yellow ribbon around the old oak tree" rejoiced when the troops came marching home. On June 8, a full-scale Victory Parade took place in downtown Washington. Men and women in their desert-camouflaged battle fatigues and their crisp blue, white or khaki uniforms marched down Pennsylvania Avenue to the President's reviewing stand in front of the White House.

I supposed the crusades in which generations of my ancestors had fought were the ones I clandestinely wished for myself. I had no desire to be on the battlefield or out in Deep Ocean; still, there was an under-the-surface aspiration to be near the center of command in battle. Working in the Bush administration and being just a block away from the Oval Office during war time had given me that opportunity. I was far removed from the process of waging war, yet I was in a place as close to the commander-in-chief as one could be. And, in spite of the hard lessons learned in the Washington political establishment, compared to other things I could have been doing with my life, I was pleased with my station.

Hangzhou, China, October 1991
Boating on West Lake with Mr. Pan during PACTECH trade mission.

★ ★

PART 6

A Promise Is Forever

★ ★

In the past, I viewed this lack of certainty in myself as a sign of weakness. I yearned for an absolute truth, an ideology, something that would cover every contingency in my life; tell me what to think and how to behave. Searching, I read great poets and philosophers—Lao-tsu, Thoreau, Tolstoy, Whitman, Shaw. I gathered them with all their inconsistencies, paradoxes, and disharmonies. I discovered that each had a piece of the truth for me, and that there is no dogma, no ideology, no absolute truth for me to fall back on.

—Richard Bode

★★★ ═══ ★★★
CHAPTER

26

THE DOMINO EFFECT

We think highly of achievement. He is a fine fellow—honorable, desirable, the perfect gentleman, but ambition is considered more of a tramp than a lady, a vixen by virtue. If her passion and power aren't creatively and constructively channeled, she could turn on the one who invoked her presence.

—Sarah Ban Breathnach

<u>SPRING 1991</u>

The previous four months of war strategy and decision-making, which had dictated Bush's schedule, were finally over, and the President held his all-time-high approval rating of 92 percent, one of only a few commanders in chief to reach this status.

The press and the people loved Bush, and there was no more mention of a weakened economy, a disorganized White House, or a crumbling Republican Party—all of which were news in the fall. Beyond any doubt, his presidency would not be challenged in 1992, and Bush would be a two-term President.

George Bush received generous compliments by the press corps, crediting him for his sharp diplomatic skills, superb political manner and articulate dialogue; even his harshest critics gave him credit for doing an extraordinary job in the Gulf. By June 8—the time of the Victory Parade—a wave of patriotism had swept across the country, and Bush was regarded as the lead figure in a resurgence of national pride and hailed as both a fine military strategist and forceful leader. He had won the hearts and respect of the soldiers and the American people. With his popularity soaring, I believe that the President was convinced the domestic agenda would eventually work itself out and that his foreign affairs successes

325

would provide the momentum needed for his reelection. By the spring of 1991, Bush was lulled into a false confidence.

DURING the fall of 1990, when things were not quite so upbeat and while the "selling" of the Gulf War was underway, the Bush administration initiated the Japan Corporate Program (JCP). The department of Commerce was designated the lead agency and Secretary Mosbacher was assigned director—with the mission to launch an overseas marketing strategy that would allow United States businessmen access to the Japanese market. At the time, no single U.S. agency-sponsored export program was given more attention than the JCP.

The Japanese economy was strong and flourishing in 1990, and American executives were curious as to how they might get their foot in the door of the Land of the Rising Sun. Asia was seen as one of the fastest-growing regions of the world, and the distance between the United States and Japan was no longer an impediment to importing and exporting goods and services. Asian trade, which American industry considered the most complex and difficult to achieve, was getting easier: Japan Air Lines, Al Nippon, and United all flew nonstop from Washington to Tokyo.

Before long, the White House would have its own agenda with Asia, and President Bush would take a senior-level trade mission to the Far East while incorporating a highly promoted State Visit to Japan. However, for the time being, the JCP, designed to boost U.S.-Japanese relations, would take on that role and, for that reason, remained under constant scrutiny by the press.

With the hope that in five years, small American businesses would have successful exporting stories to tell, the DOC chose twenty U.S. chief executive officers to participate in the Japan program. All would serve as models for individuals wanting to understand the challenges and opportunities in the Japanese marketplace.

Ten of the twenty participating companies were technology-related, and they were assigned to the office of Science and Electronics; I was appointed director of the S&E portion of the program. Pulling together ten analysts from our office (one to shepherd each company), I set out on what was to be a five-year project.

Explaining Japanese quality standards to impatient U.S. business-men was an ordeal, as was teaching international trade regulations and

★★★

protocol. Following established exporting rules meant extensive data collection, analysis, more analysis, revision and more revision. Taking action was a long twelve months away. In the meantime, patience was required, a characteristic not common to most Americans who were more inclined to dismiss the rudimentary steps and dive in. Restraint and detail had to be taught. Very slowly. Step-by-step.

By springtime, the press began to publish articles about the Japan Corporate Program, including one in the *Washington Times*, "Mosbacher, U.S. Executives to Sweet-talk Fortress Japan," by Karen Riley (April 1991):

> Mr. Mosbacher admitted that participants in the program will receive more attention than other US companies that explore trading relations with Japan, but added that they will serve as a "landmark example" for other companies. As part of their five-year commitment to the program, the companies will arrange four visits a year to Japan, including at least two by their chief executives. They have also agreed to publish their product literature in Japanese, participate in at least one trade promotion event in Japan each year and modify their products as needed to enhance sales in Japan.

While the media was focusing on the potentials of the Japan program and the positives of Operation Desert Storm, the department of Commerce became immersed in Gulf War negatives. One of the fallouts from battle was the untold destruction of land throughout the Persian Gulf region, particularly in Kuwait. Original estimates of the costs of repair were between $50 billion and $100 billion (the final figure actually would be closer to $40 billion).

War damage included the ruin of roads, the collapse of bridges and waterlines, the burning of oil wells, and the closing of electrical utility plants. Communications were touch-and-go, landmines a constant menace and living conditions horrendous. All these factors created life-threatening conditions for anyone involved in the restoration of the devastated area. During peaceful times, environmental conditions in this part of the world were far from friendly; after war, they were appalling.

In spite of the trouble and confusion raging in Kuwait, (complicated by the fact that there was a new ruling family), the possible windfall from reconstruction contracts piqued the interests of hundreds of American CEOs. Kuwait, the size of Vermont, had undergone extensive reconstruction in the 1950s when it first began to modernize, and American companies had been on the scene to offer their services. They were more than happy to do so again.

Along with the tragedies of the 1991 war came the large contracts, such as one AT&T snared for $100 million. By 1992, approximately six hundred of the one thousand contracts were signed over to U.S. businesses; over half, worth $5 billion, were earmarked for rebuilding the nation of Kuwait. Most of the agreements went to Big Business, those companies with previous ties to the region. Only the wealthiest U.S. corporations enjoyed the riches of reconstruction.

Ironically, though, once the news about job opportunities in the Middle East became public knowledge, the average American was led to believe that *he* was going to have a chance to work overseas. I know, from firsthand experience, that this never happened.

Unexpectedly, Commerce was designated as the central hub for the recruitment of citizens who wanted jobs in Kuwait. With no prior notice to DOC employees, government sources communicated that the department was opening a Gulf Reconstruction Center. Touted as being the place to find a position with an American firm going to the Middle East, Commerce was said to be parceling out more than sixty thousand jobs. Word was that U.S. companies needed employees.

The first day the office opened, more than five thousand job seekers called the department. From California to Connecticut, the phone calls poured in, overwhelming the Reconstruction Center. Immediately, the small ad-hoc team devised a system that routed incoming calls to the industry office most suitable to the caller's professional background—for example, if he was in telecommunications, engineering or computer electronics, his call would be referred to the office of Science and Electronics. Because most of the overseas jobs were technology-driven, and because most of the callers were men with technology-based skills, S&E ended up with a majority of the phone calls.

During this critical time, I had a horrid job—in fact, the most unpleasant job of those I held while working in the government. I had to inform hundreds of job-seeking callers that there were *no* jobs in the Gulf. Corporation giants, such as Bechtel, Sprint, and AT&T (which received the contracts) already had their own employees, and what was worse, they had *never* needed applicants.

★★★

Somewhere, somehow, there had been a huge communication problem between Washington and the private sector, and for months to come, the Commerce department took the brunt of it. I was unable to offer guidance to the callers, most of whom were unemployed and who relayed to me that they would go anywhere, under any conditions, at the drop of a hat. With hopelessness in their voices, these men told me of their hardships involving frustrated wives, sick children and no money in the bank. The flood of calls continued into early September, totaling over 400,000. I very much wanted to help. Of course, I could not. For the first time, I realized that wars fought in quiet desperation on the home front could be just as devastating as wars fought on the foreign battlefield.

BY May, across the nation and the world, people had tried to resume a more normal state and return to everyday lives.

In the District of Columbia, Sharon Pratt Dixon was the new mayor. After enduring the drug and sex scandal of the previous mayor, Marion Barry, the city appreciated the orderly manner by which Mrs. Pratt restored decency to the city.

On the international scene, because of my JCP work, I tracked Japanese economics and investments more closely, and took note when I saw that wealthy Japanese executives were spending billions of dollars, purchasing U.S. property, including Yosemite National Park, Music Corporation of America, and the 7-Eleven Corporation.

The European Community seemed to be on a better track now that the world trade negotiations had resumed in Geneva, and negotiators were encouraged that the General Agreement for Trade and Tariff (GATT) *would* succeed after all.

The possibility of a U.S. bilateral trade pact with Mexico, closer than ever, continued to cause concern for some Americans north of the border; potential loss of jobs was the biggest fear. Opposition against Bush and his proposed North American Free Trade Agreement was building in Congress, and the support needed for its success was lukewarm, at best. Bush would spend a great amount of time during the next year working with Congressional members on redefining the pact so that it would meet their approval. Later, I would become involved in this effort.

Besides having a difficult time promoting the Mexican accord within the opposition Party, President Bush, once again, was having a tough time integrating the differing agendas within his own Party. Conflicts continued to erupt at both the Republican National Committee and the National Republican Congressional Committee. Much to the chagrin of the White House, the NRCC had remained under the leadership of Ed Rollins. Commotion over Rollins's October memorandum to Republican House candidates—recommending that they should not hesitate to distance themselves from the President—had subsided somewhat during the Gulf War, but never had gone away. Finally, in April 1991, Rollins left the NRCC and defected to the Democratic political consulting firm of Sawyer Miller Public Relations, located in D.C. And although he was out of the limelight for the moment, he would be back to execute his most devastating blows to Bush in the 1992 campaign.

Spenser Abraham filled the position left by Rollins at the Congressional Committee. As Dan Quayle's assistant deputy and political advisor, he previously had reported to Bill Kristol. The former Michigan Republican Party chairman quickly took the helm and moved into his office in the Republican National Committee building on First Street. In his new job, while raising money to assist GOP House candidates and rebuilding relationships with the White House, he was expected to smooth over the disarray Rollins had created on the Hill. As both fund-raiser and diplomat, Abraham appeared to have the credentials, and, at last, Bush had someone at the Congressional Committee supporting his agenda.

The same could not be said for the Republican National Committee, which had been under reorganization since the fall of 1990, when Atwater was fired and Bennett declined the position. After a long and frustrating search for chairman, the White House announced that Bush's secretary of Agriculture, Clayton Yeutter, would take the seat. However, the sixty-year-old Nebraska-born lawyer and cattle rancher, who had served as U.S. Trade Representative in the Reagan administration, did not have the kind of experience needed to run an upcoming national campaign. With the wheels of the 1992 locomotive starting to roll, Yeutter—although committed to serving the President—could not simultaneously handle building the Republican Party *and* being an influential leader in the reelection. The RNC chief may have been in the right place, but it was at the wrong time.

Before the RNC chair was offered to Yeutter, it had been presented to Craig Fuller. He had turned it down—like he had the other appointments

★★★

offered to him in November 1988, after not being tapped for chief of staff. Fuller had gone to work for a D.C. lobbying firm headed by Michael Deaver. Fuller and Deaver, the two Californians who had traveled to the Reagan White House together in 1980, had worked in concert outside the walls of the Bush White House until Fuller started his own Washington lobbying group, Wexler, Reynolds, Fuller, Harrison and Schule.

In August 1990, Fuller had sold WRFH&S to the public relations firm Hill and Knowlton, owned by a British communications company. Among their many clients was the Philip Morris Company and RJR-Nabisco. According to the Federal Election Commission (Mead Data Central Inc.), from January 1989 through June 1990, Phillip Morris/RJR-Nabisco gave $1,283,000 in political action committee (PAC) money, making them Congress's second highest contributor (AT&T was first with $2,173,000). And in the months leading up to the Gulf War, the Arab government's organization named Citizen's for a Free Kuwait had retained Hill and Knowlton for the cost of $6 million, to promote their cause—in other words, influence American public opinion in the Arabs' favor.

I found it unsettling to know that Craig Fuller was promoting U.S. support for a war in the Persian Gulf while his former boss (Bush) was deciding whether or not to send U.S. forces over the Atlantic Ocean to defend Kuwait. Could it have been that the high-priced Washington firm, using Fuller, lobbied the White House to promote their own interests?

As a reflex reaction to the Hill and Knowlton purchase, Burson-Marsteller acquired the Washington lobbying group Black, Manafort, Stone and Kelly. (Paul Manafort had been Jim Baker's closest confidante when he ran the 1976 Ford campaign.) Similar to Fuller's firm, BMS&K was a small but well-known D.C. lobbying firm founded in 1980 and owned by Charlie Black. Since the spring of 1990, Black, as mentioned, had been pinch-hitting as volunteer spokesman at the RNC for his friend and former partner, Lee Atwater.

Black's firm had been accused of influencing HUD grant money during the Reagan administration regarding Section 8 housing. During the 1989 court hearings, Manafort acknowledged that he had performed work at HUD that could be termed "influence peddling." Notwithstanding, BMS&K had caught the attention of Burson-Marsteller (the group the Reagans called on for advice once they left the White House), and with the goal to expand its services into the Washington infrastructure, Burson had made the purchase just prior to Black's leaving the RNC and immediately before Operation Desert Storm.

With these two firms as illustrations, it is not difficult to deduce that the public relations business is far from being straightforward. A February 11, 1990, *Washington Post Magazine* article, "The Image Makers," by Peter Carlson put it this way:

> It's the great irony of PR: The public relations business, which is composed entirely of experts in the art of manufacturing public images, has a terrible public image. It's all those little half truths and weasel words and slick image campaigns. It's the stories about the PR guys who help elect the pols and then traipse off to do PR work for people who want something from those pols. It all combines to produce the vague feeling that nothing in politics or government is really *real* anymore. These days, the fog produced by the "foggy business" is so dense that even the so-called "insiders" have trouble telling image from reality.

Almost a year before the official '92 campaign would begin, Black and Fuller sat independently and strategically in optimal positions to take a lead position in the upcoming reelection effort.

What brought them together in March of 1991—before the campaign started—was something that brought many of us in the Bush ranks together again: the death of Lee Atwater. One of the greatest political warriors of all time had lost his battle with his last enemy—cancer.

Forgetting politics-as-usual, those of us who had known and worked with Atwater stopped whatever we were doing and grieved the loss of a man we would never forget. Craig Fuller, Charlie Black, and even Ed Rollins put political and personal passions and vendettas aside and mourned the death of their friend, adversary and colleague.

Atwater had reigned supreme in the Washington political world, and, as apropos, the celebratory service in his honor was held at the Washington National Cathedral, the castle-like structure that stood on the highest point of land in the Nation's Capital.

We all would be there.

★★★ ══════ ★★★
CHAPTER
27
WHITE FLAG OF SURRENDER

And now shall mine head be lifted
up above my enemies round about me.
Therefore will I offer in his tabernacle
sacrifices of joy; I will sing, yea,
I will sing praises unto the Lord.
—A Psalm of David: Triumphant Faith

SPRING 1991

The forty-year-old Harvey Lee Atwater died on March 29, and he was to be buried in his hometown in South Carolina. But first came the Washington memorial service.

The ultimate Bush strategist had finally lost his campaign against cancer, but on April, 4, 1991, we were there to remember how he had led us to victory. A self-admitted scoundrel and the "bad boy of politics," Atwater was sometimes referred to as a man having no scruples, morals or conscience. His enemies called him a below-the-belt-fighter and racially prejudiced, one who played on ethnic fears. Yet on this day in early spring when the cherry trees were about to burst into full bloom, Atwater was just a country boy being laid to rest in a city memorial, a shrine as lovely and prestigious as any in the world.

North of the White House on Wisconsin Avenue soared the Washington Cathedral; with its three hundred foot tower (inclosing a sixty ton carillon), the fourteenth-century Gothic-style house of worship, with its cornerstone set in 1907, still was not completed in 1991. Once finished, it would stand as the sixth-largest religious building on the planet—in America, only New York's Cathedral of St. John the Divine was larger.

In the front of the cathedral, above the altar, was a six-foot cross and a stone screen containing ninety-six statues of outstanding men and women who represented the "Company of Heaven." Some said Atwater had now joined, or at least had tried to join, this elite group.

In this Episcopal house of worship—where just over two years earlier the crowds had gathered for Bush's inaugural service —we now came to pay final tribute to Lee Atwater. Thousands crowded into the sanctuary to pay their last respects: President and Mrs. Bush, Cabinet members, hundreds who thought of Atwater as a friend or associate, as well as those who had begrudged him and his political approach.

We joined together and sang the processional: "Amazing Grace! . . . How sweet the sound, that saved a wretch like me!" I could imagine Lee "up there" wanting to be back on Earth with Isaac Hayes, Chuck Jackson and Billy Preston—so that he, with them, could get out the guitars, cymbals and drums and start singing "Life Is Like a Game." Politics was both Atwater's life and his favorite game. Under the fifty-foot cathedral dome, James Baker led the tributes:

> He's at peace; I can picture him up there in heaven now, halo askew, strumming a guitar instead of a harp, and spinning the angels on just what is involved in identifying and turning out the vote. He understood politics to be an art and not a science. And he knew that his job as an artist was to play the game of politics in the only way he knew how—by pushing it to the edge wholeheartedly and unabashedly, just the way he played the guitar and just the way he lived.

Always living on the edge, and with his rough-and-tumble tactics and charismatic personality, Atwater had seen us through the 1988 campaign, day by day, week by week, one month at a time. As our campaign manager, he had taken most of the insults from the opposition and the media, shouldering the responsibility for the campaign's "unfair political devices and negative advertising." In response to the accusations, Atwater had retorted, "What most people call negative campaigning, I prefer to call comparative campaigning; negative makes it sound as if you're beating up on the guy for no reason, which is different from choosing symbolic platforms."

Baker had stood aside during the political fray over Willie Horton, the Pledge of Allegiance and Boston Harbor—and had no trouble letting

Atwater take the heat. Disassociating himself from the tainted, and only claiming credit for the Bush triumphs, Baker was not held accountable for anything, as far as I had seen, except the pleasant/prestigious moments, even at Lee's memorial service. With thousands in attendance, Baker became the focal point.

Despite his making Lee the campaign scapegoat, during Atwater's last months, Baker had shared a good deal of time with the Southern Baptist Atwater and was said to be instrumental in converting him to Catholicism. With a newfound faith, Lee had made amends with those he felt he personally had attacked a little too hard during the 1988 campaign, particularly Dukakis, to whom, in the heat of the battle, he had made several rather raucous *personal* remarks. However, Lee never apologized for the *manner* in which he ran the campaign. Seeing George Bush catapulted into the White House had been his greatest feat, and he never had seen anything unfair in that contest, nor had he seen the need to express regret for his actions. For more than a year, having been in a struggle with the most deadly form of cancer and the most aggressive forms of treatments—causing untold pain and deformity—he still savored the memory of Election Day 1988.

Underneath Atwater's pompous rhetoric and his personal foibles, lay a set of principles and values seldom found in political warriors. Loyalty was important to Atwater. In 1981, when he was new to Washington, he had spent time figuring out how the city worked, and while learning how to "push the outside of the envelope," he became more interested in knowing people than working a crowd. He was constantly busy establishing relationships, inside the Beltway and out. Although, he may have appeared to others insensitive, I believe he saw more to life than he let on.

In the nation's capital, friendships do not hold such a high priority; a friend today is not always one the next, especially if someone better came along. It's "see ya!" Part of the unwritten political code—in the section on ambition—says that it is perfectly acceptable to step on as many people's toes as need be for *you* to get to the top. As much as Atwater loved winning, had a passion for success, and thrived on being the center of attention, he would do whatever he could *not* to sacrifice a friend. Allegiance was prized, and he gave it to those he respected.

As a youngster, Atwater had scrambled to make a name for himself and to get ahead in the world. He differed from the blueblood, Yaledegreed man he helped elect President. But underneath the diverse exteriors of these men, was a common link: their shared values of loyalty and trust. To the surprise of many, a mutual respect had grown between Bush and Atwater, one that had worked to the advantage of both.

Because of rumors about Lee's womanizing and his harsh political style, Bush initially had doubts about him as his manager. Atwater's trustworthiness was suspect because of his previous business dealings with Charlie Black (his partner, who supported Kemp in the 1988 campaign). Nevertheless, over time Atwater proved himself, and from where I stood, he became the President's strongest and most dependable advocate.

The President relied on Atwater to understand the country and the American people in a way that he could not. Spending time cruising K-Marts and Dart Drugs, chatting with Middle American folks was Atwater's gift. He was as a man "of the people"; no pollster could do the job of reading the public as well as he, and no one could tell it as straight—not even the master pollster Teeter. Atwater was one of the few to recognize what was driving the country, and, too, he knew how to feed the press. He could spin a story better than anyone, and part of his magic was getting the media to believe him.

Atwater was the President's eyes and ears, and because Bush no longer had his most savvy strategist, protector and friend who whispered to him about where on the political chessboard he should make his next move, Bush became extremely vulnerable.

While Atwater was sick, his authority had been usurped. Once he no longer was able to function as RNC chairman, Sununu and Darman had stealthily claimed his territory, transferring it from the RNC to *their* White House. Without Atwater, many ill-intentioned takers surfaced.

Even though his presence would not have guaranteed a win in '92 (Baker was much too powerful), I believe Atwater's presence would have had a curbing influence on the defeat. While he was alive, he had bridged the Republican Old Guard with the New One—as well as anyone could—and he knew best how to keep the fractured Republican squad together—as well as anyone could.

Political operatives such as Darman, Rollins, Black and Fuller as well as Rogers, Ailes and Pinkerton needed Atwater to keep them on track. Baker would always weigh in above everyone else, but with Atwater

★★★

there, he did not weigh in *quite* as heavily. The Guys, who at one time or another had been buddies with Lee, simply lost the big picture if Atwater was not around. Their individual egos, when not tempered by the guitar-strumming wiry man from South Carolina, clashed, taking them down self-serving paths. Lee Atwater rounded their sharp edges.

Atwater's situation in the Bush presidency was unique; his job was multifaceted: to be involved in campaign races, run the national convention *and* influence domestic policy. With this authority, he alone could steer both the White House political agenda and the Republican Machine. Had Atwater survived, his role as liaison between the West Wing and the campaign staff *would have* provided a cohesive mechanism for guiding the '92 troops, a situation seldom seen in an incumbent's run. More often than not, hostility between the two camps stifled the campaign process. In his RNC position, Lee was endowed with the unprecedented ability to forge an alliance between the RNC and the White House. Those individuals who knew Atwater's talents and skills agreed, including Jim Wray, Mary Matalin and Charlie Black.

Jim Wray, director of the Bush political office, and David Carney his deputy, turned to Atwater for direction. This had not been anything new for Wray; starting in 1987, he had been one of Lee's regional political directors in the campaign, going on to be national field director. Wray knew how lucky he was to have Atwater in his corner.

Ed Rogers (assistant to Sununu), had been tapped to take over Wray's job and the White House political operation in October 1990. Rogers, accustomed to taking orders from Atwater (since Reagan days), would have enjoyed the opportunity to work with his mentor again in the '92 reelection. Although a good foot soldier, Rogers was neither a leader nor a strategist. Ed needed Lee to get the work accomplished.

Mary Matalin also required Atwater to do her job. Since the 1988 win, she had reported to Lee as his chief of staff at the RNC, and like Wray had been one of Lee's regional political directors. She was dependent on Atwater to make things move ahead, and she recognized how reliant the entire Bush entourage was on Atwater for his leadership. In the *National Journal's* December 3, 1988, issue Matalin commented about the expected relationship between Atwater and the incoming White House political operatives; "He is recognized as the chief political guy, and now he is going to be the party guy. Every one of us who could have these jobs in the White House and RNC would defer to Atwater on every single issue."

Also among those recognizing Atwater as The Chief was Charlie Black, quoted in the November 23, 1988, *Washington Times,* just after Atwater took his appointment; "Lee will focus on the mechanics of Party building and winning elections on the local level, but he will also encourage candidates to support George Bush's programs, which does mean conservative programs."

Some of the Republicans not so fond of Atwater viewed him as a manipulator of power, but even they still claimed him as their colleague. Lee was able to cut across the lines of political allegiances, policy differences and personal idiosyncrasies—in a way no one else could. In 1988, Atwater had held the feuding factions off just long enough to allow for the Bush victory.

Yet, in preparing for the 1992 challenge, things had not worked out the way Atwater had predicted. The cancer had been diagnosed a brief year into his chairmanship, and he simply had not had the energy needed to face the gargantuan challenges involved in managing the RNC operations and running a reelection. The remaining Bush administration and '92 campaign would have to go on . . . but without Atwater.

Without his commanding the troops, I feared the consequences, and as I mourned the loss of Lee, the man and the politician, I sensed imminent peril for the administration that had been, in many ways, Atwater's legacy.

★★★ ▬▬▬▬ ★★★

CHAPTER

28

THE POLITICAL PULSE

The temptation in the world beyond the beltway is to blame the failures of government on the self serving tactics of the games politicians play in Washington, without considering larger flaws in our political system.

—Hedrick Smith

<u>SUMMER 1991</u>

Commuting in Washington is a nightmare.

No one arrives in the District without encountering the sixty-three-mile roadway known as the Capital Beltway, the epicenter of Washington's transportation system. Laid out in the shape of a flattened circle, the six-lane superhighway that encompasses the city and runs through the outlying areas of Virginia and Maryland handles more than twice the traffic for which it was designed. The Beltway is a conduit for sixteen and eighteen-wheelers, and it is prone to multiple accidents, caused by monstrous transport vehicles. Getting to and from work, it is not unusual to spend an hour or two sitting in the car while in a five-mile backup; with rain or snow, the time doubles.

Navigational bearings are important when maneuvering the Beltway; driving clockwise is being on the "inner loop," driving counter-clockwise is being on the "outer loop." Everything inside the inner loop is "inside the Beltway," everything outside the outer loop is "outside the Beltway." The District of Columbia lies in the middle of "inside," and most of the bordering suburbs are found "outside." It sounds either baffling or simplistic at first, but to be driving without these geographic definitions in a city where rush hour lasts twenty-four hours a day is to be a lost soul. In 1990, with the federal government employing 360,000 workers (plus another 100,000 military), not to mention the private sector workforce, and without an adequate transit system, most of us spent a good portion of the day on the road.

In bumper-to-bumper traffic for an hour-plus every morning, I listened to the radio station that reported traffic conditions and squeezed in some light rock. In the second week of April—shortly after the memorial service for Atwater—I was heading to work, in standard backed-up traffic, which meant I was late for my 9:00 Electronics Industry Association meeting at the J.W. Marriott Hotel.

Electronics executives, members of the EIA were rendezvousing in Washington for a three-day conference to be held at the end of April, and as government liaison for the affair, I was helping to coordinate portions of the annual affair, making sure there was sufficient meeting space for some four hundred people. And too, because several functions involved well-known guests and speakers, including Secretary of Defense Cheney and Vice President Quayle, arrangements had to be made for a federal security police force.

At the time I was planning for the conference, Bush was receiving an unprecedented 92 percent approval rating, and the country was euphoric over the Gulf win. Unlike Powell and Schwarzkopf, who had been dubbed the military heroes of the war, Richard Bruce Cheney, Jr., had not immediately gone on to celebrity status or received anywhere near the number of speaking engagements as had his armed services counterparts. Now, two months after the war had ended, the pragmatic, surly "behind-the-desk warrior" at Defense was beginning to evolve into a star. Two years earlier, in the *Washington Post* (March 18, 1989), Helen Dewar had written in "Cheney Confirmed for Defense" the following:

> Cheney had supported the railmobile MX missile over the smaller Midgetman, voted for new nerve gas production and expanded funding for the Strategic Defense Initiative ("Star Wars"), while opposing efforts to ban testing of antisatellite weapons and limit all but the smallest underground nuclear tests. He opposed efforts to require congressional notification—within 48 hours—of covert operations, and has questioned the constitutionality and utility of the Vietnam-era War Powers Resolution, which required congressional approval for long-term U.S. military operations.

★★★

The man viewed as the pro-war advocate on Bush's military advisory team, and only the fourth civilian with no prior military service to be secretary of Defense, Cheney had a curious background. Cheney—the man who dodged the military draft five times during Vietnam—was not the model champion for defense. Just before the EIA event, on April 3, 1991, in the *Washington Post,* Phil McCombs quoted Cheney in, "The Unsettling Calm of Dick Cheney":

> "The, uhm, I think the value of American commitments and our ability to give meaning and substance to those commitments in terms of military capability is greater today than at any other time since the end of World War II. There can't be any doubt in the minds of our allies around the world about our capacity and willingness to use force to keep our commitments, to protect our interests, to protect those of our friends and allies . . . the military itself, as an institution in the United States, stands higher today than it has at any other time since World War II. A lot of the criticism that was part and parcel of the 70's and 80's—uh, stupid generals, uh, equipment that doesn't work, uh, idiots running the Pentagon who don't know what they are doing—clearly wasn't valid."

Cheney had entered Yale in 1959, and with grades too low to continue, he withdrew in 1962. After some time building power-line transmission towers at home in Wyoming, he went back to school, this time at the University of Wyoming, where he received a B.A. and Masters; afterwards, he attended the University of Wisconsin to study for a Ph.D. that he never completed. From 1963 to '65, Cheney received four student draft deferments and, later, a fifth one for being married with a dependent child. He married Lynne in August 1964, and their first child, a daughter, was born in July 1966, seven months after his last deferment. Dick Cheney managed to dodge the draft for a total of four years, until he was 26 years old and no longer eligible.

At the EIA luncheon, Cheney spoke about the Gulf Crisis, acclaiming the work of the men and women who won the war, while pointing out the technological aspects. He made reference to 10 percent of the weapons being "smart" munitions, and said that they had proved their worth several times over during the days of combat. Cheney seemed as calm and cool as he had on television when addressing the American public about Desert Storm war issues.

On the last evening of the conference, Quayle (who recently had celebrated his forty-fourth birthday) gave the after-dinner remarks. The Vice President appeared unusually assured and instantly gained the attention of those who filled the room to capacity. He, too, had been involved in foreign affairs during the Gulf War, and on this night, he talked about the President's strengths during the days of military conflict, and how, for Bush, war had been the last choice. Bush, he said, was not prone to following the imperialist mentality of taking down foreign governments with war tactics. The EIA gathering closed on this note.

Regarding media presentation, little had changed for Quayle, and immediately after the conference, in May 1991, when Bush was hospitalized for an irregular heartbeat, the Vice President had been ridiculed mercilessly. The President's heart flutter turned out to be a symptom associated with Graves' disease, a thyroid condition that both he and Barbara acquired, and a problem that pills would easily remedy. Still, the comments about "the thought" of Quayle becoming President brought on a barrage of jokes.

JOHN Sununu was also being subjected to an inordinate amount of mockery in the spring of 1991. It was made public that Sununu had used government planes to take personal trips to such places as Aspen and Vail, Colorado, for skiing expeditions. Though not breaking the law or violating ethical guidelines, he was charged with "bad judgment," and the press ran Sununu-flight stories repeatedly; some included songs. One of the more popular tunes was printed in the *Washington Post:* "A Sununu Sing-Along," to be sung to the tune of "Chattanooga Choo Choo:"

> Pardon me George
> But are ya gonna sack Sununu?
> We trust that you care
> That we've been paying his fare.
> We will assume
> That things were fine as far as you knew
> The man's got his rights
> But he should spring for his flights....
> At least make him pay
> Whenever he may roam
> Oh, pay up, John Sununu,
> Or kindly stay the hell home.

★★★

Political travel was one thing, but treks to Colorado for skiing and excursions home to New Hampshire for dental appointments were quite another. On April 21, the *Post* printed a copy of a Pentagon log showing a list of flights on which Sununu had been the principal passenger during 1990; there were 120 entries (60 round-trips). Sununu's government jet, costing nearly $5,000 an hour to fly, cost $30,000 for *one* round-trip from Washington to Denver. For most of the jaunts, Sununu had flown in a C-20, the twelve-passenger military version of a Gulf-Stream III; the 89th Military Airlift Wing, which provided air transport for the President, Vice President and Cabinet members, cost $26,000 an hour. As an aside, the new Air Force One, a $410 million Boeing 747, equipped with 85 telephones, an anti-missile system and over one million feet of electrical wiring had been scheduled to be completed in time to take the Reagans back to California in January 1989. Although approved by Congress in 1986, the plane did not take to the air until the end of 1990, when Bush made the inaugural flight on his Thanksgiving trip to the Middle East.

The travel stories and songs about Sununu appeared comical at first, but then they turned ugly. Angered by the blitz, Sununu delivered what he deemed to be a proportionate response, and he fought back, thrusting himself into a downward spiral. His comments neither furthered his cause nor helped the position of the President.

Another senior-level Bush appointee, the third under fire at this time, was Secretary Mosbacher. Like Sununu, he was accused of flying "inappropriately," on private jets for business travel. Mosbacher had used the government planes only for high-level meetings, preferring to fly on the planes of former associates, GOP contributors and companies looking to the DOC for business enhancement. During the first eighteen months of the administration, Mosbacher logged almost eighty trips. He had flown gratis on maybe thirty; the remaining fifty or so trips had been on commercial flights or in friends' private planes. The question being asked was whether or not the complimentary trips had unduly influenced his political decisions regarding his friends and the Commerce department.

By law, Mosbacher was granted the right to solicit corporate aircraft for his trips. Since 1964, DOC officials had the legal authority to accept gifts from nongovernmental sources, as long as the donor had no business pending before the department. Although nothing was unethical about Mosbacher's actions, there was the appearance of impropriety.

Mosbacher had abided by the rules and had not abused his political position, yet reports to the contrary persisted.

Added to Mosbacher's travel trials were accusations far more serious: that he had authorized illegal exports to Iraq. Advanced technology exports licensed by the Commerce department had been a problem during the Reagan administration. Before invading Iran in 1980, Iraq had been one of the richest nations in the Middle East, with hard currency reserves somewhere around $30 billion. By 1982, these funds were gone, and by the time Saddam invaded Kuwait in 1990, his country had a foreign debt estimated to be close to $100 billion.

Just after Reagan was reelected in 1984, when the United States was anti-Iran and opposed to the Islamic Ayatollah Khomeini, the government restored full diplomatic relations with Iraq. Between 1983 and 1989, annual trade between Iraq and the United States had grown from $500 million to $4 billion. However, there were embargoes on U.S. arms shipments to both Iraq and Iran, and Iraq could not legally buy U.S.-made weapons. To get around that, Saddam purchased American "nonmilitary" computer technology.

While Reagan was President, the United States, via the Defense department, was not permitted to engage in arms sales to Iraq. However, the Commerce department *had* approved hundreds of millions of dollars in exports of sensitive technology—supposedly intended for nonmilitary purposes, "dual-use" items—equipment that could serve both military and civilian purposes. The Iraqis were imaginative in describing benign uses for gear that, on arrival in Iraq, vanished immediately into arms plants. Discovered during the U.S. bombing in the Gulf War, most dual-use exports purportedly had been diverted to missile programs and used for designing and testing weapons.

Using loans from U.S. banks, Iraq had bought $5 billion of American exports, mostly grain and technology, and the Atlanta branch of the Italian-owned Banca Nazionale de Lavoro (BNL) had been its principal source of credit. Christopher Drogoul, who ran the Atlanta BNL, later stated that the U.S. knew of the off-the-books loans . . . up to the day Saddam invaded Kuwait. Yet despite Iraq's status as a terrorist nation, the Reagan White House had been quite friendly with the nation, as both a trading partner and a political ally against Iran. Up until the time Bush took office, while Iraq was buying American exports, the U.S. had bought

$5 billion in Iraqi oil, and international relations between the two countries appeared pleasant. That changed in the Bush administration.

In 1990, unconfirmed reports showed that, for the past five years, Commerce had approved hundreds of licenses for technology shipments to Iraq, totaling $1.5 billion in sales of dual-use computers and telecom equipment. These exports were legally exported under DOC rules and had legitimate commercial applications, but they also were believed to aid in the production of chemical and biological weapons. Now, with the Gulf War over, there was concern about the U.S. having *ever* sold *anything* war-related to Iraq, and in the summer of 1991, the situation involving "legal-turned-illegal" exports escalated.

Secretary Mosbacher's attempts to clarify the dual-use items only brought that much more negative attention to him. Eventually, the story made national news and Mosbacher ended up on *Larry King Live*. Now, not only everyone in the U.S. knew about the occurrences, other nations were made aware as well, causing even more negative ramifications, in particular, with China.

For President Bush, the Iraqi-technology controversy enhanced the amount of Congressional badgering he was already suffering, and nowhere did this surface more visibly than in Chinese matters regarding Most Favored Nation (MFN) trade status. China Premier Li Peng warned the United States that, if it did not renew China's favored status, the U.S. would "suffer greatly." Chinese officials had placed an order for fifteen Boeing 737 and 757 planes, and they threatened to cancel the order if their demands were not met. American commercial aircraft manufacturers, having sold more than $700 million worth of airplanes and parts to China in 1990, supported MFN status, but it was related that most Americans opposed it.

The U.S. Congress accused the Chinese government of several infractions, including pirating copyrighted computer software (estimated to cost U.S. software companies $400 million a year), neglecting the human rights of its citizens—through prison labor, forced abortion and military violence—and illegally selling missiles and nuclear technology.

Rumors flew regarding Chinese labor camps that used prisoners to assemble commercial products, causing heated debates in the U.S. Congress and prompting attacks by congressional members on one another and on the President. U.S. relations with China, which had not been satisfactory since before Tiananmen Square, were on the brink of dissolving.

As former Ambassador to Beijing, Bush understood the Chinese culture as well as anyone, and now he looked for a way to continue diplomatically. Realizing that the termination of favored trade status would cause an immediate and damaging reduction in U.S.-China trade and, at the same time, open the door for Japan, Britain and France to increase their exports to China, Bush recommended continuing China's MFN status for another year. This proposal was not well-received.

After China's army had suppressed the student democracy movement in Tiananmen Square, everything had changed in the eyes of Congress. On June 4, 1989 (just after a State Visit by Gorbachev), student demonstrators had been told by Chinese government officials that the square needed to be cleared and that those protestors who remained would be shot. Many students stayed, and the Chinese army pulled out their submachine guns and killed five thousand students, leaving twice that number wounded. Some U.S. reporters who had been covering the Gorbachev visit had stayed on a few days and, by chance, were at the scene the moment of the outbreak. They captured the genocide on film, enraging the Chinese government, which immediately banned all broadcasts, but not before the footage was transmitted worldwide.

During the summer of 1991, the U.S. press—with the help of the Congress—assisted in keeping the Tiananmen story alive, and the memory of the student protestors gunned down remained vivid in Americans' minds. This made carving out an American-Chinese diplomatic path that much more troublesome for Bush. While he tried to find common ground between the United States and the most populous country on the globe (1 out of 5 inhabitants), the President was continually overstepped and overpowered by those on the Hill.

It was in this oppressive climate that my next assignment would take place. I unexpectedly found myself preparing for a trade mission to Hangzhou, China.

In early June, just as I was about to leave my office, I took a call from Robert Burnell of Info Catalyst in California. He wanted to talk to someone about taking a technology trade mission first to Hong Kong and then on into mainland China. Proposing that the trip be in the early fall, he suggested that if the office of Science and Electronics would recruit the

★★★ ═══

business executives to go on the mission, and if Dunn would lead the delegation, his firm would handle all the political and social arrangements in Asia. Burnell also requested that Dunn designate a point person from his office, someone with whom Info Catalyst could be in daily contact during the planning stages.

The following day, I told Dunn about Burnell's proposition, and he was rather nonchalant about the idea, but said O.K. I volunteered to be the point person, explaining that I would do the preliminary work to determine the mission's feasibility. Again, he agreed. Once Dunn released control of a project, he rarely got involved. I knew I would be on my own.

Despite Dunn's affirmative response to my request, I was certain that he would not give the idea of a trip to the South China Sea much thought; in fact, I was sure he would write it off as never happening. Actually, he had good reason. Anything having to do with China at that time—with relationships so strained—was politically in the extreme, and chances were the White House would not give its approval. The Bush administration had not sent a government-sponsored mission to China since Tiananmen Square, and as far as we knew, there were no plans to send a delegation anytime soon. Nevertheless, I tried to remain optimistic. For appointees; China is the premiere nation to visit.

ALTHOUGH the Persian Gulf victory was still regarded as a triumph among most Americans, the red, white and blue insignia was beginning to fade. And with relationships between the White House and Capitol Hill on edge, the President was starting to lose some of his popularity. However, this was not being represented in the polls, which showed him with a 90 percent-plus approval rating. As a result of Bush's war heroics, the people still had confidence in their leader, and the press persisted in its reports that Bush stood out among previous presidents. A commentary by Max Lerner in the *Washington Times* (May 1991), titled "Our Five Living Presidents," read:

> As for George Bush, he has proved the most surprising of the five [Nixon, Ford, Carter, Reagan, and Bush] in his tapping of an unexpected command of his office. He is acting out an American destiny on a stage where he stands unchallenged by any other world leader. My guess would be that we will have to wait until 1997 before casting him in the role of ex-president.

The media concluded that Bush had found his political strength and that his American Destiny would live on for another term.

At the height of the President's popularity, it seemed fitting that he would invite a dignitary to share the good times and enjoy Washington's springtime pleasantries with him. Queen Elizabeth II was the guest of choice, making this the Queen's ninth visit to the United States (her last trip had been in 1983). On the morning of Tuesday, May 14, on the South Lawn of the White House, a welcoming ceremony took place. An unusually large crowd was on hand on this spring day, and as is customary, the bands played, and the military ranks marched up and down the driveway that encircled the grounds. The attendees, myself included, attempted to find comfortable spots in which to settle, trying to stay away from the distracting press corps and find places under the gnarly, umbrella-like trees that provided shade from the warm May sun.

Standing just feet away from the podium, I observed that President Bush, wearing a dark blue suit, and Queen Elizabeth in a deep-purple suit with matching hat and white gloves, made an impressive international pair. As they stood on the welcoming platform, with the South Portico behind them, the press and the world caught, for a moment, two heads of state enjoying their place in history. They appeared as pleased with the moment as we did.

Four of the nine days of Queen Elizabeth's visit to the United States were spent in Washington, and she became the first British monarch to address Congress. With Prince Philip, she attended a Baltimore Orioles baseball game as the guest of President Bush. The following day, the royal couple traveled to Florida to meet Norman Schwarzkopf. The Queen wanted to congratulate the Army general for his Gulf War victory.

The lazy days of summer were just ahead, that time when Washington takes a break from it all, grabs a friend, and like the Queen and the President, goes to a baseball game.

★★★ ━━━━━━ ★★★
CHAPTER
29
START:
A SUMMER SUCCESS STORY

The name of "American" which belongs to you in your national capacity, must always exalt the just pride of patriotism more than any appellation derived from local discrimination.

—George Washington

<u>AUGUST–SEPTEMBER 1991</u>

Summertime in Washington is slow paced, hot and humid. Not a good time for wearing dark suits. An all-or-nothing syndrome hits around mid-June and in about a week's time, professionals go from doing it all to doing nothing. Because there is so much focus on the job ten months out of the year, the federal workforce seems to "forget it" in July and August. Many are on vacation or talking about going on vacation or just getting back from vacation. Even the President takes time off, and in the summer of 1991, the White House staff shifted into low gear while Bush was first on official travel and, then, on summer holiday.

Before Bush began his family vacation at Walker's Point (the family's summer home in Kennebunkport, Maine), he made two overseas trips; on both, he took with him a number of his seventy-five advisors and support staff. The first journey, starting in mid-July, was a combination of four State Visits and an Economic Summit. The ambitious twelve-day trek to six cities and five countries (Paris, France; Athens, Greece; the Isle of Crete; Ankara and Istanbul, Turkey; London, England) culminated in London at the gathering of the G-7. On July 11, 1991, *Washington Times* staff writer Frank Murray, in "Bush's Economic Odyssey Begins with

349

Kaifu," depicted Bush's tour this way: "President Bush begins a grueling 12-day round of diplomatic summitry today to pit his new world status as victorious war leader against the ambitious Soviets and harshly combative Japanese. Even Mr. Bush concedes that Soviet President Mikhail Gorbachev likely will steal the show at the seven-nation summit of industrial nations for the third year in a row."

The Summit was to be the highlight of the trip and the final stop before returning to Washington, and it was in London where President Bush spent time with a group of fellow heads of state, including President Gorbachev. As had been predicted, and with no apparent misgivings on the part of Bush, Gorbachev did indeed take center stage in London, where he took time to brag about the speed with which his government was making the transition from communism to capitalism and a free market system. For his recent achievements, the Soviet president was given special praise and recognition, and the Soviet Union was admitted to the prestigious International Monetary Fund (IMF) and World Bank. While in London, Bush and Gorbachev, having previously established a rather congenial relationship, delved into what was described in the press as a "productive" dialogue.

Within days of the G-7, President Bush, back in Washington, once again took flight over the Atlantic, this time to Moscow, where he and Gorbachev continued their discourse. The Soviet nation, once the Evil Empire according to Ronald Reagan, had become key in Bush's global plan for an economically linked world. Years ahead of his fellow statesmen—in Washington and around the world—Bush realized that, by establishing camaraderie with the other heads of state, an American President could more likely make peace among nations. In a non-confrontational, interconnected world, trade and financial networks could form. The Bush Plan had a harmonious nature; combative styles were not advocated, yet *for that reason,* Bush's strategy—far more civil than many in Washington's foreign affairs assemblage—was not always popular.

From a historical perspective, the 1991 Bush-Gorbachev summer meeting was momentous. The Presidents of the world's two mightiest nations signed the first treaty *ever* to slash U.S. and Soviet nuclear arsenals, by an unprecedented 30 percent. The Strategic Arms Reduction Treaty (START) was heralded as a landmark success and considered one of Bush's finest accomplishments. I believe it to be his crowning triumph,

★★★

a feat beyond all others during his four years as commander-in-chief. No other action was as significant to peace or more serving of humanity than this treaty. For Gorbachev, this achievement would also be his final one. While putting their signatures on START, Bush and Gorbachev were heroes, but unbeknownst to them at this pivotal moment, they were together on the world stage for their Final Act.

Despite Gorbachev's bragging at the London Summit, "all was well at home," the truth was, it was not. The Soviet people were angry. Their president, it was said, was not responding to their economic needs. Unexpectedly this situation exploded into a political coup—all within days of the endorsement of START.

Two weeks after Bush's return from Moscow, and while everyone in Washington was still on holiday, Gorbachev was ousted from power. The August 18, 1991, headlines in the *Washington Times*—in large, bold type—read "Gorbachev Out." The Soviet president, who had been the Communist Party chief since 1985, had, himself, been on summer vacation the day Vice President Yanayev unilaterally declared a six-month state of emergency and made himself leader. Having had no warning that Yanayev was going to issue a communiqué on August 17, Gorbachev was taken by complete surprise. Yanayev pronounced the Soviet chief unable to continue for "health reasons." The coup d'état, successful at first, would ultimately fail. However, Gorbachev would lose his presidency; this downfall would later be attributed to his being "too much of a communist" for a country with a failing economic situation.

It was true that Soviet families were struggling to keep food on their tables. But the majority did not blame Gorbachev. Adversaries faulted Gorbachev for being uninterested and unable to resolve the country's economic plight, and mocked his holiday to the United States and his party in London. Although the overthrow fell short and many in the homeland wanted Gorbachev to return, he never would regain his power. In fact, the Soviet Union, as it had been known, would soon disappear, and the fifteen Soviet republics would start declaring their independence—one by one. Russia, the largest republic, already had named Boris Yeltsin its new president.

Throughout this time, Moscow radio warned, "A fatal danger was hanging over the nation." The United States, as friend and ally, contributed $1 billion toward food and $35 million in medical aid, in hopes of alleviating some portion of the Soviet crisis.

IN contrast to Gorbachev, Bush, after the START signing, appeared to maintain most of his popularity, although his job approval rating had gone down to 75 percent. Lurking behind the declining numbers was a situation not that different from Gorbachev's: a rise in the nation's concern about the economy. Americans, as had Soviets, were placing blame for the country's present plight on their President. With the glow of the Gulf War having all but disappeared, citizens started to complain that Bush was not economically "in tune" with them and their woes.

Republicans had brushed aside fiscal issues for so many years—for so many different reasons—that it had become the norm. The Reagan White House staff had kept the numbers their little secret starting in 1981 with Stockman's attempted "revelation," and Americans had been happy enough with the way things were. Until now. The effects of the escalating deficit that had never caught up with Reagan or with Bush (in the fall of 1990), crested in the summer of 1991.

I speculate again that President Bush's favorability ratings—as good as they were—were not serving him well; in fact, during his first two and one-half years in office, I surmise his incredibly high statistics had actually worked against him. Approval ratings in the 80 and 90 percent range had bred complacency and self-satisfaction, and despite the victory in the Gulf and an economy purported to be holding steady, there *were* signs pointing in a different direction.

For sixteen months, Lee Atwater had not been around to give the President a reading on the lay of the land or to advise him where he should focus his energy. Without Atwater, who had served as the mortar that held the political team together, no one appeared to be asking, "Are the American people really happy?"…"What are their concerns?"…"Are these matters economic or social?" Because the questions were not being asked, the answers were not forthcoming.

The one exception to this dearth of data came from studies of Richard Wirthlin, a Mormon from Salt Lake City and Ronald Reagan's premiere pollster. Wirthlin, who never favored George Bush, had been pushed to the side by Baker in the 1984 Reagan reelection campaign. Baker's man, Bob Teeter, had done the polling. In 1988, Wirthlin had become Bob Dole's campaign pollster, and after Dole's loss in the primaries, he had found his way to the RNC, I assume at the invitation of the Reagan group in place there. Almost three years after the 1988 election, I read an article, "The Political Pulse Beating for Bush," by Donald Lambro that appeared in the *Washington Times* on July 15, 1991. Wirthlin, who had put together some formidable figures on the Bush presidency, told about some unusual poll results collected by his staff in the McLean, Virginia office:

> Pollster Richard Wirthlin's latest survey shows that four months after the cease-fire, the president "maintains strong public support from the American people." Moreover, his 75 percent approval score represents "the first time since Lyndon Johnson enjoyed the halo effect of following John Kennedy into office, that the job approval for a president of the United States has remained well above 70 percent for this length of time." [Nevertheless] "Despite strong public approval of his presidency, the mood of the country has turned strangely pessimistic since America liberated Kuwait. Over one-half of Americans (56%) believe the country is seriously on the wrong track, and only 39% feel things are going in the right direction."

Although Wirthlin's stats were not generally reported or acknowledged at the time (at least not by anyone I knew), I thought—as I read them—this was something Jim Pinkerton should have picked up on. Maybe because of my Boston Harbor exile situation, it never occurred to me to contact Pinkerton and ask if he had seen it. In another article, titled "Bush Aides Have Script For '92 Race," Ann Devroy (my favorite *Post* writer), reported a conversation she previously had with Wirthlin. In this piece, which came out on July 23, 1991 (just a week after Lambro's), Devroy wrote about an interview she conducted at the end of the 1984 Reagan-Bush campaign, when Wirthlin was Reagan's pollster: "Reagan wanted a general update on how he was doing, but Bush, the incumbent vice president, wanted all the numbers, the voluminous computer printouts of polling data Wirthlin kept in huge binders that Bush liked to read in detail."

It was Wirthlin's belief that Bush—despite his comments to the contrary—was interested in polling statistics. Assuming there was some truth to this, it was possible, with the present numbers showing a 75 percent favorability rating, the President felt assured of his long-term popularity. Content with his ratings, Bush was not anticipating any difficulty with his reelection. And too, because no President really wants to campaign, he was extremely slow in organizing his new team. Remembering that the '88 victory had succeeded because of Atwater's intuition and initiative, I continued to be apprehensive about Bush's political future.

Before President Bush left for Kennebunkport for Labor Day weekend, he did assemble a potential 1992 campaign staff at Camp David. Although it was said that the meeting did not produce any firm leaders, it did take on some significance for another reason, one having to do with John Sununu.

Prior to the preparations for Bush's Camp David meeting, Sununu already had gathered a group together for a reelection session *without* Bush in attendance. His guest list included aides such as Andy Card, Ron Kaufman, Ed Rogers, Robert Mosbacher, Clayton Yeutter, Bob Teeter, Charlie Black and Fred Malek. Now, in preparing for the President's meeting, Sununu did not see eye to eye with Bush over who should be present, and without the President knowing, he reportedly deleted several names, including Bush loyalists Rich Bond, Pete Teeley and David Bates. In the end, all the invitees Sununu left off the list were reinstated, but not without consequences.

Press reports about the guest list drove an even bigger wedge between the President and his chief of staff. It seems for some time, the press corps had been informed about an inside derailing of Sununu; with the reelection committee gearing up, stories had increased and speculation had escalated. There were those who wanted Sununu's authority taken away, and for sure, someone in the White House was leaking anti-Sununu stories to the press (still Kristol?); games of this type in the election cycle are deadly. Sununu was depicted as weak when he should have been projected as just the opposite. The role of the chief of staff is central to the entire campaign operation and vital to maintaining control among all the team players.

SUMMER quickly turned into fall, and soon everyone was back from vacation. The official pre-election phase was underway, and there was conjecture among the politicals about who would be tapped for the senior campaign slots; everyone was anxious about his or her presumed roles. Since July, Bob Mosbacher had been waiting to become the first formal leader; Bob Teeter and Fred Malek were expected to follow.

★★★

With primary season approaching and yet no chairman to assist in the fundraising effort ($25 million was needed) and no players on the Bush lineup, political news was sparse. Some believed Bush was following the time schedule of Reagan when he had been the incumbent. In 1984, Reagan had taken his time to campaign, based on the advice of Mrs. Reagan's astrologer, Jean Quigley.

During the fall of 1991, the most interesting news was not related to politics, but to the weather. A tempest referred to as the "Storm of the Century" was paralyzing parts of the East coast.

The first sign of Hurricane Grace was spotted in the northeast on October 26. Two days later, the Washington papers and national television displayed weather maps showing a second storm center, also brewing near Canada. Wave height near Sable Island was reported seventy feet and winds peaked at 58 knots (104 miles an hour). By October 30, another storm (a system unto itself) was caught between Hurricane Grace and the Canadian high. These three separate weather schemes converged to create a storm of gigantic proportions—something that happens, the media said, only once every one hundred years. Meteorologists referred to the 1991 tempest as "the perfect storm." "Perfect," in this case, was synonymous with the precise conditions necessary for a such a ruinous squall.

I have sometimes wondered if what I observed during my Bush years may have been "the perfect *political* storm." As opposed to the meteorological occurrence, the Bush storm was neither dictated by Mother Nature nor discernible; it was man-made and designed to unfold without notice. Just as the '91 natural storm had a disastrous effect on the people of the United States, the political storm orchestrated by Baker had a calamitous effect on them also—and the President. The fact that the Baker tempest was determined by those on the Power Pyramid and undetectable to outsiders also made it "the perfect secret."

One of the individuals in on the secret was Craig Fuller, who in Atwater's absence had smartly arranged it so that he would take Lee's place and chair the 1992 Republican National Convention. Because of his new role in the Party (he had left after chairing the Transition team), Fuller was back in the news. During the fall, with so little political data being disseminated, the site announcement of the August 17–20 Republican convention in the Houston Astrodome was portrayed more spectacularly than it would have been at some other time. And it promoted the fact that Fuller was back in the game.

IN the international news, several stories stood out. The Soviet coup was still top news, but concern over the proposed Free Trade Agreement with Mexico was, by now, turning into a major issue, and predicted to have an impact on the '92 campaign.

Bush also faced a conflict in Brussels. While shoring up U.S. troop strength in the Gulf region in the fall of 1990—a year earlier—the World Trade talks had reached a crisis point over a disagreement between the United States and the European community. The fight over farm subsidies had global trade teetering on the edge of obliteration. Negotiations had unraveled. The talks that represented the highest level of world economic cooperation appeared to be taking a giant step backwards, and there was a real possibility that international commerce in the twenty-first century was going to end in catastrophe.

The twelve-nation European confederation—made up of Belgium, Britain, Denmark, France, West Germany, Greece, Ireland, Italy, Luxembourg, the Netherlands, Portugal and Spain, in the 1990's, was attempting to form a common market, EC '92. With its birth, Europe planned on becoming an economic powerhouse; however, at present, there was only mayhem.

Unless the Europeans reduced their farm subsidies, the Bush administration refused to sign the proposed trade agreement, causing thirty thousand angry European farmers to set fires in the streets of Brussels, protesting the U.S. position and causing a stalemate in the negotiations. One hundred discouraged GATT representatives returned to their homelands—without an accord.

A good number of my fellow employees at the Trade Administration were participating in the EC '92 talks, and several were from my office. I had read their briefs referencing the fact that no one could believe negotiations at this high level actually had a chance of failing. Reports were that the (GATT) meetings, again, had failed because the United States would not endorse the conditions.

At the same time, U.S. relations with Latin America were given top billing in the press, especially because of Vice President Quayle's trip to the area in August. Accompanied by Mosbacher and chief executive officers of nine U.S. financial and business firms, Quayle led a five-day trade mission to Venezuela, Brazil and Haiti. The purpose of the tour, according to Quayle, was to show that the Bush administration had "a

★★★ ═══

definite, coordinated strategy to achieve a very stable, democratic Latin America." This was Quayle's eighth trip to the region in thirty months.

Two months before going to Latin America, Quayle had stood in for Bush on a trip to Japan after the President canceled because of his continuing involvement with the Gulf War. Relations with Japan had been and still were on edge, particularly in the trade area, and despite frequent invitations from Prime Minister Toshiki Kaifu, Bush had not yet accepted. The new Japanese Prime Minister was an aggressive, confident and popular leader, seeking world recognition. He had made six visits to the United States to see Bush, and the absence of the usual reciprocal "call" between the two heads of state had left Japanese officials feeling indignant and offended, if not incensed. The White House described the situation as "sensitive."

Quayle had been instructed to try to smooth things over with the Japanese Liberal Democratic Party leader, Kaifu, particularly with matters pertaining to automobile trade. Japan was responsible, in part, for the lingering $100 billion deficits from the Reagan administration, generating losses and layoffs in the American car manufacturers industry. Bush had been pressured by Detroit to curb Japanese automobile imports. Quayle was sent to do the job. And according to Japanese and American newspapers, he did a fine job as envoy, receiving countless compliments from his Japanese hosts, including Kaifu. Quayle spent more time with Kaifu than any other American representative had devoted to a Japanese official in recent memory. Nonetheless, the Japanese car import issue would remain problematic for the Bush White House for months to come.

Of all the international challenges at this time, it was the hostility between the U.S. and China that most distracted the President. Recently, three members of Congress, when on a visit to Beijing, had been "rattled" by Chinese security. They tried to raise a U.S. banner and place white roses in Tiananmen Square in memory of the pro-democracy protesters killed there in 1989. Nancy Pelosi (D-CA—whose son and mine were roommates at Episcopal High School), was one of the three congressional representatives involved.

Although the intent to honor the dead may have been genuine, the "Roses Ceremony" only augmented anti-U.S. sentiment in China, and Premier Li Peng signaled that he was going to further tighten governmental authority and rule more stringently than before. The

Chinese ruler was adamant that Americans were not going to interfere with or obstruct Chinese tenet.

With China taking such a hard stance, U.S. feelings worsened, and Congressional debate over liberalizing trade ties with China and granting MFN status came to an impasse.

Although U.S.–China affairs were far from amicable, I was still hoping things would calm down enough so that the October trade mission to Hong Kong and Hangzhou would fall into place. The trip looked doubtful, but so far, no one had told me to abort the plans I had been working on all summer. The dates were set for October 1–11, and the mission had been given the official name PACTECH '91. Alan Dunn would be leader and I would travel as liaison to the computer executives and their Chinese counterparts.

Over the previous weeks, I had spent endless hours trying to find U.S. technology executives who wanted to go to China. In spite of the fact that the trip would provide lucrative business opportunities for Americans looking for connections in the Pacific Rim, most of those I contacted were not interested in journeying to the Far East. I was amazed at the difficulty I had in generating any interest.

I came to realize that the recent debates in Congress over China's MFN accreditation, along with the distance and expense of the trip, made for the less-than-enthusiastic responses. The People's Republic of China, unlike Europe or South America, was viewed not only as being too far away (12,000 miles), but also as being encumbered with political, environmental, and cultural problems. However, after weeks of mailing out thousands of letters and making hundreds of phones calls, I finally secured twenty individuals, five more than necessary.

Robert Burnell kept his commitment to arrange an aggressive and extensive work-related and social agenda in both Hong Kong and Hangzhou; some two hundred Chinese representatives were now involved in the event. DOC approved Dunn's and my travel plans, and, surprisingly, the White House granted us our political clearances. Nonetheless, just as the major obstacles to the trip suddenly disappeared, Dunn informed me that he was not sure he was going to be able to leave Washington on time.

Recently, Dunn had been nominated for assistant secretary of the Import Administration (another arm within the International Trade

★★★

Administration). This was a nice promotion for him, yet because of extenuating circumstances surrounding the individual he was replacing, it was thought to be a tough appointment to get through Congress. (Dunn was replacing Eric Garfinkle, who was replacing Dennis Kloske, who just had left the DOC after his controversial testimony to Congress regarding technology exports to Iraq.) Political appointments could quickly derail, especially when they needed Senate confirmation, so Dunn, despite his busy schedule, always made time to make sure his Senate preparations were on track.

In July, when rumors started floating throughout the Commerce building that Mosbacher was leaving to become the first formal leader of Bush's reelection campaign, Dunn had been that much more attentive to his nomination. If Mosbacher were to leave, it would make it more difficult for Dunn, who needed him and his friends in Congress to get the appointment through. Under the protection of Mosbacher, who knew and liked Dunn, his promotion would most likely proceed without complications. The potential problem was that with both houses of Congress against the President's China policy, Dunn would not be viewed politically correct if he led a delegation to Hangzhou. The recent incident with Pelosi and the other Congressional representatives in Tiananmen Square had not aided Bush, but then neither had the exposure of Commerce's dual-use technology exports to Iraq. In fact, in the Gulf War's aftermath, the export of any product relating to computers or software was taken very seriously. The timing of the proposed China mission, clearly technology oriented (made up of computer/software executives), could not have been worse.

The idea of the Senate confirming a new assistant secretary who was preparing to take a delegation into China *and* promote the sale of U.S. high-tech in a communist country seemed almost unworkable under the present circumstances. The White House had to be careful about who they submitted for appointment; it was not in their best interest to send Dunn as a tainted nominee. Still, they *had* cleared him for the trip, and in my way of thinking, the "safety" issue seemed more of a problem for Dunn than the White House.

While Dunn was carefully weighing the pros and cons of the trip and tending to his confirmation, I should have been paying more attention to my own political future. With both Mosbacher and Dunn assuming new jobs, I would be left in limbo. This obviously was not a good place to be when calculating one's own security—especially at the start of a reelection campaign when people begin to be shuffled. While I unwisely concentrated on making the China trip happen, Alan Dunn prudently assessed the professional disadvantages of his leading such a mission.

Having decided that, in light of the sensitivity surrounding China, he should keep a low profile during the planning phase, Dunn would wait to see what the mood was on Capitol Hill before heading to Asia. That was playing it safe. Politicians like to increase their odds whenever possible, and Dunn was a true politician, which may have been one of the reasons why two days before we were to leave, he announced to me that he was not going to Hong Kong. He breezily explained that his appointment was going before the Senate "any day" (actually, it did not take place until two months later), and that he wanted to make sure everything was in place before he left for China. Although he had chosen to skip Hong Kong, Dunn said he would meet me and all twenty mission executives in Hangzhou. He asked me to act as leader while in Hong Kong, and then to proceed into China, assuring me that he would be in Hangzhou before PACTECH '91 officially began.

Well aware of the tremendous effort put forth by both the Hong Kong and Hangzhou teams, Dunn knew that, without his appearance, the whole mission would collapse. Hundreds of people had spent months planning for the ten days of scheduled events. Nearly one hundred Chinese government officials were flying in from Beijing and Shanghai to meet him and his delegation. Dunn simply had to be there.

★★★ ━━━━ ★★★

CHAPTER

30

REVEAL NO STATE SECRETS

I want to be at peace with myself. I want a singleness of eye, a purity of intention, a central core to my life that will enable me to carry out my obligations and activities as well as I can.

—Anne Morrow Lindberg

OCTOBER 1991

With less than a clear set of circumstances ready to unfold halfway around the world, I was assigned—without any backup support, advance team or administrative staff—to take a high-profile, senior-level U.S. delegation into Hong Kong. This was unheard of.

With bags in hand, on Monday, September 30, 1991, I took a taxi to Dulles International Airport and boarded a United Airlines flight to Los Angeles. From there I would fly directly to Hong Kong. The plane touched down twenty-three hours later, at 6:00 p.m., Hong Kong time. The flight attendant reported the temperature outside was 95 degrees.

After a quick cab ride from the airport in Kowloon to the New World Harbor View Hotel in Wanchai, I found my room on the thirty-fourth floor waiting for me. Outside my window, which was one entire wall—floor to ceiling—facing to the west, was a spectacular view. Hundreds of boats of all sizes, shapes and colors—ranging from bright yellow to deep purple—were crisscrossing the magnificent Victoria Harbor, and on this particular evening in early fall, the background for the parade of vessels was a tangerine-orange sunset.

Having lost a complete day's worth of time and a night's worth of sleep, I wearily arose the next morning and met Robert Burnell of InfoCatalysts for coffee—lots of coffee—and two croissants. Burnell was responsible for all the event planning in Hong Kong and China. Having notified the U.S. Consulate in Hong Kong that I was arriving in Dunn's place, he was ready to brief me on my newly acquired responsibilities. They started immediately.

My first meeting was at the Consulate. It was a small outpost in comparison to the embassy in Beijing or the Consulate General in Shanghai, nevertheless, it offered most of the same services and was equipped with a full-time staff. Afterward, I attended the Information and Telecommunication Technologies Conference (CENIT), a worldwide exposition being held in the Hong Kong Convention Center. The U.S. computer executives who had flown in for the mission met me there, and together, at the end of the day, we joined several Hong Kong government representatives at a local restaurant for dinner. Because Hong Kong was still under British rule (an arrangement designed to preserve its western-style freedoms) and would not return to Chinese sovereignty until July 1, 1997, most citizens understood English and spoke enough to converse quite easily with American visitors. Ordering a meal was trouble-free.

The highlight of this portion of the visit turned out to be a luncheon cruise sponsored by the Hong Kong Trade Development Council. Aboard a one hundred-foot yacht, the delegates and I spent a half-day sailing on the western side of the island. Twenty Americans and the same number of Hong Kong officials delighted in the sunny autumn day on the water, with an azure sky above. When we reached the unpopulated part of the island, near Aberdeen, we stopped for lunch and with the vessel anchored, a feast previously prepared onboard was served on the aft deck. After lunch, we again set sail.

Sophisticated and witty, as well as congenial and with a zest for fun, our Hong Kong hosts guided the conversation toward one topic after another while our craft made its way through the calm waters. By the evening, we all had joined in on the karaoke sing-along; even those who could not carry a tune found themselves in the spotlight, microphone in hand. Everyone laughed with everyone else—performers included—making for a delightful and relaxing day on the South China Sea.

Planning sessions for the trip into mainland China continued on a daily basis, with Burnell assuring me that, as long as Dunn showed up in Hangzhou, everything was "on go."

Then the night before we were leaving Hong Kong, Dunn called me from Washington. Without the slightest bit of hesitancy (or guilt), he blithely announced that he was not coming to China at all! I fell silent. Because he said nothing more—clearly not wanting to go into any explanation—I started asking questions. Dunn evaded my queries and rudely dismissed my doubts about how I was to handle the schedule in Hangzhou. He kept our conversation open-ended and non-specific, leaving me without any direction as to how I should proceed in his absence or what my role should be concerning the Chinese delegation—let alone our team of twenty computer representatives. In one quick phone call, Dunn disowned the whole affair, saying to me, "Do the best you can. See ya back in Washington."

The trip to China was not advantageous for Dunn's political career. True. However, he was still concerned about keeping in the good graces of the Chinese, who had made extensive preparations for him; he did not want to disappoint them any more than necessary. Nor did he want to let down the U.S. executives depending upon his leadership *or* the White House, which had cut some corners to approve the mission.

Dunn's problem was figuring out a way to cover all his bases, which included several: for him to stay in Washington (thereby placating Congress), for the mission to go to China (to "save face" with the Chinese), and for White House officials to know the mission was still a go. He needed to please a multitude of people, including the West Wing, Congress, China, Hong Kong, *and* the computer executives. Canceling would not work in his favor. The only answer was for someone to take his place on the mission, someone to cover for him.

Because I was the only Washington emissary available, it was not too difficult to figure out that the only way for PACTECH '91 to continue was for me to fill in for him. Already in Hong Kong, I could carry the American flag to China in his absence. I could "fix it" for him by traveling to Hangzhou (with the delegation) and assuming *his* responsibilities. Actually, these thoughts we not in my mind at the time; all I felt then was uncertainty about what was to follow in the next hour, never speculating I would be replacing him.

Dunn never asked me if I were willing to assume his job, nor did he instruct me to take it. I believe the orders purposely had been left out. By not directing me to take the leadership role, he could eliminate the possibility that I might say "no." That way, he could disassociate himself from the appointment in the eventuality that I made some egregious error while in China. Dunn did not want to be held accountable for having passed the job on to an unqualified assistant. However, when he was ready to relate to our Chinese hosts that he was unable to attend—by using the excuse about his approaching Senate confirmation—he wanted to assure them that I was capable and that the festivities would proceed. In his mind, he had come up with the ideal scheme.

While making the plan work for himself, Dunn made it almost impossible for me. He realized how extremely sensitive the mission was, and he knew how unprepared I was. And because he never directly asked me to accept his role, I took on the onerous task without ever agreeing to do so, and without the slightest idea about what was expected of me.

The thought that I, at the GS-14 level, was leading a trade mission into Communist China—alone—was beyond ludicrous. It was terribly dangerous. So many things could go wrong—politically, socially and logistically; for all these reasons, leaders always had a large advance staff with them when traveling abroad.

I had no one there to shepherd me through the ordeal. I was on my own. About as politically incorrect as one could be.

Originally, my role had been to serve as contact between the U.S. delegation executives and the Chinese technology representatives. Dunn was to handle *all* the political, diplomatic and social tasks. Had I actually realized the enormity of what was in store, I might easily have panicked. As it were, anger propelled me forward.

Just south of Shanghai, in central China, lay Zhejiag, China's smallest mainland province, renowned for its scenic beauty. To the north was a flat plain, part of the Yangtze Valley, an area crossed with many rivers and man-made canals, including the Grand Canal, which ends at Hangzhou, the provincial capital. Often referred to as the Silk City, because its factories manufactured exquisite silks, satins, and brocades, Hangzhou was home to more than a million people and was becoming known for its evolving electronics industry. Its combination of beauty and technology made it an ideal location for the PACTECH '91 conference.

On a balmy Sunday afternoon, the delegation and I flew out of Hong Kong on China Eastern Airlines and arrived on an airstrip just outside Hangzhou. After deplaning, we entered the terminal, which was not much more than a shed sitting on a dusty, abandoned stretch of land. The subtropical climate filled with humidity hit me as I stepped off the plane. It must have been 100 degrees.

★★★

Not a soul inside the airport could speak English, so I was relieved when greeted by two Chinese officials. Without claiming my luggage, I quickly was escorted to a black Lincoln Town Car adorned with a small Chinese flag on the right front hood and an American flag on the left. The U.S. executives, situated in a beige minivan, followed behind. I sat quietly on the back seat of the car-made-to-be-limousine; one official sat next to me and another sat in the front with the driver.

The four of us made our way through narrow, unmarked roads into the city, where crowds of people dressed in medium-gray, worn cotton clothing scurried across and beside the roadways. Riding bicycles, pulling rickshaws, hauling carts filled with bricks or wood or vegetables, the young and the old alike seemed unfazed as the shiny black car almost ran them down. Seemingly oblivious to his surroundings, my driver continued to honk his horn, never slowing down, and just kept driving. I felt somewhat self-conscious knowing that the American flag on the car signaled to everyone outside that an American was traveling inside. As the car flashed by, everyone tried to peer inside the windows.

Within a half hour, we reached the Shangri La Hotel, a red brick building with lots of white trim that sat on a hill among rows of jasmine trees; with its large pillared portico adorning the front entrance, it reminded me of an older, stately southern mansion. A cloth banner, the full fifty-foot length of the porch, was attached to the top of the pillars; it read, "Welcome PACTECH '91."

As I entered the hotel, I was told I had an hour to change clothes and prepare myself for a welcome ceremony and banquet. Once in my room, I found that my suitcases had magically appeared. I dressed in a simple, black silk cocktail dress, pulled my blonde-streaked hair back with a black ribbon and put on my everyday black leather heels. With my shoes on, I was just over five feet, nine inches tall. I mention this because I was taller than most of my Chinese hosts . . . by several inches.

With the delegation members, I approached the building in which the banquet was to be held, only a brief stroll from the hotel. As we approached, I could first hear a band playing, then I saw fifty-some musicians, all wearing red and white freshly pressed cotton uniforms and standing (and playing) in front of the Great Hall—the banquet hall. After arriving at the site, I was startled when one of the Chinese representatives instructed me to take the lead in a procession; some thirty others, both American and Chinese, followed.

As I walked down the forty-foot Chinese-red carpet, used as a runner on the stone walk, I focused on the group of children standing on either side, waving small American flags; they began singing to the tunes of the band. Although the music and the songs surrounded me, once I stepped onto the carpet, I do not remember hearing anything.

As I tried to gain a sense of the position I was being thrust into, for some unknown reason Queen Elizabeth came to mind. I thought to myself, "What would she do in a situation like this? How did she greet individuals in a foreign country?" In a split second, it occurred to me that I should have worn a pair of white, wrist-length gloves and a hat, like the queen had worn at the White House welcoming ceremony. With this picture in my mind, I slowly walked down the runner, trying to look as if it were something I did routinely. I waved to the children and then smiled. And smiled some more. I kept telling myself that what was happening was *not* some fantasy. Then, it occurred to me that the mission was going on as planned, without Dunn. In fact, it was proceeding as if it were intended to unfold just this way.

Without any sanctioned preparation or instruction, I had ceremoniously assumed the role of mission leader. *Never* did my Chinese hosts mention the change in plans. They were kind enough to keep their thoughts to themselves and treated me with as much respect as they would have the assistant secretary of Commerce. In the United States, the political arena, especially international trade and foreign affairs, was male dominated. In China, it was even more so, which made the present situation—at least at first—uncomfortable for all of us. In spite of this, though not without some trepidation, I began to enjoy my newfound position, and I sensed that my hosts felt more relaxed as well. Their graciousness—for whatever reason they displayed it—gave me the confidence to continue.

Before the banquet began, I attended a press conference in the ornately decorated Great Hall. In a large room filled with sizable, well-built couches covered in a worn mauve damask, I sat with twenty-or-so Chinese men who, in circular fashion, went around the room introducing themselves. Most spoke in broken English. Before I was asked to make a few remarks, television crews approached. With an interpreter by my side (the man who had ridden in the front seat of the car from the airport), I expressed my pleasure at being in their city and visiting their country.

★★★

After thirty minutes of exchanging introductory greetings, I was escorted to the banquet room.

The formal affair, given in honor of the U.S. delegation and hosted by the Chinese government, was the highlight of the five-day event and sponsored by Digital Equipment Corporation, International (one of the DEC officers was traveling with the U.S. delegation). Two hundred fifty Chinese dignitaries, university presidents, technology executives, bank officials, machine and electronic specialists, and research and development professionals were in attendance. Many had traveled to Hangzhou from Beijing that day.

I took my seat at the head table. As the guest of honor, I sat to the right of Beijing's highest-ranking official (whose name escapes me) and to the left of the vice governor of Zhejiang Province, Mr. Li Debao. Because I had been introduced to many of the Chinese notables at the press conference, I knew most at my table. In a state of elation, blended with disbelief, I gazed out onto a room filled with tables set for ten, laden with the finest crystal and china and arranged on white linen cloths. Menus, printed on thick white paper, crested at the top with the Chinese emblem and printed in Chinese, lay at each place setting.

Immediately after we were seated, an army of waitstaff attendants served the first of fourteen courses. After dinner, there were many toasts and a generous amount of rice wine—followed by shouts of "Gambe," meaning "bottoms up." I was then instructed to make a short address. Extemporaneously, I went to the microphone in the front of the room and with the help of my Chinese interpreter, I referenced my desire for a successful conference between the Chinese and American community. The press corps and television crews, again, were on hand to tape my comments for national broadcast. Before the evening was over, I was given an itinerary for the next day, and noticed that I was scheduled to deliver a speech at 10:25 in the morning. I had not written a word.

As the sun approached my second-floor hotel room early the following morning, I sat on my bed, papers strewn all around me, trying to put an address together. All I had available pertaining to China was the material I had crammed in my briefcase before leaving D.C., most of it sent to Washington by the U.S. Embassy in Beijing, and none of it, except for a few statistics, relevant. Hurriedly, I improvised from a few hand-written notes and then dashed to the auditorium.

I had decided to include a reference to the commonality of China and the United States, and speaking to the gathering, I said: "In 1970, China was admitted to the United Nations, and shortly thereafter, President Nixon made his first trip to China. Since 1979, the United States and China have enjoyed full diplomatic relations and have grown to understand one another in a way thought unattainable just two decades ago." I continued:

> Although the historical and cultural backgrounds of our two peoples are quite different, Chinese and Americans share certain characteristics: an acceptance and tolerance of outsiders and different cultures. The United States is considered to be a melting pot for various cultures; the Chinese people have been quite open to foreigners. Because of this shared openness, it seems only fitting that friendly ties be formed between the Chinese and their American counterparts. I feel there is no reason why our two countries cannot continue prosperous and dynamic cooperation and competition, particularly in the technology arena, while still maintaining respect and integrity for both nations. I am honored to be here on this occasion, the launching of PACTECH '91.

While commenting on bilateral trade conditions and potential markets on both sides of the Pacific, I mentioned that the Boeing Company ventured into China on the heels of Nixon's visit in 1972, and that in 1989, $12.2 billion worth of products were exchanged between the U.S. and China. To my delight, and thanks to an extraordinary sound system, while making my speech, I sounded much more authoritative and convincing than I thought I would.

The next four days were filled with dinners, luncheons and tours, all presenting me with occasions to become more acquainted with China and with the three Chinese men assigned to me for the duration of my stay. "My men" became indispensable. The driver, whose name I never knew; Division Deputy Director of the Zhejiang Foreign Affairs Office (the equivalent to the U.S. State department) Mr. Li, who served as my official escort; and, also from the Foreign Affairs Office, Mr. Pan, my interpreter and translator. These three men, for most of the day and into the late evening hours, never left my side. And I could not have been more pleased with my "guides." Yet, it was Mr. Pan whom I was most fond of. For understandable reasons. Without him, I would have had no voice or ability to understand my Chinese hosts. Nor they me.

A quiet young man of about twenty, Pan was the only one of the three who spoke fluid, fluent English. He made communicating effortless, a talent for which I was extremely grateful. Many times over, he saved the day for me. Pan taught me to move in unison—I should say *speak* in unison—while he translated, reminding me to slow down and speak in half-sentences. Once I learned to do that, I was able to break through the communication barrier, a key to surviving in a country where protocol and proper interpretation were vitally important.

When something went awry, Pan would make a joke about it rather than fret, a technique that had a calming effect on me. His extraordinary sense of timing made my speaking seem natural. He was my voice and ears for five days, and he allowed me to experience China in a way few seldom have the chance. Without Mr. Pan, I would have quite a different China Story to tell. His gracefulness, professionalism and good sense of humor are still vivid in my memory today and will be always.

After the frenetic pace of the first twenty-four hours in Hangzhou, I welcomed the official day-trips that became part of my schedule: visits to city parks, Chinese temples, a medicine museum, a tea farm, even a Chinese wedding in the country.

On one of these trips, with my three leading men, I experienced a piece of paradise on earth—beautiful, romantic West Lake. In 1970, while visiting Hangzhou—two years before visiting Beijing—President Nixon made West Lake a worldwide attraction by referring to it in a speech. Now, twenty-one years after that, I had the occasion to take a ride on its waters.

In a small all-wooden Chinese boat, decorated with a colorful blue-and-white striped cloth canopy fringed in blue, a rower took Mr. Pan, Mr. Li and me out to the largest island in the lake, where it was lush and green and fragrant and the lotus blossoms bloomed as far as the eye could see. By the time we returned to shore, it was sunset and the lake was calm and smooth as glass. The stone-covered bridges and the bluish purple mountains in the distance served as a backdrop for the hundreds of weeping willows that bordered the lake. Pan, Li and I took pictures of each other with my camera—pictures in which the scenery resembled the China described in history books. The China that dated back to the year 2000 B.C.

On the third evening of the mission, the mayor of Hangzhou, Mr. Lu Wenge, an unusually tall and handsome gentleman in his forties, whom I had met the night of the banquet, invited me and the delegation to a silk fashion show. My visit to a silk factory that afternoon piqued my interest in the evening's event. Before the performance began, the mayor made some opening remarks:

> Hangzhou is not only world famous for its beautiful natural sceneries, but for its political, economic, cultural and scientific research. The city government has attached great importance to the development of science and technologies in the recent years. Hangzhou now boasts twenty-one universities and colleges, nine state labs, fifty-two scientific institutes, with over ten thousand professionals and experts, thus forming a high-tech industrial park. We welcome the opportunities for cooperation which this seminar will provide.

Completing his presentation, Mr. Lu took the seat next to me, and an acrobatic performance and magic act, with cards and fresh flowers, started the program. Afterwards, the models, women in their late teens— slim and beautiful— danced onto the stage. In luxurious silks of vibrant-colored pinks, blues and reds, and with contemporary music to accompany them, the young ladies fluttered like butterflies from one corner of the stage to the other, their fine silks floating around them. They were some of China's most famous models, and they were going on tour to several other countries the following week.

On the last night of the mission, at the Hangzhou Huajashan Hotel, six Chinese officials hosted a dinner party in my honor; it was a rather intimate affair. Ten of us encircled a large round wooden table covered in a pale pink linen cloth. An oversized teak lazy-Susan was placed in the middle, where, course by course, platters were placed, and from which we served ourselves. Using chopsticks, we scooped generous portions of fish, beef, rice and vegetables onto our blue-and-white china plates. Cooked in unfamiliar spices and herbs, the Asian delicacies made for a feast.

Joining us that evening was David Murphy, a commercial representative of the U.S. Consulate in Shanghai, an American who spoke almost perfect Chinese. Seated between Mr. Pan, to my left, and Murphy, to my right, I realized I had all the interpreters I needed to join in the fun. I related a narrative about my Grandfather DuBose.

As a young Naval officer (U.S.N.A. 1913), Grandfather was stationed in Shanghai in the late 1920s. My Grandmother DuBose, as a twenty-something Navy wife with a four-year-old daughter (my mother), decided she was not going to stay at home in Annapolis while her husband was out experiencing China. The year was 1927. With haste, and I am sure many complications, Grandmother purchased a ticket for herself and my mother on a passenger ship to Shanghai. As the account goes, she did not let her husband know of her plans.

After a terribly long trip across the North American continent, by train and then across the Pacific Ocean by ship, my grandmother, with daughter, finally arrived in China and went directly to a hotel in Shanghai. In the hotel lobby, the two waited for my grandfather. Having received word at work that he was being summoned to the hotel to meet a fellow officer, the young Lieutenant Commander arrived thinking he was there for a business meeting. Instead, he discovered that his wife and daughter were waiting for him. My grandmother and mother stayed in the Shanghai hotel for several months before returning to their home next to the Chesapeake Bay, and Grandfather, when he told the tale, always attested that from the moment he saw his family in the Shanghai lobby, he was fully aware that his wife had a mind of her own.

I had always enjoyed hearing the story, and now, three-quarters of a century later and in China myself, I enjoyed relating it that much more.

During the last thirty minutes of the bon voyage dinner at the Huajashan Hotel, after much sharing and laughter (mostly at the jokes told by Murphy), the dialogue around the table turned more serious. Comments about technology transfer, software pirating, and intellectual property rights, all extremely sensitive issues for which the U.S. Congress was harassing Bush, surfaced.

The Chinese Minister of the Science and Technology Commission, Mr. Chang, and Vice President of the Zhejiang Electronics Corporation, Mr. Cai, wanted to discuss U.S. technology trade policy, and they were eager for me to understand the ways of their culture and the reasons why political change was so difficult in their country. For years, China had been denied the favored rank and had been kept out of the World Trade Organization. Now that the Chinese had acquired their preferred status, the United States Congress wanted to take it back. Was this fair?

Knowing that I was not to venture into any kind of talk involving U.S.-China policy, I politely bowed out of the discussion leading in that direction. Although I wished I could have responded differently, the U.S.

State department had briefed Dunn and me on what fell within the parameters of "authorized." While having to turn to other subjects, I felt inadequate in my replies. I do not think my hosts realized how restricted I was in what I could say; the only politically correct response for me was "No response."

One of the men at the table had drafted the Chinese reply to the U.S.'s recent threat to abolish China's MFN standing, outlining reasons why the People's Republic of China should receive it. The bill that had given China the same tariff rights as those accorded other U.S. trading partners (including Iraq), after ten years, was going to be scrapped. In fact, the vote to continue China's privileges would be put before Congress in less than a month. That night at the Huajashan Hotel, I listened with empathy, but kept my thoughts to myself.

The next day while returning to the Hangzhou airport, in what I now referred to as "my car" with Mr. Pan and Mr. Li, Pan was already planning for my return visit. I was flattered, but I knew that as much as I would have enjoyed returning someday, another visit to Hangzhou would never approach my time with the PACTECH '91 trade mission. What I had just gone through was inimitable.

On the flight from Hangzhou to Hong Kong, I had time to reflect and a chance to talk to the delegation members; because of my separate itinerary, I had seldom crossed paths with them. For their part, they had been busy forming personal and business relationships; several had entered into new ventures with Chinese companies. Surprisingly, instead of returning directly to the United States, three of the delegates flew from Hangzhou to Beijing to do further business with Chinese government representatives.

I would like to think that, by the end of the mission, both American and Chinese participants had their expectations exceeded, and were taking home with them a new friendship, a potential contract, or just better insight into an unfamiliar culture. I wanted to believe that some of our individual differences had faded and similarities grown. I looked upon the mission as a small bridge that had helped strangers who spoke different languages and lived halfway around the world from one another make a connection. For me this was politics at its best.

Few would ever know what had transpired behind the scenes in Hangzhou, China. Nevertheless, that never diminished its significance for me. Not having time to prepare for the role actually had allowed me to react with fewer restraints and less apprehension. There was not time to dwell on the "what ifs." And without a doubt, during my four years as an appointee, leading the mission to China was my most splendid accomplishment.

Dunn would eventually get his confirmation as assistant secretary, and we would continue to work together for several more months. But he *never* brought up the subject of PACTECH '91 with me; for him, it never happened. At first, I wondered about his response, then I just attributed it to the male macho thing. He knew the China Trip had been a chance of a lifetime. Secretary of State Baker and, later, secretary of Commerce Barbara Franklin would be the only other appointees to visit China during the Bush administration. And Baker's trip, taking place within weeks of mine, was a State Visit on President Bush's behalf (contentious at that), and not a substantial trade mission.

While the mid-October climate was still warm and balmy in the Far East, I made a three-day stop in Hong Kong before returning to Washington. Then, with my ruby-red silk dress from Hangzhou and my coffee-table book with pictures of Zhejiang Province (signed by everyone at dinner on the last night) carefully tucked into my suitcase, I made plans to leave my friends on the China Sea and return to those on the Potomac River. Preparations for the reelection of the forty-first President of the United States, George Herbert Walker Bush, were finally about to begin.

★★★ ═══════ ★★★
CHAPTER
31
POWER PYRAMID

And for the support of this Declaration, with a firm reliance on the protection of Divine Providence, we mutually pledge to each other our Lives, our Fortunes and our Sacred Honor.
          —United States of America Declaration of Independence

NOVEMBER 1991

After I returned to Washington from Hangzhou, my hosts sent me handwritten thank you notes in Chinese, with typed English translations. At the same time, I received a large red leather photograph album that included pictures of the events and festivities with accompanying annotation. Weeks later, a dark brown paper envelope marked "Special Assistant Joslin" was delivered, in which was a ten minute videotape of the opening night ceremonies with me speaking— footage that had gone out over the Chinese television news broadcast.

I was pleased that my new acquaintances had remembered my visit with such thoughtful gifts. And I told myself that their kind gestures far out-weighed the silent treatment I received from Dunn upon my return. I picked out copies of a book titled *Washington: The Capital City* for the eight most senior Chinese representatives and Mr. Pan, and with a personal note enclosed, I mailed the packages to China. Over the next couple of years, I continued to receive cards from several of the officials, particularly during the Christmas season, which I found to be touching.

Shortly after my China trip, Secretary Baker—who I am quite sure never knew anything about PACTECH '91—prepared for a visit of his own, to Beijing. The Chinese government, as were those on Capitol Hill, was annoyed with Bush, and for the same reason: they both felt that he was not promoting *their* interests. Bush's ongoing battle to keep the lines of communication open between Chinese officials and the U.S. Congress was becoming more and more difficult. Not desiring a face-to-face encounter with Beijing at this time, Bush sent Baker as emissary to assist him in "mending fences."

In mid-November, and with the goal to attain a more comfortable bilateral status, Baker was commissioned to carry the American flag to China; as the U.S.'s leading diplomat, he was to negate any acrimonious feelings. Stapleton Roy, ambassador to the People's Republic of China, was there to help with the effort. Born in Nanjing, China, Roy had attended Princeton University and begun his career in the United States government by entering the Foreign Service in 1956. As an intelligence analyst at the State department, he had worked his way through the ranks, to become one of this country's leading Chinese experts. In 1989, before his recent appointment as ambassador to China, Roy was Baker's executive aide at State.

Baker was the first U.S. official to visit Beijing since the Tiananmen incident, and he met with Prime Minister Li Peng, head of the Chinese State Council and one of the prime architects of the massacre. Their talks revolved around the usual: human rights, arms proliferation and trade imbalances. What was not expected were Baker's comments referring to the Chinese government as "a rigid communist regime that has alienated [the U.S.] by lashing out, and by seeking to repress an irrepressible spirit." Baker went on to tell his hosts, "we definitely do not enjoy good relations."

Secretary Baker, having arrived in China not on the most affable terms, departed on even less friendly ones. In the commentary "Coming to Trade Terms with China," in the *Washington Times* on December 11, 1991, Jesse Helms, North Carolina senator and ranking Republican on the Senate Foreign Relations Committee, referred to Baker's trip this way, "There were no friendly toasts to those who ordered Chinese young people ground into paste under tank treads."

As the U.S. Congress prepared to impose trade sanctions against Beijing, the two world powers braced for a head-on collision. Some American officials, including the President, genuinely believed that giving China MFN would facilitate trade and accelerate changes, especially those concerning human rights; Bush predicted the increased economic ties would make a positive difference. Not feeling it prudent to punish China for its infringements by withdrawing its trade status, and believing that commercial interchange was key to bringing nations together, Bush continued to maintain his wider lens view.

Congress did not see it this way. And for the first time, the United States talked about concrete retaliatory trade action. With the possibility of U.S. sanctions, Beijing threatened its own economic retaliation; major U.S. *export* items at stake were: computers and electronics ($860 million); commercial aircraft ($749 million, with Boeing, the huge Seattle aircraft manufacturer shipping thousands of 700-series airliners); fertilizer ($544 million); and wheat ($511 million). The major *imports* affected were toys (over $1 billion); petroleum ($635 million); footwear ($582 million); and sweaters/textile materials ($527 million). Based on figures from a 1990 State department study, if the United States decided to restrain Chinese imports, the economic ramifications to U.S. consumers and corporations, alike, would be disastrous. Realizing this, Congress rethought the matter, and came back with a list of conditions, as a compromise. For example, "if China abolished its practice of using prison labor, then. ..."

Just a month before, in the restaurant in Hangzhou, one of the Chinese officials at the table had said, "We wish that Americans could better understand the slowness in which policy evolves in our nation." He had spoken emphatically and directly to me, with emotion in his voice. It made sense to me that political stability and public order *had* to be the essential objectives for a nation of one billion people. No country wanted restrictions placed on its internal government practices, especially ones tied to trade. A conditional MFN would never work.

After a blitz of publicity, in the fall of 1991, predictably, China refused to accept any of the U.S. sanctions attached to the renewal of the accord, and a stalemate (such as the one with the GATT negotiations) was declared. President Bush's position had put him in a no-win situation, not only with China, but also with the American populace and the Congress.

Substantive discussions relating to trade and economic issues with the People's Republic ostensibly had broken off following Tiananmen Square, the third month Bush was in office, and talks never would resume to a comfortable level while he was President. Normalizing relations with China, for the most part, had been taken off Washington's agenda early on.

Baker, in his meeting with the Chinese leadership, had given the impression that U.S. envoys were stern, unrelenting, and unwilling to

★★★

compromise. The man known for his "smooth talk" failed the President by not conveying *his* desire...his wish for a more amicable relationship— not a more contentious one.

China trade was not the only arena in which Baker's skills appeared somewhat lacking. Within the rank-and-file of his own department there brewed an underlying feeling of resentment toward him; unless one had a personal tie with Baker, it was unlikely one had any relationship with him. For the past three years, Baker had been looking for a way to make his mark on history. Yet, while trying to establish himself as the Nation's Peacekeeper, he sometimes found it more difficult to attain peace at home than abroad. His State department was a prime example.

From the first month of the administration, the Team at Foggy Bottom had been regarded as a Baker enclave, and the association between State's bureaucracy and Baker's Praetorian Guard had been strained. Baker and his personal aides isolated themselves from the others, ignoring the department's careerists, those civil servants who would be there long after Baker left. To the bureaucrats, it often seemed the Secretary was more interested in his own publicity than in determining foreign policy, and although he had a reputation for dealing easily with those at the highest levels (business executives, congressional representatives, senior politicians and Party leaders), he failed to establish a similar rapport with the rank-and-file.

Some of the best and brightest State policy experts were not allowed to do their jobs the way they knew how. Power on the seventh floor was relegated to Baker and his top appointees: Lawrence Eagleburger, deputy secretary; Robert Kimmit, undersecretary for political affairs; Robert Zoellick, department counselor; and Dennis Ross, director of policy planning. None, outside Eagleburger, had strong foreign policy experience. Zoellick had been an aide to Baker when he was secretary of the Treasury (he had also worked with Bob Teeter). Kimmit, too, was a previous aide to Baker at Treasury and the individual who led the vice presidential candidate search, recommending Quayle. Margaret Tutwiler, Baker's spokesperson, and Janet Mullins, assistant secretary for congressional relations, were long-time Baker aides, now serving as his gatekeepers.

It was Lawrence S. Eagleburger who was the powerhouse on Baker's staff, giving Secretary Baker his influence in international affairs during the Bush administration. As previously alluded to, but worth a recap,

few had as much experience and expertise in foreign policy as
Eagleburger, Baker's aide since January 1989. The former Harvard
Professor and aide to Henry Kissinger (national security advisor to
Nixon) had stayed well within the political wake of his mentor for years.
When, in 1973, Kissinger became Nixon's secretary of State, Eagleburger
had been right there with him.

When President Ford assumed office, he agreed to keep the liberal
Kissinger as State secretary, but he made Brent Scowcroft (Kissinger's
chief deputy while he was in that office) NSC director. Eagleburger, also
remaining at State, helped Kissinger fight his fiercest adversary and most
threatening competitor, Ford's Defense secretary and archconservative,
Don Rumsfeld.

In the Reagan administration, Kissinger went back to the private
sector in New York City and Eagleburger was appointed as an assistant
secretary at State, ultimately taking on an undersecretary position. He
stayed until 1984, at the end of Reagan's first term, when, then sixty-three
years old, he joined his former boss in his New York consulting firm,
Kissinger Associates, and was anointed president. Eagleburger had
stayed at the consulting—actually lobbying—firm until 1989, when
tapped by Baker for deputy secretary of State.

Baker was lucky to have a heavyweight such as Eagleburger as his
deputy, but by relying on him alone, he shut out others. By shunning not
only those at State but also those in the other thirteen agencies *and* the
White House, Baker had alienated himself from the rest of the
administration. Nevertheless, despite this isolationist stance, he remained
the most influential member in the Bush presidency and was at the top of
the Power Pyramid—for all four years.

With one exception.

When it came to foreign affair issues, Baker had a challenger.
Another senior officer coming from Kissinger Associates recruited into
the upper ranks of the Bush administration was Lt. General Brent
Scowcroft (Ret.), national security advisor.

Scowcroft, beginning his climb up the foreign relations ladder, had
replaced Alexander Haig (deputy to National Security Advisor Kissinger)
when Haig became chief of staff to Nixon. Under Ford, Scowcroft was
head of the security agency (1975–77). The retired Air Force Lieutenant
General and member of the Church of Jesus Christ of Latter Day Saints
became accustomed to working with the domineering secretary of State,

Henry Kissinger. This had worked to his advantage, especially now that he was—again—national security advisor sharing authority with another tyrannical secretary, James Baker. Currently, Scowcroft's office, just down the street and on the opposite side of Pennsylvania Avenue from the State department, was in close proximity to Eagleburger's.

Brent Scowcroft, Baker's most ardent competitor in the Bush administration, had much in common with Lawrence Eagleburger. In many ways, during the years 1989–93, it was Scowcroft (the senior politico) versus Eagleburger (the junior politico). Both had started in the Nixon White House; both had come from under the tutelage of Kissinger; both were history professors; both had been officers at Kissinger Associates; and both had been senior appointees in four administrations.

For the most part—even with Eagleburger as Baker's deputy—Scowcroft, who liked to duel the State secretary, quietly asserted his superiority in the foreign policy domain under Bush. Unlike Baker, Scowcroft had put together a strong senior management team of foreign policy experts. The National Security Council, set up to relay vital input on foreign affairs to the President *independent* of the secretaries of State and Defense, stood well grounded while engaged in rivalry with Baker. Scowcroft ruled.

Though Baker had personal and professional ties to Scowcroft from years past and was chief Cabinet spokesman on Bush foreign policy matters, he was still a newcomer to the national security arena. Simply because Baker was not more seasoned in the international realm, he was not as able to voice a more substantive opinion. Because of Baker's lack of expertise and because Scowcroft was no longer bound by the restricting policy guidelines of the Reagan White House, Scowcroft had the opportunity to be more outspoken.

The opinions of the Utah native, differing from those prevalent in the Reagan presidency, had brought out the ire and suspicions of the arch-conservatives. Scowcroft had not been favored by the former Reaganites, who viewed him as a sharp critic of Reagan's foreign policy initiatives. The former West Point professor believed the Soviet Union was a force to be reckoned with, but not necessarily with force or by détente. Scowcroft had questioned the Star Wars program and the Strategic Defense Initiative (SDI)—going in the opposite direction from Reagan and Cheney. In 1983, when the Pentagon wanted to disband the Midgetman in favor of the ten-warhead MX missile, Reagan had appointed Scowcroft head of the commission to find a way to use the MX for deployment. In his final report, Scowcroft promoted the single-warhead mobile Midgetman—an ICBM known for its deterrent capability, which meant scratching the multi-warhead MX. Not a popular move. Now that Scowcroft was the ranking national security officer in the Bush White House, his views were of interest to many inside and outside the military.

From his small office in the OEOB, Scowcroft carried more weight than any other security or defense aide, and because Bush endowed him with virtually unlimited authority, Scowcroft's influence escalated. The President created a National Security Directive, restructuring the National Security Council. Two new subcommittees were added to Scowcroft's domain, one to review national security, the other, which included NSC deputies for the first time, to develop policy. And by virtue of his having such a close relationship with Bush, Scowcroft made staying in power more arduous for both Baker, a man terribly turf conscious, and Cheney, who liked power as much as Baker. Twelve years after the Ford administration ended, Scowcroft was again national security advisor, but this time, he had considerably more savoir-faire and control. In the Ford White House, Rumsfeld and Cheney—with complete authority—had dictated the conservative agenda, and despite Scowcroft's weighty presence, in the Bush White House, alliances previously formed as far back as in the Nixon administration could not be ignored when regarding power allocation.

When Rumsfeld had become Ford's chief of staff, Cheney had gone with him as deputy, similar to the Baker-Darman scenario. Rumsfeld had known Ford in Congress when Ford was House minority leader, but more significantly, he had established a close relationship with Nixon and his White House staff. When Vice President Ford came to power in 1974, the Ford White House remained a Nixon enclave. With an iron hand, Rumsfeld ran the West Wing and Oval Office according to former *Nixon* principles, not *Ford* philosophy.

This situation, whereby life was lived according to the mandates of Rumsfeld and Cheney, *not* President Ford, was eerily analogous to the Reagan White House run by Baker and Darman . . . and the Bush White House now being controlled once again by Baker and Darman . . . *not* President Bush!

Although Ford had not been elected to office and Bush had, the two men experienced the same phenomenon of taking the presidential oath in the wake of a predecessor. Ford's succession came under subdued conditions; Bush's under much more favorable ones. Still, the outcome was the same. Another common fate shared by Ford and Bush was that the White House aides and political appointees of their predecessors' administrations never intended to give up their power! And they never did.

Ford had Rumsfeld and Cheney to contend with; Bush had Baker and Darman *and* Cheney. Cheney knew how to run the West Wing to his advantage—as well as Baker—and felt as confident as Baker in commanding the troops and overriding a sitting President.

Because the former Nixonites had been given their authority during the Ford presidency by Rumsfeld (and then Cheney), and the Reaganites had been given theirs in the Reagan and Bush presidencies by Baker, neither contingency had looked at their President as the leader. The Reagan and Bush administrations' Men of Authority had been endowed their supremacy *before* the new President took office. As long as there was a Rumsfeld or a Cheney or a Baker or even a Darman who could protect the outgoing administration from an encroaching new one, the Old Guard was safe. They ran the show, with the father figure nothing more than a figurehead.

Ford and Reagan and Bush had never been looked upon as The President by their staffs, and because of this, these men never held the ultimate power. The Ford White House had been a seamless continuation of Nixon's second term. The Reagan White House had been an eight-year Baker presidency. And the Bush White House was a well-orchestrated Reagan third term, with Darman as captain of the team and Baker the team owner. With men like Baker and Darman overriding Bush's authority, President Bush was placed in an impossible situation. The only reason Cheney was not more influential in the Bush White House was that Scowcroft and Powell—along with the President himself—were there to temper his passion toward the extreme Republican right. Even though Scowcroft held Baker at bay in the international affairs arena, no one could or would ever completely overshadow Baker. He was *the* Republican maestro.

IN the fall of 1991, amidst skirmishes between the National Security Council and the department of State, and the U.S. and China, another scuffle emerged. It turned out to be a national scandal involving the White House nominee for Supreme Court justice. I had just returned from China, where I had heard little U.S. news, and found I was way behind the curve. Bush's candidate for Associate Justice, Clarence Thomas, was causing an uproar on Capitol Hill and throughout the country.

At the time, William Rehnquist was chief justice, and the three liberals on the Court—Thurgood Marshall, William J. Brennan, and Harry A. Blackmun—were eighty-three years old. It had been predicted, before Bush took office, that, when the justices retired, there would be a real battle between the White House and the Hill over their seats. With the replacement of Marshall, who was retiring after twenty-four years on the bench, this prediction proved true.

In the fall of 1991, the Senate Judiciary Committee was conducting congressional hearings on Thomas, an African-American who had served on the District of Columbia Circuit Court of Appeals for almost a year. At the end of September, the Committee voted to send Thomas's name to the Senate floor for a full debate. Afterwards, there was to be a vote on October 8. The Thomas hearings were anything *but* representative of most confirmations.

As part of the customary background investigation on a nominee, the FBI had contacted former employees of Thomas, including Anita Hill, who had worked for him ten years earlier, when Thomas was director of the Equal Employment Opportunity Commission (EEOC). Hill was presently a professor of law at the University of Oklahoma, and while responding to the FBI inquiry, she reported that Thomas had sexually harassed her when she worked for him at the EEOC. She also said that Thomas had engaged in inappropriate sexual game playing with other staff members.

Anita Hill *in*voluntarily gave this witness, knowing that she had far more to lose by speaking out than she had to gain. Having studied harassment in grad school, and knowing something about the subject, I do not believe Hill would have put herself in this position had she not been telling the truth.

In mid-October, after the hearings got underway—and Hill's remarks were made public—Bush was urged by some on his staff to drop the nomination. Opposing the suggestion, the President stood by his ultraconservative candidate, claiming that Thomas had been "smeared." I would have hoped that Bush, realizing the ever-present hostility of the Congress and having already experienced the savaging of John Tower by the Senate, might have decided to do otherwise. However, he did not, and America paid a price, and a heavy one, for his decision.

★★★

Enraged over the manner in which the hearing process was unfolding, Thomas denied all of Hill's allegations, and along with the Judiciary Committee members, he attacked Hill, charging her with perjury and false statements. As Americans watched the minute-by-minute proceedings on daytime television, the court scene became more and more disorderly and, at times, mired in the obscene. Sexual allegations flew, describing lewd office behavior, including pornographic language. One escapade after another was related, bordering on the underpinnings of an X-rated movie; the courtroom turned into a Congressional circus. On October 11, Thomas appeared before the committee and said, "Confirm me if you want, don't confirm me if you are so led, but let this process end." He charged that he was the victim of a "high-tech lynching."

In the 1970s and early 1980s, almost never had there been an incentive for one to file harassment charges. Red tape, backlog and lack of proof had waylaid the majority of cases; only a small portion of those filed ever went to court. If a complainant did file, she most often feared ridicule and retribution (from coworkers and the accused,) whether or not her case was tried. The Catch-22 was that if she did not take legal action, she lost all credibility later on. Such was the case with Anita Hill.

Because Hill had not filed charges against Thomas at the time of the alleged incident(s), the Senate committee now accused her of lying. This conclusion took into account neither U.S. history nor U.S. law. Title VII of the Civil Rights Act of 1964 includes the procedures set out by the EEOC whereby employees can file charges against individuals who sexually harass them, but with a time limit. Who better to understand this than Thomas himself, the former director of the EEOC—for *seven* years. Misunderstanding and misinterpretation surrounding sexual harassment in the workplace—over many decades—had made meaningful dialogue impossible, even in 1991. The Thomas incident was indicative of the country's lack of knowledge concerning sexual harassment issues.

Seldom do I find fault with decisions made by Bush, but in this case, I believe the President was mistaken in pushing the nomination of Thomas for Supreme Court Justice. If he had withdrawn the recommendation, he would have prevented an unnecessary spectacle and spared Americans from divisiveness over a subject on which they were uneducated and therefore unable to make an intelligent decision.

When all was said and done, and after the television crews had gotten their "up-close and personal" shots, Thomas was eventually confirmed, but barely—by a vote of 52 to 48. He was the first African-American to obtain the post, and the youngest Justice, only forty-three years of age. The hearings had cost the administration and the country time and an equal amount of dignity. President Bush lost political popularity, not only with liberal and civil rights groups, but also with the public, just as he had with the Tower nomination.

AFTER the Supreme Court episode calmed down, so much happened politically, it was hard to keep up. After a summer of embarrassing stories about government-funded plane trips to the dentist's office and Colorado ski slopes, Sununu was back in the headlines. Although he was portrayed as being kinder and gentler, the more somber Sununu did not appear himself. At this time, Timothy J. McBride, assistant secretary of trade development at Commerce, who headed my 500-member organization, was tapped to be his top aide.

McBride had a long and strong history with Bush, starting in 1985; while Bush was Vice President, he had served as his personal assistant. After Bush was elected President, the young college graduate, who majored in business administration at Eastern Michigan University, continued as Bush's aide in the position sometimes referred to as the "Cufflink Bearer." McBride took care of every detail of the President's official life, from making sure that Bush had the right notes at the right meeting at the right time to handing out presidential pens and cuff-links to well-wishers. He could always be counted on for total discretion, and never did he draw attention to the fact that he was always by the President's side. Despite that, the young Texan had as much day-to-day access to Bush as anyone in the White House.

Before McBride was called back to the White House to be Sununu's executive assistant, I had gotten to know him on a professional level and found him to be much like a younger Andy Card. Everyone knew Tim as a "really nice guy," someone who would do anything for the President, including taking an assignment with Sununu. Not an easy transition, especially since Sununu was in his final days at the White House.

After McBride arrived in the West Wing to work for Sununu, there was more and more talk of the COS falling from favor with the President. On November 26, 1991, in the *Washington Times,* Paul Bedard wrote an article titled "Bush Gets Message Directly to Voters." As I read it, I wondered where Sununu really stood inside the Oval Office: "In his

★★★

interview via satellite with WNBC anchor Chuck Scarborough, Mr. Bush was asked about a *New York Times* report that Chief of Staff John Sununu was losing popularity with the Bush family. 'Where they get these mischievous inside-the-Beltway things, I do not know,' said the president." Bush complained that the stories about a clash between Sununu and himself were nothing more than rumor, some kind of media attack. However, there seemed to be more behind the accounts than Bush let on, and it was reported that, because of his loyalty to Sununu (going back to the 1988 New Hampshire primary), the President was keeping him on staff.

Coming to Washington in January 1989 and working in the West Wing had never been a natural jump for Sununu. Many in the administration had accepted him. Others never had. Actually the Bush-Sununu duo had been problematic from its inception. As a staunch conservative, Sununu had opposed increased taxes and government funding, and supported states sovereignty over Washington bureaucracy. Nonetheless, Darman had transformed Sununu into a supporter of taxes and an implementer of social programs.

Even if the chief of staff had not accepted the theoretical concepts behind Darman's budget deal, he still had publicly embraced it. This decision alone had alienated him from the White House staff, Republicans on Capitol Hill and all conservative Reaganites. Sununu's temper and self-important manner had further irritated the right wing, the left wing, and those in the middle. Nonetheless, Bush, with his ingrained commitment to loyalty, would not turn his back on the man to whom he owed a good portion of his presidential victory. At least not until things reached a crisis point.

At 3:45 in the afternoon on December 3, the White House staff learned that Sununu had given his notice. I first heard about it when CNN broke into its coverage of the William Kennedy Smith rape trial to announce the news. The next day, December 4, 1991, with mixed emotions, I read Sununu's letter of resignation in the *Washington Post*. Part of it said:

> I want to thank you for the fun we have had these last three years. In a way that will be very difficult for historians to capture, this White house was an unbelievably "fun place" to work. But in politics, especially during the seasons of a political campaign, perception that can be effectively dealt with at other times can be and will be converted into real political negatives. And I would

never want to not be contributing positively, much less be a drag on your success. Therefore, as we enter the contentious climate of a political campaign, I believe it is in your best interest for me to resign as chief of staff.

I supposed the "fun" to which Sununu referred was the fighting and feuding among the various factions; his three years in the White House had added up to one big squabble.

After Sununu's resignation, there were political rumors that he had been "lynched" (newspaper language) by leaks and backstabbing coming directly from the White House staff; Budget Director Richard Darman was the chief suspect. The Baker/Darman leaks that had been so effective in the past were suspected to have worked again. It was also well known that George W. had come back to Washington specifically to help his father orchestrate an honorable way to say good-bye to his chief of staff.

By whatever means the firing had come about, justified or not, a "resignation" at Sununu's level just as the reelection process was gearing up, engendered a "who's next?" feeling among the Bush troops. Both appointees and the press corps predicted that a massive shake-up in the White House less than a year before the election would cause undue chaos and confusion in the 1992 campaign apparatus.

Within hours of the Sununu firing, another relative newcomer to Washington, Samuel K. Skinner, was appointed to take his place, effective December 15, 1991. Sununu would remain at the White House as counselor to the President until March 1, 1992.

A special edition of the White House Bulletin (faxed to all appointees) stated, "President Bush today accepted the resignation of John Sununu effective December 15. Transportation Secretary Sam Skinner will be the new Chief of Staff. One senior advisor to the White House suggested Skinner was a logical choice, in part because 'he gets along with people.' The advisor added 'That will be very important next year.'"

Not mentioned in the bulletin was the fact that the COS—who was also Bush's campaign chairman would need a lot more in the way of skills than "getting along with people." He was expected to survive the most competitive and treacherous sport on the face of the earth: the reelection of the President of the United States of America. For the man walking into this ring, more than just *his* life and reputation were at stake. There was the President's.

Vice Presidential Residence, June 17, 1988
Barbara, V.P. Bush, G.W., and Laura listening to Atwater on guitar.

★ ★
PART 7
Off with the
Rose-Colored Glasses
★ ★

For us, a man is a hero and deserves special interest only if his nature and his education have rendered him able to let his individuality be almost perfectly absorbed in its hierarchic function without, at the time, forfeiting the vigorous, fresh, admirable impetus which makes for the savour and worth of an individual.

—Herman Hesse

★★★ ═══════ ★★★
CHAPTER
32
IT'S NOT THE ECONOMY, STUPID

All the world's a stage
And all the men and women merely players;
They have their exits and their entrances;
And one man in his time plays many parts;
His acts being seven ages.
—Shakespeare

DECEMBER 1991

Beginning on December 4, 1991, the day of the Skinner/Sununu announcement, the White House bureaucracy perceptibly and publicly unraveled, never again to reunite during the Bush presidency.

For the months ahead, Sam Skinner presided over this officialdom. Having worked on the sidelines in two of Bush's previous campaigns, he was more than just an acquaintance; he was a family friend. Skinner's wife of only a short time, Honey, was close to Laura Bush, wife of George W.

Although not overconfident or annoyingly aggressive like Sununu, Skinner was a bright man; however, in his present job, intelligence had little to do with being successful. Knowing the West Wing power structure did.

The former Chicago prosecutor and IBM executive simply did not have a network of individuals to support him. Actually, without Baker's endorsement, no one holding the position had a chance of succeeding. Along with having Baker's approval, a chief of staff needed to be forceful, while at the same time not hostile. This, of course, was a fine balance, as pointed out by Ann Devroy in the *Washington Post*, on December 7, 1991, in "Bush's New High Command Shifts Gaze to Reelection Run":

One Republican outside the administration who talked to Skinner said that "by temperament and politics, he is not an ideologue but he is an activist and senses we need a sharper offense on domestic policy and the economy at the White House." "But," he said, Skinner "faces the Sununu hangover—he can't tromp in there and make wholesale changes or he'll be accused of being King John the Second. How he walks that line will be closely watched. "

As Bush's secretary of Transportation, Skinner had held his own— especially during the disastrous Exxon *Valdez* oil spill in Alaska—and he had lobbied for his present job of chief of staff. Yet within the first month of his appointment (for reasons I will go into later), President Bush seemed to question whether or not Skinner had been his best choice.

The White House staff and the President were in the unofficial throes of bracing for a tough fight in the upcoming New Hampshire primary. It had been four years since the last one. With Bush having just ousted the Granite State's favorite son from the Executive Office, his relationship with the voters was on tenuous ground, and Skinner's experience running a national campaign was nil. Having never been on the management side of a race, he had not experienced the brass-knuckle tactics inherent at the top levels of a presidential showdown .

AT present, Bush's Republican opponent, Patrick Joseph Buchanan, was in the field readying for the first skirmish, planning to make life as dreadful as possible for both Skinner and Bush. The extreme right-wing columnist and commentator, whose claim to fame was contributing to NBC's *McLaughlin Group,* CNN's *Crossfire* and *the Capital Gang* TV shows, was well known for his belligerent nature. He knew he would never be President, but by declaring his candidacy, he could pursue Bush in a way no other forum would allow. Running under the campaign umbrella, he was at liberty to go for the President's jugular.

Buchanan believed that long ago Bush had tossed aside the concerns of the Nixon and Reagan conservative confederacy, and he viewed increased taxes, minority rights, free trade and globalism as heresy. The Eastern Establishment Liberal Republicans (who had ruined the all-white, male, Catholic conservative base) deserved to be punished. In his fight for what he called "traditional values," Buchanan appealed to few—but gaining votes was not the issue.

★★★

As a 1961 Georgetown University graduate, Buchanan had also received a degree in journalism from Columbia University before starting his political career as a campaign aide to Nixon. He went to the White House and stayed until Nixon's resignation in 1973, and he had remained well connected to his Nixon cronies, including Rosemary Woods (Nixon's personal secretary), with whom he was a close friend. From 1985 to 1987, Buchanan worked in the Reagan White House; because of his conservative stance, he had been assigned the job of communications director, and although he never really fit in with some of the more moderate Reagan speechwriters, he stayed for almost two years. Peggy Noonan worked for Buchanan while she penned Reagan's speeches.

It was Buchanan's feeling that in 1991, the time was ripe to bring back the lost conservative base of the Party, and that it was he who would guide the straying Republicans back to the Right. Seeing himself as the true heir of Richard Nixon and Ronald Reagan (on his "America First" platform), he portrayed himself as the Chosen One. Wherever he found a crowd to listen, he spoke, embellishing his mission and using his standard line, "Under the Bush administration, the Reagan Revolution has gone bad and economic concerns have been tossed aside."

The economy was at the top of the Buchanan agenda. On December 15, 1991, on the editor's page of the *Washington Times,* Buchanan was quoted: "The recession is real and if the administration doesn't believe it, Mr. Bush should come to New Hampshire. [The answer is] to end the steadily rising drain of wealth and resources in Washington, to ease up on—not add to, Mr. President—the tax burden on American business, to unleash—not tie down—the genius and energy of America enterprise."

The Republican primary was scheduled for February 18, and it was true that New Hampshire, a very conservative state, was experiencing an economic downturn. Many workers were out of jobs, and a good number of those who owned businesses had difficulty securing loans. Unlike the days of the 1989 primary, the voters did not see Bush as "their defender." Buchanan, by making a three-day swing through the state before formally declaring his candidacy, began to receive the higher marks. Afterward, he remained on tour, introducing himself to people all across the state and substantially increasing his pre-primary popularity.

Former Governor Hugh Gregg, Bush's 1992 New Hampshire campaign chairman, had been sending messages to Washington saying that, unless there was some immediate response, the President would face a volatile political situation. The citizens needed reassurance that Bush was aware of their plight and was going to do something to alleviate it. Ann Devroy's article "Bush's New High Command Shifts Gaze to Reelection Run" (*Washington Post,* December 7, 1991) quoted Gregg as saying, "We want him to campaign here actively, at least 2-3 times before the primary. We have made that clear, but we have no commitments." The Bush presidential staff had a different view, saying, "Incumbent Presidents traditionally prefer to remain 'presidential' as long as they can and Bush is said to be wary of plunging directly into the political fray so early in the year and raising Buchanan's credibility going to the state."

Because Bush was not talking and Buchanan was, America listened to Buchanan. By not coming forth and addressing the looming economic problems, Bush literally handed the microphone to his adversary, and Buchanan took advantage of it.

In 1988, Bush had won the Granite State with a 15,000-vote margin, but in 1980, when then-Governor Gregg had been given total control of the primary, Bush had lost to Reagan. At that time, Gregg, having already misdirected Bush on several occasions, advised Bush's campaign team (just days before the '80 primary) to leave New Hampshire; Bush's press secretary, Pete Teeley, had reluctantly followed orders and, with Bush, left the state. Gregg's decision to banish the Bush cavalry had been problematic in that Reagan and his team were allowed to stay on and continue campaigning, giving Reagan an enormous advantage. Not surprisingly, Gregg had worked for Reagan in his '76 campaign.

In 1992, Gregg was not the only one pushing Bush to do something about a state's economic troubles. GOP governors from across the nation had forcefully reminded Bush that he had to be more concerned about the economic "non-message" he was sending the American people. *En masse,* the governors suggested that he start addressing not only economic issues, but all topics, including healthcare, environment, welfare reform and jobs.

In response, just before Christmas, Bush did invite a Manchester radio station to interview him in the White House, which gave him a chance to talk about the transportation bill he signed the day before, new legislation that meant almost $200 million for New Hampshire residents. But what may not have been too little, appeared to be too late.

★★★

The President's high national approval ratings over the previous three years (highest, 92 percent), had dipped to the mid-50s by the end of 1991, and the press most often cited the economy as the reason for the decline. Because Bush was not rectifying the pessimistic forecasts, he gave the impression that he was satisfied with the way things were. People presumed that Bush either could not correct the situation or that he simply did not care.

By the end of 1991 and the beginning of 1992, the country was still *led to believe* a recession was taking place. In truth, the "recession" had been over since April 1991. The reason for the changing economic climate in the later part of 1991 had nothing to do with a recession. Yes, the unemployment numbers were high, (hovering around 7 percent), and the economy was sluggish, but the long-term financial health of the United States was excellent.

According to the U.S. Bureau of Economic Analysis, a recession occurs when, over a six-month period, the gross national product declines for at least two consecutive quarters. In 1991, the gross domestic product was down the first quarter, up the second, down the third, and up the fourth. Looking back on the entire decade, 1990-99, economists considered 1991 the first year of an unparalleled nine-year U.S. economic expansion.

What was *actually happening* and what was *being reported* were two entirely different scenarios. In 1991, America was being fed misleading economic information.

By December, the economy had been heating up for eight months— not cooling off. And during the first quarter of 1992, domestic growth would jump from a little over 4 percent to 7 percent. Although the growth rate then receded during the second two quarters of 1992 (never going much below 5 percent), it would close in December 1992 at a phenomenal 8 percent. The sky was *not* falling, and those yelling, "It's the economy, stupid!" were stupid.

In spite of the encouraging fiscal news—that should have been presented to the nation—the Bush financial advisors, including Richard Darman, Michael Boskin and Nick Brady, did not get the word out. What is worse, they did not try. No one—no one—explained that what was taking place was a recovery. No one in the administration tried to tell Americans that the country was economically solid and heading in a positive direction. Why?

President Bush, who held friendships in high regard and who often measured people by what he wanted to believe was true, seldom took the combative path to prevail over the advice of his aides. If a disagreement meant confrontation, Bush oftentimes decided to eliminate a clash by giving in. Because he had the tendency to accept his advisors opinions—even when they went against his own better instincts—some of his greater insights and views were muted.

I see this propensity to be the diplomat—as fine a characteristic as it may be—to be Bush's greatest *strength* and his greatest *weakness*. To be fair, given the circumstances, it would have been nearly impossible for Bush to stand up for his convictions when faced with the magnitude of adversarial powers surrounding his Oval Office. Besides ignoring the "economy problem," the President had two other choices. He could fire Baker, rid the White House of the Reaganites, and start over with the re-staffing of Bush Loyals (from the '88 campaign). Or, he could keep everyone in place and fight for his own agenda. I believe the first option to be too drastic, and the second, futile. Neither would have improved his standing; in fact, they may have made circumstances worse; the system was too rigid and too ingrained, and had been operational for too many years. Jim Baker, at the top, made the rules. George Bush accepted his fate, and chose the path of least resistance and the least damaging to himself, his Party and the country. I say, "chose" because this is what I assume Bush did during the years between 1989 and 1993. Either he chose "to close his eyes," not publicly acknowledging what was happening or he simply was too naive to see it. Since Bush is a very experienced politician and an extremely intelligent man, I doubt it was the latter.

Atwater, above anyone else, may have been capable of changing the situation in early 1992, though he, too, would have faced impossible odds when trying to get Bush reelected. In 1988, although Bush was victorious, it was by chance. To those in the Reagan administration, that win was not intended nor expected to happen. The victory may even have surprised Bush. Once he was in office and running the country, Bush expected His Team to embrace the triumph as joyfully as he—the problem was His Team was *never* his.

While President Bush had been swayed by the opinions of Baker, often letting him determine what was best in accordance to what was best for Baker, Bush had not always followed this pattern of doing exactly what Baker wanted. There had been several incidents, including granting Quayle the position of Vice President, the FSX/Mosbacher struggle, the situation with Boyden Gray and his leaks, and the national security/Scowcroft power plays, in which Bush may not have actively supported his aides, yet he had not been there for Baker either. In all these cases, Bush had *not* routinely followed the preferred Baker course. Most often, the President sent Baker a message by not saying anything.

Still, I must believe that Bush did not want to antagonize Baker unnecessarily, and he did what he could to include him. That meant giving him a voice on his economic team. The one common connection among all three Bush economic aides was Jim Baker, who, as former Treasury secretary, had some financial experience of his own. Baker had put Brady on the 1984 G-6 team and helped Brady move into the Treasury position when he was leaving for the '88 campaign. Baker also had called Boskin to serve in the Bush White House as economic advisor, having first selected him to be on the '88 campaign and on the Transition team. But, most significantly, long ago, Baker had placed the liberal Darman on the Power Pyramid as number two, and it was he who controlled economic policy during the Bush years.

As the power broker in the White House and director of the office of Management and Budget, Darman had gone against some of Bush's key platform issues, including the President's fervent desire to lower taxes. As originator of the 1990 budget plan between Bush and Congress, Darman, first kowtowed to Hill representatives and then abandoned Bush, finding fault with the strategy *he,* Darman, designed and sold to Bush. Once the administration looked to be back on solid economic ground, Darman had promoted the idea of a recession hammering at the White House door.

For three years, Darman, one of a few in a tiny gang of "most-liberal," had been managing a budget of billions of taxpayers' dollars while pontificating on how it should be spent. The OMB chief had not only impaired the White House (from a Congressional standpoint), he had undercut the President's relationship with the nation.

In the spring of 1991, after a rather serious fall in front of a McDonald's, Darman spent time healing from his physical injuries while simultaneously assessing the extent of his fiscal bruises sustained in his recent skirmishes with Congress. He eventually returned to center stage, somewhat more restrained and projecting a lower profile. His powers of persuasion were said to be of a more genteel nature, and the protégé of Elliot Richardson focused his attention on the deficit. His intent was to solidify votes for the National Debt Reduction Bill, the five-year agreement to reduce the deficit by $500 billion.

House Budget Committee Chairman Leon Panetta (D-CA) appeared pleased with Darman's demeanor and with the proposed budget plan. Regrettably, the resulting amicable relations between Congress and the White House were ignored by the Bush staff. This temporary truce between Hill and Oval Office was unusual, and it would have been to the President's advantage to get some positive press out of it. Little came out of the détente. Another missed opportunity.

Chairman of the Council on Economic Advisors (CEA) Michael Boskin persistently gave a double message. He would say that things were not the way they should be, but instead of correcting them, he preferred to let them work themselves out. He saw the President's deficit-reduction plan as helpful in the overall economic forecast, but not a cure-all. With high unemployment and low consumer confidence to be reckoned with, Boskin now predicted that the economy would improve within the next six months, somewhere between January and June 1992. In Boskin's mind, any Band-Aid approach would be viewed as insufficient, and he advised Bush to wait and do nothing. Absolutely nothing. Although there was some wisdom in Boskin's theory (the economy had turned and conditions were nothing like the alarmists were portraying), his advice was not appropriate for the circumstances.

Bush needed to show he was in command of the country's state of affairs. The statistics showing the current and long-range financial prognosis as being favorable needed to be conveyed. The message in the headlines should have been, "This is the good news. . . ." Data pointing to the country's promising future should have been relayed by one of Bush's economic officials—if not by Bush himself—who was capable of speaking in clear and convincing terms. But neither the President nor anyone in the White House delivered the "good news."

The nation, restless and frustrated, therefore responded with the "bad news." Those who presumably were going to vote Bush back into office in 1992 basically let it be known that they were not going to do so unless Bush convinced them that he had a plan, one that ensured them a job and economic safety. America absolutely needed to know that the

★★★

President understood their plight. If he was going to keep his present "do nothing" message, they threatened to retreat from the Bush-led legions.

Bush had chosen Boskin for the CEA job because of his ability to speak about the economy in simple, understandable terms, while still painting a picture of the country's future. Boskin's talents may have been evident inside the White House, but they never went any further—not even at this critical time for the President. The failed savings and loan industry, coupled with a low savings rate (both inherited from Reagan), soon would aggravate Bush's problems.

The third of Bush's top financial advisors, Nicholas F. Brady, because he followed Jim Baker into the Treasury position was compared to his predecessor, and often judged as falling short of Baker's accomplishments. From his first day in office, Brady had been portrayed (by the press) as inept and unprepared for the job. All the same, Brady's loyalty to the President was indisputable.

A devoted Bush soldier for many years (including the 1988 campaign and Transition team), Brady was the one man on the squad who most resembled his leader. Regrettably, a man with such honorable intentions would never wield the power of Baker and Darman and Boskin. And that left him off the Power Pyramid and out of the ring of influence. Of the several men Bush turned to for financial consultation, Brady remained the least influential and, therefore, in terms of policy, the one with the least authority.

The other presidential fiscal advisor who fell into a category all his own and was supposed to be outside Party lines, was Federal Reserve Chairman Alan Greenspan. As has already been stated, Greenspan was not a Bush enthusiast; he had been brought into the Reagan White House by David Stockman (OMB chief) to replace Paul Volcker. Greenspan was chosen for his political leanings as a conservative and his ability to get along with the Reagan troops. However, he spent only a few months in office before Reagan left and Bush came in. I assume that Baker, who filled all the noteworthy Bush appointments, invited the former Reagan appointee to continue his four-year term as Fed chair under Bush.

Greenspan, who had supported Reagan in his "lower taxes" ideology, pontificated just the opposite once Bush assumed office; he fought for higher taxes! Then, after taxes were raised (the flip-flop), he ranted about an "imminent recession," even while he knew there was no recession. The Fed chairman had proven no more help to Bush in 1991 than he had in the past. Fully cognizant of the ramifications of his dire economic predictions, Greenspan never ceased to enlighten the public with his confidence-shattering testimonials.

Bush, wanting harmony among his economic advisors, had submerged his own ideas when contrary to theirs, and although the public seldom heard about it (his opinions were kept inside the White House walls), I am convinced that Bush had qualms about the guidance he received from his Money Experts.

It can not be overlooked that Presidents win and lose popularity and elections based on how well the nation's economy is faring or, more correctly, how it is perceived to be faring. The Bush advisors knew that an optimistic perception was imperative, yet they *never* promoted one. And because of that, citizens continued to watch the latest unemployment figures go up, their neighbors lose their jobs, and bank loan applications be rejected. If Bush had taken an aggressive posture and highlighted the nation's growing economic condition, The People, most likely, would have listened. But, to the nation, President Bush appeared as uninterested and incompetent as the financial counselors who encircled him.

WHILE the Republicans were adrift, the Democrats started to feel more and more confident. Their 1992 contenders numbered seven: Jerry Brown, Mario Cuomo, Bob Kerry, Tom Harkin, Paul Tsongas, Douglas Wilder and Bill Clinton (who two and a half years earlier, Atwater had tagged as a Bush challenger).

Already on the campaign trail, Clinton was aware the administration was not responding to questions regarding economic issues, and decided, like Buchanan, to speak out. With nothing to lose, the Arkansas governor told the country about his plan to improve Washington's financial "tragedy," claiming that with his "Covenant for Economic Change," he would boost U.S. productivity. Clinton proposed cutting taxes for the middle class, and, with those revenues, creating 45,000 new construction jobs, and he promised to encourage banks to lend money to businesses rather than calling in loans.

In December 1991, Clinton made national news with a speech he gave at Georgetown University, where he had earned his undergraduate degree. Although people listened to Clinton, some had concerns about his

★★★

personal ethics—including an unidentified woman in attendance. She asked him to explain his response to a joke Nebraska Senator Bob Kerrey (also a Democratic presidential hopeful) had made during a recent campaign function in New Hampshire. It seems, unintentionally, an open microphone had picked up comments between the Kerrey and Clinton and conveyed them to the press. When it was discovered that Clinton had responded to Kerrey's off-color, sexual joke with a similarly crude one, the two candidates had been put in an embarrassing position. Clinton answered the Georgetown woman's query by stating simply that Kerrey had apologized for the episode. He neatly sidestepped any mention of himself.

The next day, the *Washington Times* published a piece by Ronald A. Taylor, giving the full text of Clinton's Georgetown speech, including his comments afterward, "I think he (Kerrey) gave a genuine and heartfelt apology and I hope it will be accepted. I believe all of us—everybody in this room, everybody in this country—who has lived any length of time, has said something at some point in our lives we wish we hadn't said. Furthermore, I think that we should try...to learn from things like this."

Clinton's reply was typical of his future responses to questions pertaining to the less-than-desirable side of his personality. Having taken note of what his campaign manager, James Carville, had told him, Clinton tried to duck the personal stuff. Described as "burning to win and hell-bent on finding a way to do it," Carville knew that for Clinton to secure the White House, he would have to steer him away from character-related questions. Despite Carville's advice, the dark and sexually permissive side of Clinton would almost unhinge his '92 campaign.

TURNING from campaign politics to administration politics, now that Mosbacher had finally joined Sam Skinner and the reelection campaign, activity at the department of Commerce was back in the news. Barbara Hackman Franklin, at fifty-two, took Mosbacher's place, becoming the third woman appointed to the Bush Cabinet (following Carla Hills, U.S. Trade Representative, and Elizabeth Dole, secretary of Labor). As the head of forty thousand civilian employees and some one hundred appointees, the former Nixonite arrived with some fanfare. She presently ran a successful Washington-based consulting company, and while serving as director on the boards of seven major companies, she held clout with organizations like Dow and Westinghouse.

Just before Franklin was sworn in—on December 13, 1991—Dunn was promoted to assistant secretary for the Import Administration—the appointment that had interfered with the China trip. Following the swearing-in ceremony on the Hill, I and a small group of guests had been invited to a reception for him in Mosbacher's personal conference room at Commerce.

Dunn was departing the office of Science and Electronics, and I was staying. He had never suggested that I go with him to the Import Administration, and I never mentioned any interest in doing so. But now that he was leaving, I was in the awkward position of holding a job without anyone to report to. If Mosbacher had kept his position as secretary, I would have had some protection, but without him, I was left in a precarious situation. I had not built myself a political safety net. And although I had been guaranteed the option of remaining in S & E, there had been no confirmation from the White House liaison office about the continuation of my appointment.

In Washington politics, where there is no such thing as a job promise, I was guilty of not taking more responsibility to secure a slot before Mosbacher's departure. However, delays on my part were not a by-product of complacency. I had been unsure of my options. What steps did one take when her boss discarded her? My lack of initiative for finding a new position occurred more out of confusion and fear than anything else. I had no mentor, no one to turn to for advice. And, sadly, I trusted no one.

Since walking into the campaign headquarters in 1987, all my work positions had transpired without my initiation. For the past four years, it was as if I had been standing on one of those people-transport systems at the airport, where you step onto a revolving band, and without having to walk, you arrive at your destination. I had fallen into my many jobs and assignments without ever having pursued one. Not that I hadn't put effort into each job once I was there—I had—but I had not designed my own course. If I wanted to stay in the administration, I now would have to make it happen. I had to think strategy. My New Year's resolution was to find another appointment . . . as soon as possible.

But, before the new year began and I started job-searching, there was worldwide news coming from the Soviet Union. For me, it was upsetting.

Michail Gorbachev had met his political end.

On the day after Christmas 1991, the *Washington Post* headlines—in black block letters across the front page—read, "Gorbachev Resignation

★★★

Ends Soviet Era; US Recognizes Russia, Other Republics." Upon the collapse of seventy-four years of Soviet Communism, Russian President Boris Yeltsin now took over Moscow. The Soviet flag was taken down and carried through the streets, from Parliament to Red Square; the Russian flag was raised in its stead.

When the Gorbachev announcement came over the wires, Bush was at Camp David celebrating the holidays. Immediately, he returned to Washington and made a televised speech to the nation from the Oval Office. The American President praised Gorbachev and applauded his "sustained commitment to world peace." Although he was surely pleased with communism's fall, Bush, I believed, would miss Gorbachev, personally as well as politically.

Observing the two leaders over the last several years, I had found several similar characteristics between them, in strengths as well as weaknesses. Most significantly, they both dreamed of a larger, more cohesive planet, one outside their own geographic margins. That made them creative thinkers and innovators. And, too, they had shared their most defining moment together, the signing of the START agreement, which for the first time ensured limiting nuclear weapons on both sides of the globe.

Over a relatively short period, Bush and Gorbachev had overcome the political stiffness and formality so inherent in dialogue between heads of state, and had related more as friend to friend than leader to leader. As powerful national commanders, they introduced a new diplomatic style: personable, likable, and welcoming. The usually contentious relationship between President of the United States and President of the Soviet Union had softened. The humanizing element that manifested itself between Bush and Gorbachev predictably created some stir among the more protocol-correct who wanted to run international politics according to the book—with an austere and argumentative hand.

Certainly, the Baker Boys at State were not pleased that the President could conduct global matters so well—and on his own. But Bush *was* handling it. It was in his blood. It was his talent, his gift, and he shared this expertise with the world, just as one would who felt passionate about his cause. Bush had spent a lifetime relating to people of different culture, color and language, in every station of life, throughout the Earth's sphere. I judge that the Bush-Gorbachev partnership was proof enough that a global alliance had the potential to become reality.

As visionaries, Bush and Gorbachev were leaders of countries portrayed to be troubled by excessive fiscal unrest, rather than nations experiencing expected internal disturbances that were indicative of a growing society. But, neither chief seemed inclined to accept account-ability for calming their citizen's anxieties. Their mistake.

The result of this for Gorbachev was public denigration. He was taken from office by his own countrymen, and among the many commentaries published about his defeat, I found the ending of an article in the December 26 *Washington Post* to be quite poignant. Having been taught at an early age to appreciate the writings of Shakespeare, I taped this piece to the top of my office computer, where it stayed for months:

> You may my glories and my state depose;
> But not my griefs;
> Still am I king of those.
>
> (*King Richard II*, Act 1V.)

Bush, who also appeared not to care enough about the concerns of The People, unsuspectingly would follow in the footsteps of his Soviet counterpart. Yet, I doubt that Bush, whose eyes were always focused on the broader world picture, had any inkling that he was headed toward his own political oblivion. I was learning that those surrounding a President *can be*—and in the case of Bush and Gorbachev, *were* oftentimes more significant than the President himself.

★★★ ━━━━ ★★★

CHAPTER

33

UPHEAVAL IN JAPAN

White sheep, white sheep,
On a blue hill,
When the wind stops
You all stand still.
When the wind blows,
You walk away slow.
White sheep, white sheep,
Where do you go?

—Christina Rossetti

JANUARY 1992

The President's trip to Asia was planned for late December—early January. For months, there had been talk about Bush's visit to the Far East, yet, for one reason or another, it had been delayed. Those of us in the administration began to feel the Asia tour had been erected under a dark cloud. Originally scheduled to start the day before Thanksgiving, Bush's most ambitious trade mission had been postponed several times with no explanation.

Some within political circles said the latest hold-up was because of the recent Pennsylvania senatorial election in which Harris Wofford (Democrat) upset Richard Thornburg (Republican). Prior to the election, Pennsylvania Governor Casey (Democrat) had appointed Wofford to complete the term of Senator John Heinz (Republican), who had died in a plane crash. Wofford, an attorney, previously had been state Party chairman, a founder of the Peace Corps and president of Bryn Mawr College.

403

Bush attorney general Thornburg had resigned so that he could campaign for senator. As former governor of the state, he had been admired for taking thousands of people off welfare and for having had a $200 million budget surplus. Thornburg was thought to be capable of winning the Senate post with little difficulty. However, his opponent, Wofford, had hired the Louisiana politico, James Carville, who had just managed Casey's reelection campaign. Knowing the odds were against him, Carville, jumped into the fray. As a rather hard-nosed strategist, he instructed Wofford to stress the fact that Thornburg had opposed the 1991 Civil Rights bill and was a Bush insider.

On Election Day, to everyone's surprise, the Democrat—who had at one point been behind by forty-seven points—declared an upset victory over Thornburg. The Republicans, distraught, pointed fingers at Mary Matalin for being responsible. Someone on Thornburg's campaign staff believed there had been "insider trading" between Matalin at the RNC and Carville, her boyfriend. She was accused of passing confidential Party information to Wofford's camp.

Though the facts seemed to add up, nothing was proven, and the two continued their love affair up until such time as they found themselves head-to-head on the Bush–Clinton political battlefield. Thornburg's defeat gave Carville the visibility he needed to become one of the most well-recognized of all political strategists. Days after the Wofford victory, contacted by Clinton, Carville left Pennsylvania and headed south to run the Arkansas governor's presidential campaign.

The Thornburg trouncing was not a promising sign for President Bush, and the West Wing generals decided it best to allow for some time to "take stock" after the defeat. Bush's postponed visit to the East may or may not have resulted from the loss, but it was often given as one of the reasons.

The overdue trip had caused the President trouble. In the spring of '91, in the aftermath of the Gulf War, Bush had declined an invitation to Japan and sent Quayle in his place. Since then, Japanese officials had been increasingly unhappy, and shortly after the official announcement was made that the President finally would be making a State Visit, rumors coming out of Japan included a multitude of complaints: Bush was not staying long enough; U.S. business executives (traveling with the President) were not welcome; the United States was unnecessarily arguing about trade issues . . . and on and on and on. As the "lift-off" date approached, news pertaining to the trip, though of a different nature than that coming from Japan, was not encouraging.

The pre-flight medical checks showed that most of the staff traveling with the President (a large number of White House aides, secret service agents, journalists, and others) were stricken with the intestinal flu. Although they had *not* recovered by departure time, the trip went on as scheduled. Bush and his accompanying U.S. captains of industry departed Washington on December 30, 1991, with plans to visit Australia, Singapore, South Korea and Japan, in that order. It was to be a large-scale U.S. marketing tour.

For most heads of state, engaging in commercial activities—using the weight of their offices to increase export sales—was a natural phenomenon; in the United States, though applauded by individual businesses, it was often criticized. Nevertheless, with the chairmen of some of America's largest corporations (including Motorola and American Express, as well as the car giants Chrysler, Ford and General Motors), Bush was given the perfect venue during this tour to display his diplomatic skills *and* push for open markets. Bush had purposely chosen the automobile CEOs to join him in hopes of helping them increase export sales. In 1991, the U.S. automobile industry reported its worst sales year in a decade, and it was predicted that 1992 would not be much better. With the proper press, it was hoped that the giant trade mission could bring the President some kudos on the economic front, giving him a much-needed image boost. Not surprisingly, the theme of the expedition was "Jobs! Jobs! Jobs!"

The first three stops on the tour went exceedingly well, and the trade talks were encouraging. The CEO's were reported to be pleased with their negotiations and with President Bush. News filtering back to Washington was upbeat. Expectations were raised.

However, along with the heartening news, came the information that many of those who left Washington with the flu still had not improved. And after twenty hours in confined quarters aboard Air Force One (and a chartered TWA jet)—that flew the delegation to Australia—even more of the official party had fallen ill upon arriving in Sydney. In Singapore and South Korea, medical conditions persisted. With only two days left before returning to the U.S., it looked as if President Bush was one of the lucky ones not going to be affected by the outbreak.

Then things changed.

The exhausting fourteen-hour-a-day schedule—plus the dramatic alteration in weather from country to country—finally caught up with Bush on the last stop: Japan. On the first day there, Bush followed a grueling timetable. He attended the arrival ceremonies in Tokyo, visited with the emperor at the palace, conducted trade talks between U.S. and Japanese business leaders, was the guest of honor at a working luncheon, and played two sets of tennis with the emperor *before* arriving that evening with Mrs. Bush for a State Dinner at seven o'clock. At the dinner—twenty-four hours before heading home— Bush succumbed to the flu of his contagious crew.

On Wednesday morning, January 8, 1992, I was in my office at Commerce when I was told about a White House news report relating that the President had taken ill while in Tokyo. The radio and television in our front office was turned on, and I became immersed in the details—some conflicting— regarding Bush's collapse at Prime Minister Miyazawa's residence. The incident was being reported by news agencies around the world, and one particular video of the President vomiting at the dinner table and then collapsing was played and replayed on television.

To my dismay, I would find out that the film footage being shot during the State affair had been done so at a time when it was officially off-limits for reporters. From accounts in the newspapers, I later put together the sequence of events at the palace on the evening of January 8, 1991. Few seem to have picked up the full story.

During the actual dining portion of the State Dinner, a cameraman for Japan's public broadcasting network, NHK, defied a media ban and kept his camera running while he and the other reporters left the pressroom. The press staff was not allowed to return until the end of the dinner, at which time video shots could again be taken. This one unmanned NHK camera, *illegally* left on, focused on a single shot of the head table. Back at their Tokyo home base, waiting to return to the palace, the NHK crew were half-watching their monitor, but not taping. They were not expecting anything out of the ordinary to occur. Then, quite unexpectedly, Bush fell, and they immediately started to tape. Thirty seconds after Bush fell, the NHK cameras captured the now infamous image of the President of the United States on the dining room floor cradled in the arms of Prime Minister Miyazawa. A haunting picture.

★★★

The story of the President's mishap . . . a chaotic and ill-fated moment for George Bush . . . would never have reached the proportions it did had it not been for the prohibited taping. Just ten minutes after the incident, the NHK control room aired the footage for the first time. Worldwide. It would be replayed for months to come.

Ironically, sixty-seven-year-old President Bush, a man who jogged routinely and was known for being hard to keep up with on a usual day, was even more energetic on special occasions such as the Asia trade mission. On this twelve-day, four-nation Pacific tour, with activities and appointments every hour on the hour, he had been moving at a whirlwind pace, and up until the time of the dinner, U.S. press corps reports about negotiations, had been extremely encouraging. The mood of the mission participants was described as "enthusiastic." Then the State Dinner. The next day, January 9, 1992, newspapers referred to the presidential mission as "The Trip From Hell."

International trade and diplomacy issues, the reasons for making the tour, were barely mentioned. The vigorous, hard-charging, let's-not-stop President had simply gotten a case of the flu, but the press decided—with a vengeance—to come at the story from a more disparaging point of view. Their intelligence claimed everything from Bush acquiring some kind of startling new illness to his being stricken with the plague. Rumors actually escalated to the point that Bush was "Only Seconds Away From Being Declared Dead" (an actual headline), with pictures of him collapsing at the dinner table being made to correlate.

Video frames taken from the NHK camera were blown up to exaggerate every detail of the President's expression. Newspaper editions carried uncomplimentary articles way beyond the "appropriate," and the trade negotiations, which were by all accounts quite an achievement, were a thing of the past.

More press would be released about Bush falling from his chair at the Japan emperor's dinner than any other event during his presidency! Such a media frenzy, never a good thing for a politician at any time, is potentially disastrous for an incumbent in an election year. "The Dinner" pictures visually seemed to prove to Americans that the presidency was dying.

As always, the White House did little to rectify the bad press. In fact, by either not responding or joining the condemnation, they encouraged the Japan stories. Bush's rivals, as well as aides on his own staff, denounced the trip as a complete failure, giving the inside Reagan armies their first public opportunity to criticize Bush. Without Sununu, it was that much easier to openly condemn the President.

The news reporters overlooked the fact that President Bush and his entourage of prestigious corporate chairmen had traveled halfway around the world together for almost two weeks. This was nothing short of an amazing accomplishment. From balmy Australia to frigid Japan, the mechanics of the trip had remained on track; yet the unpredictable human element had derailed it. A case of the flu, combined with an unlawful tape, a hungry press corps, and—most significantly—an unresponsive White House staff, abolished what could have been a crowning economic achievement.

Doing the best he could under the circumstances, Bush declared his Pacific tour and the Japanese Summit "a success." And he left it at that.

Upon returning to Washington, the President could not spend too much time reflecting on what had been. He had to prepare for his State of the Union Address, scheduled for Tuesday evening, January 28. This particular oration was being publicized as Bush's "speech of all speeches," the one that would redeem him from his economic misjudgments. Press just the opposite of what a President wants publicized before an address. It would have been in his favor to reduce public expectations and deliver more than predicted, rather than the other way around.

While waiting for Bush to convey his domestic policy plan, the country became intent on the one message they wanted to hear: a strategy for combating the recession and priming the economy. Citizens hoped he finally had "heard" them and was ready to acknowledge their concerns.

In a *Time* article dated November 19, 1990 (after mid-terms), Nancy Gibbs wrote, "Keep the Bums In," in which she presented a description of the public's attitude toward Washington officials: "If any signal came through last week, it was a primal scream of disgust with politics-as-usual, a blunt and resounding no! No to the lies and intrigues of Washington, no to spending by the politicians who can't be trusted with the public's dollars, no to a money-greased political system dedicated to self preservation rather than leadership."

Outrage at President Bush had been evident in the fall of 1990 and was—by January 1992—at a boiling point. Americans wanted to know *how* their President was going to make life better for them. He was running out of chances to prove himself.

Before President Bush ever said a word on January 28, the bar had been set so high that it would have been almost impossible for him to hurdle it. Then standing before Congress, he declared, "This will not stand . . . [Things] are going to change . . . and change now!" In his comments, Bush suggested several recovery proposals, including a cut in the capital gains tax rate from 28 percent to 15.4 percent and a reduction of Pentagon spending by $50 billion over a period of five years (basically his deficit reduction program). In what was supposed to be the "bow" on the his economic package, Bush challenged Congress to pass an economic recovery package by March 20, 1992. But, instead of spurring enthusiasm, his proposal seemed to fall flat.

Already skeptical, Americans were not reassured by the President's State of the Union Address, and, according to the press a week later, the country remained unconvinced that Bush was in control of either his administration or their future. The question in my mind was: Who was responsible for writing the do-or-die national address? I found out that Tony Snow and Robert Teeter had penned most of it. Snow—a former *Washington Times* writer, now a Bush speechwriter—and Teeter—Bush's official 1992 campaign chairman—had written a lukewarm speech, if that. This seemed incredible to me, since there had been an entirely different angle they could have taken, one that would have *had* to catch the country's ear.

Had I been able to suggest someone to work on the President's message, I would have chosen Tom Peters, author of *In Search of Excellence*. In the *Washington Post,* on March 1992, Peters wrote a commentary, "Hey, Folks! America Isn't On The Skids," which, I believe, would have been the perfect national morale builder. Peters proposed, in spite of all the bad news about the economy, that things were *not* that bad. In fact, he suggested, we Americans had it pretty good. He admitted there were some lingering effects from a "passing recession," but he pointed out that much of the country's economy was thriving, outright booming!

The author noted that, in 1991, there had been not ten or twenty, but sixty-four new varieties of spaghetti sauce added to our grocery store shelves. And Peters cited a plethora of growing industries, ones seldom reported in the newspapers and on television, including manufacturing companies, makers of computers, software, biotech, aeronautics, and medical equipment, to mention only a few. These businesses were indicative of our country's expanding future, and in these arenas, America was better off and growing faster than any country in the world.

Having created 19 million new jobs in the 1980s, the United States was positioning itself for the upcoming millennium, *and* Peters pointed out that we were well on our way to being the most competitive nation on the planet. Trades not keeping up with the times, such as the automobile manufacturers, were being cut back to accommodate a new era of products. According to Peters, the heart of America had shifted from Bloomfield Hills, Michigan, to places like Atlanta and Orlando and Dallas and San Diego. Some bright and visionary young men and women were on the cutting edge of what he referred to as the Information Technology (IT) Age. These individuals, he predicted, would give new meaning to the way business was conducted around the world and new meaning to the idea of assets.

Another writer, Mark Kellner, wrote a similar piece, titled "Small Firms Gain as Transition Hits Computer Giants":

> Analysts predict [computer] sales will increase this year, thanks to new products that link existing computer systems and help them work together. The commerce department projects sales of $61 billion in computer hardware and software this year, up about 4% from last year's sales. "The computer industry in general is going through a major product transition," said Tom Willmott, vice president of the Aberdeen Group, a Boston consulting firm. "Users" of all types and sizes of equipment have focused more than ever on issues such as downsizing, distributed computing and software development. I think 1992 is going to be a swing year—a year when not only are we likely to start coming out of the recession, but we can also get our hands on products and services that meet users' needs. The 1992 winners will be smaller companies, those in the workstation end and those making the software and networking products.

Alas, if the Bush speechwriters had included in the State of the Union what Peters and Kellner were thinking, Bush could have said—with gusto, "The United States is not in economic trouble . . . and let me tell you why. . . ." That approach should have brought about a very different public response.

Even the staff in my office of Science and Electrics was predicting good times ahead, particularly with some of the less significant technological firms, not just the giants like IBM Corp., Apple Computer Inc., and Digital Equipment Corp., but those that soon would be among the country's future success stories. I started a newspaper file on one of them, a personal computer firm, Microsoft Corporation. Bill Gates, who started and owned the company, had already made $6.3 billion, and at thirty-six years of age, he was the youngest person to have reached that pinnacle of wealth in the United States.

Later, according to a 1992 *Forbes* magazine, this college dropout was *number-one* on the list of America's richest individuals. Gates was not only indicative of the new breed of American entrepreneurs, he was the guy Peters and Kellner referred to in their writings. His business was typical of new, economically successful American entrepreneurs. Profiting from computers using MS-DOS, Microsoft soon would become the largest software manufacturer in the world. What transpired with Bill Gates and Microsoft was proof enough that the slogan "It's the economy, stupid" was not only misleading, it was a mistruth. A lie. However, no one was paying much attention to that possibility during early 1992. Including the Bush White House.

At the first of the New Year, it would have been prudent for the President to squelch the "sky is falling" protests and carry on, but Bush did not do that any more effectively off Capitol Hill than he had on. Only as strong and capable as those who surrounded him—those he relied on for advice and support—Bush found himself in perilous waters in the winter of 1992, beginning his journey into the unknown before the campaign really got underway. He was relying on his West Wing sergeants and his campaign generals to set the tone for his reelection. An error in judgement.

Having lost connection with the American people, and having suffered the onslaught of negative publicity in the aftermath of his Asian tour, a confused President Bush found himself without allies in and out of the presidential mansion. The Japanese "death scene" was more symbolic than anyone could have imagined.

★★★ ▬▬▬ ★★★

CHAPTER

34

SAM, SAM IS A USED-UP MAN

A president can be insulated from reality. The White House, Camp David, and Air Force One are even more protected than Capitol Hill. This insulation can be compounded by a president's personal characteristics.

—Charles Peters

<u>FEBRUARY–MARCH 1992</u>

Since December 15, Sam Skinner, as the new chief of staff, had tried to improve conditions in the White House; however, he had only made them more dysfunctional. After a few short weeks, the West Wing staff was whispering in muted timbre, "When is he going to get the ax?" Skinner's biggest problem continued to worsen: he lacked connections with those on the Power Pyramid. In fact, I doubt he realized that a Baker Plan was in effect and that Darman ruled.

His deficiency in political expertise and Washington savvy—a syndrome that had afflicted both Mosbacher and Sununu—meant that, no matter how noble his intentions, Skinner was not going to survive. Although he had proven himself cool under fire as secretary of Transportation, he failed to understand how the West Wing was *really* run . . . even while ostensibly running it. He had walked into the arms of a political octopus.

During Skinner's first week in the White House, along with his deputy, Henson Moore, he declared that Bush was going to let the nation know how concerned the President was about the economy.

Under pressure to get things done NOW, Skinner repeated what he had done as secretary of Transportation: he contracted Eugene Croisant, a consultant from the private sector with whom he had worked at the

Continental Illinois National Bank. Croisant was presently working as vice president of human resources and administration at RJR Nabisco Inc. The former colleague and friend to Skinner left his job to assist with the White House "makeover."

Skinner, with intuition of his own—and now counsel to guide him—prepared to realign White House personnel, but before he did so, he had Croissant conduct an organizational study. In the January 13, 1992, *Washington Post* article "Making White House Work for Sam Skinner," Ann Devroy wrote:

> What many inside the White House and the Republican political community question is whether [Croisant's] expertise will translate to the political culture of the White House, whose chief executive is facing reelection and a nose-dive in the polls, and whose staff is still reeling from the firing of John H. Sununu as chief of staff. "We don't make widgets here," one official said scornfully. "We don't do touchy-feelie retreats and psychological profiles....We do politics. And right now we do panic." Like many people who think outsiders cannot possibly understand their work, the official said Croisant cannot understand a political operation because he hasn't been in one.

Meanwhile, as rumored for six months, Secretary Mosbacher, in mid-January, finally had taken over as general chairman of the campaign. Skinner, with Bob Mosbacher, Robert Teeter (campaign chairman) and Fred Malek (campaign manager) made up the top stratum of the reelection committee; however, it was Mosbacher, Teeter and Malek who were referred to as the Triumvirate. Skinner was not included.

Ironically, none of these three individuals had any previous campaign management experience. In the 1988 campaign, Mosbacher, the Texas millionaire, had been fund-raiser; Teeter, the Michigan swami, had been pollster; and Malek, the Marriott businessman, had been convention chairman. Malek and Mosbacher were Bush supporters (not true for Teeter), but they knew little about running a presidential campaign, let alone one for an incumbent, a factor that complicates strategy making. It was "the blind leading the blind." And, now without someone to maneuver the troops and smooth over the disagreements among top aides, an unsuccessful Bush reelection—unthinkable less than five months earlier—now seemed a real possibility.

Joining the Triumvirate was Mary Matalin; she was chosen as campaign political director. Matalin had worked in the 1988 campaign and then at the RNC with Atwater; nonetheless, she was not considered to be in the Bush high command, and she admitted to having been tapped for her present job because "they" needed a female on the lineup. What Matalin did not admit was that she had a conflict of interest: her ongoing relationship with James Carville, Clinton's campaign strategist. Matalin's lack of maturity and her cutesy smugness eventually would cause undue embarrassment to the 1992 campaign, the White House and the President.

Both Atwater and Ailes, so vital to the team four years earlier, were missing this go around. A higher power had determined Atwater's absence; Ailes was not there by choice, declining the top media spot because he was "shifting his focus to corporate and entertainment clients and getting away from political campaigns." The '92 Bush-Quayle communications crew was comprised of Michael Murphy (Michael Murphy Media), Alex Castellanos (National Media), and Don Sipple (Strategic Communications). The all-important upcoming New Hampshire primary would be their first competition.

With Croisant's organizational analysis in hand, Skinner believed that the White House staff was of "high quality, but poorly utilized," and determined the communications office to be the first place he would "adjust." Actually, under normal circumstances, he would have been right on target; however, I do not believe that Skinner had any idea that Bush personnel—the appointees in the administration—were reprocessed Reaganites. Without this data, his conclusions would never be sound; the Skinner-Croisant analysis would be flawed. By not taking into account the intricate, powerful, and often enigmatic system that was already in place, Skinner would meet his fate sooner than expected. Fred Barnes, in the January 8, 1992, *Washington Times* wrote, "White House Skinner Dipping," explaining the chief of staff's dilemma:

> Mr. Skinner is a process nut, believing a "process problem" is part of Mr. Bush's overall communications failure. Why don't folks know Mr. Bush is a domestic policy president? The White House process didn't churn out that message before now, that's why. Mr. Bush's problem isn't a sour economy or an overemphasis on foreign policy. It's a communications problem: the White House hasn't gotten its message out.

★★★

Skinner tried to rectify the communications failure by using Croisant's charts to determine which personnel stayed and which left. Rarely does any White House organization function as it is laid out on paper, including the Bush presidency; dashes showing "information flow" cannot be equated with "authority." The office of communications, for example, which housed Bush's speech-writing staff, was headed by David Demarest, and as director, he was responsible for the manner in which the President of the United States was presented to the public on all domestic policy issues. On paper, this appears to be a terribly important and pivotal position. However, in the Bush White House, Demarest played a subservient role to Sununu and Darman, having little, if any, impact on the presidency.

Skinner believed that Demarest had failed to promote Bush's domestic policies. And he wanted him fired. If Demarest actually had responsibility over his office—to oversee *all* White House communications—he may have been the suitable individual to dismiss; however, Sununu had *never* used Demarest's organization for communicating Bush's message. In fact, he had downplayed to the zero-level the office that in most administrations had taken the priority role in generating the President's public image.

As a member of the 1988 Bush campaign team, Demarest had handled logistics, *not* speech writing *or* policy *or* strategy. In the Bush White House, he ended up managing as much as he had in the campaign. If the person who placed Demarest in the highest communications position in the White House knew anything about the '88 campaign, he would have known about Demarest's limited experience and realized that he was not the person for the job. I imagine Baker knew this fact.

With Demarest and the office of communications out of the mix, Sununu had turned more and more to Fitzwater, Bush's press secretary. Having had a substantial role in Reagan's White House communications organization, Fitzwater (since first arriving from Treasury in 1985) had been in the right place at the right time. With the help of Jim Baker, his mentor, the former Environmental Protection Agency bureaucrat–turned–Reagan press secretary had out-run, out-tagged and out-smarted Bush's previous press secretary (Pete Teeley) early on. Baker, as previously mentioned, had assigned Fitzwater to be Bush's vice presidential press secretary . . . *and* Bush's presidential press secretary. What makes the moment-to-moment Washington political picture so undecipherable is that the Big Picture is seldom described so that one can understand an event from a broader perspective.

Officially, Demarest had been charged with directing Bush's communiqués, but it was Fitzwater who represented the President on domestic issues. By collaborating with his former Reagan cohort Darman, he preserved his power base in the Bush West Wing. Demarest had his authority pilfered by Fitzwater. Marlin Fitzwater, not David Demarest, was guilty of the President's inadequate responses regarding foresightedness and the economy. Assuming that Bush had "vision," which I strongly believe he did, Fitzwater had ineptly portrayed it.

Skinner did not fire Demarest, but he did demote him to chief speechwriter, and he put Tony Snow, the former editorial writer at the *Washington Times* and Sununu's favorite, in the media affairs office. At the same time, Skinner *elevated* Fitzwater to communications director, handing him Demarest's responsibilities.

Skinner's intuition about there being inept aides was correct. His decision about who they were was wrong.

Two other individuals under the communications umbrella were Dorrance C. Smith and Sig Rogich. Smith, a long time Houston friend of the Bushes and the former executive producer of ABC's *Nightline* (who had been on Demarest's staff), continued to arrange media interviews and oversee public messages for Bush, and Rogich continued to set the outside scenes for him.

After going to great lengths to rearrange the White House cast, Chief of Staff Sununu, rather than correcting the President's communications problem, had added to it. Under Skinner's authority, Fitzwater, the defiant one, took on an even greater role in the Bush White House—as pointed out in the article "Bush Staff Honed with Fitzwater's Position Expanded" in the *Washington Times*, written by Frank Murray:

> President Bush's chief of staff, Sam Skinner, driven by the theory that his boss's popularity is the victim of misunderstanding, has elevated Marlin Fitzwater to White House communications czar with the rank of presidential counselor. He will manage "all communications matters," ... [and] retain his press secretary post while formalizing already considerable clout in the Oval Office. He will help shape policy objectives and "try to make [the President's] case as best I can" by coordinating announcements, speeches and travel...

★★★

"I will still try to be an honest broker," he said. Fitzwater described the job as working with three assistants [to the president], without assuming administrative control of their departments, "kind of like being coach and general manager at the same time.…" Since taking office, Mr. Skinner repeatedly has said the president's initiatives and attention to domestic policy were not "properly communicated to the American people." He expects promotion of Mr. Fitzwater will change that. In concert with the campaign officials, Mr. Fitzwater will attempt to explain and coordinate Mr. Bush's words and actions with the Cabinet, the executive agencies and, perhaps, with party leaders.

Was there anything in the White House or the reelection campaign for which Fitzwater was not involved?

The Skinner story becomes even more intriguing.

Deeming the domestic policy office, headed by Roger Porter, to be another weak link in the Bush chain of command, Skinner again made an astute conclusion. Nonetheless, because of his inability to understand the White House power structure—he took things at face value—he again tampered with the wrong office. The organizational charts, not clearly defining the power hierarchy, made for yet another faulty course of action.

Under Sununu, Roger Porter and his staff (which included researcher Jim Pinkerton), had been subjected to the same treatment as Demarest: excluded from the White House inner loop. Darman, Fitzwater and Sununu controlled the domestic policy office as they had Demarest's. Under the new Skinner plan, Porter, like Demarest, stayed in the White House, but was demoted. As junior domestic policy adviser to Bush, he continued to supervise a staff that had nothing to do with its support function: formulate policy.

Senior to Porter's group, Skinner now created a new domestic policy position, bringing in Clayton Yeutter— RNC chairman—to fill the slot. As "counselor to the president for domestic policy," Yeutter was given the command seat. But Yeutter was in a unique position, not because he changed Porter's or Demarest's responsibilities (they, as before, remained inconsequential), but because he represented, for the first time, someone who was specifically positioned to *limit* Darman's access to President Bush.

Yeutter added another layer to the already top-heavy domestic advisors group. By giving him authority over Darman, Skinner created a situation in which something was bound to give. No one interfered with Dick Darman's agenda.

As early as December 18, 1991, immediately after assuming his new duties, Skinner had his eye on Darman, and according to Frank Murray's article, "Skinner Hints at Staff Shakeup," in the *Washington Times*, Darman would march to *his* orders:

> Richard G. Darman will no longer have special status in the Oval Office. Mr. Skinner denied "reigning in" Mr. Darman but said he would be coordinating some of Mr. Darman's Capitol Hill lobbying. "Dick Darman is one of those people—one of the people—that would be up there seeking their advice and counsel," Mr. Skinner said, adding that the task would be shared with himself, chief White House lobbyist Fred McLure and Domestic Economic Policy Director Roger Porter.

The Murray piece went on to quote Skinner, who talked about his personal IBM management style: "I think process implies discipline. Discipline! Process! Teamwork!"

Believing that he could rearrange the White House staff according to the Big Blue handbook is where Skinner was most naïve; interfering with Darman's domain made it twice as catastrophic. These blunders spelled disaster for Skinner, and within a matter of days (hours?), he was overpowered by the Inside Team. Darman had in the past, did in the present, and would in the future control 1600 Pennsylvania Ave.

Because the White House was in such a muddle while Skinner attempted to sort out managerial problems, his staff had little time to reflect on campaign strategy, allowing for Bush's opponents to be extremely successful in advancing the President's negatives.

No one pursued this course more aggressively than Pat Buchanan, who, unlike Bush, was able to communicate his message. Buchanan paraded across the country, attaching wireless microphones to his suit jackets so that the television networks could hear his every word. Buchanan, of course, had experience in the communications arena.

In the Reagan White House, in 1985, at the calling of COS Donald Regan, Buchanan had become communications chief, overseeing the speech writing staff. As a "dyed in the wool" conservative and believer in Reagan rhetoric, he had quickly become disenfranchised with the Baker-run West Wing and accused Reagan of having sold out to the moderate assembly. Buchanan was demoted and lost his job writing President Reagan's political briefs.

In February 1992, before the New Hampshire primary, one of Buchanan's commercials showed a tape of Bush's 1988 convention speech; in a rough-and-tumble cowboy kind of way, the voiceover said, "Read my lips...no new taxes," reminding Americans that Bush had broken his promise. The ad turned out to be one of the major reasons Buchanan did so well in the final New Hampshire vote, receiving 37 percent to Bush's 53. The kickoff event for the 1992 season, the high point for Buchanan, turned out to be an embarrassment for the President.

As the insurgent candidate, Buchanan, buoyed by his New Hampshire success, now prepared for the Super Tuesday contest in March. Again, he used television to air the most controversial of his commercials: a thirty-second spot portraying homosexual black men in chains and leather harnesses, casting Bush as a President who condoned federal support for pornography.

Ian Wenchel (a former Reagan aide who had tried to join Bush '92 and was turned down) was part of Buchanan's team, and he had developed the "chains and leather" footage, which included a clip from a documentary subsidized by a National Endowment of the Arts grant. By showing the clip of a group of scantily clad black men dancing across a stage, the Buchanan-Wenchel pair hoped viewers would find the ad disgusting enough that they would not vote for Bush. For rural southern voters (where many conservative evangelical Christians lived), the ad worked; however, Buchanan would not win *any* primaries. Still, the votes he would take away from Bush because of such ads exposed the deep divisions within the Republican Party, particularly the divide between the conservatives and the moderates.

During the winter of 1992, Skinner, overloaded in his job trying to reposition personnel, had little time to counter Buchanan's attacks. As a result, the President, his White House and the campaign were significantly harmed. Early on, it was evident that the Bush road to reelection was going to be filled with distractions, detours and delays.

★★★ ▬▬▬▬ ★★★

CHAPTER

35

BLACK ICE IN THE WHITE HOUSE

And lo! In meretricious dress; Forth comes a strumpet called 'THE PRESS.' Whose haggard, unrequested charms; Rush into every blaggard's arms. Ye weak, deluded minds, beware! Nought but the outside here is fair! Then spurn the offers of her sway; and kick the loathesome hag away.

—Hartford Courant, January 5, 1801

MARCH 1992

According to the 1980 census, California had added seven million new residents (75 percent of whom were Asian or Hispanic), bringing its total population to 31 million; the Caucasian population had dropped from 77 percent to 57. In the 1988 election, Bush had won by 51 percent, thereby carrying the 54 Electoral College votes—a whopping one-fifth of the total needed to win the presidency. California is a must-win for a presidential candidate.

Throughout the early months of the 1992 campaign, competitors and critics alike had been vigorously attacking the President, even those not expected to, including several notable Republicans in the most vote-heavy state in the union: California. Ronald Reagan was one of these individuals.

Ronald Reagan, always influential in the state, and who had never considered Bush his Favorite Son, had difficulty in 1988 showing support for his Vice President, but what advantage he had cast Bush's way then could be described as fervent compared to what he offered in 1992. Reagan had no interest and no time for Bush this go-around. When Bush asked to meet with him while on a fund-raising trip to California, Reagan bluntly stated, "I (have) previous commitments." It was widely publicized that Reagan had informed his friends from California and elsewhere that Bush faced reelection difficulties because he "didn't seem to stand for anything." Reagan's prediction to the press that Bush was going to lose both California and the general election had consequences, for his beliefs often set the tone for those living outside Washington. The former President had the influence to affect undecided voters, those ambivalent about Bush.

Reagan was not the only former Republican President from California who found fault with Bush. Richard Milhous Nixon decided to join in the bashing. Dating back to 1968, Bush and Nixon had carved out a rocky relationship. Nixon was the first to encourage Bush to run for the Senate; when Bush was defeated, Nixon, feeling responsible, appointed him as ambassador to the United Nations. Following that tour of duty, in 1973, Nixon appointed Bush to be chairman of the RNC. Then the real trouble began. As chairman, and while trying to hold together the Republican Party in the wake of the Watergate scandal, Bush advised Nixon to resign the presidency. This counsel had not pleased Nixon—then or ever.

Flash forward eighteen years to the winter of 1992.

Nixon had finally felt ready to make a comeback into politics. In his mind, enough time had lapsed for him to reemerge as the venerated public official and foreign relations expert. After years of preparation, and having spent months researching the recent collapse of communism in the former Soviet Union, Nixon planned to deliver his "personal observations" in a way and at a time that would attract worldwide attention. Concurrent with his "entrance," he would promote his latest book, *Seize the Moment: America's Challenge in a One-Superpower World.*

With everything in place, Nixon returned to Washington in March 1992 and hosted a foreign affairs conference at the Four Seasons' Hotel in Georgetown. He invited hundreds of the finest and brightest in international relations to join him for the two-day affair, and he had his daughter, Trisha, ask Bush to join him in making the keynote address.

The night before the gathering, unbeknownst to President Bush, portions of a Nixon memorandum just happened to appear in the *New York Times*. In the four-pager, "How to Lose the Cold War," Nixon was quoted as saying that Bush had made a "pathetically inadequate response" to both the breakup of the Soviet Union and the Russian pro-democracy movement. He warned both Bush and Baker of the dangers they might incur for having given Yeltsin such an insufficient welcome, claiming, "The hot-button issue in the 1950s was, Who lost China? If Yeltsin goes down, the question Who lost Russia? will be an infinitely more devastating issue in the 1990s."

In the March 13, 1992, *Washington Post,* Ken Adelman gave his version of the Nixon Cold War memo, "Clouded Vision of Political Realities?"

> Now Mr. Nixon blasts the Bush administration—as if it needs more flak from friends now!—in a Nixonesque way. It comes in a clandestinely circulated "memo" to friends and foreign policy gurus. American samizdat. If, it tells, Mr. Bush fails to do everything he possibly can, "a new and more dangerous despotism will take power." Mr. Nixon's predictions here are no better than those he promoted before.

The Nixon critique had been circulated countrywide to everyone— except Bush. And on the opening day of the meeting—almost before the water was poured into the glasses—Nixon began his address with even more disparaging comments regarding Bush and the Yeltsin-Soviet Union situation. To make sure he received full media coverage, Nixon had invited CNN to do live coverage of the event.

Occurring simultaneously with Nixon's seminar was another event, one that Nixon was less likely to promote: the filing of a lawsuit to release 4,000 hours of the once-secret tapes of the Nixon White House. With the threatened issue of nearly 400 hours relating to the June 1972 Watergate break-in and resulting cover-up, it seemed Nixon had reason to divert the presses attention in March 1992.

Ken Khachigian, another Californian, joined the Campaign Against President Bush. At one time, he had been Nixon's preeminent speechwriter, and in 1992, he served as campaign manager for Bruce Herschensohn (a conservative California Republican running for the Senate). Khachigian had been more influential during the Reagan administration than many realized; not only had he been Nixon's liaison to the Reagan Oval Office, he also had penned Reagan's most noteworthy speeches, including his inaugural addresses and his Bergen-Belsen speech (touted to be one of Reagan's finest).

Stuart Spencer was the man responsible for bringing Khachigian from the Nixon enclave into the Reagan group, and despite being

★★★

Nixonians to the core, Spencer and Khachigian liked to refer to themselves as "Reagan aides." Although Reaganites were stationed throughout the Bush establishment, Nixon's elite (never embraced by Baker) still had the taint of Watergate associated with them. The less mentioned about *their* President, the better.

In spite of that, three Nixon alums had been drawn into the sprawling network of Baker's Most Influential: Ken Khachigian, Jim Lake and Stuart Spencer. All were on the Power Pyramid. The political Goliath, Mr. Baker, who crossed all conviction lines, had brought together—into his confidence—men from every ideological perspective and political orientation, even some of Nixon's men. But only IF they played by his rules and only IF they remained loyal to him. They agreed with Baker's terms if they wanted to survive in Republican politics.

During this awkward time when many prominent California Republicans—Reagan, Nixon, Khachigian—were finding fault with President Bush, the Democrats started to rally around their most-likely candidate, Bill Clinton.

After the Super Tuesday contest on March 10, the Arkansas governor was his Party's frontrunner, but it had not been without a fight. Paul Tsongas, the Democratic contender from Boston, had held a sizable lead at the first of the year, having claimed a win in the New Hampshire primary. In spite of the fact that no candidate who lost New Hampshire had ever been elected President, Clinton declared himself the "Comeback Kid." However, in the March 10 Super Tuesday primaries, instead of pulling ahead, Clinton experienced another major setback, of another variety: Gennifer Flowers threatened to destroy the Clinton candidacy.

On January 16, 1992, a former cabaret singer and Arkansas state employee had sold her story to a tabloid newspaper. Flowers claimed that she had a twelve-year affair with Clinton while he was governor. She had allowed her tape-recorded telephone conversations with Clinton (during the alleged liaison) to be telecast and reprinted.

Clinton, fighting for his political life, addressed the nation on CBS *60 Minutes* (filmed earlier in the day at the Ritz Carlton hotel in Boston) on January 26, 1992, with his wife Hillary sitting next to him. Forty million viewers, at home in their family rooms, watched Clinton on television. While holding Hillary's hand, he admitted to CBS interviewer Steve Croft that "his marriage had some low spots and that he had caused pain in his marriage," but that he *never* had been involved with Flowers. "I'm not a perfect person," Clinton related. "I've made some mistakes. I regret them, but believe me, this will never happen again."

The country responded positively and seemed to give Clinton the benefit of the doubt and believe him. However, the Flowers' story, with a strange twist, did not disappear.

Because most Americans did not know Bill Clinton, the major networks, as they covered the Flowers Story, presented Clinton's total profile, as well as focusing on his political record and his speaking style. This allowed the more professional, charismatic side of Clinton to unfold. The irony was that Governor Clinton became the leading Democratic candidate in 1992 not *in spite* of the Flowers stories, but *because* of them. The assumed affair, which elevated Clinton to national recognition, unexpectedly worked to his advantage.

Still, there was another Clinton hurdle: Jerry Brown. Reemerging with his anti-establishment theme, Brown, in March, was Clinton's weightiest challenger, and the two met head-to-head at a Democratic debate in Chicago. Brown charged Bill Clinton with illegally funneling money into Hillary Clinton's law firm while trying to portray it as state business. Clinton retorted that he had never solicited business for the Rose law firm or for Mrs. Clinton. Then Brown accused Hillary of illegally representing clients before Arkansas state agencies—agencies manned by Clinton appointees. Hillary defended herself by saying, "I supposed I could have stayed home and baked cookies and held teas, but I decided to fulfill my profession and practice law." The troublesome Madison Savings & Loan problem was born out of this Chicago debate.

While Clinton was fast-talking his way out of his "weak spots," Americans became even more disgusted with everything related to politics and were described by the media as "wallowing in pessimism."

BY springtime, Sam Skinner's ineptness was evident to just about everyone, inside and outside the White House. His plan to develop *esprit de corps* among the White House regiments had been unsuccessful, and this failure manifested itself in three important primary race losses: New Hampshire, South Dakota and Georgia. On March 3, 1992, in the *Washington Times*: Skinner was quoted as saying "With the exception of David Duke, he's [Bush] got more negative coverage than anybody in government." In fact, according to a Times-Mirror poll, Bush's approval ratings had dropped to 40 percent; most of that was in protest of his handling of the economy.

Skinner never had developed a campaign strategy or launched an economic message, as he had planned (Darman stayed in control), and finally, out of desperation, impatience and anger, the chief of staff did what he knew best . . . made more White House personnel changes. He was convinced *this time* he would subdue Darman. After admitting to having made some previous miscalculations, he created yet another domestic policy committee (on top of Yeutter's): the Policy Coordinating Group (PCG). This all-encompassing office was to formulate policy in both the White House and the campaign, giving its members sweeping powers. The two new PCG directors, senior campaign advisors, were Peggy Noonan, the Reagan speechwriter, and Jim Lake, the Reagan lobbyist whom Baker had resuscitated in 1988. Skinner previously had offered Demarest's communications job to Lake, but he had refused it. Now he willingly accepted the PGC position and became "message communicator," with Noonan as "message developer." Together they would synchronize *all* the White House and campaign policy speeches.

After Skinner tapped Lake, making him deputy chairman of the campaign, Lake ran into a snag, and his joining the Bush team quickly became problematic for the White House. Scandalous press was not what Bush needed, but that is what he got when the newspaper reporters wrote about Lake's representation of Adu Dhabi Investment Co.

By representing a majority investor (77 percent) in Bank of Credit and Commerce International (BCCI), Lake had done very well for himself, earning many hundreds of thousands of dollars. Nevertheless, his BCCI client, Adu Dhabi, was accused of laundering drug money, aiding arms traffickers, secretly buying three U.S. banks, and paying $550 million in U.S. assets to settle criminal racketeering charges. The press reported the Adu story in detail, pointing out Lake's connections to the institution sometimes referred to as the Bank of Crooks and Criminals International. The press tried to show Bush's deputy campaign manager as a lawbreaker, and with the stories, Lake drew more attention to Bush than to himself.

In a *Washington Post* article by Gary Lee (executive director for the Center for Public Integrity), Charles Lewis was quoted as saying, "For a president who claims he's concerned with ethics and who says he is going to get to the bottom of the BCCI scandal, it is preposterous for him to have a top-level campaign advisor representing a major investor in the bank." Lake had responded, "We just give them [Adu Dhabi] advice on how to deal with the American media." Not until a four-year investigation took place, did the Senate conclude that the CIA, the Justice department and U.S. and British banking regulators all had failed to recognize and contain the BCCI bank fraud.

IN the polls, Bush now dropped below the 40 percent mark; it was difficult to believe that one year earlier he had been more than fifty points higher. Uncertainty about Skinner's newly organized PCG and fear about what it might do to the campaign structure was breeding poor morale throughout the administration. For the first time, those at the most senior levels publicly doubted that Bush was going to win in November; the Bush staff was protesting and griping about the President as much as the opposition.

I was reminded how different the situation had been under similar circumstances in 1988, when immediately after Bush had won the GOP nomination, the campaign had begun to falter. It had been predicted that Bush would lose the November election. The difference was in the campaign staff's attitude. As we waited out those months in 1988, we never lost sight of the fact that we were there to ensure Bush won the general election. Team spirit got us through. With a candidate we believed in and Atwater to make sure we believed, winning the White House always remained the goal. Rumblings about Bush not winning or implications that one might leave the campaign were unheard of. In fact, they would have been considered heresy and reason for instant dismissal.

That kind of political loyalty to the campaign— so evident four years earlier—had evaporated by 1992, and presently, it was difficult to say who was running the show. With so many generals, no one assumed top position, and without a Lee Atwater, there was mayhem.

The one individual who seemed to hold more authority than the rest was Robert Teeter. As pollster to every Republican President since Nixon, Teeter had plenty of experience with campaigns, and if there were such thing as a leader in the 1992 Bush ranks, it was he. Market Opinion Research (MOR) had been his company for over twenty years, and as head of the Michigan-based Coldwater Corp. (with clients like Ford Motor Co.)

Teeter had made Ann Arbor both his home and home base. Over the years, Teeter made frequent visits to the Capital to meet and greet the most powerful, yet he was not a resident of the city and because of this, it was difficult for him to be in Washington's Inner Circle. Still, he was close enough for Baker to place him near the top of the Political Ladder.

As were countless other politicos, Teeter was indebted to Jim Baker for his present status, a campaign position that brought with it more weight than he had amassed in the previous four elections. Unlike the shadow roles he had played in the Ford '76, Reagan '84 and Bush '88 campaigns, Teeter was now on center stage, and Skinner, while trying to stay above the fray, relied heavily on him for direction. With good reason.

Though not a political strategist by trade, Teeter's focus groups had guided Washington and its political elite on what they should or should not do—for decades; Teeter and his polls were said to be capable of making or breaking a presidency. While I do believe he supported Bush—to a degree—I recognize that he had other political ties, most importantly, to Baker. Teeter owed his political prominence to Jim Baker. Not Ronald Reagan. Not George Bush.

During '92, Teeter had been invited to attend top-level White House meetings, and it was widely known that he was *the* favorite in the West Wing. Malek and Mosbacher, the other two reelection generals, did not receive the same honors. Yet, as revered as Teeter was for his ability to read public opinion, during the '92 election, it seemed that he fell into one political pothole after another. Regardless of how extraordinary his data gathering may have been, the White House, I believe, squandered it through mismanagement.

With Teeter as "lead-dog," Skinner had expected something positive to happen; however, after two months on the job, there still was nothing to show, and talk about a Bush loss was growing pervasive.

In May, I had a telephone conversation with a Bush campaign volunteer in the New York field office. He said résumés from Bush appointees had been floating on the streets of New York City for over a month. And the Washington Bush/Quayle gatherings I attended (at Commerce, Capitol Hill, and the White House) were disappointing. Cabinet members, West Wing staff and/or Republican advocates were there to deliver their pep talks, but something was always missing: no one spoke with energy or conviction. In a national campaign, a staff without an inordinate amount of enthusiasm for the challenge ahead is a telltale sign the candidate is in real trouble.

In the past, when Bush faced a dilemma, he most often called for Jim Baker, as in 1988, when Baker left his Treasury position and took over. Now it was predicted that Baker would leave his post at State and come rescue the failing troops. The campaign staff chanted what they called the B-3 Slogan: "Bring Back Baker!"

But in 1992, Baker's political relationship with Bush and his role in the administration were quite different than what they had been when he was in the Reagan Cabinet orchestrating the Bush '88 campaign with the G-6. Since becoming the American Ambassador, and while focusing his energies on himself (not Bush), Baker had appeared to let the political momentum at 1600 Pennsylvania Avenue take its own course. However, Baker knew everything he needed or wanted to know pertaining to Bush and the Oval Office . . . and the campaign. Besides relying heavily on Darman, Fitzwater, Cicconi, Fuller, and Lake, Baker was closely connected to Teeter. Without leading events (or even partaking in them), Baker could easily follow White House dealings and campaign actions.

If Baker took over now, people would expect him to perform a sensational turnaround. If he waited long enough and the situation became bad enough, then not as much would be expected of him. His reputation for doing the impossible would not be tarnished; it simply would have been too late to perform miracles. Knowing more about politics, presidential image, campaign strategy and White House organization than anyone in the nation, Secretary of State Baker, in my judgment, had become uninterested in being a campaigner and supporter for George Bush.

In response to the B-3 cries, Baker's spokeswoman, Margaret Tutwiler, called the rumors "nothing but silliness." Baker did not comment, for he had headed overseas to Jordan, where he found the waters considerably calmer than those on the Potomac. The press reported that Baker planned to stay in the Middle East "on business" indefinitely.

36

TWO POLITICIANS
AND A BILLIONAIRE

Beware the jabberwock, my son!
The jaws that bite, the claws that catch!
Beware the jubjubbird, and shun
The frumious Bandersnatch!

—*Lewis Carroll*

SPRING 1992

While Baker finessed his indefinite stay on the other side of the Atlantic, it left room for another Texan to pounce onto the campaign scene. Ross Perot was making more than enough racket to fill Baker's void, while simultaneously satisfying the media's passion for bawdy political news.

During the time of titanic struggles for primary votes, Perot had appeared as a guest on *Larry King Live* and, in a rather nonsensical way, announced that if volunteers placed his name on the ballot in all fifty states, he would run for President. No one really took him seriously.

Three months later, on May 17, Perot burst onto the national scene like a Fourth of July fireworks display, taking first place in a candidate popularity poll. President Bush and Governor Clinton came in second and third, respectively. Using Perot's eccentricity and vigor to gauge what lay ahead, I predicted that anything could happen in the next six months. Just when '92 election forecasting had started to seem humdrum, it became anyone's guess.

On Junior Tuesday, March 3, seven states had held primaries and caucuses. Clinton had won his first primary, beating Tsongas, Brown and

Kerry, and Bush solidly won all the states, tromping over the renegade Buchanan. Then, on March 10, before the Super Tuesday match, Bush's approval ratings dropped to 39 percent; still, he had gone on to win all eight Republican primaries. Clinton also swept the Super Tuesday slate, and by April, Bush and Clinton had solidified their front-runner status in their respective Parties.

Sometime after his appearance on *Larry King Live* (February 20), Perot, the self-made billionaire and one of the country's richest men, who tried to present a country boy image, decided to run against the Republican and Democrat contenders. Born in Texarkana, Texas, in 1930, Perot had attended Texarkana College before graduating from the U.S. Naval Academy in 1953. Five years later, honorably discharged from the service, he went to work for IBM, and in another five years, Perot left IBM and established Electronic Data Systems (EDS).

In the early 1980s, Perot sold his successful EDS to General Motors for $2.5 billion with the provision that GM would give him an inside track to the business. That never happened, and in 1988, Perot founded another computer company, Perot Systems. Restless and angry that General Motors had reneged on their pledge to install him into their senior ranks, the master salesman wanted to try something he had never done before: campaign for public office.

On March 29 on *60 Minutes,* just hours after Perot claimed he was willing to spend up to $100 million of his own money on his campaign, he received 41,000 phone calls in support of his candidacy.

Like Buchanan, Perot turned to television to take his message to America, and like Buchanan and Clinton, the economy became his focus. In a folksy, instructional way—using multicolored charts and graphs— Perot presented his ideas about how to improve the failing economy. By mid-April, the press reported he had received 1.5 million calls. The *Houston Post* asked its readers, if given the choice between President Bush and Governor Clinton, would they rather vote for Perot? Out of 4,000 responses, 74 percent said "yes" (to Perot) and 26 percent "no." And on April 21, Texas conducted a state poll that showed Perot supported by 35 percent, Bush 30 percent and Clinton 20 percent—this was in President Bush's home state.

By April 28, the Pennsylvania primary gave Bush 77 percent of the vote, earning him enough delegates to be renominated. Nevertheless,

★★★

Perot's hoofbeats became louder and louder, and on May 17, the first nationwide survey *(Time* magazine/CNN opinion poll) showed Perot in the lead. Bush followed and Clinton came in third.

Perot named former Admiral James B. Stockdale his provisional running mate and set up an 800-number phone network. Thousands volunteered to work in his campaign; most of them had no campaign experience, but they did have zeal. Perot could not be ignored.

The nation wanted someone innovative, bright and not tied to the establishment. Perot, aware of this, proclaimed himself to be the Political Outsider. In reality, he had plenty of experience working in and with Washington, starting in 1969, when he had chartered a plane to fly supplies to prisoners of war in Vietnam. In the Nixon administration, Perot had Oval Office privileges. And in 1979, during the Carter presidency, he had rescued two of his EDS employees taken hostage in Iran. With these former political ties, it was not unusual that Perot hired two veteran White House handlers to manage his 1992 crusade: Ed Rollins and Hamilton Jordan.

Rollins, now working at the Democratic consulting firm Sawyer/Miller Group, was the Democrat-turned-Republican-turned-Democrat who served as Bush's controversial NRCC chairman. In February 1992 Rollins's wife, Sherrie, had accepted the position as head of the Bush White House public liaison and intergovernmental affairs office. With the announcement that her husband would be managing Perot's campaign, she admitted to a conflict of interest and left. Contempt for Bush and Baker had made accepting the Perot challenge that much sweeter for Rollins, who was now given carte blanche to raise havoc at 1600 Pennsylvania Avenue. On May 30, 1992, Rollins wrote, "Why I Broke with Bush," published in the *Washington Post:*

> What this country really faces is a lack of leadership. And only the most diehard partisans can fail to see the unprecedented grass-roots movement in support of Ross Perot as conclusive proof that the public's patience has finally been broken. What America needs is a catalyst for change. We need to shake off our national paralysis. We need leadership that isn't vetoed in the system or mired in partisan gridlock like Napoleon's troops in the muck of Russian winter.

Hamilton Jordan had masterminded Jimmy Carter's winning bid in 1976 and also had run Carter's second—and losing—campaign to

Reagan. The Hamilton Plan was instrumental in taking the White House away from Ford (by less than 1 percent). Just as the 1976 triumph had been credited to "Hannibel Jerkin," so was the 1980 defeat. The loss—like the win—had been marginal. I knew Hamilton from college days, which made watching the Perot campaign that much more interesting for me. "Ham," as he was called, was president of my freshman class at the University of Georgia. After graduating, Jordan had returned to his hometown of Albany, Georgia, before penning the paper considered to be Jimmy Carter's 1976 victory roadmap.

Jordan and Rollins were an unlikely pair, but both had politics in their blood, and joining the Perot brigade in the spring of 1992 was looked upon as another opportunity to become "hot shots."

Unrelentingly, the country looked for *something* from the establishment: something to end the political gridlock; something to put more money into their pockets; and something to give them confidence in their future. Nevertheless, and amazingly to those outside the White House, the stagnant situation remained. Because of the inertia, President Bush was portrayed by the press as a leader without principle, program or purpose—"wishy-washy" and "incompetent," a man who had lost interest in being President and, in fact, did not want to win in November.

Recalling the pictures from his Japan trip, some asked, "Is Bush sick?" After insisting that he *was* in good health and that he *did* want a second term, Bush—one more time—tried to address economic issues, admitting that he believed there had been a recession and consenting to the fact that raising taxes had been a mistake. The President stated that, in spite of these errors, neither incident should be viewed as fatal to his administration or to the nation. He promised no further tax increases. By now, most citizens had tuned out messages coming from Washington, particularly those from the President.

CONGRESSIONAL aides in the House (13,000 employees) and the Senate (7,000 employees) could participate in presidential campaigns. However, because of a fifty-three-year-old law limiting the partisan political actions of nearly three million federal employees, I and my colleagues could not join in the skirmish. The Hatch Act prohibited all appointees (except those on the reelection committee) from being involved, which meant that I had to just sit back and watch the next calamitous six months unfold. Skinner, having never gained any influence in the White House, had alienated himself from Darman . . . a disastrous misstep . . . and after four months in the West Wing, he was holding on by the thinnest of threads. So was the Republican National Committee.

Beginning with Atwater's illness in March 1991, the RNC had followed an unforgiving path. The Republican Committee that set the pace for all presidential campaigns and, in this case, the reelection, was in a state of flux rather than taking charge. Atwater's physical demise had been a mirror image of the breakdown of the Bush presidency and the Committee. Initially, Charlie Black had tried to keep the trains running on time, then from nowhere, Atwater had been fired; Bill Bennett and his I-will-I-won't response had turned into a Yeutter appointment, and a month after Yeutter stepped up, he was summoned to the White House to be domestic advisor to Bush.

After Yeutter's departure, Norman Cummings, who had been at the Committee since 1989, was appointed temporary chairman; he previously had served as both political director and chief of staff to Yeutter. His short RNC appointment ended with the selection of a long-standing Bush operative, Rich Bond.

Bond had been an integral part of the Baker-Atwater Team. The Big Three. The Guys who epitomized Washington War Games. Along the way, some of the mightiest warriors had disappeared, but not the heartiest; they just rotated back into the system. Some faster than others. The really crafty ones made the leap from one administration to the next—one President to the next—look as easy as jumping rocks across a stream. Atwater had done this; Bond had not.

Having suffered the devastating Iowa caucus loss in January 1988, Bond—and his reputation as being the Republican political whiz kid—had gone down in flames. Because of the Iowa mishap, he had not been invited into the 1989 Bush White House, however, his firm, Bond, Buck and Donatelli in Alexandria, Virginia, had "access."

Before Iowa '88, Bond had told Atwater that if Bush won, he wanted the top spot at the RNC. Bond remembered his glory days at the Committee as Richard Richards's deputy and thought he would make the perfect candidate for the job. Initially Atwater had agreed, but later, after Bond lost Iowa, Atwater decided that Bond was too far off the scale, and too, he concluded that *he* wanted the chairmanship. Another rift between two of the Big Three. In the fall of 1990, when Atwater was undergoing toxic remedies to maintain the size of his brain tumor, he told Bond he wanted him to have the RNC chair; but there had been another hurdle: Rich Bond had not befriended John Sununu. In fact, Bond had not even been on Sununu's short list for the position.

By February 1992, it had been over five years since the parting of Bond from the official Bush regiment, and a full two years since Atwater first suffered poor health. Bush had been left without a manager at the organization responsible for his campaign fundraising.

Certainly, Bond would be tapped *this* time. And he was. Eight months before the 1992 election, February 1992, Bond was finally where he had wanted to be since 1981: chairperson of the RNC.

Rich Bond, the tactician, the fitter of "nuts and bolts," the can-do guy, stepped forward to claim the prize he had wanted for almost a decade. His demeanor was as close to Atwater's as the Republican Party had; however, he lacked the one characteristic that made Atwater unique: vision. Atwater's ability to create a grand strategy, coupled with his "people" intuitiveness, had set him apart from the others in the Bush ranks. Bond was not a strategist, and for this reason, there would be huge gaps in his reelection line of attack. As always, Bush's biggest problems centered on the slippery slopes from within.

Richard Cohen wrote an article pertaining to this dilemma, "White House Void," in the *Washington Post* in June 1992; it was indicative of the Washington mentality at the time:

> Why seek reelection at all? After all, the polls tell us that about two out of every three Americans would choose someone else—either Bill Clinton or Ross Perot. It must both pain and confuse Bush that upwards of a third of these Americans are Republicans and that many of them do not simply prefer someone else; they actively loathe Bush. The president must feel lonely indeed. All over Washington, people who just two years ago were tub-thumping Bush supporters, now roll their eyes at the mention of his name. The right and the left are in rare agreement: Bush stands for nothing. Not even the networks seem to differ: when the president called a news conference, only one of them (CNN) came.

Since the primary season had begun, Bush, although winning votes, had exhausted his political capital, and Buchanan had stayed in the race because of the President's vulnerability, exposing Bush's weaknesses while tearing the Party further and further apart. The ultra-conservative continued to flap across the countryside pleading to Bush to give up his candidacy. Buchanan's flogging also gave the Democratic and Independent tickets a boost, augmenting Clinton's emergence and Perot's fame.

In May and June, Perot had taken the lead in the polls over both Bush and Clinton; Americans dissatisfied with Bush, especially conservatives, tended to side with Perot. By giving the Republicans another choice, Perot, more than Buchanan, divided the Party. Although Perot's campaign soon would take an unexpected turn, at the time, he was the leading force and the challenger causing the majority of Bush's tribulations, and because the Bush team had to focus so much attention on Perot (as they had earlier with the assaults of Buchanan), they ignored Clinton's mounting strength.

Having worked so closely with opposition in 1988, out of habit, I tracked Clinton's every move. I wondered, where were the Bush opposition professionals? Who was doing what Atwater and Pinkerton had done in 1988? Without a top-notch Bush offense in 1992—not to mention a defense—Clinton just kept on marching. The Bush Team *allowed* the Democratic adversary to gather his tactical muscle, despite the glaring weaknesses in Clinton's background.

The Bush campaign never made use of the Clinton liabilities—issues that mattered, issues that would have had a significant bearing on the campaign, issues that should have given them the advantage.

During the month of June, Clinton was almost as susceptible as Bush, with his polls reflecting deep snags within the camp; he was at the lowest point of his candidacy and his popularity ratings hovered around 25 percent. Questions surrounding Clinton's integrity were still being tossed around by the citizenship, and voters doubted his moral and ethical character. The positive spin Clinton received from the Gennifer Flowers publicity was on the wane, if not totally vanished. Whatever good fortune the Arkansas campaign had enjoyed during the winter had turned into one big crisis in the spring. No predicament loomed larger than the one Clinton faced with his wife.

Hillary appeared to be a hazard to her husband's frontrunner status. She was bossy and controlling and arrogant and involved with her husband's every move. This was a perfect scenario for those in the

Bush legions wanting Clinton to appear weak and hen-pecked. From the beginning, America had questioned the Clinton marriage, actually with more doubts about Hillary than Bill. The hand-in-hand television performance when Governor Clinton pleaded for the country's under-standing regarding Flowers had been forgotten, and grumblings festered.

Many Americans were disturbed by the fact that Hillary did not assume her husband's name, and went by her maiden name, Rodham. Ironically, the name "Clinton" was not Bill's given name; he was born as Billy Blythe, and had chosen to drop his birth name and call himself William Jefferson Clinton at age fifteen, against the wishes of his ex-stepfather, Roger Clinton (whom his mother had divorced). Interestingly enough, both Bill Clinton and Nancy Reagan, as teenagers, legally had changed their last names to those of their ex-stepfathers, despite the men's opposition (Nancy Reagan had changed her name from Anne Frances Robbins to Nancy Davis, her mother being Edith Luckett and her father Kenneth Robbins.)

The fact that Hillary did not use Clinton as her last name, when coupled with her haughtiness and insulting know-it-all demeanor, had an off-putting effect on many. She was being treated by the Clinton campaign staff as a liability rather than an asset, and was quickly and quietly put under wraps.

As I have alluded to with Mrs. Reagan and Mrs. Bush, the wives of the candidates play an extremely important part in their husbands' political popularity or lack thereof. Without saying a word, the spouse makes a statement, setting the tone of the marriage and defining the family parameters—so much so that, dependent on how well she presents herself, the voter may be "for" or "against" her husband.

THOUGH President Bush stood firm in his decision to keep Quayle as his '92 running mate, never publicly wavering, the White House staff hedged their support of him, and the press wrote that Quayle was a "drag" to the ticket. During the spring season, no topic of conversation outside Perot's grand entrance received more attention than did Vice President Quayle and the Potato Debacle.

A New Jersey elementary school was holding a spelling bee, and Quayle was invited to attend. At the event, in a routine press promotion,

Quayle did as his staff instructed him. In the course of the spelling bee, he was asked to spell "potato." The Vice President's cue card, standard for occasions such as this, was handwritten by a member of his own staff, and it was erroneously written to include an "e" at the end. Quayle read the word as spelled on the card—a normal response, particularly when under the lights and scrutiny of a media crew. David Beckwith and Bill Kristol had written the cue cards, and were the ones who misspelled potato, not Quayle. The tale is *that* straightforward, yet it became devastating, causing a deluge of ridicule and embarrassment for Quayle for months and years to come.

Hounded by the press on so many issues during the final five months of the campaign, Quayle became especially susceptible regarding his chairmanship of the Council on Competitiveness, a group alleged to be illegal. Several officials on the Hill and referred to it as "a secret shadow government." Ralph Nader picked up on the issue and published a report saying the council was "unduly influenced" by environmental regulators. Eventually, and after much negative publicity, California Rep. Henry Waxman charged Quayle with ethics violations and had him appear at a series of congressional hearings, where, in like fashion to the investigation proceedings regarding Reagan aides involved in the Iran-Contra Affair, he was queried. For Quayle, the nastiest was yet to come. He was soon labeled the "initiator of criticism of the cultural elite."

The "family values" issue had started when Bush promoted the idea in his May 17 speech at the University of Notre Dame. Two days later, Quayle, speaking in California, linked the April-May riots in Los Angeles to a "poverty of values," advocating what he called "traditional values." Again, with a Kristol-Beckwith script in hand, Quayle had pointed to the television show *Murphy Brown* as an example of the media encouraging lax morals.

Kristol and Beckwith had equated the TV show's message (choosing to have a child outside marriage) with the breakdown of family values, and Quayle's remarks were directed toward the title character (Brown), not Candace Bergen, who played the part; however, Bergen chose to take Quayle's comments as personal. This set off a political bonfire, melting reality and primetime together. The day after Quayle's California speech, the headlines in the *New York Daily News* read: "QUAYLE TO MURPHY BROWN: 'YOU TRAMP.'"

Bergen and her staff denounced Quayle, and the press coverage that followed led to a national feud between the two; late night television shows made jokes, night after night. Extreme and absurd teasing of Quayle over his *Murphy Brown* annotations continued throughout the campaign season.

Quayle's chief of staff, Bill Kristol, had been the author of the California *Murphy Brown* speech, using it (and Quayle) to promote the conservative values theme, and although Bush had referred to traditional family issues before Quayle, after the *Murphy Brown* incident, the President said less and less on the subject and Quayle said more and more. The more he said the more boggled the matter became.

The values topic in itself was not the problem (Clinton would eventually use it), it was the way in which Quayle was instructed to bring attention to it that caused the hoopla. The Vice President's blunders over the past years—in my estimation—had been due to Kristol-inspired antics, not Quayle defects. The same held true now.

Starting in January 1992, the *Washington Post* had run a series of complimentary articles (seven in all) on Dan Quayle. In these, the other side of Bush's Vice President was written about in glowing terms, explaining why Bush had chosen Quayle as his second-in-command. Quayle had been regarded as *the* rising star in the Senate; admired for his congressional efforts, including work in defense, arms control, and labor and human resources. He had impressed his fellow Republicans and Bush.

The *Post* mentioned that before the 1988 convention, Quayle had pursued the vice presidential slot and made his desires known to Roger Ailes and Bob Teeter, both of whom had worked on his Senate campaigns. Because of Quayle's relationships with them (and other Bush insiders), his name had been submitted as Bush's potential running mate. Submitted over Baker's objections, yet by one of Baker's aides.

Now, four years later, after a political ride he never could have imagined, Quayle was still trying to take the high road and present himself as vice presidential. Still, the media insisted on taking the low road, and instead of respecting his expertise, made a mockery of him and the office he held.

Yet, in spite of it all, in the spring of 1992, Quayle seemed to gain the favor of some of his fellow Republicans when, for the second time, he traveled to Japan on behalf of the President. Since Bush had returned from his ill-fated Asian trip in January, U.S.-Japanese relations had been described "as the worst in decades." Japan bashing in the U.S. press and U.S. bashing in the Japanese press ran rampant, and although Japan (after Canada) was America's best overseas customer, the $43 billion Japanese trade deficit fanned U.S. political flames.

Quayle returned to Tokyo in an attempt to rectify the situation. During his four-day visit, he was included in the marking of the twentieth anniversary of the return of Okinawa—the city captured by U.S. soldiers in 1945 and returned to Japanese rule in 1972. At the conclusion of his trip, Quayle received glowing reviews, this time on both sides of the Pacific. Prime Minister Miyazawa, Emperor Akihito and other top officials who met with Quayle were reportedly "delighted" with the Vice President's social and political aplomb. Their remarks were the first complimentary ones coming from the Japanese government regarding the Bush administration in over four months, since the President's ill-fated visit.

As for President Bush, he stayed in Washington, trying to avoid the quicksand that surrounded him and his Executive Office. At this point, his most fervent desire was just to stay in the race.

★★★ ══════ ★★★

CHAPTER

37

STRONG BLACK COFFEE

It matters not how strait the gate;
How charged with punishments the scroll.
I am the master of my fate;
I am the captain of my soul.
—William Ernest Henley

<u>MAY–JUNE 1992</u>

President and Mrs. Bush, in the spring, had announced that their daughter, Dorothy Bush LeBlond, was to be married on Saturday, June 27, 1992, a nice distraction from the political unrest and uncertainties. Although there had been seven children of Presidents married, there had been only two White House weddings in the last twenty-five years. Now, Bush's thirty-two-year-old daughter, divorced mother of two, was marrying Robert Petri Koch, thirty-one and single, and an aide to Democratic House Majority Leader Richard Gephardt. They would be married at Camp David.

On the evening before the wedding, a rehearsal dinner was given at the White House with nearly 60 guests; the next day, 140 invitees attended the wedding ceremony held in a small chapel at the President's retreat in the Catoctin Mountains of Maryland, less than a two-hour drive from Washington. Hidden behind wildflowers, unkempt shrubbery and towering trees, the remote setting was ideal for "the Stealth Wedding," as the press referred to it.

The bride wore white lace and peach chiffon and the First Lady dressed in lavender lace; Arnold Scaasi had designed both dresses. To add a touch of political humor to the Republican-Democrat match, the

440

groomsmen stuck "Bush-Quayle" stickers on the bottom of the groom's shoes, so that when he knelt at the altar the Republican campaign logo would be in full view of the guests.

REGARDLESS of the merriment taking place at Camp David, there was little in the way of high spirits found back in Washington. At campaign headquarters on 15th Street and at the Residence on Pennsylvania Avenue—the place to which President and Mrs. Bush would return the next day—the mood was somber.

Bush and his U.S. foreign policy officials faced copious challenges, including a new schedule of affairs with Russia and its current President, Boris Yeltsin. In June, at the time of his daughter's wedding, President Bush hosted the U.S.–Russian Business Summit. In his role as diplomat, he once again rubbed shoulders with a fellow world leader. Having learned how to push for his political agenda and at the same time develop personable relationships, the American President was one of the few who balanced commerce—U.S.-style—with the more genteel approaches of other nations.

While I was working in the Japanese, Chinese and Mexican arenas, I had found that a personal connection was often required before conducting business. Getting to know one another was the prerequisite for more substantive talk, though it was seldom the American standard. Bush, who seemed to understand and respect this custom, took time to acquaint himself with fellow envoys, immersing himself in pleasant conversation prior to more serious dialogue. His finesse in this area had been instrumental in establishing a worldwide alliance-base in the Gulf War. And due to his adroitness, America's global status had increased significantly. Bush's relationship with former Soviet President Gorbachev had exemplified his ability to blend hospitality with political skill.

Now, with the communist regime over and a new leader in place, it was time for President Bush, once again, to show off his expertise; Boris Yeltsin was making a State Visit to Washington. Despite Yeltsin's glowing reports of Russia as a "land of profits," the historic transformation of the Russian economy had not progressed suitably, and Yeltsin's trip to the United States had been prompted as much by financial need for his ailing nation as anything else.

Before his arrival, Capitol Hill representatives, not convinced the U.S. should invest so heavily in the struggling nation, had delayed the necessary action for transfer of funds to Russia. Once in America, Yeltsin addressed Congress, beseeching their approval of the $12 billion that had been earmarked to jump-start the Russian economy.

Adamant about overcoming U.S. skepticism, Yeltsin then went with Senator Bob Dole on a tour of Dole's home state of Kansas. While encouraging Wichita grain farmers to invest in or trade with Russia, the senator proudly introduced Yeltsin, who informally schmozzed with the farmers, one on one. Still, state-siders remained hesitant. Besides the high Russian crime rate and a lagging economy, Americans worried about the lingering effects of the Chernobyl explosion: the world's worst nuclear disaster.

In 1986, during a routine test, 2,000 workers had been killed in an atomic power plant explosion, leaving in its wake a radioactive cloud hovering over much of Europe and contaminating large areas of Russia. When some of my Commerce friends took trips to the former communist country, they brought back horror stories, having observed—firsthand— some of the ruined lives of thousands of radiation victims living in towns near the site. The devastating effects of the catastrophe would last for generations, and when the Soviet Union had broken apart, the wreckage, death and disease caused by the Ukraine accident had left Russia particularly susceptible. Although the new government had promised to shut down the plant, it had not; it was still operating. Russia reported that not until the West provided the $1.5 billion necessary to complete two new nuclear reactors would the plant be closed.

In spite of these difficulties, before leaving the United States, Yeltsin, with Bush, signed the U.S.-Russian Accords. This was the second set of agreements Bush had penned with the Soviets during his presidency, and this one included new ways of managing space, taxation and investment, and weapons. And although Yeltsin's visit did not have the flair of the Gorbachev 1991 trip, the 1992 Russian Business Summit was said to have "unfolded better than expected."

Having spent much of his time dwelling on the Russian state of affairs, Bush still had to deal with conflicts in the Far East. The China trade situation had not improved. However, as bad as American-Chinese relations were, there had been a fair amount of media hype describing the recent China-McDonalds union, whereby the U.S. fast-food giant was building their largest-ever hamburger store on Beijing's busiest

★★★

intersection, not far from Tiananmen Square. Unfortunately, this multi-million dollar deal had not helped the President in his trade relations.

On June 2, Bush, having asked Congress one more time to renew China trade benefits, one more time, had been turned down. In "Bush Faces Opposition on Renewal of Trade Benefits for China" by Don Oberdorfer, published in the June 3, 1992 *Washington Post*, Bush—appealing to Congress—was quoted: "It is wrong to isolate China if we hope to influence China. Maintaining a constructive policy of engagement with China has served U.S. interests. Positive, if limited, development in our human rights dialogue are insufficient and have left the United States deeply disappointed." The Oberdorfer article went on, "Senate majority Leader George J. Mitchell (D-ME) said in a statement that Bush's policy toward China has failed and that his decision is inconsistent with American values and contrary to America's best interest."

Along with other Bush critics, such as Nancy Pelosi (D-CA), Mitchell lambasted the White House for not taking a harsher stand on human rights and nuclear weapons, and he promised to defeat Bush's request to grant Most Favored Nation status to China. For the third year in a row, the President, who, according to his opponents, was too lenient in his international approach, continued to fight, and ultimately, he *did* overcome Congress. The Hill was not able to come up with the necessary two-thirds majority to override him. Although this win was noteworthy, it left the relationship between the Executive Office and the legislative branch in a less-than-desirable state, and trade between the People's Republic of China and the United States of America remained unstable.

Shortly after the U.S.-Russian Business Summit (and while China's MFN status was being determined), a summit of another kind was held: the United Nations Conference on Environment and Development. In the months leading up to the symposium, tagged "the most ambitious environmental conference ever," there had been much speculation as to how President Bush would present the United States' point of view. He had been under pressure to lend the prestige of his office to set the pace of the conference, held in Rio de Janeiro and referred to as the Earth Summit. President Bush, who spent two days at the event, did not lose politically because of his involvement, yet he did not gain either.

The Rio meeting was the third of its kind in over three decades, and before it started, there were those who predicted it was going to be a problematic conference for Bush. On Wednesday, May 13, 1992, the *Washington Post* printed, "Bush to Attend Rio 'Earth Summit' in June" by Michael Weisskopf:

> For Bush, the road to Rio was full of turns. After inviting negotiators to begin global warming talks here in 1990, he continued to stress the "scientific uncertainty" of the threat and to call for no more than a "framework" treaty. With Rio looming, however, the president faced a dilemma, administration officials said. He could not afford to avoid the meeting without damaging his environmental image in the reelection campaign, but blocking an agreement could expose him to criticism at the summit.

Bush *did* block a significant treaty: the Biological Diversity Accord. This pact, which dealt with the protection of a large variety of the world's plants and animals, was the most contentious of those addressed in Rio. And of all the nations represented, including Japan and the twelve European countries, only the United States did not support it. Bill Reilly, administrator of the Environmental Protection Agency (and former conservationist), had advised Bush to sign the pact, but because the President believed it would harm U.S. biotechnology interests, he refused. For his decision, Bush was harshly criticized for putting industrial concerns before the environment.

Clayton Yeutter responded to the President's critics with a statement in the *Washington Post* on June 15, 1992, in "Letters to the Editor." The White House domestic counselor stated that the biodiversity treaty . . .

> . . . asks the United States and other developing nations to put up money that developing countries would spend as they see fit. The American public is already unhappy with foreign aid programs where *we* decide how to spend our money. The people would be doubly unhappy if asked to help finance agreements where someone else makes the spending choices. The proposal demands the transfer of our technology to the developing world. We believe it also could lead to the pirating of technology (intellectual property—patents and copyrights) that we do not transfer voluntarily.

During the twelve-days in Rio, the Intergovernmental Panel on Climate Change (IPCC) distributed a 365-page document on global warming to the 110 heads of state, and although there were those who said the report lacked scientific data (including those from the U.S.), it was signed into law as the Climate Change Accord. As the centerpiece of the summit, this treaty limited greenhouse gases (carbon dioxide emissions from power plants) believed to cause a rise in global temperatures, with potentially dangerous consequences. Going beyond the determinants of previous years, clean air standards now called for a reduction of sulfur dioxide, nitrogen oxide, mercury and carbon dioxide. The United States insisted that no specific targets or timetables for reductions be included. For many American executives, this was not good enough.

On the other hand, the American President pleased many conservationists when he sponsored the Forest Preservation Accord, not a binding treaty, but a significant one. Bush, who for two years had been promoting the idea of a forestry convention, committed to planting one billion trees a year in the United States for the next decade. And while focusing on safeguarding the planet's shrinking forests, Bush proposed $150 million to assist in preserving tropical forests. The majority of the industrialized countries hoped that one day a treaty would be signed; the poorer countries, which possessed most of the forests, fought the idea, feeling that an accord would intrude upon their territorial rights.

After the Rio gathering concluded, the *Washington Times,* on June 14, 1992, printed a statement that Bush had given at an earlier news conference: "We're the leaders, we're not the followers. The U.S. fully intends to be the world's pre-eminent leader in protecting the world environment."

Up until 1992, the U.S. environmental stance had been determined by the EPA and considered to fall exclusively under the domestic umbrella. During the Bush presidency, an important alteration was made: for the first time, policy was redesigned as an international topic, to be monitored by a number of federal agencies, including the departments of State and Commerce.

AT the end of January 1992, Barbara Franklin had been confirmed by Congress and sworn into office as Commerce secretary. Shortly after she arrived, I tried to meet with someone on her staff to discuss my appointment situation. Through the grapevine, I had heard that trade development (TD) was cutting back on political appointees and that S&E was combining forces with the office of Aerospace. Some politicals would be squeezed out.

Larry Ryan, the incoming deputy assistant secretary of Aerospace, would eventually direct all S&E operations, as well. The former vice president of D.C. operations at Bell Aerospace Textron, Ryan was a newcomer to Commerce and to politics, and understandably, wanted his own appointees with him. Overnight, the promises made to me that I could stay in my present position were forgotten. Appointee slots were becoming scarcer, and White House personnel were no more accommodating now than any previous time. I started to worry.

Not wanting to leave the administration, I knew I needed a plan—an aggressive one. Most appointees in this situation would have picked up the telephone and started networking, asking those they knew—and anyone else who would listen—for their help. However, I did not have those kinds of connections, and without contacts to people in "higher places," I readily could be subjected to exile.

I decided to write some letters.

Using my Pelican pen and blue-black ink—and scripting in my best handwriting—I sent notes to one hundred appointees, including those in Commerce, in the other thirteen lead agencies and in the twenty smaller ones. All my notes (except for Commerce) were written to the White House liaisons. I also mailed messages to members of President Bush's senior staff, whose names and titles I looked up in my White House phone directory. My goal was to let as many influential people as possible know of my intention to secure another appointment. On each single piece of Crane paper, I wrote:

> As you may know, the office of Trade Development in the International Trade Administration here at Commerce is being reorganized and downsized. My political position as special assistant to the former deputy assistant secretary for Science and Electronics (GM-14) is being eliminated. Since February 1989, it has been my pleasure and privilege to serve in the Department under Secretary Mosbacher. My commitment to the Bush Administration is unquestionable and my job performance, as special assistant, has consistently been appraised at the highest level in the outstanding ranks. If you have any suggestions or advice as to how I might explore other political openings and continue to serve in the Bush Administration, I would be most appreciative. Enclosed, please find my résumé, which I hope you will find helpful. Thank you for your consideration.

★★★

No responses were forthcoming from Commerce, where I most wanted to stay. Nevertheless, the letter did generate several replies; I was invited by seven White House liaisons to interview in their agencies. Although none of them anticipated an immediate opening, I still scheduled five meetings—at Education, State, Interior, Labor and Treasury—deciding to take advantage of the opportunity to broaden my contact base.

Unexpectedly, I also received a response from the White House regarding an opening in personnel; Constance (Connie) Horner asked me to meet with her to discuss the position of director of Presidential Boards and Commissions. The job entailed placing individuals on part-time committees, of which there were hundreds.

I was scheduled to visit Horner in her West Wing office on Saturday, March 28. Although I had been in the White House on several occasions, this was the most personal trip. My encounter with Horner ended up going beyond the "hello-how-are-you" meetings I had experienced over the past couple of weeks with the liaisons.

Wearing a bright salmon-pink tailored suit, with a long, black dress-coat over it, I entered the White House's Pennsylvania Street entrance. After checking in with the security guards at the front gate, I proceeded down the walkway to the entrance of the West Wing. The short distance between Pennsylvania Avenue and the low-lying West Wing annex is a singular spot and where news reporters gather and give their six o'clock reports. On this particular day, their equipment, protected in white canvas covers, was sprawled on the lawn to the left of the walkway.

Even in the winter, maybe especially in the winter—because the Executive Mansion is not obscured by the mammoth trees in bloom—the majesty of the grounds surrounding the presidential quarters is breathtaking. I tried to absorb everything around me, taking pleasure in the solitude, assuming I might never again have the chance. There is no way to fully describe my elation at that moment.

Upon first entering the building, I thought how small the West Wing appeared, and while waiting in the Presidential Reception Room (called the Appointments Lobby, which, in 1969, had been created from the former press lobby), I realized I was sitting there with no distractions. I was the only one in the room. The interior was one of understated elegance, and because of the room's miniature size, it felt cozy and more reassuring than I would have thought. There was a hush throughout the complex, which, on this day, reminded me of being in a small chapel, and because of the dim lighting, I had a sensation of reverence. I quietly surveyed every object around me as if I were in a museum; two handsome Chippendale sofas, reproductions of originals in the Governor's Palace in Williamsburg; above one was a portrait of *George Washington in the Battle of Princeton,* painted by Charles Peale Polk. On the longest wall was an exquisite English breakfront-bookcase, and on another was an inlayed Hepplewhite-style clock.

The high-key pace of the West Wing staff, usually unobservable to guests, takes place behind heavy closed doors, as was true in the OEOB. This being a Saturday, staffers were not caught up in the usual workweek frenzy; only a few were on hand. Unlike the Residence proper, the West Wing's ceilings are low, the hallways narrow and the wooden stairs—as one proceeds to the upstairs offices—are creaky, like those in an eighteenth–century colonial home. On my visit with Horner, I walked up these stairs for the first time.

In her office, equivalent to a small study, Horner and I sat side by side on a contemporary sofa, and after some small talk, she asked me about my interest in rejoining presidential personnel. During our two-hour discussion, I related specifics about my previous jobs with Transition, my work in the campaign and my professional background, including my appointment in the exporting arena. She was both courteous and gracious with her time, explaining the complexities of working in the White House and reassuring me that because I had "been there," it would not be as difficult the second time around. Compared to most employer-applicant job interviews, my one with Horner was unusually pleasant. Connie said that she would get back to me within a week.

Subsequent to this meeting, and without warning, I received another call from the White House, this one from Lucy Muckerman, special assistant to Sig Rogich, the President's advisor for special events. Because Rogich was out of town, she called in his place to ask what kind of a position I was interested in finding, and she said that although they were not hiring in their office at the time, Mr. Rogich had wanted to suggest that I call him after he returned to Washington. At that time, he would be glad to assist me. Again, this rejoinder was uncommon, and I felt flattered.

★★★

Clayton Yeutter, assistant to President Bush for Domestic Policy, was the third individual in the White House to offer job search assistance. Former trade representative and secretary of Agriculture, Yeutter temporarily had chaired the Republican National Committee before moving over with Skinner in January. He responded to my letter by arranging an interview for me at the International Affairs Agency at the department of Agriculture. They had an opening.

Being previous Secretary of that agency, Yeutter was aware that the Foreign Agricultural Service (the FAS is equivalent to State's Foreign Service) was looking for someone with an international trade background to manage their private sector advisory committees. The office of Congressional Affairs needed a liaison to direct its 700-some private sector advisors, those individuals acting as agricultural trade counsels to Bush. Presently, the group, comprised of chief executive officers, was advising the President on the North American Free Trade Agreement, the accord being sent to Capitol Hill for approval in November.

After several interviews with the FAS staff, including one with the four heads of the International Affairs Agency, the review board offered me the position of director of Advisory Committees on International Trade; I would be working in the office of Congressional Affairs. The administrator and head of the FAS was Dr. Duane Acker, an admired and highly respected man, to whom I would be reporting. It was in his well-appointed office on the third floor of the Agriculture building that the official bid was made. Along with the offer, I was assured that I would receive a promotion to deputy assistant secretary (a notch above my present GS-14, but still at the junior end of the political pecking order) as soon as the Trade Bill passed. Projecting NAFTA to be completed just after Bush started his second term (trying to stay optimistic), I looked forward to a promotion by spring '93.

Working in the White House, in any position, is an honor and privilege. Nevertheless, I had been ambivalent about the boards and commissions position, feeling that I would prefer to stay in the trade area rather then go back into personnel. My impression was that the international field had greater potential in the world outside the administration. I let Connie Horner know of my decision.

Interestingly, all three individuals who had gone beyond the expected formalities of responding to my letter—Connie Horner, Sig Rogich and Clayton Yeutter—were in senior positions at the White House and none of them knew me. Actually, they were the last group of people I thought I would hear from. However, it was with their encouragement that I became more resolute than ever in my desire to stay with President Bush for as long as he was in the White House. I would always remain grateful to Clayton Yeutter for taking time to find my next appointment.

The International Trade Administration was a better known organization than the Foreign Agricultural Service, yet the clout behind the FAS, unbeknownst to me, was renowned in U.S. international trade circles. Although Agriculture, with over 200,000 employees, was five times the size of Commerce, it did not receive the same political stature in the eyes of appointees. My friends laughed about my leaving an office where policy centered on computer chips and entering one where discussions revolved around potato chips. In spite of the jokes, the job, which started in mid-April, thrust me into an arena where the trade issues were ostensibly the same, but, in many ways, more multifaceted.

Agricultural products represented America's most noteworthy export, making trade deliberations regarding fruit, flour, sugar, cotton and apple industries (to name a few) among the most contentious during the NAFTA talks. For the remainder of his presidency, Bush would spend more time and give more attention to Mexico and NAFTA than to any other foreign affairs matter—despite the importance of the events taking place in Europe, China, Japan and Russia.

Not without controversy, the U.S. effort to unite with Canada and Mexico in a hemisphere of free trade became the centerpiece of Bush's international policy platform in the '92 election. If successfully negotiated, NAFTA would free trade from Alaska to Cape Horn, involving over 350 million people and creating the largest market in the world. Conversely, if NAFTA were to be viewed as the thrust behind the loss of U.S. jobs, Bush would have a long, hard fight in proving its worth. Although some of the nation's leading economists forecast that, given time, NAFTA would be worth trillions of dollars to American exporters, that prediction was not all that convincing to a select number of business segments.

My job was to help promote the success of NAFTA and to ensure that the President's position received the backing of the chiefs of the major agricultural industries. I would facilitate the U.S. agriculture committee talks, in which the singular purpose was to agree on how to rally behind the specifics in the Mexico-Canada accord while supporting President Bush.

I believed then—and still believe—that free trade, when carried out in the manner intended, is both fair and beneficial to those with the superior goods and services. And as director of the Advisory Committees on International Trade, I made it my goal to do whatever I could to make NAFTA happen. With twenty-four government-appointed commissions —and 700 participants—to "care for," I suddenly found myself engulfed in the inner workings of the trade negotiations.

Each morning, I met with the Agriculture department's senior trade negotiators, an elite and intelligent group of civil service employees who were the best and brightest in their field. The toughness of the Ag envoys was softened by their sense of humor, which in no way compromised their penchant for challenging work.

In these meetings, I sat with The Trade Guys on folding metal chairs around an old wooden table in an unpretentious closet-sized office stuck off a back hallway of the FAS wing. Not what you would picture as a setting for men of this caliber and meetings of this consequence, especially in a government agency that took up two city blocks. They talked while I listened, but because of my eavesdropping, I stayed current with the trade proceedings, which helped me immensely in my position as the congressional contact. The NAFTA chapters that this crew was responsible for were grueling to finalize and write, but the negotiators knew that Bush was counting on them for the passage of his 1,038-page North American Free Trade Bill, and they rallied to the occasion.

In January 1991, Bush had requested the Hill members to give NAFTA "fast track" status, agreeing not to attach other bills or amend-ments to the legislation, and thereby giving it a greater chance of passing sooner. Under this system, Congress also could not amend the accord from the floor. Before presenting NAFTA, Bush was given three months to negotiate with the Mexican government; after such time, the Hill representatives would have ninety days to vote the bill "up" or "down."

Since my visit to Mexico City in 1990, I had put together a good amount of information on Mexico, including recent material on the Free Trade Agreement, and now that Mexico was so relevant to my work, I sorted through the data looking for pertinent articles. One by Hobart Rowan in the February 21, 1991, *Washington Post* described the present situation in "Trade Fight At the Rio Grande":

> A bitter fight over President Bush's proposal for a free trade zone with Mexico is shaping up—with the outcome uncertain.

Organized labor and Democrat liberals are leading the battle against the idea, fearful that low wages in Mexico will accelerate the relocation of American plants there, adding to unemployment here. There's no doubt a free trade agreement with Mexico will wipe out some American jobs in the short run. The question is whether that will be outweighed by benefits—economic and political—to the United States of a larger and more advanced Mexican economy.

I was curious to read in this piece a quote from one of the Mexican Cabinet Ministers I had met while on the trade mission in 1990. Secretary of Commerce Puche argued that the U.S. would not lose jobs:

> Mexican Secretary of Commerce Jaime Serra Puche argues if it were not for the availability of cheap labor in the *maquiladora* [near the American border], the American companies that settled there— unable to compete in the States—would have left North America entirely. "Most importantly, this has *not* resulted in a net loss of jobs for the American economy: it is estimated that for every job created in Mexico's *maquiladora* industry, there is at least one created in the U.S." Puche said.

Despite the Democrats vehemently opposing NAFTA, Bush's request to extend fast track authority passed with a majority votes in both the House and Senate. Nonetheless, getting the bill signed into law before the end of the year looked more and more doubtful. With the argument against free trade becoming a campaign lightning rod, the timing for Bush was dreadful. Perot and Buchanan, as well as Clinton, assailed the President for what they snidely referred to as the "Bush Accord."

Conversely, NAFTA proponents claimed the agreement to be one of Bush's most successful diplomatic initiatives. In a relatively short amount of time, they touted, Bush had overcome geographic, cultural and political impediments, not only assembling a strong alliance with Mexico and Canada, but also building relationships with China and Russia. Trade barriers, Bush believers said, were no longer appropriate tools for constructing nations of universal strength and stature, and trade accords—that encouraged commerce—were seen as vehicles by which countries looking to the twenty-first century could prosper. Bush's vision of a global neighborhood, his advocates cheered, was his finest contribution, so far, to creating an affluent and authoritative America.

White House, Washington, D.C., March 1993
As close as I could get to the West Wing after the 1992 election.

★ ★

PART 8

The Light Brigade

★ ★

Half a league, half a league; Half a league onward;
All in the valley of Death; Rode the 600
Forward, the Light Brigade! Charge for the guns! he said;
Into the valley of Death; Rode the 600

—Lord Alfred Tennyson

★★★ ═══════ ★★★
CHAPTER

38

FREE FIRE ZONE

Since men don't as a rule consider women rivals for power, they have no way of mentally fitting them into the existing local power structure. Men are seldom inclined to see them as rivals, male chauvinist pride being what it is.

—Michael Korda

<u>JUNE 1992</u>

In spite of those who saw past the accusations that Bush had no foresight, the Vision Thing, as it was referred to, was a perpetual obstacle for Bush. Describing America as he envisioned it in the year 2000 and explaining how America was going to get from "here to there" seemed simple enough, yet Bush never made it happen. More correctly, the Bush *staff* never made it happen.

Evidence continued to support my Crazy Conspiracy Theory. In the White House, the Darman/Baker Inferior Plan had worked well. The more unsophisticated and inexperienced the individuals who were being placed in the political mainstream, the more Darman and Baker reigned supreme.

With a vast network of persons under his authority, Baker maneuvered them like chess pieces. In his subtle manner, he quietly, sometimes covertly, gave orders—nothing obvious and almost always behind the scenes by way of a one-on-one conversation in the hallway, in a closed-door telephone call, or in an inconspicuous small group assembly. Baker continued to run Political Heaven.

In the spring of '92, Mary Joe Matalin became Bush's new campaign political director. Thirty-eight-year-old Matalin had bounced around Washington for years, going from one job to another; the "special

455

assistant" had secured most of her positions by being in the right place at the right time. But she never had authority of her own, and she was best known for her foul language, wisecracks and party-time behavior.

On one hand, it surprised me when the Bush White House named her to *manage* political strategy in the reelection, yet, on the other hand, it did not. The Inferior Plan was working. Matalin was placed with Charlie Black, who had been moved from the RNC to the reelection committee in February and was now supervising the Bush political shop while directing opposition research. By whatever means or methods Matalin was singled out for this job, in my opinion, her appointment was a major mistake. Matalin, herself, thought she had been assigned the slot because there were no visible females in the Bush lineup. Little did any of us know just how visible she would become in the following months.

Still in love with James Carville (Clinton's political strategist), Matalin jokingly referred to him as her "Ragin' Cajun," while he called her his "Ragin' Croatian." Although the two tried to convince the public they were not continuing their romance while in the throes of campaign battle, Mary and James, in their respective camps (Washington and Little Rock), found time to compare notes every evening by phone. The liaison that previously had been described as "steamy," was now "stormy." At least, that was what the two tried to portray. For a while, Washington went Hollywood. The Matalin-Carville saga was like a bad—very bad—comedy.

In a *Washington Post* article, the affair was described this way: "Carville and Matalin aren't just working in opposing campaigns, they're going mano a mano every day in a war of messages, sound bites—and nerves—that promises to become nuclear as November approaches." The media frenzy regarding their relationship heightened as the two politicos, begging to be in the public eye, took the campaign to its lowest common denominator.

Things got absurd when Matalin started sending a barrage of fax memos to Carville. One in particular, meant to resemble a press release, listed twenty-two questions, one of which was, "Which campaign had to spend thousands of taxpayer dollars on private investigators to fend off 'bimbo eruptions?'" In response, the Clintonites in Little Rock sent back "the Clinton campaign" as their answer. It was assumed that Matalin had coined the phrase "bimbo eruptions," but, she had not; unbeknownst to most everyone (including Clintonites), Clinton's opposition research director, Betsey Wright, had been the first to use it. While strategizing on how to eradicate predictable Clinton "sexual liaison" stories, Wright had come up with the term to describe these Clinton affairs.

Because Matalin was mistakenly credited with authorship, a slew of anonymous hate mail arrived at the Bush headquarters—ironically, from the Clinton encampment. One of the memos, written in all caps, said: "YOU'VE GOT 86 DAYS TO TURN BOZO BUSH AND HIS PIT BULL DUMMY DAN INTO A VIABLE, BELIEVABLE DYNAMIC DUO!!" Because of Matalin's unauthored quip, Clinton staffers accused Bush of running a negative attack, and they demanded that Matalin be dismissed. CBS News reported the "bimbo" goings-on as "new evidence that the Bush campaign is out of control." NBC News called it a "public relations fiasco." I contend that Matalin was used by the Clinton campaign to their candidate's advantage and to discredit the President.

Contrary to what one might have expected—given their positions—Matalin and Carville seemed to love the public attention, and the more they enjoyed it, the more ridiculous their actions became. Finally, Matalin was forced to make an apology to Bush, offering to resign, but he said "no." Admitting now that she was aware the President had stipulated no personal references to Clinton ("This is not how I want to run a campaign," Bush was quoted), Matalin vowed to back off.

THROUGHOUT the spring, the Bush communications team had grown and grown and grown. The list of message chiefs included nine: Marlin Fitzwater, Sam Skinner, David Demarest, Sig Rogich, Jim Lake, Peggy Noonan, Fred Malek, Dick Darman, and Will Ellis. Now Victoria Clarke, called Torie, was the newest addition, making the total ten. Clarke's campaign position (Sheila Tate's in 1988) was equivalent to Marlin Fitzwater's in the White House, and as campaign press secretary, she was responsible for delivering the presidential communiqué. In other words, thirty-two year old Clarke was in charge of presenting *the* Bush message. Her appointment, as had Matalin's, fit the Baker Plan.

Aside from taking photographs of Bush when he was Vice President, Clarke had no White House experience. Pittsburgh-bred and nearly six feet tall, she had started her career as a photographer for the *Washington Star,* and after the paper shut down in 1981, she had taken official pictures of Bush for a short time. From 1982–1992, Clarke had various jobs, including press secretary to Senator John McCain and Trade Representative Carla Hills.

Clarke had not wanted the '92 Bush press secretary position, and when asked, "Why take it?" she replied, "Because I didn't want to find a dead horse head at the bottom of my bed." Only after being coaxed by Robert Teeter, among others, did Clarke accept. She was quoted in an April 13, 1992, *Post* article titled "Bush's Stealth Spokeswoman" as saying: "There is just so much we can do with the national press corps; so much we can do to influence their views. When you work for the incumbent, you know they're gunning for you. So I focus quite a bit on second-tier media and local press." "That's about as visionary as it gets," summed up the reporter.

Of late, Fitzwater had unexpectedly admitted to burnout, and he seemed to have little interest in Bush, the White House and the campaign. Inevitably, Clarke, from her 15th Street office, was unilaterally directing presidential spin, and as both media advisor and spokesperson, she epitomized the ham-fisted Bush campaign machine. As Matalin's ally, she contributed to the childish campaign antics, plunging the Bush reelection operation into further pandemonium . . . until it was revealed that Baker would soon be on the premises. According to an August 1992 *Post* article, The Girls were "reining themselves in with the anticipated arrival of James Baker, a man not known to have a high appreciation for operatives, other than himself, who attract the limelight."

The "Bring Baker Back" chant was louder and stronger than ever, and for the State secretary, everything was going according to plan: chaos governed, Bush needed him, and the timing for an entrance was perfect— he had waited long enough to ensure a Bush defeat. In addition, his rules of power were working flawlessly: gain the trust of the President, assemble the best and brightest as your Loyals, and place mediocre competitors in positions where you want to maintain clout.

Not knowing The Rules, Skinner had proven virtually incompetent as chief of staff. Here, as elsewhere, Baker had let the weak and ineffective "dig their own hole," so to speak. And after twelve years of manning the levers of power, Baker had learned that, at times, being absent could have more of an impact than being present. By keeping a safe distance from the West Wing and the campaign, he had been able to proceed with a much heavier hand in orchestrating disorder.

All the while, the Clinton campaign grew in strength and numbers. Besides establishing their Little Rock communications headquarters, they had set up a large office in Washington (at 1317 F Street N.W., ninth floor), housing some 3,500 volunteers—1,500 more people than at the Bush headquarters. The Clintonites could smell blood in the White House, and like a pack of animals fighting over its prey, they circled and attacked, circled again and attacked harder.

George Stephanopoulos was Clinton's campaign director. The former aide to Rep. Dick Gephardt had not forgotten what he considered to have been the unfair campaign tactics waged by Bush in the 1988 campaign. Nor had he forgiven Lee Atwater (even after his death) for what he described as his "ruthless attacks." In Stephanopoulos's thinking, George Bush had illegitimately taken the Oval Office away from Michael Dukakis, and in 1992, he determined that Clinton would not be treated in the same manner. Stephanopoulos was going to make the White House pay for their injustices. Bush *would not* take the victory away from another Democratic governor.

Stephanopoulos, thirty-three and a northern liberal, and Carville, the same age but a more conservative southerner, were in charge of the Little Rock crowd, and they delighted in the campaign warfare scene, encouraging the fight and flaunting the battle atmosphere whenever possible. In the words of Stephanopoulos, they were "relentless, intimidating and unpredictable."

Bush continued to flounder, causing, of course, more Skinner-directed personnel shifts. Heads rolled. Torie Clarke, press secretary, was the first to leave. According to the chief of staff, communications was still Bush's most significant problem. Clarke had not fit the bill (despite what Teeter said), and Skinner scoured the Republican ranks to find another person for the job, offering it to one candidate after another. Lobbyist Jim Lake was the first to receive and decline the offer. Following him were Robert Grady (Darman's number-one at OMB), Robert Zoellick (Baker's man at State) and Bill Kristol (Quayle's chief of staff). All refused the position.

Finally, Steven Provost was selected as Bush's new communications director. Bob Teeter, again, had his candidate placed in the most recognizable and central position in the campaign, only this time around, Teeter suggested that Provost not only assume the press secretary job, but that he also become chief speechwriter. So it was. Provost took over David Demarest's job, as well. And Demarest, having just been placed as head speechwriter (by Skinner), was moved over to take Sherrie Rollins's position as director of public relations.

All this meant that Provost would leave his present job as spokesman for Kentucky Fried Chicken. (Prior to this, he had been communications director to New Jersey Governor Thomas Kean.) Provost had never worked in a national campaign, never been involved in presidential politics and never met Bush; still, Teeter assigned Provost to this most discernible White House position, with innumerable respons-ibilities attached to it—ones Provost knew nothing about. The Baker Plan continued to hold its own.

As I read Ann Devroy's article, "Bush Communications Chief Named: Critics Call Kentucky Fried Chicken Official Too Inexperienced," in the *Washington Post* in July 1992, I thought what a joke campaign appointments had become:

> Yesterday, some administration officials and advisors were sharply critical of Skinner for opting for an inexperienced candidate for so critical a job. "This is absolutely ludicrous," said one official. "I'm sure he is fine, maybe great in what he does, but this is a presidential campaign. This is a crisis. You don't go out and get a guy who's never laid eyes on the president or tried to maneuver through this horrible White House bureaucracy to be your chief speechwriter and communications director. It is totally ridiculous."

While it was improbable that, at this near zero hour, Bush could recapture the trust of the American people and win a second term, I thought, perhaps naively, that it was not *impossible*. Four years ago, when Bush had been at the lowest ebb of his campaign, he *had* come back, overcoming a seventeen-point deficit. Under the present circumstances, the 1992 Bush Brigade should have been a lot more brawny than '88, and the President's position as incumbent should have been that much more gainful. This was not the case.

True, Atwater—the master strategist—was not there, and Roger Ailes—the media guru—was absent. But, Baker and Teeter and Darman and Fuller and Fitzwater, all on the Power Pyramid, were in places of prominence. They were the ones who received the campaign medals; were they not capable of turning failures into successes? Yes, they could

★★★

have organized the troops, if they had wished. But, all five of them wanted Bush to lose, and if that was their desire, no one—absolutely no one—could have overcome their strategic plan to take Bush out of the Oval Office.

Along with the rest of the citizenry, I watched the *most perfectly orchestrated* made-to-look-like-it-was-failing campaign in presidential history. The goal was to lose. And with that as their objective, Baker and Team were winning.

At this point, some of the President's advisors suggested that, rather than avoid a "sleaze campaign," Bush should pursue one. But that was not the course the President wished to take. And so, the Clintonites, having been successful in pushing their narrowly focused campaign, kept going. By rendering Bush as an ineffectual and irresolute commander and chief, the opposition repeatedly brought up one particular issue more than any other: the economy.

Despite its inaccurate message, no Clinton campaign slogan harmed Bush more than "It's the Economy, Stupid!" Relentlessly, the fellows in Arkansas bellowed it over and over and over. It was THE slogan; they had it pasted in bold letters across their Little Rock war room, and by focusing on that theme only, they were able to drown out Bush's feeble attempts to talk about recovering economic conditions—as well as everything else.

The Bush campaign *gave* the Democrats that catchphrase, they, therefore, *gave* them control and allowed them to escalate their attack. Clinton assailed Bush, while the President tried to ignore the assault. In some ways, what Clinton was doing was similar to what Bush did in the fall of 1988, when he had kept going on the offensive and Dukakis paid no heed, not wanting to "lower himself." I was inclined to agree with a *Washington Post* editorial published in August 1992:

> Mr. Bush seems to be pretending that the Clinton campaign has not attacked him personally, and that he will not resort to sleaze. The Democrats have been relentlessly attacking Mr. Bush personally, including class warfare. Mr. Bush can also choose a substantive attack. Most Americans say they are for educational choice, or vouchers. [Bush supported a government-funded voucher system to let poorer children go to private schools.] Two years ago, Mr. Clinton was for the idea. Now he's not. Why? He has caved in to the monopolistic National Education Association. "Slick Willie" here

has been "Spaghetti-Spine Clinton." Let Mr. Bush gird himself to say so. The Bush campaign has to start some time.

Even if Bush had chosen to go strictly positive, and not negative, there would have been several strategies that would have worked. But, designing winning strategies in 1992 was not in the Reaganite game plan. Destroying Bush was.

By June, Clinton had won enough primary votes to claim the delegates needed for nomination. Of the thirty-eight states, he won twenty-eight, receiving 52 percent of the total votes cast. (Bush had won all thirty-eight states, with 63 percent of the votes.) Then in mid July, the Democratic Convention brought most of the Clinton clan from Little Rock and Washington to New York City. The crossover point in the campaign, when Clinton assumed the lead, took place during this time.

The Democrats, with Governor Bill Clinton and Senator Al Gore taking center stage, held a charismatic and highly successful convention, with over four thousand delegates participating. The superb celebration was coordinated by Democratic National Committee Chairman Ron Brown. Paul Tsongas, Jerry Brown, Bob Kerrey and Tom Harkin (all of whom Clinton had run against in the final primaries) appeared in a united front and established "Family Values" as their theme (ironically, the Republican initiative led by Dan Quayle). Making a special plea to remember "our forgotten middle class," Clinton, forty-six, and Gore, forty-five, were the first presidential ticket of post–World War II baby boomers and would be the youngest ever to command the White House.

According to the CBS/*New York Times* and Gallup/*USA Today*/CNN polls, Bush had been slightly ahead up until the Democratic Convention. Afterwards, he was behind, and from then on, Clinton and Gore would never lose their lead. Additionally, Clinton would enjoy the largest post-convention popularity boost of any candidate since 1944, with an approval rating of 55 percent. (Concurrently, after the Democrats convention, Bush's popularity plummeted to 31 percent.)

While the New York convention assembled, two unusual political events occurred, neither having to do with the Democrats. Both took place in the Perot camp. On June 25, the polls showed Perot with a remarkable 408 electoral votes. He could actually win! Then weeks after launching his invigorating and sweeping campaign, Perot and Perotmania came to an abrupt halt.

★★★

Ed Rollins, with his Mob Squad (operatives like Joe Canzari), had told Perot that unless *he* was in charge, he was leaving. Shortly thereafter, Perot, while addressing the Nashville NAACP on July 11, read a line from his own handwritten speech referring to the crowd as "you people." A colossal mistake. The next day, Perot fired Rollins, the man known to shift Parties and allegiances faster than most people change the oil in their car, and press reports indicated that the wildcard candidate and his team had run into some "differences of opinion." The fact was that Perot, who had never met either Rollins or Jordan before they became his advisors, quickly realized he did not like either of them.

Within days, Perot found himself in a free fall, running third in the polls. In the media's glare, he hastily announced that continuing his candidacy "would be too disruptive to the national campaign" and he withdrew. On July 16, while holding a 25 percent favorability rating, Perot, who had never officially entered the race, announced that he would not run. It was interesting to look back to a month earlier (on June 20) and read the *U.S. News and World Report* cover story on Perot:

> Ross Perot, the spunky Texas billionaire who attracts controversy the way spilled milk draws flies . . . has become the Davy Crockett of our time, an honest-to-God folk hero who broke horses as a roughneck kid, took on the North Vietnamese, the Ayatollah and GM, and stands for bedrock American values embodied in the Declaration of Independence, the *Boy Scout Handbook* and the paintings of Norman Rockwell . . . At 58, the 5-foot, 7-inch, 148-pound stick of high-grade dynamite with the bent nose and large cockeyed ears, throws himself into his adventures with patriotic fervor.

Just because Perot withdrew from the race did not mean he was going to stop bombarding President Bush; if anything, he escalated his attacks. He had previously collected "investigative" material on Bush (since Bush's vice president days), and now Perot looked for ways to use it. There had never been warm feelings between the two men, at least not since Bush (during Reagan days) had been appointed to halt Perot's badgering the White House about his Vietnam schemes to recapture the MIAs and POWs. Nothing had changed.

In 1992 Perot hired lawyers to look into Bush's past for possible wrongdoings: tax deductions, Iran-Contra, under the table deals . . . anything would do. But because nothing turned up, Perot decided to go after the President's sons, George W. and Neil. Each had a shadowy story that Perot used in his fight against their father. This tactic was seldom touted as evenhanded. That did not stop Perot.

As managing partner of the Texas Rangers baseball team, Governor George W. Bush had returned to Washington in April 1992 to assist his father in his faltering campaign. Just beforehand, he had sold stock in a Texas energy firm with oil drilling interests in the Middle East; because he sold his allocations a week before the value of the firm's shares plunged, Perot asserted there had been insider trading.

Next, Perot attacked Bush's younger son, Neil, portraying him as the poster child of "greed, mismanagement and excess." From 1985 to mid-1988, Neil had served as director to the Denver thrift, Silverado Banking, Savings and Loan Association, where he managed the Office of Thrift Supervision (OTS). Just a few months after he resigned, the S&L collapsed, causing an estimated $1 billion loss. Blamed for conflicts of interest and disregarding his fiduciary duties, Neil had been accused of authorizing an illegal $900,000 line of credit to friend and business partner, Kenneth Good, so that Good's company, in 1986, could invest in an oil and gas venture in Argentina. Whether or not Perot pushed this story, Neil would continue to suffer from the "made for news" accounts.

A candidate's children—even as adults—were usually off limits during a presidential race, and in 1992, Bush labeled Perot's actions as "beyond the pale." However, that did not deter Perot from attempting to discredit the President. He claimed that the Republican Party was responsible for putting together a "Dark Cabal" and that with its "top secret" data, the White House was planning to interfere with his daughter's upcoming wedding. Those "dirty tricksters," as Perot referred to Bush White House aides, were out to get him and his family. The West Wing responded by saying that Perot was "paranoid and risky." Perot countered that the Bush staff was "Mickey Mouse tossed salad."

Sniping between Perot and Bush became so commonplace and so silly that most citizens tried to tune out their quibbling. Unfortunately, though, all three presidential candidates and their staffs had already set a tone for the race, and it was anything but presidential.

Despite his formal exit from the campaign ranks, Perot's influence on the 1992 campaign was far from over. He would not disappear. In fact, the Perot Factor would become one of the most divisive and decisive factors in the outcome of any presidential election to date.

★★★ ═══════ ★★★

CHAPTER

39

SIXTY-THREE POINTS DOWN,
AND COUNTING

*It's interesting that when you are in public life, people are always trying to put you into
a conventional mold, to categorize you, but they seldom look beneath the surface to see
what's in your heart.*

—George Herbert Walker Bush

JULY–AUGUST 1992

Ross Perot was not the only one trying to dig up the dirt on President Bush. Michael McCurry, previous Dukakis supporter now Democratic National Committee (DNC) chief spokesman, was doing his best to uncover "the goods," but, so far, no such luck. After opposition director Betsey Wright failed in her attempt to find any evidence showing Bush to be self-serving or prone to take care of his own (government favors), McCurry turned to outside sources. Subsequent to spending $30,000 on private investigators and hired researchers, he still was unable to locate something meaningful.

Hiring from the private sector was most unconventional in campaign procedures, and it represented the first time the DNC opposition research unit had to employ private firms to do their spy work. David Tell, head of Bush opposition, disparaged the DNC's hiring of consultants and stated that the Republican team "never has and never will" use private investigators. I thought back to 1988 and my uncovering the data on Boston Harbor, an investigation that had not cost the campaign a dime.

During the summer of 1992, campaign research was receiving quite a bit of press, mainly because of a reversal in thinking. Negative tactics

465

that once had tainted the '88 Bush team now were described as having been executed with "extraordinary effectiveness." The Democrats, in 1992, were trying to replicate Republican tactics—the same ones they had been condemning for four years. Michael Isikoff's article in the July 1992 *Washington Post*, "Democrats Hire Firms to Investigate Bush: Move Reflects Growing Use of Opposition Research by Both Parties" reflected this growing interest, "The Republicans success with opposition research in large part spurred the DNC to develop its own capability during this year's election. From a two-person unit that mainly did speechwriting in 1988, the DNC's research department has grown into a staff of six with a budget more than three times its former congressional budget."

Behind the polished exteriors and carpeted hallways of the Bush national campaign headquarters, the crew that may have had the appearance of laboring was accomplishing little. The surroundings at 1030 15th Street N.W. were far superior to those we'd had in the Woodward Building, there was a more pleasing layout and a collection of much better equipment. Four years earlier, a computer was something to be fought over; now, they were plentiful. Fax machines had not been available; now, everyone had access.

However, the 1992 quarters lacked the 1988 characters: Atwater and his battalions. To my knowledge, only Jim Pinkerton was capable of creating another Atwater-like assault. Unfortunately, the former director of research and "idea man," who recently had moved from his policy position in the White House to counselor at the Bush/Quayle reelection committee, was still fighting with OMB director Richard Darman. E. J. Dionne's description of the ongoing Darman-Pinkerton tiff was as follows:

> The Darman-Pinkerton tussle is full of delightful contrasts. Darman's roots are in the staid but steady Republican moderation of Elliot Richardson. Pinkerton's are in the freewheeling libertarian movement, which wanted to abolish as much government as possible. Darman is more East Coast and Harvard. Pinkerton went to Stanford and is, culturally speaking, a Californian. Darman's main guru is Secretary of State James A. Baker III, whom Darman helped mightily by mastering the details of the White House bureaucratic politics. Pinkerton's is Lee Atwater, the general chairman of the Republican Party, whom Pinkerton served as a researcher. In a paradigm-less administration, the New Paradigm could be king, which would make Pinkerton, not Darman, the court philosopher of the Bush Era. (December, 1990 *Washington Post*)

★★★

The one thing Dionne had left out was that the Darman Plan reigned supreme over the Pinkerton Paradigm. Darman had made sure he thwarted Pinkerton's rise to fame, which, of course, ensured his place at the top of Washington's intellectual hierarchy and at the top of the Power Pyramid. He was not going to be toppled by Pinkerton, Atwater's underling. Still, during the 1992 resurrection of campaign articles, Pinkerton's name was most often mentioned, and in July '92 the *Washington Post* published yet another 1988-related article:

> The 1988 campaign saw perhaps the best-known product of the Republican opposition research in Willie Horton . . . The "discovery" of Horton—or more precisely, the idea of using him as a campaign issue—has been largely credited to Jim Pinkerton, the research director for the Bush campaign. Pinkerton has said he first got wind of the case when Senator Albert Gore Jr. (Tennessee) briefly referred to it during a Democratic primary debate the following April.

Dick Darman thrived in acrimonious surroundings and, in one way or another, he forced anyone who got in the way to succumb. Darman and Pinkerton were bound to reach a crisis point. It was inevitable. Darman, while guarding the '92 campaign chairman's empty chair and waiting to be appointed deputy to Baker, kept his eagle eye on Pinkerton, who recently had written an alternative "vision" thesis for President Bush: "Fourth American Revolution" was Pinkerton's second attempt to bring themes into a themeless campaign.

While attempting to put forward the conservative cause—from an original perspective—Pinkerton suggested in his writings that Bush re-create himself as an "agent of change," promising that in the next four years he would look toward the future. Pinkerton theorized that Americans had grown suspect of an all-encompassing government, and for Bush to be reelected, he would have to initiate a first-class marketing plan, selling to the electorate the idea that *he, the President,* would be the new agent of change.

Darman, of course, would have no part in sponsoring Pinkerton's treatise, and as head of the Campaign A-Team (comprised of Teeter, Malek and Mosbacher), he smothered Pinkerton's ideas. Again. Darman, who sought to be the smartest guy in town, ignored Pinkerton during the summer of 1992, referring to his views as "old hat, having been tried in the 60s, and failed."

I believe that, if Bush had heard about Pinkerton's concepts, he would have supported them, as he had in July 1988 at the meeting in Kennebunkport. But, that would not happen, and Darman, the primal force behind both the reelection committee and the West Wing, encouraged Bush to wait "just a little longer" before he put forth any initiatives; pertaining to fiscal concerns, he told Bush that a strong economy would manifest itself soon enough. I believe that Darman, realizing better than anyone that Bush needed to get out a strong economic message, was somehow able to persuade the President to wait and wait—and wait—long enough, until there was no time left. The doubly exasperating part of the "don't tell America anything yet" arrangement was that the economy was showing signs of robustness.

By all statistical gauges and monetary meters, financial systems had been heating up since April 1991, and President Bush, with the full backing of his economic team, should have delivered this news way before the summer of 1992. If the facts, as they stood at the time, had been revealed—and had they been tied to Pinkerton's policy themes—Bush would have had a *very* positive message to deliver. And the country *just may have had* their faith renewed in their leader. But that never came to be, and the days of Bush being the 92 percent champion were long gone and fast forgotten.

Would a positive economic statement have been enough to win? Probably not, not without Baker's consent. But *had* Baker reversed his thinking and supported the reelection, even at this late date, then yes, I believe that Bush might have had time to do the impossible. The political phenomenon that had occurred during the 1988 New Hampshire primary had convinced me anything was possible *if* the effort and desire were there. But Bush's Economic Brain Trust, had misled him. For months. For years. And, seven months after his State of the Union, Bush still was not delivering the truth. His only strategy during the summer months was to hunker down and wait for the gale to blow over.

Of course, it never would. It would only worsen.

First, though, there would be thirty-one scorching days of August to contend with, during which time, Bush—while losing his lead to Clinton and undergoing Party problems at the National Convention in Houston— would finally be forced to do what he usually did when all his chips were gone: beckon for Baker.

★★★

DURING early 1992, a clever sixty-second advertisement was broadcast across six continents into the homes of millions of television viewers in more than one hundred nations around the earth. Voices of men, women and children were chanting a message of global cooperation: Asian children, desert Bedouins, Indian women, African tribesmen, a Buddhist monk, a Catholic priest, and a young blond girl wearing a bikini.

Sent out by the Coca-Cola Company via satellite, the commercial was one that only a giant multinational corporation could create or afford. But beyond the slick production, this form of advertising was both inspirational and groundbreaking. Coke sent a message to a world population that would understand its meaning in just the same way. It emphasized how alike we are, rather than how different, and crossed all boundaries of cultural disparity and geographical distances. Quite simply, the ad gave the impression that we were related because we all drank Coca-Cola.

True or not, this kind of thinking was an important new way of viewing the international community in the early 1990s. The distance between one country and another was shrinking dramatically; the other side of the Atlantic or Pacific Ocean was as close as a thirty-second fax. Commerce between a company on one continent and another thousands of miles away was touted to be as easy as clicking onto a Web page.

The United States computer industry and its clever young techies were leading this communication boom. In April 1992, Apple Computer, Inc. announced it had signed an agreement with a start-up company to use their online information technology. The partner—located in Vienna, Virginia, just a few miles from my home in McLean—was relatively unknown: America On Line, Inc. And Apple had just them paid $15 million for the project. AOL, with only 150 employees at the time, considered hiring a "few extras" to work on the contract. Many people in the early '90s were doubtful about computers and the internet, thinking the information technology craze would soon be over. Conversely, just the opposite would occur, and what some had previously considered to be a fad, would turn out to be the world's premiere communication system.

AS the summer months of the campaign rolled on, a group of conservative freelancers with the Presidential Victory Committee emerged on the scene. The PVC was legally entitled to raise and spend as much money as it wished, on any candidate it desired. The present director, thirty-five-year-old, six-feet, six-inch tall, Floyd Brown, had been Midwest field director for Bob Dole in the 1988 primaries. With Dole's defeat, he had joined a political action committee comprised of Republican conservatives that turned out to be the forerunner of his own PVC, Citizens United. In 1988, Brown, as chairman of the Fairfax City, Virginia, PAC, had produced $10 million on behalf of the Bush campaign, claiming 100,000 members and a $5 million budget. From this success, Brown had gained some influence in the Party, and being a former employee of Roger Ailes had only elevated his status.

In 1992, Brown, who was turned away from the Bush campaign, favored Buchanan. However, when Buchanan stumbled, Brown decided to reverse his decision and favor President Bush, which, in itself, was fine. Erroneously presenting himself as a moneymaking arm of the Bush campaign was not so fine. Despite White House pleas to back off, Brown had produced some provoking anti-Clinton ads, including telephone advertisements described as "interactive, sexy, racy, vile and voyeuristic." After dialing a telephone number and paying $4.99 by credit card, a caller could listen to a recorded telephone discussion between Gennifer Flowers and Bill Clinton. These taped conversations had been unveiled by Flowers at a New York news conference in January 1992; she had hoped that they would support her assertions of having had a twelve-year affair with Clinton. After acquiring legal copies of the tapes, Brown had put together his commercials, with an intro that was transcribed in the July 10, 1992, *Washington Times:* "'Get to know Bill Clinton the way Gennifer Flowers did,' an announcer intones dramatically, sounding like a promo for the tabloid *A Current Affair.*"

Bush campaign spokesperson Tony Mitchell responded to the Brown ads with, "We don't want to be associated with commercials that we have no participation in or influence over but might be linked to us." In the article "Dennis the Menace," published in the same *Times* edition, Judith Colp quoted Bush aide Bobby Burchfield as saying, "Your group has neither asked for nor received permission to solicit funds using the name of George Bush. The President strongly disapproves of this misleading use of his name."

At the same time, Jack Anderson and Michael Binstein wrote an article quoting a Democratic strategist: "I think they'll [the Bush campaign] hurt us as badly in '92 as they did in '88. Clinton's so undefined with the electorate, he's a sitting duck. They can plant seeds of doubt about him even more than they did to Dukakis."

The above Clinton supporter did not seem to realize that the 1988 team was no longer in place. Had the original team been there in '92, his scenario might have been more reality than fantasy. As distasteful as the Brown commercials were, they did tap into the Clinton character issue—his weakest, most vulnerable spot, and I agreed with Brown when he said:

> Here's a guy [Clinton] who has some very serious ethical problems. It's not just one thing. It's the infidelity, smoking marijuana, avoiding the Vietnam draft and his wife getting special deals from the state. All of these things are like ornaments on a Christmas tree. You get them all together, and you guarantee Bill Clinton won't be elected president of the United States.

On November 2, 1992, in the *Washington Times,* Mona Charon's thoughts also made sense:

> What the press frequently calls negative campaigning is merely identifying for voters that one's opponent is a liberal, or mentioning that he voted for every tax increase he saw while in the legislature, or noting that he has told several inconsistent stories about his military service. All of that is useful information for voters. Here's the odd part: The press rewards its own people handsomely with Pulitzer and other prizes for digging up such damaging information about politicians. Why, then, do they sniff and scowl when politicians do the same thing?

Having informed facts about the opponent and *not* using them is as much a transgression as lying. It is misinforming the public. The Bush Bunch never advanced important and relevant data on Clinton's defects, and without waging an aggressive, credible offense, they allowed the weak—yes—weak Clinton campaign to override them. Brown, who did advance some of the negatives, had not produced his ads with integrity, and for that reason, they boomeranged. Exhibiting extremely bad taste, the Brown commercials turned the voters against the President. The public, thinking that the Flowers advertisements were a product of the Bush campaign became even more hostile and slipped even further away from the President's grasp. George Bush approached his darkest hour.

On August 4, President Bush's approval rating, once at 92 percent, fell to 29 percent. Bush sustained the largest decline in popularity ever recorded for an American President! Sixty-three points!

According to an August 17, 1992, *Washington Post* article, Bush had held the highest job approval rating of any President since Truman. The Gallup *Washington Post*-ABC News poll showed that in March of 1991, immediately after the Gulf Crisis, Bush had reached the 92 percent mark. Remembering that Ronald Reagan never reached 70 percent in the polls and John F. Kennedy never saw his ratings go above 80 percent, the Bush 63-point tumble was an unprecedented calamity.

Yet, the 33 percent held by Bush after the Houston convention was not something unheard of. Johnson, Carter and Reagan had all been there at one time, and Nixon, the only President since Eisenhower to go below that level, had Watergate to blame. Outside Carter, however, Bush was the only incumbent to seek reelection with such a low rating. No sitting President with a Gallup approval rating of less than 30 percent had ever been reelected.

It was not surprising that during the last week of August, Bill Clinton reached the high point of his campaign, and one of the individuals responsible for his climb to 55 percent was Mandy Grunwald, his campaign media consultant. She did more for the Arkansas governor's affirmative image than anyone on his staff.

Daughter of former *Time* editor-in-chief Henry Grunwald, Mandy graduated from Harvard in 1979 before joining the Sawyer-Miller Group in New York City. Her stint with one of the country's top political consulting firms had gained her a reputation as the "Lee Atwater in a Chanel suit." She fought tough. In 1987, Grunwald had been a consultant to Wallace Wilkenson, the Kentucky gubernatorial candidate who had started as the underdog and ended up winning. Carville, working on the same campaign, had met Grunwald in Kentucky.

By 1991, dissatisfied with her work at Sawyer-Miller, Grunwald took a position with a Georgetown (D.C.) firm, working for Frank Greer, among whose clients was presidential candidate Bill Clinton. Grunwald's only other campaign experience had been with Dukakis, where she supposedly had written the response to the Bush Boston Harbor ad, one that never aired. This had not stopped her from seizing the Clinton account in early 1992. With her Madison Avenue background and former

Democratic consulting skills, she attempted, with great determination, to transform Clinton from frog to prince.

Grunwald insisted that Clinton fight off the Slick Willie factor by repeatedly saying, "The media is trying to make this election about a woman I never slept with and a draft I never dodged." She also suggested that Clinton take advantage of public appearance opportunities and call Don Imus, the radio disc jockey who referred to Clinton as "Bubba," and offer to be on his program. And it was Grunwald who originated the idea that Clinton go on the *Phil Donahue Show* and chitchat on daytime television. She even convinced Clinton to play the saxophone on the *Arsenio Hall Show.*

All these unconventional antics were attempts to moderate Clinton's less-than-pristine image. And they worked. In an article on August 10, 1992, Howard Kurtz of the *Washington Post* remarked:

> Grunwald's challenge was to end-run the establishment press, to find ways of painting a more personal picture of Bill Clinton in the era of the 7.3-second sound bite. The result was the Arsenio strategy, hitting every talk show this side of MTV. "The nature of what makes it to the evening news is an attack or proposal," she says. "The question is how you reach people who don't care about the evening news and don't read the *New York Times.*"

Grunwald had tapped into a category of younger Americans who got their news through mediums other than the "Six o'clock news," and by doing so, she built a base for Bill Clinton. However, of all the far-out ideas Grunwald devised while attempting to build the softer side of her candidate, her real coup was getting Bill Clinton, with Hillary and Chelsea, on the cover of *People* magazine during the week of the Democratic convention. The article headline read, "Hillary and Bill Talk about Tag-Team Parenting, Their Bruising Run for the White House and Staying in Love." It took. The public liked it. The Clintons liked it. And now America liked the Clintons. With Grunwald's temerity and tenacity, Bill Clinton passed by his Republican opponent in July 1992 and never looked back.

In mid-August, while Clinton was forging ahead, the Republicans converged on the Astrodome in Houston, for their convention. For President and Mrs. Bush, Houston was more than just a gathering site; it was their adopted hometown, the city in which Bush had managed his prosperous oil business and from which he was first elected to the House of Representatives.

Rich Bond, as RNC chairman, was officially responsible for the '92 Republican affair, but since the winter of 1991 (when tapped by Baker), Craig Fuller had been in charge of making all the arrangements. While Fuller was chairman, Kenneth Lay, head of Enron Corporation, was appointed co-chairman. (There soon would be an "Enron Prize for Distinguished Public Service" at the Baker Institute at Rice University in Houston.)

Fuller had been given eighteen months to prepare for the Houston rendezvous, and during that time, he had ample support staff and funds to put together a first-class recoronation of Bush. Through his associations with Baker, Darman, and Teeter, he had a ready-made advantage and could create any sort of macro Republican get-together he wished. Houston should have been a well-managed, professionally polished American Show.

In August, the state delegates converged on the Lone Star State as the ninety-plus degrees bore down, and the humidity wilted everything from their linen suits to their leather luggage. Once settled indoors and enjoying the fifty-degree temperatures, the 2,000 delegates, 15,000 journalists and 1,000 foreign correspondents breathed a sigh of relief. Houston was the most air-conditioned city in the world. All 750 television cameras and 50 satellite trucks stayed close by . . . waiting.

The convention was considered a "do or die" for Bush, as Alan McConagha wrote in his article in the *Washington Times*:

> The Grand Old Party changed the way the nation talks to itself, presided over seismic global changes and offered the country the most popular politician of his time in Ronald Reagan. Now, however, President Bush, the man at the wagon's reins, drives a road pocketed with such potholes as a carping press, disheartening polls, mutinous party members and disheartening economic statistics.

Not feeling very grand, but appearing old and tired, the 132-year-old Grand Old Party began a week of lackluster galas and festivities. Many Republican officeholders and candidates had chosen to skip the event entirely, opting to stay in their home states and watch from afar. Their absence added to the prevalent notion that support for Bush, even among

★★★

his own ranks, was, at best, lukewarm. In the same *Washington Times*, Jim Clardy and Todd Spangler quoted one of these representatives, "'You have a lot of people shying away from Bush, away from the Republican ticket, who say they don't want to be any part of it,' said Virginia state delegate Clinton Miller of Shenandoah. 'I sense a general unease and frustration about the presidential campaign in general,' said Mr. Miller."

The convention was a disaster from the start. Republican chairman Rich Bond, behind the podium, before any warm introductory remarks were made, started lambasting Hillary Clinton and accusing her of comparing marriage to slavery. Bond had taken a quote (out of context) from a legal article Mrs. Clinton had written years earlier referring to a woman's legal standing before the laws were changed. Using it, Bond tried to make the argument that women were better off before the Equal Rights Amendment.

Although hard to believe, Pat Buchanan was a bigger humiliation than Bond. For months, he had been out of the campaign, with only his sister, Bay, remaining on his staff. During this time, Buchanan had tried to get a spot on the convention agenda, and was finally granted permission to speak on opening night. Picking up where Bond left off, he callously criticized the ERA and a woman's right to choose. Buchanan's discourses against women were beyond passé; they were appalling. Next, he assailed—no, ravaged—Bill and Hillary Clinton and Al and Tipper Gore, doing exactly what President Bush had asked Party members *not* to do. Even the delegates became perturbed with his diatribe. And as they viewed the uncompromising Buchanan from their homes, Americans were both dismayed and disgusted. The ghastly part was that Buchanan ended up dominating the convention—for all four days.

Despite everything, on August 19, Bush, for the second time, was nominated to be President of the United States. Lynn Martin, Secretary of Labor, did the honors. After securing the state delegation votes and being introduced by Senate Minority Leader Bob Dole, President Bush gave his acceptance speech, requesting that Americans trust that he would not repeat his tax increase mistake; he promised to ask Congress to cut taxes across the board. Bush went on, saying:

> In this election, you'll hear two visions of how to do this; theirs is to
> look inward and protect what we already have. Ours is to look
> forward, to open new markets, prepare our people to compete, to

> restore our social fabric—to save and invest—so we can win. We
> believe that now that the world looks more like America, it is time
> for America to look more like herself. And so we offer a policy that
> puts faith in the individual, not the bureaucracy.

Many of those who earlier had watched the Houston highlights by
now had turned off their television sets . . . before Bush took the podium.
Bond and Buchanan had set the mood of the convention: hostile,
unyielding and ultra-conservative. For an assemblage with a reputation
for being convivial and organized—to a fault—the Republicans made a
poor showing in 1992. Houston was more than a disappointment. It was
a disgrace.

For Quayle, the situation actually was better than it had been in
1988. With no media feeding frenzy this time, he was left in good shape;
nonetheless, talk about replacing him on the ticket still surfaced.
Having learned to brush aside as much of the heckling as possible,
Quayle had found ways to enjoy the challenges Bush put
before him, including managing several foreign policy projects (in
particular fostering democracy in Central America) and directing the
Competitiveness Council.

During much of the '92 campaign, the Vice President's prime focus
had been on the importance of family values, the theme picked up by the
Democrats. Although the Clinton campaign had tried to replicate the
issue in their platform, Quayle was still the official champion of the cause,
and a number of middle-American voters had rallied around him.
Because Bush continued to struggle on the economic front, these
traditional principles had taken on added significance.

Since the *Murphy Brown* uproar, the press never had treated Quayle
or his ethics concern seriously, and criticism persisted no matter how
succinctly Quayle spoke. Published in the *Washington Times* during
convention week was an article by Paul Beddard, saying, "At a time when
Mr. Bush is so far down in the popularity polls that he can't even attract
protesters to campaign rallies, Mr. Quayle remains a steady draw on the
stump. Many officials attribute that to voter curiosity, while others say
Mr. Quayle's message is sharper than Mr. Bush's."

The euphoric feeling of being on Bush's team four years ago was
completely gone. I had no teammates in the administration. The Team was
not THE TEAM. It never had been. Not since 1988. What was worse was

★★★

that I had no one to talk to about the situation. No one to agree or disagree with me. I trusted no one, and had no option other than accept the circumstances—as they were. Or leave.

After the Houston convention—and unexpectedly—Bush managed to rebound in the polls, coming within five points of Clinton. A week later, Bush tumbled.

With 64 percent of the country saying they were unhappy with Bush, it was predictable that the White House, for the umpteenth time, would make personnel changes. What was not quite so predictable was that Skinner was one of those included this time.

For eight months, the chief of staff had struggled to maintain order, but in a White House where the Darman Plan was to create chaos, Skinner was predetermined to fail. No matter how hard he tried nor how good his intentions, Sam Skinner would never have been able to alleviate the President's problems.

Skinner was dismissed and appointed chairman of the RNC—a position that since Atwater's demise, no one seemed to hold for longer than a few months. Rich Bond was dethroned almost before he'd had time to hang his political pictures behind his desk. In Houston, Bond had not showed the polish expected of a Republican Party Chairman. For him, it was Iowa 1988 all over again.

In addition to Skinner's transfer, there were two other personnel moves involving senior positions: Janet Mullins took the top political affairs spot (replacing Mary Matalin) and Clayton Yeutter (after a six-month period as the President's domestic counselor) was moved to Team A, the senior campaign staff, joining Teeter, Mosbacher, Malek, Darman, Fitzwater, Black and Lake.

And on August 13, the announcement finally came that Jim Baker would be Bush's new chief of staff and would assume his responsibilities the third week in August. Lawrence Eagleburger, Baker's deputy at State, would remain at the department as acting secretary. The next day, the caption on the front page of the *Washington Post,* in one-inch block letters, read: "President Names Baker Chief of Staff: 4 Assistants to Assume Top White House Jobs." Below the headline was an article by Ann Devroy, including the following, "Appearing in the White House pressroom to announce a move that had been urged on him for months by worried Republicans, Bush said he asked Baker to join him to 'help me build on what we started by developing an integrated second-term program of domestic, economic and foreign policy.'" Devroy continued, "It is unprecedented for a secretary of State to give up the senior Cabinet post to move to a White House staff job." And it was. Everyone knew that, but no one felt it like Bush. His call for help was a desperate measure, but these were desperate times.

In the same edition of the *Post,* Dan Balz wrote, "Seasoned Political Captain Will Face Difficult Terrain: Baker's 1988 Success Hard to Duplicate," explaining the Baker move this way, "Bush's decision to tap Baker once again to run his campaign is an extraordinary action by a sitting president, because of what it says about his political weakness and what it conveys about the White House team that has served him and the country for most of the year."

Although Baker had the reputation for saving George Bush, I sensed that in August 1992, he had little interest in trying to do so. Coming to Bush's rescue no longer had the pay off it used to, and the super strategist, who, at one time, relished the attention he received while standing in Bush's corner, no longer was attracted to the role. Taking on the State position was as much as he would get out of being the President's friend. There was no need to put forth any more effort.

After months of speculation and anticipation about whether Baker, as Bush's chief of staff, had enough chutzpah to resurrect the dying campaign, The Man, himself, finally—and again—assumed an office in the West Wing of the White House. It had been eight years since he left as Reagan's chief of staff.

Accompanying Baker to the West Wing were four of his top-line assistants at State, all of whom immediately took on the leadership roles at the White House and in the campaign. Margaret Tutwiler (Baker's closest aide and State presswoman) became head of communications, Robert Zoellick (aide to Baker at Treasury and State) was made deputy to Baker, Dennis Ross took over policy planning, and Janet Mullins was the new chief of political affairs.

On the campaign trail and during his public appearances, George Bush had left a more off-putting impression of himself than of Clinton. The President looked tired, and he appeared to have lost all interest in the campaign, in the job and in Washington. The White House sergeants and campaign generals had Bush looking, acting and talking in a befuddled and non-presidential manner. Repeatedly. The communications problem had never been resolved.

Just three months earlier, the one man on the President's team most qualified to handle communications—in particular, media presentations—had been expelled by Teeter. Sig Rogich, after serving three years as Bush's events coordinator, had been dismissed and placed as ambassador to Iceland. However, Baker now decided to bring him back to the White House to supervise the November Group, a troop of Madison Avenue advertising executives. Baker also summoned GOP strategist Mitch Daniels to assist Rogich with press relations.

President Bush appeared to believe that his team was doing its best and were steadfast in their loyalty to him, conveying that somehow, someway *he* was letting *them* down. Of course, it was just the opposite. His own closest advisors had been, and were now, in the process of betraying him.

Fall was around the corner, and a nor'easter was brewing, one that would soon turn into a full-blown hurricane. It was time to get out the foul-weather gear and hold tight.

★★★ ━━━━ ★★★

CHAPTER

40

HURRICANE WEATHER

A mature hurricane is by far the most powerful event on earth; the combined nuclear arsenals of the United States and the former Soviet Union don't contain enough energy to keep a hurricane going for one day. A typical hurricane could provide all the electric power needed by the United States for three or four years.

—Sebastian Junger

<u>SEPTEMBER 1992</u>

The weather on Thursday, September 10, 1992, in downtown Washington was partly sunny and humid with a high temperature of eighty-eight degrees. Four days earlier, Hurricane Andrew, the largest natural disaster in American history and the third environmental catastrophe to strike during the Bush presidency (the first being the 1989 Exxon-Valdez oil spill and the second being the 1991 Perfect Storm), hit the East Coast of the United States.

The "most powerful event on earth" devastated Florida and Louisiana and left in its wake, for Florida alone, ruins estimated at $20 billion. With a congressional appropriation of $8 billion for repair costs, Bush initiated the immediate construction of temporary shelters and the rebuilding of schools, hospitals, roads and public facilities. The hurricane-distressed areas slowly would rebuild; however, the Bush campaign apparatus shared no such hopeful future.

After Labor Day, and in the wreckage of Hurricane Andrew, President Bush and Governor Clinton began their sprint down the final lap to Election Day. In spite of his lead, and Grunwald's efforts, Clinton still ran into one calamity after another, including press regarding his former denunciation of the Vietnam War.

During the late 1960s, Clinton, as a college student at the University of Arkansas, made a commitment to join the ROTC. Later, he reneged, and in 1969, while a Rhodes Scholar in London, he led anti-draft demonstrations and organized anti-Vietnam War protests. In a letter he had written to Colonel Holmes, the ROTC director, explaining why he opposed the war, Clinton described himself as "loathing" the military, saying that he wished to avoid the draft because he "vehemently" opposed the Vietnam War, declaring that it was a "disservice to be in the service." The full text of the letter was published on September 17, 1992, in the *Washington Times.* A portion read:

> I have written and spoken and marched against the war. One of the national organizers of the Vietnam Moratorium is a close friend of mine. After I left Arkansas last summer, I went to Washington to work in the national headquarters of the Moratorium, then to England to organize the Americans here for demonstrations Oct. 15 and Nov. 16. Because of my opposition to the draft and the war, I am in great sympathy with those who are not willing to fight, kill and maybe die for their country.

In the 1988 campaign, Dan Quayle had been gouged by the press for not entering the Vietnam War (he had been in the National Guard), and the media had portrayed him as a coward and without patriotic values. Conversely, in 1992, Clinton's 1960s anti-American protests turned out to be almost a non-issue. However, the press corps did bring to light another Clinton matter, one that resulted in a great deal of negative publicity. The character issue was back.

During the last week in October, the November issue of *Penthouse* magazine was on the stands, and in it was a ten-page-plus interview with Gennifer Flowers, who emphatically declared (with stories and pictures to back her up) that she'd had a long-term affair with Clinton. Before *Penthouse* was on the newsstands, I and the other appointees were sent copies of the sexually explicit article, but with text only—the accompanying pictures of Flowers had been cut out.

Due to both a failure of the Bush team and a turnaround in pre-election absolutes, in four years time, presidential campaign theory had reversed itself. On October 6, the *New York Times* came out with "What Worked in 1988 Is No Aid to Bush Now ":

If 1988 is remembered as the year they wrote the book on negative campaigning, 1992 may be the year the book was sent back for revision. Putting together a successful negative campaign is a lot like putting together a winning movie promotion; the point is to put out the same message through the press, paid commercials and eventually word of mouth. This kind of coordination requires a lot of teamwork and a lot of luck.

The White House staff, having *no* coordination abilities, worsened the situation by repeatedly issuing misleading and erroneous information. Nowhere had this been more obvious than with economic matters. In the *Washington Times* "Political Week" column, Elizabeth Kolbert wrote:

> Further complicating the President's efforts to get some negative synergy going between his campaign and the press coverage is the economy. Whenever the economy is on the news, which is often, it tends to work against the President's paid advertising and for his opponent. "The national economic news is an on-going anti-Bush ad."

And in the November 5, 1992, *Washington Times,* in the article "Campaign Kept Focused on the Economy," Donald Lambro explained the Clinton strategy this way, "More than any other issue in the 1992 election, more than all of the campaign tactics he employed, [the economy] was the dominant factor in Mr. Clinton's campaign [success]." In the same paper, Mona Charon, promoting a pro-Bush stance, wrote, "George Bush has a point: The candidates who run for office by running down the country have done us a disservice. It is difficult to know just how demoralized the nation has become as a consequence of this false economic information, but the damage may be profound." And Paul Craig Roberts, in the November 2, *Washington Times* penned an insightful piece, "Exaggerated Woes That Mislead Us," addressing Bush and the economy this way:

> Candidates and pundits have portrayed the deficit as the monster that ate the nation's savings, leaving the economy unable to invest or grow. The fault has been placed on George Bush's White House doorstep . . . The IMF indicators of economic performance don't support this rhetoric of doom. In 1992, U.S. growth in real gross

domestic product and real fixed private investment exceeded the G-7 average. Moreover, the IMF projects that the United States will have the highest investment rate in 1993. George Bush has been unable to respond effectively to his opponents because his own economic team agrees with his critics that the deficiency is our biggest problem.

That last sentence bears repeating, "George Bush has been unable to respond effectively to his opponents because *his own economic team* agrees with his critics that the deficiency is our biggest problem."

All Presidents have a responsibility to ensure that a truthful and accurate message regarding the nation's well-being is identified and publicized; they must be honest with the citizenship as well as reassuring. A leader builds trust by responding to the constituents concerns. In the 1992 contest, President Bush did not do this because he was not "allowed" to. And because of purposeful neglect, the Clinton team only did what was natural: make the most of Bush's failure.

Months earlier, in the Little Rock headquarters, Stephanopoulos and Carville had launched the "It's the economy, stupid" slogan. When the Bush campaign did not instantly retaliate, the Clintonites *must* have wondered why. But Carville and Stephanopoulos approached the campaign as warriors would warfare, and when they saw an obvious safe clearing on the battlefield, they confidently marched on, though they would have *had to know* that the Bush team was giving them the signal to advance. Not stopping to ask, "why isn't the Bush army fighting back?" they then did what soldiers would do when conquering the enemy: crush them. The Clinton posse, without opposition, continued to perpetuate the notion that America's dwindling economy and escalating debt, due to Bush's defects, was ruinous to the nation's future. Unceasingly, they reminded the voters how Washington had "deceived them," and how Clinton was there to "save" them from economic ruin. It took.

In this regard, in the days before the election, the relationship between Bill Clinton, presidential candidate, and George Mitchell, Senate majority leader, was an unusual one. A *Washington Times* editorial on November 2, 1992, pointed out that Clinton and Mitchell had "been in regular communication, in personal meetings and on the phone, discussing and coordinating campaign and legislative issues." Even more disturbing was this excerpt:

                                                                    ★★★

Mr. Clinton owes Mr. Mitchell, and owes him big time. To begin
with, he owes him for helping to dampen the economic recovery, to
maintain government gridlock and to make President Bush look
bad in general. Every bill that might have improved the economy
was larded with pork or soaked with tax hikes so that Mr. Bush
would be caught in a jam: Either he was ignoring the economy or
he was breaking his tax pledge.

In September 1992, the Democrats pushed a book (selling for $7.99)
written by Clinton and Gore, *Putting People First: How We Can All Change
America.* An ad promoting the publication was printed in the *Washington
Post,* and read, "Before You Decide, Get It In Writing... The only book that
details the Democratic program—as articulated by the candidates
themselves. Here is what Bill Clinton and Al Gore mean when they
say it is time to 'put people first'—a comprehensive plan to revitalize
America that is neither liberal nor conservative, neither Democratic
nor Republican."

With tome in hand, Clinton took steps to woo corporate executives
and academic leaders from across the country. Two hundred, now Clinton
supporters, published an open letter that was printed in the November 2
New York Times, saying, "Without a national economic strategy, this
country has been allowed to drift. With Bill Clinton as President, we can
work together to respond in practical and constructive ways to what
Abraham Lincoln called 'the better angels of our nature.'"

Clinton's recruitment of Big Business resulted in the migration of
Bush corporate sponsors into Democratic territory. The stampede was
reflected in some of the Washington headlines: "For Clinton's High-Tech
Plan, Corporate Cheers—CEOs Applaud Increased Government Role,"
"400 Listed as CEO's for Clinton," "The Democrat Finds Executive
Endorsements in GOP Stronghold." In the fall of 1992, there were
Republicans in the private sector who felt Bush's approach to directing
the country's competitive race was not adequate, and that his industrial
policy approach was "lackadaisical." Louis Cabot of Cabot Corp., John
Sculley of Apple Computer, and John Young of Hewlett-Packard were no
longer tolerant of the Bush Method, and the September 17, 1992,
Washington Post quoted Young as saying, "Most people are trained to
think about a separation of the public and private sectors, but I just don't
think that's what's going to work in the competitive world today."

★★★

Political, economic and foreign policy issues soon intertwined with trade and NAFTA concerns. Free trade, the cornerstone of Bush's international campaign platform, was being criticized by Big Business for the same reason as his economic policy: it was "insufficient." It was difficult for me to believe there was any truth behind these accusations, given that statistics proved them wrong.

In 1992, the United States had the world's most productive economy and was the world's largest exporter. During the Bush presidency, America had become an exporting superpower. The higher the number of exports, the belief is, the stronger the economy, and in August 1992, U.S. exports were $35.1 billion. When Bush took office in January 1989, the country's total exports had been $26.2 billion. This meant that during the Bush presidency, exports had grown by 34 percent. Bush viewed the North American Free Trade Agreement as a means to increase U.S. exports and *further* build the economy; however, because politics was tied to economic and trade interest, the President found himself fighting on an unleveled playing field.

Earlier in the summer, Clinton had sidestepped the trade issue by presenting himself as neither protectionist nor free-trader. Ensuing arguments between business and labor revolved around whether or not moving U.S. companies' operations to Mexico would negatively affect the American workforce. Bush argued it would generate jobs; Clinton said the opposite. And while he tried to shelter the labor vote for himself and, at the same time, berate Bush for harming the U.S. workforce with *his* trade agreement, Clinton declared he wanted no part of NAFTA.

Nonetheless, a month after Bush concluded negotiations with Mexico (August 12), Clinton decided to reconsider his position. His anti-free trade posture had not received the business support he expected, and his earlier veto of the agreement was now a "well, maybe." Just before the election, Clinton would begrudgingly embrace the accord.

ROSS Perot, responding to a question from Reuters regarding his possible comeback as a presidential candidate, was quoted in the *Washington Post* on September 17, 1992, as saying, "This is like saying how likely am I to jump over a tall building in a single bound—unlikely. This is like asking is lightning going to strike here in the next two seconds—I don't think so." Then, only days later, on October 1, declaring Bush and Clinton "hopeless," Perot, in his usual unconventional Rough Rider form, said he "could stand it no longer" and jumped back into the race. In the seventy days he was absent, Perot had spent upward of $11 million to maintain a presence in the state organizations. Yet, he still was not an authorized candidate. Eleven weeks after he had withdrawn from a race he had never officially entered, Perot returned, in full force, yelling his "United We Stand America" campaign chant.

Perot lambasted Bush for his economic policies, referring to them as the "failing Reagan-Bush approach." With the use of color-coded graphs and classroom pointers, Perot, on television once again, addressed the nation with thirty-minute infomercials. Weighed down with more figures than in a statistics textbook, he attempted to explain—in a series of lectures—what was wrong with America and ended with a gloomy conclusion: if the United States continued on the same Bush course, the country could expect an even more ominous future.

Perot and his running mate, retired Navy Admiral Stockdale, had leaped back into the political fray just in time to join Bush and Clinton in the presidential debates scheduled to begin October 11. The first of three debates took place in St. Louis and rattled on for ninety minutes, with neither Bush nor Clinton gaining any ground and Perot adding a touch of humor. In a second debate from Richmond, Virginia, on October 15, Clinton looked at ease as he answered questions from the audience; Bush looked at his watch, as if to imply he was bored; and Perot simply looked on. East Lansing, Michigan, hosted the last debate, which aired on October 19. The expected squabbles came from all three this time, but concluded with nothing out of the ordinary.

The one vice presidential debate was held on October 13, and it quickly turned into a three-ring circus, with Quayle mocking Clinton for his lack of integrity, Gore lambasting Bush for his *non*-economic policy, and Stockman just there, seemingly out of place.

Overall, the debates brought an uneventful two weeks of hype that did little to damage or enhance the candidates standing. Clinton, at 50 percent, was ahead of Bush (holding 30 percent) by almost twenty points, and Perot followed with 10 percent.

Then, without warning, a week after the debates ended, on October 25, the polls showed Perot's numbers surging. Having estimated that he would spend $75 million on his campaign (as compared to the $60 million spent by the Bush and Clinton campaigns), Perot watched his investment start to pay dividends. He quickly moved up to 17 percent, while Bush took 37 percent. With a twist, Clinton slid back to 42 percent.

While his numbers were increasing, Perot made an unannounced appearance on CBS's *60 Minutes* (as he was accustomed to doing by now), and revealed that he was suspending his presidential campaign. Again.

With the final countdown to Election Day about to begin, Bush, having concluded his formal negotiations with Mexico, focused on getting the agreement to the Hill for Congressional approval. Before the December 5 deadline. Some of the more controversial sections of the 1,038-page document still needed polishing, and most of the unfinished portions related to the department of Agriculture.

Staying involved with NAFTA was really the only means I had to show my support for Bush. I had found that keeping up with the menagerie of trade members was a full-time task, and coordinating two to four ATAC meetings a day was a challenge, yet it kept me engaged so that I had that much less time to fret about the campaign happenings.

Along with putting the finishing touches on NAFTA, the Agriculture department became headline news in October because of yet another administration scandal: Iraqgate. For months, accusations had percolated about U.S. firms selling high-tech equipment to Iraq before the Persian Gulf War (Mosbacher's predicament), then the rumors escalated into a bigger and more damaging indignity: U.S. agencies were trying to cover up the information.

A *Los Angeles Times* article, reprinted in the *Washington Post* on June 1992, stated, "The House Judiciary Committee has asked President Bush to provide documents and witnesses to explain his administration's prewar assistance to Iraq, moving a step closer to seeking a criminal investigation of the policy and setting the stage for a political showdown." Bush repeatedly had denied that U.S. companies transferred military technology to Saddam Hussein's war machine, but gossip persisted.

In the November 22, 1922, issue of *Insight* magazine, an article contained a list of questions, and an "expert" answered them: "Did U.S. taxpayers help pay for Saddam Hussein's military expansion?" "Maybe." "To the tune of billions and billions of dollars, as many Iraqgate theories have it?" "Doubtful." Nevertheless, there was evidence showing both prior extensions of farm credit diverted for military purposes and approval of one billion dollars in credits to Iraq. A significant portion (borrowed by Iraq) had been used to buy U.S. agricultural products, and a smaller amount to buy technology items. The Iraqgate allegations and their resultant suppositions fueled a major confrontation between United States security advocates and free trade promoters. A similar rift to the one conceived out of NAFTA. Mosbacher was brought into the spotlight again.

The Senate Banking Committee dismissed Bush's claims that he had not exported dangerous technology to Iraq and, a week before the election, they summoned National Security Advisor Brent Scowcroft and former secretary of Commerce Mosbacher to appear as witnesses at a congressional hearing. Mosbacher was accused of giving U.S. companies licenses for illegal export and of wrongful behavior. What still seemed strange to me about the continuing dual export hoopla during the Bush presidency was that for four of the five years cited, a Reagan appointee— not Mosbacher—had been secretary. From January 1985 until February 1989, the Commerce department was directed *only* by Reagan officials.

None of this seemed to matter now. Any facts, figures or records with the potential to present Bush in a favorable light were quickly snuffed. My Conspiracy Theory was appearing to be less and less crazy.

CHAPTER

41

DEFEAT

I have seen Him in the watch-fires of a hundred circling camps;
They have builded him an alter in the evening dews and damps;
I can read His righteous sentence by the dim and flaring lamps;
His day is marching on.
                                                    —*Julia Ward Howe*

<u>NOVEMBER 1992</u>

Among the four top aides Baker brought with him to the West Wing
was Margaret Tutwiler, his State department press secretary. She was
now President Bush's communications director: the last in a long line of
presidential message chiefs. With Baker's full endorsement, the previous
campaign scheduler almost effortlessly had risen to her place on the
Power Pyramid. In the fall of 1992, the forty-one-year-old University of
Alabama graduate and Birmingham debutante out-ranked everyone,
except maybe Bob Teeter.

Although endowed with authority—by virtue of her proximity to
Baker and family fortune (her father was said to be "very" wealthy)—
Tutwiler had as much flair and flamboyance as her cohort Fitzwater. In
the Style section of the *Washington Post* on September 23, 1992, Megan
Rosenfeld published "The Fabulous Baker Girl: Margaret Tutwiler, Right
Hand To the President's Right Hand," that described Tutwiler's press
briefings during the Persian Gulf War:

> Her daily briefings, broadcast around the world (during the Persian
> Gulf War), brought her a kind of fame unknown to aides-de-camp.
> That fame was not unconditionally favorable. Reading flatly and
> nasally from prepared "guidelines," she provoked a wave

of international cringes as she massacred the pronunciations of Middle Eastern countries, repeatedly referring to I-raq and I-ran. She refused to deviate from her written text—she was a dour schoolmarm.

Tutwiler never should have been Bush's chief communications aide in the last weeks of the campaign, but she came with the territory, so to speak. In spite of her southern drawl and mispronounced words, she got people's attention, and because she was Baker's voice, they listened to what she had to say.

Bush's final campaign hurrah was designed by Tutwiler: she, with the other Bush communications and public relations experts, had arranged for the President to make a 485-mile train trip on the World War II–era *Spirit of America*. While standing at the rear of the caboose and implementing the good old-fashioned stump speech, Bush rumbled through thirty-six southern towns, meeting the local residents and letting them know he was one of "them." It was his last chance to connect. However, instead of befriending his fellow Americans, Bush, *one more time*, came across as out-of-touch. The reason for the unfortunate outcome was mostly due to an incident that took place at a grocers' convention.

While at this gathering, Bush was shown a grocery store checkout scanner, and instead of recognizing the device that was a part of everyday life for most Americans, Bush, seeing a scanner for the first time, appeared astonished at the "new invention." This story, surpassing all others along the train route, was picked up by the traveling press corps and instantaneously transformed into national headlines. The whistle-stop tour was one more indication of how poorly the White House and campaign staffers handled spin, particularly the damage control variety.

The political goings-on in October, although outwardly full of activity, had inwardly slowed to a crawl. In my office, the phone was not ringing as often; the many executives arriving for trade advisory meetings were not quite so ingratiating; my fellow appointees no longer wanted to talk politics; the Bush-Quayle committee had not planned a Christmas party; the White House liaison office had not said anything about the promotion I was supposed to receive in January, and while no one admitted writing a résumé, everybody was.

It was customary during the last few days before a national election for the press to observe a moratorium, a brief period when political

★★★

attacks ceased and the candidates caught their breath before the final vote; nonetheless, this critical time in a presidential campaign can be treacherous. For President Bush, it was hard to believe that things could get any worse. But they did.

As with most unforeseen events during the Bush administration, the final episode had at its core Reagan's Men written all over it. The weekend before the vote, the 1980s' Iran-Contra Affair was reintroduced, and events from six years earlier were dredged up and promoted by the press corps to be the true measure of Bush's inadequacies as President. How was it that in the final hours before the election, this situation arose? After juggling names, dates, and legal facts, this is what I seamed together.

The Iran part goes this way. Days before the 1980 election, Reagan's campaign staff made a deal with the Iranians *not* to release the fifty-two American captives. Not yet. Not until Reagan was pronounced President. For their cooperation, the Iranians were paid millions of dollars—in weapons. Weeks before the election, in October, Carter had attempted to rescue the hostages; his failure ended with eight Americans killed. After Carter lost his reelection and Reagan was sworn into office, the hostages were released. Just *twenty minutes* later. Starting in March 1981, President Reagan, making good on his agreement, began making arms shipments to Muslims in Iran.

The contra portion of the tale begins with a dictator named Somoza and his National Guard. The extremely poor and oppressed inhabitants of Nicaragua, led by the Sandinista Marxist military, finally rallied to defeat him. Strangely enough, the United States, under President Reagan, rescued and reassembled the National Guard, renaming them contras, or counterrevolutionaries. After training and arming the contras, Reagan put them back in Nicaragua to overcome the new leadership, and at President Reagan's insistence, these strongmen were given whatever they needed to continue their battle. This action was in clear violation of the Boland Amendment, in which Congress had emphatically prohibited aid. After a decade of more bloodshed—much of it initiated by the United States—the contras had won and the Nicaraguan government had folded.

This civil war had been the showpiece of Reagan's foreign policy; however, because of these illegal actions, America's intelligence operations had been jeopardized, and Reagan's Iran-Contra support was tagged one of the most flagrant abuses of presidential power—if not *the* most flagrant—ever. Nicaraguans had endured almost fifty years under a dictatorship, and much of it had been supported by the United States. This scheme became public knowledge after being published in the CIA's *Freedom Fighters Manual*. In 1989, when George Bush was elected President and the Nicaragua infighting had recommenced, Bush reversed Reagan's strategy, abandoning the Nicaraguan civil war and no longer providing for the insurgent contras.

To another, but directly related topic, one that is central to the events of November 1 and 2, 1992. Donald P. Gregg, National Security Advisor to Bush while he was Vice President, had worked at the CIA when Bush was director. Before that time, in 1979, Gregg had been appointed to the national security staff of President Carter and headed the White House directorate that reviewed covert activities. Ten years later, in September 1989, having spent thirty years in the intelligence community (eighteen in Asia), Gregg was confirmed as Bush's ambassador to South Korea.

I had worked with Gregg's wife, Meg, at the campaign headquarters in late 1987, while I was assisting with the volunteers. Always pleasant, she was a nice addition during those crunch times. I knew nothing about her husband and did not know about his relationship with Bush until I read the newspaper articles regarding his controversial appointment.

Gregg's confirmation had passed in the Senate, but not that easily. Because of his previous involvement with Iran-Contra, there had been some questions. Democrats argued that during the Reagan administration, Gregg, as NSA to Vice President Bush, had not been a credible witness when testifying to the Senate about his (and Bush's) involvement with the contra affair. Gregg had testified that he first learned of the clandestine maneuvers on August 8, 1986, after a conversation with friend and former CIA agent, Felix Rodriguez. This was long after Congress had banned aid (October 1984) and before Rodriquez had been recruited by Oliver North to supervise the aerial delivery of arms to the resistance in September 1985. Gregg also testified that Bush's first knowledge of the contra operation was in December 1986; until then, he said, Bush had been kept in the dark about North's activities in aiding the rebels.

Gregg's accusers said this just was not possible. "Hard to comprehend," said Senator Alan Cranston (D-CA) in the *Washington Post* on May 13, 1989. Nonetheless, the majority of Congress wanted to put

Iran-Contra behind them and move on. Case closed. Gregg had been confirmed, but, more importantly, the credibility of George Bush, who was then President, was on solid ground.

Under a statute enacted by Congress in 1978 to investigate and prosecute wrongdoing by high-ranking administration officials, Lawrence E. Walsh had been appointed the nation's eighth independent counsel in 1986. He was handpicked by a special court to investigate the legality of Reagan appointees involved in the diversion of arms profits from Iran to giving aid to the Nicaraguan contras. Walsh had been given lots of latitude while investigating. However, by spring of 1992, having spent over $30 million, he had little to show for his efforts: ten convictions, two of which were dismissed on appeal, and only one of which required a prison sentence. On technical grounds, the Supreme Court had overturned the convictions of Oliver North (Reagan's National Council security aide) and retired Admiral John M. Poindexter (Reagan's National Security Advisor), two men who had delivered damaging testimony about Reagan.

Then, in June 1992, Casper W. Weinberger, Reagan's secretary of Defense (who opposed the Reagan arms sale), had been indicted, charged by Walsh with perjury and obstruction of justice. On June 22, 1992, the *Washington Post* printed an after-the-fact article by Sharon La Franiere, "Independent Counsel Law Increasingly Beset," which stated:

> Republicans in the administration and on Capitol Hill now characterize Walsh as the embodiment of everything that is wrong with the statute: no limits on how long an independent counsel can investigate or how much one can spend, no oversight, no assurance the prosecutor meets the Justice Department's threshold for seeking indictments.

Four months later—less than a week before the election (October 28, 1992)—John Barrett, the prosecutor preparing for the Weinberger indictment, informed Walsh that he had come upon evidence pertaining to Bush's involvement in the Iran arms sale. In a diary note dated January 7, 1986, Weinberger had written that Bush knew about the affair *and* that he had favored the arms sale. In all these years, this was the first corroboration of Bush misconduct Walsh had been able to uncover, and the discovery had been purely accidental.

Walsh's staff suggested that, with the Weinberger trial scheduled for January 1993, he wait until after the election to disclose the potentially incriminating report on Bush. But, Walsh, who had never believed Bush was innocent of contra involvement and who had a soft spot for Reagan (a man he thought was "basically honorable"), actually despised Bush. If there were ever an opportunity for him to move in for the kill, it was now.

Even though independent prosecutors are not supposed to be swayed by political philosophy or allegiance in any way, on Friday, October 30—just seventy-two hours before the election—Walsh released his evidence. What better time to attack an archenemy than when he least expected it: in this case, the weekend before the election, when the candidates were taking advantage of the "truce."

To make the '92 Iran story even more attention-grabbing, on the same Friday—just before the Walsh announcement—polls showed Clinton suddenly making a plunge downward while Bush surged upward. In spite of all that had occurred over the previous twelve months, a dead heat (somewhere between 35 and 40 percent) was projected to occur by election time. But . . . once the contra story—with mention of the Weinberger note—hit the newswires, everything changed. Pandemonium broke loose, and the press made it sound as if Bush were being indicted. Right then! While he was President! Before the election!

ON that cold, rainy Halloween weekend following the Walsh revelation, I read one newspaper account after another. All reported that President Bush previously had known about the arms-for-hostages arrangement. Weinberger's handwritten message said so. The newsstands and airwaves were flooded with The Story, each, in their own way, informing America that Bush *had been caught*. He had been caught in his own lie. In less than twenty-four hours, the President, who had appeared (with the dead heat prognosis) to be making a New Hampshire–style rally, fell to 33 percent, likened to a rabbit snared in a trap. And Clinton, who jumped on Bush and the Iran-Contra report like a tiger pounces on a powerless prey, watched his ratings move up to 40 percent. Bush was devoured.

The morning of November 3, Election Day, rolled in like dark clouds before a storm. I spent my lunch hour sitting on the steps of the Lincoln Memorial, gazing out across the Reflecting Pool to the Washington Monument in the distance. It was hard to go back to work that afternoon and even harder to watch the election returns that night. A mega-gathering of Republicans was being held in the Washington Hilton's ballroom, but at the last minute, I decided not to attend. I chose instead to spend the evening at home in front of the fireplace, watching the returns with friends—who later told me that they had voted for Perot. At 11:15 P.M., it was announced that Bill Clinton was projected to receive 286 electoral votes, which surpassed the required 270 (of 538), making him the winner in the race for President of the United States.

Clinton received 19,858,745 popular votes, and became the fourteenth President elected with less than 50 percent of the popular vote, yet he had two million more ballots cast his way than Bush. President Bush received 17,848,340 votes, making him the ninth incumbent in U.S. history to be defeated for reelection. And Ross Perot secured 7,878,801 popular votes, the highest number ever cast for an independent or third-party candidate . . . almost 8 million Americans voted for a man who never was an official candidate—of any Party! Perot's total number had been substantially boosted by votes that had fallen away from Bush. The final statistics showed: Clinton 44 percent, Bush 39 percent, and Perot 17 percent.

I knew that the real defeat of President Bush had little to do with Perot, the strategy of the opposing Clinton camp, their candidate, the supposed economic slump or even Lawrence Walsh. I would have preferred that one or all of them could have been the decisive factor. But, they were not.

From the beginning of this book, I have promoted the idea that certain members of the Republican Party were not loyal to President Bush—that Bush was ambushed. And throughout this narrative, I have repeatedly tried to prove my thesis by corroborating my beliefs with those of reputable reporters.

I may not have been in the Oval Office, but I was a "stone's throw" away—watching, reading, researching and simply doing my job. At Campaign Headquarters, the Republican National Committee, the Transition Team, the White House, the International Trade Administration, and the Office of Congressional Affairs, I always was cognizant of the people around me, whether I knew them or only knew "of" them.

In the days after the 1992 election, I continued to study the administration's activities, and kept on observing fellow Republicans discrediting President Bush. One last story to demonstrate. A friend told me that young conservatives working at the Washington, D.C., Heritage Foundation had taken a silver platter, placed a plastic mask of Bush in the center, poured ketchup all over it and paraded the platter around the room. True? I think so.

It is my adamant belief that George Bush was overpowered because Jim Baker and his former Reaganite cronies did not want Bush reelected. The 1992 defeat was as simple and as intricately complex as that. The concept is now fact for me. The Power Pyramid jigsaw puzzle told the story. Piece by piece by piece, I fit the sections together, and as I arrive at the end of my writing odyssey, I feel more convinced than ever that my Crazy Conspiracy Theory is as close to the truth as anything yet proposed.

Earlier, I suggested that the media had not stopped the Baker Plan because the conspirators themselves had fed the media; and that the government had not stopped The Plan because the conspirators themselves were the government. The more junior Reagan appointees acted as agents, not knowing about The Plan; they voluntarily (and cheerfully) acted in blind obedience to their superiors. The Baker-Fuller–led Transition team gave them the same autonomy they had been endowed with when Baker was Reagan's COS. Only those at the very top of the Bush Power Pyramid truly knew what was happening; Cheney and Cicconi, Fitzwater and Fuller, Teeter and Tutwiler, Darman and whoever else Jim Baker had anointed.

All the while, there were countless links between people and places, campaigns and cohorts, all crisscrossing, sometimes canceling or deflecting each other's agenda. But, most times, they had reinforced one another's self-interests—one another's greed and reprisal of Bush. With punishment, revenge, and retribution. Those on the Power Pyramid had never wanted nor anticipated Wimpy George winning in 1988. The ultimate fluke. He may have slid under the bar in 1988, but he *would not* in 1992. And he had not. Bush was the loser, and in actuality, Baker, *not* Clinton, was the winner!

STANDING on the South Lawn of the White House the day after the election, with hundreds of others from the administration, I waited for the arrival of President Bush, who had just returned from Houston; the family had listened to the election returns in their home state. The skies overhead were a deep, clear blue with just a few fluffy clouds gracefully waltzing above us. The November temperatures had brought cool, crisp air to the Capital, but the sun above felt more like September. On the grounds of the mansion, a platform had been set up where the presidential helicopter usually landed.

Then, coming into view, exiting from the southern entrance of the White House, was Bush, who walked up onto the makeshift stage and addressed those of us assembled to greet him. As in November 1988, at the hangar at Andrews Air Force Base when Bush returned as President-elect, I held my small American flag, but unlike the celebratory mood four years earlier, this day was one of distress, and I waved it more out of nervousness than anything else. Bush presented himself as he had the night before, when giving his concession speech on television. Calm and composed, he spoke with dignity: "I can think of nothing other to say except let's finish this job with style, let's get the job done. We will support the new President and give him every chance to lead this country to greater heights."

As I stood there observing the President's surrender, I had questions in my mind. If truth (and the virtues that come with it such as trust and respect) is an illusion, then is truth relevant? If the world no longer mandated that principle and character were necessary in a leader, then what did that say about today's American political and military leaders? Had America's most influential figures been raised to know about honor and honorable intentions? And if it turned out that the world was more immoral than moral, was it possible for one to keep to a code of high merit and still survive . . . at the top? And lastly, if through media techniques, the guys in the black hats could present themselves in such a way as to convince others that they wore the white hats, then what happens to the guys who *really* wear the white hats?

These disturbing thoughts would run through my mind for a long time—way past the day I stood on the South Lawn listening to Bush speak about "getting the job done." I feared then, as I do today, that the United States, not President Bush, had lost something far greater in November 1992. America had started to lose its soul, and with that, its mark of distinction. President Theodore Roosevelt once said: "To educate a man in mind and not in morals is to educate a menace to society."

Having watched all the events unfold between 1987 and 1993, I probably should have gained political savvy. Yet, the more I learned, the more complex the assumptions and the more numerous my inquiries. Today, over a decade after the Bush presidency ended, I have trouble defining words like politics, government and democracy, just as I do Republican and Democrat. And, I reluctantly admit that these terms have lost some of their significance. At these times, I go back to Thomas

Jefferson's tradition of rules and virtues and my military family's laws of character. For when all else fails, these truths ground me and remind me that integrity, pride, and love of God and Country are—must be—real.

On November 4, 1992, with the White House in front of me and the President within feet, I saw many familiar faces, and some not so familiar. For the last time, the President's team was together on the prestigious grounds, and everyone was pushing against one another, hoping that when Bush left the stand to meet the crowd they would have a chance to shake his hand. I saw Craig Fuller in the second row. A shiver went down my spine. Bob Dole, Lamar Alexander, Andy Card (named to oversee the regime change), and Baker's aide Robert Zoellick were in the front lines.

But James Baker was missing. The President's chief of staff and "best friend" had decided he would stay in Texas and ready himself for a hunting expedition he was hosting at his ranch in Wyoming. After ten weeks of being chairman of the reelection committee, he'd had enough.

For the most part, the individuals I saw on the South Lawn were the men and women whom I have written about in this account, and having crossed paths many times over the preceding five years, we now departed the White House grounds. While walking across the thick, newly mowed lawn, I asked myself, "Will I ever see these people again?" And then, instead of paying attention to those who were swarming around me, I was reminded of those who *were not* there: the Real Bush Team. The 1988 Campaign Team.

Momentarily, I was back on "another" lawn belonging to the Bushes. It was July 1988, and the staff had gathered for a picnic at the Vice President's Residence at the Naval Observatory. In retrospect, the memory of that informal get-together on *this* day of Bush's concession meant more to me than ever before. Many of those hard-working revelers were missing now; they had not received appointments in the administration, yet they were the ones who had dedicated themselves to a Bush victory and who had remained loyal to the Vice President, even during the dark days.

On the night of the 1988 summer picnic, all of us had the opportunity to share time with the Vice President, his wife, children and grandchildren—as if we had been neighborhood guests invited over for a spur-of-the-moment barbecue. The '88 picnic could just as easily have been a Houston gathering, like in the days when Bush gathered with Baker and Mosbacher and their families in their backyards drinking beer, barbecuing beef, and throwing horseshoes. Those were the old days—the

★★★

oil days, after Bush had abandoned his Connecticut blue-blood lifestyle and learned to like ribs and pork rinds.

In Washington D.C., during the summer of 1988—over hotdogs and keg beer—the Bush Team had celebrated being together, working for a common cause; I had felt we were bound together in mission and purpose. We all had wanted George Bush to be the President of the United States. And although, at the time, his ratings were far from desirable, it had not deterred our optimism or ability to have fun. We *never* spoke about any finale other than Bush being elected President in November 1988.

A barbecue, whether held in Texas or Washington, always needs country music; it naturally brings people together, especially when it is the toe-tapping kind that makes you feel good and brings a smile to your face. The kind Atwater had played on that sultry, humid evening at the Naval Observatory. From the Residence porch, strumming his electric guitar, Lee had made his political musical debut. With his Hawaiian shirt hanging outside his white Levis, and in his raspy, edgy voice that did not always carry the correct tune, he had sung his favorite songs. And months later, when cutting the CD of his '89 inaugural concert, Atwater had written inside the *Red, Hot and Blue* CD cover:

> I don't think anything is more helpful to the body politic or to the people in general than music. It is a uniting force, a gentle force. Music is harmony and harmony is what we are seeking in politics and in life. There is nothing more beautiful than a perfect chord, whether it is a good chord in music or in the concert of human relationships. Nothing brings people together as much as when you play in a band, and when you sing together, and tap your feet and dance.

Atwater believed that music was the salve that mended all and healed in a way nothing else could.

Walking out of the White House gates for the last time, on November 4, 1992, I wanted to believe that had Atwater been there under these same circumstances—a Bush defeat—he would have stepped forward to rally a party, get out his guitar and start strumming B.B. King songs. With Atwater on stage, one more time, maybe, just maybe, the Real Team would have had a chance to sing together, tap their feet . . . and dance.

Vice Presidential Residence, June 17, 1988
Atwater jammin' at the campaign picnic . . .
with the Real Team.

★★★ ACKNOWLEDGMENTS ★★★

My gratitude to the special people who contributed to *AMBUSHED:*

Amory Weld, valued advice, brilliant copy editing, and most loyal supporter
Ann Devroy, gifted journalist whose articles I found to be my greatest confirmation
Barbara Garaygordobil, dear cousin and #1 go-getter who inspires and energizes
Barbara Gee, writer with marvelous intuition and flair for crafting a unique script
Betsy & Jack Dunham, sister and her husband, lawyers who kept my words "legal"
Betty Hackmann, teacher/editor whose valued opinions launched the second draft
Beverly Herter, editor and proofreader whose work reflects the highest standards
Bing West, author and ally who trudged the writer's trail before I, enlightening me
Carnes & Meredith Lord, fellow writer and Republican friends who know the game
Catherine Boisseau, fine writer and talented actress whose judgments I respect
Dan Connelly, indexer, whose expert judgment created a credible "list" of characters
Doug Logan, read the first draft and had the grace not to tell me it should be my last
Gregg Madden, converted a 528-page text into a "hot off the press" political memoir
Jim & Jane Moore, dear friends whose opposing viewpoints are always prized
John Pantalone, talented editor/writer generous with his time, counsel & convictions
Joan Wilson, knows the meaning of friendship and sharing, and has professional flair
J. P. Trousilek, for his protocol expertise, good counsel and vision of "what it takes"
Justin Katz, accomplished writer, editor and tech guru, whose efforts saved the day!
Kimberly Spear & Shawn Dixon, my "whiz kids," creators of superb graphic art
Newport Restoration Foundation, my FUN and well informed Rough Point crew
Nina Dotterer & Bob Cooper, supreme friends who have been with me since day one
Paul & Dorcas Taylor, their considered opinion sustained me during revision times
PDQ Newport, for copying thousands & thousands of pages and always with a smile
Pro & Mary Lyon, whose wise editorial counsel and forthcoming insight inspired me
Redwood Writing Group, where collaborative efforts help writers cross the finish line
Rich Schlegel, his prompt and pleasing manner launched *AMBUSHED* on the Web
Robert Singleton, whose verification gave me the fortitude to publish "on my own"
Rob Walker, a valued source of information whose attitude toward life I admire
Tom D'Evelyn, with his vision, the underpinnings of a political memoir were born
Trinity KGroup, always providing sustenance, commentary and fellowship

And too, a personal thank you to my children, Lance and Joslin—the reason for my writing the book—who, with little complaining and an inordinate amount of support (emotional, technological, and editorial) put up with their mother throughout her nearly decade-long writing marathon. And who, at the beginning of each year, queried, "Is this the year that you are going to finish the book and get a real job ... one that pays you?"

It is only with the assistance and encouragement of these many individuals who were there along the way—in fact, who happened to come into the project at just the right moment to keep it alive—that I was able to complete my dream: the writing of my first book. I am truly grateful to all of them.

★★★ QUOTATIONS ★★★

Part 1
p.1, Michael Korda, *Power;* p.3, Richard Bode, *Beachcombing at Miramar;* p.16, Sun Tzu, *The Art of War;* p.26, Unnamed, "Moy Castle"; p.34, Forrest McDonald, *The American Presidency;* p.50, Herman Hesse, *The Glass Bead Game*

Part 2
p.67, Hendrick Smith, *The Power Game;* p.69, Paul Boller, *Presidential Campaigns;* p.81, Michael Korda, *Power;* p.94, Edgar Allan Poe, "The Raven"; p.105, Chin-Ning Chu

Part 3
p.121, Sun Tzu, *Art of War;* p.123, Carl M. Brauer; p.132, Richard Bode, *Beachcombing at Miramar;* p.146, Carl G. Jung; p.158, Hedrick Smith, *The Power Game;* p.169, Tom Wolf, *The Right Stuff*

Part 4
p.181, Arlington National Cemetery, Kennedy Gravesite; p.183, Hedrick Smith, *The Power Game;* p.197, George Herbert Walker Bush, Boy Scout National Jamboree Speech, August 7, 1989; p.218, Paul Light; p.228, Sun Tzu, *The Art of War;* p.242, Emily Dickenson, "I Am Nobody"; p.251, Eric Alterman, "Mother Jones," Anne Devroy's quote

Part 5
p.263, George Reedy; p.265, Rudyard Kiping; p.273, Stephen Covey, *Seven Habits of Highly Effective People;* p.287, Dag Hammarskjold; p.298, William Shakespeare, "Sonnet 94"; p.308, Herman Wouk, *The Winds of War*

Part 6
p.323, Richard Bode, *Beachcombing at Miramar;* p.325, Sarah Ban Breathnach, *Simple Abundance;* p.333, "A Psalm of David; Triumphant Faith"; p.339, Hedrick Smith, *The Power Game;* p.349, George Washington, *Farewell Address;* p.361, Anne Morrow Lindberg, *Gift From the Sea;* p.374, U.S. of America Declaration of Independence

Part 7
p.387, Herman Hesse, *The Glass Bead Game;* p.389, William Shakespeare, *As You Like It;* p.403, Christina Rossetti, "Clouds"; p.412, Charles Peters, *How Washington Really Works;* p.420, *The Hartford Courant,* January 5, 1802; p.429, Lewis Carroll, "Jabberwocky"; p.440, William Ernest Henley

Part 8
p.453, Alfred, Lord Tennyson, "The Charge of the Light Brigade"; p.455, Michael Korda, *Power;* p.465, Hedrick Smith, *The Power Game;* p.469, George Herbert Walker Bush; p.480, Sebastian Junger, *The Perfect Storm;* p.489, Julia Ward Howe, "Battle Hymn of the Republic"

★★★ INDEX ★★★

★★★

★★★